SAGE PUBLISHING: OUR STORY

We believe in creating fresh, cutting-edge content that helps you prepare your students to make an impact in today's ever-changing business world. Founded in 1965 by 24-year-old entrepreneur Sara Miller McCune, SAGE continues its legacy of equipping instructors with the tools and resources necessary to develop the next generation of business leaders.

- We invest in the right **authors** who distill the best available research into practical applications

- We offer intuitive **digital solutions** at student-friendly prices

- We remain permanently independent and fiercely committed to **quality, innovation, and learning**.

To my colleagues

Sara Miller McCune founded SAGE Publishing in 1965 to support the dissemination of usable knowledge and educate a global community. SAGE publishes more than 1000 journals and over 800 new books each year, spanning a wide range of subject areas. Our growing selection of library products includes archives, data, case studies and video. SAGE remains majority owned by our founder and after her lifetime will become owned by a charitable trust that secures the company's continued independence.

Los Angeles | London | New Delhi | Singapore | Washington DC | Melbourne

Organizational Ethics

A Practical Approach

Fourth Edition

Craig E. Johnson
George Fox University

$SAGE

Los Angeles | London | New Delhi
Singapore | Washington DC | Melbourne

SAGE

FOR INFORMATION:

SAGE Publications, Inc.
2455 Teller Road
Thousand Oaks, California 91320
E-mail: order@sagepub.com

SAGE Publications Ltd.
1 Oliver's Yard
55 City Road
London EC1Y 1SP
United Kingdom

SAGE Publications India Pvt. Ltd.
B 1/I 1 Mohan Cooperative Industrial Area
Mathura Road, New Delhi 110 044
India

SAGE Publications Asia-Pacific Pte. Ltd.
3 Church Street
#10–04 Samsung Hub
Singapore 049483

Acquisitions Editor: Maggie Stanley
Content Development Editor: Lauren Holmes
Editorial Assistant: Alissa Nance
Production Editor: Nevair Kabakian
Copy Editor: Rachel Keith
Typesetter: C&M Digitals (P) Ltd.
Proofreader: Ellen Brink
Indexer: Jean Casalegno
Cover Designer: Candice Harman
Marketing Manager: Amy Lammers

Copyright © 2019 by SAGE Publications, Inc.

All rights reserved. No part of this book may be reproduced or utilized in any form or by any means, electronic or mechanical, including photocopying, recording, or by any information storage and retrieval system, without permission in writing from the publisher.

Printed in the United States of America

Library of Congress Cataloging-in-Publication Data

Names: Johnson, Craig E. (Craig Edward), 1952- author.

Title: Organizational ethics : a practical approach / Craig E. Johnson, George Fox University.

Description: Fourth edition. | Los Angeles : SAGE, [2019] | Includes bibliographical references and index.

Identifiers: LCCN 2017046099 | ISBN 9781544327853 (pbk. : alk. paper)

Subjects: LCSH: Business ethics. | Corporate culture.

Classification: LCC HF5387 .J645 2019 | DDC 174/.4—dc23
LC record available at https://lccn.loc.gov/2017046099

This book is printed on acid-free paper.

18 19 20 21 22 10 9 8 7 6 5 4 3 2 1

BRIEF CONTENTS

List of Case Studies, Self-Assessments, Ethical Checkpoints, and Contemporary Issues in Organizational Ethics — xii

Introduction: Making the Case for Studying Organizational Ethics — xv

Acknowledgments — xxiii

About the Author — xxiv

PART ONE • PRACTICING PERSONAL ETHICS IN THE ORGANIZATION — 1

CHAPTER 1 • Ethical Competencies and Perspectives — 2

CHAPTER 2 • Components of Personal Ethical Development — 33

CHAPTER 3 • Ethical Decision Making and Action — 59

PART TWO • PRACTICING INTERPERSONAL ETHICS IN THE ORGANIZATION — 93

CHAPTER 4 • Ethical Interpersonal Communication — 94

CHAPTER 5 • Exercising Ethical Influence — 121

CHAPTER 6 • Ethical Conflict Management — 155

PART THREE • PRACTICING LEADERSHIP, FOLLOWERSHIP, AND GROUP ETHICS — 189

CHAPTER 7 • Leadership and Followership Ethics — 190

CHAPTER 8 • Improving Group Ethical Performance — 228

PART FOUR • PRACTICING ETHICS IN ORGANIZATIONAL SYSTEMS   257

CHAPTER 9 • Building an Ethical Organization   258

CHAPTER 10 • Ethical Marketing, Finance, Accounting, and Human Resource Management   295

CHAPTER 11 • Promoting Organizational Citizenship   327

CHAPTER 12 • Ethics in a Global Society   355

Notes   384
References   393
Index   438

DETAILED CONTENTS

List of Case Studies, Self-Assessments, Ethical Checkpoints, and Contemporary Issues in Organizational Ethics	xii
Introduction: Making the Case for Studying Organizational Ethics	xv
Acknowledgments	xxiii
About the Author	xxiv

PART ONE • PRACTICING PERSONAL ETHICS IN THE ORGANIZATION   1

CHAPTER 1 • Ethical Competencies and Perspectives   2

Developing Ethical Competencies	2
Defining Organizational Ethics	5
Ethical Perspectives	8
Utilitarianism: Do the Greatest Good for the Greatest Number	8
Kant's Categorical Imperative: Do What's Right Despite the Consequences	10
Rawls's Justice as Fairness: Balancing Freedom and Equality	12
Aristotelian Ethics: Live Well	14
Confucianism: Building Healthy Relationships	16
Altruism: Concern for Others	20
Chapter Takeaways	25
Application Projects	26

CHAPTER 2 • Components of Personal Ethical Development   33

Component 1: Discovering Vocation	33
Discovering Your Personal Gifts	34
Barriers to Obeying Our Callings	35
Component 2: Identifying Personal Values	38
Component 3: Developing Character	39
Positive Psychology and Virtues	39
Direct Approaches to Character Development	41
Indirect Approaches to Character Development	41
Component 4: Creating a Moral Identity	46
Component 5: Drawing Upon Spiritual Resources	47

Caring for the Soul	48
Spiritual Well-Being	50
Chapter Takeaways	52
Application Projects	52

CHAPTER 3 • Ethical Decision Making and Action — 59

Components of Ethical Behavior	59
Component 1: Moral Sensitivity (Recognition)	60
Component 2: Moral Judgment	64
Component 3: Moral Motivation	71
Component 4: Moral Character	74
Decision-Making Formats	77
The Lonergan/Baird Method	79
The Moral Compass	81
The Foursquare Protocol	82
Five Timeless Questions	83
The Five "I" format	85
Chapter Takeaways	86
Application Projects	86

PART TWO • PRACTICING INTERPERSONAL ETHICS IN THE ORGANIZATION — 93

CHAPTER 4 • Ethical Interpersonal Communication — 94

Dialogue: An Ethical Framework for Interpersonal Communication	94
Ethical Communication Competencies	96
Mindfulness	97
Effective Listening	98
Self-Disclosure	102
Confirmation	105
Emotional Intelligence	106
Trust Building	111
Moral Argument	113
Chapter Takeaways	115
Application Projects	116

CHAPTER 5 • Exercising Ethical Influence — 121

Questions of Power	122
Question 1: Are Some Forms of Power More Ethical Than Others?	122
Question 2: Is It Possible to Have Too Much Power?	125
Question 3: Should I Play Politics?	127
Question 4: What Factors Contribute to Empowerment?	130
Question 5: How Do I Overcome Barriers to Empowerment?	131

Ethical Issues in Influence 133
    Framing 133
    Proactive Tactics 134
    Impression Management 136
    Deception 141
    Emotional Labor 143
    Communication of Expectations 145
Chapter Takeaways 148
Application Projects 149

CHAPTER 6 • Ethical Conflict Management 155

Conflict in Organizational Life 155
Becoming an Ethical Conflict Manager 158
    Step 1: Recognize the Differences Between Functional and Dysfunctional Conflicts 158
    Step 2: Manage Your Emotions 158
    Step 3: Identify Your Personal Conflict Style 160
    Step 4: Develop Conflict Guidelines 162
    Step 5: Employ Collaborative Conflict Management Tactics 163
    Step 6: Be Prepared to Apologize 163
Resolving Conflict Through Ethical Negotiation 165
    Ethical Issues in Negotiation 165
    Adopt an Integrative Approach to Negotiation 168
Combating Aggression and Sexual Harassment 171
    Types of Aggression 171
    Sources of Aggression 173
    Resisting and Reducing Aggression 176
    Preventing Sexual Harassment 177
Chapter Takeaways 181
Application Projects 182

PART THREE • PRACTICING LEADERSHIP, FOLLOWERSHIP, AND GROUP ETHICS 189

CHAPTER 7 • Leadership and Followership Ethics 190

Ethical Leadership 191
    The Ethical Challenges of Leadership 191
    The Shadow Side of Leadership 194
    Stepping Out of the Shadows: Normative Leadership Theories 200
Ethical Followership 204
    The Ethical Challenges of Followership 204
Meeting the Moral Demands of Followership: Principles and Strategies 210
Chapter Takeaways 219
Application Projects 220

CHAPTER 8 • Improving Group Ethical Performance   228

Acting as a Morally Responsible Team Member   229
- Adopting a Cooperative Orientation   229
- Doing Your Fair Share (Not Loafing)   231
- Displaying Openness and Supportiveness   234
- Being Willing to Stand Alone   237

Responding to Ethical Danger Signs   238
- Groupthink   238
- Polythink   241
- Mismanaged Agreement   242
- Escalating Commitment   244
- Excessive Control   246
- Moral Exclusion   247

Chapter Takeaways   250
Application Projects   251

PART FOUR • PRACTICING ETHICS IN ORGANIZATIONAL SYSTEMS   257

CHAPTER 9 • Building an Ethical Organization   258

Making Ethics Matter   258
Components of Ethical Culture   260
- Formal Elements   261
- Informal Elements   274

Cultural Change Efforts   278
- Ethical Drivers   278

Chapter Takeaways   286
Application Projects   287

CHAPTER 10 • Ethical Marketing, Finance, Accounting, and Human Resource Management   295

Ethical Marketing   296
- Ethical Issues in Marketing   296
- Ethical Principles and Strategies   297

Ethical Finance and Accounting   302
- Ethical Issues in Finance and Accounting   302
- Ethical Principles and Strategies   305

Ethical Human Resource Management   311
- Ethical Issues in Human Resource Management   311
- Ethical Principles and Strategies   314

Chapter Takeaways   319
Application Projects   320

CHAPTER 11 • Promoting Organizational Citizenship   327

   The Organization as Citizen   327
      Components of Organizational Citizenship   328
      Corporate Social Responsibility   332
      Corporate/CEO Activism   335
      Sustainability   337
      The Stages of Corporate Citizenship   340
   Promoting Organizational Citizenship   343
      Adopting a Stewardship Mind-Set   343
      Measuring Social Performance   345
   Chapter Takeaways   347
   Application Projects   348

CHAPTER 12 • Ethics in a Global Society   355

   The Dangers of Globalization and the Challenges of Ethical Diversity   355
   Developing Cross-Cultural Ethical Competence   357
      Coming to Grips With Ethnocentrism   357
      Becoming a World Citizen   359
      Understanding Ethical Diversity   360
      Finding Moral Common Ground   370
      Resolving Ethical Cross-Cultural Conflicts   375
   Chapter Takeaways   377
   Application Projects   378

Notes   384
References   393
Index   438

LIST OF CASE STUDIES, SELF-ASSESSMENTS, ETHICAL CHECKPOINTS, AND CONTEMPORARY ISSUES IN ORGANIZATIONAL ETHICS

CASE STUDIES

CASE STUDY 1.1	Federal Employees Behaving Badly	27
CASE STUDY 1.2	National Security or Computer Security?	29
CASE STUDY 1.3	Is This Any Way to Run a Prison?	30
CASE STUDY 2.1	Character Development at West Point	53
CASE STUDY 2.2	Taking Down the Monuments: Erasing History?	55
CASE STUDY 2.3	A Different Kind of Pope	56
CASE STUDY 3.1	White Collar Crime: The Gap Between Perpetrators and Victims	87
CASE STUDY 3.2	Scenarios for Analysis	89
CASE STUDY 4.1	Everyone's Favorite Professor	117
CASE STUDY 4.2	Unfairly Taking the Blame	118
CASE STUDY 4.3	The Stem Cell Account	119
CASE STUDY 5.1	Moving Beyond Empowerment at Morning Star	150
CASE STUDY 5.2	Hiding the Real Story at Midwestern Community Action	152
CASE STUDY 5.3	Flying the Unfriendly Skies	153
CASE STUDY 6.1	Any Way You Look at It, You Lose: Longshore Workers versus International Container Services Inc.	183
CASE STUDY 6.2	Negotiating the Plant Reopening	184
CASE STUDY 6.3	When Football Comes First: Sexual Assault at Baylor University	186
CASE STUDY 7.1	Failing to Serve Those Who Served	221
CASE STUDY 7.2	Challenging the Chancellor	223
CASE STUDY 7.3	Putting Fraud Before Family	225
CASE STUDY 8.1	Team Denial	252
CASE STUDY 8.2	Groupthink in the Sweat Lodge	254

▶ CASE STUDY 8.3	To Loan or Not to Loan?	256
▶ CASE STUDY 9.1	Winning at All Costs at Uber	288
▶ CASE STUDY 9.2	Wells Fargo: Getting the Ethics You Pay For	290
▶ CASE STUDY 9.3	GM's Deadly Ignition Switch	292
▶ CASE STUDY 10.1	Boosting the Cost of the EpiPen: Price Gouging or Good Business?	321
▶ CASE STUDY 10.2	Accounting/Finance Ethics Scenarios	323
▶ CASE STUDY 10.3	Regulating Love at the Office	324
▶ CASE STUDY 11.1	Why the Circus No Longer Comes to Town	349
▶ CASE STUDY 11.2	Facebook Takes on Fake News	351
▶ CASE STUDY 11.3	The Public Benefit Corporation and Profit-With-Purpose Businesses	353
▶ CASE STUDY 12.1	The Right to Be Forgotten	379
▶ CASE STUDY 12.2	Goldman Sachs and Hunger Bonds	380
▶ CASE STUDY 12.3	Scenarios for Analysis	382

SELF-ASSESSMENTS

▶ SELF-ASSESSMENT 1.1	Attitudes Toward Business (and Organizational) Ethics	3
▶ SELF-ASSESSMENT 1.2	Organizational Citizenship Behavior Scale	21
▶ SELF-ASSESSMENT 2.1	Preferred Roles	36
▶ SELF-ASSESSMENT 2.2	Spiritual Well-Being Questionnaire	50
▶ SELF-ASSESSMENT 3.1	Moral Sensitivity Scenarios	63
▶ SELF-ASSESSMENT 3.2	Key Self-Knowledge Questions	78
▶ SELF-ASSESSMENT 4.1	Mindful Attention Awareness Scale (MAAS)	99
▶ SELF-ASSESSMENT 4.2	Listening Styles Profile	103
▶ SELF-ASSESSMENT 5.1	Personal Power Profile	123
▶ SELF-ASSESSMENT 5.2	Political Skill Inventory	129
▶ SELF-ASSESSMENT 6.1	Conflict Style Inventory	161
▶ SELF-ASSESSMENT 6.2	Negative Acts Questionnaire	172
▶ SELF-ASSESSMENT 7.1	Servant Leadership Questionnaire	202
▶ SELF-ASSESSMENT 7.2	Followership Role Orientation Scale	212
▶ SELF-ASSESSMENT 8.1	Class Project Social Loafing Scale	232
▶ SELF-ASSESSMENT 8.2	Concertive Control Scale	247
▶ SELF-ASSESSMENT 9.1	Ethics Audit Questions	279
▶ SELF-ASSESSMENT 9.2	Socialization Scale	285
▶ SELF-ASSESSMENT 10.1	Skepticism Scale	308
▶ SELF-ASSESSMENT 10.2	Organizational Justice Scale	316
▶ SELF-ASSESSMENT 11.1	Four Stages of Issue Maturity Scale	331
▶ SELF-ASSESSMENT 11.2	Covenantal Relationship Questionnaire	344
▶ SELF-ASSESSMENT 12.1	Individualism/Collectivism Scale	362
▶ SELF-ASSESSMENT 12.2	Moral Foundations Questionnaire	369

ETHICAL CHECKPOINTS

▶ **ETHICAL CHECKPOINT 1.1**	Facebook Etiquette	19
▶ **ETHICAL CHECKPOINT 2.1**	Character Strengths	40
▶ **ETHICAL CHECKPOINT 3.1**	Rational Remedies for Cognitive Biases	70
▶ **ETHICAL CHECKPOINT 4.1**	Listening Skills	101
▶ **ETHICAL CHECKPOINT 4.2**	Emotional Analysis Questions	110
▶ **ETHICAL CHECKPOINT 4.3**	Building Blocks of Organizational Trust	112
▶ **ETHICAL CHECKPOINT 5.1**	Impression Management Tactics	137
▶ **ETHICAL CHECKPOINT 6.1**	What *Not* to Do in a Conflict	157
▶ **ETHICAL CHECKPOINT 6.2**	Five Ways to Avoid Lying During a Negotiation	167
▶ **ETHICAL CHECKPOINT 7.1**	The Whistle-Blower Checklist	218
▶ **ETHICAL CHECKPOINT 8.1**	Social Loafing in Virtual Teams	235
▶ **ETHICAL CHECKPOINT 9.1**	Sample Mission Statements	262
▶ **ETHICAL CHECKPOINT 9.2**	Integrity-Based Governance	269
▶ **ETHICAL CHECKPOINT 10.1**	The Geometry of Financial Fraud	304
▶ **ETHICAL CHECKPOINT 11.1**	Stakeholder Approach to CSR	334
▶ **ETHICAL CHECKPOINT 11.2**	CERES Principles	338
▶ **ETHICAL CHECKPOINT 12.1**	United Nations Global Compact: The Ten Principles	372

CONTEMPORARY ISSUES IN ORGANIZATIONAL ETHICS

▶ **CONTEMPORARY ISSUES IN ORGANIZATIONAL ETHICS 1.1**
Extreme Altruism — 24

▶ **CONTEMPORARY ISSUES IN ORGANIZATIONAL ETHICS 2.1**
The Dangers of Workplace Spirituality — 49

▶ **CONTEMPORARY ISSUES IN ORGANIZATIONAL ETHICS 3.1**
Reason versus Intuition — 72

▶ **CONTEMPORARY ISSUES IN ORGANIZATIONAL ETHICS 4.1**
The Trait Approach to Emotional Intelligence — 108

▶ **CONTEMPORARY ISSUES IN ORGANIZATIONAL ETHICS 5.1**
"Honest" Ingratiation — 140

▶ **CONTEMPORARY ISSUES IN ORGANIZATIONAL ETHICS 6.1**
Cyberbullying — 175

▶ **CONTEMPORARY ISSUES IN ORGANIZATIONAL ETHICS 7.1**
Guerrilla Bureaucrats — 206

▶ **CONTEMPORARY ISSUES IN ORGANIZATIONAL ETHICS 8.1**
Premature Abandonment — 245

▶ **CONTEMPORARY ISSUES IN ORGANIZATIONAL ETHICS 9.1**
Cyberloafing — 266

▶ **CONTEMPORARY ISSUES IN ORGANIZATIONAL ETHICS 10.1**
The Robin Hood Effect — 319

▶ **CONTEMPORARY ISSUES IN ORGANIZATIONAL ETHICS 11.1**
The Rise of Consumer Boycotts — 336

▶ **CONTEMPORARY ISSUES IN ORGANIZATIONAL ETHICS 12.1**
Cultural Appropriation: When Does Borrowing Become Exploitation? — 358

INTRODUCTION
Making the Case for Studying Organizational Ethics

Figure 0.1

Source: Dilbert cartoon, July 25, 2013.

Evidence for the importance of organizational ethics is all around us. Scarcely a day goes by without revelations of a new organizational scandal. We read and hear about ethical failures in every sector of society—business, education, social service, environmental, entertainment, military, medicine, religious, government. Here is just a small sample of the prominent organizations accused of immoral behavior:

- Wells Fargo Bank: creating fake customer accounts, mortgage fraud
- General Motors: failure to correct a defective ignition switch
- National Football League: player misconduct, including DUIs, domestic violence, and murder; disregard for player safety
- KPMG: failure to uncover illegal sales practices and corruption in client firms; collusion with government regulators
- FIFA (soccer's governing body): bribery and corruption
- Sterling Jewelers (Kay and Jared jewelry chains): sexual harassment, gender discrimination

- Trump University: deceptive advertising; overcharging for courses
- National Security Administration (NSA): illegal surveillance of U.S. citizens
- Baylor University: sexual assaults
- Dean Foods: insider trading
- St. Jude Medical: shipping faulty heart defibrillators
- Petrobras (Brazil's national oil company): bribery, money laundering, kickbacks
- United Nations Haitian peacekeeping force: child sexual abuse and rape
- Samsung: influence peddling
- U.S. Department of Veterans Affairs medical system: falsifying wait times for patient care
- Takata: manufacturing faulty airbags
- Volkswagen: circumventing emissions tests
- Fox News: sexual harassment
- Atlanta school system: falsifying student test scores
- Federal Bureau of Alcohol, Tobacco, Firearms and Explosives (ATF): operating a secret slush fund

We all pay a high price for unethical organizational behavior. Offending organizations suffer damaged reputations; declining revenues, earnings, donations, and stock prices; downsizing and bankruptcy; increased regulation; and civil lawsuits and criminal charges. Their members may lose their jobs, see their retirement savings shrink, and end up doing jail time. Outsiders who have a stake or interest in the fallen organization also suffer. For example, patients taking drugs with undesirable side effects face a higher risk of death; neighbors near a polluting manufacturing plant have to live with environmental damage; investors victimized by fraud see their net worth decline; and needy citizens must do without important services when taxpayer funds are wasted. In addition, society as a whole suffers because trust in many of our basic institutions is lost. According to the 2017 Edelman Trust Barometer, there has been a worldwide "implosion of trust." In two-thirds of the countries surveyed, the "distrusters" outnumber the "trusters," with more than half of the respondents saying they don't trust their governments, nongovernmental organizations (NGOs), businesses, and the media to do what is right.[1] Such low trust levels threaten the stability of countries around the world.

Preventing significant harm is one reason why organizational ethics is worthy of your time and attention; the fact that you will constantly be faced with ethical choices is another. As a member of an organization, you will make ethical decisions on nearly a daily basis. Some are obvious, such as whether or not to clock in for a coworker or to lie to customers. Yet even routine decisions involving hiring, accounting, planning, manufacturing, and advertising have an ethical dimension. Take the case of a supermarket produce buyer deciding which fruits and vegetables to sell in her local stores, for instance. She must weigh several ethical considerations when making these determinations. For example, should she stock only organic products? Should she use suppliers who treat their workers poorly? Should local growers be given priority over distant producers even if the cost is higher? Is price or quality a more important consideration? Should she use her bargaining power to take advantage of growers or negotiate agreements that benefit all parties?

Not only will you continually make ethical choices, but those decisions can also determine your success or failure in your career. Technical skills alone are not enough to guarantee you a productive future. For instance, accountants at the now defunct Arthur Andersen accounting firm had all the proper professional certifications. But, to keep their clients happy and to generate consulting revenue, they signed off on fraudulent financial statements at Waste Management, the Baptist Foundation of Arizona, Sunbeam, Enron, and WorldCom. In the end, the company, which was one of the world's largest and most respected accounting firms, failed.[2]

Business ethics professor Lynn Paine argues that moral thinking is "an essential capability for effective managers and organizational leaders."[3] She contrasts moral reasoning, which is concerned with ethical principles and the consequences of choices, with strategic or results-based thinking, which focuses on reaching objectives such as increasing revenue, finding new distributors, or manufacturing products. Though distinct, these two strands of reasoning intertwine. As a manager making strategic choices, you ought to consider important moral principles and weigh potential ethical consequences or outcomes. If you don't, your organization (like Arthur Andersen) may lose the right to operate in a modern society. Conversely, you must be a good strategic thinker to make wise moral decisions. You have to understand marketing, production, and organizational design, for example, to implement your ethical choices.

There's one final reason that you should focus on understanding ethics in organizations—you have a duty to do so. I believe that when we enter organizations as managers, workers, or volunteers, we assume the ethical burden of making them better places. *Organizational Ethics: A Practical Approach* is designed to help us carry out that task. But as we take on that responsibility, we need to clear out some misunderstandings that serve as barriers to ethical change. I call the first of these myths "There's nothing to it." Those who fall victim to this misconception believe that changing ethical performance is easy or that making moral choices is just common sense. They are seriously mistaken. Acting morally can be a tough task, as you've probably discovered when you tried to do the right thing in the face of peer pressure or were punished for telling the truth. At times you will be called upon to put aside your self-interest to meet the needs of others, to stand alone, and to endure criticism. You could risk losing your job because you "aren't a team player" or because you have to bring organizational wrongdoing to the attention of outside authorities (see Chapter 7). Further, ethical decisions are complex and often without any clear answers. They may require choosing between what appear to be two "rights" or two "wrongs."

The second myth is "It won't do any good." This myth comes out of widespread cynicism about organizations and stands at the opposite end of the spectrum from the first misconception. According to this perspective, change is too hard, not too easy. The individual can have little impact on the ethical climate of an organization. Organizations are too complicated and have a life of their own. Even people with high personal moral standards leave their scruples at the door when they go to work. They end up following company dictates, no matter how immoral.

This misconception contains an element of truth. Situational pressures are important determinants of ethical versus unethical behavior. In recognition of that fact, a great deal of this text is devoted to how we can reshape the ethical climates of our groups and organizations. There is little doubt that many of us do act contrary to our personal convictions due to outside pressures. However, this myth overlooks the fact that organizations are the products of choices. Organizations become embroiled in scandals because individuals and groups decide to lie, steal, abuse their positions and power, and cover up crimes. The same members that create and sustain unhealthy practices, values, and structures can develop more productive alternatives.

Granted, your ability to make significant systemwide changes will be limited if you are a college graduate entering your first job. Nevertheless, you do have the power to manage your own behavior, and your coworkers will note how you react to ethical issues. Your influence will likely grow over time, as those with undergraduate and graduate degrees generally end up in management positions.

If you question the ability of one person to make a difference, consider the humble origins of Barack Obama. He was the son of a white mother and African father who abandoned his family. As a child, Obama spent time in both Indonesia and Hawaii, living either with his mother and sister or with his grandparents. He admits experimenting with drugs in high school as he struggled to find his identity. It wasn't until he enrolled in law school that Obama began to emerge as a leader, becoming the editor and then the first African American president of the *Harvard Law Review*. Later he moved to Chicago to become a community organizer and teach constitutional law. He was elected to the Illinois State Senate and then to the U.S. Senate (after first being defeated by a two-to-one margin in a race for a congressional seat). From there he went on to be elected and reelected as the first African American president of the United States.

The third myth is "Too little, too late." Proponents of this view—including some university faculty—argue that our ethical values and standards are set in childhood. Studying ethics in college or on the job is a waste of time if that's the case. If we don't have strong values by the time we are adults, coursework will do little good.

Research doesn't support this argument. Neuroscientists report that brain structures are malleable, which means that we can improve our moral functioning throughout our life-spans.[4] Psychologists have established that moral development, like physical and psychological development, continues beyond childhood.[5] Discussing ethical issues in the classroom does increase moral reasoning abilities all the way through graduate school. Most of us, whatever our stage in life, can point to ways that our views on moral issues like the death penalty, cloning, gay marriage, stem cell research, and recycling have changed over a period of years.

The fourth myth is "It all depends." This myth sometimes comes up at the beginning of ethics courses and workshops. One or more participants point out that ethical standards differ between cultures. They argue that what they will learn about ethics in the upcoming class or training session is of limited use in a global society where the right behavior depends on the cultural setting. They believe that there are no universal moral standards and that we should set aside our particular values to fit into the local culture. Those who adopt this stance are correct in noting that ethical standards vary between cultures. However, as we'll see in Chapter 12, there do appear to be universal moral standards. We shouldn't go along with some local practices, such as bride burning and female circumcision. Further, there are guidelines to help us determine when we should accept or reject local customs.

The fifth myth is labeled "Yes but." Proponents of this view acknowledge that while ethics is important, it is not as important as other topics. They argue that time devoted to studying organizational ethics would be better spent on other subjects (e.g., public administration, management, financing, accounting, entrepreneurship, marketing). They object to offering a stand-alone ethics course. As recent scandals indicate, however, more, not less time, should be spent on moral decision making. An Ethics Resource Center survey found that misconduct is common in the workplace. Forty-one percent of business employees reported observing unethical conduct in the past year (managers were most often the perpetrators), and 26% said the misconduct is ongoing in their organizations.[6] Ethics deserves the same attention as, say, topics focused on the bottom line.

The sixth and final myth I've titled "We can't afford it." The argument here is that adopting high ethical standards is too costly. Adherents believe that ethical organizations can't compete in the modern marketplace. Groups that do the right thing, like refusing to bribe foreign officials to gain contracts, lose out to less scrupulous competitors. Proponents of this view also point out that unethical behavior often goes undetected and that good intentions, by themselves, are no guarantee of organizational success.

There is no doubt that ethical behavior can be costly. Unethical behavior frequently does go unpunished, and careful planning and execution must back lofty goals. However, there is evidence that ignoring ethics is costlier than pursuing ethics. Business ethicists report that, more often than not, it pays to be ethical. High moral standards and outstanding performance often go hand in hand. Many ethical strategies and actions—empowering employees, creating a sense of shared mission and values, demonstrating concern, truth telling, rewarding moral behavior—can improve employee commitment and productivity. The productivity of the entire organization improves as a result. In addition, there is evidence that organizations that strive to be good citizens are frequently (but not always) more successful. Winners of the prestigious Baldrige Performance Excellence award, for instance, must demonstrate ethical and social responsibility. Companies adopting the Dow Jones Sustainability Index (DJSI) standards for social and environmental performance reported a higher gross profit margin and higher return on investment than similar non-DJSI firms.[7]

LOOKING AHEAD

This version of *Organizational Ethics: A Practical Approach* incorporates substantive changes from previous editions. Material on ethical competency has been moved to Chapter 1. Separate chapters on ethical leadership and followership are combined into Chapter 7, which now comes before the discussion of ethical group performance. A new feature titled "Contemporary Issues in Organizational Ethics" has been added to every chapter. This box highlights special topics, trends, and controversies in the field. Half of the previous case studies have been replaced, and many of those that remain have been updated to reflect the latest developments. New cases deal with computer hacking, fake news, Uber, the Barnum and Bailey Circus, Confederate monuments, Morning Star, Wells Fargo, Goldman Sachs, Theranos, the EpiPen, the University of Missouri, and Baylor University. Several self-assessments have been replaced with new instruments. Material on corporate social activism, consumer boycotts, framing, redefining the followership role, polythink, self-disclosure, universal dilemmas, and other topics has been added.

The fourth edition also retains several features found in earlier editions. First, as the title suggests, this is a book about the practice of ethics in all sorts of organizations (not just businesses). Second, there are plenty of opportunities for the application of concepts through practical suggestions and chapter-end projects. Third, the text retains its interdisciplinary focus. In recent years, a significant number of social scientists have begun to examine ethics in the organizational setting. I cite findings from the fields of management, moral psychology, education, communication, neuroscience, marketing, human resources, organizational behavior, accounting, finance, and social psychology in addition to philosophy. This research is cited in the notes as well as in the comprehensive reference section at the end of the book.

Fourth, I emphasize self-examination and reflection. There are two self-assessments in each chapter. Fifth, my goal is to write in a reader-friendly style to make the discussion of ethics less intimidating. Sixth, I don't hesitate to reveal my biases. You are likely to take issue with some of my conclusions. I hope you do. Discussion and dialogue are essential to the learning process.

Seventh, *Organizational Ethics: A Practical Approach* is organized around levels or concentric circles of organizational behavior as depicted in Figure 0.2, starting with the individual and then moving outward. However, in practice, these levels are permeable, as reflected by the dotted lines that separate them. Each level influences, and is influenced by, the other levels. A dishonest employee, for example, can undermine interpersonal communication, promote defective group decision making, and help create an unethical organizational culture. Conversely, a corrupt organization can corrupt otherwise honest groups and individuals. The organization and its members operate in a global society. Cultural values and practices shape the ethical behavior of organizations and the people that inhabit them. At the same time, organizations can help reshape the values of the larger society. Each level is covered separately in the pages to come, but don't lose sight of their interdependence.

Part I, "Practicing Personal Ethics in the Organization," examines the skills and knowledge we need to function as ethical organizational members. Many of the concepts introduced in this section play an important role in the later sections of the text. Chapter 1 describes ethical competencies and important ethical perspectives. Chapter 2 surveys personal moral development, including character development. Chapter 3 describes moral reasoning and intuition as well as decision-making processes and formats. Part II, "Practicing Interpersonal Ethics in the Organization," looks at the moral issues raised by our connections to other organizational members. Chapter 4 outlines an ethical framework for interpersonal communication. Chapter 5 addresses questions of power and influence in organizational settings. Chapter 6 examines the practice of ethical conflict management and negotiation, providing strategies for dealing with aggression and sexual harassment. Part III, "Practicing Leadership, Followership, and Group Ethics," focuses on the ethical dilemmas that are part and parcel of leadership and followership (Chapter 7) as well as organizational groups and teams (Chapter 8). Part IV, "Practicing Ethics in Organizational Systems," examines organizations as integrated units. Chapter 9 looks at the components of ethical organizational culture and cultural change efforts. Chapter 10 identifies ethical issues that arise when carrying out critical organizational functions—marketing, finance and accounting, and human resources. Chapter 11 discusses tactics for promoting corporate citizenship. Chapter 12 addresses the challenges of practicing ethics in an increasingly global society.

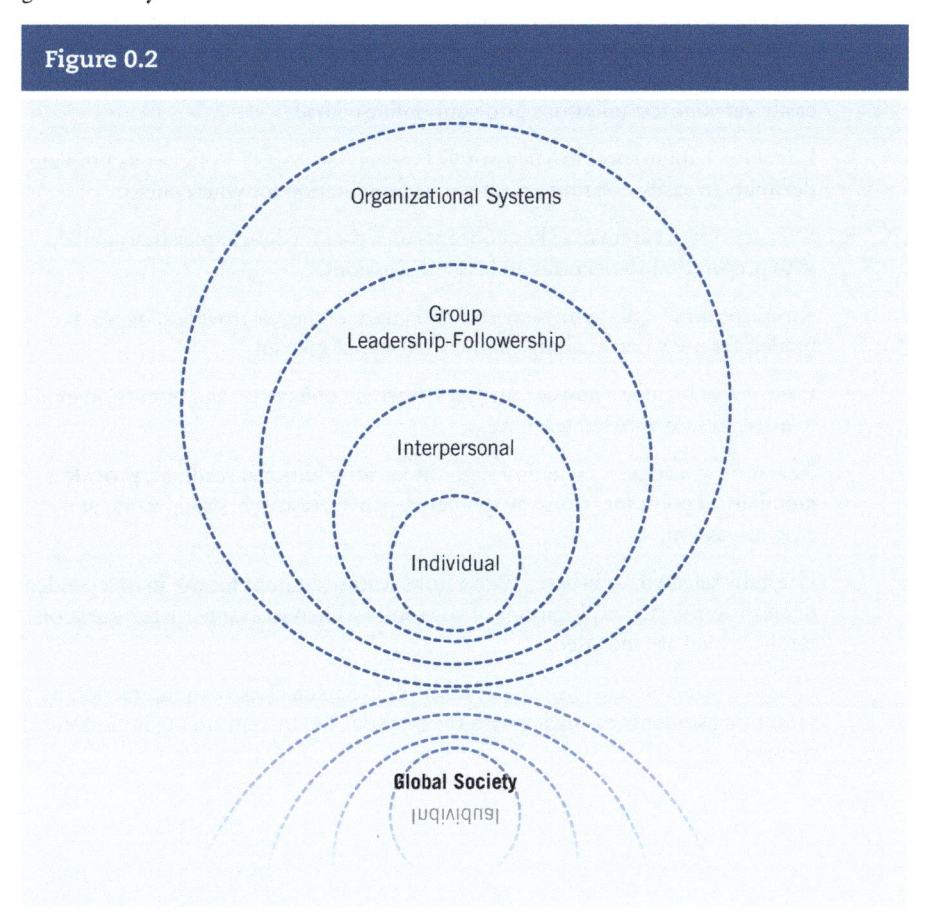

Figure 0.2

Organizational Systems

Group
Leadership-Followership

Interpersonal

Individual

Global Society

DIGITAL RESOURCES

SAGE Study Site for Instructors

A password-protected instructor resource site at **edge.sagepub.com/johnson4e** supports teaching with high quality content to help in creating a rich learning environment for students. The SAGE edge site for this book includes the following instructor resources:

- A **Microsoft® Word® test bank** is available containing multiple choice, true/false, and essay questions for each chapter. The test bank provides you with a diverse range of pre-written options as well as the opportunity for editing any question and/or inserting your own personalized questions to effectively assess students' progress and understanding.

- An **ExamView electronic test bank** is available and can be used on PCs. The test bank contains multiple choice, true/false and essay questions for each chapter and provides you with a diverse range of pre-written options as well as the opportunity for editing any question and/or inserting your own personalized questions to effectively assess students' progress and understanding. ExamView is also compatible with many popular learning management systems so you can easily get your test questions into your online course.

- Editable, chapter-specific Microsoft® **PowerPoint® slides** offer you complete flexibility in easily creating a multimedia presentation for your course.

- **Lecture notes** summarize key concepts on a chapter-by-chapter basis to help with preparation for lectures and class discussions.

- **Sample course syllabi** for semester and quarter courses provide suggested models for use when creating the syllabi for your courses.

- **Case notes** include synopses, analyses, learning objectives, and discussion guides to assist with case-based teaching.

- **Teaching strategies,** including suggestions for additional readings, provide a jumping-off point for course assignments, papers, research, group work, and class discussion.

- Carefully selected, web-based **video links** feature content for use in independent or classroom-based explorations of key topics. When relevant, related questions for discussion are included.

- **Chapter-specific discussion questions** help launch classroom interaction by prompting students to engage with the material and by reinforcing important content.

ACKNOWLEDGMENTS

Writing this text would have been impossible without assistance at every stage of the project. Rob Bohall and other reference librarians helped me gather information. Students enrolled in my undergraduate and graduate business ethics classes were the first to try out cases, self-assessments, and other chapter material. Colleagues in the College of Business answered my questions on topics ranging from accounting and economics to marketing and corporate social responsibility. Colleagues around the university have given me a greater appreciation of what it means to live in an ethical community.

Several reviewers offered helpful critiques on the fourth edition of this text. These reviewers are Denise Cumberland, University of Louisville; Joe Gerard, West New England University; Glen E. Chapius, Saint Charles Community College; Laura Gow-Hogge, Eastern Oregon University; John Tichenour, Stetson University; Amy Jordan, Loyola University Chicago; Lynn Tovar, Lewis University; Joel Mackey, University of San Francisco; Robert Bass, Thomas Edison State University; Kathryn Woods, Austin Peay State University; and Pam Meyers, University of Louisiana at Lafayette. I have incorporated their insights whenever possible into this revision. The editorial and production staff at SAGE skillfully guided me through the final publication stages.

I am grateful to all the individuals and groups named above. Thanks, too, to my wife, Mary, who is all too aware of the demands that writing makes on my time but supports my efforts nonetheless.

Finally, I want to acknowledge the ethics scholars whose research and analysis provide the foundation of this book. Their ongoing efforts make me optimistic about continued progress in the study and practice of organizational ethics.

ABOUT THE AUTHOR

Craig E. Johnson (PhD, University of Denver) is professor emeritus of leadership studies at George Fox University, Newberg, Oregon, where he taught undergraduate and graduate courses in leadership, ethics, and management. During his time at the university, he served as founding director of the George Fox Doctor of Business Administration program and chair of the Department of Communication Arts. Johnson continues to teach part time in the college's Doctor of Business Administration program and served as chair of the International Leadership Association's Ethics Learning Community. He is the author of *Meeting the Ethical Challenges of Leadership* (also published by SAGE) and coauthor, with Michael Z. Hackman, of *Leadership: A Communication Perspective*. He has published research findings, instructional ideas, and book reviews in the *Journal of Leadership Studies*, the *Journal of Leadership and Organizational Studies*, the *Journal of Leadership Education*, the *Academy of Management Learning and Education*, the *International Leadership Journal*, *Communication Quarterly*, *Communication Reports*, and other journals. When not teaching or writing, he enjoys volunteering, working out, reading, fly-fishing, watching sports, and spending time with family.

PART ONE

PRACTICING PERSONAL ETHICS IN THE ORGANIZATION

CHAPTER ONE

ETHICAL COMPETENCIES AND PERSPECTIVES

Chapter Preview

Developing Ethical Competencies
Defining Organizational Ethics
Ethical Perspectives
    Utilitarianism: Do the Greatest Good for the Greatest Number
    Kant's Categorical Imperative: Do What's Right Despite the Consequences
    Rawls's Justice as Fairness: Balancing Freedom and Equality
    Aristotelian Ethics: Live Well
    Confucianism: Building Healthy Relationships
    Altruism: Concern for Others
Chapter Takeaways
Application Projects

Before we can raise the ethical performance of ourselves and our organizations, we need to be equipped for the task. In this first section of the text we'll focus on the knowledge and tools we need to make better ethical decisions ourselves while encouraging others to do the same. This chapter introduces ethical competencies and perspectives as well as an overview of organizational ethics. Chapter 2 addresses the components of personal moral development. Chapter 3 examines how to make and follow through on moral choices.

DEVELOPING ETHICAL COMPETENCIES

For the study of organizational ethics to make a positive difference to us, to our organizations, and to society as a whole, we must put our knowledge to work. That calls for an applied or practical approach. A practical approach to organizational ethics is founded on the premise that we can develop our ethical expertise or competency just as we develop our abilities to manage, do cost accounting, and oversee operations.

University of Notre Dame psychologist Darcia Narvaez argues that we can master the knowledge and skills that can help us behave more like moral experts. She points

SELF-ASSESSMENT 1.1

Attitudes Toward Business (and Organizational) Ethics

Instructions

Reflect on the following statements. Indicate your position regarding each by writing a number in the blank before each statement.

1 = Strongly disagree 2 = Disagree 3 = Not sure
4 = Agree 5 = Strongly agree

1. The only moral of business is making money.
2. Act according to the law, and you can't go wrong morally.
3. Moral values are irrelevant to the business world.
4. The lack of public confidence in the ethics of businesspeople is *not* justified.
5. As a consumer making an auto insurance claim, I try to get as much as possible regardless of the extent of the damage.
6. When shopping at the supermarket, it is appropriate to switch price tags on packages.
7. As an employee, I take office supplies home; it doesn't hurt anyone.
8. I view sick days as vacation days that I deserve.
9. In my grocery store every week, I raise the price of a certain product and mark it "on sale." There is nothing wrong with doing this.
10. The business world has its own rules.
11. True morality is first and foremost self-interested.
12. You should *not* consume more than you produce.

Scoring

If possible, have a classmate, friend, or colleague take this questionnaire and compare your ratings on each item. Explain your responses. Take the assessment again after completing the text and course. Compare your before and after answers and determine how much they have changed and why.

Source: Adapted from Preble and Reichel (1988), pp. 947–948. Used by permission.

out that ethical authorities, like experts in other fields, think differently than novices.[1] First, they know more about the ethical domain. Their networks of moral knowledge are more developed and connected than those of beginners. They note commonalities and differences, are more sensitive to moral cues, and understand the moral standards of the culture and group.[2] Second, they see the world differently than novices. While beginners are often overwhelmed by new data, those with expertise can quickly identify and act on the relevant information. They are able to "think about their thinking" (demonstrate metacognitive ability), knowing what moral knowledge to apply in a particular situation. Morally mature individuals also understand their personal moral standards and use their self-understanding to evaluate their options (e.g., "is this action consistent with my image of myself?") Third, experts have different skill sets. They are better able to define the moral problem and then match the new dilemma with previous ethical problems they have encountered. "Unlike novices," Narvaez says, "they know *what* information to access, *which* procedures to apply, *how* to apply them, and *when* it is appropriate."[3] As a result, they make better moral decisions faster, sometimes even automatically.

Experts become expert by learning in situations that reward the behaviors that lead to success in that domain, building on the knowledge of previous generations and putting forth sustained effort. A professional violinist, for example, spends years taking lessons, completing classes in music theory, practicing hours daily, and performing in recitals and concerts. You must follow similar strategies if you want to become less of an ethical novice and more of an ethical expert. Learn in a well-structured environment where correct behaviors are rewarded and where you can interact with mentors and receive feedback and coaching. Master both moral theory and skills. Familiarize yourself with how previous experts have dealt with moral problems and why some choices are better than others. Gain experience so that you'll not only get better at solving ethical problems but can better explain your choices. Finally, practice, practice, practice. You will have to put in the necessary time and concentrated effort. Ethical progress takes hours of practice wrestling with moral dilemmas. To get started, complete Self-Assessment 1.1 to determine how you feel about ethical behavior in business and other organizational settings.

Organizational Ethics: A Practical Approach incorporates all of the developmental components outlined above. The book is designed for use in a college or university classroom where ethical knowledge and behaviors are encouraged and professors and classmates provide feedback. You will be introduced to the insights of ethical experts both past and present and see how some behaviors are more effective than others. The text supplies you with plenty of opportunities to practice your problem-solving abilities and to defend your decisions. You'll be provided with lists of steps or actions you and your organization can take. Cases provide opportunities to apply what you've read, and the self-assessments in each chapter measure your (or your leader's or organization's) performance on an important behavior, skill, or concept. The Takeaways sections at the end of each chapter review important concepts and their implications. The Application Projects sections ask you to engage further reflection, analysis, and implementation. You can complete some of these activities on your own; others require group participation.

Scholars describe a variety of competencies we need to develop if we hope to become more expert. Daniel Menzel, former president of the American Society of Public Administration, identifies five key competencies for those serving in government, which also apply to other professions. These can serve as one yardstick for measuring your ethical progress. First, be committed to high standards of personal and professional behavior. Second, understand the ethics codes and laws that relate to your profession and organization. Third, demonstrate your ability to engage in ethical reasoning when confronted with moral dilemmas. Fourth, identify and then act on important professional values. Fifth, be committed to promoting ethical practices and behaviors in your organization.[4]

Wright State University business ethics professor emeritus Joseph Petrick outlines three types of competencies that can serve as another yardstick by which to measure your ethical development. *Cognitive decision-making competence* means demonstrating "abilities to recognize, understand, analyze, and make responsible judgments about moral matters" in business and other organizational contexts.[5] *Affective prebehavioral disposition competence* encompasses ethical emotions, attitudes, and motivations. Becoming more of an expert in organizational ethics should not only improve your problem-solving abilities but also prompt you to develop your character and increase your motivation to follow through on your choices. *Context management competence* involves the managerial skills needed to build ethical organizational environments. You need to help create ethical settings that encourage members to demonstrate their cognitive and affective competence. You should also be able to encourage your organizations to meet the needs of stakeholders, protect the environment, honor the rights of overseas workers, and so on.

DEFINING ORGANIZATIONAL ETHICS

The first step toward expert mastery is defining the field of study. In the case of organizational ethics, that means identifying the unique characteristics of organizations and determining what sets ethical choices and actions apart from other forms of decision making and behavior. Organizations consist of three or more people engaged in coordinated action in pursuit of a common purpose or goal. They function as socially constructed, structured, interconnected systems.[6] Let's look at the elements of this definition in more detail.

> *Three or more people.* The presence of three or more persons sets the stage for the formation of an organization, allowing for the development of structure, coalitions, shared meanings, and so forth. Organizational membership is generally voluntary, which sets organizations apart from families. We choose which organizations we want to join; we don't have a choice about which family we are born into. Organizations are generally more stable than small groups due to substitution of personnel. Members leave—retire, quit, pass away—but the organization continues as new people take their places.
>
> *Coordination of activities.* Completion of any complex project, whether it be making a film, repairing a highway, or starting a health club, requires the coordination of people and units that carry out specialized tasks. Coordination, in turn, produces synergy. Synergy describes the way in which organizations are greater than the sum of their parts. The achievements of an organization as a whole are much greater than could be reached by a collection of individuals working on their own.
>
> *Goal directed.* Organizations don't form by chance. Instead, they are intentionally formed to meet specific needs and to serve specific purposes like educating elementary school children, developing and selling automobiles, passing legislation, and combating crime. These objectives focus the collective energies of members.
>
> *Socially constructed.* Organizations are human creations shaped through the collective decisions and actions of their members. These creations then shape

the thoughts and behaviors of their makers. For example, those who make a policy, such as one forbidding romantic relationships between superiors and subordinates, are bound by this rule. The socially constructed nature of organizations is particularly apparent in their cultures. No two organizations are exactly alike. Every group has its unique way of seeing the world and culture developed through shared meaning and experiences. New employees often undergo a form of culture shock as they move into an organization with a different language, customs, and attitudes about work and people.

Structured interaction. The word *organization* frequently conjures up images of organizational charts, policy manuals, discipline policies, articles of incorporation, and other official documents. Bureaucratic organizations in particular do their best to leave nothing to chance, spelling out everything from how to apply for sick leave and retirement benefits to the size of office cubicles. They also carefully detail how tasks like processing auto insurance payments and registering students are to be managed. However, some of the most important elements of structure aren't formalized. Communication scholars, for instance, study communication networks, which are patterns of messages sent between individuals and organizational units. These networks may have little resemblance to the flow of information outlined in the official organizational chart.

Roles and hierarchy are two particularly important aspects of structure. Roles are sets of expectations, responsibilities, and duties associated with organizational positions. Failure to meet role expectations generates sanctions in the form of criticism, reprimands, lower wages, and termination. Hierarchy grants certain individuals and groups more power, status, and privileges, and there are one or more centers of power that review and direct organizational performance. Differences in status and power are part of every interaction between organizational members. The degree of structure helps set organizations apart from groups. Groups also have three or more members, may be goal directed, and delegate various roles. Nonetheless, they lack many of the formal elements—written policies, job descriptions, job titles—common to organizations.

Interconnectedness (systems). Organizations function as interconnected systems. Consider all the departments involved in the introduction of a new product, for instance: research and development, design, purchasing, production, marketing, finance, human resources. The success of a product introduction depends on each division doing its part. Marketing can do an effective job of promoting the new item, but first purchasing must secure the necessary components at the right cost and production must meet manufacturing deadlines. Because organizations function as systems, a change in any one component will influence all the others. A new accounting system, for example, will change the way that every department records expenses, books revenue, and determines profits.

Ethics involves judgments about the rightness or wrongness of human behavior. To illustrate this point, I've collected definitions of the term from a variety of sources. Notice how each highlights the evaluative nature of ethical study and practice.

"Ethics is concerned with how we should live our lives. It focuses on questions about what is right or wrong, fair or unfair, caring or uncaring, good or bad, responsible or irresponsible, and the like."[7]

"Ethics deals with individual character and with the moral rules that govern and limit our conduct. It investigates questions of right and wrong, fairness and unfairness, good and bad, duty and obligation, and justice and injustice, as well as moral responsibility and the values that should guide our actions."[8]

". . . the principles, norms, and standards of conduct governing an individual or group."[9]

"Ethical judgments focus . . . on degrees of rightness and wrongness, virtue and vice, and obligation in human behavior."[10]

"Ethics refers to the rules or principles that define right and wrong conduct."[11]

"Ethics basically refers to issues of right, wrong, fairness, and justice."[12]

"[An ethical act or decision] is something judged as proper or acceptable based on some standard of right and wrong."[13]

There are some scholars who make a distinction between ethics and morals, drawing in part on the origins of each word.[14] *Ethics* comes from the Greek term *ethos*, which refers to "custom" or "usage" or "character." *Moral* is derived from the Latin *mos* or *moris*, which refers to "conduct" or "way of life." From this perspective, ethics has to do with the systematic study of general principles of right and wrong behavior. Morality and morals, on the other hand, describe specific, culturally transmitted standards of right and wrong ("Thou shalt not steal"; "Treat your elders with respect"). Maintaining this distinction is becoming more difficult, however. Both ethics and morality involve decisions about right and wrong. When we make such evaluations, we draw upon universal principles as well as upon our cultural standards. Further, scholars from a number of fields appear to use the terms *ethics* and *morals* interchangeably. Philosophers interested in ethics study moral philosophy, for example, while psychologists examine moral reasoning and educators promote moral education. For these reasons, I will use the terms synonymously in the remainder of this text. You, of course, are free to disagree. You may want to engage in a class discussion about whether these two concepts should be integrated or treated separately.

Organizational ethics applies moral standards and principles to the organizational context. Organizations are well suited for ethical analysis because, as we've seen, they are the products of conscious, goal-directed behavior. Whatever form they take (small, family-owned restaurants; community-based nonprofits; large multinational corporations; international relief agencies), all employers share the common features described above. These shared elements mean that members in every type of organization face some common ethical temptations and dilemmas. Further, a common body of theory, principles, strategies, and skills can be used to address these moral challenges.

I am convinced there is much to be gained in looking at ethical problems and solutions across organizational boundaries. No matter what particular type of organization we belong to, we can learn from the experiences of others in different settings. Knowing how corporate managers communicate important values, for instance, can be useful to those of us working in the federal government. (For a closer look at some of the ethical issues facing federal employees, see Case Study 1.1.) If we work in business, we can gain important insights into how to empower employees from watching how nonprofit executives recruit and motivate volunteers.

ETHICAL PERSPECTIVES

Ethical theories are critical to developing our ethical competence. Ethical perspectives are tools that help us identify and define problems, force us to think systematically, encourage us to view issues from many different vantage points, and provide us with decision-making guidelines. We'll return to them again and again throughout the rest of this text. I'll briefly summarize each perspective below and then offer an evaluation based on the theory's advantages and disadvantages.

Resist the temptation to choose your favorite approach and ignore the rest. Use a variety of theories when possible. Applying all six approaches to the same problem (practicing ethical pluralism) is a good way to generate new insights about the issue. You can discover the value of ethical pluralism by using each theory to analyze Case Studies 1.2 and 1.3 at the end of the chapter (see Application Project 9). You may find that some perspectives are more suited to these problems than others. Combining insights from more than one theory might help you come up with a better solution. At the very least, drawing from several perspectives should give you more confidence in your choice and better prepare you to defend your conclusions.

Utilitarianism: Do the Greatest Good for the Greatest Number

Many people weigh the advantages and disadvantages of alternatives when making significant decisions. They create mental balance sheets listing the pluses and minuses of each course of action. When it's a particularly important choice, such as deciding which job offer to accept or where to earn a graduate degree, they may commit their lists to paper to make it easier to identify the relative merits of their options.

Utilitarianism is based on the premise that our ethical choices, like other types of decisions, should be based on their outcomes.[15] It is the best-known example of *consequentialism*, a branch of moral philosophy that argues that the rightness or wrongness of an action is dependent on its consequences. The goal is to maximize the good effects or outcomes of decisions. English philosophers and reformers Jeremy Bentham (1748–1832) and John Stuart Mill (1806–1873) believed that the best decisions (1) generate the most benefits relative to their disadvantages, and (2) benefit the largest number of people. In other words, utilitarianism is attempting to do the greatest good for the greatest number of people. *Utility* can be defined as what is best in a specific case (act utilitarianism) or as what is generally preferred in most contexts (rule utilitarianism). We can decide, for example, that telling a specific lie is justified in one situation (to protect a trade secret) but, as a general rule, believe that lying is wrong because it causes more harm than good.

Utilitarians consider both short- and long-term consequences when making ethical determinations. If the immediate benefits of a decision don't outweigh its possible future costs, this alternative is rejected. However, if the immediate good is sure and the future good is uncertain, decision makers generally select the option that produces the short-term benefit. Utilitarians are also more concerned about the ratio of harm to benefit than the absolute amount of happiness or unhappiness produced by a choice. In other words, a decision that produces a great amount of good but an equal amount of harm would be rejected in favor of an alternative that produces a moderate amount of good at very little cost. Further, the utilitarian decision maker keeps her or his own interests in mind but gives them no more weight than anyone else's.

Making a choice according to utilitarian principles is a three-step process. First, identify all the possible courses of action. Second, estimate the direct as well as the indirect costs and benefits for each option. Finally, select the alternative that produces the greatest amount of good based on the cost-benefit ratios generated in step two. Government officials frequently follow this process when deciding whether to impose or loosen regulations. Take decisions about regulating genetically modified foods (GMOs), for example. The benefits of GMOs include increasing the food supply (thus helping to reduce world hunger), improving quality and taste, making crops more disease resistant, and reducing the need for pesticides and herbicides. Costs include introducing allergens and toxins, increased human resistance to antibiotics, lower nutrient content, and creation of herbicide-resistant "super weeds." After balancing the costs and benefits, the United States has approved the use of genetically modified food without labeling (60% to 70% of processed foods in U.S. grocery stores have genetically modified ingredients). The European Union, on the other hand, largely bans their use, arguing that the risks to human health and the environment are too great.[16]

Evaluation

Few could argue with the ultimate goal of utilitarianism, which is to promote human welfare by maximizing benefits to as many people as possible. We're used to weighing the outcomes of all types of decisions, and the utilitarian decision-making rule covers every conceivable type of choice, which makes it a popular approach to moral reasoning. Utilitarian calculations typically drive public policy decisions, such as where to set speed limits. In fact, Bentham and Mills introduced utilitarianism to provide a rational basis for making political, administrative, and judicial choices, which they felt previously had been based on feelings and irrational prejudices. They campaigned for legal and political reforms, including the creation of a more humane penal system and more rights for women. Utilitarian reasoning is also applied in emergency situations, such as in the wake of earthquakes and tsunamis. In the midst of such widespread devastation, many medical personnel believe they ought to give top priority to those who are most likely to survive. They argue it does little good to spend time with a terminal patient while a person who would benefit from treatment dies.

Despite its popularity, utilitarianism suffers from serious deficiencies, starting with defining and measuring "the greatest good."[17] Economists define utility in monetary terms and use such measures as the gross national product to determine the greatest benefit. But the theory's originators, Bentham and Mills, define the greatest good as the total amount of happiness or pleasure, abstract concepts that are hard to quantify. Sometimes identifying possible consequences can be difficult or impossible as well. Many different groups may be affected, unforeseen consequences may develop, and so on. Even when consequences are clear, evaluating their relative merits can be challenging. Being objective is difficult because we humans tend to downplay long-term risks in favor of immediate rewards and to favor ourselves when making decisions.

Due to the difficulty of identifying and evaluating potential costs and benefits, utilitarian decision makers may reach different conclusions when faced with the same dilemma. Not all medical experts agree on how to prioritize patients for medical treatment in emergency situations; the sickest patients might survive, for example. During Hurricane Katrina, medical personnel at one New Orleans hospital were accused of mislabeling patients as "Do not resuscitate" or terminal. As the hospital was emptied, a doctor and two nurses then allegedly engaged in mercy killing by injecting these DNR patients an overdose of morphine.[18] (Case Study 1.2, "National Security or Computer Security?" provides another example of how groups come to competing conclusions when faced with the same moral issue.) Ironically, one of the greatest strengths of utilitarian theory—its concern for collective human welfare—is also one of its greatest weaknesses. In focusing on what's best for the group as a whole, utilitarianism discounts the worth of the individual. The needs of the person are subjugated to the needs of the group or organization. This type of reasoning can justify all kinds of abuse. For example, a number of employees accuse Walmart of refusing to accept medical absences to cut labor costs for the greater good of the company.[19] Then, too, by focusing solely on consequences, utilitarianism seems to say that the ends justify the means. Most of us are convinced that there are certain principles—justice, freedom, integrity—that should never be violated.

Kant's Categorical Imperative:
Do What's Right Despite the Consequences

Like the Utilitarians, German philosopher Immanuel Kant (1724–1804) developed a simple set of rules that could be applied to every type of ethical decision. However, he reached a very different conclusion about what those principles should be. Kant argued that moral duties or imperatives are *categorical*—they should be obeyed without exception. Individuals should do what is morally right no matter what the consequences are.[20] His approach to moral reasoning falls under the category of deontological ethics. Deontological ethicists argue that we ought to make choices based on our duty to follow universal truths, which we sense intuitively or identify through reason (*deon* is the Greek word for "duty"). Moral acts arise out of our will or intention to follow our duty, not in response to circumstances. Based on this criterion, an electric utility that is forced into reducing its rates is not acting morally; a utility that lowers its rates to help its customers is.

According to Kant, "what is right for one is right for all." We need to ask ourselves if the principle we are following is one that we could logically conclude should be made into a universal law. Based on this reasoning, certain behaviors, like honoring our commitments and being kind, are always right. Other acts, like cheating and murder, are always wrong. Kant cited borrowing money that we never intend to repay as one behavior that violates what he called the *categorical imperative*. If enough people made such false promises, the banking industry would break down because lenders would refuse to provide funds.[21] That's what happened during the collapse of the U.S. housing market. A number of borrowers never intended to pay their home loans back, which helped generate a wave of foreclosures. Home loans then became much harder to get. Deliberate idleness is another violation of Kant's principles, because no one would exercise his or her talents in a culture where everyone sought to rest and enjoy themselves.

Kant also argued for the importance of "treating humanity as an end," or respect for persons, which has become one of the foundational principles of Western moral philosophy. Others can help us reach our objectives, but they should never be considered solely as a means to an end. We should, instead, respect and encourage the capacity of others to choose for themselves. It is wrong, under this standard, for companies to expose manufacturing workers to hazardous chemicals without their consent or knowledge. Managers shouldn't coerce or threaten employees, because such tactics violate freedom of choice. Coworkers who refuse to help one another are behaving unethically because ignoring the needs of others limits their options.

Respect for persons underlies the notion of moral rights. Fundamental moral or human rights are granted to individuals based solely on their status as persons. Such rights protect the inherent dignity of every individual regardless of culture or social or economic background. Rights violations are unethical because they are disrespectful and deny human value and potential. The rights to life, free speech, and religious affiliation are universal (always available to everyone everywhere), equal (no one has a greater right to free speech than anyone else, for instance), and cannot be given up or taken away.[22] (I provide one list of universal human rights in Chapter 12.)

Evaluation

Kant's imperative is a simple yet powerful ethical tool. Not only is the principle easy to remember, but making sure that we conform to a universal standard should also prevent a number of ethical miscues. Emphasis on duty builds moral courage. Those driven by the conviction that certain behaviors are either right or wrong no matter the situation are more likely to blow the whistle on unethical behavior (see Chapter 8), to resist group pressure to compromise personal ethical standards, to follow through on their choices (see Chapter 3), and so on. Recognizing that people are intrinsically valuable is another significant ethical principle. This standard encourages us to protect the rights of employees, to act courteously, to demonstrate concern for others, and to share information. At the same time, it condemns deceptive and coercive tactics.

Critiques of Kant's system of reasoning often center on his assertion that there are universal principles that should be followed in every situation. In almost every case, we can think of exceptions. For instance, many of us agree that killing is wrong yet support capital punishment for serial murderers. We value our privacy but routinely provide confidential information to secure car loans and to order products online. Then, too, how do we account for those who honestly believe they are doing the right thing even when they are engaged in evil? "Consistent Nazis" were convinced that killing Jews was morally right. They wanted their fellow Germans to engage in this behavior; they did what they perceived to be their duty.

Conflicting duties also pose a challenge to deontological thinking. Complex ethical dilemmas often involve competing obligations. For example, we should be loyal both to our bosses and to our coworkers. Yet being loyal to a supervisor may mean breaking loyalty with peers, such as when a supervisor asks us to reveal the source of a complaint when we've promised to keep the identity of that coworker secret. How do we determine which duty has priority? Kant's imperative offers little guidance in such situations.

Rawls's Justice as Fairness:
Balancing Freedom and Equality

Limited organizational resources make conflicts inevitable. There are never enough jobs, raises, corner offices, travel funds, laptop computers, iPads, and other benefits to go around. As a result, disputes arise over how to distribute these goods. Departments battle over the relative size of their budgets, for example, and employees compete for performance bonuses, promotions, and job titles. Participants in these conflicts often complain that they have been the victims of discrimination or favoritism.

Over the last third of the 20th century, Harvard philosopher John Rawls developed a set of guidelines for justly resolving disputes like these that involve the distribution of resources.[23] His principles are designed to foster cooperation in democracies. In democratic societies, all citizens are free and equal before the law. However, at the same time, citizens are unequal because they vary in status, economic standing, talents, and abilities. Rawls's standards honor individual freedom—the foundation of democratic cultures—but also encourage more equitable distribution of societal benefits. Rawls offered a political theory focused on the underlying structure of society as a whole. Nevertheless, I hope to demonstrate that his principles also apply to organizations and institutions that function within this societal framework.

Rawls rejected the use of utilitarian principles to allocate resources. He believed that individuals have rights that should never be violated no matter what the outcome. In addition, he asserted that seeking the greatest good for the greatest number can seriously disadvantage particular groups and individuals. This can be seen in decisions to outsource goods and services to independent contractors. Outsourcing reduces costs and helps firms stay competitive. Remaining employees enjoy greater job security, but some employees lose their jobs to outsiders.

As an alternative to basing decisions on cost-benefit ratios, Rawls argued that we should follow these two principles of justice:[24]

> ***Principle 1:*** Each person has an equal right to the same basic liberties that are compatible with similar liberties for all.

> ***Principle 2:*** Social and economic inequalities are to satisfy two conditions: (a) they are to be attached to offices and positions open to all under conditions of fair equality of opportunity, and (b) they are to be to the greatest benefit of the least advantaged members of society.

The first principle, the *principle of equal liberty*, has priority. It states that certain rights are protected and must be equally applied to all. These liberties include the right to vote, freedom of speech and thought, freedom to own personal property, and freedom from arbitrary arrest. Invading employee privacy and pressuring managers to contribute to particular political candidates would be unethical according to this standard. So would failing to honor contracts, since such behavior would reduce our freedom to enter into agreements for fear of being defrauded.

Principle 2a, the *equal opportunity principle*, asserts that everyone should have the same chance to qualify for offices and jobs. Job discrimination based on race, gender, or ethnic origin is forbidden. Further, all citizens ought to have access to the training and education needed to prepare for these positions. Principle 2b, the *difference principle*, recognizes that inequalities exist but that priority should be given to meeting the needs of the disadvantaged.

Rawls introduced the concept of the *veil of ignorance* to support his claim that these principles should guide decision making in democratic societies like Great Britain, the United States, and Canada. Imagine, he said, a group of people who are asked to come up with a set of guidelines that will govern their interactions. Group members are ignorant of their own characteristics or societal position—they may be privileged or poor, employed or unemployed, healthy or sick, and so on. Faced with such uncertainty, these individuals will likely base their choices on the *maximin rule*. This rule states that the best option is the one whose worst outcome is better than the worst outcomes of all the other options. Or, to put it another way, the best choice is the one that guarantees everyone a minimum level of benefits.

Rawls argued that individuals standing behind the veil of ignorance would adopt his moral guidelines because they would ensure the best outcomes even in the worst of circumstances. Citizens would select (1) equal liberty, because they would be guaranteed freedom even if they occupied the lowest rungs of society; (2) equal opportunity, because if they turned out to be the most talented societal members, they would not be held back by low social standing or lack of opportunity; and (3) the difference principle, because they would want to be sure they were cared for if they ended up disadvantaged.

Evaluation

Rawls became one of the most influential philosophers of his time because he offered a way to reconcile the long-standing tension between individual freedom and social justice. His system for distributing resources and benefits encompasses personal liberty as well as the common good. Individual rights are protected. Moreover, talented, skilled, or fortunate people are free to pursue their goals, but the fruits of their labor must also benefit their less fortunate neighbors. Applying Rawls's principles would have a significant positive impact on the moral behavior of organizations. High achievers would continue to be rewarded for their efforts, but not, as is too often the case, at the expense of their coworkers. All of an organization's members (including those, for example, employed in low-income jobs in the fast food industry) would be guaranteed a minimum level of benefits, such as a living wage and health insurance. Everyone would have equal opportunity for training, promotion, and advancement. The growing gap in compensation between the top and bottom layers of the organization would shrink.

Rawls's theory addresses some of the weaknesses of utilitarianism outlined earlier. In his system, individuals have intrinsic value and are not to be treated as means to some greater end. Certain rights should always be protected. The interests of the organization as a whole do not justify extreme harm to particular groups and individuals.

Stepping behind a veil of ignorance does more than provide a justification for Rawls's model; it can also serve as a useful technique to use when making moral choices. Status and power differences are an integral part of organizational life. Nonetheless, if we can set these inequities aside temporarily, we are likely to make more just decisions. The least advantaged usually benefit when status differences are excluded from the decision-making process. We need to ask ourselves if we are treating everyone fairly or if we are being unduly influenced by someone's position or relationship to us. Classical orchestras provide one example of how factoring out differences can improve the lot of marginalized groups. Orchestras began to hire a much higher percentage of female musicians after they erected screens that prevented judges from seeing the gender of players during auditions.[25]

Rawls's influence has not spared his theory from intense criticism. Skeptics note that the theory's abstractness limits its usefulness. Rawls offered only broad guidelines, which can be interpreted in a number of different ways. Definitions of justice and fairness vary widely, a fact that undermines the usefulness of his principles. What seems fair to one group or individual often appears grossly unjust to others. Take, for instance, programs that reserve a certain percentage of federal contracts for minority contractors. Giving preferential treatment to minorities can be defended based on the equal opportunity and difference principles. Members of these groups claim that they should be favored in the bidding process to redress past discrimination and to achieve equal footing with whites. On the other hand, such policies can be seen as impinging upon the equal-liberty principle because they limit the freedom of Caucasians to pursue their goals. White contractors feel that these requirements unfairly restrict their options. They are denied the opportunity to compete for work based on the criteria of quality and cost.

By trying to reconcile the tension between liberty and equality, Rawls left himself open to attack from advocates of both values. Some complain that he would distribute too much to the have-nots; others believe that his concern for liberty means that he wouldn't give enough. Further, philosophers point out that there is no guarantee that parties who step behind the veil of ignorance would come up with the same set of principles as Rawls. They might not use the maximin rule to guide their decisions. Rather than emphasizing fairness, these individuals might decide to emphasize certain rights. Libertarians, for instance, hold that freedom from coercion is the most important human right. Every individual should be able to produce and sell as he or she chooses, regardless of the impact of his or her business on the poor. Capitalist theorists believe that benefits should be distributed based on the contributions each person makes to the group. They argue that helping out the less advantaged rewards laziness while discouraging productive people from doing their best. Because decision makers may reach different conclusions behind the veil, critics contend that Rawls's guidelines lack moral force and that other approaches to distributing resources are just as valid as the notion of fairness.

Aristotelian Ethics: Live Well

Aristotle (384–322 BC) would appear on any list of the most influential thinkers in history. Here are just some of the topics he wrote about: logic, philosophy, ethics, zoology, biology, chemistry, astronomy, botany, language, rhetoric, psychology, the arts, and politics. One biographer summed up his achievements this way: "He bestrode antiquity like an intellectual colossus. No man before him had contributed so much to learning. No Man [or woman] could hope to rival his achievements."[26] A student of Plato, Aristotle founded a school for young scholars (the Lyceum) in Athens and served as an adviser to Alexander the Great. His surviving works are not in polished book form but consist of collections of lectures and teaching notes.

Bentham, Mills, Kant, Rawls, and most other moral philosophers argue that we make the right choices by following rules or principles. Not so Aristotle. He contends that we will make ethical decisions if we develop character traits or virtues.[27] These virtues are both intellectual (prudence and wisdom that give us insight) and moral (e.g., courage, generosity, justice, wisdom). To make ethical determinations, virtuous people find the mean or middle ground between the extremes of too little (deficit) or too much (excess) in a given context, which some refer to as the "Golden Mean." For instance, the entrepreneur who refuses to invest in any project, fearing loss, is cowardly. But the overoptimistic entrepreneur who ignores risks is foolish. The courageous entrepreneur recognizes the risks but invests when appropriate. Aristotle admits that finding this balance is difficult:

> Hence also it is no easy task to be good. For in everything it is no easy task to find the middle . . . anyone can get angry—that is easy—or give or spend money; but to do this to the right person, to the right extent, at the right time, with the right aim, and in the right way, *that* is not for everyone, nor is it easy; that is why goodness is both rare and laudable and noble.[28]

According to Aristotle, we cannot separate character from action: "Men [and women] become builders by building, and lyre-players by playing the lyre, so too we become just by doing just acts, temperate by doing temperate acts, brave by doing brave acts."[29] Good habits are voluntary routines or practices designed to foster virtuous behavior. Every time we engage in a habit—telling the truth, giving credit to others, giving to the less fortunate—it leaves a trace. Over time, these residual effects become part of our personality, and the habit becomes "second nature." In other words, by doing better, we become better. We also become more skilled in demonstrating the virtue. Practicing self-restraint, for instance, improves the ability to demonstrate self-restraint under pressure. (I'll have more to say about character-building habits in the next chapter.) Conversely, practicing bad habits encourages the development of vices that stunt character development. Lying once makes it easier to lie again, helping to undermine our integrity.

For Aristotle, the exercise of virtues is designed to serve a higher purpose. To describe this purpose, he uses the term *eudemonia*, which has been variously translated as "happiness," "success," and "flourishing." Eudemonia is the ultimate goal in life for which we strive through our actions and choices. We are happiest when living well—effectively using our abilities to achieve our purpose. Aristotle rejects the notion that happiness comes from pleasure—food, wine, entertainment—and is critical of those who pursue wealth solely to purchase these items. In fact, fixating on pleasure puts us at the level of animals. It is our ability to reason and to apply reason to higher goals that sets us apart from other creatures. Aristotle urges us to focus more on goods of the soul that include the mind (knowledge, contemplation) as well as our relationships with others (love, friendship). Because people are social or political in nature, we flourish when working together in community. Good (high-character) individuals create a good society.

Evaluation

Aristotle's enduring popularity can be traced, in large part, to the fact that he addresses some of humankind's most important concerns: What is my purpose in life? What is success? What does it mean to be human? What kind of person do I want to become, and how can I become that person? How can I live my life in the most satisfying manner possible? Modern scholars are still wrestling with these timeless questions. Happiness remains an important topic of investigation, for example, and many researchers and organizations are dedicated to determining what makes people satisfied with their lives. Aristotle's emphasis on the goods of the soul is more relevant than ever in modern materialistic societies that equate wealth with success and are driven by consumer spending on clothing, automobiles, cars, cosmetics, fine dining, and other pleasures. Aristotle contends that flourishing or living well doesn't rest on external goods (though he agreed that we need some of these) but on developing high character and working with others to create a healthy society. He seems to take direct aim at businesspeople who excuse immoral behavior by saying "business is business" and care only about generating profits. Business ethicist Robert Solomon summarized Aristotle's message to businesspeople this way:

> The bottom line of the Aristotelian approach to business ethics is that we have to get away from "bottom line" thinking and conceive of business as an essential part of the good life, living well, getting along with others, having a sense of self-respect, and being part of something one can be proud of.[30]

Virtue ethicists who follow Aristotle's lead recognize that ethical decisions are often made under time pressures in uncertain conditions.[31] Individuals in these situations don't have time to apply rules-based approaches by weighing possible consequences or selecting an abstract guideline to apply. Instead, they respond based on their character. Those with virtuous character will immediately react in ways that benefit themselves, others, and the greater good. They will quickly turn down bribes, reach out to help others, and so on. Character is shaped through repeated actions or habits. Patterns of behavior (good or bad) tend to continue over time and are hard to break.

Those looking for specific guidance from Aristotle will be disappointed. He offers only general thoughts about what it means to "live well," leaving us to define happiness for ourselves. Since Aristotle provides no rules to follow when making ethical choices, we must determine what is right based on our character. Further complicating matters is the fact that the exercise of virtue is determined by the specifics of the situation. Finding the middle ground or mean is difficult (as Aristotle himself points out) and varies between contexts. Individuals will likely disagree as to the correct course of action. What is courageous to one person may appear rash to another.

Aristotle privileges reason as humankind's highest achievement and treats emotion with suspicion. As we'll see in Chapter 3, modern researchers are discovering that feelings play an important role in making wise ethical choices. Finally, it should be noted that some people would never be able to live well according to Aristotle. Certain individuals lack reasoning ability, for example. Others (like many around the world who live on a dollar a day) must put all their efforts into acquiring external goods like food, shelter, and water. They have little time and energy to engage their minds in the reflection and contemplation Aristotle considered so essential to eudemonia.

Confucianism: Building Healthy Relationships

China's emergence as an economic superpower has focused the attention of Western scholars on Chinese culture and thought. Ethicists have been particularly interested in Confucianism. Confucius (551–479 BCE), the son of a low-level official, was born into a turbulent period of Chinese history. Wars, palace coups, and power struggles were common as the ruling Zhou dynasty collapsed into competing states. Confucius wanted to restore order and good government. He believed that the ideal society is based on a series of harmonious, hierarchical relationships (starting in the family and extending all the way up to the pinnacle of government) marked by trust and mutual concern. Ideal citizens are individuals of high character who engage in lifelong learning and always strive to improve their ethical performance. Ideal leaders govern by setting a moral example.[32]

Confucius apparently served a brief period as a government minister but spent most of his life working outside the political system, offering his ideas to various rulers. After his death, a number of his disciples, most notably Mencius, spread his ideas; Confucianism gained a foothold in Korea, Japan, and Vietnam. The philosophy's most important guidebook, *The Analects*, is a collection of the founder's (Master's) sayings. Confucianism was adopted as the official state doctrine of the Han dynasty, but throughout Chinese history Confucian thought has undergone periodic attack, most recently during Mao's Cultural Revolution of the 1970s. However, since that time Confucius has regained his popularity. Some 300 Confucius institutes have been formed in 87 countries. Several highly successful businesses in mainland China, Taiwan, and Korea operate according to Confucian principles, including Weizhan Garment Co., Sinyi Real Estate, financial services conglomerate Ping An Insurance, and electronics giant LG.[33]

Several key components of Confucianism are particularly relevant for modern business and organizational ethics, starting with the philosophy's emphasis on relationships.[34] Confucius argued that humans don't exist in isolation but are social creatures connected to others through networks of relationships. Because organizations consist of webs of relationships, it is critical that these connections be based on trust and benefit all parties. Organizations must also establish relationships with other organizations, as in the case of a firm that moves into a new foreign market. This company must enter into agreements with shippers, suppliers, local distributors, banks, and other business partners in the new country. The firm's expansion plans will fail if its relational partners don't live up to their responsibilities.

Confucianism emphasizes that policies, norms, procedures, and rituals—referred to as etiquette, or *li*—maintain relationships within and between organizations. These practices also prevent ethical misbehavior. It is easier to trust others if we operate under the same guidelines, and we are less likely to cheat or steal if there are clearly stated rules against such activities. (We'll take a closer look at the formal and informal elements of ethical culture in Chapter 9.) However, Confucius was quick to point out that rules and codes are not enough, by themselves, to maintain good relationships and ethical behavior. Individuals have a moral duty to take their roles and duties seriously. They should follow the Golden Rule ("Do not do to others what you do not want them to do to you") in all of their dealings.

Confucius, like Aristotle, puts a high priority on personal virtues or character.[35] That's because virtuous behavior is essential to maintaining healthy relationships and fulfilling organizational duties. The most important Confucian virtue is that of humaneness or benevolence. Benevolence goes beyond displaying compassion. It also means treating others with respect and promoting their development through education and other means. In addition to benevolence, the key virtues of Confucianism are honesty, trust, kindness, and tolerance. Virtuous people put the needs of others above their own. They seek the good of the organization as a whole and of the larger society. Consider profit taking, for instance. While they do not condemn profit, Confucian thinkers argue that profit should never take precedence over moral behavior or concern for others. The ideal person strives first for virtue, then for profits. In instructing the king, Mencius emphasized that commercial activities should serve the needs of society:

> Your majesty . . . What is the point of mentioning the word "profit"? All that matters is that there should be benevolence and rightness . . . If the mulberry is planted in every homestead, then those who are fifty can wear silk; if chickens, pigs and dogs do not miss their breeding season, then those who are seventy can eat meat; if each field is not deprived of labor during the busy season then families with several mouths to feed will not go hungry . . . When those who are seventy wear silk and eat meat and the masses are neither cold nor hungry, it is impossible for the prince not to be a true king. (Mencius I, 3, I, A, 1, 1, A, 3)[36]

Finally, Confucians recognize the reality of status and power differences in society as well as in organizations. Individuals occupy various roles and levels in the organizational hierarchy, and humaneness demands that we treat every person, whatever his or her role or position, with love and concern. At the same time, Confucius recognized the important role played by those at the top of the hierarchy. Executive-level management plays a key role in establishing moral organizational climates by setting an ethical example and expecting ethical behavior from followers. For example,[37]

> The Master said, "When a prince's personal conduct is correct, his government is effective without issuing orders. If his personal conduct is not correct, he may issue orders, but they will not be followed." (*Analects*, XIII, vi)

> The Master said, "The superior man seeks to perfect the admirable qualities of men, and does not *seek to* perfect their bad qualities." (*Analects*, XII, xvi)

Evaluation

Confucianism highlights the fundamental truth that organizations, economies, and societies are built on relationships. As the global economy grows, fostering ethical relationships will become even more important. People who never meet each other in person now conduct much of the world's business. Confucius offers a blueprint for fostering trusting, healthy relationships that we can put into practice. We need to institute rules and procedures that create ethical organizational climates. As Ethical Checkpoint 1.1 illustrates, etiquette still has an important role to play in a technological society. However, codes and policies are not enough. We have to develop personal character to equip us to take our duties seriously and follow the Golden Rule. Every person, no matter what that individual's status, is worthy of our respect and should be treated as we would want to be treated. Putting the interests of others ahead of our own concerns can keep us from taking advantage of them or pursuing profit above people. Confucian thought also recognizes that the leader shapes the ethical climate of the organization by setting a moral example.

The strengths of Confucianism can become weaknesses if taken too far.[38] Take the philosophy's emphasis on social connections, for example. Placing too much importance on relationships can undermine justice or fairness. Jobs and promotions in China often go to family members, friends, and associates instead of the most qualified individuals. In China, *guanxi*, which is the practice of favoring those with social connections, has led to

ETHICAL CHECKPOINT 1.1
Facebook Etiquette

Blogger Brett McKay notes that etiquette has not kept pace with technology. He hopes to encourage manners on Facebook by offering these friendly reminders:

> *Use discretion when wall posting.* Don't use the Facebook wall for lengthy conversations but for brief notes. Don't post anything personal on others' walls, as these are public spaces.
>
> *Take it easy on the application invites.* Most of your friends don't want to be invited to participate in games.
>
> *Use appropriate language when writing on someone else's wall.* Don't use off-color comments and check for spelling and grammatical errors. Consider the kind of impression you want to make.
>
> *Keep photos of yourself to a minimum.* Avoid pictures of yourself by yourself. Posting lots of these is a mark of vanity.
>
> *Do not break up with a person through Facebook.* Only a jerk would use the relationship status feature to break up with someone. Be mature—meet them face-to-face to tell them your relationship has ended.
>
> *Remove compromising photos of yourself.* Try to avoid these kinds of pictures in the first place. But if one shows up, ask the poster to take it down (or the tag of you at a minimum).
>
> *Join Facebook fan pages with discretion.* Be careful which pages you join (this reveals a lot about you). Also, don't join lots of pages.
>
> *Avoid "oversharing" in your status update.* Beware of information overload. Post updates that others might care about, not personal grooming habits or pet peeves. Be careful not to post items that could get you in trouble with friends, employers, family members (like your mom), or other people.
>
> *Don't "friend" someone you don't know or hardly know.* Be sure to include only those who really are friends, not just contacts. Ignore strangers who try to befriend you.
>
> *Respond to people's Facebook wall posts and messages.* Reply if you can within twenty-four hours. When overwhelmed with Facebook messages, let others know to contact you some other way, such as email.
>
> *Default rule*: Apply the same courtesy, respect, and decorum you would in real life. The same guidelines you would use in face-to-face encounters (treating others with courtesy and respect) apply in online communities as well.

Source: McKay (2014).

---

corruption. Local and foreign firms try to establish *guanxi* through bribes to win public works contracts, commercial deals, and bank loans. Placing too much emphasis on hierarchy and submission to the collective good can foster authoritarian leadership where leaders impose their will and employees have little freedom but blindly submit to authority. Critics also point out that pursuing harmony at any cost can suppress individual rights and silence dissent. Many Confucian thinkers have been reluctant to endorse the existence of universal human rights like those described earlier.[39]

Altruism: Concern for Others

Altruism is based on the principle that we should help others regardless of whether or not we profit from doing so.[40] Assisting those in need may be rewarding (we may feel good about ourselves or receive public recognition, for example). Nevertheless, altruistic behavior seeks to benefit the other person, not the self. The most notable cases of altruism are those that involve significant self-sacrifice, as when a soldier jumps on a grenade to save the rest of his platoon or when an employee donates a kidney to another worker in need of a transplant. The word *altruism* comes from the Latin root *alter*, which means "other." Advocates of altruism argue that love of one's neighbor is the ultimate ethical standard.

Some philosophers argue that altruism doesn't deserve to be treated as a separate ethical perspective because altruistic behavior is promoted in other moral theories. Utilitarians seek the good of others, Kant urges us to treat others with respect, and Confucius identifies compassion as a key element in maintaining proper social relations. However, I believe that altruism deserves to be considered on its own merits and demerits. To begin with, altruism often calls for self-sacrificial behavior, whereas utilitarianism and the categorical imperative do not. Kant warns us never to treat people as a means to an end. Altruism goes a step further and urges us to treat people as if they *are* the ends. Then, too, there is significant debate over the existence of prosocial behavior. One group of evolutionary biologists believe that humans are conduits of "selfish genes."[41] For instance, they believe that anything we do on behalf of family members is motivated by the desire to transmit our genetic code. Some skeptical philosophers argue that people are egoists. Every act, no matter how altruistic on the surface, always serves our needs, such as helping others because we expect to get paid back at some later time.

In response to the skeptics, a growing body of research in sociology, political science, economics, social psychology, and other fields establishes that true altruism does exist and is an integral part of the human experience.[42] In fact, altruistic behavior is common in everyday life:

> We humans spend much of our time and energy helping others. We stay up all night to comfort a friend who has suffered a broken relationship. We send money to rescue famine victims halfway round the world, or to save whales, or to support public television. We spend millions of hours per week helping as volunteers in hospitals, nursing homes, AIDS hospices, fire departments, rescue squads, shelters, halfway houses, peer-counseling programs, and the like. We stop on a busy highway to help a stranded motorist change a flat tire, or spend an hour in the cold to push a friend's—even a stranger's—car out of a snowdrift.[43]

Care for others appears to be a universal value, one promoted by religions the world over. Representatives from a variety of religious groups agree that every person deserves humane treatment, no matter what his or her ethnic background, language, skin color, political beliefs, or social standing.[44] Western thought has been greatly influenced by the altruistic emphasis of Judaism and Christianity. The command to love God and to love others as we love ourselves is the most important obligation in Judeo-Christian ethics. Since humans are made in the image of God, and God is love, we have an obligation to love others no matter who they are and no matter what their relationship to us. Jesus drove home this point in the parable of the Good Samaritan. In this tale, a generous businessman stops (at great risk to himself and his reputation) to befriend a wounded Jewish traveler—a person he could have considered his enemy.

Concern for others promotes healthy relationships like those described by Confucius. Society functions more effectively when individuals help one another in their daily interactions. This is particularly apparent in organizations. Many productive management practices, like empowerment, mentoring, and teambuilding, have an altruistic component. Researchers use the term *organizational citizenship behavior* to describe routine altruistic acts that increase productivity and build trusting relationships.[45] Examples of organizational citizenship behavior include an experienced machine operator helping a newcomer master the equipment, a professor teaching a class for a colleague on jury duty, and an administrative assistant working over break to help a coworker meet a deadline. Such acts play an important if underrecognized role in organizational success. Much less work would get done if members refused to help out. Take the case of the new machine operator. Without guidance, he or she may flounder for weeks, producing a number of defective parts and slowing the production process. Caring behaviors also break down barriers of antagonism between individuals and departments. Communication and coordination increase, leading to better overall results. You can determine your likelihood to engage in organizational citizenship behavior by completing the test in Self-Assessment 1.2.

SELF-ASSESSMENT 1.2

Organizational Citizenship Behavior Scale

Instructions

As an employee, rate yourself on each of the following items on a scale from 1 = never to 7 = always.

1. Help others who have been absent.
2. Willingly give your time to help others who have work-related problems.
3. Adjust your work schedule to accommodate other employees' requests for time off.
4. Go out of the way to make newer employees feel welcome in the work group.
5. Show genuine concern and courtesy toward coworkers, even under the most trying business or personal situations.
6. Give up time to help others who have work or nonwork problems.
7. Assist others with their duties.
8. Share personal property with others to help their work.

Scoring

Total up your responses. Possible scores range from 8 to 56. The higher your score, the more likely you are to go beyond your job description to help other employees succeed.

Source: K. Lee and Allen (2002), p. 142. Used by permission.

The Ethic of Care

Altruism provides the foundation for the *ethic of care*, which developed as an alternative to what feminists deem the traditional, male-oriented approach to ethics.[46] The categorical imperative and justice-as-fairness theories, for example, emphasize the importance of acting on abstract moral principles, being impartial, and treating others fairly. Carol Gilligan, Nel Noddings, and others initially argued that women take a different approach (a "different voice") to moral decision making that is based on caring for others. Instead of expressing concern for people in abstract terms, women care for others through their relationships and tailor their responses to the particular needs of the other individual. Subsequent research has revealed that the ethic of care serves as a moral standard for many men as well as for many (but not all) women.[47]

The ethic of care incorporates both attitude and action.[48] Caring individuals are alert to the needs of others. They value those who demonstrate care and concern as well as groups and societies that tend to the needs of their members. Care is also an activity.[49] To practice care, we must first recognize or be attentive to the needs of others. We then have to take responsibility for meeting those needs. Providing good care depends on having the right skills, such as listening, counseling abilities, and medical training. As caregivers, we should recognize that receivers of care are in a vulnerable position, and we must not take advantage of that fact.

Philosopher Virginia Held identifies five key components of the care ethic that separate it from other moral philosophies.[50]

1. *Focuses on the importance of noting and meeting the needs of those we are responsible for.* Most people are dependent for much of their existence, including during childhood, during illness, and near the end of life. Morality built on rights and autonomy overlooks this fact. The ethic of care makes concern for others central to human experience and puts the needs of specific individuals—a child, a coworker—first.

2. *Values emotions.* Sympathy, sensitivity, empathy, and responsiveness are moral emotions that need to be cultivated. This stands in sharp contrast to ethical approaches that urge decision makers to set aside their feelings to make rational determinations. However, emotions need to be carefully monitored and evaluated to make sure they are appropriate. For example, caregivers caught up in empathy can deny their own needs or end up dominating the recipients of their care.

3. *Gives priority to specific needs and relationships over universal principles.* The ethic of care rejects the notion of impartiality and believes that particular relationships are more important than universal moral principles like rights and freedom. For instance, the needs of our immediate coworkers should take precedence over the needs of distant employees or society as a whole (though we should be concerned for members of those groups as well). Most moral theories see ethical problems as conflicts between two extremes: the selfish individual and universal moral principles. The care ethic falls somewhere in between. Persons in caring relationships aren't out to promote their personal interests or the interests of humanity; instead, they want to foster ethical relationships with specific individuals. These relationships benefit both parties. Family and friendships

have great moral value in the ethic of care, and caregiving is a critical moral responsibility.

4. *Breaks down the barriers between the public and private spheres.* In the past, men were dominant in the public sphere while relegating women to the "private" sphere. Men largely made decisions about the exercise of political and economic power while women were marginalized. As a result, women were often economically dependent and suffered domestic violence, cut off from outside help. Previous moral theories focused on public life and ignored families and friendships, but the ethic of care addresses the moral issues that arise in the private domain. It recognizes that problems faced in the private sphere, such as inequality and dependency, also arise in the public sphere.

5. *Views persons as both relational and interdependent.* Each of us starts life depending on others, and we depend on our webs of interpersonal relationships throughout our time on Earth. These relationships help create our identity. Unlike liberal political theory, which views persons as rational, self-interested individuals, in the ethic of care individuals are seen as "embedded" in particular families, cultures, and historical periods. Embeddedness means that we need to take responsibility for others, not merely leave them alone to exercise their individual rights.

Adopting the ethic of care would significantly change organizational priorities. Employers would use caring as a selection criterion, hiring those who demonstrate relational understanding and skills.[51] Managers would be evaluated based on how well they demonstrated care and concern for employees. Organizations would help members strike a better balance between work and home responsibilities, provide more generous family leave policies, expand employee assistance programs, and so on. Those directly involved in caregiving—assisted-living attendants, nursery school teachers, hospice workers, home health caregivers—would receive more money, recognition, and status.

Evaluation

Altruism has much to offer. First, concern for others is a powerful force for good. It drives people to volunteer to care for the dying, to teach prisoners, to act as Big Brothers and Sisters, to provide medical relief, and to answer crisis calls. Every year CNN television honors "ordinary heroes"—those devoted to helping others and the environment.[52] Recent honorees include a Columbian with cerebral palsy who provides services to disabled young people, a cyclist who coaches cycling teams for at-risk youth, a woman who rescues and provides homes for older dogs, a Kenyan providing free medical services near the Somali border, and a designer who provides living spaces for former foster kids. Second, following the principle of caring helps prevent ethical abuses. We're much less likely to take advantage of others through accounting fraud, stealing, cheating, and other means if we put their needs first. (We'll return to this theme in our discussion of servant leadership in Chapter 7.) Third, altruistic behavior, as we've seen, promotes healthy relationships and organizations. There are practical benefits to acting in a caring manner.

Fourth, altruism lays the foundation for high moral character. Many personal virtues, like compassion, hospitality, generosity, and empathy, reflect concern for other people. Fifth, adopting an ethic of care would make our workplaces more humane and provide caregivers with the rewards they so richly deserve. Finally, altruism is inspiring. When we hear of the selfless acts of Gandhi, Desmond Tutu, and the Rwandans who risked their lives to save their neighbors from genocide, we are moved to follow their example.

While compelling, altruism suffers from serious deficiencies. All too often, our concern for others extends only to our immediate families, neighbors, or communities.[53] On the other hand, it may be possible to take altruism too far (see Contemporary Issues in Organizational Ethics 1.1). Sadly, well-intentioned attempts to help others can backfire. They fail to meet the need, have unintended negative consequences, or make the problem worse. A large proportion of the money donated to some charities pays for fund-raising expenses rather than for client services. Government agencies can create dependence by providing welfare assistance.

Altruism is not an easy principle to put into practice. For every time we stop to help a stranded motorist, we probably pass by several others who need assistance. Our urge to help out a coworker is often suppressed by our need to get our own work done or to meet a pressing deadline. Common excuses for ignoring needs include the following: (1) "Somebody else will do it, so I don't need to help"; (2) "I didn't know there was a problem" (deliberately ignoring a coworker's emotional upset or someone's unfair treatment); (3) "I don't have the time or energy"; (4) "I don't know enough to help"; (5) "People deserve what they get" (disdain for those who need help); (6) "It won't matter anyway, because one person can't make much of a difference"; and (7) "What's in it for me?" (looking for personal benefit in every act).[54] There's also disagreement about what constitutes loving behavior. For example, firing someone can be seen as cruel or as caring. This act may appear punitive to outsiders. However, terminating an employee may be in that person's best interests. For someone who is not a good fit for an organization, being fired can open the door to a more productive career.

The ethic of care often conflicts with the ethic of justice. Take the allocation of jobs and resources, for instance. The ethic of care suggests that job openings and organizational funds should go to those closest to us—family, friends, acquaintances, coworkers. The ethic of justice holds that such determinations should be impartial, based on qualifications, not relationships (see our earlier discussion of Confucianism). Care and justice often clash in the legal system as well. Some advocate that jails should focus on rehabilitation; others (likely the majority) argue that the prison system should focus on punishment, seeing that criminals get the treatment they deserve. Case Study 1.3, "Is This Any Way to Run a Prison?" describes one nation that takes a caring approach to incarceration. You may find this approach unjust to victims and society.

CONTEMPORARY ISSUES IN ORGANIZATIONAL ETHICS 1.1

EXTREME ALTRUISM

Over forty years ago Australian ethicist Peter Singer wrote a provocative essay in which he posed two scenarios. In the first he asked readers to imagine that they were walking by a shallow pond and saw a child drowning. Rescuing the child might mean ruining a new pair of shoes, however. Nearly all would agree that saving the child should take precedence over the shoes. In the next scenario, he asked his audience to imagine that they had been asked to send money to save the life of a child in a poor nation. According to Singer, we are just as morally obligated to send the contribution as we are to rescue the drowning child. Singer went on to urge wealthy world citizens to forgo luxuries like movie tickets and give the money to humanitarian aid instead.

Some scholars use the term "extreme altruism" to describe the kind of sacrifices Singer suggests. Extreme altruists take concern for others beyond normal limits. They are willing to put the needs of others above their own needs and the needs of their families. *New Yorker* writer Larissa MacFarquhar interviewed a number of such "radical do-gooders" in her book *Strangers Drowning: Grappling With Impossible Idealism, Drastic Choices, and the Overpowering Urge to Help*. The title for her book comes from another thought experiment that asks: "Should you save your mother from drowning or save two strangers?" Most of us would save our mothers. But not extreme altruists. They make the calculation that saving two lives is better than saving one. As a consequence, MacFarquhar's interviewees were willing to sacrifice their loved ones on behalf of larger causes. One couple, for example, put their children in danger from wild animals and disease to start a leprosarium in an Indian jungle. A missionary risked the life of her son, who had a heart condition, to serve in Mozambique. Others sacrificed personal comfort, giving nearly all their money to the poor, donating kidneys to complete strangers, and adopting multiple children with significant disabilities.

MacFarquhar reports that even radical do-gooders have to set limits (stop adopting children or living on the streets) in order to save themselves. Saving others does not always bring happiness, because some in her sample couldn't forget the world's misery. She concludes that extreme altruism is not always healthy, but radical do-gooders make the world a better place.

Many of us probably share MacFarquhar's mixed feelings about extraordinary altruists. They make us feel uncomfortable (we feel guilty for not giving more) and we couldn't, or perhaps shouldn't, follow their example. Yet we admire radical altruists for their sacrifices. Their example may prod us into doing more for others.

Sources: MacFarquhar (2015). Moyn (2015). P. Singer (1971, 2017). Wilson (2015).

CHAPTER TAKEAWAYS

- Developing ethical competencies is essential to taking a practical approach to organizational ethics.

- Ethical experts know more about the ethical domain, see the world differently than novices, and have different skills sets. To become more of an ethical expert, learn in a well-structured environment, master moral theory and skills, and practice, practice, practice.

- One list of ethical competencies includes commitment to high standards of personal and professional behavior, understanding ethics codes and laws, engaging in effective moral reasoning, identifying important professional values, and demonstrating a commitment to promoting ethical practices and behaviors in the organization. An alternative list identifies three key capacities: (1) cognitive decision-making

- competence—demonstrating the ability to solve moral problems; (2) affective prebehavioral disposition—being motivated to follow through on choices; (3) context management competence—using managerial skills to create ethical organizational environments.

- Organizations are made up of three or more persons engaged in coordinated action in pursuit of a common purpose or goal. Ethics is concerned with the rightness or wrongness of human behavior. Organizational ethics applies moral standards to the organizational context.

- Ethical theories or perspectives are critical tools for developing competence. Each ethical perspective has its weaknesses, but each makes a valuable contribution to moral problem solving.

- Utilitarian decisions are based on their consequences. The goal is to select the alternative that achieves the greatest good for the greatest number of people.

- Kant's categorical imperative is based on the premise that decision makers should do what's morally right no matter what the consequences. Moral choices flow out of a sense of duty and are those that we would want everyone to make. Always respect the worth of others when making ethical decisions.

- Justice as fairness theory provides a set of guidelines for resolving disputes over the distribution of resources. Ensure that everyone in your organization has certain rights, such as freedom of speech and thought; is provided with a minimum level of benefits; and has the same chance at positions and promotions. Try to make decisions without being swayed by personal or status considerations.

- Aristotelian ethics rejects rules-based approaches and urges us to develop virtues that lead to wise moral choices. You'll need to find the middle ground between extremes (not deficiency or excess) and focus your choices and actions on your ultimate purpose, which is happiness or flourishing. Live well by pursuing goods of the soul (development of the mind and relationships with others), not wealth or pleasure.

- Confucianism focuses on the importance of creating healthy, trusting relationships. You can help build such connections by establishing ethical organizational practices, taking your responsibilities seriously, following the Golden Rule, demonstrating humanity toward others, and seeking the good of others over your own interests.

- Altruism seeks to benefit the other person, not the self. By making caring for others the ethical standard, you can encourage practices—empowering, mentoring, teambuilding, organizational citizenship behavior—that build trust and increase productivity. The ethic of care specifically rejects abstract, universal moral principles in favor of meeting the needs of specific individuals.

APPLICATION PROJECTS

1. Outline a plan for developing your ethical competence. What skills/abilities do you want to develop? How will you incorporate the components of ethical development described in this chapter into your plan?

2. Reflect on one of your ethical decisions. Which approach(es) did you use when making your determination? Evaluate the effectiveness of the approach(es) as well as the quality of your choice. What did you learn from this experience?

3. Form a group and develop a list of behaviors that are always right and behaviors that are always wrong. Keep a record of those behaviors that were nominated but rejected by the team and why. Report your final list, as well as your rejected items, to the rest of the class. What do you conclude from this exercise?

4. Join with classmates and imagine that you are behind a veil of ignorance. What principles will you use to govern society and organizations?

5. What does happiness mean to you? How is your education helping you (or not helping you) to flourish and live well?

6. How would your organization operate differently if it were governed by the ethic of care?

7. During a week, make note of all the altruistic behavior you witness in your organization. How would you classify these behaviors? What impact do they have on your organization? How would your organization be different if people didn't engage in organizational citizenship behavior? Write up your findings.

8. Write a case study based on an individual or group you admire for its altruistic motivation. Provide background and outline the lessons we can learn from this person or persons. As an alternative, create a case study on an organization based on Confucian principles.

9. Apply all six ethical perspectives presented in the chapter to Case Study 1.2 and Case Study 1.3. Keep a record of your deliberations and conclusions using each one. Did you reach different solutions based on the theory you used? Were some of the perspectives more useful in this situation? Are you more confident after looking at the problem from a variety of perspectives? Write up your findings.

CASE STUDY 1.1

Federal Employees Behaving Badly

Ethics officials at the U.S. Department of Defense (DoD) believe that the best way to avoid ethical failures is by learning from the moral failures of others. With that premise in mind, the DoD's Office of General Counsel created the *Encyclopedia of Ethical Failure*. This training manual provides real examples of federal employees who, intentionally or unintentionally, violated standards of conduct. It also describes the sanctions the offenders received as a result. The manual identifies 18 different categories of ethical violations ranging from abuse of position and conflicts of interest to misuse of government resources and travel monies. Here are a few of the cases described in the *Encyclopedia*:

- A supervisory special agent for the Department of the Treasury presented her credentials to a police officer during a traffic stop to get more favorable treatment. The agency determined that she was using her position for personal gain and demoted her.

- A former Alcohol, Tobacco, and Firearms (ATF) chief provided his nephew with access to ATF equipment and employees (20 in all) for his school project on the agency. Under direction of the chief, staffers conducted research for the nephew, ushered him on tours, and let him use the ATF's film studio and camera for interviews with ATF employees. The nephew earned an A for his project, while his uncle was found guilty of misusing his position and government resources.

- A U.S. Postal Service (USPS) employee accepted free golf games from a vendor involved with a $100 million contract with the agency. He pled guilty to bribery charges.

(Continued)

(Continued)

- A supervisor in the Bureau of Indian Affairs purchased large quantities of overpriced lightbulbs from a North Dakota company and received $21,000 in kickbacks. The scheme earned him up to 21 months in prison.

- An Army brigadier general lobbied on behalf of a contractor while seeking a position with the same company. He also skipped meetings and billed the government for unauthorized expenses as he conducted his job search. He was fined but allowed to retire at his current pay grade.

- An assistant secretary of telecommunications and information in the Department of Commerce informed ethics officers that she was going to have a small dinner party at her house. However, she failed to mention that the party was for 60 to 80 people from companies she was responsible for regulating. She was found in violation of department regulations but avoided criminal charges.

- An accountant with the National Science Foundation (NSF) used her government-issued travel card to make personal purchases and unauthorized cash withdrawals. The accountant—who managed the NSF's travel card program—then unsuccessfully tried to purge her illegal transactions from the records. She was fired, banned from future federal employment, and sentenced to 20 weekends in jail as part of her two-year probation.

- A service officer appeared in her uniform on the website of an outside organization that identified her as a board member. This gave the impression that she was participating in an official capacity or that the federal government endorsed the organization. She received verbal counseling, and the picture was altered to hide the uniform.

- An Army staff sergeant falsely claimed the higher housing allowance for married soldiers after his divorce. He was court-martialed for receiving more money than he was entitled to.

- A top Department of Homeland Security border officer flew a DHS helicopter to his daughter's elementary school and landed it on the school yard. His supervisor gave him permission to use the multimillion-dollar machine, but his actions were considered unethical because federal employees are expected to use their own judgment when making moral choices. They cannot rely totally on the opinions of their superiors.

- At first glance, two executives at the Naval Undersea Warfare Center had exemplary work records, taking very little vacation time. Investigators soon discovered that the two employees were taking "religious compensatory time" instead. Yet their absences fell not on traditional religious holidays but on days when they had golf tournaments, sightseeing trips, and medical appointments. The inspector general concluded that the two had conspired to defraud the government, and they were forced into retirement. (Note: Religious compensatory time is available to federal employees for religious observances, but workers must make up this time later.)

Discussion Probes

1. Do you agree with the Department of Defense that, when it comes to teaching ethics, bad examples are more effective than good ones?

2. Which example of unethical behavior described above is the most offensive? Least offensive? Why?

3. Should government employees—local, state, and federal—be held to a higher ethical standard than those working for businesses and corporations? Why or why not?

4. What similarities do you see between the ethical dilemmas faced by public employees and those who work in private business? What differences?

5. If you were going to create your own *Encyclopedia of Unethical Behavior* based on your experiences in work and other organizations, what examples would you include?

Source: Department of Defense (2011).

CASE STUDY 1.2

National Security or Computer Security?

In 2017, the world was rocked by massive computer attacks, the largest hitting 2,000 organizations in 65 countries. Hackers shut down hospitals in Britain, the Chernobyl nuclear site, Ukraine's national bank, a Russian energy company, Merck pharmaceutical, and the Danish shipping company Maersk. They locked up computer files at a number of U.S. businesses, releasing the information after users paid a ransom.

The cyber weapons used in these assaults were developed by the National Security Agency. Computer experts at the NSA used flaws in the Microsoft operating system and other tools to spy on other nations and to carry out secret operations. They gained access to Iran's air defense systems and infrastructure and disrupted its nuclear program, for example. They also interfered with North Korea's nuclear missile launches and attacked Islamic State militants. The agency kept knowledge of software vulnerabilities to itself. Thus, officials didn't notify Microsoft so the company could develop a patch to protect users from a computer program called EternalBlue. According to one security expert, "For many, many years, while it was secret, the NSA could use [EternalBlue] to unlock any door of any computer network in the world. It was the ultimate cyberweapon for espionage."[1]

NSA's cyber cover was blown when the secret weapons were leaked to a group called the Shadow Brokers, which posted some of the tools on the Web. (At that point the NSA notified Microsoft of the EternalBlue program.) Hackers then modified them to carry out their attacks. Experts predict that the attacks will escalate, wreaking even greater havoc as perpetrators move from targeting individual organizations to

(Continued)

(Continued)

shutting down entire systems—medical, production, banking, government, transportation, power.

Victims and technology companies are critical of the NSA for failing to warn the public. Microsoft President Brad Smith urged the agency to "consider the damage to civilians that comes from hoarding these vulnerabilities and the use of these exploits."[2] However, according to security experts, the NSA apparently has no plans to release additional vulnerabilities, calculating that national security should take precedence over civilian computer security.

Discussion Probes

1. Has your organization been victimized by ransomware or other computer hacks? How did it respond? What steps are you and your organization taking to improve computer security?
2. Should national security take priority over the computer security of citizens?
3. What are the costs of keeping information about software vulnerabilities secret? The costs of releasing this information?
4. What are the benefits of keeping information about software vulnerabilities secret? The benefits of releasing this information?
5. Based on the costs and benefits, is the NSA justified in keeping information about cyber weaknesses to itself?

Notes

1. S. Sheth (2017).
2. Perloth and Sanger (2017).

Sources: D. Goodwin (2017). Shadow Brokers group (2017). Szoldra (2017).

CASE STUDY 1.3

Is This Any Way to Run a Prison?

Halden prison in Norway has all the amenities you would expect at an expensive resort and then some. Prisoners can take advantage of a sound studio, a climbing wall, jogging trails, a "kitchen laboratory" for cooking classes, and two-bedroom homes for hosting their visiting families. They live in dormitory-style rooms complete with flat-screen televisions and mini-refrigerators. (There are no bars on the cells.) Furnished with stylish furniture and artwork, Halden placed second in an interior design competition, losing only to a spa hotel. At Balstøy, another Norwegian prison, murderers, rapists, and other felons enjoy the beach, horseback riding, and tennis. They also grow organic vegetables and raise their own livestock for food.

The Halden and Balstøy prisons reflect the guiding principles of the Norwegian penal system. National leaders believe that repressive prisons do not work. They operate under the premise that treating inmates with respect and giving them responsibilities reduces the chances that they will end up back in jail. According to the Halden prison governor, "In the Norwegian prison system, there's a focus on human rights and respect. When they [inmates] arrive, many are in bad shape. We want to build them up, give them confidence through education and work and have them leave as better people."[1]

Caring relationships between staff and inmates are essential to carrying out the prison system's mission. At Halden, prison guards (half of them female) don't carry guns, and they routinely eat meals and participate in sports with their charges. They strive to create a sense of family for inmates, who often come from poor home situations. Many staff members choose to work at the prison to transform lives. Said one, "Our goal is to give all prisoners—we call them our pupils—a meaningful life inside these walls."[2]

There is evidence that the Norwegian approach is effective. Prison violence is rare, and within two years of release, only 20% of Norway's prisoners end up back in prison, compared with 50% to 60% in the United Kingdom and the United States. Observers point out, however, that the imprisonment rate in Norway, a small, equalitarian, and prosperous country, is much lower than in the United States (69 per 100,000 compared to 753 per 100,000). Norway's total prison population is between 3,000 and 4,000, which makes it much easier to focus on rehabilitation. And the system is expensive. It costs twice as much to house an inmate at Halden than in Great Britain prisons.

Norway's commitment to rehabilitation rather than punishment was sorely tested after Anders Behring Breivik killed 77 of its citizens in 2011. Breivik first set off a series of bombs near government offices in downtown Oslo, killing eight. Then, dressed as a policeman, he went to an island where he systematically hunted down and shot children and adults at a camp. Breivik never repented for his actions and declared that he would kill again if freed. For his crimes he was sentenced to 21 years (an average of four months per victim), but he is unlikely to ever be released because judges can add additional 5-year extensions to his sentence. He may end up spending some of his days in Halden with access to exercise facilities, computers, classes, and other perks.

While many around the world were offended by what they saw as a lenient sentence, most Norwegians appear comfortable with the court's decision in Breivik's case. They see it as a reflection of their values. "We don't talk much about revenge," said Halden's deputy governor.[3] A survivor of the shooting stated, "If he is deemed not to be dangerous any more after 21 years, then he should be released. That's how it should work. That's staying true to our principles, and the best evidence that he hasn't changed our society."[4]

Norway's prisoners expressed their solidarity with the victims of Breivik's murderous rampage. Inmates at two facilities collected money and sent flowers to Norway's Royal Ministry of Justice and the Police, which had been attacked. According to the Justice minister, "They seemed to feel that it was their ministry that had been bombed." When asked how ministry personnel responded to the prisoners' gifts, he replied, "We cried."[5]

Discussion Probes

1. Is it fair to crime victims (and to society) to treat prisoners so well?

2. Do Norwegian prisons reward criminals for their bad behavior?

3. Should prisons focus on punishment or on rehabilitation?

4. Do you think that the Norwegian prison model is ethical?

5. Was Breivik's sentence too lenient? Should he be released if he is rehabilitated after serving his sentence?

6. Could the Norwegian prison model work in the United States or other countries? Why or why not?

(Continued)

(Continued)

Notes

1. W. L. Adams (2010), p. 14.
2. W. L. Adams (2010).
3. Nixey (2012), pp. T4, T5.
4. Lewis and Lyall (2013).
5. Nixey (2012).

Sources: Crooks (2011). Fouche (2009). Gentlemen (2012), p. 25. Lowe (2012). Soares (2007).

CHAPTER TWO

COMPONENTS OF PERSONAL ETHICAL DEVELOPMENT

Chapter Preview

Component 1: Discovering Vocation
    Discovering Your Personal Gifts
    Barriers to Obeying Our Callings
Component 2: Identifying Personal Values
Component 3: Developing Character
    Positive Psychology and Virtues
    Direct Approaches to Character Development
    Indirect Approaches to Character Development
Component 4: Creating a Moral Identity
Component 5: Drawing Upon Spiritual Resources
    Caring for the Soul
    Spiritual Well-Being
Chapter Takeaways
Application Projects

In this chapter we add to the body of knowledge and skills we need to improve ethical performance. We'll focus on the components of personal moral development that are critical to ethical decision making and action. Vocation provides a sense of direction; values determine moral priorities; character and moral identity guide moral choices and behavior; and spirituality can serve as a resource for personal and organizational ethical improvement.

COMPONENT 1: DISCOVERING VOCATION

Any strategy for personal ethical development ought to address the question "Where am I headed?" A number of authors suggest that we can best determine our life direction through understanding our vocation or calling. In popular usage, the word *vocation* refers to a job or occupation. However, the original meaning of the term was much broader. The English word is drawn from the Latin *vocare*, which means "to call" or "calling."[1] Discovering our vocation means determining our purpose in life.

Calling is important to a great many students and working adults. In one study of 5,000 undergraduates, over 40% reported that having a calling to a particular career was true for them.[2] A similar percentage of working adults also view their work as a vocation.[3]

College students who sense a calling are more comfortable with their employment choices, place greater importance on their careers, and are more satisfied with their educational experiences and their lives as a whole. Working adults with a sense of vocation find their work and lives more meaningful, tend to be more satisfied and committed to their teams and organizations, are more productive, and have more rewarding relationships at work.[4]

Researchers report that calling isn't limited to those in high-status jobs (e.g., executive, doctor, lawyer, engineer). Those in less prestigious positions, such as administrative support staff, zookeepers, and janitors, are almost as likely to feel a sense of calling as those in higher-status roles.[5] For many of us, the work we do is essential to fulfilling our vocation. At times, however, the pursuit of vocation has little to do with paid employment. Some use the money they earn from their jobs to pursue their vocations—working with homeless youth, performing music, inventing, researching—in their spare time. Others, such as stay-at-home parents, retirees, and the voluntarily unemployed, follow their callings without earning a salary. Career experts suggest that we will play a variety of roles over our lifetimes, most of them not work related (e.g., child, student, citizen, homemaker, retiree). The prominence of each role will vary depending on our age and stage in life.[6] The student role is more important through our early twenties, for example, but we generally become more focused on work as we get closer to age 30. Retirement and homemaking will take priority after we end our careers. Vocation guides us as we carry out all of our roles, both work related and not work related, no matter how young or old we are.

Finding our calling produces significant ethical benefits. First, having a sense of meaning fosters perseverance, buffering us from the effects of stress and allowing us to overcome obstacles. Second, when we are using our abilities and interests, we enjoy a feeling of personal satisfaction or self-actualization. This sense of satisfaction increases our level of commitment and reduces the likelihood that we will poison the ethical climate of the organization. Third, having a clear direction makes us better stewards. Instead of wasting time and energy on tasks that aren't central to our purpose, we can focus on more meaningful projects that make effective use of our abilities. Fourth, vocation equips us for service to others. Both secular and religious descriptions of calling emphasize its other-centeredness. Those who are called find meaning in serving the community and significant causes, not in making money. This outward or other focus is captured in writer Frederick Buechner's description of vocation as "the place where your deep gladness and the world's deep hunger meet."[7] Because we are more productive when pursuing our vocation, we are better able to serve others, whether as engineers, architects, graduate students, software developers, nursing home administrators, or scientists.

Discovering Your Personal Gifts

Philosophy professor Lee Hardy offers practical advice for discovering how you can use your gifts to serve others in the workplace.[8] The first step is to determine your unique gifts. Pay particular attention to past experiences. Ask yourself these questions:

- What have I done and done well?
- What kinds of skills did I make use of?
- What kind of knowledge did I acquire?

- What kinds of objects did I work with?
- In what capacity was I relating to others?
- Was I working in a position with a lot of freedom and responsibility, or was I working in a highly structured situation where my activity was thoroughly and carefully structured?

Hardy suggests that you try out a variety of jobs. Even if you don't like a particular position, you will learn from the experience. Identify the roles you enjoy (see Self-Assessment 2.1) and get feedback about your strengths and weaknesses from those who know you well.

Professor Hardy's second and third steps to finding vocation consist of identifying your specific concern for others and your interests. You may be concerned about the housing needs of immigrant populations, for instance, or environmental and educational problems. Your interests—like art, music, literature, bird watching, hiking, photography, film production, or current events—can motivate you to develop skills and knowledge that later can be employed in service. For example, one of my colleagues was prompted by his boyhood hobby of collecting baseball statistics into pursuing a career as a professor of mathematics.

The final step is to find the right job fit. Locate a place where your gifts, concerns, and interests can be put to best use. According to Hardy, finding the right fit goes beyond matching your talents to the job description. It should also include an evaluation of the values and goals of the work setting. You may be well suited for a position (for example, a job writing copy for tobacco ads) yet refuse it on moral grounds.

Barriers to Obeying Our Callings

Sadly, the call of vocation often falls upon deaf ears. Ambition is one significant barrier to obeying our callings. Following our heart's desires may put us in direct conflict with what the world defines as success. We may want to study art, protect wildlife, or teach, but our culture encourages us to pursue other objectives, like making money, getting promoted, and achieving status. Emory University professor Brian Mahan argues that to follow our vocation, we must "forget ourselves on purpose."[9] After determining what is most satisfying and meaningful to us, we then need to discover what is preventing us from hearing its call. We can uncover our preoccupations by asking "What is keeping me from living fully for the thing I want to live for?" Setting aside distractions enables us to acknowledge that pride and the trappings of success are constant temptations. By understanding their power, we can begin to break their hold over us. Then we are ready to respond to our life purpose.

Avoidance is another obstacle to vocation. Like the biblical figure Jonah, who headed in the opposite direction when God sent him to the city of Nineveh, many of us resist our call. We may do so out of a sense of caution, doubts about our own abilities, self-imposed limitations, or compliance with orders from authority figures. Resistance can take these forms:

- Waiting for just the right moment
- Analyzing the call to death

- Lying to ourselves
- Replacing one call with another, more socially acceptable one
- Sabotaging our own efforts
- Filling our lives with other activities[10]

To overcome resistance, we need to break free of our low self-esteem. Fortunately, our chances of success are much greater when we respond to a genuine call. That realization should make it easier to leave our self-doubts behind and move forward.

Circumstances beyond our control can also be significant barriers to responding to our callings. We may become sick or injured, find ourselves caring for ailing relatives, or fail to find the job we want in a down economy. In those cases, we can focus on those aspects of our work and life roles that fit with our purpose. We can recraft our jobs to make them meaningful, for example. The power of recrafting or reframing can be seen in a study of cleaning staff at one hospital.[11] All the staff members had the same basic job description but viewed their roles very differently. One group concentrated on cleaning rooms, rarely interacted with others, and did the bare minimum. These cleaners believed they were stuck in low-skill positions and disliked their jobs. Members of the other group were convinced that they played a critical role in the healing process. They took on extra tasks and interacted frequently with patients, nurses, and visitors. They did their best to help the entire work unit function more smoothly. These more proactive workers believed they were highly skilled and liked their jobs.

SELF-ASSESSMENT 2.1

Preferred Roles

Career counselors Kevin and Kay Marie Brennfleck classify roles according to the following categories. *Preferred roles* are those that feel the most natural and enjoyable to you and can play a role in determining your life's purpose. Read through the list and identify the two or three roles you most prefer. Then consider the following questions:

- What do my preferred roles have in common?
- What gifts and skills do I need to carry out these roles and how can I further develop these abilities?
- Would people who know me well agree that I am effective in playing these roles?
- What do my preferred roles suggest about my possible vocation?

Roles emphasizing CREATING

Designer/creator: Enjoys coming up with new solutions, bringing visions into reality, or generating something new (artworks, poems, music, computer programs)

Performer: Enjoys using speaking, singing, music, and other skills in front of an audience

Roles emphasizing LEADING/CONTRIBUTING

Coordinator: Enjoys being the key person who connects people and resources to reach a goal

Contributor/investor: Enjoys giving money and resources to people and projects

Leader: Enjoys creating a vision or direction for a group or organization

Manager: Enjoys coordinating people, departments, and groups toward accomplishing goals

Team or group leader: Enjoys working with and directing a small group toward goals and building team cohesion

Roles emphasizing PERSUADING

Negotiator: Enjoys helping groups or individuals come to an agreement or solution

Promoter: Enjoys promoting the merits of someone or something

Recruiter: Enjoys influencing others to get involved in a cause, project, or event

Seller: Enjoys convincing others to purchase or invest their money

Roles emphasizing HELPING/INSTRUCTING

Counselor: Enjoys helping people deal with their problems and improve their situations

Mentor/coach: Enjoys interacting with a mentee to help that person grow personally and/or professionally

Reconciler: Enjoys bringing harmony and healing to both individual and group relationships in organizations

Teacher/trainer/speaker: Enjoys helping others learn

Roles emphasizing HELPING/ASSISTING

Caretaker (people): Enjoys providing personal care to needy individuals (children, the elderly, the disabled, the sick or injured)

Caretaker (things): Enjoys being in charge of particular things or areas and overseeing upkeep and maintenance

Host/hostess: Enjoys helping people feel welcomed and comfortable

Organizer: Enjoys organizing information, people, and things

Record keeper: Enjoys entering data, maintaining records, and keeping track of people and data

Roles emphasizing ANALYZING/SOLVING PROBLEMS

Evaluator: Enjoys assessing the quality of a person, process, or product

Troubleshooter: Enjoys assessing and then solving problems, sometimes in crisis situations

Other Roles

Specialist: Enjoys performing specific, specialized skills based on training and experience (e.g., carpentry, painting, landscaping)

Source: Adapted from Brennfleck and Brennfleck (2005), pp. 53–57. Used by permission.

COMPONENT 2: IDENTIFYING PERSONAL VALUES

Personal moral values are "desirable goals, varying in importance, that serve as guiding principles in people's lives."[12] Values drive a good deal of our decision making and behavior on the job, including how hard we work, how we treat coworkers and subordinates, how we evaluate performance, and so on. For example, those who put a high value on responsibility are rarely late to work and may show up even when they are sick. Those who place more value on enjoying life may skip work to go skiing or to the beach. We also use our values as standards to determine right from wrong and to set our priorities.

One way to identify or clarify the values you already have is by sitting down and generating a list. The odds are good that you'll have no trouble coming up with at least a few of your core values. Nevertheless, there may be some potentially important values that you overlook. For that reason, you might want to consider rating a list of values supplied by values experts. Duane Brown and R. Kelly Crace developed a widely used values system called the Life Values Inventory.[13] They identify the following as important values that drive decision making and behavior:

Achievement (challenges, hard work, improvement)

Belonging (acceptance, inclusion)

Concern for the environment (protecting and preserving)

Concern for others (well-being of people)

Creativity (new ideas and creations)

Financial prosperity (making money, buying property)

Health and activity (staying healthy and physically active)

Humility (modesty)

Independence (making own decisions and choosing own direction)

Loyalty to family or group (following traditions and expectations)

Privacy (time alone)

Responsibility (dependability, trustworthiness)

Scientific understanding (employing scientific principles in problem solving)

Spirituality (spiritual beliefs; connection to something greater than the self)

As an alternative to generating a list of values or selecting from a standardized list, some counselors suggest that you clarify your values by more indirect means. For example: (1) describe what you admire or dislike in others (these judgments are based on your values); (2) examine how you spend your discretionary time and money as well as how you feel about the activities you enjoy or don't enjoy; (3) reflect on experiences with the environment (watching a sunset, for instance) that have been satisfying or dissatisfying; or (4) complete unfinished sentences about what makes you mad, happy, or sad.[14]

Industrial psychologists report that values play a critical role in person–organization fit.[15] *Person–organization fit* describes the degree of compatibility between an employee and his or her work environment. Those who share values in common with their organizations have greater commitment and motivation, feel more successful, and experience less work stress and anxiety. They are also convinced that their organizations are more ethical. As a consequence, you should give careful attention to how your values mesh with those of your organization. (See Application Project 3.) If your values priorities agree with those of the larger group, you are well fitted to your organization. As a consequence, your job satisfaction is likely to be high.

One final note on personal values. Beware of placing too much importance on acquiring wealth and material possessions. Those driven by materialistic (external) values like financial success, status, fame, and personal image generally have a lower quality of life.[16] For example, they tend to be more depressed and anxious, experience more physical problems like backaches and headaches, are at higher risk for drug and alcohol abuse, have more trouble establishing lasting relationships, and suffer from low self-esteem. Materialistic individuals are also more likely to lie and manipulate others while ignoring the needs of the community and the environment. To avoid the dangers of materialism, focus on intrinsic values that are naturally satisfying and promote psychological health. These include values related to self-acceptance/personal growth (choosing what to do, following your curiosity), relatedness/intimacy (expressing love, forming intimate relationships), and community feeling/helpfulness (making other people's lives better, making the world a better place).

COMPONENT 3: DEVELOPING CHARACTER

As we saw in Chapter 1, Aristotle and Confucius argue that character plays an important role in ethical decision making and behavior. Your chances of making wise decisions and following through on your choices will be higher if you demonstrate positive moral traits or qualities. Modern scholars define virtues as "deep-rooted dispositions, habits, skills, or traits of character that incline persons to perceive, feel, and act in ethically right and sensitive ways."[17] It takes a long time for such qualities to develop. Being virtuous increases sensitivity to ethical issues and encourages moral behavior. While a virtue may be expressed differently depending on the situation, as Aristotle argued, a virtuous person doesn't abandon his or her principles to please others or act civilly to some people but not to others. Christians added faith, hope, and love to Aristotle's original list of virtues.[18] Later lists of virtues include compassion, generosity, empathy, hospitality, modesty, and civility.

Positive Psychology and Virtues

In recent years, virtues have also attracted the attention of positive psychologists. Positive psychologists take issue with the traditional approach of psychology, which tries to fix the weaknesses or deficiencies of people. They argue, instead, that it is more productive to identify and build on the strengths of individuals. Positive psychologists define virtues as morally valued personality traits. Introversion would not be considered a virtue because, although it is a personality trait, it is not considered ethically desirable or undesirable. Kindness, on the other hand, would be considered a virtue because compassion is honored in most cultures.[19] Positive organizational psychologists have identified six broad categories of character strengths, which share much in common with the lists of virtues described above. These character strengths (which are described in more detail in Ethical Checkpoint 2.1) include (1) wisdom and knowledge—cognitive strengths that involve the acquisition and use of knowledge; (2) courage—emotional strengths that exercise the will to reach goals in the face of external and internal opposition; (3) love—interpersonal strengths that involve caring for and befriending others; (4) justice—civic strengths that make healthy community life possible; (5) temperance—strengths that protect against excess; and (6) transcendence—strengths that forge connections to the larger world and help supply meaning.[20]

ETHICAL CHECKPOINT 2.1

Character Strengths

1. Wisdom and knowledge
   Creativity: thinking of novel and productive ways to do things
   Curiosity: taking an interest in all ongoing experience
   Open-mindedness: thinking things through and examining them from all sides
   Love of learning: mastering new skills, topics, and bodies of knowledge
   Perspective: being able to provide wise counsel to others

2. Courage
   Authenticity: speaking the truth and presenting oneself in a genuine way
   Bravery: *not* shrinking from threat, challenge, difficulty, or pain
   Perseverance: finishing what one starts
   Zest: approaching life with excitement and energy

3. Humanity
   Kindness: doing favors and good deeds for others
   Love: valuing close relations with others
   Social intelligence: being aware of the motives and feelings of self and others

4. Justice
   Fairness: treating all people the same according to notions of fairness and justice

   Leadership: organizing group activities and seeing that they happen
   Teamwork: working well as a member of a group or team

5. Temperance
   Forgiveness: forgiving those who have done wrong
   Modesty: letting one's accomplishments speak for themselves
   Prudence: being careful about one's choices; not saying or doing things that might later be regretted
   Self-regulation: regulating what one feels and does

6. Transcendence
   Appreciation of beauty and excellence: noticing and appreciating beauty, excellence, and/or skillful performance in all domains of life
   Gratitude: being aware of and thankful for the good things that happen
   Hope: expecting the best and working to achieve it
   Humor: liking to laugh and joke; bringing smiles to other people
   Religiousness: having coherent beliefs about the higher purpose and meaning of life

Source: C. Peterson and Pakr (2009), p. 28. Used by permission.

Direct Approaches to Character Development

Strategies for fostering character development can be classified as direct or indirect. Direct approaches are specifically designed to promote virtues. For instance, a number of schools offer character education programs.[21] The most effective character education efforts don't tell children how to behave but instead engage students in debate, dialogue, case studies, role plays, self-evaluation, and problem solving. They introduce students to ethical issues suitable to their ages and stages of development. Teachers model desired behaviors, and character education is central to the school's purpose and mission. The integrated education (IEE) model, used in Minnesota and elsewhere, ties character development to skill development.[22] Educators cultivate virtues by leading students through four levels of instruction. At Level 1, they help pupils recognize basic patterns by engaging them in a variety of activities. At Level 2, they focus students' attention on concepts and details to help them build a knowledge base. At Level 3, they coach the students, helping them set goals and practice their skills while solving problems. At Level 4, students begin to act on their own. They integrate their knowledge and skills to solve problems in a variety of situations. Building perseverance provides one example of the IEE model in action. To foster this virtue, instructors (1) assign pupils to find examples of individuals who demonstrate perseverance, (2) encourage learners to examine how their self-talk can help them succeed, (3) assign class members to interview adults about their perseverance, and (4) ask students to develop strategies for helping themselves reach an important goal.

For college and university students, experiential learning (particularly service learning) plays an important role in character development. Hands-on experience, coupled with reflection on those experiences, makes participants more sensitive to moral issues, broadens their perspectives, and increases their commitment to the community.[23] (Case Study 2.1 describes the efforts of one university to promote the character development of students.)

Like educators, positive psychologists take a direct approach to character development.[24] The specific tactics they use vary depending on the particular virtue they want to build. For example, to foster optimism, they encourage clients to identify their negative thoughts ("I am a loser") and then convert them into more constructive thoughts ("I may have failed in this case, but I am successful in other activities"). To foster courage, they expose individuals to low-level threats and then expose them to progressively greater dangers. To foster humility, they encourage counselees to realistically assess their weaknesses as well as their strengths.

Indirect Approaches to Character Development

While the direct methods described above build character, virtues often develop indirectly as well, as a by-product or outcome of other activities. These indirect methods include developing habits, finding role models, telling and living collective stories, and successfully navigating the passages in our organizational lives.

Habits

If habits are the primary tools for building character, as Aristotle argued, then what kinds of habits should we practice? Examples of character-building habits include being honest in every transaction, no matter how small; never hiding the bad news from the boss; and treating every person with respect. Stephen Covey described seven habits that characterize highly effective, ethical individuals.[25] Each habit incorporates knowledge ("what to do" and "why"), skill ("how to do"), and desire ("want to do"). These principles have been adopted by thousands of businesses, schools, and nonprofit organizations. You can use Covey's list of habits as you strive to develop your character on the job.

Habit 1: Be proactive. Proactive people realize they are in charge of their lives; they can choose how they respond to events. When faced with a career setback, they try to grow from the experience instead of feeling victimized by it. Proactive individuals also take the initiative by opting to attack problems instead of accepting defeat. Their language reflects their willingness to accept rather than avoid responsibility. A proactive employee makes such statements as "Let's brainstorm some possible solutions" and "I can develop new sales leads." A reactive worker makes comments such as "My boss won't go along with that idea," "I can't learn the new software program," and "That's just who I am." Those with a proactive orientation also seek to expand the circle of people they can influence.

Habit 2: Begin with the end in mind. This habit is based on the notion that "all things are created twice." First we get a visual picture of what we want to accomplish (a mental creation), and then we follow through on our plans (a physical creation). Inadequate mental creation is the cause of many organizational failures. Entrepreneurs fail to anticipate start-up costs, for instance, or to correctly identify markets for their products and services. On a personal level, if we're unhappy with the current direction of our lives, we can generate new mental images and goals, a process Covey calls *rescripting*. Discovering our vocation and identifying our values help to isolate the results we want and thus control the type of life we create. Covey urges leaders to center their lives on inner principles such as fairness and human dignity rather than on such external factors as family, money, friends, or work.

Habit 3: Put first things first. Our time should be organized around priorities. Unfortunately, though, most of us spend our days coping with emergencies, mistakenly believing that urgent means important. Meetings, deadlines, and interruptions place immediate demands on our schedules, but other, less pressing activities, such as relationship building and planning, are more important in the long run. To be effective, we need to carve out time for significant activities by identifying our most important roles, selecting our goals, creating schedules that enable us to reach our objectives, and modifying plans when necessary. We can create space for important but not urgent items by learning to say no to requests that don't fit our priorities. We'll also need to delegate more, outlining the results we want but letting others determine the methods they'll use to achieve these objectives.

Habit 4: Think win-win. Adopt a win-win perspective that reflects a cooperative orientation to communication. (I'll have more to say about cooperation in Chapter 8.) Be convinced that the best solution benefits both parties. The win-win habit is based on these dimensions: character (integrity, maturity, and a belief that the needs of everyone can be met); trusting relationships committed to mutual benefit; performance or partnership agreements that spell out conditions and responsibilities; organizational systems that fairly distribute rewards; and principled negotiation processes in which both sides generate possible solutions and then select the one that works best.

Habit 5: Seek first to understand, then to be understood. Put aside your personal concerns to engage in empathetic listening. Seek to understand the other party, not to evaluate, advise, or interpret. Empathetic listening is an excellent way to build a trusting relationship. Covey uses the metaphor of the emotional bank account to illustrate how trust develops. Principled individuals make deposits in the emotional bank account by understanding the other person, showing kindness and courtesy, keeping commitments, clarifying expectations, demonstrating personal integrity, and sincerely apologizing when they make a withdrawal. These strong relational reserves help prevent misunderstandings and make it easier to resolve any problems that do arise. Being understood is also important. You can't enter into win-win agreements unless the other party understands your position.

Habit 6: Synergize. Synergy creates a solution that is greater than the sum of its parts and uses right-brain thinking to generate a third, previously undiscovered alternative. Synergistic, creative solutions are generated in trusting relationships (those with high emotional bank accounts) where participants value their differences. You can eliminate those negative forces—distrust, fear—that block change by creating a setting where it is safe to talk about these forces and to come up with an agreement.

Habit 7: Sharpen the saw. Sharpening the saw refers to continual renewal of your physical, mental, social or emotional, and spiritual dimensions. Care for your body through exercise, good nutrition, and stress management. Promote your mental development by reading good literature and writing thoughtful messages and journal and blog entries. Create meaningful relationships with others, and nurture your inner or spiritual values through study or meditation and time in nature. Renewal should be balanced, addressing all four elements of the self. Be careful not to focus your efforts entirely on one dimension (say, physical fitness) because you will neglect your mental, social, and spiritual development.

Role Models

Virtues are more "caught than taught" in that they are often acquired through observation and imitation. We learn what it means to be courageous, just, compassionate, and honest by seeing these qualities modeled in the lives of others. Role models can be drawn from the people we know (managers, friends, teachers); historical figures; or contemporary political, business, and military leaders. For example, those interested in careers in government can turn to a set of exemplars provided by the American Society for Public Administration.[26] These examples of virtue include Harvey W. Wiley, the chief chemist of the U.S. Department of Agriculture, who engineered passage of the Food and Drug Act in 1906; Elmer Staats, former U.S. comptroller general (1966–1981), who used the General Accounting Office to root out corruption and inefficiency; William Ruckelshaus, the U.S. attorney general who refused to follow President Nixon's orders to fire the independent prosecutor investigating the Watergate scandal; former surgeon general C. Everett Koop, who fought against smoking and for treatment of AIDS as a medical, not moral, problem in the 1980s; and Marie Ragghianti, a Kentucky official who, in 1977, uncovered a scheme by the governor of Kentucky to sell paroles.

Government ethics expert David Hart argues that it is useful to differentiate between different types of moral examples or exemplars.[27] Dramatic acts, such as when Captain

Chesley ("Sully") Sullenberger safely landed his plane on the Hudson River shortly after takeoff, capture our attention. However, if we're to develop worthy character, we need examples of those who demonstrate virtue on a daily basis. Hart distinguishes between moral episodes and moral processes. *Moral episodes* are made up of moral crises and moral confrontations. *Moral crises* are dangerous, and Hart calls those who respond to them "moral heroes." Tuvia and Zus Bielski are two such heroes. These two Belorussian brothers saved more than 1,000 of their fellow Jews from Nazi extermination squads by creating a hidden village in a forest. *Moral confrontations* don't involve physical danger, but they do involve risk and call for "moral champions." Researcher Jeffrey Wigand emerged as a moral champion when he revealed that the tobacco industry had suppressed evidence that smoking was harmful.

Moral processes consist of *moral projects* and *moral work*. Moral projects are designed to improve ethical behavior during a limited amount of time and require "moral leaders." A moral leader sets out, for example, to reduce gang activity, to feed the victims of a famine, or to provide more affordable housing for low-income residents. In contrast to a moral project, moral work does not have a beginning or an end but is ongoing. The "moral worker" strives for ethical consistency throughout life. This moral exemplar might be the elementary school lunchroom supervisor who befriends her young diners or the retiree who faithfully delivers meals to shut-ins several times a week.

Hart believes that the moral worker is the most important category of moral exemplar because, as he points out, most of life is lived in the daily valleys, not on the heroic mountain peaks. Since character is developed over time through a series of moral choices and actions, we need examples of those who live consistent moral lives. Those who engage in moral work are better able to handle moral crises like war and genocide.

Stories

Narrative is one of humankind's primary tools for understanding and experiencing the world. We tell stories, read stories, watch stories, think in story form, and star in our dream stories. Narratives not only help us make sense of the world but also promote desired behavior.[28] The narratives told by our families, schools, and religious bodies are designed to impart values and to encourage caring, self-discipline, and other virtues. When we learn of the bravery of a distant relative, for instance, we get a better grasp of our family's heritage. At the same time, we are encouraged to follow his or her example in order to maintain the family name. A similar process unfolds in the organizational setting. The story of a coworker who went to extraordinary lengths to serve a customer inspires us to do likewise. (See Chapter 9 for more information on organizational stories.)

Character growth comes not only from hearing narratives but also from "living up" to our roles in the stories we share with others.[29] (See Case Study 2.2 for an example of a conflict over how to interpret a shared narrative.) When we align ourselves with an organization, we become actors in its ongoing narrative. We should seek out organizations that will bring out the best in us or try to change the collective story of which we are a part.[30]

Literature can also enhance character development. Educator Stephan Ellenwood notes that literature mirrors the complexity of real life. Literature and biography introduce us to complicated individuals who, like us, must make judgments in specific situations. Wrestling with fictional moral dilemmas or reading about the struggles of historical figures can prepare us for the ethical issues we face both on and off the job. According to Ellenwood,

> Sound moral choices depend on reflection, taking time, and active communication about nuances, connotations, understandings, and implications. In that context literature is an especially rich resource for truly understanding moral issues because good authors attend carefully to details and complexity. Good stories do not provide quick fixes or simplistic solutions.[31]

When it comes to moral development, the best narratives are both vivid and vexing. Vivid stories, whether in literature, film, television, or video games, introduce characters we care about; vexing stories place characters in ethical situations that are difficult and challenging. These narratives provide us with opportunities to practice moral reflection and judgment in complex settings before we encounter them in life, much as simulators prepare pilots for flight emergencies.[32] They help us understand our possibilities and limits while escaping our old ways of thinking and acting.[33]

Passages

Intense experiences—those that push us out of our comfort zones—play a critical role in character development. These crossroads events, called *passages*, often result in failure. Important passages include diversity of work experiences (joining a company, accepting a major new assignment); work adversity (significant failure, losing a job, coping with a bad boss); diversity of life experiences (living abroad, blending work and family into a meaningful whole); and life adversity (death, divorce, illness).[34]

All types of passages offer significant potential for character growth if we negotiate them successfully through a nine-step process:

Step 1: Learn resilience. Don't define yourself as a failure when things go wrong, but remain optimistic and self-confident. Learn from your mistakes.

Step 2: Accept personal responsibility. Don't blame others or the organization for problems. You can learn and grow only if you take personal responsibility.

Step 3: Reflect. When confronted with a life passage, ask yourself why this happened, whether you contributed to the event, how you might have acted differently, and how you could go back and change something you said or did.

Step 4: Seek support from your partner, family, friends, and professionals. Avoid isolating yourself, which can lock you into a negative mind-set. Instead, be vulnerable to others and seek out emotional support.

Step 5: Develop and use a professional network. Networks can be sources of information, advice, and insights. Take advantage of these connections by asking questions and seeking help.

Step 6: Seek refuge. Passages are intense, so take time to get away to a relaxing location or immerse yourself in an enjoyable activity like sports, meditation, or yoga. You'll have more energy and insights when you return.

Step 7: Gain perspective. Use the pain of a passage experience to step back and take a broader perspective. Putting some distance between yourself and immediate issues can help you put difficult experiences into context. A bad boss may not be so threatening if you step back and realize that you are not defined by your job, for instance.

Step 8: Retirement. Mastering a series of passages should provide you with the self-understanding and maturity you need to take on the next phase of life beyond work. This transition is much more difficult, though, if you have invested all your energies in your career.

Step 9: Pass on your experience. Take what you have learned and the character qualities you have developed, such as empathy and authenticity, and use them to help others who are going through similar passages.

COMPONENT 4: CREATING A MORAL IDENTITY

We are not likely to seek to discover our vocations, identify our values, or develop our character unless motivated to do so. The term *moral identity* describes one powerful motivating force behind ethical behavior. Psychologists treat moral identity as either a generalized personality trait or as a cognitive framework. Antonio Blasi and others argue that those with high moral identity define themselves in terms of their ethical commitments and act consistently regardless of the situation. Moral principles and character traits are at the core of their being.[35] They feel compelled to act in ways that are consistent with their self-definitions, demonstrating highly developed willpower and integrity activated by a strong desire to do the right thing. For those with strong moral identity, to betray their ethical commitments is to betray themselves. They follow in the footsteps of Protestant reformer Martin Luther. When called upon to defend his radical religious beliefs in front of the Catholic hierarchy at the Diet of Worms, Luther declared, "Here I stand; I can do no other." (See Case Study 2.3 at the end of the chapter for a closer look at a modern Catholic leader who demonstrates a strong moral identity.)

Moral exemplars like those described earlier have extremely high moral identities. Anne Colby and William Damon studied 23 contemporary moral exemplars and found no separation between these individuals' morality and their core identity.[36]

> Over the course of their lives, there is a progressive uniting of self and morality. Exemplars come to see morality and self as inextricably intertwined, so that concerns of the self become defined by their moral sensibilities. The exemplars' moral identities become tightly integrated, almost fused, with their self-identities.[37]

Participants in the Colby and Damon study were very clear about what they believed and then acted (often spontaneously) on their convictions. Most drew their moral beliefs from religious faith or faith in a higher power. They had a positive approach to life and defined success as pursuing their life mission. Their moral commitments extended well beyond those of ordinary citizens. They were devoted to significant, far-reaching causes like feeding the world's poor children and campaigning for human rights.

Colby and Damon offer some clues about how we might develop a high moral identity like the exemplars in their study. They note that some in their sample didn't take on their life's work until their forties and beyond. This suggests that our moral identities can continue to develop well beyond childhood. The researchers also found that working with others on important ethical tasks or projects fosters moral growth by exposing participants to different points of view and new moral issues. We, too, can benefit by collaborating with others on significant causes, such as eliminating sexual slavery, building affordable housing for seniors, or fighting malaria. The key is to view these tasks not as a burden but as an opportunity to act on what we believe. Adopting a joyful attitude will help us remain optimistic in the face of discouragement.

Other psychologists view moral identity as only one of many identity frameworks. Instead of having one unitary "self," we have a variety of selves or identities that we activate depending on the context. At home, our child or parent self-identity is most important, for example, while our professional identity is more salient while at work. Unlike the trait researchers who focus on moral exemplars, these scholars are more interested in improving the moral motivation of average individuals. They suggest that elements of the situation can prime or activate our sense of moral identity.[38] When our moral identities are activated, we place more importance on behaving ethically, are more aware of demonstrating character traits like compassion and fairness, make better moral choices, and are less likely to excuse or justify our unethical behavior. Organizations can enhance the moral motivation of their members by (1) creating climates where close, cooperative relationships can flourish, (2) providing opportunities for moral discussion and reflection, (3) continuously emphasizing values and mission, and (4) encouraging ongoing involvement in the local community.

COMPONENT 5: DRAWING UPON SPIRITUAL RESOURCES

Spirituality can play a significant role in our personal moral development as well as in the ethical development of our organizations. As we noted above, faith provides the foundation for the moral identity of many moral exemplars. Investigators have also discovered a number of links between spiritual values and personal and organizational performance. They report that spirituality enhances the following qualities:[39]

Ethical sensitivity

Commitment to mission, core values, and ethical standards

Moral reasoning

Altruism

Organizational learning and creativity

Job satisfaction (even under adverse workplace conditions)

Morale

Job involvement and commitment

Collaboration

Job effort

Loyalty

Quality of life

Trust

Employee well-being

Willingness to mentor others

Sense of community

Social support

Meaningfulness of work

Productivity and profitability

Given the relationship between spirituality and personal and collective performance, it's not surprising that there has been a surge of interest in spirituality in the workplace among both academics and practitioners. The *Leadership Quarterly*, *Journal of Organizational Change*, *Journal of Business Ethics*, and other academic sources carry articles devoted to the topic. Thousands of Bible study and prayer groups meet in corporate settings. Spiritual seekers can find business and spirituality courses at a number of colleges and universities or attend conferences and seminars devoted to the subject. Tom's of Maine, Herman Miller, TD Industries, Medtronic, Bank of Montreal, HealthEast, and Reell Precision Manufacturing are just a few of the companies that base their organizational cultures on spiritual values. (See Contemporary Issues in Organizational Ethics 2.1 for information on the dangers of organizational spirituality.)

Ashmos and Plowman offer one definition of workplace spirituality as "the recognition that employees have an inner life that nourishes and is nourished by meaningful work that takes place in the context of community."[40] The *inner life* refers to the fact that employees have spiritual needs (their core identity and values) just as they have emotional, physical, and intellectual wants, and they bring the whole person to work. *Meaningful work* describes the fact that workers are generally motivated by more than material rewards. They want their labor to be fulfilling and to serve the needs of society. *Community* refers to the fact that organization members desire connection to others. A sense of belonging fosters the inner life. It should be noted that religion and spirituality overlap but are not identical. Religious institutions encourage and structure spiritual experiences, but spiritual encounters can occur outside formal religious channels.[41]

Caring for the Soul

Spiritual values need to be nurtured. Psychotherapist and best-selling author Thomas Moore uses the phrase "caring for the soul" to describe the ongoing process of cultivating the inner emotional and spiritual self.[42] In an organizational setting, Moore says you can feed your soul through the following:

Intimacy (closeness and connection). Organizations foster intimacy through encouraging friendship, repeating the history of a business to foster employee attachment, opening up contact between departments, storytelling, creating a sense of family, and being sensitive to the community.

Creative work. Creativity is a drive or impulse that needs to be supported by allowing people to work in their own ways and by accepting their failures. Even routine tasks are creative because they produce products and profits, further careers, and generate new organizational structures.

Nature and beauty. Refreshment comes through encounters with nature, whether in the form of landscaping, interior design, a park, or the countryside. Nature is a provider of what every soul must have—beauty. Unfortunately, by focusing on success, the modern organization sacrifices beauty for efficiency. Colors, textures, and sounds are essential to the soul but are often forgotten in the rush to build drab, inexpensive, and efficient buildings. Stopping to contemplate beauty is seen as a barrier to progress instead of as a vital way to nourish the soul.

Spirituality. The term *sacred* need not be reserved solely for personal beliefs. Work can be dedicated to higher purposes, as we've seen. In addition, business activity is sacred because it has a dramatic impact on the lives of individual workers, the community, and the economy as a whole. Corporations attuned to the soul recognize that making a profit can work in harmony with other important values like concern for the poor and the environment. These groups establish a strong business identity and earn the trust of outsiders. (We'll take an in-depth look at organizational citizenship in Chapter 11.)

CONTEMPORARY ISSUES IN ORGANIZATIONAL ETHICS 2.1

THE DANGERS OF WORKPLACE SPIRITUALITY

Despite its benefits, there are reasons to be cautious about incorporating spirituality into the workplace. First, there is a danger of proselytizing, as managers and entire companies try to convert workers to their particular religious or spiritual doctrines. This can lead to coercion, favoritism, and discrimination. Second, not all members will feel comfortable with incorporating spirituality into the workplace and may consider it a personal issue or an invasion of privacy. Others may sense a threat to their power and status. The third problem is the risk of using interest in spiritual topics as a management tool to manipulate employees or of treating spirituality as the latest management fad. Spirituality then becomes another way for leaders to exert power, power that extends into the personal lives of employees. Because spirituality appears to enhance productivity, it is tempting for leaders to focus on spiritual values not because they speak to inner needs but because they motivate employees to work

(Continued)

(Continued)

harder. Fourth, authoritarian leaders may use spirituality to foster dependence in followers. There are ways to address the potential dangers of bringing spiritual concerns into the workplace. These include (1) accommodating the spiritual requests of all employees from all religious traditions; (2) respecting the spiritual diversity of employees; and (3) making openness and respect for diversity the center of organizational attention, allowing all employees the freedom to express their values and feelings.

Source: Boje (2008). Tourish (2013).

Spiritual Well-Being

Workplace spirituality expert John Fisher and his colleagues offer a model of spiritual health as a way to track our spiritual progress.[43] They believe that spiritual health is key to overall health and well-being. It is linked to, and ties together, the other dimensions of well-being—physical, mental, emotional, social, vocational. Spiritual health, in turn, is made up of four domains. The *personal* domain addresses an individual's meaning, purpose, and values in life and creates self-identity. The *communal* domain deals with the depth and quality of interpersonal relationships and ties to morality and culture. Communal values include love, justice, hope, and faith in humankind. The *environmental* domain incorporates care and nurture for the natural world, a sense of awe and wonder, and connection with the environment. The *transcendental* domain describes the relationship between the self and some-thing or some-One beyond humanity, a Transcendent Other (e.g., God, cosmic force). This domain is reflected in faith and adoration for this larger force.

Many people place priority on one domain over the others. *Personalists* see the personal domain as their measure of spiritual health. They rely on themselves and focus on discovering their own purpose and values. *Communalists* focus on harmony in relationships with others. To these individuals, spiritual health is built through relationships. *Environmentalists* see nature as the measure of spiritual health. They are in tune with nature and are inspired by it. (Many indigenous peoples would fall into this category.) *Religionists* focus on the transcendental domain. Faith is key to them and they are most interested in communicating with a larger force. According to Fisher and his colleagues, those with the best spiritual health score high in all four dimensions. Complete the Spiritual Well-Being Questionnaire in Self-Assessment 2.2 to assess your level of spiritual well-being.

SELF-ASSESSMENT 2.2

Spiritual Well-Being Questionnaire

Instructions

This questionnaire explores your views on the term "spiritual." Assess each item against the question: "How much is this a component of spirituality?" For each item, respond using a five-point scale: *very little* (1), *little* (2), *medium* (3), *much* (4), or *very much* (5).

1. Celebrating significant moments

2. Zest for life
3. The place of obedience in living
4. Valuing personal instincts
5. Awareness of life's mysteries
6. Appreciating life as it happens
7. Justice
8. Honesty
9. Experiencing drama
10. Experiencing art
11. Trust between individuals
12. Forgiveness between individuals
13. Appreciating the natural environment
14. Moments of solitude
15. Appreciating beauty
16. Having responsibilities
17. Scientific understanding of the universe
18. Admiring something
19. Religious belief
20. Belonging to a faith community
21. Perception of living as a response to God (Other)
22. Personal relationship with God (Other)
23. Reverence to God (Other)
24. Admiring God (Other)

Source: Fisher, Francis, and Johnson (2000).

Scoring

Add up your score for each domain and then add up the domain scores to come up with a total score. Higher scores indicate that you give priority to that domain. Your total score reflects your overall spiritual well-being.

Personal well-being: items 1–6 _____ (range 6–30)

Communal well-being: items 7–12 _____ (range 6–30)

Environmental well-being: items 13–18 _____ (range 6–30)

Transcendental well-being: items 19–24 _____ (range 6–30)

Total well-being _____ (range 24–120)

It is also possible to measure the spiritual health of our workplaces. The following values are markers of spiritual progress. The more your organization demonstrates these commitments, the greater its level of spiritual well-being.[1]

- *Benevolence:* kindness toward employees; desire to promote their happiness and well-being
- *Generativity:* interest in leaving something worthy behind for those who follow; mentoring; active care for the environment
- *Humanism:* practices and policies that promote personal growth; concern for the entire person; blurring of work and family life
- *Integrity:* focus on wholeness; alignment of personal and organizational values; consistent policies
- *Justice:* fair treatment of employees; impartial decision-making processes
- *Mutuality:* feelings of interconnection and interdependence; meaningful work; cohesive work groups with control over their goals/tasks
- *Receptivity:* flexible thinking; open-mindedness; creativity
- *Respect:* demonstration of consideration and concern for others; valuing employees
- *Responsibility:* independent follow-through on goals; empowerment; ability to overcome obstacles
- *Trust:* confidence in fellow workers and the organization as a whole

CHAPTER TAKEAWAYS

- Components of personal moral development are essential to improving ethical performance.

- Discovering your vocation means determining your purpose in life, which is based on a clear understanding of your unique skills, abilities, and desires. Following your vocation produces greater self-fulfillment, makes you a better steward, and equips you for more productive service to others. To hear your call, you'll need to set aside ambition, distractions, and resistance based on fears and low self-esteem. If circumstances interfere with your ability to follow your vocation, you may need to recraft your job or role to better fit your purpose.

- Moral values serve as guiding principles that drive behavior and help us determine right from wrong. If your principles agree with those of your organization, you will experience a better fit, helping you feel more committed to the group and more satisfied with your job.

- Materialistic or external values generally lead to a lower quality of life. Focus instead on internal values related to self-acceptance/personal growth (choosing what to do, following your curiosity), relatedness/intimacy (expressing love, forming intimate relationships), and community feeling/helpfulness (making other people's lives better, making the world a better place).

- High moral character will better enable you to make wise ethical choices. Direct approaches to character building include formal character education programs and psychological interventions designed to develop specific virtues. You can also foster the virtues that make up character though such indirect means as (1) developing moral habits, (2) observing and imitating ethical role models, (3) telling and living collective stories, and (4) learning from passage experiences.

- Moral identity motivates ethical behavior. From a traits perspective, those with high moral identity define themselves in terms of their ethical beliefs and feel compelled to act on those commitments. You can foster your moral identity throughout your life. Work with others on important ethical projects and join organizations that heighten your awareness of your ethical values. From a cognitive perspective, moral identity is one of our many "selves" that can be activated by elements of the situation, such as close relationships, moral discussion, focus on mission and values, and involvement in the community.

- Spirituality can play an important role in your moral development and that of your organization. Organizational spirituality recognizes the importance of inner needs, meaningful work, and community. Nourish your soul through intimacy (closeness and connection), exposure to nature and beauty, and recognition of the sacred nature of work.

- You can determine your personal spiritual health along four dimensions: personal, communal, environmental, and transcendent. You can measure your organization's spiritual progress by its policies and practices that support spiritual values.

- When addressing spirituality in the workplace, don't impose one particular set of spiritual values but respect and foster religious and spiritual diversity.

APPLICATION PROJECTS

1. Use the steps outlined in the chapter to identify a job that fits your vocation. Identify distractions that might be keeping you from hearing your calling. Determine how you might put these pressures and preoccupations aside.

2. With classmates, create a list of six to eight virtues that you think are most important in the workplace. Present your list and defend your choices to the rest of the class.

3. How do your values impact your behavior at work? What values conflicts do you have with coworkers? How good is the match between your values and those of your employer? Write up your conclusions.

4. What habits do you want to develop? How will you go about developing them?

5. Analyze a popular television drama from an ethical perspective. Identify the issues raised by the program, the values it promotes, and the virtues and vices demonstrated by the important characters.

6. Identify some key passages in your life. What have you learned from these experiences?

7. Develop a case study based on someone you consider to be an outstanding moral example. How does this person demonstrate character and high moral identity? What factors contributed to this person's moral development? What do you learn from this person's example that can help you develop your character and moral identity?

8. Choose two strategies for nurturing your soul and implement them on a daily basis for two weeks. Note any changes in your attitudes and behavior.

9. Complete Self-Assessment 2.1. What do the results tell you about your vocation and where you might be most productive? Discuss your conclusions with a friend. Or complete Self-Assessment 2.2. What do your results reveal about your spiritual well-being? Do you score higher in one domain than the others? How did you rate your overall spiritual health?

10. Evaluate the spiritual health of an organization you belong to using the values described in this chapter.

CASE STUDY 2.1

Character Development at West Point

The United States Military Academy at West Point takes character development very seriously, seeking to graduate soldiers who are honorable, courageous, loyal, patriotic, just, and caring. Their efforts are centered around this 12-word honor code: "A cadet will not lie, cheat, steal, or tolerate those that do." New students receive 12 hours of training on the code their freshman year, and cadets are in charge of administering the code. They conduct investigations, rule on violations, and oversee the code training program.

There are seven components to the West Point character development program. First, all students have to take courses in ethics, psychology, and military law that introduce ethical issues. Professors provide opportunities for students to practice ethical behavior through unproctored exams and take-home graded assignments. Second, faculty, administrators, and students provide values instruction through ongoing training programs taking place over four years. Third, all students are required to participate in at least one contact sport and take a swimming course to overcome personal fears. When it comes to intramural sports, demonstrating character is more important than

(Continued)

(Continued)

winning. (It is possible to win a game and later forfeit due to poor sportsmanship.) Fourth, from the sophomore year on, cadets are placed in leadership positions where they have to exercise moral judgment and demonstrate virtues. Fifth, faculty and administrators are recruited to be role models and are trained to focus on cadet character development. Sixth, students are assigned both academic advisers and professional mentors. Seven, physical structures on campus reinforce important virtues. Buildings are named after successful graduates and there are statues of George Washington, Dwight Eisenhower, and other role models. Plaques with the names of Medal of Honor graduates are scattered around campus.

Action learning is an underlying theme of the Academy's character development efforts. Cadets are constantly placed in situations where they have to put their ethics into action—on the athletic field, in their leadership roles, in the classroom, and in the dorm. They then have an opportunity to reflect on what they learned through these hands-on experiences.

The last part of the honor code, called the nontoleration clause ("or tolerate those that do"), plays a particularly important role in molding character. Many cadets have been dismissed from the Academy for observing unethical behavior but keeping silent. The nontoleration clause makes students accountable to one another. Cadets have to turn in their friends if they lie or cheat. However, a number of cadets report that obeying the nontoleration clause actually improves relationships. Said one, "If somebody is truly your friend, they won't ever put you in that position to tolerate and to choose between being your friend and doing the right thing."

Source: Dufresne and Offstein (2012).

Skeptics could argue that West Point has an advantage because it admits only students who are morally advanced. However, this does not appear to be the case. Academy officials report that approximately 80% of incoming freshmen admit to having cheated at least once in high school, which is consistent with results from other colleges. One study found that the moral judgment of West Point freshmen was no higher than that of a sample of incoming students at a comparison group of liberal arts colleges.

Discussion Probes

1. Should all colleges and universities make character development an important component of their mission? Why or why not?

2. Should character be a criterion for hiring faculty at other colleges and universities? Should faculty be expected to be moral role models?

3. Does your school have an honor code? How effective is this code? What role do students play in administering it?

4. Does participation in athletics build character, as West Point believes?

5. Do you think the nontoleration clause is too demanding?

6. What are the strengths of the United States Military Academy character development program? What are its weaknesses?

7. What elements of the West Point character development program could be implemented at your college or university?

CASE STUDY 2.2

Taking Down the Monuments: Erasing History?

Those seeking evidence for the power of lived stories need look no further than the battle over the removal of Confederate monuments. Following the shooting of nine black church members in South Carolina by white supremacist Dylann Roof, there has been a push to remove Confederate symbols from public view. South Carolina voted to take the Confederate flag from statehouse grounds and Alabama removed the flag from its state capitol. Other states stopped making specialty Confederate license plates.

As part of the South's effort to confront its past, the city government of New Orleans, led by mayor Mitch Landrieu, voted to remove four Confederate memorials. These included an obelisk commemorating a white supremacist attack on the city's Reconstruction Era integrated police force, and statues of Confederate president Jefferson Davis, Confederate general (and first head of the Ku Klux Klan) P. G. T. Beauregard, and Robert E. Lee. The statues will be released to nonprofits or governments who will accept them, as long as they are not publicly displayed. The markers will be replaced with fountains and United States flags. After the removal of the Robert E. Lee statue, Landrieu, who is Caucasian, said:

> It's not good to continue to revere a false version of history and put the Confederacy on a pedestal. We as a nation are far enough from this that we ought to acknowledge that the Confederacy was on the wrong side of history.[1]

Due to death threats, removal of the first three statues was carried out at night without advance notice by masked workmen wearing bulletproof vests and guarded by snipers. (The Lee statue had to be removed in daylight for fear of hitting power lines.) Company names on worker vehicles were covered up following death threats and the firebombing of a contractor's car. Republicans in the Louisiana legislature proposed a bill to stop the further removal of Confederate monuments. The State of Alabama passed a law imposing $25,000 fines for taking down Confederate memorials.

Opponents of monument removal argue that the memorials are important historical reminders that honor proud Southern heritage. Taking them down erases an important part of United States history, critics say. They complain that removal is political correctness run amok, a power play that deliberately humiliates millions of southerners who had nothing to do with the Civil War. To opponents, felling Confederate monuments is a "cultural purge." The problem of racism isn't limited to the South, they note, but is nationwide. Less strident opponents point out that the New Orleans monuments were important neighborhood markers and that leaving them up would be a better way to spark conversation about the South's racist legacy. Some have ancestors who fought in the Civil War. They claim that Robert E. Lee and General Beauregard apparently softened their bigotry later in life. (Beauregard left the Ku Klux Klan when it shifted from police force to white supremacist group.)

(Continued)

(Continued)

Proponents of removal see the statues as symbols of oppressive racism and an attempt to glorify the South's participation in a shameful attempt to retain slavery. Mayor Landrieu calls those lobbying to keep the monuments members of the "Cult of the Lost Cause."[2] Historians report that many of the statues were put up well after the war in an attempt to burnish the South's image and to promote the idea that southerners shouldn't feel guilt for supporting slavery and succession. Some scholars believe that putting the monuments in museums is a better way to promote discussion about the past. In response to those who have relatives who fought in the Civil War, Tulane history professor Randy Sparks argues, "My ancestors were slave owners who fought for the Confederacy. I take no pride in that, nor am I ashamed of it. They were men of their time and place. But this is *our* time, and *our* place."[3]

Debates over how to treat racist historical figures are not limited to the South. Princeton University removed the name of John Calhoun, a U.S. vice president and a proponent of slavery, from one of its residential colleges. The University of Oregon took the name of a former Ku Klux Klan leader off a dormitory but refused demands by black students to rename another facility, determining that the building's namesake had a less offensive legacy.

Discussion Probes

1. What values are in conflict in the battle over monument removal?
2. Is the removal of Confederate symbols a form of "cultural cleansing"?
3. Does taking down Confederate statues make it less likely that people will confront the past? Where should the monuments be housed if they are removed?
4. How should we deal with the unsavory, shameful aspects of the stories of our organizations, communities, and cultures?
5. What guidelines should governments, colleges, and nonprofits follow when deciding when to remove monuments or to change the names of buildings?
6. Did New Orleans make the right decision to remove its Confederate monuments? Why or why not?

Notes

1. Associated Press (2017b).
2. "New Orleans Confederate" (2017).
3. Chotiner (2017).

Sources: J. D. Davidson (2017). Hesse (2016). D. Moore (2017). Newsome (2017). Smithers (2015). Sterling (2015). Theen (2017).

CASE STUDY 2.3

A Different Kind of Pope

Pope Francis is certainly not your typical pontiff. Since being elected to head the Catholic Church in 2013, Pope Francis (formerly Argentine archbishop Jorge Mario Bergoglio) has deliberately set himself apart from his predecessors. He refuses to live in the papal apartment, living instead in a modest bungalow on the Vatican grounds. He eats his dinner with priests and visitors, taking any available seat. He refers to cardinals as "brother cardinals" instead of "your lordships," as is the custom. Extremely frugal, the pontiff drives a 1984 Renault instead of the Mercedes Benz cars driven by other modern popes. At his installation Mass, he pledged to serve "the poorest, the weakest, the least important." He is the first pope chosen from the Jesuit order, which emphasizes service, and the first from Latin America.

Pope Francis acts more like a parish priest than the traditional leader of a billion-member organization that some believe is the richest institution in the world. He routinely greets visitors (posing with one group for a "selfie"), travels about in an open-air vehicle for public appearances, and is quick to wade into crowds to shake hands and hold babies. Perhaps nothing has endeared him more to the public than his habit of spontaneously calling people, which earned him the nickname "Cold-Call Pope." He called to cancel his newspaper subscription and to talk to his cobbler in Buenos Aires. On New Year's Eve he left a message at a Spanish nunnery, jokingly asking the nuns where they were that evening. He also talks to ordinary citizens who write him with their problems. In one case he consoled a pregnant Italian woman whose boyfriend had abandoned her (he offered to do the baby's baptism if no one else would). In another he chatted with a young gay man. In a third instance he offered his support to an Argentine woman who had been raped by a police officer. He even goes so far as to call his opponents, dialing an Argentine journalist who took issue with the pontiff's plans to meet with the outgoing Argentine president.

The pope's more humble, accessible style, along with his attempts to shift focus away from such controversial issues as gay marriage, abortion, and contraception, have renewed the faith of many in the Church. Said one Italian Catholic, "I feel like I am a new Catholic since he became pope . . . I feel he is very close to us ordinary people. His words touch anybody's heart."[1] Pope Francis also makes efforts to reach out beyond the church. He gave a surprise TED talk via video link where he urged leaders to act humbly. Francis noted that his family immigrated to Argentina and he could have ended up as one of the "discarded people" (the sick, migrants). He asks himself, "Why them and not me?"[2]

Some observers in the Catholic Church, while applauding his style, doubt that Francis can have a lasting impact on the Vatican. The pope is a political leader as well as a spiritual one. He serves as the head of a global empire headquartered in the world's smallest sovereign state, located in Rome. The Vatican government resembles a medieval court, with lower-level officials often scrambling for power. It has been described as "an ancient monarchy in which the pope is treated like a king, branches of the hierarchy are run like medieval fiefs and suppliants vie for success and influence."[3] In recent years the Vatican has been plagued by banking and money-laundering scandals. Failure to root out this corruption apparently was a factor leading to the decision of Pope Benedict, Francis's predecessor, to resign his post. He was the first pontiff to resign his post in 600 years. Recently, Australian cardinal George Pell, the man appointed by Pope Francis to oversee and reform the Vatican's financial operations, was charged with sexually abusing children.

Discussion Probes

1. What virtues does Pope Francis demonstrate? How does he demonstrate a strong moral identity?

(Continued)

(Continued)

2. What are the advantages and disadvantages of Pope Francis's leadership style?
3. Would Pope Francis be more effective if he acted like a more traditional leader?
4. Do you think Pope Francis will be able to change the culture of the Vatican?
5. Should the Pope put down his cell phone or continue his cold calls? Why?

Notes

1. Donadio (2013).
2. Kilpatrick (2017).
3. Donadio and Yardley (2013).

Sources: Berlinger and Smith-Spark (2017). D. Burke (2015). L. Goodstein (2013). Povoledo and Bilefsky (2013). Preston (2013). Romero and Neuman (2013). Speciale and Gibson (2013). Yglesias (2013).

CHAPTER THREE

ETHICAL DECISION MAKING AND ACTION

Chapter Preview

Components of Ethical Behavior
    Component 1: Moral Sensitivity
      (Recognition)
    Component 2: Moral Judgment
    Component 3: Moral Motivation
    Component 4: Moral Character
Decision-Making Formats
    The Lonergan/Baird Method
    The Moral Compass

The Foursquare Protocol
Five Timeless Questions
The Five "I" Format
Chapter Takeaways
Application Projects

Now that we've examined ethical competencies, ethical perspectives, and the components of personal moral development, we're ready to put them to use. This chapter focuses both on the how (the processes) and the how-to (the formats) of moral thinking and action drawing from the first two chapters. Our chances of coming up with a sound, well-reasoned conclusion and executing our plan are greater if we understand how ethical decisions are made and take a morally grounded, systematic approach to problem solving. As you'll see, ethical abilities, moral principles, values, character, and spiritual resources all come into play when making ethical decisions.

COMPONENTS OF ETHICAL BEHAVIOR

Breaking the process down into its component parts enhances understanding of ethical decision making and behavior. Moral psychologist James Rest identifies four elements of ethical action. Rest developed his four-component model by asking, "What must happen psychologically in order for moral behavior to take place?" He concluded that ethical action is the product of these psychological subprocesses: (1) moral sensitivity (recognition); (2) moral judgment or reasoning; (3) moral motivation; and (4) moral character.[1] The first half of the chapter is organized around Rest's framework. I'll describe each factor and then offer some tips for improving your performance on that element of Rest's model.

Component 1: Moral Sensitivity (Recognition)

Moral sensitivity is the recognition that an ethical problem exists. Such recognition requires us to be aware of how our behavior impacts others, to identify possible courses of action, and to determine the consequences of each potential strategy. Moral sensitivity is key to practicing individual ethics. We can't solve a moral dilemma unless we know that one is present. For that reason, raising ethical awareness is an important goal of many ethics courses and programs. (Test your moral sensitivity by responding to the scenarios in Self-Assessment 3.1.)

Perspective skills are essential to identifying and exploring moral issues. Understanding how others might feel or react can alert us to the potential negative effects of our choices and makes it easier to predict the likely outcomes of various options. For example, the central figure in the first scenario of Case Study 3.2, "Is It Better to Ask Permission or to Ask Forgiveness?" understands the perspective of the neighbors. He realizes that he faces an ethical problem as a result. Emotions such as anger, disgust, and guilt give us the energy to identify ethical problems.[2] (I'll have more to say about moral emotions later in the chapter.)

According to University of Virginia ethics professor Patricia Werhane, many smart, well-meaning managers also stumble because they are victims of tunnel vision.[3] Their ways of thinking or mental models don't include important ethical considerations. In other words, they lack moral imagination. Take the case of the Nestlé Company. This European food producer makes a very high-quality infant formula, which the firm successfully marketed in North America, Europe, and Asia. It seemed to make sense for the company to market the formula in East Africa using the same communication strategies that had worked elsewhere. However, Nestlé officials failed to take into account important cultural differences. Many East African mothers could not read label directions and were so poor that, to make the product last longer, they overdiluted it, and they used polluted water to mix it. In a society that honors medicine men, parents felt pressured to use the formula because it was advertised with pictures of men in white coats. As a result, many poor African mothers wasted money on formula when they could have breastfed their children for free. Thousands of their babies died after drinking formula mixed with polluted water. Nestlé refused to stop its marketing campaign despite pressure from the World Health Organization and quit only when faced with a major boycott. Company leaders hadn't considered the possible dangers of marketing to third-world mothers and failed to recognize that they were engaged in unethical activities.

To exercise moral imagination, managers and employees step outside their current frame of reference (disengage themselves) to assess a situation and evaluate options. They then generate creative solutions. Werhane points to Chicago's South Shore Bank as an example of moral imagination at work. In the early 1970s, a group of investors bought a failing bank in the impoverished South Shore neighborhood and began loaning money for residential restoration. Few people in the area qualified for traditional bank loans, so South Shore managers developed a new set of criteria. Loan officers gave credit to individuals of limited means who had good reputations. The bank prospered and, at the same time, the neighborhood became a desirable place to live. South Shore's morally imaginative owners and managers envisioned a profitable financial institution in a depressed, poverty-stricken area. They disproved traditional "bank logic" by demonstrating that they could make money in a responsible manner under tough conditions.

Moral muteness, like lack of moral imagination, interferes with the recognition of moral issues. Managers can be reluctant to talk about their actions in ethical terms. They may want to avoid controversy or may believe that keeping silent will help them appear practical, efficient, powerful, and capable of handling their own problems.[4] Describing a situation in moral terms breaks this ethical code of silence. Such terms as *values*, *justice*, *immoral*, *character*, *right*, and *wrong* encourage listeners to frame an event as an ethical problem and to engage in moral reasoning.[5]

A number of researchers believe that elements of the ethical issue itself are key to whether or not we recognize its existence. They argue that problems or dilemmas differ in their degrees of *moral intensity*. The greater an issue's moral intensity, the more likely we are to notice it. The components of moral intensity include the following six elements:[6]

1. *Magnitude of consequences.* The moral intensity of an issue is directly tied to the number of harms or benefits it generates. Moral dilemmas attract more attention when they have significant consequences. For example, denying someone a job because of his or her race raises significant ethical concerns; rescheduling an employee's vacation dates does not. A massive oil spill generates stronger condemnation than a minor one.

2. *Social consensus.* Moral issues are more intense if there is widespread agreement that they are bad (or good). Societal norms, laws, professional standards, and corporate regulations all signal that there is social consensus on a particular issue.

3. *Probability of effect.* Probability of effect is "a joint function of the probability that the act in question will actually take place and the act in question will actually cause the harm (benefit) predicted."[7] For instance, selling a gun to a gang member has a much greater likelihood of causing harm than does selling a gun to a law-abiding citizen.

4. *Temporal immediacy.* Issues are more intense if they are likely to generate harm or good sooner rather than later. That helps explain why proposals to immediately reduce social security benefits attract more attention than proposals to gradually reduce them over a long period of time.

5. *Proximity.* Proximity refers to social, cultural, psychological, or physical distance. We tend to care more about issues involving people who are close to us in terms of race, nationality, age, and other factors; we care less about issues involving people who are significantly distant from us or significantly different from us. (Case Study 3.1 describes executives who stumbled because of the distance between them and their victims.)

6. *Concentration of effect.* Causing intense suffering violates our sense of justice and increases moral intensity. Thus, we are more likely to take note of policies that do severe damage to a few individuals than to take note of those that have minor consequences for large groups of people. For instance, cutting the salaries of 10 people by $20,000 each is seen as more problematic than reducing the salaries of 4,000 employees by $50 each.

Moral intensity has been correlated not only with moral sensitivity but also with the other components of Rest's model—moral judgment, moral motivation, and moral behavior.[8] Not only are decision makers more likely to recognize morally intense issues, but they also respond more quickly and appropriately. In addition, decision makers faced with intense issues are more motivated to follow through on their choices. However, investigators are still trying to determine if some components of moral intensity are more critical to problem recognition and resolution. At this point, magnitude of consequences and social consensus appear to have the strongest relationship to moral sensitivity. Individuals are most likely to notice ethical dilemmas if they generate significant harm and if there is widespread agreement that these issues have a moral dimension.

Tips for Enhancing Your Ethical Sensitivity

Engage in active listening and role playing. The best way to learn about the potential ethical consequences of choices, as well as the likely response of others, is through listening closely to what others have to say. (See Chapter 4 for a closer look at the process of active listening.) Role play can also foster understanding. Taking the part of another individual or group can provide you with important insight into how the other party is likely to react.

Pay attention to your feelings. Emotions can signal the presence of an ethical issue. Look further to determine if this is indeed the case.

Speak up. Don't hesitate to discuss problems and your decisions in ethical terms. Doing so will help frame arguments as ethical ones for you and your colleagues.

Challenge mental models or schemas. Recognize the dangers of your current mental models and try to visualize other perspectives. Distance yourself from a situation to determine if it indeed does have moral implications. Remember that you have ethical duties that extend beyond your group or organization.

Adapt to the situation. Consider whether there is a general consensus about an ethical issue and whether or not you have the power to address the problem. Choose your strategy accordingly.

Be creative. Look for innovative ways to define and respond to ethical dilemmas; visualize creative opportunities and solutions.

Crank up the moral intensity. Frame issues to increase their intensity and thus improve problem recognition. In particular, emphasize the size of the problem—how many people are affected, how much the company or environment will be damaged. Point out how even small acts like petty theft can have serious consequences. Also, highlight the fact that there is consensus about whether a course of action is wrong (illegal, against professional standards, opposed by coworkers) or right. As a group, develop shared understanding about the key ethical issues facing your organization.

SELF-ASSESSMENT 3.1

Moral Sensitivity Scenarios

Instructions

Read each of the following vignettes and determine if the scenario poses an ethical dilemma. Then turn to Application Project 2 to determine if you agree with the researchers who developed the scenarios.

Vignette 1

A manager in your area, Terry, drives a company car. Company policy states that corporate cars are to be inspected every 3,000 miles without exception. Terry last had her car inspected about 5,000 miles ago—she says that she "just doesn't want to be bothered that often." Today, Pat, a coworker of Terry's, asked Terry for the keys to the car so she could deliver some artwork to a few customers. While she was driving on the highway, the car's brakes malfunctioned. The car spun out of control and came to rest in a ditch on the side of the road. Pat's forehead struck the steering wheel, and she had to go to the hospital to get 18 stitches.

Vignette 2

One of DenComp's manufacturing facilities contains five very large and very noisy pressing machines. The facility manager has always followed state and federal regulations about noise control that apply to those machines, but the noise effects can never be completely eliminated. Doug, a longtime DenComp electrician who regularly works right next to the pressing machines (and always wears the proper equipment), came to your office and told you that his doctor has informed him that he has lost 80% of his hearing in his right ear, probably because of the work he does near the machines.

Vignette 3

Earlier today, a DenComp salesman who works in Iowa called you and told you about an experience that he had last week. One of his customers placed a small order of about $1,500 worth of product from DenComp's corporate headquarters. DenComp immediately shipped the package through a freight company, and it arrived the next day at the freight company's warehouse in Iowa. The salesman went to the warehouse just as it was closing and talked to one of its managers. The manager said that everyone had gone home for the day, but he assured him that the package would be delivered directly to his office the next day. The salesman knew that the customer did not need the materials for at least another three days, but he didn't want to wait. He placed a twenty-dollar bill on the counter and asked the warehouse manager one last time if there was anything he could do. The manager found the paperwork, got the product from the back of the warehouse, and brought it out to the salesman.

Vignette 4

Last Monday, you were sitting at your desk examining a request that a customer had just faxed you. The customer was proposing a project that would make a tremendous amount of money for your company but had an extremely demanding time schedule. Just as you were about to call the customer and accept the project, one of your employees, Phil, knocked on the door. He entered your office, politely placed a letter of resignation on your desk, and told you that he was sorry, but in two weeks, he would be moving to another state to be closer to his ailing parents. After he left, you thought about the proposed project and determined that even though Phil would be gone, you could still meet all of the customers' deadlines. You called the customer and accepted the project.

Source: Modified version of S. J. Reynolds (2006), pp. 242–243. Copyright © 2016 by the American Psychological Association. Used by permission.

Component 2: Moral Judgment

After determining that there is an ethical problem, decision makers then choose among the courses of action identified in Component 1. They make judgments about the right or wrong thing to do in this specific context.

Moral judgment has been studied more than any other element of the Rest model. There is far too much information to summarize it here. Instead, I'll focus on three topics that are particularly important to understanding how problem solvers determine whether a solution is right or wrong: cognitive moral development, unhealthy motivations, and cognitive biases.

Cognitive Moral Development

Before his death, Harvard psychologist Lawrence Kohlberg was the leading champion of the idea that individuals progress through a series of moral stages just as they do physical ones.[9] Each stage is more advanced than the one before. As individuals develop, their reasoning becomes more sophisticated. They become less self-centered and develop broader definitions of morality.

Preconventional thinking is the most primitive level and is common among children as well as those suffering from brain damage to emotional regions of the brain. Individuals at Level I decide on the basis of direct consequences. In the first stage, they obey to avoid punishment. In the second, they follow the rules in order to meet their own interests. Stage 2 thinkers believe that justice is giving a fair deal to others: You help me and I'll help you.

Conventional (Level II) thinkers look to other people for guidance for their actions. They strive to live up to the expectations of family members and significant others (Stage 3) or recognize the importance of going along with the laws of society (Stage 4). Kohlberg found that most adults fall into Stages 3 and 4, which suggests that the typical organizational member looks to work rules, leaders, and the situation to determine right from wrong.

Postconventional or principled (Level III) thinking is the most advanced type of reasoning and relies on universal values and principles. Stage 5 individuals are guided by utilitarian principles, seeking to do the greatest good for the greatest number. They recognize that there are a number of value systems within a democratic society and that regulations may have to be broken to serve higher moral purposes. Stage 6 thinkers operate according to internalized, universal ethical principles like the categorical imperative or justice as fairness. These principles apply in every situation and take precedence over the laws of any particular society. According to Kohlberg, only about 20% of Americans can be classified as Stage 5 postconventional moral thinkers. Very few individuals ever reach Stage 6.

Kohlberg's model has drawn heavy criticism from philosophers and psychologists alike.[10] Some philosophers complain that it draws too heavily from Rawls's theory of justice and makes deontological ethics superior to other ethical perspectives. They note that the theory applies more to societal issues than to individual ethical decisions. A number of psychologists have challenged the notion that people go through a rigid or "hard" series of moral stages. They argue instead that individuals can engage in many ways of thinking about a problem, regardless of their age.

Rest (who was a student of Kohlberg's) responded to these criticisms by replacing the hard stages with a staircase of developmental schemas. *Schemas* are general structures or patterns in our memories. We use these patterns or structures when we encounter new situations or information. When you enrolled in college, for example, you probably relied on high school experiences to determine how to act in the university classroom. Rest and his colleagues contend that decision makers shift upward, adopting more sophisticated moral schemas as they develop. Rest's group redefined the postconventional stage to make it less dependent on one ethical perspective. In their "neo-Kohlbergian" approach, the most advanced thinkers reason like moral philosophers.[11] Postconventional individuals look behind societal rules to determine if they serve moral purposes. These thinkers appeal to a shared vision of an ideal society. Such a society seeks the greatest good for the entire community and ensures rights and protections for everyone.

Rest developed the Defining Issues Test (DIT) to measure moral development. Subjects taking the DIT respond to six scenarios and then choose statements that best reflect how they went about making their choices. The statements—which correspond to the levels of moral development—are then scored. In the best-known dilemma, Heinz's wife is dying of cancer and needs a drug Heinz cannot afford to buy. He must decide whether or not to steal the drug to save her life.

Over 800 studies have been conducted using the DIT.[12] Among the findings:

- Moral reasoning ability generally increases with age.
- The total college experience, both inside and outside the classroom, increases moral judgment.[13]
- Those who love learning, taking risks, and meeting challenges generally experience the greatest moral growth while in college.
- Ethics coursework boosts the positive effects of the college experience, increasing moral judgment still further.
- Older students—those in graduate and professional school—gain a great deal from moral education programs.
- When education stops, moral development plateaus.
- Moral development is a universal concept, crossing cultural boundaries.
- There are no consistent differences between the moral reasoning of men and that of women.
- Principled leaders can improve the moral judgment of the group as a whole, encouraging members to adopt more sophisticated ethical schemas.

Destructive Motivations

No discussion of moral judgment is complete without consideration of why this process so often breaks down. Time after time, very bright people make very stupid decisions. Former President Bill Clinton illustrates this sad fact. By all accounts, Clinton was one of the country's brightest leaders. Not only was he a Rhodes scholar with a nearly photographic memory, but his former adviser, David Gergen, reports that Clinton could hold conversations with aides and visitors while completing the *New York Times* crossword puzzle. Somehow, the former chief executive thought he could have sex with an intern and keep the affair quiet despite constant media scrutiny. Further, he didn't think he would suffer any serious consequences if word got out. He was wrong on both counts.[14]

The moral stupidity of otherwise intelligent people can be explained in part by the power of their destructive motivations. Three motivating factors are particularly damaging: insecurities, greed, and ego.

1. *Insecurities.* Low self-esteem and inner doubts can drive individuals to use others to meet their own needs, and insecure people fall into the trap of tying their identities to their roles. Those plagued by self-doubt are blind to larger ethical considerations, and, at the same time, they are tempted to succeed at any cost.

2. *Greed.* Greed is more likely than ever to undermine ethical thinking because we live in a winner-take-all society.[15] The market economy benefits the few at the expense of the many. Consider the inequity of the salary structure at most fast food chains. Average fast-food workers make around $9 an hour, while the CEO at Yum! Brands (owner of KFC, Taco Bell, and Pizza Hut) took home $22 million in 2014 and the CEO of McDonald's earned $7.7 million. According to the Demos public policy group, the fast-food industry has the greatest pay disparity of all sectors of the U.S. economy, exceeding 1,000 to 1.[16] A winner-take-all culture encourages widespread cheating because the payoff is so high. In addition, losers justify their dishonesty by pointing to the injustice of the system and to the fact that they deserve a larger share of the benefits. When greed takes over, altruism disappears, along with any consideration of serving the greater good.

3. *Ego.* Even the most humble of us tend to greatly overestimate our abilities (more on this shortly).[17] Unless we are careful, we can become overconfident, ignore the risks and consequences of our choices, take too much credit when things go well and too little blame when they don't, and demand more than our fair share of organizational resources. Inflated egos become a bigger problem at higher levels of the organizational hierarchy. Top managers are often cut off from customers and employees. Unlike the rest of us, they don't have to wait in line for products or services or for a ride to work. Subordinates tell them what they want to hear and stroke their egos. All these factors make it easier for executives to excuse their unethical behavior—outrageous pay packages, diversion of company funds to private use—on the grounds that they are vital to the organization's success.

The formidable forces of insecurity, greed, and ego become even more powerful when managers and subordinates adopt a short-term orientation. Modern workers are under constant time pressures as organizations cut staffing levels while demanding higher performance in the form of shorter product development cycles, better customer service, and greater returns on investment. Employees are sorely tempted to do what is expedient instead of what is ethical. As ethics expert Laura Nash puts it, "Short-term pressures can silence moral reasoning by simply giving it no space. The tighter a manager's agenda is, the less time for contemplating complex, time-consuming, unpragmatic issues like ethics."[18]

Stress also generates unpleasant feelings, focusing managers solely on their own needs. They then adopt a lower level of moral reasoning. The conventional thinker, for example, might revert to preconventional reasoning.[19]

Time-pressed supervisors lose sight of the overall purpose of the organization and fail to analyze past conduct. They don't stop to reflect on their choices when things are going well. Overconfident, rushed decision makers are only too willing to move on to the next problem. Eventually, they begin to make mistakes that catch up with them. In addition, short-term thinkers begin to look for immediate gratification, which feeds their greedy impulses.

The damage caused by rushing to judgment can be seen in the results of a study by Ohio State professor Paul Nutt.[20] Professor Nutt examined 400 poor organizational decisions over a period of 20 years, including construction of Ford's failure to recall the Pinto and NASA's decision to launch the Challenger space shuttle. Adopting a short-term perspective helps to account for many of the decision-making blunders he uncovered. Nearsighted decision makers (1) overlooked important ethical questions, (2) came to premature conclusions, (3) failed to consult with important stakeholders, (4) lacked a clear direction, (5) limited their search for information, (6) demonstrated little creativity, and (7) learned little from either their successes or their failures.

Cognitive Biases

Harvard professor Max Bazerman and his colleagues believe that unethical choices are more often the product of perceptual and cognitive biases than of unhealthy motivations. These unconscious distortions cause us to participate in or approve of "ordinary unethical behaviors" that we would normally condemn.[21] Examples of common biases include the following:

1. *Overestimating our ethicality.* When it comes to ethics, the majority of us have a "holier than thou" attitude.[22] We believe that we are more caring, loyal, fair, and kind than the typical person and are quick to condemn others for their moral failings. In addition, we predict that we will behave more ethically in the future than we actually do and believe that we have behaved more ethically in the past than we actually have.

2. *Forgiving our own unethical behavior.* We want to be moral and to behave ethically. So, when we behave in an unethical fashion, we feel a sense of psychological tension called *cognitive dissonance* because our actions and self-images don't match. To relieve this distress, we either change our behavior or use a variety of tactics to excuse what we've done. One minimizing strategy is *moral disengagement*. In moral disengagement, organizational members convince themselves that their questionable behavior was really morally permissible because (1) it served a worthy purpose, (2) it was driven by outside forces ("My boss told me I had to it"), (3) it did not have any damaging consequences, or (4) the victims had it coming (dehumanizing them).[23] Another strategy is *motivated forgetting*. We have selective recall, remembering events in a way that supports our decisions. In particular, we forget that we have violated moral rules. Permissive work environments (those that excuse immoral behavior) encourage

moral disengagement and moral forgetting. However, reminding employees that ethical choices are important reduces the use of both tactics.[24]

3. *Overlooking other people's unethical behavior.* As noted above, we generally judge others more harshly than ourselves. But not always. There are times when we excuse others' unethical behavior.[25] We are tempted to forgive the ethical shortcomings of others when we benefit from their choices. Board members handpicked by the CEO are less likely to object to her/his decision to divert company funds for personal use. By the same token, we excuse the unsavory recruiting methods of the coach of our favorite basketball team if he or she has a winning record. Observers are less likely to hold people and organizations accountable if they delegate unethical behavior, as in the case of a manager who avoids blame by assigning a project and then declaring that employees should complete it "by any means possible." Merck used an indirect approach to shift blame when it sold the cancer drug Mustargen to another pharmaceutical company. The smaller firm raised the price of the medication tenfold. While Merck kept manufacturing the product, it deflected public criticism toward the other company. Gradual changes also encourage observers to ignore unethical behavior. We are less likely to notice declines in moral standards if they occur slowly over time; this is referred to as the *slippery slope.* Overlooking minor infractions like taking change from the cash register can lead to ignoring more serious offenses like stealing equipment.

4. *Implicit prejudice.* Implicit prejudice is different from conscious forms of prejudice like racism and sexism. This type of bias comes from our tendency to associate things that generally go together, like gray hair and old age or pickup trucks and blue-collar workers.[26] These associations are not always accurate (some young people go gray, and some blue-collar workers drive luxury cars). When it comes to personnel decisions, false associations discriminate against marginalized groups. For instance, those who hold unconscious gender stereotypes are less likely to hire women who demonstrate stereotypically "masculine" traits like independence or ambition for jobs requiring interpersonal skills and other stereotypically "feminine" qualities.

5. *Favoring members of our own group.* It's only natural to do favors for people we know who generally come from the same nationality, social class, religion, neighborhood, or alma mater as we do. We may ask the chair of the business department to meet with the daughter of a neighbor or recommend a fraternity brother for a job. Trouble is, when those in power give resources to members of their in-groups, they discriminate against those who are different from them.[27] A number of universities reserve admissions slots for the sons and daughters of alumni, for instance. Since Caucasians make up the vast majority of college graduates at most schools, white applicants may be selected over more qualified minority students who are not the children of graduates.

6. *Judging based on outcomes rather than on decision-making processes.* Employees are typically evaluated based on results, not on the quality of the decisions they make.[28] We determine that a choice is good if it turns out well and bad if it

generates negative consequences. However, just because a poorly made decision had a desirable outcome in one case doesn't mean that a similar decision won't turn out badly in the future. In fact, poor decision-making processes eventually produce bad (ineffective, unethical) results. Take the case of the university that depended on the recommendations of a popular administrator when hiring new staff. Relying totally on his advice—which circumvented the usual hiring process involving group input—led to several successful searches. However, the process broke down when the administrator recommended a candidate who was under indictment for embezzling hundreds of thousands of dollars from a local business. An embarrassed university quickly fired the new hire.

Tips for Improving Your Moral Judgment

Stay in school. The general college experience (including extracurricular activities) contributes greatly to moral development. However, you'll gain more if you have the right attitude. Focus on learning, not grades; be ready to take on new challenges.

Be intentional. While the general college experience contributes to moral development, focused attention on ethics also helps. Take ethics courses and units, discuss ethical issues in a group, and reflect on the ethical challenges you experience in internships.

Reject ethical pessimism. Ethical values and thought patterns are not set in childhood, as pessimists claim, but continue to grow and develop through college and graduate school and beyond.

Take a broader view. Try to consider the needs and positions of others outside your immediate group; determine what is good for the community as a whole.

Look to underlying moral principles. Since the best ethical thinkers base their choices on widely accepted ethical guidelines, do the same. Draw upon important ethical approaches such as utilitarianism, the categorical imperative, and justice as fairness for guidance.

Acknowledge your dark side. Before coming to a conclusion, try to determine if your decision is shaped by feelings of self-doubt and self-interest or your need to feed your ego. If so, then reconsider.

Step outside yourself. We can't help but see the world through our own selfish biases. However, we have a responsibility to check our perceptions against reality. Consult with others before making a choice, consider the likely perspective of other parties (refer back to our earlier discussion of role taking), and double-check your assumptions and information.

Keep your ego in check. Stay close to those who will tell you the truth and hold you accountable. At the same time, don't punish those who point out your deficiencies.

Take a long-term perspective. In an emergency (when lives are immediately at stake, for example), you may be forced to make a quick decision. In all other situations, provide space for ethical reflection and deliberation. Resist the temptation to grab on to the first solution. Take time to reduce your level of stress, consult with others, gather the necessary data, probe for underlying causes, and set a clear direction. Adopting a long-term perspective also means putting future benefits above immediate needs. In most cases, the organization and its clients and consumers are better served by emphasizing enduring relationships. You may make an immediate profit by selling low-quality products, but customers will be hurt and refuse to buy again, lowering corporate performance.

Apply rational remedies to overcome your cognitive biases. Use the conscious strategies outlined in Ethical Checkpoint 3.1 to avoid the traps posed by your unconscious biases.

ETHICAL CHECKPOINT 3.1

Rational Remedies for Cognitive Biases

- Don't overestimate your ethical abilities.

- Prepare ahead of time (imagine how you will respond to questions, for example) so that you don't engage in unethical behavior under pressure.

- Publicly commit to an ethical course of action, or make such a commitment to someone who is important to you. (This increases the likelihood that you will follow through on your choices.)

- Recognize and resist your tendency to excuse your immoral actions.

- Create organizational climates that punish unethical behavior.

- Remind yourself and others of the importance of acting ethically (e.g., have students sign honor codes; post regulations and corporate values statements).

- Don't be lenient toward others because you are benefiting from their unethical behavior.

- Don't try to shift blame by delegating to others or excuse groups and individuals that take this approach.

- Don't ignore even minor ethical infractions, which can lead to much more serious transgressions.

- Put yourself in environments that challenge your implicit biases or stereotypes.

- Audit your organization to determine if it is trapped by in-group biases; eliminate initiatives that perpetuate the tendency to admit, hire, and promote those of similar backgrounds, like alumni children admission programs or rewards for employees who recommend people they know for jobs at the organization.

- Generate more equitable choices by pretending that you don't know what group you belong to when making decisions and by imagining how a policy change will impact different groups.

- Evaluate the quality of the decision-making process, not the outcome; don't condemn those who make good-quality decisions only to see them turn out badly.

Component 3: Moral Motivation

After reaching a conclusion about the best course of action, decision makers must be motivated to follow through on their choices. Moral values often conflict with other important values like job security, career advancement, social acceptance, and wealth. Ethical behavior will result only if moral considerations take precedence over competing priorities.

Moral hypocrisy demonstrates how competing values can overcome our commitment to doing the right thing. In moral hypocrisy, individuals and groups want to appear moral but don't want to pay the price for actually behaving morally.[29] Self-interest overwhelms their self-integrity. For example, participants in experimental settings say that dividing pleasant tasks equally with a partner is the moral course of action. However, when they believe that their partners will never find out, subjects assign themselves the majority of pleasant tasks, in violation of their moral standard. The same pattern is repeated in real-life settings. Sellers often use privileged information to take advantage of purchasers. They might hide the fact that the car they are selling was in a serious accident or needs a new transmission. Companies may use public relations campaigns and marketing to maintain their ethical reputations while continuing to engage in unethical activities. Tobacco giant Philip Morris provides one example of corporate moral hypocrisy in action. The firm spent much more money publicizing its charitable contributions ($108 million) than it did on the charitable contributions themselves ($60 million).

People are more likely to engage in moral hypocrisy when there is a high cost for behaving ethically, when they can disguise their actions, when they are in a powerful position, and when they can easily justify their inconsistent behavior by claiming that they are acting out of self-defense or are serving the greater good.

Three factors—rewards, emotions and duty orientation—play an important role in ethical follow-through. It is easier to give priority to ethical values when rewarded for doing so. Conversely, moral motivation drops when the reward system honors inappropriate behavior.[30] Individuals are much more likely to act ethically when they are evaluated on how well they adhere to important values and when they receive raises, bonuses, promotions, and public recognition for doing so. On the other hand, they are motivated to lie, steal, act abusively, take bribes, and cheat when offenders prosper. Before the housing crisis which led to a global recession, far too many lending officers at mortgage companies generated large commissions by lying to borrowers. They misled homeowners about the terms of their loans and steered them into loan products they couldn't afford. (Reward and performance evaluation systems will be discussed in more detail in Chapter 10.)

Moral emotions are another significant influence on motivation. Moral emotions are the product of living in human society (they are social in nature) and are elicited by the violation of moral standards.[31] (See Contemporary Issues in Organizational Ethics 3.1 for more information on the role of emotions in the decision-making process.) They are focused on the needs of others, not the self. Moral feelings encourage us to take action that benefits other people and the good of the community. Sympathy, empathy, and compassion are prosocial or *other-suffering* emotions. They are elicited when we perceive suffering or sorrow in our fellow human beings. Such feelings encourage us to comfort, help, and alleviate the pain of others. We might call our congressional representative to protest cuts in the federal food stamp program or send money to a humanitarian organization working with displaced persons. Humans are also sensitive to the suffering of other creatures, leading to efforts to prevent cruelty to animals and to care for abandoned pets.[32]

Shame, embarrassment, and guilt are self-blame or *self-conscious* emotions that encourage us to obey the rules and uphold the social order. These feelings are triggered when we violate norms and social conventions, present the wrong image to others, cause harm, fail to live up to moral guidelines, or receive unfair benefits. Shame and embarrassment can keep us from engaging in further damaging behavior and may drive us to withdraw from social contact. Guilt generally motivates us to action—to repair the wrongs we have done, to address inequalities, and to treat others well.

Anger, disgust, and contempt are other-blaming or *other-condemning* emotions. They are elicited by unfairness, betrayal, immorality, cruelty, poor performance, and status differences. Anger can motivate us to redress injustices like racism, oppression, and poverty. Disgust encourages us to set up rewards and punishments to deter inappropriate behaviors like betrayal and hypocrisy. Contempt generally causes us to step back from others who, for instance, are disrespectful or irresponsible.

Gratitude, awe, and elevation are *other-praising (positive)* emotions that are prompted by the good actions of other people. For instance, someone may act on our behalf, we may run across moral beauty (acts of charity, loyalty, and self-sacrifice, for example), or we may hear about moral exemplars. Gratitude motivates us to repay others; awe and elevation encourage us to become better persons and to take steps to help others.

Duty orientation is one other factor linked to moral motivation.[33] Duty drives some individuals to make and act on ethical decisions based on their loyalty to the group. To fulfill their obligations, they are willing to give up some of their free choice and to make sacrifices. Duty orientation, in turn, is made up of three dimensions: (1) duty to members, (2) duty to mission, and (3) duty to codes. Duty to members involves supporting and serving others in the group, even at a cost to the self. Members of combat units are often highly motivated by their loyalty to their fellow soldiers. They are willing to risk their own lives to ensure the safety of other team members. Duty to mission is support of the group's purpose and work, going beyond minimum requirements to ensure that the team or organization succeeds (e.g., coming in to work on weekends or learning a new computer program so the team can complete a project). Duty to codes involves adherence to group codes and norms. Formal codes of ethics (see Chapter 9) lay out rules for behavior both inside and outside the organization ("treat other employees with respect"; "avoid gossiping about the competition"). Norms are the unwritten guidelines for behavior (e.g., "everyone pitches in to complete the project"; "don't be afraid to ask for help"; "share the credit for success"). Shame comes from violating either formal codes or informal norms.

CONTEMPORARY ISSUES IN ORGANIZATIONAL ETHICS 3.1

REASON VS. INTUITION

There's been a seismic shift in how scholars understand the process of ethical decision making. In the past, philosophers, moral psychologists, ethicists, and ethics educators assumed that individuals consciously use logic and reason to solve ethical problems through careful deliberation. Researchers largely ignored emotions or viewed them with suspicion because feelings could undermine moral reasoning and action. Now, however, a growing number of investigators in a variety of fields argue that emotions are central to ethical decision making. Cognitive neuroscientists, for instance, highlight the important role that emotional regions of the brain play in ethical thinking. One group of scientists employs the medical case study method to demonstrate how brain deficits undermine moral reasoning. These researchers study individuals with brain damage who engage in antisocial and unethical behavior as a result of their injuries. Patients who suffer damage to the regions of the brain that govern emotion engage in antisocial and unethical behavior as a result of their injuries. For instance, "Elliott," who had a brain tumor, scored above average on intelligence tests but reported no emotional responses to pictures of gory accidents—though he knows he used to have strong emotional reactions to similar events. He lost his job, put all of his money in a bad business investment, and was divorced twice. Through it all he remained calm. Those studying Elliott concluded that he failed not because he couldn't reason but because he couldn't integrate emotions into his judgments. He could know but not feel.

Another group of neuroscientists uses neuroimaging to determine which areas of the brain are activated when we are confronted with moral issues. Researchers place study participants in magnetic resonance imaging (MRI) machines and present them with ethical dilemmas. Active brain cells (which require more oxygen than inactive ones) "light up," indicating which parts of the brain are functioning when volunteers are responding to moral problems. Neuroimaging studies reveal that ethical decision making is not localized in one region of the brain but involves several different locations. Both cognitive and emotional areas of the brain are activated.

While neuroscientists believe that we can't make wise choices unless we engage our feelings, some psychologists go a step further. They claim that emotion, not logic, plays the dominant role in moral reasoning. Jonathan Haidt is a leading proponent of the affective approach to ethical decision making. He argues that we quickly make ethical determinations and then use logic after the fact to justify our choices. Haidt points to *moral dumbfounding* as evidence that moral decision making is the product of intuition, not deliberation. In moral dumbfounding, people have strong opinions about right and wrong but can't explain why they feel as they do. For example, when surveyed, most Americans are disgusted with the idea of having sex with a sibling, even if there is no danger of pregnancy or sexually transmitted disease. They know that this behavior is wrong but are at a loss to explain why they feel this way.

Haidt contends that automatic processes are the elephant and cognition is the rider. The elephant is more powerful and generally goes wherever it wants to go, but the rider can occasionally steer the beast in a different direction. Our instantaneous, affective intuitions about right and wrong are the products of our cultural backgrounds and other social forces. For instance, Americans typically reject the idea of eating the family dog. But, in other cultures, which don't treat pets as family members, respondents would approve of eating a dog for dinner. Haidt doesn't completely eliminate reason from his model. Other people may challenge our intuitions, introducing new information and arguments that lead us to change our initial positions. Or we may modify our attitudes after reflecting on them.

The debate over the relative importance of logic and emotion still rages and will likely continue until we learn more about the physiological and psychological bases of moral reasoning. In the interim, a number of experts advocate a dual-process approach. The dual-process approach is based on the premise that both logic and emotions are important to making good decisions. However, the relative importance of each varies with the type of moral dilemma. Emotions or intuitions are dominant in situations involving life and death, bodily/personal harm, and deeply held beliefs like "incest is always wrong" or "do not play God by cloning humans." We respond immediately and automatically in these dilemmas. Cognition is more important when situations call for balancing competing claims and values or abstract reasoning, such as deciding whether it is ethical for your firm to download pirated software.

Sources: Boksem and De Cremer (2009). Casebeer (2003). Greene (2005). Haidt (2001, 2012). Lapsley and Hill (2008). Monin, Pizarro, and Beer (2007a, 2007b). Prehn and Heekeren (2009). S. J. Reynolds (2006). Salvador and Folger (2009).

Tips for Increasing Your Moral Motivation

Put moral integrity above moral hypocrisy. Reduce the cost of ethical behavior (reward whistle-blowers instead of punishing them, for example). Put principle above self-interest. Promote transparency, which makes it harder to hide choices; for instance, make sure that both buyers and sellers, employees and management, have access to the same data. Reject the tendency to justify your unethical behavior by identifying the costs of your immoral choices. And take a hard look at yourself and your motivations, making sure that you are motivated by your moral standards and not solely by the desire to look good.

Seek out ethically rewarding environments. When selecting a job or a volunteer position, consider the reward system before joining the group. Does the organization evaluate, monitor, and reward ethical behavior? Are rewards misplaced? Are organizational leaders concerned about how goals are achieved?

Reward yourself. Sometimes ethical behavior is its own best reward. Helping others can be extremely fulfilling, as is living up to the image we have of ourselves as individuals of integrity. Congratulate yourself on following through even if others do not.

Harness the power of moral emotions. Moral emotions can be powerful motivators, pushing you to act on your ethical decisions. Recognize their power and channel them toward worthy goals like helping others and serving the common good.

Component 4: Moral Character

Carrying out the fourth and final stage of moral action—executing the plan—requires character. Moral agents must overcome active opposition, cope with fatigue, resist distractions, and develop sophisticated strategies for reaching their goals. In sum, they must persist in a moral task or action despite obstacles.

Persistence can be nurtured like other positive character traits (see Chapter 2), but it is also related to individual differences. Those with a strong will, as well as confidence in themselves and their abilities, are more likely to persist. So are individuals with an internal locus of control.[34] Internally oriented people (internals) believe that they have control over their lives and can determine what happens to them. Externally oriented people (externals) believe that life events are beyond their control and are the product of luck or fate. Because internals take personal responsibility for their actions, they are motivated to do what is right. Externals are more susceptible to situational pressures. As a consequence, they are less likely to persist in ethical tasks.

Successful implementation demands that persistence be complemented with competence. A great number of skills can be required to take action, including, for instance, relationship building, organizing, coalition building, and public speaking. Pulitzer Prize–winning author and psychiatrist Robert Coles discovered the importance of ethical competence during the 1960s.[35] Coles traveled with a group of physicians who identified widespread malnutrition among children of the Mississippi Delta. They brought their report to Washington, DC, convinced that they could persuade federal officials to provide more food. Their hopes were soon dashed. The secretaries of agriculture and education largely ignored their pleas, and southern senators resisted attempts to expand the food surplus program. The physicians were skilled in medicine, but they didn't understand the political process. They got a hearing only when New York senator Robert Kennedy took up their cause. A highly skilled politician, Senator Kennedy coached them on how to present their message to the press and public, arranged special committee meetings to hear their testimony, and traveled with them to the South to draw attention to the plight of poor children.

Moral Potency

Developing *moral potency* is one way to nurture character and improve ethical follow-through.[36] Moral potency is a psychological state marked by a sense of ownership or responsibility for personal ethical behaviors and the actions of colleagues. Those with moral potency see their groups, organizations, and communities as extensions of themselves, which increases their obligation to act in an ethical manner. A sales manager who identifies strongly with her company, for example, may see sales tactics as representative of her own ethicality. She has a strong motivation to see that her sales force doesn't mislead customers. Moral courage and moral efficacy reinforce moral ownership. Moral courage provides the impetus to act despite external pressures and adversity. Moral efficacy is the belief or confidence in the ability to act. The sales manager might want to fire a high-performing sales representative for lying to customers but likely won't do so unless she believes that she has the support of her bosses or if she believes she can effectively confront the individual.

Moral potency can be developed. To foster ownership in yourself and others, clarify the ethical duties associated with each organizational role and emphasize personal responsibility for acting on these responsibilities. Identify with professional codes and values while encouraging others to do the same. (Doctors, for example, tie their identities to the medical code "do no harm to one's patients.") Develop moral courage by looking to courageous role models and act as a role model yourself. Build in cues—mission statements, codes of ethics—that promote courageous action. Develop moral efficacy by taking on increasingly difficult ethical challenges and then reflect on how you handled them. Participate in case studies, simulations, and training. Learn from how others respond to these dilemmas.

When it comes to implementing our choices, knowing how to stand up for our values is a particularly important competency. All too often we know what is right but fail to speak up due to peer pressure, opposition, fear, and other factors. We go along with inflating quarterly revenues, overselling product features, and lying to donors. Mary Gentile, director of the Giving Voice to Values program, argues that the first step to acting on personal moral standards (developing our "moral muscle") is to conduct a thought experiment.[37] Ask "What if you were going to act on your values—what would you say and do?" Gentile then outlines seven assumptions or foundational concepts that equip us to act on our ethical choices:

1. *Certain values are widely shared.* Identifying commonly held values like compassion, courage, integrity, and wisdom can help us clarify our differences

with others, understand their positions, and communicate our values more effectively. Shared values can also provide a foundation for working together to do the "right" thing in a variety of cultural settings.

2. *Acknowledge the power of choice.* Most of us can think of a time when we acted on our ethical convictions or, conversely, failed to do so. Telling the stories of these events reveals that we have the power to choose. Such narratives help us identify those factors that contributed to success (enablers) or failure (disablers). Some common enablers include finding allies; approaching the right audiences at the right time; gathering information; asking questions; understanding the needs, fears, and motivations of the audience; and reframing (offering a new interpretation of a situation, as in redefining ethical misbehavior as a financial risk and turning competition into a win-win negotiation). Disablers are often the absence or the reverse of enablers. We fail because we act alone, don't have enough information, misunderstand our audiences, and so forth.

3. *Treat values conflicts as normal.* Expect disagreements about moral choices in your organization—they are a natural part of doing business. Recognizing that fact should keep us from being surprised and help us remain calm. We'll find it easier to appreciate the viewpoints of other parties instead of vilifying them. We can develop strategies for dealing with the most common conflicts we'll face in our work.

4. *Define your personal and professional purpose.* Before values conflicts arise, ask "What am I working for?" Consider the impact you want to have in your job and career. Reflecting upon why we work and the mission of our organizations can provide us with new arguments to use when voicing our values. We'll feel more empowered to speak up, and others may be attracted to our purpose.

5. *Play to your personal strengths.* We are more likely to speak up if we create a self-story or personal narrative based on self-knowledge. Voicing values then arises out of our core identity and our desired self-image. Consider your purpose, the degree of risk you are willing to take, your personal communication style, where your loyalties are, and your image of yourself. (See Self-Assessment 3.2 for a list of questions that can help you identify each of these factors.) Your self-story should build on your strengths, helping you to see that you can make hard choices and follow through on your decisions.

6. *Find your unique voice.* There are many ways to speak out about values in the work setting. For example, you might directly confront your boss or prefer to ask questions instead. Or you might work within the existing hierarchy or go outside the regular chain of command. Find and develop your unique voice by reflecting on your experience, practice (each time you speak up, you build moral muscle), and coaching from mentors and peers.

7. *Anticipate reasons and rationalizations for unethical behavior.* Consider the most likely arguments that others will use to support immoral behavior. Two

common arguments are "everyone does this, so it's really standard practice" and "this action doesn't really hurt anyone." Then consider how you might best respond. The "everybody is doing it" argument is an exaggeration because (1) not everyone engages in the practice, and (2) if it were standard practice, there wouldn't be law or policy against it. The "nobody is hurt" rationalization overlooks the fact that some practices are wrong (stealing, for instance), no matter how small their impact.

Tips for Fostering Your Moral Character

Take a look at your track record. How well do you persist in doing the right thing? How well do you manage obstacles? Consider what steps you might take to foster the virtue of persistence.

Believe that you can have an impact. Unless you are convinced that you can shape your own life and surroundings, you are not likely to carry through in the midst of trials.

Take personal responsibility. Resist the temptation to excuse your unethical behavior or to shift the blame to someone or something else.

Watch your language. Avoid euphemisms that mask or sanitize poor behavior. Recognize the power of talk to dehumanize others.

Master the context. Know your organization, its policies, and important players so you can better respond when needed.

Be good at what you do. Competence will better enable you to put your moral choice into action. You will also earn the right to be heard.

Develop your voice. Anticipate values conflicts and prepare for them. Identify those factors that enable you to speak out or prevent you from doing so. Find the approach that works best for you and practice it to build your moral muscle. Develop arguments to overcome justifications for immoral behavior.

DECISION-MAKING FORMATS

Decision-making guidelines can help us make better moral choices both individually and as part of a group or organization. Formats incorporate elements that enhance ethical performance while helping us avoid blunders. Step-by-step procedures ensure that we identify and carefully define ethical issues, resist time pressures, acknowledge our emotions, investigate options, think about the implications of choices, and apply key ethical principles. I'll introduce five decision-making formats in this second half of the chapter. You can test these guidelines by applying them to the scenarios described in Case Study 3.2. You'll probably find one format more interesting and useful than the others. Which format you prefer is not as important as approaching moral problems systematically.

SELF-ASSESSMENT 3.2

Key Self-Knowledge Questions

According to the Giving Voice to Values program, answering these questions can help you build your self-knowledge, resulting in a self-story that will help you voice your values. Based on your answers to these questions, develop a list of your strengths that can equip you to stand up for your values.

Questions of Personal Purpose

- What are your personal goals?
- Your professional goals?
- What is your personal purpose for your business or career?
- What impact do you want to have through your work? On whom?
- What do you hope to accomplish?
- How do you want to feel about yourself and your work, both while you are doing it and in the end?

Questions of Risk

- Are you a risk taker, or are you risk-averse?
- What are the greatest risks you face in your line of work?
- What levels of risk can and can't you live with?

Questions of Personal Communication Style and Preference

- Do you deal well with conflict, or are you nonconfrontational? Under what circumstances?
- Do you prefer communicating in person or in writing?
- Do you respond best in the moment, or do you need to take time out to craft your response?
- Do you assert your position with statements, or do you ask questions to get your points across?

Questions of Loyalty

- Do you feel the greatest loyalty to family, work colleagues, your employer, or other stakeholders, such as customers?
- How do different conditions and different stakes affect your sense of loyalty?

Questions of Self-Image

- Are you most comfortable in the role of a learner or of a teacher?
- Are you most comfortable in the role of an autonomous, individual contributor or a team member?
- Can you think of circumstances where you have surprised yourself?
- What may have been unique or different about those circumstances, such that they drew out a different side of you?

Source: Condensed from Gentile (2010), pp. 116–117. Used by permission.

The Lonergan/Baird Method

Twentieth-century philosopher Bernard Lonergan (1904–1984) believed that all humans follow the same basic pattern of cognitive operations in order to make sense of the world.[38] People act like natural scientists. First they observe at the physical or *empirical* level (perceive, sense, move, speak). Next, they process this information on an *intellectual* level by asking questions, expressing relationships, developing hypotheses, and coming to an understanding. Then they put together arguments and come to a judgment on the truthfulness and certainty of the hypotheses or propositions at the *rational* level. Finally, individuals move to the *responsible* level. At this stage they determine how to act on their conclusions, evaluating various courses of action and then carrying out their decisions. These processes can be condensed into the following steps: Be attentive. Be intelligent. Be reasonable. Be responsible.

Ethics expert Catharyn Baird uses Lonergan's method as a framework for making ethical choices and has developed a set of questions and guidelines for each of his four levels.[39]

Step 1: Be Attentive—Consider What Works and What Doesn't

The first stage sets the parameters of the problem by asking these questions:

- Who is the ethical actor? An individual or organization must carry out every ethical decision. Make sure the person or group with the authority to carry out the decision makes the final determination.

- Who are the stakeholders in the conflict? All moral decisions have a relational component. Consider all the stakeholders who could be impacted by the choice. In a company this would be shareholders, employees and customers, competitors and vendors, and members of the larger community. (I'll have more to say about stakeholders in Chapter 11.)

- What are the facts of the situation? Be aware of personal biases and try not to prejudge the situation. Describe the situation in neutral language. Consider the history of the issue, important players, conflicts between parties, and so on.

Step 2: Be Intelligent—Sort Through the Data

Begin to make sense of the information gathered in Step 1 by asking:

- Is this an ethical question? Some issues involve conflicts between core values, while others are aesthetic (matters of taste) or technical (differing strategies for completing a task or reaching a goal).

- For this question, what is the very specific issue to be resolved? Put the problem in the form of a question if possible. Identify which values are in conflict in this particular situation. According to Baird, many conflicts arise along two axes. The first axis is autonomy versus equality. Those who favor autonomy believe that individuals should have as much freedom as possible to determine how they live. They demand privacy on the job and resist workplace restrictions on cell phone and Internet use. Those valuing equality want to make sure everyone is treated fairly. As employees they are concerned that the workload, profits, and benefits are fairly distributed. Baird's other continuum is rationality versus sensibility. Those who put a priority on rationality know what is expected and follow the rules. They focus on safety and economic security (minimum wage laws, overtime rules). Those who value sensibility, on the other hand, are flexible, adapting to each new situation. They don't want to be tied down by a long-term commitment to any one organization.

Choosing among options is the final component of Step 2. The best solutions creatively integrate competing interests and values. Consider the example of a company that decided that all employees needed photo ID cards for security reasons. One longtime employee, a Muslim woman, objected to having her picture taken without her veil. To balance her right of autonomy against the corporate need for security, the firm had two pictures taken—one with her in a veil and another without. A woman photographer took the facial photo. Only female security guards were allowed to check her facial ID card.

Step 3: Be Reasonable—Evaluate the Options

Making responsible decisions involves critical evaluation of the options:

- Follow the analytical rules that bring the best result. Hone your critical thinking skills. Rigorously examine all assertions and assumptions; make sure that supporting evidence is accurate and relevant. Apply the same critical standards to your own reasoning as you do to the reasoning of others.

- Evaluate the problem against core principles and values. Apply the ethical perspectives described in Chapter 1.

- Reasonably apply moral principles and values. Consider how best to carry out the decision. Employ both the head and the heart, reason and emotion, to make responsible choices. Use imagination to envision an outcome that balances competing interests and values.

Step 4: Be Responsible—Act With Courage

To act responsibly, incorporate the following:

- Correct for bias through ethical maturity. Ethically mature individuals use reason effectively, nourish relationships, make proper use of power, and strive for integration that models ethical wholeness to others.

- Attend to the common good. Consider how your actions will impact the larger community and generations to come.

- Act with courage. Make the most thoughtful choice possible given the limited information available. Remember, "choosing not to act *is* acting."[40]

The Lonergan/Baird model involves continuous improvement based on a constant cycle of action and reflection. Mature ethical agents act and then evaluate the results of their decisions. They determine which principles and strategies worked well and which did not. Based on their reflection, they are better equipped to tackle the next moral issue.

The Moral Compass

Ethics professor Lynn Paine offers a four-part "moral compass" for guiding managerial decision making.[41] The goal of the compass is to ensure that ethical considerations are factored into every organizational decision. Paine believes that we can focus our attention (and that of the rest of the group) on the moral dimension of even routine decisions by engaging in the following four frames of analysis. Each frame or lens highlights certain elements of the situation so that they can be carefully examined and addressed. Taken together, the lenses increase moral sensitivity, making it easier for organizational members to recognize and discuss moral issues.

Lens 1: Purpose—Will This Action Serve a Worthwhile Purpose?

The first frame examines end results. Proposed courses of action need to serve worthy goals. To come up with the answer to the question of purpose, we need to gather data as well as make judgments. Consider what you want to accomplish and whether your goals serve a worthy purpose. Examine possible alternatives and how they might contribute to achieving your objectives.

Lens 2: Principle—Is This Action Consistent With Relevant Principles?

This mode of analysis applies ethical standards to the problem at hand. These guidelines can be general ethical principles, norms of good business practice, codes of conduct, legal requirements, and personal ideals and aspirations. Determine what norms are relevant to this situation and important duties under these standards. Make sure any proposed action is consistent with organizational values and ideals.

Lens 3: People—Does This Action Respect the Legitimate Claims of the People Likely to Be Affected?

This third frame highlights the likely impacts of decisions. Identifying possible harm to stakeholder groups can help us take steps to prevent damage. Such analysis requires understanding the perspectives of others as well as careful reasoning. Determine who is likely to be affected by the proposed action and how to respect their rights and claims. Be prepared to compensate for harm and select the least harmful alternative.

Lens 4: Power—Do We Have the Power to Take This Action?

The final lens directs attention to the exercise of power and influence. Answers to the questions raised by the first three lenses mean little unless we have the legitimate authority to act and the ability to do so. Consider whether your organization has the authority, the right, and the necessary resources to act.

Paine uses the example of a failed product introduction to illustrate what can happen when organizational decision makers don't take moral issues into account. In the early 1990s, Lotus Development and Equifax teamed up to create a product called Lotus Marketplace:

Households. This compact disc and software package was designed to help small businesses create targeted mailing lists from their desktop computers. For $695, purchasers could draw from a database of 80 million households (created from credit information collected by Equifax) instead of buying one-time mailing lists from list brokers. Businesses could then tailor their mailings based on income, gender, age, marital status, and lifestyle.

Criticism began as soon as the product was announced to the public. Many consumers didn't want to be included in the database due to privacy concerns and asked if they could opt out. Others worried that criminals might misuse the information—for instance, by identifying and then targeting upper-income single women. The system didn't take into account that the information would soon be outdated and that data could be stolen. The two firms tried to address these issues by allowing individuals to remove their names from the list, strengthening privacy controls, and improving security. Lotus and Equifax failed to sway the public, and the project was scuttled. Equifax subsequently stopped selling credit information to marketers.

The Foursquare Protocol

Catholic University law professor and attorney Stephen Goldman offers another decision-making format designed specifically for use in organizational settings. He calls his method a *protocol* because it focuses on the procedures that members use to reach their conclusions.[42] Following the protocol ensures that decisions are reached fairly.

Protocol Element 1: Close Description of the Situation

Ethical decision making begins with digging into the facts. Goldman compares the process to how a physician generates a diagnosis. When determining what is wrong with a patient, the doctor gathers information about the patient's symptoms and relates them to one another to identify the problem. In the same way, we need to get a complete account of the ethical "patient," or problem. Gather data and identify the relevant facts.

Protocol Element 2: Gathering Accumulated Experience in Similar Situations

Doctors rely on their past experience when treating patients; organizational decision makers should do the same. Use important ethical principles but, at the same time, look to past experiences with similar problems. How did the organization respond to cases of sexual harassment in the past, for instance? Explore how other managers have responded to related dilemmas. To be fair, similar cases should be treated the same way. Also consider how others will talk about your decision. Remember that how you respond to the issue will shape the group's ethical culture going forward. For instance, if you excuse those who engage in sexual harassment now, you can expect more cases of harassment in the future.

Protocol Element 3: Recognize the Significant Distinctions Between the Current Problem and Past Ones

Identify the important differences between the current situation and past incidents. Some distinctions are insignificant, while others are critical. The ability to discern which is which separates average ethical decision makers from the really good ones. For example, companies may want to modify their drug policies in light of the fact that some states have legalized the use of medical and recreational marijuana.

Protocol Element 4: Situating Yourself to Decide

Once the facts are gathered and sorted, it is time to make the choice. To "situate" yourself to make the decision, consider three factors. First, what, if any, self-interest do you have in the choice that might compromise your judgment? You might have a financial stake in a course of action, or you may be faced with disciplining an employee who is also a friend. Second, imagine that you are on the receiving end of your decision, which is likely to be costly to some groups. Consider how you would respond if you were to be laid off, for instance. Third, determine what your moral instincts or intuitions are telling you to do. For example, does your gut tell you that it is wrong to lay off those with the longest tenure? That protecting the organization's diversity by retaining minority employees is the right thing to do? Use your instincts to test the choice you make through the application of ethical principles like utilitarianism.

Five Timeless Questions

Harvard business professor Joseph Badaracco notes that managers face "gray area" problems.[43] These moral dilemmas don't have clear black or white, right or wrong answers. He describes them as "dense tangles of important, complicated, and uncertain considerations." Successfully resolving a gray area problem requires the use of managerial skills (working with others, gathering information, analyzing data) and the desire to resolve it as a person or human being (adopting a humanistic perspective).

Badaracco draws upon the insights of Machiavelli, Aristotle, Sun Tzu, Buddha, and other thinkers to identify five questions that have guided decision making through the centuries. These timeless questions encourage decision makers to be both analytical and humanistic. In addition to describing the questions, Badaracco provides guidelines for responding to each query.

> *Question 1. What are the net, net consequences?* This first question draws upon the utilitarianism of Bentham and Mill. Since anticipating consequences is so difficult (see our discussion in Chapter 1), make sure to get the process of decision making right. Don't jump to conclusions; get the right people with the right expertise involved in the deliberations. List all possible options in as much detail as possible. Make sure to hear dissenting viewpoints.
>
> *Question 2. What are my core obligations?* This question highlights the fact that we have obligations to one another as human beings. It forces managers to think about what is most important. To answer this query, look beyond maximizing profit by highlighting duties to stakeholders—employees, communities, customers. (Don't forget who might be impacted in the future.) Use moral imagination to generate new perspectives. Always treat people with respect. Ask "What is hateful?"—imagine how you would feel if you were negatively impacted by the decision.

Question 3: What will work in the world as it is? Question 3 acknowledges the complexity and danger of organizational life. A good ethical plan is one that "will actually work," keeping in mind that members often protect their own interests. Developing a workable plan begins with considering the power and interests of organizational members (including yourself). Be modest about what you can control, be flexible, and take advantage of opportunities as they arise. Adapt the approach to unfolding events. Instead of playing it safe, be ready to assert authority and use power when necessary.

Question 4: Who are we? This query highlights the context of decision making and should be asked only after the first three questions have been answered. Managers are part of larger organizations and communities, so choices should reflect collective norms and values. Shift from analysis to sensing the entire situation, thinking in terms of what the group should or would do. Reflect on the messages carried by organizational and personal stories (see Chapters 2 and 9). Imagine having to explain the decision to the group impacted by the choice—how would they respond? Look for solutions that are simple yet recognize the complexity of the situation.

Question 5: What can I live with? The fifth and final question focuses on the internal process of decision making. This is where "tempered" intuition—considered reflection based on character and experience—comes into play. Take time to deliberate; answer all five questions, not just a preferred one; apply a variety of perspectives. Recognize that deciding may involve struggle and that the outcome will likely not be perfect. When possible, make a trial decision and consider how a respected third party would respond. Finally, make the actual decision, communicate the choice, and move ahead.

Badaracco illustrates his method through the use of both bad and good examples. In one case of poor decision making, Internet provider Yahoo released the name of a dissident associated with an email account to Chinese authorities. The dissident was then arrested and sentenced to prison. Founder Jerry Yang and other company officials failed to anticipate the situation (which was very likely to arise), to develop a process for dealing with Chinese requests based on company values, and to think about how difficult it would be to live with their choice. (The firm came under heavy criticism in the Western press.) In contrast, Biogen and its leader Jim Mullen took a more disciplined and humane approach when deciding how to market the multiple sclerosis drug Tysabri. The drug, which dramatically improved the lives of patients during clinical trials, appeared to trigger a rare, fatal brain infection in a few individuals. Biogen then had to decide whether to go forward with its marketing plans or to withdraw the medication. Clearly the product posed a significant danger to a small minority, but MS sufferers and their doctors continued to demand the drug (and the company was geared up to supply it). Biogen decided that its primary obligation was to patients. The company provided them with information on the possible side effects, temporarily suspended sales of the drug, and spent a year gathering information with the help of experts and regulators from a number of countries. Later Biogen reintroduced Tysabri after determining who was at most risk and setting up monitoring protocols for those patients. One hundred thousand patients gained relief from their symptoms, but there were still undesirable consequences. Five hundred individuals contracted the brain infection and 100 died. Nonetheless, the firm developed a practical, medically acceptable decision by combining managerial skills with concern for people.

The Five "I" Format

Remembering all of Baird's and Paine's subsidiary questions or all the details of Goldman's protocol and the timeless questions would be difficult without referring to a book or a handout. Sometimes, we need to make decisions without access to our notes. For that reason, I offer the easily memorized five "I" format as a guide. This approach incorporates elements of the first two models into the following sequence:

1. Identify the Problem

Identification involves recognizing that there is an ethical problem to be solved and setting goals. Check in with your feelings and clearly identify the problem. Describe what you seek as the outcome of your deliberations. Will you be taking action yourself or on behalf of the group or organization? Developing recommendations for others? Dealing with an immediate issue or setting a long-term policy?

2. Investigate the Problem

Investigation involves two subprocesses: problem analysis and data collection. "Drill down" to develop a better understanding of the problem. Determine important stakeholders as well as conflicting loyalties, values, and duties. Develop a set of criteria or standards for evaluating solutions. This is the time to introduce important ethical perspectives. You may decide that your decision should put a high value on justice or altruism, for instance. In addition to analyzing the issue, gather more information. Knowing why an employee has been verbally abusive, for example, can make it easier to determine how much mercy to extend to that individual. You will likely be more forgiving if the outburst appears to be the product of family stress (divorce, illness, rebellious children). There may be times when you can't gather more data or when good information is not available. In those cases, you'll need to make reasonable assumptions based on your current knowledge.

3. Innovate by Generating a Variety of Solutions

Resist the temptation to reach quick decisions. Instead, continue to look for a third way by generating possible options or alternative courses of action that could reach your goals and meet your criteria.

4. Isolate a Solution

Settle on a solution using what you uncovered during the investigation stage. Evaluate your data, weigh loyalties and duties, consider the likely impact on stakeholders, and match the solution to your ethical criteria. The choice may be obvious, or you may have to choose between equally attractive or equally unattractive alternatives. When it comes to decisions involving truth and loyalty, for instance, there is no easy way out. Lying for a friend preserves the relationship at the expense of personal integrity; refusing to lie for a friend preserves the truth but endangers the relationship. Remember that you are looking not for the perfect solution but for a well-reasoned, carefully considered one.

5. Implement the Solution

Determine how you will follow through on your choice. If you are deciding alone, develop an action plan. If you are deciding in a group, make sure that every team member knows her or his future responsibilities.

CHAPTER TAKEAWAYS

- Moral behavior is the product of moral sensitivity, moral judgment, moral motivation, and moral character. You'll need to master each of these components in order to make and then implement wise ethical decisions.

- You can enhance your ethical sensitivity through active listening, being attentive to your emotions, challenging your current ways of thinking, looking for innovative ways to solve problems, and discussing decisions in moral terms. Increase the moral intensity of issues by emphasizing their consequences and by pointing out that there is widespread agreement that they are problematic.

- Your moral judgment can be impaired if you look only to others for guidance or blindly follow the rules of your organization. Try to incorporate universal ethical principles into your decision-making process.

- Beware of major motivational contributors to defective decision making: insecurities, greed, and ego.

- Recognize the unconscious cognitive biases that lead to unethical choices. These include (1) overestimating your ethicality, (2) forgiving your own unethical behavior, (3) overlooking other people's unethical behavior, (4) implicit prejudice, (5) favoring members of your own group, and (6) judging based on outcomes rather than on the quality of the decision-making process.

- You will be more likely to put ethical values first if you resist the temptation to engage in moral hypocrisy, if you are rewarded for putting moral considerations first, if you harness the power of moral emotions, and if you have a sense of duty toward your group and organization.

- To succeed at implementing your moral choice, you'll need to be both persistent and competent. Believe in your own ability to influence events, master the organizational context, develop the necessary implementation skills, and learn to give voice to your values.

- Decision-making formats can help you make better moral choices. Which format you use is not as important as approaching moral problems systematically. The Lonergan/Baird method builds on the process that individuals use to make sense of the world; the moral compass factors ethical considerations into every organizational decision; the foursquare protocol ensures that decisions are reached fairly; the five timeless questions combine managerial skills with humanism; and the five "I" format offers a shorthand approach that incorporates elements of the first four sets of guidelines.

APPLICATION PROJECTS

1. Use the suggestions in the chapter to develop an action plan for improving your moral sensitivity, judgment, motivation, and character.

2. Compare your answers to the vignettes in Self-Assessment 3.1 with those of ethics researchers. How do your responses compare to theirs?

What factors did you consider when making your determination? Can someone cause harm without violating moral standards? Answer key: Vignette 1: harm caused/ethical violation. Vignette 2: harm caused/no ethical violation. Vignette 3: little harm caused/ethical violation. Vignette 4: no harm/no violation.

3. Select a moral issue and evaluate its level of moral intensity using the components described in the chapter. Or choose an ethical dilemma that you think deserves more attention. What steps could you and others take to increase this issue's level of moral intensity?

4. Describe how your college career has influenced your moral development. What experiences have had the greatest impact?

5. Which of the cognitive biases described in the chapter poses the most danger to moral judgment? Defend your choice in a small-group discussion.

6. How do you use both emotions and reason when you make moral choices? Provide examples.

7. Apply one of the decision-making formats to an ethical dilemma found at the end of this chapter or to another one that you select. Keep a record of your deliberations and your final choice. Then evaluate the format and the decision. Did following a system help you come to a better conclusion? Why or why not? What are the strengths and weaknesses of the format you selected? Would it be a useful tool for solving the ethical problems you face at school and work? Write up your findings.

8. Using the material presented in this chapter, analyze what you consider to be a poor ethical decision made by a well-known figure. What went wrong? Why? Present your conclusions in a paper or in a presentation to the rest of the class.

9. Develop your own set of guidelines for ethical decision making. Describe and explain your model.

CASE STUDY 3.1

White Collar Crime: The Gap Between Perpetrators and Victims

When a prominent business leader ends up in prison, we often ask: "Why would a successful person with so much to lose risk it all by engaging in criminal activity?" Harvard professor Eugene Soltes sets out to answer this question in his book *Why Do They Do It?* In addition to reviewing what experts have to say on the subject, he interviews executives serving jail time for insider trading, manipulating interest rates, backdating stock options, falsifying financial statements, and stealing from investors. Soltes points out that while he analyzes the failures of prominent executives, we can learn from their example to avoid a similar fate.

Soltes reports that two common explanations for white collar crime—personality weaknesses and judging that the benefits outweigh the costs—don't explain the actions of his subjects. For the most part, the convicted executives didn't have poor self-control or lack empathy. (One exception was Bernie Madoff, who seemed to lack feeling even for his own family.) And they didn't carefully weigh the costs and benefits of their actions. Scott London, a KPMG senior partner who provided inside trading information to a friend, noted, "At the time this [securities fraud] was going on, I just never really thought about the consequences" (p. 99). London made little

(Continued)

(Continued)

money from providing the information to his friend but had to pay a high cost. In addition to going to jail, he lost his CPA license and his job (which paid $650,000 to $900,000 a year) and had to resign from three charitable boards.

Professor Soltes puts much of the blame for corporate crime on the disconnect between the action and the harm. In large companies, perpetrators are separated physically and psychologically from their victims. Their misbehavior is eased by the fact that they are distanced from the harm caused by their crimes. The CFO of ProQuest, for example, illegally boosted earnings, which cost shareholders $437 million when the scam was discovered. However, he didn't think he did much damage because he carried out his crime on a computer and didn't target a particular individual or group. In addition, perpetrators are often rewarded for misbehavior (get promoted or honored for making the numbers) before they are caught. According to Soltes:

> Each kind of corporate misconduct has facets that make it resonate less intuitively. With financial reporting fraud, the effects are not felt until long into the future and the victims are often applauding the perpetrator's behavior until the deception is revealed. With insider trading, it's difficult to identify precisely which investors are harmed. And with tax evasion, the reduction to government coffers make the harm to specific individuals so diffuse that it no longer feels salient to say it harmed any individual person. (pp. 128–129)

Many of the disgraced executives didn't consider the moral implications of their actions. They saw themselves as solving immediate business problems under time pressures in order to further their careers. They relied on their intuitions, which lacked a moral component. No one then challenged their choices. Executives at Symbol Technologies, for example, were convicted of booking sales for equipment that wasn't shipped in order to continue to reach earning projections. Said one executive engaged in the scheme: "We always came up with solutions . . . Whatever it took, you did it and you got success from it." (p. 189)

Soltes concludes by offering suggestions to reduce corporate misbehavior in ourselves and others. (Financial fraud costs the United States nearly $400 billion a year.) He argues that we need "uncomfortable dissonance" if we are to avoid falling victim to faulty intuition. To engage in deliberate reasoning, we need to hear more dissenting opinions when making choices, something that his leaders failed to do. Along with dissonance we need to be humble, to appreciate "our lack of invincibility—our inherent weakness and frailty" (p. 329). Doing so will encourage us to stop and reflect. However, moving toward greater humility may not be easy. The former executives interviewed by Soltes didn't appear all that humbled by their experiences. Instead, they believed that what they did wasn't so bad and that others were more at fault. According to Soltes: "Virtually every one of the former executives I spoke with pointed out, even complained, that it was not he who was the true villain—it was always someone else" (p. 329).

Discussion Probes

1. What steps can organizations take to reduce the physical and psychological distance between financial crimes and the harms they cause?

2. What might be other reasons that executives commit white-collar crimes?

3. How can we help ensure that moral considerations are factored into important organizational decisions?

4. How open are you to "uncomfortable dissonance?" How can you ensure that you will hear from those with different opinions?

5. Why do so many disgraced executives excuse their behavior?

6. What are some strategies for recognizing our "inherent weakness and frailty?"

Source: Soltes (2016).

CASE STUDY 3.2

Scenarios for Analysis

Scenario 1: Is It Better to Ask Permission or to Ask Forgiveness?

Anselmo Escobar is the owner of Stately Homes, a small residential contracting firm. Stately Vistas is the company's biggest project yet. Escobar is eager to begin building this new subdivision after a series of costly delays caused by a backlog in the city zoning office. He plans to remove nearly all the mature trees in the area so that he can build more homes and recoup his losses. However, the contractor knows this move will be unpopular with current residents, who believe that the trees enhance the neighborhood and improve property values.

Escobar is under no legal obligation to consult with the neighborhood association about his plans. Further, he fears that notifying neighbors might lead to additional delays. A successful protest could force Anselmo to retain some of the trees scheduled for removal. Yet the builder feels uneasy about moving ahead without talking to neighborhood representatives. Taking unilateral action could generate negative publicity and increase opposition to future Stately Homes developments. More important, Escobar wonders about his responsibility to current residents. He knows that he would be upset if another contractor removed trees in his neighborhood without notifying anyone.

As he ponders what to do, Anselmo is reminded of the old saying, "It is easier to ask for forgiveness than to ask for permission." He is torn between consulting with the neighbors before removing the trees (asking for permission) and removing the trees and then dealing with the fallout (asking for forgiveness).

What should Escobar do?

Scenario 2: When the Good News Is Bad News

Employees and administrators at Kentucky College were excited to hear that the incoming freshman class was the largest in the small private school's history. Years of slumping enrolment had left the college, which depends heavily

(Continued)

(Continued)

upon tuition dollars, strapped for cash. Now the school's leadership could add new staff, increase faculty salaries, and improve facilities.

Unfortunately, what was good news for the Kentucky College as a whole was bad news for some freshmen. There weren't enough rooms available to house everyone. New students were placed in study rooms and in double rooms that were converted to "triples" by adding an extra bunk bed. All students paid the same price for room and board regardless of their housing arrangements. A few freshmen complained, arguing that they should pay less because their living arrangements weren't equal to those of other students. The housing director refused their request. Less revenue would mean fewer repairs to dorms and apartments. In addition, he believed that conceding to such demands could set a bad precedent. Some dorms are older and more run-down than others. Residents living in these facilities might also claim that they should pay less.

Was Kentucky College wrong to admit more students than it could house comfortably?

Was the housing director justified in refusing to reduce fees for those students forced to live in substandard conditions?

Scenario 3: Mercy for Margaret?

Receptionist Margaret Simpson was one of the first employees hired at T Rex Manufacturing when the company opened 20 years ago. The first two years of operations were difficult ones, and Simpson accepted late paychecks on more than one occasion to help keep the company afloat. For two decades she has been the face of the company to visitors and a friendly voice on the phone for suppliers and employees alike. Company president Gregg Smith often praises Margaret at employee meetings, citing her as an example of what the "T Rex family" is all about.

Sadly, Margaret's job performance has begun to slip. Over the past few months, she has often been late to work and has become cold and distant. Outsiders and coworkers alike complain about how difficult the new Margaret is to deal with. They resent her rude comments and brusque manner. Earlier this month, President Smith took the receptionist aside to confront her about her poor performance, but to no avail. If anything, she is more unpleasant than ever. Smith did discover, however, that Simpson plans to retire in three years but that the value of her retirement savings plan has declined dramatically.

Smith knows that he must come to a decision about Margaret soon. In fact, she would have been fired earlier if she had been almost any other employee. However, the T Rex executive knows that the choice is a difficult one, given Margaret's loyal service, her age and lack of retirement savings, and his desire to foster a familylike atmosphere at the plant.

What action should Smith take?

Scenario 4: Making Losers Into Winners

Laura Salmon was recently elected president of the board of the South Side Youth Soccer Association. South Side, run by volunteers, operates a soccer program for kids ages 6 to 12 in four suburban communities. The organization collects fees from parents and then uses those funds to pay operating costs. Most of the monies go toward renting playing fields, hiring officials, and buying uniforms. In addition, the association purchases trophies that go to the members of the winning teams.

Trophy expenditures make up a relatively small portion of South Side's budget but are causing the biggest headache for Laura. A group of parents is pressuring the board to expand the award program. All players would receive a trophy for participating, even if their teams had a losing record. Supporters of participation trophies argue that children should be rewarded for their efforts and treated equally, not divided into winners and losers. They point to other youth sports and music programs that guarantee that every child receives an award. Another group of parents is adamantly opposed to participation trophies. They argue that too much recognition can cause children to underachieve, that young children are motivated by the fun of playing and don't need awards, and that kids need to learn how to lose gracefully. The board is scheduled to meet next week to decide whether or not to expand the award program for the coming year. The other members are looking to Laura for guidance on this issue.

Should Laura recommend that the award program be expanded to include all participants?

Scenario 5: Guns and Coffee

Thomas Odonga is the owner of Hot Coffee, a small coffee shop located downtown in a major U.S. city. Hot Coffee does a brisk business despite being surrounded by coffee stores operated by Starbucks, Peet's, and other major chains. A number of locals want to support small businesses like Hot Coffee, and Odonga actively supports community activities. However, national debate over gun control has put Hot Coffee at risk. Gun laws vary from state to state, but businesses have a right to ban weapons on their private property. Peet's bans all guns from its premises. Starbucks requests that gun owners voluntarily refrain from bringing their weapons into their stores but doesn't forbid them from doing so, noting that weapons make other customers uncomfortable.

Now Hot Coffee customers are asking Thomas about his gun policy. He stands to lose business no matter what choice he makes. Community leaders—who regularly meet at his shop—want to limit guns to prevent them from falling into the hands of criminals and gang members. Odonga is sympathetic to their position because his brother was wounded during a robbery. Nevertheless, the right to bear arms is considered a birthright by the majority of the state's citizens. A number of Hot Coffee's most loyal customers have permits to carry concealed weapons.

What should Hot Coffee's gun policy be?

PART TWO

PRACTICING INTERPERSONAL ETHICS IN THE ORGANIZATION

CHAPTER FOUR

ETHICAL INTERPERSONAL COMMUNICATION

Chapter Preview

Dialogue: An Ethical Framework for Interpersonal Communication
Ethical Communication Competencies
   Mindfulness
   Effective Listening
   Self-Disclosure
   Confirmation
   Emotional Intelligence
   Trust Building
   Moral Argument
Chapter Takeaways
Application Projects

Communication is a logical starting point for any consideration of ethical relationships because organizational partnerships are created through verbal and nonverbal messages. If we want to establish and maintain healthy relationships, we must adopt a moral stance toward our communication with others and master communication skills that foster ethical interactions and decisions.

DIALOGUE: AN ETHICAL FRAMEWORK FOR INTERPERSONAL COMMUNICATION

The outcome of any conversation is largely dependent upon the attitude we bring to the encounter. Consider how you respond to a request from a coworker you respect as compared to one you distrust, for instance. You're likely to be more friendly and helpful to the former than to the latter. The 20th-century German philosopher Martin Buber argued that our attitudes also set the moral tone for our conversations. He identified two primary human attitudes or relationships: I-It and I-Thou.[1] Communicators in I-It relationships treat others as objects. Centered on their own needs, they are not really interested in the ideas of their conversational partners. Participants in I-Thou (I-You) relationships, in contrast, treat others as unique human beings. They are genuinely committed to understanding the perspectives of their fellow communicators.

Buber identifies three types of communication that reflect varying degrees of interest in the self or the other. *Monologue* is self-centered, I-It communication. At its worst, monologue is characterized by deception, exploitation, coercion, and manipulation. *Technical dialogue* reflects a more neutral stance toward self and other. In this type of interaction, the focus is on gathering and processing information. *Dialogue* is the product of an I-Thou relationship. Dialogue occurs between equal partners who focus on understanding rather than on being understood. Together they create meaning.

All three forms of communication have their place in the organization. There are times when we legitimately engage in monologue to meet our needs, such as when we desire emotional support. Technical dialogue enables us to get our work done, and we spend the vast majority of our time sending and receiving information-centered messages. However, dialogue has the most potential to build productive relationships and organizational communities. Entering into I-Thou relationships heightens self-esteem by reaffirming the worth of both parties, strengthens interpersonal bonds, and promotes understanding and learning. Yet, before we can pursue dialogue, we need to clear up some common misconceptions about this form of communication, clarify its unique characteristics, and identify the ethical demands it makes of us.

Dialogue is frequently misunderstood. It is *not* merely venting one's feelings (that is a form of monologue). Successful dialogue focuses on what happens between communicators based on the meanings and understandings they jointly develop. For that reason, dialogue can't be forced, only encouraged, and it may occur infrequently. Communication scholar John Stewart urges us to "open a space" for dialogue.[2] Opening this space takes three elements. First, we need to develop the right competencies, including a willingness to engage in dialogue and to seek continuous improvement. Second, we should enter encounters with what Stewart terms a *default dialogue index*, which means we should employ behaviors associated with I-Thou communication, like committing ourselves to being good listeners and treating others with respect, even when engaged in technical dialogue. Third, when the other person appears open to engaging in dialogue, we need to take advantage of this opportunity.

Dialogue is not limited to friendly interactions between friends or intimates. Instead, dialogue is most powerful when acquaintances profoundly disagree but remain in an I-Thou relationship. Buber urged discussants to walk "a narrow ridge" between extreme positions, avoiding the temptation to take up residence in one opposing camp or another.[3] They should stand by their convictions while remaining open to the positions of others. Buber had this type of relationship with Mahatma Gandhi. The two disagreed about whether violence should be used against the Third Reich in World War II. Gandhi urged nonviolent tactics, while Buber (who suffered persecution as a Jew) was convinced that such strategies would not sway the Nazis. Finally, it should be noted that dialogue does not assume that all people are good. Buber recognized that every person has a dual nature that consists of good and evil. Engaging in dialogue is one way to nurture the positive dimension of persons.

Communication experts Kenneth Cissna and Robert Anderson outline the following as characteristics of interpersonal dialogue:[4]

- *Presence.* Partners in dialogue are less interested in a specific outcome than in working with others to come up with a solution. Their interactions are unscripted and unrehearsed.

- *Emergent unanticipated consequences.* Dialogue produces unpredictable results that are not controlled by any one party.

- *Recognition of "strange otherness."* If dialogue is to flourish, discussants must refuse to believe that they already understand the thoughts, feelings, or intentions of others, even people they know well. Instead, they are tentative, continually testing their understanding of the perspectives of other group members and revising their conclusions when needed.

- *Collaborative orientation.* Dialogue demands a dual focus on self and others. Participants concentrate not on winning or losing but on coming up with a shared, joint solution that preserves the relationship.

- *Vulnerability.* Dialogue is risky because discussants open their thoughts to others and may be influenced by the encounter. They must be willing to change their minds and to be changed as persons.

- *Mutual implication.* Speakers engaged in dialogue always keep listeners in mind when speaking. In so doing, they may discover more about themselves as well.

- *Temporal flow.* Dialogue unfolds over time—drawing from the past, filling the present, and leading to the future. It is a process that can't be cut into segments and analyzed.

- *Genuineness and authenticity.* Participants in dialogue give each other the benefit of the doubt, assuming that the other person is being honest and sharing from personal experience. While speakers don't share all their thoughts, they don't deliberately hide ideas and feelings that are relevant to the topic and to the relationship.

We have to make several ethical commitments if we hope to engage in the kind of conversation described by Cissna and Anderson.[5] First, we must be committed to the good of others in order to treat them as unique beings. Second, we need to value relationships and the common good, recognizing that organizations are made up not of autonomous individuals but of people living in relation to one another. Third, we have to be open to influence and be willing to take criticism. Fourth, we ought to allow others to hold and express opinions different from ours. Fifth, we have to commit ourselves to honesty, not just during dialogue but also when we engage in monologue and technical dialogue. We often need to get others to follow our directions or to change their opinions. However, let's not disguise our motives by pretending to engage in dialogue when we really only want to get our way. Sixth, we need to invest ourselves in the hard work of dialogue. Focusing on the needs and positions of others takes a good deal of time and energy, as does mastering the necessary communication competencies to make dialogue successful.

ETHICAL COMMUNICATION COMPETENCIES

While dialogue can't be forced, it is much more likely to take place when we have the necessary competencies. Productive communication behaviors that foster I-Thou relationships include mindfulness, effective listening, appropriate self-disclosure, confirmation, emotional intelligence, trust building, and moral argument. These strategies can also help us make better choices. When used in conjunction with the principles and practices of sound moral reasoning introduced in the last chapter, they further increase our likelihood of coming up with a well-reasoned ethical conclusion.

Mindfulness

Dialogue demands our complete attention. Not only is it unscripted, unrehearsed, and unpredictable, but this type of interaction also requires that we simultaneously focus on our own thoughts as well as on the positions of our conversational partners. Psychologists use the term *mindfulness* to describe the process of devoting full attention to the task at hand, to being fully present in the moment. Mindfulness takes the form of a trait and a state.[6] Some individuals are naturally more mindful—that is, exhibit more of this trait—than other people. (Determine your level of mindfulness by completing Self-Assessment 4.1.) However, mindfulness can vary depending on the situation (state), such as when an ordinary drive to work turns dangerous due to a major pile up on the freeway. In this case, we instantly shift from a mindless state (where our attention is divided between the road and thoughts of the day's activities and the radio) to a mindful one (where our focus is on the threat and our response).

Researchers report that mindfulness produces a number of positive effects. Mindful individuals are more likely to experience positive moods and are less likely to suffer from depression and anxiety. At the same time, they recover more quickly from negative events. Mindful people are better able to control their behavior in order to complete their tasks, reach their goals, and follow through on their ethical choices. Such individuals also enjoy better physical health because they deal more effectively with pain and stress and can better manage the symptoms of chronic illness.[7]

Mindfulness stands in sharp contrast with *mindlessness*, which is inflexible, thoughtless activity. Individuals acting mindlessly don't take in useful information, or they misinterpret the data they do receive.[8] As a result, they behave inflexibly, overlook alternative choices, and become locked into a single course of action. Mindlessness can be costly. People get stuck in current roles and self-perceptions, stop developing intellectually, engage in unintended cruelty by rationalizing immoral behaviors, lose control of their choices to advertisers and other outsiders, give in to helplessness when they can control the situation, and limit their potential.

The benefits of mindfulness carry over into interpersonal relationships both on and off the job. Researchers report that mindfulness promotes relational connection and closeness because (1) communicators are more receptive to the messages being sent by their relational partners, and (2) they are more aware of, and thus in more control of, their own responses. In addition, mindful individuals aren't as concerned about their egos, so they feel less threatened by rejection and more compassionate toward others.[9]

Ellen Langer identifies three psychological processes of information processing in a mindful state of being that can help us reap the benefits of mindfulness while sidestepping the dangers of mindless behavior in our interpersonal relationships.[10] The first psychological process is the *creation of new categories*. Being mindful breaks us out of our old rigid categories and makes us more sensitive to differences. These distinctions enhance our thinking and relationships. We become better problem solvers when we realize that moral reasoning can be broken down into smaller stages, as we saw in Chapter 3. We're much less likely to stereotype individuals and act in a prejudiced manner if we refuse to lump people into broad categories based on age, race, sexual orientation, or role.

The second psychological process involves *welcoming new information*. In mindful communication, we seek new information as we closely monitor our behavior along with the behavior of others. These data allow us to revise our conclusions and adjust our responses. Mindless communication, on the other hand, closes us off to new information. As a result, we make costly mistakes and fail to adjust to changes in our environments. We assume that others hold our ethical values when they don't, settle on the first solution when a better one might be available, fail to meet the changing expectations of our audiences, and so on.

The third psychological process is *openness to different points of view*. Any event or behavior can be viewed from more than one perspective. What seems like thoughtless, hurtful behavior on the part of a coworker may have been intended as playful or harmless. Exploring multiple perspectives gives us more options, reduces the probability that we will get locked into an extreme position, and equips us to change our behavior. For instance, we are more likely to change the way we act when we realize that others take offense at what we're currently doing.

It's easy to identify situations that clearly demand a mindful state: dealing with strangers and people of other cultural backgrounds, public presentations, brainstorming sessions, interviews, performance reviews, strategy meetings, change efforts. You can prepare for these encounters by considering your expectations (avoid negative self-fulfilling prophecies like "the interviewer is going to think I am too young or old for the position"); what your intentions are (what you want to get out of the encounter); and visualizing your performance. During the interaction, note your thoughts ("What evaluations and assumptions am I making?") and feelings ("Why am I feeling uncomfortable?") After the interaction, reflect on your behaviors to make sense of what happened. You may identify hidden assumptions, habits or emotional triggers that kept you from being successful. Learn from these and you'll be better prepared for similar events.[11]

While some contexts clearly require mindfulness, even routine interactions like casual conversations with coworkers can be enhanced with mindful awareness. You can practice shifting your thinking modes by deliberately paying more attention during common communication events. For example, approach a classroom lecture with a mindful attitude, noting elements of delivery, audience response, and other factors you usually overlook. Or you might analyze a film from more than one point of view (see Application Project 2). Foster your inclination to be mindful in a variety of situations (your trait mindfulness) both through meditation and by taking time each day to focus your attention on yourself. Set aside five minutes at work to take stock of your thoughts, emotions, and physical sensations. Consider the impact these elements are having on your well-being. Accept them as reality (even if negative) and let them go.[12]

Effective Listening

Listening is key to coming to mutual understanding through dialogue. We can't come up with a joint, shared solution or speak to the needs of the other party unless we

SELF-ASSESSMENT 4.1

Mindful Attention Awareness Scale (MAAS)

Instructions

Below is a collection of statements about your everyday experience. Using the 1–6 scale below, indicate how frequently or infrequently you currently have each experience. Answer according to what really reflects your experience rather than what you think your experience should be. Please treat each item separately from every other item.

1 = Almost always

2 = Very frequently

3 = Somewhat frequently

4 = Somewhat infrequently

5 = Very infrequently

6 = Almost never

1. I could be experiencing some emotion and not be conscious of it until some time later.
2. I break or spill things because of carelessness, not paying attention, or thinking of something else.
3. I find it difficult to stay focused on what's happening in the present.
4. I tend to walk quickly to get where I'm going without paying attention to what I experience along the way.
5. I tend not to notice feelings of physical tension or discomfort until they really grab my attention.
6. I forget a person's name almost as soon as I've been told it for the first time.
7. It seems I am "running on automatic," without much awareness of what I'm doing.
8. I rush through activities without being really attentive to them.
9. I get so focused on the goal I want to achieve that I lose touch with what I'm doing right now to get there.
10. I do jobs or tasks automatically, without being aware of what I'm doing.
11. I find myself listening to someone with one ear, doing something else at the same time.
12. I drive places on "automatic pilot" and then wonder why I went there.
13. I find myself preoccupied with the future or the past.
14. I find myself doing things without paying attention.
15. I snack without being aware that I'm eating.

Scoring

Add up your scores and divide by 15 to create an average for the 15 statements. The higher the average, the higher your trait level of mindfulness. Scores range from 1 to 6. The typical average score is approximately 3.86.

Source: K. W. Brown and Ryan (2003). Copyright © 2003 by the American Psychological Association. Reproduced with permission.

comprehend the other party's perspective. Skillful listening is also essential to processing the informational messages that make up technical dialogue. According to Judi Brownell of Cornell University, communication is best understood as listening centered, not speaking centered.[13] She offers the multistage HURIER model to describe her listener-focused approach to communication. This model consists of the following six components:

Component 1: Hearing. The environment is filled with all kinds of stimuli. Listening begins when we focus on one or more of these elements—music, a podcast, the voice of a friend, a supervisor's phone call. What we choose to hear is dependent on our perceptual filters, which are made up of our cultural background, beliefs and values, past experiences, interests, family history, and other factors. Consider how you and a friend respond to the same stimuli, for example. If you are an avid skiboarder, you'll listen carefully to the morning radio report on mountain snow conditions. Your conversational partner (who is not interested in heading for the slopes) may change stations when this segment comes on.

Component 2: Understanding. Once the message is received, it must be processed. Like reading comprehension, listening comprehension is based on the literal meanings of the words and signals received. Shared language and vocabulary greatly increase the likelihood of understanding.

Component 3: Remembering. Memory allows an individual to retrieve information in order to come up with an appropriate response. Memory, like hearing, is especially influenced by our perceptual filters. Information we're interested in is retained; other messages are quickly forgotten.

Component 4: Interpreting. During this stage, meaning is assigned to the message based on words and nonverbal cues like context (location, previous events, participants), vocal qualities, and body language.

Component 5: Evaluating. At this stage, the receiver makes a judgment about the accuracy and truthfulness of the message by evaluating evidence and reasoning, source credibility, the situation, emotional appeals, and other factors.

Component 6: Responding. We can respond appropriately only if we've successfully completed the first five steps of the model. Since listening is continuous, we must also adjust our messages even as we're speaking. If a coworker gives us a puzzled look while we're explaining a new technical process, for instance, we need to pause to ask if he or she understands our directions.

Listening can fail at any stage of the HURIER model. We might tune out important messages or fail to comprehend their meanings, forget essential data, come up with an inaccurate interpretation, misjudge the message, or formulate the wrong response. Unwillingness to suspend our own needs likely causes the most problems when it comes to listening in interpersonal relationships.[14] Instead of suppressing our urge to talk, we fool ourselves into thinking we really are listening when we aren't. We interrupt to relate a similar story, react with excessive sympathy (which takes over the conversation), offer unwanted advice, joke around, tell them that he/she shouldn't feel the way they do, and blame the other person for bringing the same topics up again. To increase our listening effectiveness, we need to be more selfless. In addition, we need to approach conversations with a mindful attitude and incorporate the skills outlined in Ethical Checkpoint 4.1.

ETHICAL CHECKPOINT 4.1

Listening Skills

Hear Messages: Focus Attention and Concentrate

- Take a sincere interest in other people and ideas.
- Listen to new and difficult information.
- Stay active by taking notes, paraphrasing, and so on.
- Manipulate the physical environment to make listening easier.
- Use the thought-speech differential (extra time generated by the ability to process speech faster than it is delivered) wisely.

Understand What You Hear

- Listen to the entire message.
- Distinguish main ideas from details.
- Recognize your personal assumptions and meanings.
- Increase your vocabulary.
- Check your perceptions.

Remember Messages

- Improve your short-term memory.
- Learn long-term memory techniques and use them regularly.

- Create associations.
- Use visual imagery.

Interpret Messages

- Develop empathy.
- Increase awareness of and sensitivity to nonverbal cues.
- Take into account the speaker's background attitudes and other variables.
- Take into account the communication context.
- Strive to be a high self-monitor (monitor the impact your behavior has on the other person).

Evaluate What You Hear

- Consider the speaker's credibility.
- Recognize personal bias.
- Understand persuasive strategies.
- Analyze logic and reasoning to identify logical fallacies.
- Recognize emotional appeals.

Source: Brownell (2003). Reprinted with permission of Dr. Judi Brownell.

Understanding how we prefer to listen can also improve our performance as listeners. Listening consultants Larry Barker and Kittie Watson identify four listening preferences.[15] Each has its own unique combination of strengths and weaknesses. Knowing the downside of our listening profiles can help us avoid listening errors. (Discover your preferred listening style by completing Self-Assessment 4.2.)

- *People-oriented listeners* put a priority on maintaining relationships. They are concerned, caring, and nonjudgmental and provide clear feedback. However, these communicators can get overly involved with others and may overlook their faults.

- *Action-oriented listeners* concentrate on the task and are good at keeping meetings on topic while encouraging speakers to organize their thoughts. Unfortunately, they often come across as impatient, quick to jump to conclusions, and disinterested in relationships.

- *Content-oriented listeners* (often those in technical fields) evaluate messages carefully, even highly complex ones, and explore all sides of an issue. Their weaknesses include getting bogged down in details and taking forever to come to a decision.

- *Time-oriented listeners* value effectiveness and efficiency. They are good at saving time (theirs and others') but tend to interrupt, look at clocks and watches, and limit creativity by setting time limits.

While most people have one or two preferred styles, effective listeners know how to match their preferences or habits to the communication context. The action-oriented style works well in processing business proposals, for example, but is not so effective in the break room, where messages are not likely to be clearly structured. Time-oriented executives often get in trouble when they take this style home to conversations with their spouses and children. In these cases, effective listeners would adopt a people-centered approach. Conversely, a content-oriented style works better than a people-focused preference when the listener is engaged in technical processes like debugging software and creating engineering designs.

Self-Disclosure

Dialogue rests upon the sharing as well as the receiving of information. Not only do we need to listen effectively, we also need to engage in self-disclosure, sharing appropriate information about ourselves. Sharing personal information fosters the collaboration, "strange otherness," vulnerability, genuineness, and authenticity that characterize I-Thou communication. Self-disclosure also builds long-term relationships. We generally respond favorably to those who disclose to us because we learn more about them. As an added bonus, disclosure leads to better self-understanding, such as when talking about a problem gives us insight into solving it. Sharing our reactions also lets us test our perceptions against reality.[16]

SELF-ASSESSMENT 4.2

Listening Styles Profile

Instructions

Indicate how well each of the following statements applied to you based on the following scale:

0 = Never

1 = Infrequently

2 = Sometimes

3 = Frequently

4 = Always

1. I focus my attention on the other person's feelings when listening to them.
2. When listening to others, I quickly notice if they are pleased or disappointed.
3. I become involved when listening to the problems of others.
4. I nod my head and/or use eye contact to show interest in what others are saying.
5. I am frustrated when others don't present their ideas in an orderly, efficient way.
6. When listening to others, I focus on any inconsistencies and/or errors in what's being said.
7. I jump ahead and/or finish thoughts of speakers.
8. I am impatient with people who ramble on during conversations.
9. I prefer to listen to technical information.
10. I prefer to hear facts and evidence so I can personally evaluate them.
11. I like the challenge of listening to complex information.
12. I ask questions to probe for additional information.
13. When hurried, I let the other person(s) know that I have a limited amount of time to listen.
14. I begin a discussion by telling others how long I have to meet.
15. I interrupt others when I feel time pressure.
16. I look at my watch or clocks in the room when I have limited time to listen to others.

Scoring

Add up your scores for each of the four listening styles to identify your listening profile.

People-Oriented Listener	Action-Oriented Listener	Content-Oriented Listener	Time-Oriented Listener
Item 1	Item 5	Item 9	Item 13
Item 2	Item 6	Item 10	Item 14
Item 3	Item 7	Item 11	Item 15
Item 4	Item 8	Item 12	Item 16
Total	Total	Total	Total

Source: **Adapted from Watson and Barker (1995). Used by permission.**

You might have discovered that self-disclosure can backfire. Sharing too much personal information (or disclosing sensitive information too soon) makes others uncomfortable. Conversely, not sharing enough can also be problematic. Others expect that disclosure will be reciprocated. Failure to share when the other party is vulnerable breaks trust and raises the fear that one person will use the personal information against the other.

Management experts Lisa Rosh and Lynn Offerman identify five types of executives who engage in inappropriate self-disclosure. While they gear their description to leaders, the same types can be found at all levels of the organizations.[17]

Oblivious disclosures have an unrealistic view of themselves and thus reveal information that appears insincere. For example: the highly task oriented leader who shares stories about how much she cares about others.

Bumblers have greater self-understanding but don't realize how they come across to others. They can't decipher body language or facial expressions and their disclosures are out of place. For example: the colleague who tells a humorous personal story when the office is coping with a series of lay-offs.

Open books never shut up. In sharing too much they break trust. For example: the new employee who talks about his divorce the first day of work; the newly appointed leader who describes her failure on the last project.

Inscrutable disclosures rarely share anything about themselves at work. They appear remote and inaccessible and have trouble establishing long-term relationships. For example: the CEO who tries to inspire through statistics rather than through personal experiences.

Social engineers try to encourage disclosure in others but don't disclose themselves. Because they fail to model self-disclosure, they rely on others to do so. For example: the manager who hosts an annual teamwork retreat while keeping his thoughts and experiences to himself the rest of the year.

Self-disclosure experts make the following suggestions for revealing information about the self.[18] These suggestions not only help foster I-Thou dialogue, they are critical for improving technical dialogue as well. Self-disclosure reveals what each party wants to accomplish when collaborating, identifies past experiences that apply to a current project, prompts additional effort, and so on.

1. Make it relevant. Information should be related to the topic and task at hand.

2. Consider the likely the impact of the disclosure. Will it make the other person uncomfortable? Will it foster dialogue and strengthen the relationship?

3. Make it gradual. Increase the breadth (the number of topics covered) and depth (the significance of the information) as the relationship develops.

4. Look for reciprocity. Continue to share only if the other party responds in kind.

5. Understand the context. Be sensitive to the disclosure patterns of your organization. (Is it okay to talk about problems with children, for example? Do

people talk about their interests outside of work?) Keep in mind the cultural context as well. Members of individualistic societies like the United States expect to share more personal information than employees from collectivist societies like Japan and China.

6. Avoid unnecessary risks. Some people in your organization likely should not be trusted. (See our discussion of trust to follow.) With these individuals, keep your reactions and personal information largely to yourself.

Confirmation

Treating the other person as a unique human being is at the heart of dialogue. Buber used the term *confirmation* to describe the process of recognizing and acknowledging the presence and value of others. He made this recognition of personhood the defining characteristic of human society:

> The basis of man's life with man is twofold, and it is one—the wish of every man to be confirmed as what he is, even as what he can become by men; and the innate capacity in man to confirm his fellow men in this way.... Actual humanity exists only where this capacity unfolds.[19]

Confirmation occurs when we value ourselves more after interacting with another person; disconfirmation takes place if we value ourselves less. Confirming behaviors (1) express recognition of the other person's existence, (2) acknowledge a relationship or affiliation, (3) express awareness of the significance or value of the other, and (4) accept or "endorse" the other person's experience or way of seeing the world. Disconfirming behaviors send the opposite messages.[20]

Examples of disconfirming and confirming responses are outlined below. Ethical communicators try to avoid the first category of remarks and engage in the second set of behaviors.

Disconfirming Responses

- *Impervious:* Failing to acknowledge the messages of the other person; ignoring; shunning

- *Interrupting:* Cutting the other speaker short; beginning before he or she is finished

- *Irrelevant:* Responding in a way that seems unrelated to what the other person has just said

- *Tangential:* Acknowledging the previous message but immediately taking the conversation in a new direction

- *Impersonal:* Conducting a monologue, speaking in an overly intellectual or impersonal way

- *Ambiguous:* Responding with messages containing multiple or unclear meanings
- *Incongruous:* Engaging in nonverbal behavior that is inconsistent with the verbal content of the message, as when a speaker denies being angry even as his voice rises and his face turns red

Confirming Responses

- *Recognition:* Responding to the presence of the other person; treating the other person with respect
- *Acknowledgment:* Providing a direct, relevant response to the message of the other person; asking questions, disagreeing, paraphrasing
- *Endorsement:* Accepting the feelings of the other party as legitimate; letting the other person "be" without trying to analyze, blame, or change him or her

Researchers initially studied confirmation in the family setting. They discovered that confirming communication increases marital satisfaction and intimacy, helps build positive father–son relationships, and encourages children to have higher perceptions of their self-worth, appearance, intellectual capacity, and physical appearance.[21] More recently, investigators have begun to explore the effects of confirmation in the organizational context, focusing on the relationship between teachers and students. They point out that teaching has a relational component.[22] Professors not only want students to learn course content but to also have fulfilling interactions with them. For their part, college students want to learn and earn good grades. However, students have other goals as well, like feeling good about themselves and believing they have significant ideas to contribute.

According to confirmation researcher Kathleen Ellis, teacher confirmation is critical to helping students establish their identities. She discovered that teachers communicate confirmation through four behavioral patterns.[23] First, they are supportive of students' questions and comments by, for example, expressing appreciation for student input and listening attentively. Second, confirming instructors demonstrate interest in students and their learning both inside and outside of class. They make themselves available to answer questions before and after class sessions and make an effort to get to know students. Third, confirming professors use an interactive teaching style, which employs a variety of strategies and exercises to improve learning. Fourth, they avoid such disconfirming behaviors as embarrassing students in class or refusing to listen to those who disagree with them.

Instructor confirmation has a strong positive influence on the student–teacher relationship.[24] Students with confirming instructors learn more and develop a positive attitude toward the subject matter and the teacher and are less likely to complain. They also prepare more for class, participate more frequently in class sessions, interact more with one another, and are more likely to talk one on one with the instructor. Professors who engage in confirmation behaviors receive higher teaching evaluations. (Case Study 4.1 describes one professor who developed strong relationships with students through his confirming behaviors.)

Emotional Intelligence

Understanding and responding to emotions plays a critical role in building relationships. Emotionally sensitive individuals get along better with people in general, experience few negative interactions with friends, and are more supportive team members. In addition, they make better choices because they recognize how their moods influence their thinking, and they manage their feelings instead of falling victim to them. Researchers use the term *emotional intelligence (EI)* to describe the capacity to identify and influence emotions in others and in the self. Psychologists Peter Salovey, John Mayer, and David Caruso tie emotional intelligence to how individuals process information, describing EI as "the ability to engage in sophisticated information processing about one's own and others' emotions and the ability to use this information as a guide to thinking and behavior."[25] This intelligence is made up of the following four skill sets.[26] Each skill set is increasingly difficult and builds on the levels that come before. (See Contemporary Issues in Organizational Ethics 4.1 for a broader definition of emotional intelligence.)

1. *Identifying emotions.* Emotions provide important data about what's happening to us, to others, and in the environment. Effective communication depends on accurately reading these signals and on accurately conveying how we feel. Unfortunately, research suggests that when it comes to interpreting emotional expressions, we are not as skilled as we think.[27] Most people can pick out intense emotional expressions but are less adept at identifying slight or partial displays of the same feelings. Accurate decoding is further complicated by the fact that facial displays of emotion during conversation last only a short time (generally from half a second to two and a half seconds). Skillful communicators have mastered these challenges and can

    - Recognize their internal emotional states
    - Talk about their feelings
    - Communicate internal emotional states so that their feelings are understood as intended
    - Accurately read people even when people try to disguise or repress their emotions
    - Pick up on the emotional meaning of messages sent through body language, vocal cues, and facial expressions

2. *Using emotions.* Emotions, as we saw in Chapter 3, play an important role in reasoning and can enhance our thinking. Positive moods promote new ideas and risk taking; negative moods focus attention on details and possible errors.[28] Our chances of coming up with a good solution are greatest when we employ both modes of reasoning. For that reason, we might put ourselves in a positive frame of mind for a brainstorming session but wait until the next day to evaluate our ideas when we're not so optimistic and can do a better job of catching potential problems. Those with high emotional intelligence can

    - Demonstrate creative thinking and imagination
    - Inspire and motivate others
    - Closely monitor events that generate strong emotions
    - Match their emotions to the task and select tasks based on their mood

3. *Understanding emotions.* Emotions aren't chaotic but have underlying causes and follow progressions. Annoyance leads to anger and then to rage, for example, but not the other way around. If we understand these patterns, we can better forecast how others will respond to events and plan accordingly. Emotionally sensitive individuals can do these things:

   - Make correct assumptions about how others will behave
   - Have an extensive emotional vocabulary that enables them to accurately communicate what they are experiencing
   - Appreciate emotional complexity—the fact that communicators can experience contradictory emotions at the same time
   - Accurately predict how others will respond and choose the right message

4. *Managing emotions.* Emotions (even the unwelcome ones) need to be factored into reasoning, evaluation, and behavior. However, we need to manage our feelings instead of being controlled by them. Emotions can generate more productive outcomes if they are integrated into our thinking. Emotionally intelligent people can do these things:

   - Resist unhealthy impulses
   - Know when to follow their feelings and when to set them aside temporarily
   - Are open to their own feelings and the emotions of those around them
   - Let emotions activate productive behavior, like fighting against injustice when angry and avoiding risks when afraid
   - Regulate their moods to achieve their goals; for example, getting "pumped up" before a class presentation or consciously shifting attention from a source of irritation to preparing for an upcoming meeting
   - Establish genuine interpersonal connections
   - Manage the feelings of coworkers in appropriate ways (cheer them up, calm them down)

CONTEMPORARY ISSUES IN ORGANIZATIONAL ETHICS 4.1

THE TRAIT APPROACH TO EMOTIONAL INTELLIGENCE

Many writers define emotional intelligence as a collection of traits. For example, Daniel Goleman, who is credited with introducing EI to popular audiences, identifies 20 EI abilities, including such traits as empathy, self-confidence, achievement drive, trustworthiness, communication, conflict management, and organizational awareness. He claims that EI is more important than traditional IQ in determining who emerges as "star" organizational performers.

A number of critics point out that the trait approach to emotional intelligence has serious weaknesses. It is not clear why some competencies are considered part of emotional intelligence while others are left out. Including so many traits makes EI less useful as a teaching, training, and research tool. Then, too, EI traits, like those identified by Goleman, seem to include everything from self-perceptions, attitudes, and behaviors to motivations and moral virtues. Further, proponents of the traits approach often overstate the importance of EI in the workplace. Researchers report that there is a link between emotional sensitivity and job performance (as well as with leadership emergence and leader effectiveness). However, there is little evidence to support claims that emotional intelligence is the most important factor in determining job success.

Sources: Goleman (1998, 2001). Mayer, Salovey, and Caruso (2008). O'Boyle, Humphrey, Pollack, Hawver, and Story (2011). Walter, Cole, and Humphrey (2011).

Salovey, Mayer, and Caruso developed the Mayer-Caruso-Salovey Emotional Intelligence Test (MCSEIT) to measure their four skill sets.[29] The instrument asks respondents to complete a variety of tasks, including labeling facial displays of emotion, comparing emotions to physical sensations, and responding to emotional scenarios. Follow-up studies reveal that those who score higher on this test have more productive work relationships.[30] In one study employees with high EI scores were rated by their colleagues as easier to work with and were credited with helping to create a positive work environment. Their leaders rated them as more interpersonally sensitive and sociable. In another project, managers who scored high on the MCSEIT were seen as engaging in more effective behaviors like communicating clearly and mentoring. Employees also noted that these supervisors supported the overall goals of the organization. In a third study, researchers found that customers were more satisfied when working with claims adjusters with high emotional intelligence. In a fourth project, British teachers able to regulate their emotions experienced greater job satisfaction and less burnout.

The four skill sets of emotional intelligence, taken together, provide an "emotional blueprint" for dealing with organizational relationships of all kinds. This blueprint can be used to analyze past encounters or to prepare for important or difficult situations (client presentations, performance evaluations, termination interviews). One way to raise your emotional intelligence quotient is by evaluating a past conversation from the vantage point of emotion using the set of questions found in Ethical Checkpoint 4.2. You can also use these same queries to analyze an upcoming event.

Participating in emotional intelligence training is another way to raise your emotional intelligence and to help raise the EQ of your entire organization. Ameriprise Financial (formerly American Express Financial Advisors) has a long running emotional intelligence training program, one that has been held up as a model for other

ETHICAL CHECKPOINT 4.2

Emotional Analysis Questions

Think of a recent communication encounter, and apply the following questions both to yourself and to the other person involved. Respond to each query. Then, apply the same questions to an upcoming conversation. Summarize your conclusions.

1. Questions to Help You Identify Emotions
   - How aware were you (the other party) of your (his or her) emotions?
   - Were you aware of how you felt during this situation?
   - How do you feel right now?
   - How did you feel during this interaction?
   - How emotional were you?
   - Did you express your feelings to others? Appropriately so?
   - Were you expressing your true feelings or trying to cover them up?
   - Were you focused only on your feelings, or were you aware of the other person's feelings?

2. Questions to Help You Use Emotions
   - Did it help you (the other party) to feel this way?
   - Did your mood focus you on the issue or away from it?
   - Did you find yourself feeling negative or positive about things?
   - Did your mood help you see the other person's point of view?
   - Were you able to feel what the other person was feeling?
   - How much did you pay attention to the problem?
   - Did you try to feel the emotions or block them out?

3. Questions to Help You Understand Emotions
   - Why did you (the other party) feel this way?
   - What caused you to feel the way you feel?
   - Describe the intensity of your feelings.
   - How will you feel next?

4. Questions to Help You Manage Emotions
   - What did you (the other party) want to happen?
   - What did happen?
   - What did you do?
   - How did it work out?
   - Was there a better way to have handled it?
   - Why didn't you handle it better?
   - How satisfied were you with the outcome?
   - How satisfied do you think the other person was with the outcome?
   - What could you have done differently?
   - What did you learn from this situation?

Source: Caruso and Salovey (2004). Copyright © 2004. Reprinted with permission of Jossey-Bass, an imprint of John Wiley & Sons, Inc.

organizations.[31] The training builds competency in self-awareness, self-regulation, empathy, and social skills using lectures, exercises, small-group discussion, demonstrations, and role plays. Managers are taught how to be "emotional coaches" for their direct reports. Enhanced emotional intelligence has improved the company's organizational performance.

Trust Building

Interpersonal trust is often the "glue" that binds organizational members together. Those in trusting relationships feel a greater sense of interdependence, help one another, and are more willing to learn and to take risks, including the risk of engaging in dialogue. A group whose members trust each other makes higher-quality decisions, is more productive, and operates more efficiently.[32]

Trust is defined as "a psychological state comprising the intention to accept vulnerability based upon positive expectations of the intentions or behavior of another."[33] A cluster of attitudes and behaviors defines trusting relationships. First, trust involves optimistic expectations. Trusting individuals believe that the other party will carry through on promises and commitments. Second, those who trust put themselves in a vulnerable position. They depend on the behavior of others and have much to lose if these individuals break their commitments. Third, trust is willingly offered. Participants entering into trust relationships hope to increase cooperation and generate benefits, not only for themselves, but also for the group as a whole. All organizational stakeholders gain from such partnerships. Fourth, trust is hard to enforce. Organizations try to ensure cooperation through contracts, legal requirements, and other means. However, formal enforcement mechanisms don't have much impact on informal relationships between group members and can't, by themselves, create a trusting climate. Fifth, trust imposes an obligation or duty to protect the rights and interests of others. The target of trust is expected (1) not to harm the other party and (2) to act in a way that benefits both individuals.

Interpersonal trust, because it involves obligation or duty, has a moral dimension.[34] More than just a strategy for ensuring cooperation and better results, trust also imposes ethical demands. We have a moral responsibility to protect and promote the interests of those who rely on us (put themselves in a vulnerable position). Breaking trust can be considered unethical because interpersonal trust serves the greater organizational good.

Earning the trust of others starts by demonstrating the character virtues described in Chapter 2. We need to express concern, to act in a consistent manner, and to be honest, open, and loyal. In addition, we need to demonstrate our competence. Others are more likely to trust us when we display knowledge and expertise by turning out high-quality work, responding to questions, completing assignments on time, and so on.

As a leader, you can take steps to help create organizations that encourage the development of trusting interpersonal relationships. Foster an atmosphere that encourages openness and sharing, be consistent in your behavior, and focus attention on the organizational mission by communicating vision and values. These steps are described in more detail in Ethical Checkpoint 4.3.

> ## ETHICAL CHECKPOINT 4.3
> ### Building Blocks of Organizational Trust
>
> *Dialogue of Openness and Sharing*
>
> - Be honest with yourself and others (share humanness).
> - Don't harbor hidden agendas.
> - Let others know that what they say will not be used against them.
> - Make people feel valued for their contributions.
> - Make people feel safe in expressing honest opinions.
> - Don't withhold information for power.
> - Hold a basic belief that all people have good potential.
> - Be willing to listen.
> - Be willing to be vulnerable.
>
> *Consistency in Behavior*
>
> - Say it and do it.
> - Do the right thing.
> - Be consistent in how decisions are made.
> - Keep promises and commitments.
>
> *Everyone Committed to the Mission*
>
> - Know where the organization is headed.
> - Make sure people know and believe in organizational goals.
> - Encourage teamwork.
> - Encourage dialogue to establish shared values.
>
> Source: Adapted from Bruhn (2001), p. 82. Used by permission.

Despite our best efforts, we are likely to betray the trust of others and to be betrayed ourselves. Betrayal can be classified as major or minor, intentional or unintentional.[35] Major betrayals generate intense feelings of distress and disappointment; minor betrayals are less disruptive but can seriously undermine trust if they accumulate over time. Intentional betrayal is deliberate, consciously aimed at harming others. Unintentional betrayal is a byproduct of other actions and activities. Major intentional betrayals include deliberately withholding information, sharing corporate secrets, and sabotaging equipment. Major unintentional betrayals include layoffs resulting from restructuring and pay freezes produced by slumping sales. Minor intentional betrayals include gossiping, backbiting, blaming (see Case Study 4.2), and accepting credit for another person's work. Minor unintentional betrayals include consistently showing up late for work and regularly missing scheduled appointments.

When we experience betrayal, we need to work through our painful feelings and move forward. Consultants Dennis and Michelle Reina offer seven steps for healing.[36]

First, observe and acknowledge what has happened. In this initial step, take note of what happened and how you are feeling as a result (i.e., depressed, angry, betrayed). Second, allow these feelings to surface—work through the pain but refuse to wallow in worry and guilt. Third, get support by reaching out to family, friends, and coworkers who can act as "trusted advisers." Fourth, reframe the experience; try to figure out why this event happened and what you learn from it. Fifth, take responsibility by considering if you played a role through your actions and choices; think about what you could do differently next time. Sixth, forgive yourself and others; forgiveness promotes our healing and provides insight into the motivations of the betrayer. Seventh, let go and move on; make a choice to take what you have learned, and use those insights to improve your future work relationships.

Moral Argument

Disagreement puts dialogue to the test. Buber encouraged disputants to walk the narrow ridge between opposing points of view. However, when we disagree, we tend to set up camp on one side of the ridge or the other. Remaining in dialogue during such encounters is never easy, but we are more likely to succeed if we follow guidelines for moral argument. The German philosopher Jürgen Habermas provides one set of ground rules, called *discourse ethics*, for engaging in argument.[37] Habermas believes that communities—towns, societies, organizations—develop their policies and moral norms through making and refuting claims and assertions. For community standards to be valid, Habermas argues that everyone affected by the decision must be allowed to freely participate in the discussion without fear of coercion. Every idea presented must be open to challenge, and all participants must have roughly the same power to influence one another. Individuals engaged in these discussions should be prepared to justify the claims they make during the argument. They must demonstrate that their statements are logically true, morally right, and sincerely offered.

Communication professor Rebecca Meisenbach offers a set of five steps for "enacting" discourse ethics in the organizational context.[38] The first step is to make a statement about actions or decisions that will have an impact on others. Not every decision needs to be guided by the rules of moral argument, only those that affect other organizational members, the local community, and the larger society. A proposal to reduce company contributions to an employee retirement plan would meet these criteria, for example.

The second step is to identify those who may be affected by the decision. In the case of modifying a retirement plan, this might include board members, stockholders, government regulators, and financial institutions, in addition to current and past employees.

The third step is to communicate to the parties identified in the second step. Interpersonal conversations, employee meetings, and Internet conferences could be used as channels for discussing the retirement plan changes.

The fourth step is to fully debate the consequences of the proposal (in this case, reduction of the current retirement plan) and decide if they are acceptable. Ensuring that all parties have an equal opportunity to be heard is critical in this stage.

The fifth and final step is to make a judgment about the claim and its consequences, determining if it is acceptable to all groups and therefore ethical. If the parties can reach a consensus that the retirement plan should be restructured, then the decision to make the changes is a moral one. (For another example of how moral argument can be applied in the organizational setting, turn to Case Study 4.3, "The Stem Cell Account.")

Discourse ethics sets a high standard for argument that is difficult to reach. For example, the hierarchical nature of organizations makes it difficult for all participants to have an equal voice; coercion is all too common. Nevertheless, you can take steps to improve your ability to promote and engage in moral argument. Practice perspective taking by imagining how others will be impacted by decisions. Make an effort to locate and involve everyone who has a stake in the decision, and involve these individuals in the decision process. Engage in active listening to better understand the claims of others. Try to ensure that all groups and individuals have a roughly equal voice in the decision process. Most importantly, develop your ability to make valid claims and to evaluate the claims of others. Valid arguments are based on sound evidence and reasoning. Evidence consists of the information—facts, conditions, opinions, beliefs—used to support a position. For instance, if you are arguing that more of your company's manufacturing process should be outsourced, then you might point to the fact that the firm has been losing money the last two years as evidence that your employer needs to cut costs. The strongest evidence has these characteristics:[39]

- *Reliability:* Comes from a trusted source that has been accurate in the past, like a respected industry analyst.

- *High in expertise:* Comes from sources knowledgeable about the topic at hand.

- *Objectivity:* Draws from unbiased sources that don't have distorted judgment or prejudice related to the topic.

- *Consistency:* Does not conflict with other sources of information or with other information provided by the same source.

- *Recentness:* Reflects the latest developments.

- *Relevance:* Directly relates to the claim being made.

- *Accessibility:* Reflects the source's firsthand knowledge of, or access to, the topic being discussed.

Like evidence, reason or logic can be used to support your position and to dispute the arguments of others. Common patterns of reasoning include (1) analogical (making comparisons between two objects or cases), (2) inductive (generalizing from one or a few cases to many cases), (3) deductive (moving from a larger category to a smaller one), and (4) causal (arguing that one situation or event causes another). Be alert to the potential weaknesses in each form of reasoning when constructing your argument or when analyzing the arguments of others.

Analogies hold only if the similarities between the two items being compared outweigh their differences. Take the case of comparisons between two schools, for example. You might be able to draw valid analogies between two neighboring small colleges, but it will be harder do so when comparing a small college and a major research university.

Generalizations must be made with care because a particular example may not hold for others in the same class or category. For instance, one graduate from a particular university may be a poor worker, but that doesn't mean that others from the same school will be poor performers, too.

Deductive arguments falter when communicators falsely assume that qualities from the larger group apply to every case within that category. Just because some neighbors object to a new plant doesn't mean that everyone in the area feels the same way, for instance.

Finally, causal relationships are often hard to establish. A sales decline is generally the product of several forces (new competition, an economic downturn, poor marketing), not just one. Be wary of inferring that chronological order means that the first event caused the second. A case in point: The university where I work has quadrupled in size since I was hired. However, it would be a mistake to say that my presence on campus accounts for the school's growth!

CHAPTER TAKEAWAYS

- Our attitudes set the moral tone for organizational conversations. Treat others as unique human beings (I-Thou) rather than as objects (I-It).

- Technical dialogue (information-centered speech) makes up the majority of communication in organizational settings. However, open a space for dialogue to occur by developing your communication skills and taking advantage of opportunities for I-Thou interaction.

- To engage in dialogue, you will need to commit yourself to (1) seeking the good of others, (2) valuing relationships and the common good, (3) being open to influence, (4) allowing others to hold differing opinions, (5) practicing honesty, and (6) being willing to invest time and energy in the process.

- Learn to be mindful; give your full attention to an encounter. Create additional categories in order to make greater distinctions, to welcome novel information, and to be open to new points of view.

- Understand communication as listening centered, not speaking centered. Keep in mind that listening is a multistage process made up of hearing, understanding, remembering, interpreting, evaluating, and responding (HURIER). This process can break down at any step along the way. Master listening skills and avoid listening errors by understanding the weaknesses of your listening profile.

- Dialogue rests upon the sharing as well as the receiving of information. Make sure that your self-disclosure is relevant, considers the context and likely impact, takes place over time, avoids unnecessary risks, and is reciprocated.

- Confirmation is the process of recognizing and acknowledging the presence and value of others. You can affirm others by recognizing the other person, by acknowledging your relationship with that individual, by signaling your awareness of the other's significance, and by accepting the other person's experience and perspective.

- Master the four skill sets of emotional intelligence in order to get along better with others, to become a more effective manager, and to make wiser choices. These skills include (1) accurately identifying emotions, (2) using emotions to enhance reasoning, (3) understanding the causes and progressions of emotions to predict events, and (4) managing emotions to generate productive outcomes.

- Trust means putting ourselves in a vulnerable position, expecting that the other party will carry through on promises and commitments. We have a moral obligation to protect others who are relying on us, and we can build our trustworthiness by demonstrating moral virtues and competence.

- If you violate trust, you will need to accept responsibility for what has occurred and engage in trust repair with the other party.

- Moral argument involves everyone who would be affected by a decision, and each organizational member freely participates without fear of coercion. As a participant in a moral discussion, speak from the conviction that your arguments are right, and be consistent with your other statements and actions.

- Develop your ability to make valid claims and to evaluate the claims of others. Employ strong evidence, and be alert to potential weaknesses in analogical, inductive, deductive, and causal reasoning.

APPLICATION PROJECTS

1. Describe a time when you engaged in dialogue. When did it occur and with whom? What did each party say and do? What was the outcome of your encounter? How did both parties feel when it ended? What did you learn from the experience?

2. As a group, select a film, and assign each member to view it from a different point of view. Then discuss the film based on each perspective. What insights do you gain from this perspective? What does this project reveal about the value of being open to many different points of view?

3. Develop a strategy to increase your mindfulness during an important communication encounter—job interview, class presentation, first date, important meeting, performance review.

4. Based on the HURIER listening model, what are your strengths and weaknesses as a listener? What skills do you need to develop to become more effective? What does your listening style profile (Self-Assessment 4.2) suggest about your listening habits and how they might hurt or help your relationships with other organizational members?

5. As a small or large group, discuss Buber's assertion that confirmation (recognizing one another's personhood) is the defining characteristic of humankind.

6. Write up your responses from Ethical Checkpoint 4.2. Compare your current perspective to your thinking before you completed this exercise. How has your understanding of the past conversation changed? How might you prepare differently for the upcoming encounter?

7. Describe a time when trust was broken and then restored in one of your work relationships. Outline the effects of the breach of trust, how you worked through the painful feelings (if you were the victim), and how trust was restored.

8. Employ Habermas's moral argument guidelines in an ongoing disagreement. Report on the success (or the lack of success) of your efforts.

CASE STUDY 4.1

Everyone's Favorite Professor

As a student at Brandeis University in the 1970s, sportswriter and author Mitch Albom developed a special relationship with sociology professor Morrie Schwartz. Mitch was attracted by the diminutive professor's warmth and kindness. Morrie encouraged Mitch from the first day of class, saying that he hoped that the two would become friends. Later he told Mitch that he reminded him of a younger version of himself. Professor Schwartz was a memorable figure on campus. One time he helped negotiate a settlement between striking black students and campus administration. At a basketball game, he silenced the cheer "We're number one" by standing up and asking "What's wrong with being number two?" He was a regular at Wednesday night dances where, dressed in black sweatpants and a white T-shirt, he would twist and turn with students under flashing lights to every kind of music—rock and roll, big band, the blues. His classes were heavy on personal development. Morrie encouraged students to find a meaningful purpose in life and to avoid the lure of money.

Mitch took every course that Morrie taught and began referring to the professor as "Coach." The two became friends, talking regularly outside of class. Mitch signed up to do a senior thesis so he could spend more time with his mentor.

The pair lost touch after Mitch graduated. That all changed in 1995, when Morrie went on national television to talk about his struggle with ALS disease, a neurological condition that first paralyzes the legs and moves up the body, ending in death by suffocation. Albom got in touch with his former mentor and once again became a student of Schwartz's. The two began meeting every Tuesday in Morrie's bedroom to work on their "final thesis." Over the last 14 weeks of Morrie's life, the old professor shared his thoughts on topics ranging from culture, family, and forgiveness to aging and death. Mitch recorded these conversations in the book *Tuesdays With Morrie*. Albom originally hoped to sell enough books to help Morrie pay for his medical bills. However, *Tuesdays* (which was rejected by several publishers) became a surprise hit, selling an estimated 35 million copies. It became required reading for courses at colleges around the country.

Readers were drawn both by Morrie's message and by the man himself. His conversations with Mitch were filled with short bits of wisdom. For example:

- When you learn how to die, you learn how to live.
- Love is the only rational act.
- If you've found meaning, you don't want to go back. You want to go forward.
- Do the kinds of things that come from the heart. When you do, you won't be dissatisfied.
- Love is how you stay alive, even after you are gone.
- Invest in the human community. Invest in people.

(Continued)

(Continued)

- Forgive yourself before you die. Then forgive others.
- Love is when you are as concerned about someone else's situation as you are about your own.

Morrie challenged Mitch to express his emotions and to reconcile with his brother, who was also terminally ill. Morrie also posed tough questions of Mitch and readers, asking: "Have you found someone to share you heart with?" "Are you giving to your community?" "Are you at peace with yourself?" "Are you trying to be as human as you can be?"

Morrie was an extraordinary communicator even in the midst of a slow death. Rather than being overwhelmed by self-pity, Morrie was able to give visitors (hundreds of former students streamed to his bedside during his final months) his full attention. "I believe in being fully present," Morrie told Mitch. "That means you should be with the person you're with." (p. 135). According to Mitch,

> I believe many visitors in the last few months of Morrie's life were drawn not because of the attention they wanted to pay to him but because of the attention he paid to them. Despite his personal pain and decay, this little old man listened the way they always wanted someone to listen. (pp. 135–136)

Morrie asked that the inscription on his tombstone read "Teacher till the last." And indeed he was. In the final act of his life he offered lessons in living, dying, and dialogue to Mitch and millions of readers.

Discussion Probes

1. Have you read *Tuesdays With Morrie*? How did you respond to the story of Mitch and Morrie?
2. Have you ever had an instructor who became a mentor and a friend? How did the instructor encourage this relationship? How did you encourage the relationship?
3. What ethical communication competencies did Morrie demonstrate?
4. What characteristics of dialogue do you see in the conversations between Morrie and Mitch?
5. Do you think visitors came to help Morrie or to be helped by Morrie?
6. How do you account for Morrie's ability to be present even in the face of death?

Source: Albom (1997).

CASE STUDY 4.2

Unfairly Taking the Blame

Tom Loveless is director of strategic planning for SandFan, a rapidly expanding regional sandwich chain. In this role he selects the sites for new locations. He works closely with Dave Bonner, the company's property manager. Bonner is in charge of negotiating leases for the new locations in addition to managing the facilities of existing stores.

Tom's ability to select good locations and Dave's skill at negotiating reasonable leases with commercial property managers are key to the chain's success. The two work well together and share a mutual interest in golf. On occasion they will spend a Saturday afternoon at the local public course.

The duo's string of successes was recently broken when SandFan had to close a store in a new market. Traffic to the store was lower than expected and the lease payments were higher than at other locations. Tom and Dave agreed that fault for the closure was a combination of these two factors.

SandFan founder Marjorie Oliphant met first with Dave to discuss the store's closing because Tom was traveling. When Tom met with Marjorie upon his return, he was surprised to learn that Dave blamed him for the closure. Dave told Marjorie that the terms of the lease were reasonable but that Tom had chosen a poor location, making it impossible to generate a profit.

Feeling betrayed, Tom plans to drop by Dave's office tomorrow morning.

Discussion Probes

1. Why do you think that Dave decided to put the blame on Tom for the failed location?

2. What should Tom say to address this breach of trust when he meets with Dave?

3. How should Dave respond?

4. How can Loveless and Bonner restore their relationship? Or can they?

5. Can you think of times when your trust was betrayed on the job? How did you respond? What would you do differently (if anything) the next time a similar event occurs?

CASE STUDY 4.3

The Stem Cell Account

Tim O'Shannon is the owner of a small public relations agency located in the capital city of a midwestern state. Much of his firm's business comes from representing builders, solid waste haulers, and other groups to state agencies and lobbying on their behalf when the legislature is in session. Recently, he was approached by the local branch of the Stem Cell Research Alliance to lobby on behalf of a bill that would fund stem cell research in the state.

Tim knows that stem cell research is highly controversial and anticipates that he will have employees on both sides of the issue.[1] Supporters want to use human embryos to generate tissue

(Continued)

(Continued)

that can be used to fight Parkinson's disease, ALS (Lou Gehrig's disease), diabetes, and other illnesses. Opponents of stem cell research argue that embryos are humans and that using them for research is murder.

As the owner of the agency, O'Shannon knows that he alone could make the decision to accept or reject the stem cell account. Nonetheless, he worries that an arbitrary decision on his part could seriously damage morale and split the agency into warring factions. (Tim himself doesn't have a strong opinion on the issue but does have a brother who suffers from diabetes.) Further, he has always been committed to empowering employees and giving them a voice in the operation of the firm.

After letting the account proposal sit on his desk for several days, O'Shannon decides to involve his employees in the decision-making process. He will abide by the group's conclusion. He wants to set some ground rules, though, to ensure that the discussion, which could get very heated, is conducted fairly. He is open to bringing people from outside the agency into the discussion as well.

Discussion Probes

1. What groups are affected by this decision?
2. Who should be involved in the discussion?
3. How should the discussion take place? What communication channels should be used?
4. How can O'Shannon make sure that all participants are heard?
5. What instructions should Tim give the participants?
6. What kinds of claims could be made for or against accepting the account?
7. What types of evidence and reasoning could be used to support these claims?

Note

1. For more information on the stem cell research controversy, see: H. Gardner (2010). Herper and Langreth (2006). Munrol (2002). Vogel (2001).

CHAPTER FIVE

EXERCISING ETHICAL INFLUENCE

Chapter Preview

Questions of Power
    Question 1: Are Some Forms of Power More Ethical Than Others?
    Question 2: Is It Possible to Have Too Much Power?
    Question 3: Should I Play Politics?
    Question 4: What Factors Contribute to Empowerment?
    Question 5: How Do I Overcome Barriers to Empowerment?
Ethical Issues in Influence
    Framing
    Proactive Tactics
    Impression Management
    Deception
    Emotional Labor
    Communication of Expectations
Chapter Takeaways
Application Projects

On the job, you can expect to devote much of your time to influencing others. Over the course of a day, you may find yourself urging the mail room to ship your package first, asking a subordinate to complete a project on time, convincing a customer to place another order, and persuading your boss to increase the budget for your department. The exercise of influence is not an option in the workplace. We must influence others if we are to fulfill our roles. If we don't, our work groups and organizations (not to mention our careers) will suffer.

While we don't have much choice as to whether or not we exert influence, we do have control over *how* we go about modifying the behaviors of others. These choices will go a long way toward determining the ethical health of our organizations. In this chapter, we'll address ethical questions that arise when influencing others. We'll begin with a look at power and then address moral issues related to framing, proactive influence tactics, impression management, deception, emotional labor, and the communication of expectations.

QUESTIONS OF POWER

The exercise of ethical influence is founded on an understanding of power, the capacity to control the behavior of others. Power is the foundation for influence. The greater the power we have, the more likely that others will comply with our wishes no matter what particular strategy we employ. However, to wield power ethically, we need to answer some important questions.

Question 1: Are Some Forms of Power More Ethical Than Others?

Power comes from a variety of sources. The most popular power classification system identifies five power bases:[1]

1. *Coercive power* is based on penalties or punishments—for example, verbal warnings, wage cuts, staffing reductions, and student suspensions.

2. *Reward power* depends on being able to deliver something of value to others, whether tangible (bonuses, health insurance, grades) or intangible (praise, recognition, cooperation).

3. *Legitimate power* resides in the position. Supervisors, judges, police officers, and instructors have the right to control our behavior within certain limits. A professor sets the requirements in her course, for example, but has no influence over what we do in our other classes.

4. *Expert power*, in contrast to legitimate power, is based on the characteristics of the individual regardless of his or her official position. Knowledge, skills, education, and certification all build expert power. As a result, those who are not in positions of authority can be very influential because they possess valued information.

5. *Referent (role model) power* rests on the admiration one individual has for another. We're more likely to do favors for a peer we admire or to agree to work over the weekend for a supervisor we respect.

No form of power is inherently immoral. In fact, we need to draw from a variety of power sources. The manager who is appointed to lead a task force is granted legitimate power that enables her to reward or punish. To succeed, she'll also have to demonstrate her knowledge of the topic, skillfully direct the group process, and earn the respect of task force members through hard work and commitment to the group. The effective use of one form of power can increase other power bases.[2] A widely admired employee who demonstrates expertise is more likely to be promoted. Conversely, the boss who has more access to information is better equipped to solve problems and thus will appear more expert. (Complete the Personal Power Profile in Self-Assessment 5.1 to determine how you prefer to influence others.)

SELF-ASSESSMENT 5.1

Personal Power Profile

Instructions

Below is a list of statements that describe possible behaviors of leaders in work organizations toward their followers. Carefully read each statement, thinking about *how you prefer to influence others*. Mark the number that most closely represents how you feel.

I Prefer to Influence Others by:	Strongly Disagree	Disagree	Neither Agree Nor Disagree	Agree	Strongly Agree
1. Increasing their pay level	1	2	3	4	5
2. Making them feel valued	1	2	3	4	5
3. Giving undesirable job assignments	1	2	3	4	5
4. Making them feel like I approve of them	1	2	3	4	5
5. Making them feel that they have commitments to meet	1	2	3	4	5
6. Making them feel personally accepted	1	2	3	4	5
7. Making them feel important	1	2	3	4	5
8. Giving them good technical suggestions	1	2	3	4	5
9. Making the work difficult for them	1	2	3	4	5
10. Sharing my experience and training	1	2	3	4	5
11. Making things unpleasant here	1	2	3	4	5
12. Making work distasteful	1	2	3	4	5
13. Helping them get a pay increase	1	2	3	4	5
14. Giving them the feeling that they have responsibilities to fulfill	1	2	3	4	5

(Continued)

(Continued)

I Prefer to Influence Others by:	Strongly Disagree	Disagree	Neither Agree Nor Disagree	Agree	Strongly Agree
15. Providing them with job-related advice	1	2	3	4	5
16. Providing them with special benefits	1	2	3	4	5
17. Helping them get a promotion	1	2	3	4	5
18. Making them feel like they should fulfill their job requirements	1	2	3	4	5
19. Providing them with needed technical knowledge	1	2	3	4	5
20. Making them recognize that they have tasks to accomplish	1	2	3	4	5

Scoring

Record your responses to the 20 questions in the corresponding numbered blanks below. Total each column, and then divide the result by 4 for each of the five types of influence.

	Reward	Coercive	Legitimate	Referent	Expert
	1	3	5	2	8
	13	9	14	4	10
	16	11	18	6	15
	17	12	20	7	19
Total					
Divide by 4					

Interpretation

A score of 4 or 5 on any of the five dimensions of power indicates that you prefer to influence others by using that particular form of power. A score of 2 or less indicates that you prefer not to employ this particular type of power to influence others. Your power profile is not a simple addition of each of the five sources. Some combinations are more synergistic than the simple sum of their parts. For example, referent power magnifies the impact of other power sources because these other influence attempts are coming from a respected person. Reward power often increases the impact of referent power because people generally tend to like those who can give them things. Some power combinations tend to produce the opposite of synergistic effects. Coercive power, for example, often negates the effects of other types of influence.

Source: Modified version of Hinken, T. R., & Schreisheim, C. A. (1989). Development and application of new scales to measure the French and Raven (1959) Bases of Social Power. *Journal of Applied Psychology, 74*, 561–567. Copyright © 2016 by the American Psychological Association. Reproduced with permission.

Ultimately, the morality of a particular power source depends on the ends or goals that it serves. We need to ask if our exercise of power serves worthy objectives. However, arguing that no form of power is unethical in and of itself should not obscure the fact that some types of power are more likely to be abused. *Hard* power linked to organizational position (coercive, reward, and legitimate) is more dangerous than *soft* power linked to the person (expert, referent). Positional power gets immediate results, securing compliance and boosting short-term performance—but at a high cost. The use of legitimate, reward, and coercive power reduces trust and lowers task satisfaction and performance over the long term.[3] Of the three forms of positional power, coercive tactics pose the greatest risk. Extreme coercion can be devastating to individuals, attacking their dignity and value while threatening their mental and physical health.

To sum up, select your power bases carefully. Positional power should be used with caution. Reduce your reliance on authority, reward, and coercion by developing your skills and knowledge while modeling the behaviors you want to see in others. Coercion should be employed only as a last resort. It is best used for preventing and punishing incivility, dishonesty, aggression, discrimination, criminal activity, sexual harassment, and other destructive behaviors.

Question 2: Is It Possible to Have Too Much Power?

Concentration of power produces a wide range of unethical behavior, as Britain's Lord Acton noted in the 1800s. "Power corrupts," asserted Acton, "and absolute power corrupts absolutely." Lord Acton could have been commenting on the organizational scandals of our day. In case after case, powerful individuals abused their positions and put their organizations at risk. John Bolton, former U.S. ambassador to the United Nations, was accused of treating his bosses with respect while bullying subordinates. Movie director James Cameron is known for driving his employees hard. He allegedly used a nail gun to attach the cell phones of staffers to the wall while filming *Avatar*.[4] Former Theranos president Sunny Balwani acted as an "enforcer" who chastised any employee who had doubts about the company's faulty blood-testing system and threatened legal action against anyone talking publicly about the firm.[5] (See Case Study 7.3 in Chapter 7 for more information about the scandal at Theranos laboratories.)

Positional power is most susceptible to abuse. Lord Acton probably had this type of control in mind when he noted power's corrosive effects. History's most infamous leaders—Nero, Stalin, Hitler, Pol Pot, Milosevic, Amin—used their lofty positions to darken the lives of followers through purges, torture, murder, and other means. However, many of these same leaders also misused their personal power. Followers believed that these leaders were endowed with special gifts and looked to them as role models.

There are a number of possible explanations for why unfettered power is so susceptible to misuse. To start, powerful individuals are free to project their insecurities on others. Second, powerful people are more susceptible to judgment biases.[6] They typically devote little attention to finding out how others think and feel. As a consequence, they are more likely to hold and act on harmful stereotypes, which justify their lofty positions. In addition, they believe they deserve their high status because those who are powerless aren't as capable as they are. Third, powerful people protect their positions by attacking those they perceive as threats. Fourth, those in power often ignore the needs of others. They see subordinates as a means to achieving their ends. Fifth, powerful individuals are tempted to rely upon positional power. Rather than build personal power bases, they employ coercion. Power holders are more likely to order subordinates to complete a task when a softer tactic (making a request, offering a reason) would achieve the same result at less emotional and relational cost.[7]

If you have considerable power, be open to influence. Influence needs to be reciprocal; leaders exert power but, at the same time, respond to the influence attempts of followers. Enact formal mechanisms like appeals procedures, subordinate feedback, recalls, and elections to encourage yourself to be responsive to your less powerful colleagues.[8]

Having too little power also poses ethical dilemmas.[9] Powerless members can't achieve worthy objectives and feel as if they have no control over their environments. They focus on maintaining the little power they have instead of on achieving collective goals. Along with taking out their frustrations on other employees, they harm the organization through work slowdowns, breaking equipment, calling in sick, and other aggressive behaviors. Powerlessness also impairs cognitive functioning, making errors more likely. If you find yourself in a low-power position in an organizational relationship, here are some ways to address your situation.[10]

- *Highlight your interdependence.* Help the high-power person recognize that your help is essential if he or she is to succeed. Take the case of the high-level executive and the lowly IT specialist, for example. The executive has significantly more organizational power but, in order to get her work done, relies on the specialist to keep her computer and mobile devices running properly.

- *Be persistent.* Be patient and remain calm. Carefully analyze the problem at hand and offer a credible solution. Oftentimes the higher-power person gives in to the lower-power individual just to get him or her to go away.

- *Stay actively engaged.* Resist the temptation to disconnect or to use the destructive tactics described above. Instead, speak up and state your values, beliefs, and priorities. Reflect your values through your actions.

Question 3: Should I Play Politics?

In organizational politics, members accumulate and use informal power to achieve personal and organizational objectives. Political behavior is not officially sanctioned by the organization and operates outside the formal power structure.[11] Examples of engaging in organizational politics include lobbying for a higher salary, forming a coalition with other managers to push through a project, or doing a favor for someone in another department in hopes that this individual will reciprocate in the future.

Most of us associate "playing politics" with hidden agendas, selfishness, backroom deals, manipulation, and deceit. More often than not, those who engage in politics get what they want while more deserving, nonpolitical individuals do not. Members who perceive that they work in highly political organizational climates are less satisfied with their jobs and less committed to their organizations. At the same time, they report higher stress levels and are more likely to leave the group.[12]

Given its poor reputation, it would appear that engaging in organizational politics is unethical. But that is not always the case. Sometimes going outside formal channels is the only way to achieve worthy objectives like getting top management to deal with safety problems, to introduce innovative new products, or to keep the organization going when formal authority breaks down.[13] Then, too, informal power is an inescapable fact of organizational life. It is most frequently used in lateral or peer relationships to promote projects, to allocate resources like people and equipment, and to coordinate work flow. Dwight Eisenhower used his political skill to organize the successful invasion of Europe in World War II. Earlier in his career, he developed a network of friendships with George Patton, George Marshall, and Omar Bradley, generals who were to play a critical role in the assault. From a young age, Eisenhower was skilled at settling disputes and getting classmates to focus on a shared goal, abilities that were to serve him well as he planned the Normandy landing.[14]

Ensuring that our political behavior generates positive outcomes begins with a shift in our mind-set. Organizational behavior experts Ronnie Kurchner-Hawkins and Rina Miller argue that we need to abandon our negative image of organizational politics and begin to think of the use of informal power as an opportunity to foster cooperation and collective achievements.[15] In Figure 5.1, they contrast the "dark side" of political power on the left side of the continuum with the bright, or positive, mind-set on the right side.

Negative politics is self-centered, focused on achieving individual goals like promoting one's job or career; positive political action supports the vision and values of the group. In positive politics, power is no longer used to control others but is used to serve them instead. While negative politics relies on controlling through intimidation and manipulation, positive politics focuses on achieving a shared vision and living out shared values. Negative political behavior focuses on winning at all costs; positive politics stresses collaboration and working together (win-win). Negative organizational politics often ignores ethical standards and focuses only on efficiency ("doing things right"). Positive political strategies, on the other hand, recognize the importance of considering the ethical implications of actions and following moral standards ("doing the right things").

Figure 5.1 Political Mind-Set Shift Continuum

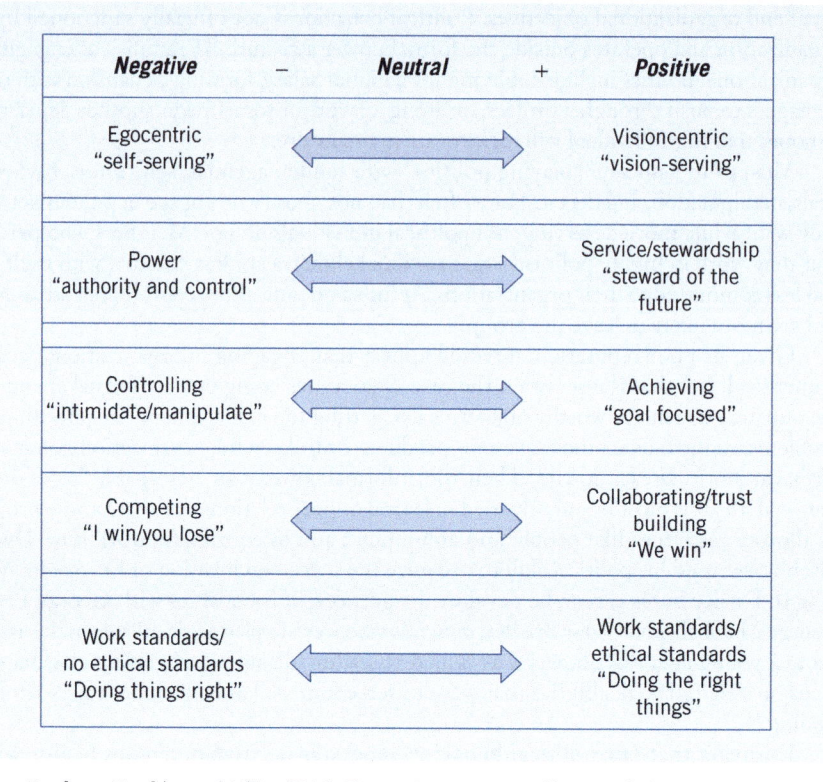

Negative	− Neutral +	Positive
Egocentric "self-serving"	⟷	Visioncentric "vision-serving"
Power "authority and control"	⟷	Service/stewardship "steward of the future"
Controlling "intimidate/manipulate"	⟷	Achieving "goal focused"
Competing "I win/you lose"	⟷	Collaborating/trust building "We win"
Work standards/ no ethical standards "Doing things right"	⟷	Work standards/ ethical standards "Doing the right things"

Source: Kurchner-Hawkins and Miller (2006), Figure 19.1, p. 332. Used by permission.

Achieving our goals through positive political means takes four skills.[16] You can determine if you have these abilities by completing Self-Assessment 5.2.

1. *Social astuteness.* Politically skilled people are keen observers of other people and know how to interact in social situations. They might decide that now is not a good time to approach a supervisor who has had a stressful week, for example. They are also highly self-aware, knowing how they come across to others, presenting themselves and their work in a positive light.

2. *Interpersonal influence.* Those with political skills can adapt their behaviors to the specific situation. They know which ideas will be of most interest to a particular leader, for instance, and what arguments will be most effective when approaching individual colleagues.

3. *Networking ability.* Politically skilled individuals know how to make friends, form alliances, build coalitions, and make connections with powerful people. Their

networks form social capital that can be drawn upon when promoting ideas or projects. These members are frequently good negotiators and deal makers who are skilled at conflict management.

4. *Apparent sincerity*. When it comes to sincerity, perception is more important than reality. Even the most sincere person will be distrusted if he or she is seen as manipulative. Those skilled at positive politics communicate that that they don't have ulterior motives and can be trusted.

SELF-ASSESSMENT 5.2

Political Skill Inventory

Instructions

Using the following 7-point scale, please place the number before each item that best describes how much you agree with each statement about yourself.

1 = Strongly disagree

2 = Disagree

3 = Slightly disagree

4 = Neutral

5 = Slightly agree

6 = Agree

7 = Strongly agree

1. I spend a lot of time and effort at work networking with others.
2. I am able to make most people comfortable and at ease around me.
3. I am able to communicate easily and effectively with others.
4. It is easy for me to develop good rapport with most people.
5. I understand people very well.
6. I am good at building relationships with influential people at work.
7. I am particularly good at sensing the motivations and hidden agendas of others.
8. When communicating with others, I try to be genuine in what I say and do.
9. I have developed a large network of colleagues and associates at work whom I can call on for support when I really need to get things done.
10. At work, I know a lot of important people and am well connected.
11. I spend a lot of time at work developing connections with others.
12. I am good at getting people to like me.
13. It is important that people believe I am sincere in what I say and do.
14. I try to show a genuine interest in other people.
15. I am good at using my connections and network to make things happen at work.

(Continued)

(Continued)

16. I have good intuition or am savvy about how to present myself to others.
17. I always seem to instinctively know the right things to say or do to influence others.
18. I pay close attention to people's facial expressions.

Scoring

To determine your networking ability, add up your scores on items 1, 6, 9, 10, 11, and 15 (range 6–42).

To determine your interpersonal influence skill, add up your scores on items 2, 3, 4, and 12 (range 4–28).

To determine your social astuteness, add up your scores on items 5, 7, 16, 17, and 18 (range 5–35).

To determine your apparent sincerity score, total your scores on items 8, 13, and 14 (range 3–21).

To determine your total score, add up your scores for each dimension (range 18–126).

The higher the score, the greater your perceived political skills.

Source: Adapted from Ferris et al. (2005). Used by permission.

Question 4: What Factors Contribute to Empowerment?

There are both ethical and practical reasons for giving power away. Distributing power to others supports such important ethical values as individual autonomy, fairness (equality), and concern for others. At the same time, empowering followers boosts the bottom line. Researchers report that empowered individuals and groups perform better. People like their jobs more, work harder, take more responsibility, and are more committed to their organizations when they feel that they have a significant voice in shaping decisions.[17] They're more likely to cooperate as well. Paradoxically, you gain more power by distributing it to others.[18] The performance of the group increases as a result (as do perceptions of your power). Empowerment also fosters the personal growth of followers. Sharing power can help them learn new skills, tackle new challenges, and find greater fulfillment. (Turn to Case Study 5.1 at the end of the chapter to see how one company takes power sharing to a new level.)

Psychological empowerment refers to increased motivation to carry out tasks associated with work roles. According to organizational scholars Kenneth Thomas and Betty Velthouse, this heightened motivation is the product of four factors:[19]

1. *Meaning.* Meaning is the value placed on a task, goal, or purpose based on personal standards. The better the fit between the purpose of the task and our standards, the greater our motivation to do the job.
2. *Competence.* Competence is the belief that we can do the job required. It is part of a broader sense of personal power or self-efficacy. Self-efficacy is the conviction

that we can deal with the events, people, and situations at work and in other environments.[20]

3. *Self-determination.* Self-determination is the sense that we have a choice in how we carry out our jobs—when to start, how fast to work, how to prioritize tasks.

4. *Impact.* Impact is the extent to which we can influence the larger organizational environment. Those with a high sense of impact believe that they make a difference in the work group's operating procedures, plans, and goals.

All four of the cognitive components of empowerment are shaped by elements of the work group environment. As a consequence, we can boost perceptions of empowerment as managers by modifying the setting where work occurs, including reward systems, job duties, organizational structure and work flow, rules, and physical layout. Elimination of situational factors that create feelings of powerlessness is an excellent place to start. Get rid of petty regulations, authoritarian supervision, and strict routines. Next, shift more decision-making authority to followers. Allow those assigned to do the task a great deal of leeway in how the task gets done. Invite employees into organizational decision-making processes. At the same time, supply resources. Completing a task depends on having adequate funds and supplies, sufficient time to devote to the job, and a place to work. The support of leaders is essential for major projects. The introduction of new products, accounting systems, and software programs requires the endorsement of important individuals who also encourage other leaders to buy into initiatives.[21]

Information may be the most important resource for empowerment. Data about the competition, consumers, and strategy help members see the "big picture." They gain a better understanding of their roles in the organization and how their efforts help achieve collective goals. Access to information builds self-efficacy and enables individuals to make better decisions while exerting influence over the direction of their work units. Newly empowered followers, in particular, need information in order to carry out more demanding assignments. At one pet supply manufacturer, managers gave employee teams the power to shut down the production line and set production schedules. To prepare workers for this added responsibility, they provided employees with production schedules and information on customer requirements. The company developed a set of criteria for shutdowns, trained teams to diagnose line malfunctions, and told them how much it cost to shut down and restart production. Workers discussed case studies involving line shutdown decisions. They then exercised their new powers for three months with review by managers. At the end of that period, they controlled the production process entirely on their own.[22]

Question 5: How Do I Overcome Barriers to Empowerment?

Empowerment efforts face significant obstacles. Keeping, not sharing, authority is rewarded in traditional, top-down organizations. Managers in these systems are afraid to let go of their power for fear of failure. Adopting any new approach is risky, particularly when it comes to empowerment. Managers lose control and have to rely on the efforts of team members. They may be punished if their subordinates fail to produce. Success in a more equalitarian system also requires a different skill set. Empowering managers must provide resources instead of direction, share information, and facilitate the group process. Newly empowered followers are anxious, too. They're used to having one person make the final decision and must take on greater responsibilities. Some are not eager to learn new skills and are afraid of making mistakes.

Management professor and consultant Alan Randolph admits that empowerment is hard to put into practice but notes it has been successfully implemented at such companies as the Marriott Corporation, General Electric, AES, Springfield Remanufacturing, and Pacific Gas and Electric. Companies who want to take "the long journey to empowerment" must pass through three stages.[23]

Stage 1: Starting and orienting the process of change. Any major empowerment initiative must begin not with a grand vision but with practical answers to personal concerns. People want to know why the change is needed and what's wrong with the way things operate now. Further, they want to understand how the change will impact them and how they stand to gain (or lose). Providing information—financial statements and projections, data on market changes—motivates members to do a better job. At the same time, managers need to set boundaries so members don't feel overwhelmed. Boundaries can be established through setting goals and by providing training that equips employees to reach those objectives. Most successful empowerment efforts replace hierarchy with self-directed work teams.

Stage 2: Making changes and dealing with discouragement. In this stage, the focus shifts to concerns about implementation and impact. Workers wonder what they need to do to be empowered, where to go for help, and why the process is so difficult. They also question whether the effort is worth it and doubt that any progress is being made. Once again, members desire data, this time about how to proceed. They need to know where to get help, what to do if things go wrong, and whether the initiative is producing results. Instead of backing off empowerment efforts, leaders need to expand boundaries further. Work teams ought to be given even more responsibility for work flow, not less. The good news is that once results begin to appear, members will promote the advantages of empowerment to their colleagues. One key during this step is to change performance appraisal systems to reward collaboration instead of individual efforts.

Stage 3: Adopting and refining empowerment to fit the organization. At this stage, a culture of empowerment emerges. Concerns turn to collaboration and refinement. Individuals in this final step want help getting everyone involved in the process because they know empowerment works. They also want to learn how to perform even better. Managers and teams share data with each other about how to make improvements. Employees internalize commitment to the values and goals of the organization.

Organizational empowerment has its share of critics.[24] Some complain that empowerment is just a management fad and that far too many organizations give it lip service only, resisting any meaningful change efforts. Employees then become disillusioned and resentful as trust breaks down. Others complain that managers and employees understand the term *empowerment* differently. Empowered employees may expect to be treated equally, while managers view empowerment as a means for better getting the work done. The most cynical observers believe that empowerment is a form of exploitation. In participative systems, workers contribute more ideas and energy but don't get rewarded for their additional efforts.

These criticisms are valid. Empowerment can be faddish and exploitive. Yet it doesn't have to be. Truly empowering organizations back up their talk with their walk, following through on their commitment to change. These groups recognize that genuine empowerment benefits both workers and management. They boost compensation for those who accept more responsibility.

ETHICAL ISSUES IN INFLUENCE

Selecting the appropriate tactic is one of the most important choices we make when exerting influence. Ethical considerations should always play a central role in this determination. In the remainder of this chapter we'll look at the ethical issues raised by six widely used organizational influence strategies: framing, proactive tactics, impression management, deception, emotional labor, and the communication of expectations.

Framing

Successful influence often begins with creating the right frame. Frames are mental pictures or interpretations that shape understanding of reality.[25] Interpretive frames have much in common with picture frames:

> . . . the way a photograph is matted and framed brings out some aspects of the photo more than others. Certain mat colors and frame shapes can drastically alter the appearance of a photograph. Particular aspects of the photograph can be made central, others made peripheral and still others cut out entirely by the placement of the frame. A cognitive, interpretive frame operates the same way: a held frame may privilege certain aspects and angles of an entity, issue or event, and de-emphasize or ignore other aspects. By employing one frame verses another, our interpretation of that reality may be drastically altered, and our future action influenced.[26]

Politicians recognize the power of frames. For example, some congressional representatives refer to estate taxes as "death taxes." This frame makes it appear as if the government is waiting for citizens to die to unfairly collect from their descendants. Such an interpretation makes it easier to reduce or to eliminate these taxes. The Trump administration uses the "crossing a red line" metaphor to frame the U.S. response to North Korea's nuclear missile program. If at some point the North Koreans cross this line, the U.S. is prepared to take strong action.

Success or failure often rests on convincing others to adopt the desired frame.[27] A study of how cardiac surgery departments responded to a new, less invasive way to conduct heart operations illustrates this fact. The new procedure not only required surgeons, nurses and other members of the surgery team to learn new equipment, but it also required more coordination among team members. When implementation failed, it was because departments adopted a performance frame. Guided by this frame, which focused on getting the job done, team members believed that the new procedure was not that different from the previous method. They thought they knew what to do and failed to coordinate their activities. Team members operated independently and the surgeons treated everyone else as subordinates. When implementation succeeded, cardiac departments adopted a learning frame—to learn as much as possible to anticipate what to do next. Guided by this frame, surgery team members viewed the new practice as a challenge and an opportunity to try new things. They spent time practicing the procedure. They saw themselves as interdependent, and the surgeons told the nurses that they were valued resources.[28]

Gail Fairhurst urges communicators to morally position themselves when framing by tying into the ethical codes and values of their organizations.[29] These codes (see Chapter 9) keep framers from pursuing selfish interests while acknowledging that others also have legitimate concerns. She cites the example of three CEOs to illustrate the contrast between selfish and morally positioned framing. When asked about the consequences of moving jobs overseas, then Cypress Semiconductor CEO T. J. Rodgers framed his response in economic terms, saying some American jobs "didn't have a right to exist." When asked to defend his compensation, former Scott Paper and Sunbeam-Oster CEO Al Dunlap framed his response in terms of superior ability. He claimed that he was one of the "superstar executives" who deserved to be paid extremely well. When asked whether employees at a soon-to-be-closed Alabama plant deserved their fate, then Van Huesen CEO Bruce Klatsky framed his response in moral terms instead. He replied that these employees didn't deserve what was to happen. He was "scared to death for them," which made it hard for him to sleep.

The importance of creating ethical frames is highlighted by the fact many organizational miscues come from frames that ignore ethical considerations. Consider the case of a major US life insurance company found guilty of deceptive sales practices during the 1990s. Sales people falsely promised customers "free insurance" by claiming that annual dividends paid by policyholders would always cover the cost of future premiums. They also engaged in "churning," continually putting customers into new products that generated higher commissions. A number of frames embedded in the corporate culture—none of which took ethical behavior into account—led to this misconduct. These frames were related to (1) products (the dividends were virtually guaranteed), (2) customers (buyers were underinsured and needed more coverage), and (3) insurance regulations (compliance with external requirements was a meaningless ritual).[30]

Proactive Tactics

Proactive influence tactics are focused on achieving immediate objectives by convincing targets to go along with requests. Gary Yukl of the State University of New York at Albany and his associates have identified the following as proactive influence strategies commonly used in organizations.[31]

- *Rational persuasion:* Offering explanations, factual evidence, and logical arguments to demonstrate that a proposal or request will attain task and organizational objectives. Examples: "Research shows that there is a need for a new hospital." "Hiring a new finance professor will draw more students to the major."

- *Apprising:* Explaining how compliance with the request will benefit the target (e.g., help a career, make a job more interesting). Examples: "Taking the sales training will help you make your sales quota." "Accepting a position at company headquarters should get you promoted faster."

- *Inspirational appeals:* Creating enthusiasm by appealing to ideals and values; arousing emotions. Examples: "Investing in the new engineering software will make our product the highest quality in the industry." "Joining our research team will put you on the front lines in the fight against cancer."

- *Consultation:* Soliciting support by seeking suggestions for improvement; asking for input when planning strategy, an activity, or a change. Examples: "How do you think we can attract more qualified job applicants?" "Take a look at these plans for the new store and let me know you think."

- *Collaboration:* Providing resources and assistance if the target of the request complies. Examples: "If you can provide the staffing, I can get the necessary funds to complete the project." "I could go with you to talk to your boss about the proposal."

- *Ingratiation:* Generating positive feelings by the use of flattery and praise either before or during a request; expressing confidence in the target's ability to satisfy a difficult request. Examples: "Since you know the product much better than I do, you should make the sales call." "You are the only person on the team who can create the phone app."

- *Personal appeals:* Appealing to feelings of loyalty and friendship when requesting something. Examples: "As a friend, do me a favor, and switch shifts with me." "We've worked together for a long time, so I am counting on you to vote for me when I run for union steward."

- *Exchange:* Providing something the target wants in return for compliance; trading favors; promising to reciprocate later or to share the benefits when the job is completed. Examples: "If you support my request for highway funds for my legislative district, I'll support your request for your district." "If you invest more in our startup now, you will have a bigger share of the company when it goes public."

- *Coalition tactics:* Enlisting the help of others or using the support of coworkers to convince the target to go along with the request. Examples: "The divisional vice-president supports this policy change." "Your friend Sue from accounting really likes this idea."

- *Legitimating tactics:* Claiming the right or authority to make a request; aligning the request with the organization's rules, policies, and traditions. Examples: "The policy manual states that I can't be forced to work overtime two weekends in a row." "Your company signed a lease stating that you would pay $5,000 a month for the space."

- *Pressure:* Demanding, threatening, checking up; persistent reminders. Examples: "If you don't pay the rent on time, we'll evict you." "Have you had a chance to read that report yet?"

Legitimating and pressure tactics, which are based on hard power, are more likely to be abused. Soft power strategies—rational persuasion, consultation, collaboration and inspirational appeal—pose less danger. Nevertheless, as we noted in our earlier discussion of power, the morality of a particular strategy depends on our ends or goals. Rational persuasion and inspirational appeal can support legitimate or illegitimate requests, for example. Legitimating tactics and pressure may be necessary when pursuing important organizational goals or when enforcing safety regulations. Determining an ethical-emotional threshold is one way to determine when harder tactics are justified.[32] This threshold is based on the level of negative emotions that influencers are willing to generate. Normally the threshold is high. In other words, persuaders are reluctant to create anger and other negative emotions when influencing others. However, the threshold should be set lower if necessary. Be willing to generate negative feelings when dealing with destructive behaviors like aggression and stealing. Don't hesitate to claim authority or to threaten to end these unethical and illegal activities

Impression Management

In the organizational setting, you'll have little chance of getting what you want unless you create the desired image. Want a raise? Then you must convince your supervisor that you are hardworking and productive. Want to be assigned to be a project leader? Then you must be seen as competent and able to manage others. Want to make a sale? Then customers must perceive that you are honest and trustworthy. Want more staff for your work group? Then you'll have to convince the management team that your group is critical to the organization's success.

Scholars use the term *impression management* to describe how people try to control the images others have of them through their behaviors.[33] Impression management is a part of all human interaction, but it is particularly evident in the organizational setting. In a very real sense, organizations act as stages. On the organizational stage, members perform a variety of roles for different audiences. Consider the average professor, for example. Faculty members are typically evaluated on their teaching, scholarship (research), and service. To succeed, our instructor will have to perform well in the classroom, write for scholarly publications and present papers to academic peers, and demonstrate leadership at the university and in the local community. Each of these audiences requires a different performance. The highly technical jargon of the academic journal or presentation won't work well, for instance, with community audiences. The ability to accurately evaluate student work is essential to a successful teaching performance but has little relevance to research and service.

There are a variety of ways to manage the image that others have of us in the organizational setting, ranging from what we say and wear to the layout of our dorm rooms and offices. These tactics can be divided into two major categories: *acquisitive impression management* and *protective impression management*.[34] Acquisitive tactics are attempts to be seen in a positive light; protective tactics are attempts to avoid looking bad. Both sets of tactics, in turn, can be directly or indirectly applied. Parties use direct tactics during interactions, while indirect tactics involve the process of association. If Dan wants to convince Mary that he deserves a raise, he might point out how hard he works. Or he might take a more indirect approach, counting on her to remember that he was part of the team that launched the company's hottest new product. A catalog of organizational impression management tactics is provided in Ethical Checkpoint 5.1.

ETHICAL CHECKPOINT 5.1

Impression Management Tactics

Acquisitive/Direct Tactics

1. *Ingratiation*

   Goal: To appear more likeable and attractive

   Examples: Expressing similar attitudes, doing favors, flattering, complimenting, publicizing one's desirable qualities

2. *Self-Promotion*

   Goal: To appear competent

   Examples: Claiming relevant work experience on a résumé, mentioning a high grade point average in a job interview

3. *Intimidation*

   Goal: To gain social power and influence by appearing dangerous

   Examples: Using coercive power to ensure follower compliance, using counterpower (lawsuits, a tough image) to intimidate superiors

4. *Exemplification*

   Goal: To generate impressions of integrity and morality

   Examples: Publicizing self-sacrifice (working over the weekend or while sick), going beyond the call of duty

5. *Supplication*

   Goal: To secure help by appearing incompetent

   Examples: Asking for help with a new computer program, claiming lack of experience to get someone else to take the lead on a project

Acquisitive/Indirect Tactics

1. *Acclaiming*

   Goal: To highlight a relationship or association with a successful occurrence

   Examples: Claiming to be responsible for success (softball team victory, higher sales), maximizing the value of a positive event (noting that not only did you graduate from college, you graduated from one of the country's top-rated universities)

2. *Nonverbal Impression Management*

   Goal: To encourage liking through nonverbal behaviors

(Continued)

(Continued)

Examples: Smiling and leaning forward during a job interview, renting expensive office furniture to create an image of financial stability

Protective/Direct Tactics

1. *Accounts*

   Goal: To lessen or repair the damage after a failure has occurred

   Examples: Making excuses—admitting that an action is wrong but denying responsibility for it ("It wasn't my fault"); offering justifications—accepting responsibility but claiming that the event wasn't as bad as it seemed or that the behavior was justified

2. *Disclaimers*

   Goal: To lessen the potential damage that might be caused by an upcoming failure event

   Examples: Claiming credentials to make racist comments ("some of my best friends are . . . "), claiming an exception to the rules, asking for a suspension of judgment

3. *Self-Handicapping*

   Goal: To put self-imposed barriers in place when outcomes are uncertain, in order to maximize the value of success and minimize the penalties for failure

   Examples: Claiming to be coming back from an injury prior to a racquetball game with a coworker, mentioning an illness that prevented you from doing as much research as you wanted

4. *Apologies*

   Goal: To obtain pardon by admitting responsibility and blame

   Examples: Expressions of remorse, offers of restitution, requests for forgiveness

Protective/Indirect Tactics

1. *Blaring*

   Goal: To disassociate from a negative event or person

   Examples: Publicizing a lack of connection with the occurrence or individual ("I had nothing to do with that project"; "I was always suspicious of him")

2. *Blasting*

   Goal: To exaggerate the bad qualities of a person to whom we are connected but don't want to be

   Examples: Pointing out the poor work habits of another team member, claiming that a supervisor is abusive

Source: Rosenfeld, Giacalone, and Riordan (1995).

Some observers equate impression management with manipulation. To them, impression managers are phonies who try to deceive others by projecting a false image when they should strive to reflect their "true" selves instead. They note that competent performers get passed over in favor of employees who ingratiate themselves with the boss. (Contemporary Issues in Organizational Ethics 5.1 takes a closer look at the ethics of ingratiation.)

It is easy to see why impression management would be viewed with suspicion. We probably have all encountered individuals who are "all style and no substance." These coworkers are all too ready to change their behaviors and standards to conform to the wishes of others. They get ahead by projecting a good image instead of through hard work. Our academic and work careers may have languished because professors and supervisors played favorites. Those focused on self-enhancement may even be less productive because they spend so much energy on self-presentation. To maintain a competent image, self-promoters may refuse the help they need to complete their tasks.

Research confirms that we are right to be concerned about the ethics of impression management. Skilled impression managers are more likely to be hired and promoted regardless of ability. This puts women, who are more likely to rely on their performance to get ahead, at a disadvantage. Careerists who care little about coworkers and organizational goals use self-promotion to advance themselves at the expense of others.[35] Deceit can quickly turn impression management into manipulation, as in the case of job applicants who overstate their skills and background. One study reported that 95% of college students were willing to make at least one false statement in order to get a job. More than 40% of the respondents in the same study had already done so. This happens despite the fact that falsifying credentials and past accomplishments can serve as grounds for dismissal. Padded résumés cost Steve Masiello a $5 million contract to coach men's basketball at the University of South Florida and cost Scott Thomson his job as CEO of Yahoo. The principal of a Pittsburg, Kansas, high school had to resign when students from the school newspaper discovered that she had purchased her university degree from a diploma mill and was not licensed to teach in the state.[36] (We'll take a closer look at the ethics of deception in the next section.)

Recognition that impression management is prone to abuse does not mean we should abandon this form of influence. In fact, it would be impossible to do so. Impression management is found in every culture. Whatever the particular setting, humans want to achieve their goals and to be seen in a favorable light. Impression management is also hard to eliminate because it can occur at the unconscious or semiconscious level. For example, you may not have given much thought to why you brushed your teeth this morning or chose a particular shirt or top to wear. Yet both of these activities help shape the impressions you make on others throughout the rest of the day. Other organizational members are forming impressions of us, whether we are intentional about our behaviors or not. Even our attempts to avoid impression management tactics influence the impressions of others. Take the example of the job applicant who thinks that dressing up for an interview is "fake." His sloppy appearance manages the impressions of the employer, only in a negative manner. The interviewer may think that the applicant doesn't understand what the business world is like, that he didn't care enough about this job to make an effort to look good, or that his work habits may match his appearance.

Impression management serves many useful purposes Creating positive impressions on coworkers fosters cooperation and team satisfaction. More often than not, individuals use it to project an image that is congruent with who they think they are. Rather than deceiving or manipulating others, they want to accurately reflect their identities. Impression management is also essential to accomplishing moral objectives. Convincing management that a department legitimately needs more resources benefits both the work unit and the total organization. Department members will feel fairly treated and produce more. Organizational performance will likely increase because budget and personnel will be strategically allocated.

Organizational impression management experts Paul Rosenfeld, Robert Giacalone, and Catherine Riordan offer the following standards for determining whether impression management is beneficial or detrimental to an organization.[37] Beneficial impression management (1) facilitates positive interpersonal relationships both inside and outside the organization; (2) accurately portrays positive people, products, and events to insiders and outsiders; and (3) facilitates effective decisions. Dysfunctional impression management (1) inhibits or obstructs internal and external relationships; (2) inaccurately casts persons, events, and products in a bad light; and (3) distorts information, which leads to erroneous conclusions and decisions.

Under these standards we have a responsibility to generate accurate images. For example, it would be unethical to wear the college pin of the job interviewer to imply that we went to the same school as he did. At times we may have to correct wrong impressions. In the case of the interviewer, if he has the mistaken impression that we attended the same school, we have a responsibility to make it clear that we did not.[38] We also need to resist the temptation to exaggerate by, for instance, claiming more than our fair share of the credit for a class group project or overstating how much we like the boss's ideas.

Self-interest should always take a back seat to the interests of others, which means that impression management ought to be a tool for carrying out our roles in a way that benefits both the organization and its constituencies. Consider the impact of your tactics on coworkers.[39] Behaviors that generate positive outcomes for you might have negative consequences for others. Ingratiation and supplication may get you better job assignments and raises but leave fewer desirable tasks and less money for workmates. Even exemplary behaviors might have unintended negative consequences for coworkers. Coming in early and staying later may "raise the bar" for colleagues, making it harder for them to reach excellent performance levels.

Targets of impression management tactics have an ethical responsibility to ensure that agents aren't unduly or unfairly shaping decisions and outcomes. Job interviewers and human resources personnel ought to use objective criteria in hiring decisions. Managers should be aware that they are susceptible to influence and encourage followers to disagree and to tell them the truth.[40] (If supervisors suspect they are being manipulated, they probably are.) They need to beware of playing favorites and also base personnel decisions on objective criteria, knowing that women in particular may not trumpet their accomplishments as much as men do. Careerists should be confronted. Their success should be tied to how well they cooperate in a group, not on how well they promote themselves.

CONTEMPORARY ISSUES IN ORGANIZATIONAL ETHICS 5.1

"HONEST" INGRATIATION

Ingratiation is one of the most popular impression management techniques. That should come as no surprise, given that flattery, agreeing with the other party, and doing favors are highly effective in influencing others, particularly in organizational settings. Ingratiation puts the target in a positive frame of mind and makes the recipient feel obligated to return the favor. The influencer appears more attractive and communicates liking for the target. Feeling liked, the target generally responds in kind.

While effective, ingratiation has a bad reputation. Business journals warn of the "sneaky tactics" subordinates use to manipulate their bosses. We recognize transparent attempts to "kiss up" to a supervisor or teacher, as in the case of the student telling the instructor she is "the greatest professor he has ever had" right before grades are due.

A number of ingratiation tactics appear devious. These include: (1) lying about the good qualities of the target, or pretending to support or disagree with her or him; (2) obscuring the intent to ingratiate by disagreeing on minor matters while agreeing on important ones; (3) yielding by disagreeing at first and then changing to agreement to avoid appearing to be a "yes man" or "yes woman;" (4) flattering someone through someone else (telling the boss's administrative assistant how great the boss is); (5) and using a series of ingratiation tactics over time to get one's way.

Despite its poor reputation, experts suggest that ingratiation has its place in the organization. It can facilitate relationships, increase harmony and collaboration, counter stereotypes, help "outsiders" become "insiders," and bind organizational members together. Ingratiation may be the only way for some subordinates to enhance their power, reducing the power differential between them and their supervisors. However, when the difference in power is great, the supervisor is more attune to insincere ingratiation attempts and such tactics are more likely to backfire, damaging impressions of the follower.

The same standards should be used to evaluate ingratiation as other impression management strategies—accuracy, service to the organization and others, and so forth. In addition, it is possible to engage in "honest" ingratiation. There are likely elements of a supervisor that we honestly admire and are worthy of praise. There are times when we do agree with the boss's ideas. We should change our opinions when we have been convinced to do so. It's okay to tell others we like our boss if our intent is to express our judgments and not to manipulate. Doing favors is not always manipulative but, as we saw in Chapter 1, can serve as a form of altruistic organizational citizenship behavior.

Sources: Grant (2013). Liu et al. (2014). Rosenfeld, Giacalone, and Riordan (1995).

Deception

Deceit, as noted above, is often used when influencing others. Deception is defined as knowingly trying to mislead others. While deception can occur when parties keep secrets or reveal only part of the truth (see Case Study 5.2), lies are the most obvious example of messages designed to convince others of something we ourselves don't believe. Liars (1) are aware that the information is false and (2) knowingly deliver a message with (3) the intent to mislead someone else.

Explanations for the causes of organizational lying generally fall into two categories: self-interest and role conflict.[41] Members lie for personal benefit—to cover up a mistake, save money, further a career, or avoid conflict with the boss. They also lie in order to relieve tension between the various roles they play. For example, a contractor who is unable to complete two remodeling projects at the same time may falsely claim to be waiting for materials in order to placate one homeowner while working at the other job site.

The combination of role conflict and self-interest is more likely to result in deceit than is either factor on its own. Role conflict acts as a stimulus, providing the reason to lie; rewards then provide the motivation or encouragement to engage in lying. The contractor in our example feels caught between two sets of role obligations, and his lie pays off by buying him more time to complete (and to get paid for) both tasks.

Most moral thinkers concur that lying is wrong.[42] Deontological theorists (and some theologians) generally prohibit lying on the basis that such behavior violates moral law or duty. If everyone lied, we would lose our confidence in verbal commitments and in the value of speech itself. Many utilitarians point out that lies typically cause more harm than good. Even if the benefits of a particular lie outweigh the harm (telling "white" lies to protect the feelings of a coworker, for instance), the practice of lying generates more costs than benefits. Virtue ethicists note the damage done to the character of the person who lies. Habitual lying becomes second nature, driving out such virtues as honesty, consistency, and integrity.

Researchers who study lying in the organizational context note that lying is costly to organizational performance. Lies not only undermine trust, they corrupt the flow of information essential to organizational decisions and coordination. Deception damages the reputation of the organization, lowers job satisfaction, drives out ethical employees, and encourages further dishonesty.[43]

While the preponderance of evidence suggests that lying and related forms of deception are unethical, there are a number of exceptions to this general rule. The law allows police officers to lie to suspects in order to obtain confessions, for instance, and we applaud investigators who go undercover to uncover fraud and corruption. Organizations maintain trade secrets, and nations attempt to dupe each other during war.

Ethicist Sissela Bok offers the *principle of veracity* as a way to affirm our commitment to the truth while acknowledging that deceit may be justified in special circumstances.[44] She contends that truth should function as the moral standard. Liars must assume the burden of proof if they want to violate this standard, establishing that deceit is justified. In particular, they need to look at the lie from the target's point of view. Deception might be justified from the liar's vantage point, but it's much more difficult to defend lying when taking the other person's perspective. Targets of deception typically feel victimized even by well-intentioned lies.

What special circumstances might permit lying? Bok doesn't offer a definitive list but suggests that deception might be justified when (1) there is significant threat to life and safety; (2) society has publicly agreed that certain forms of deceit can be used, like unmarked patrol cars, surprise audits, and random drug tests; and (3) both parties acknowledge that the situation calls for mutual deceit (a poker game, bargaining at a foreign bazaar).

The principle of veracity would outlaw many common lies and other forms of deception, like overstating a company's income, offering an unrealistically optimistic status report on a project, or padding résumés and expense accounts. Salespeople would have a duty to tell the entire truth about their products (including possible hazards) and to refuse to steer customers toward purchases that might harm them.[45]

You may think Bok's guideline is too restrictive. Or you may hold a deontological position that outlaws any exceptions to total honesty. Nevertheless, the principle of veracity does address the need for truth telling while acknowledging that lying can pose complex ethical dilemmas. It also encourages us to take a closer look at how we might promote truthfulness in organizational relationships.

As a leader, you can reduce the frequency of deception in your organization because you determine both the roles that employees play and the rewards they receive. Reduce the pressure of role conflicts through clarifying expectations and chains of command, opening up lines of communication to resolve role issues, and making sure that you don't set unreasonably high expectations that tempt workers to lie. "Teach" employees that honesty pays by rewarding integrity while punishing offenders. Further, make honesty a core value, highlighting it in mission statements while promoting truthful interactions with all constituencies.

Emotional Labor

Emotional labor is a special form of impression management that is increasingly common in the modern economy, in which an estimated 8 out of every 10 workers are employed in service industries.[46] In emotional labor, frontline workers—baristas, restaurant servers, sales representatives, counter staff, receptionists, retail clerks—manage their feelings so that they can present the desired bodily and facial displays to the public. Service personnel may have to hold back their anger at obnoxious clients, project enthusiasm to everyone entering the store, or answer the same questions with "smiles in their voices" time after time after time. Emotional labor is different from other forms of impression management because (1) control of feelings is done for pay; (2) emotional laborers interact with outsiders, not with other organizational members; and (3) this form of influence raises its own special set of ethical issues.

Sociologist Arlene Hochschild, who coined the term *emotional labor*, studied the emotional performances of Delta flight attendants who had to project a warm, helpful persona to passengers, even rude ones. (See Case Study 5.3 for a look at the challenges facing contemporary flight attendants.) Subsequent researchers examined the emotional labor of frontline service workers in a wide variety of settings, including, for example, convenience stores, schools, hospitals, fast food restaurants, a cruise ship, Disneyland, door-to-door insurance sales, and a 911 call center.[47] Investigators discovered that emotions can be managed for neutral or negative displays as well as for "nice" ones. For example, psychiatric workers try to remain calm in the face of abuse, and police officers and bill collectors express irritation and anger to intimidate suspects and to collect delinquent accounts.[48]

Emotional labor works. Employees who express positive moods through greeting, smiling, and eye contact encourage customers to develop positive feelings about the organization and its products and services. These feelings, in turn, prompt customers to buy.[49] Emotional contagion helps account for much of the relationship between positive emotional displays, sales, and satisfaction. In service encounters, the happy affect of employees often spreads to customers, who return greetings, smile, and make eye contact. Emotional influence is particularly powerful because it often operates below the level of consciousness. We are often unaware that our emotions (in this case, positive moods) have been aroused and that they are influencing our behavior. Since we don't realize that our emotions are being managed, we can't counteract their effects by, say, reminding ourselves to think more carefully about the possible disadvantages of a product or service.

Because emotional labor is so effective, organizations go to great lengths to control the emotional behavior of their frontline workers. Managers ("emotional supervisors") may only hire individuals deemed to have "friendly, outgoing" personalities. Once hired, new employees go through orientation and training sessions that introduce them to the corporation's guidelines and formulas for customer service. Emotional routines or scripts tell workers both what to say and how to act. They are given lines like "Welcome to Burger King" "How is your day today?" and "Have a great day!" These lines are packaged with uniforms (smocks, aprons, name tags, blazers), smiles, eye contact, attentive posture, and vocal enthusiasm.

The practice of emotional labor raises a number of important ethical issues. To begin, all these programmed emotional displays can be costly to employees. Emotions, traditionally considered the worker's private concern, are now "owned" by the organization.[50] As service providers, we feel the tension between wanting to maintain our ideal or authentic selves and following organizational rules. Being forced to display emotions that aren't felt (or that contradict feelings) can produce dissonance. This dissonance may lead to stress, cynicism, burnout, low self-esteem, illness, job turnover, and difficulties in work relationships. Intrusive emotional scripts threaten the dignity of the individual and can reinforce gender stereotypes. Women programmed to be flirtatious, outgoing, and friendly, such as waitresses at Hooters restaurants, run a higher risk of becoming the targets of sexual harassment.

Not everyone is convinced that emotional labor harmful.[51] Some researchers defend these performances. They point out that service providers aren't robots. Front-line employees sometimes fight the organization's attempts to control their feelings and can adjust their performances when needed. Convenience store clerks are friendlier during slow periods, for instance. When lines develop, they adopt a more efficient manner. Emotional labor can also be enjoyable. One group of 911 dispatchers reported that emotional work was the highlight of their jobs, providing comic relief and excitement.

The amount of damage done by emotional labor depends in large part on whether employees engage in *surface* or *deep acting*. In surface acting, workers experience a disconnect between their feelings and their emotional expressions, which is stressful. In deep acting, workers embrace their roles and display what they genuinely feel. They experience little or no dissonance as a result. Then, too, employees engaged in surface acting can find their moods shifting to fit their performances. There is some evidence that acting cheerful, even when we are not feeling particularly cheerful, reduces levels of stress hormones and increases resistance to disease. Further, in some roles, like nursing, positive affect is a form of altruistic behavior. We expect nurses to express optimism and concern for patients in order to alleviate their suffering and promote healing.[52]

As we can see, emotional labor can have both negative and positive effects on employees. Emotional labor is most damaging when employees (1) experience a great deal of dissonance between their felt and expressed emotions (when surface acting), (2) are not suited for service roles, (3) must suppress negative emotions, (4) become emotionally exhausted from high levels of customer interaction, (5) must deal with aggressive clients, and (6) receive little emotional support from coworkers and the organization.

Organizations can reduce the damage done by emotional labor by recognizing their moral obligation to members. This might mean doing the following:

- Providing potential employees with a realistic preview of the emotional demands of the job.

- Hiring applicants who are emotionally sensitive and expressive.

- Relying less on scripts.
- Providing more opportunity for workers to develop personal performance styles.
- Protecting employees from rude and aggressive customers.
- Providing opportunities to discuss the emotional demands of the job.
- Limiting the amount of acting required during a work shift.
- Encouraging supervisors to be supportive of emotional laborers.
- Encouraging peer support networks.
- Providing adequate compensation for emotional laborers.
- Allowing for expression of negative emotions when appropriate.

Organizations also have a moral obligation to consider the impact of emotional labor on outsiders as well as on employees. As noted earlier, positive moods created through emotional work unconsciously influence buying decisions. The emotional labor provided by frontline employees should therefore benefit the consumer as well as the organization. In addition, customers, like employees, can experience emotional dissonance.[53] Consider the tensions inherent in the pleasant service encounter, for instance. All displays of positive emotion in this setting, no matter how authentic they appear, are suspect because they are designed to sell products and services. These emotional routines are logically and ethically inconsistent because they attempt to standardize "personal" service. In addition, service recipients who are offered pleasant performances might not want to respond in kind if they suspect they are being manipulated or are in a foul mood. Most of us play along, acting the role of the "good customer," even when we don't feel very friendly or are having a bad day. But a few consumers resist. When dining out, for instance, they complain to management when the wait staff is too attentive and friendly. They may use put-down or sarcastic lines like "What's the worst thing on the menu?" or "Hi, my name's Dave, and I'll be your customer tonight."[54] Those who play along run the risk of lying about how they really feel—unhappy, tense, angry. Those who resist may maintain their integrity but little else. They come across as mean spirited and have minimal impact on organizational policy. Instead, resisters make the job of the emotional laborer (who is generally underpaid and overworked) all the harder. As an alternative, we could strive for personal consistency and authenticity in the consumer role by responding tactfully but honestly to emotional displays: "I'm not doing too well today, but thanks for asking"; "I appreciate your friendliness, but it is a little overwhelming this early in the morning."

Communication of Expectations

The communication of expectations is a powerful organizational influence tool. That's because we have a tendency to live up to the expectations others place on us. Researchers refer to this phenomenon as self-fulfilling prophecy, or the Pygmalion effect, after the sculptor of Greek mythology. Pygmalion created a statue of a beautiful woman, whom he named Galatea. After the figure was complete, he fell in love with his creation. The goddess Aphrodite took pity on the dejected prince and brought Galatea to life.

Evidence of the Pygmalion effect has been discovered in a variety of organizational settings. For example:[55]

- Nursing home residents are less depressed and less likely to be admitted to hospitals when staff members believe that these clients will respond more favorably to rehabilitation.
- Industrial trainees designated as "high-aptitude personnel" learn more quickly and are less likely to drop out.
- Patients in medical experiments improve when they receive placebos because they believe they will get better.
- The high expectations of teachers lead to higher student test and IQ scores as well as better performance on cognitive tasks.
- Subordinates can improve the performance of their supervisors by expressing high upward expectations (the reverse Pygmalion).
- Military personnel labeled as having high potential perform up to the expectations of their superiors. Those told that they can succeed are more likely to volunteer for dangerous special duty.
- In international relief agencies, the positive expectations of headquarters aid workers can improve the performance of local staff members.

The Pygmalion effect is more pronounced with some individuals than others. Disadvantaged groups (those stereotyped as low achievers) tend to benefit most from positive expectations, as do those who lack a clear sense of their abilities or find themselves in a novel situation. Men seem to be more influenced by the expectancies of their managers than are women.[56] Negative expectations also have an impact on performance. This is sometimes referred to as the Golem effect (*golem* means "dumbbell" in Yiddish). Unless counteracted, these reduced expectancies lower performance.[57]

Verbal persuasion is the straightforward way to communicate expectations—for example, offering compliments, assuring others that they have the necessary ability, and stating that you expect great things from them. However, self-fulfilling prophecies are most often communicated indirectly through these four channels:[58]

1. *Climate.* Climate describes the social and emotional atmosphere individuals create for others. Communicators act in a friendly, supportive, accepting, and encouraging manner with people they like. This is done through using nonverbal behaviors that portray respect and warmth while avoiding behaviors that communicate disrespect, coolness, and superiority. Supervisors, for example, signal positive expectations by giving adequate time to employees, holding appointments in pleasant surroundings, sitting or standing close to workers, nodding and smiling, making frequent eye contact, and using a warm tone of voice.

2. *Input.* Positive expectations are also communicated through the number and type of assignments and projects given to workers. High expectations create a

positive performance spiral. As employees receive and successfully complete more tasks, they gain self-confidence and the confidence of superiors. These outstanding performers are then given further duties, which they are more likely to complete as well.

3. *Output.* Those tagged as high performers are given more opportunities to speak, to offer their opinions, and to disagree. Superiors pay more attention to these employees when they speak and offer more assistance to them when they're solving problems. In the classroom, teachers call on "high achievers" more than "low achievers," wait less time for low achievers to answer questions, and provide fewer clues and follow-up questions to low achievers.[59]

4. *Feedback.* Supervisors give more frequent positive feedback when they have high expectations of employees, both praising them more often for success and criticizing them less often for failure. In addition, managers provide more detailed performance feedback to high-expectation employees. Just the opposite occurs with those labeled as poor performers. Supervisors praise their minimal performance more, reinforcing the impression that they expect less from these employees.

Pygmalion investigators wrestle with the ethical implications of this influence strategy, beginning with the use of deception. Experimenters typically deceive leaders by informing them that groups differ in abilities, even though they have been randomly assigned. Such tactics could be used in the organizational setting by telling managers that selected subordinates have more potential when, in reality, there are no data to support that assertion. Some researchers argue that this deceit would be justified because the organization would benefit from the superior performance of those described as high performers. Nonetheless, to carry off this deception, managers would have to be misled by their supervisors or staff personnel, which would undermine trust. Deliberately privileging one group of people is unjust and might result in lawsuits.

Even when deception isn't involved, the separation of groups into different ability groupings is problematical. Organizations routinely label some individuals as exceptional employees according to some set of criteria. These members are then given extra training, assigned to mentors, placed into more challenging assignments, and so on. These measures generate the Pygmalion effect for the chosen few and the Golem effect for everyone else. Those labeled as average or low performers receive fewer benefits and may live down to reduced expectations.

Communicating high expectations to everyone in the organization is an ethical alternative to deception and ability grouping.[60] Such an approach not only maintains integrity, it encourages everyone to function at his or her best. Strategies for improving organizationwide performance include (1) building follower self-efficacy (a sense of personal power) through breaking down tasks into manageable segments, role modeling, and verbal persuasion; (2) encouraging a learning orientation that emphasizes improvement over perfection; (3) creating a friendly atmosphere; (4) raising consciousness of the impact of negative expectations; (5) creating opportunities for employees to start anew in different departments and assignments; and (6) fostering a culture that demands high productivity.

Even if our organization doesn't adopt a high-expectations orientation, we can do so as individuals. The power of self-fulfilling prophecy places a moral burden upon us. If others are to reach their full potential, we need to communicate positive expectations to them, not negative ones. We should carefully monitor our behavior to reduce inequities, particularly subtle ones, in our treatment of others. The strategies outlined above for communicating high expectations can be employed in our peer relationships and organizational units. Also, we can use the Galatea effect to insulate ourselves from the negative expectations of our leaders. The Galatea effect (named after the statue in the Greek myth) refers to the tendency for high self-expectation to produce high performance. High self-expectancies can keep us from lowering our performance when others expect little of us. We can encourage leaders to raise their expectations of us by meeting and exceeding standards.

CHAPTER TAKEAWAYS

- While the exercise of influence is not optional in the workplace, you do have control over how you go about modifying the behaviors of others.

- No form of power is inherently immoral, but positional power (legitimate, coercive, reward) is more likely to be abused than person-centered power (expert, referent).

- Use a variety of power sources when pursuing worthy objectives.

- Concentration of positional power (in yourself or others) is dangerous, producing a wide range of unethical behavior.

- Adopt a positive mind-set toward organizational politics—the use of informal or unofficial power. Positive political behavior supports the organization's vision and values, serves others, focuses on achieving shared goals, fosters collaboration, and meets widely accepted ethical standards.

- Increase psychological empowerment—the motivation of others to carry out tasks, based on meaning, competence, self-determination, and impact—by modifying the work setting and supplying adequate resources.

- Overcome barriers to empowerment by managing the journey through the three stages of the empowerment process: (1) starting and orienting the process of change, (2) making changes and dealing with discouragement, and (3) adopting and refining empowerment to fit the organization.

- Create frames (mental pictures or interpretations that shape reality) that are tied into organizational codes and values. Highlight the importance of ethical considerations when framing events.

- When trying to convince others to go along with your requests, try to use "soft" power compliance-gaining tactics—rational persuasion, consultation, collaboration, inspirational appeal—whenever possible. However, when combating unethical and dangerous behaviors, be willing to generate negative feelings through your influence tactics.

- Use impression management tactics to build positive relationships, to accurately portray your personal image and that of your organization, and to facilitate effective decisions. Ensure that others don't manipulate you through their use of impression management strategies.

- Truth telling should be the moral standard. If you decide to lie, the burden of proof is on you. Reduce the frequency of lying and other forms of deception in your organization by limiting role conflicts and rewarding truth telling.

- Emotional labor—the management of feelings by frontline workers that leads to facial and bodily displays—can pose significant dilemmas for employees and customers. Take steps to reduce the emotional dissonance that workers experience and provide them with organizational support.

- Communication of positive expectations can be one of your most powerful influence tools. Encourage those around you to live up to their full potential. Generate positive self-fulfilling prophecies (the Pygmalion effect) through creating a warm emotional climate, providing valuable assignments, giving opportunities for others to express their opinions, and offering frequent positive feedback. Have high expectations of your own behavior (employ the Galatea effect) even if others don't.

APPLICATION PROJECTS

1. Analyze a leader's use of power. Determine whether this leader acted ethically or unethically. Explain why. Write up your findings.

2. Debate the following propositions:

    Empowerment takes advantage of workers.

    Impression management is unethical.

    Frames don't tell us what to think; they tell us what to think about.

    Telling the truth isn't as important as it used to be.

    Nothing good can come from playing organizational politics.

    The costs of emotional labor are overstated.

    Communicating positive expectations to everyone in a work group is impossible.

    Communicating high expectations to people you don't like is unethical.

3. Identify a significant change taking place at your college or place of employment. How has this development been framed? What tools have been used to create this frame? What are the competing frames? Which frame, if any, is morally positioned and takes ethical considerations into account? How would you frame this event? Write up your analysis.

4. Write up a summary of your results on Self-Assessment 5.1 or Self-Assessment 5.2. What do your scores reveal? What steps can you take to act on this information?

5. Create a case study based on an organization's attempts to empower its employees. What went right? What went wrong? What conclusions can you draw from this organization's experience? As an alternative, create an organizational politics case study. Describe how political skill was exercised in this situation and what happened as a result. Determine whether this is an example of negative or positive politics, and highlight the lessons you take from this situation.

6. Keep a log of your proactive influence attempts over the course of a day. What requests did you make? What tactics do you use? Do you consider your proactive strategies to be ethical or unethical?

7. Invite emotional laborers to be interviewed in front of the class. Ask them to describe their experiences. Possible interview questions include: What characteristics did you have to demonstrate to land your jobs? What training did you receive, and what scripts did you have

to follow? What did it take to be successful? What were the costs of your performances? What were the benefits of engaging in emotional labor? What do you conclude about the ethics of emotional labor?

8. Under what circumstances is lying justified? See if you can reach a consensus in a small group and report your conclusions to the rest of the class.

9. Have you ever been the victim of low expectations (the Golem effect)? How did you respond? What happened as a result? Share your story orally or in writing.

CASE STUDY 5.1

Moving Beyond Empowerment at Morning Star

Some companies don't believe in empowerment because they are convinced that empowerment doesn't go far enough. To these firms, empowerment implies that managers give or grant power to employees. They strive to give all employees power by eliminating managers instead. Workers manage themselves, operating in teams (circles, cabals) that continually form and reform. Flat organizations go under a variety of names, including holography (Zappos, ARCA), lattice management (Gore and Associates), and self-management/self-leadership (Orpheus Chamber Orchestra, individual Whole Foods stores).

The world's largest tomato processor, Morning Star, has been committed self-management since it started 1970 as a trucking company delivering tomatoes to canneries. Founder Chris Rufer discovered that the management theories he learned as an MBA at UCLA didn't work well in his new company. "How do you manage truck drivers?" he wondered. "Put a supervisor in every truck? It was just, I do my thing; everyone else do your thing. That seemed to work."[1] He continued that philosophy as his firm grew to a $700 million business employing 400 people (up to 2,200 in the peak processing season). The company is now the largest tomato processor in the world, producing canned tomatoes and tomato sauces for pizzas and pastas. Employees earn 10% to 15% more than those working for comparable firms and have 35% higher benefits.

The Morning Star model is founded on the company's vision that states that all employees "will be self-managing professionals, initiating communications and the coordination of their activities with their colleagues, customers, suppliers, and fellow industry participants, *absent directives from others*" (italics added). Every worker is responsible for creating a personal mission statement that outlines how she or he will help meet the corporate mission of producing quality tomato products and services and get the resources and training to do so. Each employee annually negotiates a Colleague Letter of Understanding (CLOU) with the associates most impacted by her or his work. A CLOU serves as an operating plan for fulfilling the personal mission and may take discussions with 10 or more associates (each conversation can take 20 to 60 minutes). CLOUs can cover as many as 30 activities. At last count, there were 3,000 CLOUS spelling out relationships at the company. Business units also negotiate annual customer–supplier agreements with other company units.

Morning Star employees are free to purchase the tools they need or hire the staff they require without a sign-off from purchasing or a senior executive. According to Rufer, "I don't want anyone

150   PART TWO · PRACTICING INTERPERSONAL ETHICS IN THE ORGANIZATION

at Morning Star to feel they can't succeed because they don't have the right equipment or capable colleagues."[2] Since roles are flexible, employees can take on greater and greater responsibilities. Ideas come from anyone in the company.

There are no promotions at Morning Star. Instead, colleagues who have signed off on CLOU agreements rate one another. An elected compensation committee then determines compensation levels based on self-assessments presented by workers. Disputes about whether CLOU commitments have been fulfilled are settled through the use of a mediator and a peer committee.

Morning Star promotes transparency by providing detailed financial statements, available to all employees, twice a month. Each CLOU includes detailed metrics called "steppingstones" that employees use to track their progress in meeting the needs of colleagues. Such transparency fosters accountability. According to Rufer:

> Everyone's a manager here. We are manager rich. Everyone is a manager of their own mission. They are managers of the agreements they make with colleagues, they are managers of the resources they need to get the job done, and they are managers who hold their colleagues accountable.[3]

Business units are held accountable through performance reports and strategy sessions. Each unit defends its prior year's performance in front of the entire company and outlines a plan for the coming year.

Morning Star's approach to self-management encourages workers to take initiative, develop their expertise, and exercise better judgment. Since there are no bosses or promotions, there is less competition between employees and more cooperation. But it takes a long time for new hires to adjust, and many experienced managers from other companies fail to make the transition. Quality suffers when colleagues fail to confront low performers and hold them accountable. It remains to be seen if the system could work at much larger companies, like PepsiCo and Intel. Indeed, not all self-management experiments work. Internet content provider Medium gave up on the model, calling it a "tax" on productivity. Zappos is struggling to implement self-management, having lost 18% of its workforce during the conversion to circles. However, organizations could benefit from elements of self-management even if they don't eliminate managers altogether. Personal mission statements, CLOUs, and self-managing teams are ways to empower employees while retaining hierarchy.

Discussion Probes

1. What would you like most about working under Morning Star's model? Least? Why?
2. Is everyone a manager at Morning Star, as CEO Rufer claims?
3. What do you see as the ethical benefits of self-management? Possible ethical dangers?
4. Is there value in retaining some managers?
5. Do you think that really large organizations could adopt self-management? Can they adopt parts of the model?

Notes

1. Buchanen (2013).
2. Hamel (2011).
3. Ibid.

Sources: Bernstein, Bunch, Canner, and Lee (2016). Reinghold (2016).

CASE STUDY 5.2

Hiding the Real Story at Midwestern Community Action

Recently, life at Midwestern Community Action has been anything but smooth. The nonprofit runs a variety of programs in a midsized city, including preschools, teen drop-in centers, a food pantry, a medical clinic, and low-income housing. Health problems forced founding executive director Sally May, who was well loved by staff, to quit after 20 years in her position. The board then appointed Josiah Lang, who had served as the manager of a local government service agency, as the next executive director.

When Lang arrived at Community Action, he discovered that May had been a hands-off leader. She allowed coordinators to run their programs without much supervision. Used to operating on their own, they resisted Lang's efforts to institute performance evaluations, to evaluate the effectiveness of each program, and to reallocate funds between programs. It didn't help that Lang made little effort to get to know his subordinates and has an abrasive personality. Three coordinators and a half dozen front-line staff quit. Lang has the support of the board, which believes that the organization needs more structure and accountability, but staff morale is low. Employees have lost faith in the organization's leadership. However, they remain committed to helping the disadvantaged and to Community Action's mission. For that reason, they largely keep their frustrations to themselves and are careful to protect the organization's public image. Community Action continues to be well regarded by clients, government officials, donors, and the public at large.

This week Community Action will interview an applicant for its housing coordinator position, a vacancy created when the previous coordinator left in frustration. This is the most important open position to fill. The housing coordinator oversees three apartment complexes with 200 tenants and manages the most employees. Failure to fill the vacancy soon could reduce Community Action's outreach to the homeless. The applicant, Albert Singh, appears to be highly qualified. If he takes the position, Singh will move his family from out of state. He has no idea that Community Action is dealing with significant conflict and poor morale.

Singh will make a brief presentation to the entire staff during his visit and then meet for an extended time with the current program coordinators. During this session, the coordinators (without the director present) will question him and present an overview of Community Action. Albert will also have an opportunity to ask questions of the coordinators.

Discussion Probes

1. What ethical duties are in conflict in this situation?

2. Are Community Action employees justified in keeping their concerns "in house," out of the public eye? Why or why not?

3. If you were one of the current program coordinators, how much would you reveal about the turmoil at Community Action to Singh?

4. As a coordinator, what would you say if Singh asked why the previous housing coordinator quit? How would you answer if asked your opinion of the executive director?

5. Is withholding the truth as damaging as lying? Why or why not?

CASE STUDY 5.3

Flying the Unfriendly Skies

Changes in the airline industry have put added strain on passengers and flight crews alike. Fliers pass through long lines at security checkpoints at crowded airports and are faced with more flight delays and cancellations. Planes are filled to near capacity, seats are smaller, and passengers battle for luggage space in overhead bins. (Some airlines now charge for carry-on bags on economy flights.) Free meals and movies are things of the past. Said one frequent flyer: "My expectations for travel have gotten so low that the highest praise I can bestow upon a trip is that it was 'uneventful.'"[1]

Frustration with the airlines reached a new high (or low) when Chicago airport police took a paying passenger off an overbooked United flight, removing him to make room for United employees. Video of the incident shows Dr. David Dao being dragged down the aisle of the plane, screaming while blood runs down his face. (He lost two teeth in the incident.) Witnesses can be heard expressing their shock and displeasure. At first United seemed to blame Dao, claiming that he refused to leave the aircraft when asked, so security had to be called. (Dao said he had patients to see the next morning.) Later, United CEO Oscar Munoz offered his "deepest apology" and announced a new policy banning employees from taking the place of ticketed passengers on overbooked flights. He vowed that what happened in Chicago would "never happen again." Many used the incident to voice their criticism of the airlines. Said one, "the airlines are seemingly forever coming up with new and innovative ways to coddle an increasingly small group, while treating the majority of fliers with greater and greater contempt."[2]

Customers aren't the only ones stressed by conditions in the sky. Underpaid flight attendants, who may start at $20,000 a year and earn an average of $32,000 to $38,000, now must serve more passengers, some of whom are in a bad mood or intoxicated. They often find themselves mediating disputes between customers about legroom and unruly children as well as dealing with fliers who refuse to turn off their electronic devices.

Given the stresses of flying, it is not surprising that a number of passengers have experienced emotional meltdowns. One flyer attacked a flight attendant who told him to put away his duty-free alcohol before landing in New York. Another threw a cell phone and scratched an attendant. Actor Alec Baldwin was taken off a plane after he refused to stop playing an electronic game on his phone. He called the flight crew "inappropriate names" and then locked himself in a lavatory. Ivana Trump was also removed from a plane after she launched a diatribe against small children on the flight.

Flight crews have also made the news for their emotional outbursts. A Jet Blue attendant briefly became a hero to service workers everywhere when he got on the plane's intercom to berate passengers, grabbed a couple of beers, and exited via an inflatable emergency chute. (Later he agreed to a plea deal that required him to receive mental health counseling and to repay the airline $10,000 for deploying the chute.) An American Eagle flight attendant yelled at passengers over the public address system after enduring abuse from belligerent customers angry about a five-hour delay. An American Airlines flight attendant had to be subdued by

(Continued)

(Continued)

passengers and crew after ranting about a possible crash over the PA.

Of course, the vast majority of passengers and flight attendants play their roles, ensuring pleasant customer service interactions. But the stresses of flying set the stage for further emotional breakdowns. Airports and planes will continue to be crowded as additional Americans fly and airlines consolidate and seek greater profits. Nevertheless, passengers and flight crews can reduce the frequency of these incidents by recognizing and avoiding behaviors that irritate the other party. A USA Today online survey found that passengers are most bothered by flight attendants with a "surly demeanor," followed by "gabbing in the back," "refusal to deal with unruly passengers," a "schoolmarm attitude," and "slowness in serving drinks and food."[3] For their part, members of the Association of Professional Flight Attendants union identified the following as their top 10 peeves about passengers:[4]

1. Walking around without shoes
2. Changing diapers on seats or tray tables
3. Clipping fingernails or toenails while flying
4. Talking to crew members with earphones on
5. Speaking to flight attendants in a condescending and angry tone
6. Hanging arms or legs out into the aisles, blocking the food and beverage cart
7. Standing and exercising in the galley and restroom areas
8. Keeping electronic devices on after being told to turn them off
9. Bringing smelly food onto the plane
10. Carrying a bag onto the plane that you can't lift into the overhead bin

Discussion Probes

1. What is your attitude toward flying? Are you satisfied when nothing unpleasant happens at the airport or during the flight?
2. What is your biggest complaint about flight attendants? Or, if you are a member of a flight crew, what is your biggest complaint about passengers?
3. Have you engaged in any of the irritating behaviors identified by flight attendants?
4. What moral obligations do passengers have to flight crews? What moral obligations do flight crews have to passengers? How can each side meet its obligations in this service industry?
5. What can airlines do to help their flight crews avoid emotional breakdowns? What can they do to lessen the stress on passengers?

Notes

1. Stoller (2011).
2. Engle Bromwich (2017).
3. Yancey (2010b).
4. Stoller (2011).

Sources: "Antonio Ynoa, JetBlue Passenger" (2011). Fussell (2017). "Jose Serrano, American Eagle Flight Attendant" (2012). Kaye (2010), p. C10. Stern (2012). D. Victor and Stevens (2017). Yancey (2010a), p. 11B. Yoshino and Blankstein (2011).

CHAPTER SIX

ETHICAL CONFLICT MANAGEMENT

Chapter Preview

Conflict in Organizational Life
Becoming an Ethical Conflict Manager
    Step 1: Recognize the Differences Between Functional and Dysfunctional Conflicts
    Step 2: Manage Your Emotions
    Step 3: Identify Your Personal Conflict Style
    Step 4: Develop Conflict Guidelines
    Step 5: Employ Collaborative Conflict Management Tactics
    Step 6: Be Prepared to Apologize

Resolving Conflict Through Ethical Negotiation
    Ethical Issues in Negotiation
    Adopt an Integrative Approach to Negotiation
Combating Aggression and Sexual Harassment
    Types of Aggression
    Sources of Aggression
    Resisting and Reducing Aggression
    Preventing Sexual Harassment
Chapter Takeaways
Application Projects

CONFLICT IN ORGANIZATIONAL LIFE

Conflict is a daily occurrence in every organization. Managers estimate that they spend between 20% and 40% of their time dealing with disagreements. Common sources of organizational conflict include these:[1]

Interests: Benefits, budgets, organizational policies, office location, and other wants and needs

Data: The best sources of information; the reliability or the interpretation of data

Procedures: How to solve problems; how to make decisions; how to solve conflicts

Values: How to prioritize interests and options; determining organizational direction

Dysfunctional relationships: Those marked by distrust, disrespect, lack of integrity, and lack of mutual concern

Roles: Expectations related to organizational roles; power imbalances between roles

Communication: How something was said; emotions triggered by words; withholding information

Some observers believe that we can expect even more conflicts in the years to come.[2] They note that there is growing pressure on organizations to innovate, change, and adapt. These pressures increase workloads and generate job insecurity. In a global society, the workforce is increasingly diverse, which produces more conflicts between those of different cultural backgrounds. Organizational members now work in different geographical locations and communicate over the Internet rather than face to face. These developments mean that miscommunication is more likely. As organizations empower groups to carry out projects, team members must manage the conflicts that come from working collaboratively.

Conflict experts Joyce Hocker and William Wilmot define conflict as "an expressed struggle between at least two interdependent parties who perceive incompatible goals, scarce resources, and interference from others in achieving their goals."[3] Conflict begins when the parties express their thoughts and feelings to each other through their behaviors. They engage in conflict because they depend to some degree on one another. The choices of one party affect the options of others, as when one employee's choice of vacation time interferes with the vacation plans of a fellow worker. Hocker and Wilmot believe that the sources of conflict identified earlier can be condensed into two general categories. Conflict can be over perceived incompatible goals (if I get promoted, then you don't) or over scarce resources like office space, staffing, or funding for new projects. Interference sets the stage for conflict. Goals may be incompatible and resources scarce, but conflict develops only if we perceive that the other party is interfering with our efforts to achieve our goals and get the resources we want.

Many of us fear and avoid conflict because of our past experiences. Early struggles cost us relationships and left us feeling bruised and battered. Chances are, one or both parties behaved unethically by making threats, engaging in ridicule and sarcasm, losing their tempers, and so on. (Ethical Checkpoint 6.1 describes some of the behaviors that make conflicts destructive.) Aversion to conflict is counterproductive, however. To begin with, organizational conflict is inevitable. Trying to avoid conflict means that we are not equipped to deal with it when it arises. Further, conflicts can promote personal and relational growth. Resolving a conflict successfully builds our skills and generates a sense of accomplishment. Often, conflict over an idea or a proposal produces a higher-quality solution.

The objective of this chapter is to help you become a more ethical, competent conflict manager. I'll identify important steps you need to take to achieve this goal and help you recognize the ethical issues you'll face if you decide to use negotiation to resolve differences. Then we will shift our focus to aggression, which deserves special attention because it is the most destructive type of organizational conflict. We will examine ways to reduce aggression and to prevent sexual harassment.

ETHICAL CHECKPOINT 6.1

What Not to Do in a Conflict

Sometimes learning what to avoid is the first step to improvement. Conflict resolution expert Dana Caspersen identifies strategies that lock participants into destructive conflicts. According to Casperson, steer clear of the following tactics if you want to engage in healthy conversations that lead to positive outcomes.

Make Listening and Speaking Difficult

1. Hear attack. Ignore any additional information being offered by the other party.
2. Attack the other person and begin destructive communication patterns.
3. Provoke the other person's worst self; speak to their worst qualities.
4. Confuse needs and interests (which can be met in many different ways) with strategies that insist on one particular path to reach the need or interest.
5. Ignore emotions or act them out destructively.
6. Assume acknowledgment means agreement; don't acknowledge what the other person is saying.
7. Make suggestions instead of listening to the other person.
8. Judge people. Try to pass off your evaluations of others as observations.
9. Act on your assumptions without testing them; be unwilling to change your assumptions.

Ensure Stagnation or Destructive Escalation

1. Adopt a rigid stance that doesn't try to understand other viewpoints.
2. Assume that meaningful dialogue is impossible and that the interaction can't get better.
3. Ignore your contribution to creating the problem. Make things even worse through attacking and overreacting.
4. Pin the blame on someone else. Prevent full understanding of the situation from emerging.

Prevent Positive Developments

1. Ignore conflict. Talk to the wrong people (not the other party in the conflict), complain or avoid addressing the real problem.
2. Assume there are no good options. Rush to a solution and settle for an unsatisfying outcome.
3. Make vague agreements or don't make any agreement at all.
4. Ignore the possibility that there could be further conflicts. Don't develop strategies for dealing conflicts when they arise.

Source: Casperson (2015).

BECOMING AN ETHICAL CONFLICT MANAGER

Investigators have identified six steps you can take to increase the odds that you will behave ethically when engaged in conflict. Your ability to ethically manage conflict will depend on recognizing the difference between productive and unproductive conflicts; identifying your personal conflict style; managing your emotions; setting up guidelines for conflict resolution; using collaborative communication tactics; and being willing to apologize.

Step 1: Recognize the Differences Between Functional and Dysfunctional Conflicts

Several factors distinguish between productive and unproductive conflicts.[4] Functional conflicts focus on the content of messages—ideas, values, beliefs, proposals, procedures, budgets, and so on. Participants in these kinds of conflicts are out to solve the problem, not to damage the other party. They make supportive comments, engage in effective listening, signal that they want to collaborate to come up with a solution, and avoid verbal abuse. Dysfunctional conflicts often center on the personalities of those involved. Strong negative emotions as well as verbal attacks (e.g., threats, sarcasm, name calling) characterize these encounters. Discussants locked in unproductive conflicts engage in fight-or-flight responses. They either escalate the conflict or try to avoid it. Conflict spirals when each party retaliates at successively higher levels. An employee who feels unjustly treated may retaliate by trying to undermine the authority of her supervisor, who, in turn, may retaliate against the subordinate by reducing her work hours. Avoidance, as we noted earlier, is the other common destructive pattern. Participants may reduce their dependence on one another, refuse to cooperate, withdraw, harbor resentment, and complain to third parties. In doing so, they leave conflicts unresolved and poison the relationship. (See Case Study 6.1 for an example of a dysfunctional conflict in action.)

While task-oriented conflicts are to be preferred over relational ones, it would be a mistake to assume that constructive conflict always produces positive outcomes.[5] Even productive disagreements about ideas can frustrate members if they drag on too long, and conflicts can divert energy from other priorities. Healthy conflicts can quickly turn nasty when strong emotions are sparked by a poor choice of words or doubts about the other party's motivations. Our task, then, is not only to avoid relational conflicts but to prevent task conflicts from deteriorating or transforming into dysfunctional exchanges. We also need to be alert to the possibility that some emotional conflicts may masquerade as substantive ones, such as when group members who dislike each other disguise their relational problems as criticism of ideas.[6]

Step 2: Manage Your Emotions

Chapter 4 introduced the components of emotional intelligence that are critical to maintaining positive interpersonal relationships. These skill sets are particularly important in conflict settings, where the potential for misunderstanding is high and we need to predict how the other party will react. Since conflict can spark intense feelings of anger and frustration that can derail even healthy disputes, managing our emotions takes on added importance.

Eckerd College conflict experts Craig Runde and Tim Flanagan offer a three-phrase model specifically designed to help us keep our negative emotions from getting out of control.[7] This approach can keep us from turning task conflict into relational conflict or help us convert a dysfunctional dispute into a collaborative problem-solving effort.

Phase 1: Cooling down. Determine what makes you angry. Hot buttons, behaviors that upset us, vary from person to person. For you, it might be coworkers who don't put in a full day's work. For me, it might be supervisors who are disorganized. Just reflecting on your hot buttons reduces their power over you. Also, determine how you can better respond when these buttons are pushed. You might concentrate on not clenching your fists or not raising your voice when someone irritates you, for example.

Phase 2: Slowing down. Have a backup strategy (plan B) if you can't keep your cool and you find yourself getting mad and defensive. If you can, withdraw from the encounter to give your negative emotions time to dissipate. Deep breathing and thinking about more pleasant topics and places can help you relax. When you begin to slow down, determine why you feel so strongly, and consider that the other party may have logical reasons for his or her behavior, instead of assuming that the other person is out to hurt or upset you.

Phase 3: Engaging constructively. Once you have your emotions under control, you are ready to actively resolve the conflict. Consider the other person's perspective. Listen carefully to determine the other party's point of view (this also defuses the tension). Disclose how the conflict is making you feel. If the conversation has stalled, reach out to restart the communication. Approach the other party, point out the impasse, and encourage the resumption of talks. Once reengaged, you and the other person can create win-win solutions that meet the needs of both of you. Solutions are more likely to emerge because you have controlled your negative emotions, defused the tension, and you and the other person have a clearer understanding of each other's logic and feelings.

In addition to managing your own emotions, try to avoid sparking negative emotional reactions in the other party. Emotionally charged conflicts usually involve identities.[8] Identities are made up of the characteristics—beliefs, values, customs, allegiances, important experiences—that define individuals and groups. Respect for the identity of others promotes cooperation because the parties feel free to be themselves and enjoy connection with others. Threats to identity trigger strong protective emotions that undermine collaboration. In particular, be careful not to threaten the identity of the other party by violating important taboos and attacking what they view as sacred. Muslim anger has been stirred by Western attacks on the Prophet, which is considered blasphemy, and desecration of the Koran, which is considered holy. Taboos and the sacred are not limited to those with strong religious identities, however. Take the manager who identifies with her company, for instance. For her, speaking ill of the firm's founder may be taboo and corporate values are sacred. Attacking the founder and making fun of the company's mission statement is likely to generate a negative emotional response and escalate the conflict.

Step 3: Identify Your Personal Conflict Style

Conflict styles describe the ways that individuals typically approach conflict situations. Researchers report that there are five approaches to conflicts.[9] (Complete Self-Assessment 6.1 to determine which style you prefer.) Conflict styles are based on two dimensions: (1) concern for one's own needs and (2) concern for the needs of others:

- The *avoiding* style is low on both concern for self and concern for others. Avoiders steer clear of conflict by keeping their distance from other disputants, changing topics, withdrawing, and so on.

- The *accommodating* style reflects low concern for self and high concern for others. Accommodators give in while helping other parties reach their goals.

- The *compromising style* demonstrates moderate concern for self and others. Compromisers call for concessions from everyone in order to reach an agreement.

- The *competing style* puts the needs of self first with little concern for the other side. Competitors are aggressive and focused on meeting their own needs, often at the expense of other parties.

- The *collaborative style* reflects a high degree of concern for both the self and others. Collaborators listen actively, stay focused on the issues, and hope to reach solutions that meet the needs of both sides.

Avoiding, competing, compromising, and accommodating can be effective and ethical in certain situations.[10] Avoiding works best when there is danger of physical violence. It is ethically appropriate when an organization is temporarily dealing with more significant moral issues. Accommodation can maintain relationships and may be the morally right choice for a follower when a leader is more knowledgeable about an issue. Compromising can generate quick solutions and is ethically justified when both parties have valid interests and want to avoid a stalemate. Competing also produces rapid results and may be an ethical approach when implementing unpopular decisions.

In contrast to the other conflict styles, collaboration appears to be the most successful and ethical option across a variety of contexts. Collaboration has the greatest chance of producing agreements, improves decisions, and leads to greater satisfaction with outcomes.[11] It is the only approach that incorporates high regard for both the self and the other party. There also appears to be a direct link between an individual's level of moral development and his or her choice of conflict style.[12] Those in the lowest stage of moral development (see Chapter 3) tend to use the dominating and avoiding approaches. Those who display a moderate level of moral reasoning rely heavily on compromise. Those who engage in the highest level of moral reasoning are more likely to take an integrative or collaborative approach.

Since collaboration is more effective and ethical, seek to meet the needs of both sides whenever possible. Look to collaborate first, but adopt another style if the situation warrants.

SELF-ASSESSMENT 6.1

Conflict Style Inventory

Think of an organizational setting (school, work, nonprofit) where you have conflicts or disagreements with others. With this setting in mind, complete the following scale. Rate each item on the following scale:

1 = Never

2 = Seldom

3 = Sometimes

4 = Often

5 = Always

1. I avoid being "put on the spot"; I try to keep conflicts to myself.
2. I use my influence to get my ideas accepted.
3. I usually try to "split the difference" in order to resolve an issue.
4. I generally try to satisfy the other's needs.
5. I try to investigate an issue to find a solution acceptable to both of us.
6. I usually avoid open discussion of my differences with the other.
7. I use my authority to make a decision in my favor.
8. I try to find a middle course to resolve an impasse.
9. I usually accommodate the other's wishes.
10. I try to integrate my ideas with those of others to come up with a joint decision.
11. I try to stay away from disagreement with others.
12. I use my expertise to make decisions that favor me.
13. I propose a middle ground for breaking deadlocks.
14. I give in to the wishes of others.
15. I try to work with others to find solutions that satisfy both our expectations.
16. I try to keep my disagreement to myself in order to avoid hard feelings.
17. I generally pursue my side of an issue.
18. I negotiate with others in order to reach a compromise.
19. I often go with others' suggestions.
20. I exchange accurate information with others so we can solve a problem together.
21. I try to avoid unpleasant exchanges with others.
22. I sometimes use my power to win.
23. I use "give-and-take" so that a compromise can be reached.
24. I try to satisfy others' expectations.
25. I try to bring all our concerns out in the open so that the issues can be resolved.

Scoring

Add up your scores on the following questions:

(Continued)

(Continued)

	Avoidance	Competition	Compromise	Accommodation	Collaboration
	1. ____	2. ____	3. ____	4. ____	5. ____
	6. ____	7. ____	8. ____	9. ____	10. ____
	11. ____	12. ____	13. ____	14. ____	15. ____
	16. ____	17. ____	18. ____	19. ____	20. ____
	21. ____	22. ____	23. ____	24. ____	25. ____
Total					

Source: From Hocker and Wilmot (2014), pp. 147–148. Adapted from Rahim and Magner (1995).

Step 4: Develop Conflict Guidelines

Guidelines can help both sides engage in collaborative conflict management and generate better outcomes. Organizational communication expert Pamela Shockley-Zalabak offers one set of conflict strategies. When it comes to your participation in conflict, she recommends the following:[13]

Monitor your personal behavior and the behavior of the other party for signs of destructive conflict. Be alert to behaviors that indicate that you or the other party is contributing to escalation or avoidance cycles.

Identify common goals and interests. Think about what both parties have in common and want to achieve. Consider overlapping needs, concerns, goals, and fears.

Develop norms to work on problems. Rules of behavior can be developed for both individual- and group-level conflicts. Relational partners may want to agree to take "time-outs" when discussions get too heated (see our earlier discussion of emotion management), meet in a neutral location, and avoid personal attacks. Groups may want to encourage dissent, seek consensus rather than vote on a solution, and resist speedy outcomes that fail to take advantage of productive conflict over ideas.

Focus on mutual gain. Identify and state what everyone can gain from working through the conflict. Think win-win rather than win-lose. One party does not have to win at the expense of another. Try to expand the resource "pie" instead so that both parties can get what they want.

Create a process for productive conflict. Set up procedures that encourage parties to constructively engage with one another to resolve the issues. Call a meeting to work on the problem. Involve everyone in generating alternatives and selecting a solution. Commit to the solution by developing an implementation plan. Follow up by monitoring the implementation process.

Step 5: Employ Collaborative Conflict Management Tactics

Conflict guidelines set the stage for collaboration, but it is what we say during a conflict episode that generates mutual gains. Collaborative messages reflect a high level of concern for the interests of both parties as well as for the health of the relationship. Collaborative tactics are either analytic or conciliatory. Analytic remarks include the following:[14]

- *Descriptive statements:* Nonevaluative comments that report on observable events surrounding the conflict. ("I was short with you yesterday when you turned in that report.")

- *Disclosing statements:* Nonevaluative statements about conflict events that the partner can't observe—thoughts, feelings, intentions, past history, motivations. ("I didn't intend to criticize you in front of the rest of the staff.")

- *Qualifying statements:* Remarks that qualify the nature and the boundaries of the conflict. ("Tensions between our departments are greatest near the end of the fiscal year, when both groups are swamped with work.")

- *Solicitation of disclosure:* Nonhostile queries that seek information from the other party that can't be observed, like thoughts, feelings, intentions, past history, and motivation. ("What was your goal in raising this issue at this time?")

- *Solicitation of criticism:* Nonhostile questions aimed at soliciting criticism of the self. ("Does it frustrate you that I don't get the sales figures in every Monday?")

Conciliatory verbal messages include the following:

- *Supportive remarks:* Statements that reflect positive affect, understanding, and acceptance for the partner along with shared interest and goals. ("I appreciate the stress you must be under in your new job.")

- *Concessions:* Comments that signal flexibility, a willingness to change, a conciliatory attitude, and concern for reaching mutually acceptable solutions. ("I would be willing to extend the due date for the project an additional month.")

- *Acceptance of responsibility:* Remarks that attribute responsibility to one or both partners. ("I'll admit that I overreacted at first.")

Step 6: Be Prepared to Apologize

Sometimes saying "I'm sorry" is the best way to defuse conflict. As evidence of that fact, a growing number of organizations are seeing tangible benefits from apologizing to clients and customers. The University of Michigan Health System and University of Illinois Medical Center at Chicago saw steep declines in the number of malpractice suits after doctors started admitting their mistakes. Toro's product liability settlement costs dropped by two thirds when the company began expressing empathy to any customers injured by its products, whether that injury was due to user error or a product defect.[15]

As individuals we can also benefit from the power of apology. However, our motivation for apologizing should be based on our ethical obligations, not on hope of personal gain.[16] If we have harmed others through our actions, we have moral responsibility to admit our culpability and to try to repair the damage. Doing so helps to restore the dignity of our victims and acknowledges that we have violated widely ethical standards.

Unfortunately, a great many apologies fall short. After his company was found cheating on the emissions tests of 11 million diesel cars, Volkswagen CEO Matthias Mueller began his apology tour of the United States by denying that the company had deceived regulators. He blamed the cheating on a "technical problem" and said he couldn't understand why Americans thought there were ethical issues in his company. Michigan governor Rick Snyder took responsibility for the state's failure to act to prevent lead poisoning in the Flint water supply and pledged to take care of city residents. Yet the state cut off financial assistance to citizens of Flint before all corroded pipes were replaced.[17]

According to apology expert Aaron Lazare, complete (ethical) apologies contain the following elements:[18]

1. *Acknowledgment.* Any effective apology begins by acknowledging the offense. Identify your role, specify the offensive behaviors you committed, acknowledge the negative effects of your behaviors, and confirm that you broke norms against lying, cheating, using abusive language and so on. Don't be vague ("I apologize for anything I did"); use the passive voice ("Mistakes have been made"); make the offense conditional ("If mistakes have been made"); question whether the victim was injured ("If anyone was hurt"); or minimize the offense ("I have nothing or little to apologize for").

2. *Remorse.* Express your regret for the harm you caused and indicate that you intend to act differently in the future. How you offer the apology is critical. Your attempt at seeking forgiveness will probably be rejected if your words, voice, and body language fail to communicate shame, humility, and sincerity.

3. *Explanation.* Offer an explanation for your behavior because those you offend want to hear why you behaved the way you did. Unethical explanations reduce the seriousness of the harm. Avoid the following statements: "It was an accident"; "That wasn't the 'real me'"; "I was under a lot of pressure to meet the deadline."

4. *Reparations.* Make an effort to repair the damage. Sometimes the remorse and sincerity of the apology itself is enough to address the harm you have caused. At other times, follow up is required. For example: offer to restore lost wages and benefits, provide missing information, pledge to treat subordinates with respect, consult coworkers before making budget decisions, and so forth. In the case of Governor Snyder, his apology would have carried more moral weight had the state completely fulfilled its commitment to Flint residents.

At times you will find yourself on the receiving end of an apology. In these situations the conflict will likely continue unless you offer forgiveness. Many families, for example, can cite instances where relatives continued to feud for decades because neither party was willing to forgive the other. Forgiving is **not** forgetting past wrongs or reducing the seriousness of offenses. Instead the wronged party acknowledges that she or he has been unjustly treated but decides to let go of resentment and revenge in a process that unfolds over time.[19] Like seeking forgiveness, offering forgiveness is a moral obligation. Forgiving prevents the escalation of dysfunctional conflict and can result in reconciliation. Refusing to forgive can provoke cycles of aggression and retaliation. Contrast the experience of Germany and Japan following World War II, for instance. The German government offered a number of heartfelt apologies for its wartime aggression and atrocities. Germany's relationships with its European neighbors have never been better. Japanese officials have offered only weak apologies for the nation's invasion of China and the slaughter of Chinese citizens. Relations between the two nations remain uneasy.

RESOLVING CONFLICT THROUGH ETHICAL NEGOTIATION

Negotiation is one common method of resolving organizational conflicts. For instance, employees negotiate with supervisors for higher salaries and promotions; workers bargain with each other when they need to switch work schedules; corporate purchasing agents and outside suppliers settle on the price of goods and services; members of production and marketing departments haggle over product features and delivery dates; and store owners bargain with property companies over lease agreements.

In negotiation, parties settle their disputes by generating a joint agreement or solution.[20] The negotiation process highlights the interdependent nature of conflicts. Bargainers must have some common goal, or they wouldn't negotiate. On the other hand, at least one issue must divide them, or they wouldn't need to negotiate to reach an agreement. Consider management and union relationships. Both sides share a common interest in seeing the company survive and prosper. However, management wants to keep labor costs as low as possible, while union workers want wage and benefit increases and job security. Management and union representatives will have to successfully negotiate their differences to keep the company in business. Similar disagreements can be found in project teams. Everyone in the group wants the project to succeed, but members will have to negotiate assignments, timelines, and a host of other details.

Because negotiation is so widely used, it is important to recognize the moral dilemmas inherent in this form of conflict resolution and to highlight the ethical benefits of taking an integrative approach to bargaining.

Ethical Issues in Negotiation

Ethical issues in negotiation typically fall into one of three categories: the choice of tactics, the distribution of benefits, and the impact of the settlement on those who are not at the bargaining table.[21]

When approaching a negotiation, bargainers have decisions to make about which tactics they will use when interacting with the other party. Most of these tactical dilemmas involve deceit. Do I share what I am really willing to settle for, or do I argue for a higher price? Do I lie when asked if I have other offers when I don't? Do I reveal problems (e.g., upcoming lawsuits, hidden debts) when negotiating with someone who wants to buy my company? Is it okay to bluff by threatening to walk out of the auto dealership when I don't really intend to?

Some argue that deception is okay because both parties know that deceit is to be expected in negotiation settings. They treat bargaining like a poker game. Just as we expect players to hide their cards and bluff, those who enter negotiations know to expect deceit. They agree with the British statesman Henry Taylor, who claimed, "Falsehood ceases to be falsehood when it is understood on all sides that the truth is not expected to be spoken."[22] Bargaining thus meets one of the standards of the principle of veracity described in Chapter 4, which is that lying is permissible in situations where parties know that deception is the norm.[23] However, it is not clear that everyone understand the "rules" of negotiation. A cooperative negotiator operates by a different set of assumptions than a competitive one. Those from other cultures play by different sets of rules, which are unclear to visitors. (For example, should a foreign tourist haggle with every street vendor in Kenya?) By its very nature, deceit shows disrespect for the worth of the other party and thus violates Kant's imperative to treat people as ends and not as the means to our ends.[24]

David Lax and James Sebenius suggest that we ask ourselves the following questions when determining whether or not to use deceit as a bargaining tactic.[25] Responding to these queries can help us determine if we should tell the truth. (Turn to Ethical Checkpoint 6.2 for a description of concrete ways to avoid lying during a bargaining session.)

- Will you be comfortable with yourself the next morning? Would you want friends and family to know what you have done? The public?

- Does this tactic conform to the norm of reciprocity—that we treat others as we would like to be treated? How would you feel if the roles were reversed?

- Would you be comfortable counseling someone else to use this strategy?

- If you were to design a negotiation system from scratch, would you allow this strategy? How would you rule on this tactic if you were an outside arbitrator?

- What if everyone used the same method? Would this tactic create a desirable society?

- Are there alternative tactics you can use to avoid lying and deception?

- How can you create value instead of claiming what you think is rightfully yours?

- Does using this tactic further poison the ethical atmosphere for this type of negotiation or in this industry?

You can also take steps to encourage honesty in the other party, who may be dishonest in order to protect him or herself, fearing that you might exploit any weaknesses.[26] Overcome suspicion and fear by building a climate of mutual trust. Building such a climate requires acting in a trustworthy fashion and demonstrating trust in the other person. This can be accomplished through five strategies. (1) Build a sense of benevolence—goodwill and moral commitment. Highlight any similarities in family, community ties, ethnic background, and so on. Set up preliminary face-to-face meetings in neutral locations before the negotiation starts to build rapport. (2) Create opportunities for displaying trust. Break the negotiation process into stages and provide low risk ways for both parties to prove themselves willing to trust. (3) Demonstrate trustworthiness. Keep even small promises, provide access to information about your position, be candid about issues that might arise, and stand behind your claims (with warranties, for example). (4) Put the negotiation in a longer-term context. Emphasizing that the parties have an ongoing relationship reduces the temptation to take advantage of the other negotiator. (5) Bring in mutually respected intermediaries. Find someone who can vouch for your reliability and punish dishonest behavior.

ETHICAL CHECKPOINT 6.2
Five Ways to Avoid Lying During a Negotiation

Harvard business professor Deepak Malhotra believes that we can tell the truth at the bargaining table without suffering significant losses. He offers the following five "ethically superior alternatives" to lying.

1. *Don't succumb to time pressures.* Many lies come when negotiators are caught off guard and resort to deception when responding to unanticipated questions. Pretend that you are selling a business, for instance. You can expect to be asked, "Do you have any other offers for your company?" Prepare your answer for this question before the talks start. You might point out that you haven't advertised your business for sale yet or that the market for your kind of company is strong.

2. *Refuse to answer certain questions.* Despite preparation, you may still be taken by surprise by a tough question. You may need to tell the other party that you are not authorized to answer or need to gather more information. There may also be certain questions that you will never feel comfortable answering (nor would other parties if they were in your shoes). For instance, you may not want to reveal to a purchasing agent the production cost of an item you are selling. Instead, you might offer to share other information, such as the details of the manufacturing process and the quality control systems you have in place.

3. *Adopt the logic of exchange.* When you exchange important information, you should receive similar privileged information in return. If you reveal your timeline for completing a deal, you should expect to learn the time constraints of the other party, for example.

4. *Eliminate the lie by making it true.* Reduce the temptation to lie by reshaping reality prior to bargaining. For instance, a lawyer might ask her client to limit the concessions she, the lawyer, can make during a mediation session, or a department head may ask for more time to gather information instead of submitting an inflated budget request.

5. *Observe the shadow of the future.* Focus on building long-term, trusting relationships through truth telling. You are less likely to lie if you and the other negotiator have a truthful relationship. Further, if you both have been truthful in the past, this pattern will generally continue into the future.

Source: Malhotra (2004).

The next set of ethical issues in negotiation stems from the distribution of outcomes. Unequal settlements raise questions of fairness. For example, most of us feel uneasy if one party appears to take advantage of the other, as in the case of a buyer who convinces an elderly widow to sell her house at well below market value, or a giant food processing firm that squeezes the absolutely lowest price out of a small farmer. Determining exactly what is fair can be difficult, but making sure that both sides benefit is a good starting point.[27] Also, some of the questions outlined above can be applied to determining fairness as well. Does the settlement violate norms of reciprocity? Would you counsel others to follow the same approach? What if everyone claimed a disproportionate amount of the benefits; what kind of society would that create?

The third set of ethical concerns shifts the focus beyond the parties directly involved in the negotiation process. Decisions made by bargainers can have a negative impact on outside groups. For instance, when a public utilities commission negotiates higher power rates with power companies, members of the community have to pay larger utility bills. Then, too, settlements can adversely affect the environment and future generations. Take the case of landowners who negotiate mineral rights with mining companies. The property owners get generous settlements, and the firms gain access to the materials they need to generate significant profits. However, extracting the minerals can cause environmental damage that will scar the landscape for decades to come. One way to minimize the potential damage is to keep the interests of outside stakeholders—current and future—in mind. Weigh the benefits generated at the negotiation table against the harms that will be caused to outsiders. Consider the legacy you want to leave behind. (Do you want to be known and remembered for the terms of this settlement?)[28]

Conflicts of interest arise in negotiations when bargainers act as agents for outside parties. Lawyers negotiate on behalf of clients, real estate agents on behalf of sellers, union representatives on behalf of the union membership. Negotiation agents often face conflicting interests. On the one hand, they are being paid to get the best deal possible for their clients. On the other hand, there may be an incentive to settle for an outcome that benefits them rather than their employers. A lawyer may urge her clients to accept a smaller settlement so she can collect the fee that she might lose if the plaintiffs continue their lawsuit. By the same token, a real estate agent may encourage buyers to purchase a less desirable property so that he can collect his commission. Lessen potential conflicts of interest by aligning your incentives with those of your employer (e.g., a bonus if you generate a better settlement for your client). Avoid even the appearance of a conflict of interest. For instance, don't accept trips and golf outings from suppliers lest you be tempted to make a deal that is not advantageous for your firm.

Adopt an Integrative Approach to Negotiation

Bargainers typically adopt either a distributive or integrative approach to negotiation. Distributive negotiators adopt the win-lose conflict management style described earlier. Their basic assumption is that they are engaged in a battle over a fixed "pie," or value. As a result, whatever one party gains is at the expense of the other. Integrative negotiators take a win-win approach. They are convinced that the pie can be expanded and that both parties can benefit. They view the negotiation as a joint problem-solving session. Table 6.1 offers a summary of the behaviors that come from adopting each perspective.

Table 6.1 Behaviors Corresponding to Distributive and Integrative Approaches to Negotiation

Integrative Negotiation	Distributive Negotiation
Open sharing of information	Hidden information
Trade of valued interests	Demand of interests
Interest-based discussion	Positional discussion
Mutual goals	Self-goals
Problem solving	Forcing
Explanation	Argument
Relationship building	Relationship sacrificing
Hard on problem	Hard on people

Source: Spangle and Isenhart (2003), p. 15. Used by permission.

In comparing the two approaches, it is clear that distributive bargainers are more likely to engage in unethical negotiation behavior. They are tempted to deceive, generate unfair settlements, fall victim to conflicts of interests, and generate solutions that benefit them at the expense of outsiders. As a result, we should adopt an integrative perspective whenever possible. However, there do appear to be times when the rules call for a win-lose approach, such as when buying a motorcycle. We also risk being taken advantage of if we come to the table with an integrative approach and the other party is out to get as much as he or she can.

Harvard negotiation experts Roger Fisher and William Ury outline one widely used integrative approach that enables negotiators to take a win-win approach while protecting themselves from being victimized. They call their problem-solving approach the *principled negotiation model*.[29] Here are the four steps of principled negotiation. You can practice these steps by applying them to Case Study 6.2, "Negotiating the Plant Reopening," at the end of the chapter.

1. *Separate the people from the problem.* Make sure that you address the human dimension of negotiation. Set the stage for productive discussions by building a working relationship. Think of yourself as working side by side to reach an agreement that is good for both of you. Once in the negotiation, address three types of people problems: perception, emotion, and communication. Don't blame the other party, but try to understand her or his perspective. Recognize and address the emotions both sides feel; don't react to emotional outbursts, but reach out to build positive emotional connections. Address the other party directly (not third parties), actively listen, and use "I" language ("I was disappointed in your response") rather than "you" language ("You lied to me").

2. *Focus on interests, not positions.* A bargaining position is the negotiator's public stance (i.e., "I want to hire two new employees for my project"). An interest, on the other hand, is the reason why the negotiator takes that position ("I need additional help so that my team can finish the project on time"). Focusing on positions can blind participants to the reality that there may be several ways to meet an underlying need or interest. The company in the example above might decide not to hire additional staff yet meet the project leader's need for help by reassigning current employees to his team.

   The Camp David peace treaty between Egypt and Israel demonstrates how separating interests from positions can generate productive settlements. When the two nations began negotiating with the help of President Jimmy Carter in 1978, they argued over ownership of the Sinai Peninsula, which Israel seized from Egypt during the Six-Day War in 1967. Egypt took the position that all occupied lands should be returned immediately. Israel took the position that only some of the Sinai should be returned to Egyptian control, fearing that Egyptian tanks would be stationed on its border. As a result, the talks went nowhere. However, once the parties realized that Israel's real interest was national security and that Egypt's interest lay in regaining sovereignty over her land, an agreement was reached. Israel gave back the occupied territory in return for pledges that Egypt would not use the Sinai for military purposes. Tensions in the region continue, but the two nations have remained at peace.

3. *Invent options for mutual gain.* Spend time expanding the pie before trying to divide it. In other words, generate solutions that can meet the needs of both negotiators. Brainstorm a variety of possible ideas (either on your own or with the other party) that you can draw from later on, look for shared and complementary interests that can lead to creative outcomes, and develop options that will be attractive to the other side. Fisher and Ury offer the following example of a creative solution that met the interests of both parties.

   Consider Mary Follett's story of two men quarreling in a library. One wants the window open, and the other wants it closed. They bicker back and forth about how much to leave it open: a crack, halfway, three quarters of the way. No solution satisfies them both.

   Enter the librarian. She asks one why he wants the window open: "To get some fresh air." She asks the other why he wants it closed: "To avoid the draft." After thinking a minute, she opens wide a window in the next room, bringing in fresh air without a draft.[30]

4. *Insist on objective criteria.* Avoid a test of wills when reaching the final agreement. If you pit your will against theirs, one of you will have to back down. One party may force the other into accepting an unsatisfactory solution as a result. Instead, agree on a set of criteria when determining a settlement. Employ fair standards (market value, industry standards, replacement costs, scientific findings) and fair procedures (taking turns, letting another party decide). Negotiators typically accept agreements that are in line with widely accepted principles.

COMBATING AGGRESSION AND SEXUAL HARASSMENT

Types of Aggression

Aggressive behavior is the most destructive form of conflict at work. Interpersonal aggression consists of conscious actions that hurt or injure. Such behavior can take a variety of forms, from refusing to return phone calls to screaming at employees to murder. One widely used typology categorizes aggression along three dimensions: (1) physical-verbal (destructive words or deeds); (2) active-passive (doing harm by acting or by failing to act); and (3) direct-indirect (doing harm directly to the individual or indirectly through an intermediary and by attacking something the individual values).[31] Examples of behaviors that fit into each of these categories are outlined in Table 6.2.

Interpersonal workplace aggression is all too prevalent. An estimated 2 million U.S. workers are physically assaulted yearly; 16 million are threatened with violence; 6 million experience physical assault; and homicide is one of the leading causes of death on the job.[32] In fact, the term "going postal" has entered the national vocabulary to describe workplace shootings. The term was coined after several postal worker killings between 1986 and 1993, though subsequent research revealed that postal employees are less likely to be killed on the job than others in the workforce. (Retail employees and taxi drivers are in much greater danger.)[33]

Table 6.2 Types of Aggression

Type of Aggression	Examples
Physical-active-direct	Punching, kicking, stabbing, shooting another person
Physical-active-indirect	Sabotaging a piece of equipment so that another person will be hurt; removing tools and supplies
Physical-passive-direct	Physically preventing another person from obtaining a desired goal or performing a desired act (e.g., by failing to move out of the person's way when asked to do so)
Physical-passive-indirect	Refusing to perform necessary tasks (e.g., refusing to provide information or help needed by a coworker)
Verbal-active-direct	Insulting or derogating another person in some manner
Verbal-active-indirect	Spreading malicious rumors or gossip about another person
Verbal-passive-direct	Refusing to speak to another person or refusing to answer questions posed by this person
Verbal-passive-indirect	Failing to speak up in another person's defense when he or she is unfairly criticized

Source: Adapted from Baron (2004), p. 29. Reprinted by permission of John Wiley & Sons, Inc.

While violence attracts the most media attention, milder forms of workplace aggression, such as *incivility* and *bullying*, are far more common. Incivility consists of rude, discourteous actions that disregard others and violate norms of respect. Examples of workplace incivility include leaving a mess for custodians to clean up, making a sarcastic comment about a peer in front of coworkers, and claiming credit for someone else's work.[34] Bullying involves repeated, unwanted actions and behaviors carried out over weeks, months and years, which are designed to humiliate victims and cause them psychological distress.[35] Examples of bullying include shouting, name-calling, insults, threats, unsafe job assignments, cruelty, sabotage, and spreading harmful rumors. In Europe, 3% to 4% of workers report being the victim of bullying behavior at least once a week and 10% to 15% say they have been targeted for psychological aggression in the past six months. In the United States, 10% to 12% of those sampled report being bullied in the past year while at work. (You can determine if you have been a victim of bullying by completing Self-Assessment 6.2.)

Mobbing is a type of bullying carried out by groups. The term comes from animal behavior where a group of birds or animals targets one specific individual in order to drive it away. In human organizations, groups of employees target coworkers to remove them because they either underachieve (and keep the team from reaching its goals) or overachieve and thus are seen as threats.[36]

Not surprisingly, bullying and other forms of aggression can do extensive damage to both individuals and the organization as a whole.[37] Victims may be injured, experience higher stress levels leading to poor health, become fearful or angry or depressed (leading in some cases to thoughts of suicide), lose the ability to concentrate, and feel less committed to their jobs. Observers who witness aggressive incidents may suffer some of the same negative outcomes. They, too, experience more anxiety and a lowered sense of well-being and commitment. Family members may be impacted, as victims take out their frustrations at home. At the organizational level, performance drops as a result of aggressive actions. Workplace aggression, whether in person or online (see the Contemporary Issues in Organizational Ethics box), is correlated with lower productivity, higher absenteeism and turnover rates, lawsuits, and negative publicity.

SELF-ASSESSMENT 6.2

Negative Acts Questionnaire

Think of your workplace over the past six months. Indicate how often you have experienced the following behaviors on this scale

0	1	2	3	4
None	Now and then	Several times per month	Several times a week	Almost daily

1. Having someone withhold information, which affects your performance.
2. Being humiliated or ridiculed in connection with your work.
3. Being ordered to do work below your level of competence.
4. Having key areas of responsibility removed or replaced with more trivial or unpleasant tasks.

5. Having gossip and rumors spread about you.
6. Being ignored or excluded.
7. Having insulting or offensive remarks made about your person, attitudes or your private life.
8. Being shouted at or being the target of spontaneous anger.
9. Being the target of intimidating behaviors such as finger-pointing, invasion of personal space, shoving, blocking your way.
10. Receiving hints or signals from others that you should quit your job.
11. Getting repeated reminders of your errors or mistakes.
12. Being ignored or facing a hostile reaction when you approach.
13. Receiving persistent criticism of your errors or mistakes.
14. Having your opinions ignored.
15. Being subjected to practical jokes carried out by people you don't get along with.
16. Being given tasks with unreasonable deadlines.
17. Having allegations made against you.
18. Being subjected to excessive monitoring of your work.
19. Receiving pressure not to claim something to which by right you are entitled (e.g. sick leave, holiday entitlement, travel expenses).
20. Being the subject of excessive teasing and sarcasm.
21. Being exposed to an unmanageable workload.
22. Receiving threats of violence or physical abuse or actual abuse.

Scoring

Scores can range from 0 to 88. The higher the score, the greater your exposure to bullying at your workplace. Scores on individual items indicate the severity of the bullying behavior, which can range from mild (withholding information, having opinions ignored) to highly stressful (being threatened, physical intimidation).

Source: Adapted from Einarsen, Hoel, and Notelears (2009), pp. 32. Used by permission.

Sources of Aggression

Aggressive behavior is the product of a number of factors—personal, social, and situational—outlined below.[38]

Personal Causes of Aggression

Type A personality. Type A behavior-pattern people are extremely competitive, generally in a hurry, and highly irritable. Such individuals are more likely to engage in hostile actions both on and off the job (child and spousal abuse, for instance).

Hostile attributional bias. Those with this perceptual bias tend to assume the worst in others. They believe that peers and subordinates are out to hurt them, and then they respond accordingly. For example, an employee with a hostile perspective who doesn't get notice of an important meeting will assume that his boss deliberately snubbed him, even if this omission was a harmless oversight. He may refuse to answer questions from his supervisor the next time they meet.

Inflated (or deflated) self-esteem. Those who hold extremely high views of themselves are particularly sensitive to negative feedback, which threatens their self-image. They are more likely to respond with anger and nurse grudges. Individuals with low self-esteem are more prone to seeking revenge.

Low self-monitoring. High self-monitors pay close attention to situational cues and then modify their behavior to act appropriately. Low self-monitors, on the other hand, pay more attention to their inner attitudes and feelings. As a result, they are more likely to escalate conflict and misinterpret motives.

Social Causes of Aggression

Frustration. Interference with the pursuit of goals produces anger and hostility. Frustration is most likely to cause aggression when the interference is seen as illegitimate. An employee turned down for a promotion, for instance, will be more upset if he thinks that the job went to a much less-qualified candidate.

Direct provocation. Aggression begets further aggression. Most people respond to verbal and physical assaults by retaliating with more extreme measures of their own.

Displaced aggression. If it's too dangerous or costly for a member to retaliate against someone who provokes her (the boss, for example), she may then take frustrations out on someone else—subordinates, friends, family members.

Triggered displaced aggression. Sometimes a weak provocation will trigger a strong aggressive response. This may occur because the individual recently experienced a much stronger provocation. For instance, an employee may lash out at a peer who suggests minor modifications to a project after being subjected to severe criticism about the same project from her supervisor.

Aggressive models. Aggressive individuals act as role models for other organizational members. Observers learn new ways to aggress that are often more subtle, like stalling initiatives or quietly sabotaging the work of another department. Seeing aggression also "primes" hostile thoughts. Coworkers begin to think about the wrongs they have suffered at the hands of others. Finally, role models demonstrate that aggression is a legitimate means for dealing with frustration or provocation. Soon an organizational culture of aggression emerges.

Contextual Causes of Aggression

Oppressive supervision. Employees are more likely to strike out against their supervisors when they (1) sense that they have little influence over the workload and work pace, (2) are the victims of bullying bosses, and (3) feel overly controlled (given little power, monitored extremely closely).

Job stressors. Layoffs, demanding performance standards, role ambiguity, conflicts, increasing competition, and other job factors produce stress that can sow the seeds of aggression.

Use of alcohol. Alcohol weakens resistance to anger and aggression. Intoxicated people can still restrain themselves but are more likely to go along with suggestions to harm others and to attack helpless victims.

Perceived unfairness. Individuals are more likely to retaliate when they perceive that they have been treated unjustly. They may take issue with how resources are distributed (distributive injustice) and how decisions are reached (procedural injustice). However, being treated with disrespect (interactional or informational injustice) appears to be the strongest determinant of aggression. (For more information on organizational justice, see Chapter 10.)

Unpleasant working conditions. Extremely high or low temperatures, crowding, noise, and other uncomfortable environmental factors generate negative emotions and increase aggressive behavior. As a result, attempts to save money by cutting back on the quality of the work environment—shutting down the air conditioning, lowering the thermostat in the winter, removing carpet—often backfire, lowering productivity while producing more aggression.

CONTEMPORARY ISSUES IN ORGANIZATIONAL ETHICS 6.1

CYBERBULLYING

Electronic communication has expanded the reach of bullies, allowing them to attack their targets even when they are off the job. Categories of cyberbullying include:

Flaming—sending angry, rude, and cruel messages about a person to an online group and/or target via email or text messaging

Online harassment—repeatedly sending offensive messages electronically directly to the victim

Cyberstalking—threats of harm and intimidation delivered online

Denigration—posting harmful, untrue messages about a target online or sending them to other people

Masquerade—pretending to be somebody else and posting or sending items that make the victim appear bad

Outing—sending or posting private, sensitive, or embarrassing information about a person (includes forwarding private messages or pictures)

Exclusion—deliberately excluding someone from an online group

(Continued)

(Continued)

Organizations have been slow to address cyberaggression, partly because they aren't aware that it is going on. Bullies operate online (out of sight) and often carry out their attacks on their own time on their personal electronic devices. Nonetheless, the problem appears to be widespread. A Pew Research Center study found that roughly 40% of adult Americans have been harassed online; 18% were targeted for such severe behaviors as physical threats and sexual harassment. One out of five Australian government employees say they have experienced or witnessed cyberbullying. Further, such abuse has the same impact as cyberabuse among teenagers, which has attracted more media attention. The cofounder of the anticyberbullying charity The Cybersmile Foundation notes: "Adult cyberbullying in the workplace can be more subtle [than teen bullying], but is equally distressing. The outcomes are often the same—to humiliate, undermine and distress the person being targeted."[1]

Experts say that employers can discipline employees for online activities. (Workers have been fired for posting critical comments about their bosses and companies on websites and social media platforms.) However, authorities encourage employers to first develop clear, written polices stating that such behavior can be punished, whether on or off the job. They encourage victims to print copies of all harassing messages and to report the cyberbully to the employer, Internet provider, and even the police, if the messages contain threats. Targets should cut off the cyberaggressor's access by shutting down current social networking sites and email accounts and opening new ones.

Note

1. Shearman (2017).

Sources: "Cyberbullying in the Workplace" (2016). S. Gordon (2016). F. Lawrence and Lidstone (2016). Li (2007). Pew Research Center (2017). Schimmel and Nicholls (2014).

Resisting and Reducing Aggression

Offering resistance to bullying and harassment can be risky. Bullies generally have more power and status; those who object to their behavior are often punished or find themselves out of a job. When confronted by their victims, bullies often escalate the abuse. Nonetheless, targets of bullying often do resist, convinced they have a moral duty to do so. They want to confront the unethical behavior and keep harassers from hurting others.[39] Third parties who observe bullying may intervene as well. Those with the strong moral identity described in Chapter 2 are most likely to recognize this type of injustice and are motivated to act by moral anger.[40]

If you find yourself the victim of harassment, you can resist by following these steps:[41]

Step 1: Examine your behavior to ensure that you are not seen as bullying others (which provokes an aggressive response from the harasser).

Step 2: Manage your work-related behaviors by improving your work performance (if needed) in order to meet high standards and adhere to group norms.

Step 3: Build your power by forming alliances with others; by increasing the bully's dependence on your skills and knowledge; and by developing your expertise in an area of vital importance to the organization.

Step 4: Calmly confront the bully, focusing specifically on the harassing behavior and communicating that it needs to stop immediately.

Step 5: Report the bully to the internal authorities like the human resource department or a supervisor (be sure to document the abuse).

Step 6: Go outside the organization, bringing legal action on the basis of assault, battery, emotional distress, and so on.

Step 7: Look for another job in an organization that discourages bullying.

The difficulty of resisting ongoing aggression either as a victim or as an observer makes a strong case for preventing aggression before it starts. Strategies for reducing aggression must address its personal, social, and contextual origins.[42] Careful screening of potential employees is a good place to start. Try to weed out individuals with aggressive tendencies and strong Type A personalities through interviews, testing, and reference checks. Ask applicants how they responded when unfairly treated or what they would do in a difficult job-related situation. Careful reference checks can identify individuals who should not be hired because of their patterns of abusive behavior. For current employees, provide training in social skills. Some workers get caught up in aggressive interactions because they unwittingly provoke others. They may not understand that their behavior irritates their peers and generates negative feelings.

Next, address social factors. To reduce frustration, establish legitimacy for decisions and actions by providing background information and rationale to your employees. Short-circuit the development of a climate of aggression by eliminating aggressive role models and punishing offenders. Effective punishment is prompt, highly certain, strong, and justified.

Finally, reduce negative contextual factors. Cut back on tight supervision, eliminate unnecessary rules, and avoid intrusive monitoring practices. Give your employees more control over how they complete their tasks, and outlaw drinking on the job (even at lunch). Reduce the impact of stressors by lowering work demands, by providing physical and emotional outlets (recreation areas, nap rooms, office celebrations), and by supplying stress management training. Create pleasant working environments with adequate space, comfortable temperatures, soundproofing, attractive furnishings, and so on. Prevent perceptions of injustice by treating others with respect, using the communication skills described in Chapter 4.

Preventing Sexual Harassment

Sexual harassment is a distinctive form of aggression based on biological sex, gender identity, or sexual orientation. Male harassment of women is by far most common but it should be noted that women do harass men (though much less frequently than men harass women), and both men and women can harass others of the same sex, as in the case of a gay or lesbian supervisor demanding sexual favors from an employee of the same sex. Sexual harassment is a global problem that has drawn the attention of the European Union, International Labour Organization, and the United Nations.[43] There are three types of sexual harassment behaviors.[44] The first is *gender harassment*, which consists of gender-based (nonsexual) comments and behaviors designed to demean women. For example, a supervisor may claim that a woman can't do a job defined as "men's work." The second form of harassment consists of *unwanted sexual attention*. This category includes both verbal (repeated requests for dates) and nonverbal behaviors (gestures, touching, kissing). The third is *sexual coercion*, which is forcing employees into sexual activity through promises or threats. A boss might promise a promotion to a subordinate who sleeps with him or threaten to fire her if she does not.

In the United States there are also legal definitions of sexual harassment, which is prohibited by law. Title VII of the Civil Rights Act of 1964 forbids discrimination in employment based on "race, color, religion, sex, or national origin." The Equal Employment Opportunity Commission (EEOC) enforces this statute, as do the Americans with Disabilities Act and the Equal Pay Act. State laws also apply to harassment cases. The EEOC has extended the sex discrimination provisions of Title VII to protect lesbian, gay, bisexual and transgender (LGBT) employees from unfair treatment in the workplace.[45] Examples of LGBT sex discrimination include denying family health coverage to a female employee with a female spouse, firing individuals making the transition from male to female, failing to provide equal access to restrooms corresponding to gender identity, denying a promotion to a gay or straight employee because of sexual orientation, and harassing bisexuals in the workplace.

According to the EEOC and a number of court decisions, there are two forms of sexual harassment under the law.[46] The first is called *quid pro quo*, which is a legal term roughly meaning "something for something." Plaintiffs in quid pro quo cases claim that they were coerced into providing sexual favors to their supervisors in return for keeping their jobs or getting promotions and raises. This constitutes discriminatory behavior because victims were required to submit to conditions not placed on other workers. The second type of harassment involves the creation of a "hostile work environment." Plaintiffs in hostile work environment cases claim that working conditions interfere with their job performance. The following have been identified as components of a hostile work environment:

- *Harassment aimed at one gender (or gender identity).* For instance, comments or slurs directed at only one gender, not the other, or toward transgender persons.

- *Severe and sustained negative behavior.* Generally, a pattern of behavior must be established, like a series of lewd comments and offensive gestures, not just one isolated remark.

- *Negative effects of behavior on the receiver.* Behavior is considered harassing when it offends the recipient, regardless of the expressed intent of the perpetrator. A male worker may put up a sexual poster "for fun," for instance, but this display is illegal because it makes his female coworkers uncomfortable.

- *Violation of the "reasonable woman" standard.* The behavior must violate what the typical woman would see as appropriate. A business lunch between a male and female colleague would not be seen as harassment under this standard.

Harassment would occur, however, if a supervisor kept asking a subordinate for a date despite her repeated refusals.

- *Significant damages.* Claimants must establish that the behavior had a significant negative impact (caused discomfort, lowered work performance).

- *Unwelcome behavior.* Consensual behavior is not illegal, but unwanted behavior is. Researchers have discovered that men and women often interpret the same behavior differently. Males often see "friendly" behavior on the part of women as sexual in nature. They are more likely to be flattered by sexual attention, whereas females find it offensive. Conversely, men are less likely than women to define teasing sexual remarks, jokes, and suggestive looks and gestures as harassing behavior.

Examples of both quid pro quo and hostile work environment sexual harassment (male to female) can be seen at Fox News. Network president Roger Ailes was forced to resign after the company paid $20 million to settle claims by former network anchor Gretchen Carlson and 20 other women. He reportedly told Carlson that they "should have had a sexual relationship a long time ago" and squeezed the buttocks of a young intern. In another suit, the plaintiff who was applying for an anchor position alleges that Ailes asked her to turn around for him, as it was important for on-air females "to look good head to toe." He reportedly contacted a former boyfriend to ask if the applicant would "put out" sexually. When the boyfriend said no, she was turned down for the job. Fox also settled harassment claims involving the network's leading star, Bill O'Reilly. Former *O'Reilly Factor* contributor Juliet Huddy reported that the anchor tried to forcibly kiss her, made sexually appropriate remarks over the phone (sometimes while apparently masturbating), took her to dinner and the theater, and, when she returned a key to his hotel room, opened the door in his boxer shorts. When Huddy rebuffed his advances, O'Reilly removed her from the show.[47]

Sexual harassment, while unique, does have elements in common with other forms of workplace aggression. Like other aggressive behavior, it occurs with distressing frequency. An analysis of 55 surveys involving more than 86,000 women found that 58% had experienced potentially harassing behaviors at work.[48] Harassment is most frequent in male-dominated, blue-collar jobs (construction worker, machinist), but female doctors, lawyers, and other professionals are not immune from being targets of such behavior. Neither are women students. The rate of harassment among female college students is roughly that of female workers; approximately 50% report having been targeted for such harassing actions as insulting remarks, propositions, bribes, threats, and sexual assault. The U.S. Department of Education began releasing the names of colleges it was investigating for failure to adequately handle rape and sexual assault complaints. More schools are requiring that all students complete sexual assault awareness programs.[49] (Case Study 6.3 describes how one college failed to address sexual violence on its campus.) Like bullying, sexual harassment has found a home online. In one well-publicized case, male Marines posted nude photos of their female colleagues on men-only Facebook sites along with "sexually aggressive" comments.[50]

The costs of sexual harassment mirror those of other aggressive behaviors. The work performance of targets suffers due to stress, decreased morale, damaged relationships, withdrawal, and career changes. Many victims quit their jobs or are fired for filing complaints. Targets experience headaches, sleep loss, weight loss or gain, nausea, sexual dysfunction, and eating and gastrointestinal disorders. Negative psychological effects include depression, a sense of helplessness and loss of control, fear, detachment, and decreased motivation.[51]

Many of the same personal, social, and contextual factors that promote other forms of aggression also contribute to harassment. Offenders are more likely to harbor hostility and to be low self-monitors. Men may be frustrated because they believe that women as a group are taking away their privileges, and they retaliate. Perpetrators also take their cues from others who model harassing behavior.

In addition to these general factors, there are unique determinants of harassment.[52] First, male sexual aggressors hold more traditional (less egalitarian) views of females. They expect women to function in nurturing roles and believe that some professions should be closed to females. Harassment punishes those who violate these prescriptions and victimizes women while reinforcing the masculine image of the perpetrator. Second, violators hope to win sexual favors and other payoffs, like reduced competition for jobs. Third, rates of sexual harassment are substantially higher in organizations that don't take complaints seriously, fail to investigate charges or punish offenders, and retaliate against whistleblowers. Fourth, harassment preserves male-dominated organizational systems that give men power over women.

You can take a number of steps to prevent sexual harassment, beginning with creating a zero-tolerance organizational climate. Adopt a written policy that condemns such actions, spells out what types of behavior qualify as harassing, encourages victims to come forward, identifies penalties, and prohibits retaliation. Then back up the policy with an effective investigation procedure using an impartial third party who interviews all participants. Attack gender stereotypes through training, which also encourages men to understand how women perceive behavior that men interpret as harmless. Increase the proportion of women in the organization to reduce the likelihood of harassment. Set boundaries on workplace romances (see Chapter 10) so that they don't result in sexual harassment.

University of Arkansas business professor Anne O'Leary-Kelly and her colleagues suggest that paying more attention to the moral dimension of sexual harassment would also reduce its frequency.[53] Clearly, such behavior, which is harmful, selfish, and unfair, is unethical as well as illegal. The stronger the employees' sense that harassment has a moral component (the higher its degree of *moral intensity*—see Chapter 3), the more likely it is that those workers will avoid sexually aggressive actions and intervene when they observe harassment. Professor O'Leary-Kelly suggests that you can increase the moral intensity of sexual harassment through the following actions:

1. *Make aggressors aware of the effects of their actions.* Some individuals, as noted earlier, aren't aware that their actions are harmful. Others may think they are hurting only the target of their sexual advances or remarks. Perpetrators need to learn that their actions are destructive not only to the target but to other women, the work team, and the entire organization. This is particularly important in light of the fact that the majority of victims do not file complaints for fear of retaliation. Offenders therefore get the mistaken notion that their behavior is not harmful.

2. *Encourage consensus about the definition and immorality of sexual harassment.* Create a shared understanding of what harassment might be in your particular organization, and develop clear standards of behavior that highlight the unethical nature of harassing actions. Promote discussion about situations that make participants uncomfortable.

3. *Shorten the time between conduct and consequences.* Moral intensity drops when there is a substantial delay between a behavior and its consequences. Immediate response is difficult in hostile-environment harassment cases, since a pattern of behavior must be established. Offenders feel distanced from their harmful actions as a result. Try to shorten this psychological distance by investigating and responding promptly. Begin investigations immediately after complaints surface, and come to a quick resolution.

4. *Emphasize similarities.* Our sense of moral obligation is highest when we perceive similarities between others and ourselves. Even though harassment is based on the differences between agents and targets, build a sense of similarity by emphasizing shared organizational goals and values. Provide opportunities for men and women to discuss their similar personal values, goals, and dreams.

5. *Promote individual responsibility.* Moral intensity is heightened by acknowledgment of personal accountability. Harassers will more likely desist if they stop trying to diffuse responsibility by blaming the work environment or the behavior of their colleagues. Highlight the fact that sexual harassment damages the character of the perpetrator and is inconsistent with such personal values as equality, respect, and concern for others.

CHAPTER TAKEAWAYS

- Conflict is an inevitable and increasingly common fact of organizational life. Conflict arises when interdependent parties perceive incompatible goals and scarce resources and believe that others are keeping them from reaching their objectives.

- Don't try to avoid conflict; instead, learn how to ethically manage disagreements.

- Functional or productive conflicts focus on the content of messages and are designed to solve problems. Dysfunctional or unproductive conflicts center on personalities and generate strong negative emotions, which produce escalation or avoidance behaviors.

- Managing your emotions can help keep constructive conflicts from becoming destructive. Take steps to cool down your emotions and let them dissipate; reengage constructively with the other person. Don't trigger negative emotions in the other party. Respect his or her identity; don't attack taboos or what the other person holds as sacred.

- Adopt a collaborative personal conflict style as your first option; employ other conflict styles when the situation calls for it.

- Put conflict guidelines in place that foster problem solving and mutual gains.

- Defuse conflict by apologizing when you have harmed others. An ethical apology includes acknowledgment of the offense, expression of remorse, an explanation for the behavior, and offering reparations. Be prepared to offer forgiveness as well.

- Negotiation resolves conflict by generating joint agreements or solutions. When negotiating, you will encounter three types of ethical issues: choice of tactics, distribution of benefits, and the impact of the settlement on outsiders.

- Distributive bargainers take a win-lose approach to negotiation, which encourages unethical behavior; integrative bargainers view negotiation as a process of joint problem solving.

- Take an integrative approach to negotiation by following the steps of principled negotiation. Separate the people from the problem, focus on interests and not positions, invent options for mutual gains, and insist on the use of objective criteria.

- Aggression, which is aimed at hurting others, is the most destructive form of conflict, damaging victims, observers and the organization as a whole.

- Incivility (rudeness and disrespect), bullying (repeated attempts to do psychological damage to targets), and mobbing (groups ostracizing individuals) are common forms of aggression. Resisting bullying can be risky but you can increase your chances of success by strengthening your power base (develop expertise, recruit allies) and turning to authorities in the organization for help.

- Reduce aggression by addressing its personal, social, and contextual origins: (1) Screen out potential offenders. (2) Provide interpersonal skills training for employees. (3) Share your rationale for decisions. (4) Punish offenders and eliminate aggressive role models. (5) Cut back on intrusive management practices. (6) Reduce stressors. (7) Empower workers. (8) Create pleasant working conditions.

- Sexual harassment is a special form of aggression based on biological sex, gender identity or sexual orientation. You can prevent quid pro quo and hostile-environment sexual harassment by creating a zero-tolerance climate, by training, by hiring more women, and by raising awareness that this type of behavior is immoral.

APPLICATION PROJECTS

1. Conduct a conflict inventory. Identify the sources and types of conflict common to your organization and how these disputes are typically resolved. What does this inventory tell you about the organization's conflict patterns and how effectively members deal with conflict?

2. Reflect on the results of Self-Assessment 6.1. Record your responses to the following questions: What is your conflict style? Why do you think you take this approach to conflict? How has this style been effective? Ineffective? What are the ethical strengths and weaknesses of this approach? What steps can you take to develop a more collaborative conflict style?

3. Create a set of conflict guidelines (a conflict covenant) for your small group. These guidelines should outline the procedures you will follow in conflict situations, what type of comments members may and may not make, and so on.

4. Try to employ collaborative guidelines and tactics in an ongoing conflict. Report on the success (or lack of success) of your efforts.

5. Analyze the apology of a public figure or an organization. How well does it fulfill each of the four elements of ethical apologies outlined in the chapter?

6. Evaluate your ethical performance in a recent negotiation. Based on material from the chapter, identify the ethical issues you faced. Describe how you responded to these dilemmas. What, if anything, would you do differently next time? Write up your analysis and reflections.

7. Prepare for an upcoming negotiation using the steps of principled negotiation. Determine how you will deal with people issues, focus on interests, invent a variety of solutions, and identify objective criteria you can use when reaching an agreement. As an alternative, apply the steps to Case Study 6.2.

8. Create a case study dealing with workplace aggression. What factors contributed to this incident, and how could they be reduced or eliminated?

9. How often have you been the victim of bullying behavior based on your response to Self-Assessment 6.2? How did you feel and respond? What suggestions would you make to others who might be victims? Write up your conclusions.

10. Evaluate your organization's sexual harassment policies and procedures.

CASE STUDY 6.1

Any Way You Look at It You Lose: Longshore Workers versus International Container Terminal Services Inc.

For 30 years the city of Portland, Oregon, operated a container-shipping terminal that handled agricultural products, machine parts, clothing, and other goods largely being shipped to and from Asia. After losing money 28 of those years, in 2011 the city decided to contract with a private company, International Container Terminal Services Inc. (ICTSI), to run the facility. For the first year, relations between the longshore workers who load and unload the box containers and ICTSI appeared to be friendly. Then the International Longshore and Warehouse Workers Union (ILWU) local began to complain that ICTSI was badly managed and driving shippers away through its poor business practices. The union accused the company of creating dangerous working conditions. Union leaders claimed that its members, not members of the electricians union, should plug and unplug and monitor refrigerated containers called reefers. Longshore workers hold these positions at other West Coast ports, but ICTSI's contract with the Port of Portland specified that the company must employ electricians as the port had done in the past. ICTSI denied that conditions were unsafe, though the Occupational Health and Safety Administration fined the company for minor safety violations.

The conflict soon escalated. Longshore workers engaged in work slowdowns to protest working conditions and the use of electricians. ICTSI took the union before the National Labor Relations Board, which ruled that the longshore workers had engaged in a series of unfair labor practices, including deliberate work slowdowns and threatening ICTSI officials. In 2015, a new five-year labor agreement between the international longshore union and West Coast ports

(Continued)

(Continued)

was signed. But this agreement did little to ease tensions at the Port of Portland. The first Sunday after the settlement, ICTSI Oregon CEO, Elvis Ganda, accused ILWU workers of being "engaged in an illegal work stoppage" when union members failed to show up for work. A union representative fired back: "ICTSI arbitrarily fired entire crews of workers this week and then complained that no one was working."[1]

The ongoing strife prompted the Port's biggest shipper, Hanjin, to pull its freight, followed by other companies. Soon the terminal was empty. Longshore workers were idled and the city of Portland ended its relationship with ICTSI. The terminal shutdown had a ripple effect, costing Oregon exporters an estimated $15 million a year to truck to other ports. Since many of the state's exports can be purchased elsewhere, growers and manufacturers risk losing their markets in China, Korea, and other Asian nations.

The bitterness lingers on even though the terminal is idle. ICSTI plans on bringing legal action against the union. The city of Portland wants to attract new shipping companies, but the history of labor strife might discourage potential shippers from signing lease agreements. Some businesses that used to ship through Portland may never return, relying on other West Coast ports instead.

Discussion Probes

1. What signs of dysfunctional conflict do you see in this case? What unethical behaviors do you note?
2. Can you think of other conflicts that ended with both sides losing?
3. What steps could have been taken to prevent this conflict from escalating?
4. Was it ethical for one union (longshore workers) to try to take jobs away from another union (electricians)?
5. Should ICSTI have renegotiated its contract with the city to allow longshore workers to take the jobs of electricians?
6. What responsibility, if any, did the company and the union local have to farmers and businesses that were hurt by their dispute?

Note

1. Harbarger (2015b).

Sources: **Harbarger (2015a).** Isidor (2015). Njus (2012, 2017). Weise and Woodyard (2015).

CASE STUDY 6.2

Negotiating the Plant Reopening*

For decades Brilliance Glass Manufacturing was the pride of the small town of Husker, Nebraska. Brilliance is one of the few companies making specialty colored glass for stained glass windows, figurines, and other artwork. Its products are used by some of the top artisans in the world. The plant is the largest employer in Husker and plant tours are featured in tourist brochures.

In the past few months, Husker pride in Brilliance Glass has turned to concern. Following reports that another specialty glass manufacturer on the East Coast was releasing dangerous levels of cadmium, arsenic, chromium, and lead into the air, state and federal environmental officials tested the air and soil around the Brilliance plant. They found abnormally high levels of lead in the soil in the surrounding neighborhood, including at a daycare center. Ingesting enough lead can cause permanent brain damage and is especially dangerous to children. Officials issued an order temporarily shutting down the plant, and panicked parents had their children tested for lead poisoning. Fortunately, no children had dangerous levels of the metal in their systems. Press coverage highlighted the lax enforcement of environmental regulations that could have prevented the toxic emissions.

Nearly all Brilliance employees were laid off as a result of the closure. Plant managers installed a new pollution control system that should eliminate 99% of all toxic metal emissions. The company also promised to greatly reduce its use of toxic metals in the production process, though doing so will reduce the quality and variety of the glass it produces.

Imagine that the Brilliance CEO has appointed you to head up negotiations to reopen the plant. If a satisfactory agreement cannot be reached, he will close the plant or move production to China or Mexico, where environmental restrictions are much looser. Others participating in the negotiations include the following:

- Representatives from the state department of environmental quality and the federal Environmental Protection Agency.
- The chair of the neighborhood association, a parent of two small children, who represents neighbors living close to the plant.
- The town's mayor.
- The director of the regional tourist bureau.

You have two days to prepare for the first negotiation session.

Discussion Probes

1. How can you encourage participants to take an integrative approach to negotiation?
2. How might you separate the people from the problem?
3. What are the interests of each party?
4. What possible solutions could meet the interests of all parties?
5. What criteria could be used to determine the terms of the final settlement?
6. What ethical issues might arise during the negotiations and how might you deal with them?

*Inspired by actual events.

CASE STUDY 6.3

When Football Comes First: Sexual Assault at Baylor University

Baylor University has made a name for itself as a major athletic power. Notable achievements of the Waco, Texas, Christian school include national championships in women's basketball (twice), tennis, equestrian, acrobatics, and tumbling as well as a Big 12 football title. Baylor's Brittney Griner was named women's basketball player of the year, and Robert Griffin III won college football's Heisman Trophy. The recent success of Baylor athletics is all the more notable because of the school's previous history as a perennial loser, particularly in football. The Bears won only six conference football games in Baylor's first nine seasons in the Big 12 conference. Said one former player: "Imagine year after year seeing your program just get demoralized, embarrassed. Opposing teams looked at us like, oh, that's a win. They were lining up to schedule us."[1] When the team began winning, the board of regents chairman told a reporter that he "didn't think I'd ever live to see something like this."[2] Boosters rewarded the football team's accomplishments by erecting a $260 million stadium.

Success on the football field hid a much darker reality. An investigation by the Pepper Hamilton law firm revealed that between 2011 and 2016, 17 women on campus said they were victims of sexual and domestic assaults—including gang rapes—by football players. (Baylor officials later said that they were reviewing 125 reports of sexual assault or harassment, some committed by students not on the football team.) According to Pepper Hamilton, the school failed to comply with Title IX requirements designed to prevent sex discrimination in education. The report found the football program "hindered enforcement of rules and policies, and created a cultural perception that football was above the rules."[3] Pepper Hamilton offered 105 recommendations for improvement.

Sexual assault victims received little help from campus authorities. Baylor police often failed to take action or discouraged victims from filing reports. Police officers seemed to blame them for what happened by asking if they were drinking or what they were wearing at the time of the assaults. Others who sought help at the counseling center were put on waiting lists. Victims claim they were denied academic assistance, like receiving extra time to finish assignments or to take exams, which is required by Department of Education regulations.

The university didn't have the required Title IX coordinator to ensure fair treatment of women until 2014, and even then the coordinator they hired left in frustration a couple of years later, claiming that authorities kept her from doing her work. Assailants continued to take classes so victims would run into their abusers on campus. Such encounters not only brought back the trauma (one freshman said that she fled to the bathroom to throw up the first time she saw her attacker walking a few feet away) but also put the women in further danger.

Athletic officials, administrators, and the Baylor and Waco police departments appeared more interested in protecting the image of the football team than in protecting coeds. When Coach Art Briles learned that a female student-athlete was gang-raped by five players, he responded: "Those are some bad dudes. Why was she around those guys?"[4] When one of his players threatened a female student-athlete with a gun, he texted an assistant coach with the message, "What a fool—she reporting to authorities."[5] The athletic director texted Briles that it would be "great" if authorities kept quiet about a player's death threats. Defensive end Sam Ukwuachu was allowed to transfer to Baylor from Boise State in 2013 after assaulting a woman. While waiting out a year to play, he was convicted of raping a Baylor student and eventually removed from the team. However, the team and the university kept his trial secret and never explained why Ukwuachu was no longer on the roster. He was allowed to complete his degree after he served a short prison sentence.

Baylor regents responded to the Pepper Hamilton report by firing Briles and the athletic director and demoting university president Kenneth Starr to faculty status. (He later resigned.) Baylor launched a number of new initiatives to address sexual violence, including doubling its number of counselors; providing trauma training to staff; setting up an assault hotline; forming task forces to implement the recommendations of the Pepper Hamilton report; working with Baylor police to develop new protocols; hiring additional compliance personnel; and refocusing on the school's Christian mission. Yet, some on campus were reluctant to acknowledge the extent of the problem. Baylor fans lined up to buy T-shirts with the initials CAB (Coach Art Briles) at one home game. Women's basketball coach Kim Mulkey said she would "smack" anyone who said that Baylor wasn't a good place to send their daughters. She complained that the school was being unfairly targeted and that the press should shift its attention elsewhere. (Mulkey apologized for her comments the next day.)

The costs of the scandal continue to mount. The Big 12 conference voted to withhold one quarter of Baylor's shared revenue—$7.5 million annually—until the university can establish that it has implemented better practices for dealing with sexual violence. The Southern Association of Colleges and Schools issued a warning to the university that it will closely monitor the school's compliance with accreditation standards. The state's top law enforcement agency, the Texas Rangers, is looking into possible criminal charges. The Department of Education is investigating civil rights violations and could withdraw funding. Baylor settled lawsuits with two women but faces additional legal action.

The victims, many of whom dropped out of Baylor, continue to suffer. Said one: "I still think about it every day. It's taken a lot for me to move on, get a job, have a life."[6] Press reports about the scandal bring back disturbing memories. Victims who did graduate from the school feel betrayed. They welcome the changes being implemented on campus but are skeptical. "It's something," said a Baylor education graduate. "But it's not enough, really. It's not enough to take away the past."[7]

Discussion Probes

1. As a woman, would you be concerned about attending Baylor? Would you send your daughter to Baylor?

2. Did Baylor's historic record of athletic failure, particularly in football, make it more susceptible to covering up sexual assaults once the school became successful?

3. What additional penalties, if any, should Baylor face?

4. When scandals break at Baylor and other organizations, why do some members refuse to admit there is a problem?

5. How can universities prevent football and other sports from becoming too important?

6. What procedures does your school have in place to respond to sexual violence? Are they adequate?

(Continued)

(Continued)

Notes

1. Bishop (2012).
2. Ibid.
3. Axon (2016).
4. "Art Briles Denies" (2017).
5. "The 8 Biggest Recent" (2017).
6. "Breaking Down the Baylor cases" (n.d.).
7. Ibid.

Sources: "Accreditation Group" (2016). Associated Press (2017a). "Baylor Fans" (2016). Creech (2016). D. Goodwin (2017). Moskovitz (2015). Powell (2016). "Timeline: Baylor" (2017). M. Tracy (2016). Watkins (2015, 2016).

PART THREE

PRACTICING LEADERSHIP, FOLLOWERSHIP, AND GROUP ETHICS

CHAPTER SEVEN

LEADERSHIP AND FOLLOWERSHIP ETHICS

Chapter Preview

Ethical Leadership
    The Ethical Challenges of Leadership
    The Shadow Side of Leadership
    Stepping Out of the Shadows: Normative Leadership Theories

Ethical Followership
    The Ethical Challenges of Followership
Meeting the Moral Demands of Followership: Principles and Strategies
Chapter Takeaways
Application Projects

Leaders are critical to the ethical performance of any organization. They are largely responsible for determining mission and values, developing structure, and creating ethical climates. As a consequence, leaders deserve a good deal of credit for ethical success and a good deal of the blame when groups fall short. That's why names of prominent leaders are linked to well-publicized ethical successes (former Starbucks CEO Howard Schultz and Patagonia CEO Yvon Chouinard, Southwest Airlines president emeritus Colleen Barrett, Container Store founder Kip Tindell, Special Olympics founder Eunice Shriver) and failures (Fox News CEO Roger Ailes, Theranos CEO Elizabeth Holmes, Uber founder Travis Kalanick, Wells Fargo CEO John Stumpf). However, while leaders largely determine the ethical direction of organizations, this does not excuse followers from their moral responsibilities. Followers have a choice whether or not to follow a particular leader, to maintain the status quo or to work for change, to obey commands or to object, to draw attention to wrongdoing or to keep silent. More attention is shifting to followership ethics as the power and influence of followers appears to be increasing.[1] Consider for example, how average citizens around the world took to the streets in support of women's rights and protests led to the ouster of South Korean president Park Geun-hye and Brazilian president Dilma Rousseff on corruption charges. In the United States, the standing of leaders has weakened as organizations adopt flattened hierarchies and move away from traditional command and control structures. As you can see, both leaders and followers are important. With that in mind, we'll examine the ethical duties associated with being a leader and a follower. We'll survey the challenges faced by both and then consider principles, theories and strategies we can use to master these obstacles.

ETHICAL LEADERSHIP

The Ethical Challenges of Leadership

Leadership is the exercise of influence in a group context.[2] Leaders engage in furthering the needs, wants, and objectives shared by leaders and followers alike. Because leadership is exercised in the group setting in pursuit of common goals, leaders and followers function collaboratively. They are relational partners who play complementary roles. Leaders take more responsibility for the overall direction of the group; followers are more involved in implementing plans and doing the work itself. While leaders and followers work together, they face different sets of ethical demands based on the roles they play.

Leaders, by virtue of the fact that they exert greater influence and have broader responsibility for organizational outcomes, face six principal ethical challenges: power, privilege, responsibility, information management, consistency, and loyalty. These challenges are described below.

The Challenge of Power

I talked at length about power and influence in Chapter 5. However, it is worth noting that power is of greater concern to leaders because (1) they generally have more of it, and (2) power is the tool or currency that leaders use to exercise influence over the direction of the group. All too often leaders abuse power. A total of 90% of those who responded to one survey reported that they had experienced disrespect from a boss at some point in their careers. Fifty-four percent of employees in another survey reported that they didn't regularly get respect from their leaders.[3] Leaders are particularly prone to engage in bullying behavior (see Chapter 6). Bully bosses feel the strong urge to put others down in order to feel good about themselves. Angry and bitter, they frequently threaten and lash out at others, particularly when they feel threatened (which is much of the time). Engaging in hostile, denigrating, verbal personal attacks is one of their favorite tactics.[4]

Concentration of power, which tends to corrupt power holders, is also an issue. Media giant Viacom's former CEO Sumner Redstone (who was still in office in his 90s) knew firsthand the seductive nature of power. He reportedly advised Disney CEO Michael Eisner (who was later removed from his post) to hang on to his job despite the efforts of stockholders who opposed him. Redstone told Eisner, "Once you've had this kind of power, Michael, let's face it, nobody wants to give it up."[5] Top leaders like Redstone and Eisner are particularly likely to think themselves godlike, believing that they are omniscient (all knowing), omnipotent (all powerful), and invulnerable (safe from all harm).[6] They mistakenly conclude that they know everything they need to know because they have access to many different sources of information and are used to having followers look to them for answers. They are convinced they can do whatever they want because they have so much power. Surrounded by subservient followers, they believe that they will be protected from the consequences of their actions.

The Challenge of Privilege

Power and privilege generally operate in tandem. The more power a leader has, generally the greater the privileges he or she enjoys. Evidence of this fact can be found in the wide gulf between the pay of top executives and of the average worker. The pay gap between the median pay of large company CEOs and median workers is 204 to 1, with some bosses earning over a 1,000 times more than the average worker in their firms. Expedia CEO Dara Khosrowshahi took home $94.6 million in 2016, followed by Leslie Moonves of CBS ($56.4 million), and Philippe Dauman of Viacom ($54.1 million). The enormous chasm between the haves and the have-nots extends well beyond organizational boundaries. According to the Economic Policy Institute, the top 1% of Americans own 34% of the country's wealth; 10% of the population controls 76% of the nation's total net worth. The gap between the richest and poorest Americans is much larger than it was a few decades ago. Economic inequality in the United States is now greater than in Europe and in a number of Latin American countries.[7]

Leaders probably deserve higher salaries and more benefits because they shoulder greater responsibility for the success or failure of the organization as a whole. At the same time, it is clear that far too many leaders get more than they deserve. We must answer such questions as these: How much should top managers be paid? How many additional privileges should they enjoy? What should be the relative difference in pay and benefits between employees and supervisors? What can be done to narrow the current gap in wages and benefits between the top and bottom organizational layers?

The Challenge of Responsibility

Leaders are accountable for the entire group (a sports franchise, a nonprofit, a public relations agency), while followers are largely responsible for their own actions. Determining the extent of a leader's responsibility is difficult, however. That becomes evident when ethical standards are violated. Should growers be held responsible for unwittingly using undocumented workers to harvest their crops? Can we hold the editor of a newspaper responsible for reporters who plagiarize stories? What should be the penalty for military officers if they sanction prisoner abuse in Afghanistan? Should they receive the same sentences as the soldiers who followed their orders, or harsher ones? How do we respond to business and nonprofit managers who fail to follow the codes of ethics they write for their employees?

Answers to these questions can vary depending on the particular situation. Nevertheless, there are some general expectations of leaders. If we hope to be considered responsible leaders, we must take the following steps:

- Admit our duties to followers
- Take reasonable steps to prevent crimes and other follower abuses

- Acknowledge and try to correct ethical problems
- Take responsibility for the consequences of our orders and actions
- Hold ourselves to the same standards as our followers

The Challenge of Information Management

Leaders generally have access to more information than do followers. They network with other managers, participate in task forces, keep personnel files, receive financial data, get advance notice of new programs, and so forth. Being "in the know" is a mixed blessing. Leaders need lots of data to carry out their tasks. Yet possessing knowledge raises some sticky ethical dilemmas. The most obvious is deciding whether to tell the truth or to conceal it. Leaders must also determine whether to reveal that they have important information, when to release that information, and to whom. Consider the case of the manager who gets early notice of increases in employee health insurance costs. He is asked to keep this knowledge to himself until the official announcement is made. In the meantime, his subordinates are angered by rumors that health coverage is going to be cut altogether. Does he let it slip that he knows what will happen? Does he immediately try to squelch the rumors, or does he maintain his silence? Finally, how information is gathered is yet another concern. For example, leaders of virtual teams must be careful about how they monitor the online behavior of group members.

You can use the following behaviors as signs that you or your leaders are failing to meet the ethical challenge of information management:

- Lying, particularly for selfish ends
- Using information solely for personal benefit
- Denying having knowledge that is in one's possession
- Gathering data in a way that violates privacy rights
- Withholding information that followers legitimately need
- Sharing information with the wrong people
- Releasing information at the wrong time (too early or too late)
- Putting followers in moral binds by insisting that they withhold information that others have a right to know

The Challenge of Consistency

In an ideal world, leaders would treat all followers equally, and all followers would respond in an identical fashion. This is not the case, of course. All too often, leaders act inconsistently, giving more favorable treatment—extra pay and time off, special attention, longer deadlines—to their friends and their favorite subordinates. Followers react to leaders in a variety of ways because of diverse backgrounds, skill levels, and personalities. Those from individualistic cultures respond well to personal rewards, while members of collectivist groups (where group unity is prized) do not. Some followers are better at their tasks than others. In addition, tactics that motivate certain individuals will backfire on others. Wise coaches, for instance, know that there are some players who work harder when yelled at in practice and others who get discouraged. The latter group responds better when quietly taken aside for private instruction.

Obviously, a one-size-fits-all approach to managing followers doesn't work. Throw in the fact that rules may have to bend to fit changing circumstances like weather emergencies and flu epidemics, and you can see why consistency puts ethical demands on leaders. They have to determine (1) how to adapt to individual needs while acting justly, (2) when to bend the rules and for whom, (3) how to adjust to the reality that some followers are going to be more competent than others, and (4) how to be fair to those who aren't as close to them.

Some degree of inconsistency appears inevitable, but leaders generate resentments when they seem to act arbitrarily and unfairly. To be a consistent leader, respond to the individual preferences of each constituent while supporting the principle that all followers deserve the same level of respect and attention. Go out of your way to treat "fringe" subordinates—those who are less skilled, less committed, and less connected to you—justly and compassionately, providing equal access to promotions and other benefits. Also, try to be evenhanded in your dealings with outsiders; treat your opponents as well as your friends with respect.

The Challenge of Loyalty

Leaders have to balance a variety of loyalties, weighing their commitments to employees, suppliers, families, investors, their professions, the larger society, and the environment. To be a model leader, put the needs of the larger community ahead of selfish interests. Reject decisions that benefit you and your organization at the expense of such outside constituencies as consumers, neighborhoods, local governments, and fellow professionals. You will also face the challenge of honoring the loyalty that followers and others place in you. Followers trust leaders to act in their best interests, and the public trusts leaders to act as responsible members of the community. Many organizational leaders fail to live up to this challenge. Release of the Panama Papers revealed that wealthy leaders were betraying public trust by hiding assets in offshore accounts, allowing them to evade taxes in their home countries. Managers at the Imperial Food Products chicken-processing plant betrayed the trust of workers by padlocking exit doors and failing to install a sprinkler system. When fire broke out in 1991, 25 employees died and 56 were injured. Severely damaged, the plant closed down, and the town of Hamlet, North Carolina, lost its largest employer.[8]

The Shadow Side of Leadership

As we've seen, failure to meet the ethical challenges of the leadership role can lead to a variety of misbehaviors—abuse of power and privilege, irresponsibility, deception, invasion of privacy, injustice, and misplaced and broken loyalties. Recognizing the dark or "shadow" side of leadership can help us become more ethical leaders.[9] By understanding the nature and origins of destructive leadership, we are less likely to cast shadows ourselves (see Chapter 2). In this section, we'll examine three perspectives on the negative face of leadership.

Bad Leadership

Harvard political scientist Barbara Kellerman is critical of the positive bias of most leadership research and training. To scholars and laypeople alike, leadership has a positive connotation. After all, we wouldn't take leadership classes and attend leadership workshops if we thought that to be a leader was undesirable! Kellerman believes that limiting our idea of leadership solely to good leadership ignores the reality that a great many leaders engage in destructive behaviors.[10] Until we acknowledge that reality, our attempts to become better leaders are likely to fall short. "I take it as a given that we promote good leadership not by ignoring bad leadership," Kellerman says, "nor by presuming that it is immutable, but rather by attacking it as we would a disease that is always pernicious and sometimes deadly."[11]

According to Kellerman, bad leaders can be ineffective, unethical, or both ineffective and unethical. She identifies seven types of bad leaders:

Incompetent leaders. These leaders don't have the motivation or ability to sustain effective action. They may lack emotional or academic intelligence, for example, or may be careless, distracted, or sloppy. Some can't function under stress, and their communication and decisions suffer as a result. Federal Emergency Management Agency (FEMA) director Michael Brown was widely considered to be an incompetent leader following Hurricane Katrina. Under his leadership, FEMA's slow, inadequate response led to unnecessary deaths and widespread lawlessness. Yahoo's Marissa Mayer was criticized by some for failing to change the company's culture and to engineer a turnaround. (The firm was purchased by Verizon.)

Rigid leaders. Rigid leaders may be competent, but they are unyielding and cannot accept new ideas, new information, or changing conditions. Thabo Mbeki is one such leader. After becoming president of South Africa in 1999, he insisted that HIV did not cause AIDS and withheld antiretroviral drugs from HIV-positive women. These medications would have dramatically cut the transmission of the disease to their babies. Leaders in the U.S. banking industry proved inflexible prior to the mortgage crisis. They believed that home prices would continue to rise despite evidence that the housing market was overpriced and overbuilt.

Intemperate leaders. Intemperate leaders lack self-control and are enabled by followers who don't want to intervene or can't. Marion Barry Jr.'s political career demonstrates intemperate leadership in action. Barry served as mayor of Washington, DC, from 1979 to 1991. He ignored widespread corruption in his administration, perhaps in part because he was busy cheating on his wife and doing drugs. Barry was convicted of possessing crack cocaine and served six months in jail. After being released from prison, he was elected to the city council in 1992 and was reelected as mayor in 1994. Former Congressman Anthony Weiner blamed his "destructive impulses" for ending his political career and marriage. He sent sexually explicit pictures to women and then to a 15-year-old girl, which led to a guilty plea on a federal obscenity charge in 2017.

Callous leaders. The callous leader is uncaring or unkind, ignoring or downplaying the needs, wants, and wishes of followers. Former hotel magnate Leona Helmsley personified the callous leader. She earned the epithet "The Queen of Mean" by screaming at employees and firing them for minor infractions like dirty fingernails. Helmsley later served time for tax evasion. (She once quipped, "Only the little people pay taxes.") BP oil executive Tony Hayward appeared callous during the Gulf oil spill. Several weeks into the crisis, he complained that he "wanted his life back," a comment that came across as extremely insensitive to the families of the victims who had died in the oil rig explosion that triggered the spill. Later, he took time off to participate in a yacht race with his son.

Corrupt leaders. These leaders and at least some of their followers lie, cheat, and steal. They put self-interest ahead of public interest. Former Detroit mayor Kwame Kilpatrick is an exemplar of this type of leader. Unlike Mayor Barry, who ignored corruption, Kilpatrick actively promoted corruption. He shook down contractors, took kickbacks, and stole money from a nonprofit fund for needy kids to pay for travel, golf clubs, and camps for his children. He didn't cause the city's subsequent bankruptcy but made the crisis worse. Kilpatrick received 28 years in prison for using city government to enrich himself, family, and friends. Bernie Madoff bilked billions from investors, spending a portion of the money on maintaining his lavish lifestyle (he owned a penthouse in Manhattan, a mansion in Florida, and a villa in France).

Insular leaders. The insular leader draws a clear boundary between the welfare of his or her immediate group or organization and that of outsiders. Chinese officials have insulated themselves from those fleeing repression and starvation in North Korea, sending them back to face torture and imprisonment. Leaders in Central Europe rejected pressure from the European Union to accept more refugees fleeing chaotic conditions in the Middle East.

Evil leaders. Evil leaders commit atrocities, using their power to inflict severe physical or psychological harm. Ugandan warlord Joseph Kony is one example of an evil leader. His Lord's Resistance Army (LRA) kidnaps young boys and turns them into killers who torture and dismember their victims. Syria's Bashar al-Assad is another example of evil leadership in action. He has drawn international condemnation for using chemical weapons against his citizens during the country's civil war and bombing hospitals in rebel held areas.

Kellerman makes several suggestions to leaders who want to be both effective and ethical:

1. *Limit your tenure.* If we stay in power too long, we are more likely to become complacent, overreach, lose touch with reality, and lose touch with our moral foundation.
2. *Share power.* Centralized power is more likely to be abused. Delegate and collaborate instead.
3. *Don't believe your own hype.* Far too many leaders begin to believe press accounts of their greatness. They forget that they are fallible human beings.
4. *Get real and stay real.* Bad leaders block out reality, ignoring corruption in their organizations as well as their addictions, self-destructive behaviors, and crimes.

5. *Compensate for your weaknesses.* Recognize your limitations, and surround yourself with followers and other leaders who can help you compensate for these deficiencies.

6. *Stay balanced.* Avoid becoming a workaholic. Spend time with family and friends.

7. *Remember the mission.* Put the mission of the organization (particularly if it is focused on serving others) above your own desires.

8. *Stay healthy.* Take care of your physical and mental health, and seek professional counsel when needed.

9. *Develop a personal support system.* Don't drive off friends, family, and associates who will always tell you the truth.

10. *Be creative.* Don't get stuck in the past, but think of new options for solving problems.

11. *Know and control your appetites.* Don't let your hunger for power, money, success, or sex take over your life.

12. *Be reflective.* Take time for self-refection. Get to know yourself, and develop self-control and good habits.

Toxic Leadership

Claremont University professor Jean Lipman-Blumen introduces the term *toxic* when addressing the shadow side of leadership.[12] Toxic leaders engage in the destructive behaviors and demonstrate the dysfunctional characteristics described in Table 7.1. These behaviors and qualities cause significant harm to leaders, groups, organizations, and societies. Toxic leaders appear in every segment of society and in every region of the globe. Examples of toxic corporate leaders include "Chainsaw" Al Dunlap, former CEO of Sunbeam, who ruthlessly eliminated costs and personnel; "Junk Bond King" Michael Milken, whose illegal financial activities ruined the firm Drexel Burnham Lambert; and A. Alfred Taubman, chairman of the auction house Sotheby's, who engaged in price fixing. Toxic nonprofit leaders include former Westboro Baptist pastor Fred Phelps, who picketed the funerals of military personnel with signs proclaiming "Thank God for dead soldiers," as well as priests who abused children and the bishops who protected them. Toxic political figures include former FBI chief J. Edgar Hoover and Zimbabwe's President Mugabe. Mugabe presides over a country where 80% of the population is unemployed, the life expectancy is 52 years, and 1.7 million residents out of 50 million are infected with AIDS.

Lipman-Blumen is most concerned with how followers can keep themselves from being taken in by toxic leaders (see the discussion of toxic followership in the next section of the chapter). However, she does make suggestions that can help us recognize the early signs of toxicity in ourselves. Ask yourself these questions:

- Do I inflict harm on my enemies or competitors first and then on others in the organization?

- Do I demonstrate disdain for others?

Table 7.1 The Behaviors and Personal Characteristics of Toxic Leaders

Destructive Behaviors	Toxic Qualities
Leaving followers worse off	Lack of integrity
Violating human rights	Insatiable ambition
Feeding followers' illusions; creating dependence	Enormous egos
Playing to the basest fears and needs of followers	Arrogance
Stifling criticism; enforcing compliance	Amorality (unable to discern right from wrong)
Misleading followers	Avarice (greed)
Subverting ethical organizational structures and processes	Reckless disregard for the costs of their actions
Engaging in unethical, illegal, and criminal acts	Cowardice (won't make tough choices)
Building totalitarian regimes	Failure to understand problems
Failing to nurture followers, including successors	Incompetent in key leadership situations
Setting constituents against one another	
Encouraging followers to hate or destroy others	
Identifying scapegoats	
Making themselves indispensable	
Ignoring or promoting incompetence, cronyism, and corruption	

Source: Adapted from Lipman-Blumen (2005).

- Have I changed my lifestyle and circle of friends, avoiding my old acquaintances and colleagues?
- Do I keep my own counsel or take advice from just a few others in my inner circle?
- Do I use others to do my dirty work and then get rid of them?
- Have I begun to mistreat the lowest or weakest members of the group?
- Have I begun to engage in excess (lavish spending and lifestyle)?
- Have I become evasive, denying accountability for results?
- Do I blame others for my decisions and actions?

- Am I acting in my self-interest instead of the organization's interest?
- Do I attempt to disguise unethical behavior as noble and altruistic?

Selfish Leadership

Concern for others is essential for ethical leadership, since leaders exercise influence on behalf of others. Unfortunately, leadership roles, which call for selfless behavior—like understanding and meeting the needs of followers, taking personal risks, and self-sacrifice—are also highly attractive to selfish individuals who focus on their own needs instead.[13] Using their positions for personal gain, they steal, lie, bully, and dominate followers, break promises, and so on. Selfish leaders can be classified as impulsive, narcissistic, or Machiavellian.

Impulsive, selfish people are more likely to seek powerful positions and to be identified as leaders by others. They are often extroverts who come across as charismatic and energetic. Once in power, impulsive individuals are free to fill their selfish desires. They consume more of the group's resources, are more likely to engage in sexual aggression, and frequently violate social norms. Selfish leaders justify their actions by narrowly defining morality. They put more emphasis on individual rights and freedoms than on obligations and duties to others. They want to allocate resources based on contributions (which favors them) rather than according to needs (which favors less powerful individuals) and typically fail to take into consideration other points of view when deciding on ethical issues. Sadly, organizational environments can reinforce the selfish tendencies of leaders. Powerful leaders often silence the criticisms of followers. Unchallenged, they are able to exert even more control over subordinates. Over time, low-power individuals adjust their emotions and attitudes to match those of powerful people.

Narcissism, like impulsiveness, is common among leaders.[14] The word *narcissism* has its origins in an ancient Greek fable. In this tale, Narcissus falls in love with the image of himself he sees reflected in a pond. Like their ancient namesake, modern-day narcissists are self-absorbed and think highly of themselves. They are attracted to leadership roles because they like to be the center of attention. They are often named to leadership positions because they are socially skilled; they make a positive first impression because they come across as bold and self-confident. Once in power, they are effective at holding on to their authority (which they believe they deserve). Narcissistic leaders engage in a wide range of unethical behaviors. They claim special privileges, demand admiration and obedience, dismiss negative feedback, respond defensively and aggressively if their egos are threatened, abuse power for their personal ends, ignore the welfare of others, and exercise an autocratic leadership style. Their unrealistic visions and expectations put the organization at risk. For example, some retiring CEOs want to "go out with a bang," so they involve their firms in mergers and acquisitions that may undermine the long-term health of their firms.[15]

Machiavellianism is a third manifestation of self-centered leadership. Psychologists Richard Christie and Florence Geis first identified Machiavellianism as a personality factor in 1970. Christie and Geis named this trait after the Italian philosopher Niccolò Machiavelli, who argued in *The Prince* that political leaders should maintain a virtuous public image but use whatever means necessary (ethical or unethical) to achieve their ends.[16] Highly Machiavellian individuals are skilled at manipulating others for their own ends. As a result, they are more likely to end up in leadership roles. They have a better grasp of their abilities and of reality than narcissists but, like their narcissistic colleagues, they engage in lots of self-promotion and are emotionally cold and prone to aggressive behavior.

Machiavellian leaders often engage in deception because they want to generate positive impressions while they get their way. They may pretend to be concerned for others, for example, or assist in a project solely because they want to get in good with the boss. Machiavellians often enjoy a good deal of personal success—organizational advancement, higher salaries—because they are so skilled at manipulation and at disguising their true intentions. Nonetheless, Machiavellian leaders put their groups in danger. They may be less qualified to lead than others who are not as skilled in impression management. They are more likely to engage in unethical practices that put the organization at risk because they want to succeed at any cost. If followers suspect that their supervisors are manipulating them, they are less trusting and cooperative, which can make the organization less productive.[17]

Combating selfishness is an important ethical responsibility. To start, we need to look for selfish tendencies in ourselves, asking why we want to take leadership roles and exercise power. We need to determine if we are overestimating our abilities, demanding admiration and obedience, dismissing negative feedback, manipulating followers for our own purposes, and so on. We also need to keep selfish individuals from assuming leadership roles.[18] Impulsive individuals, narcissists, and Machiavellians all have excellent self-presentation skills, so we need to be careful not to be taken in by initial impressions. Employ objective criteria when making hiring and promotion decisions (see our discussion of impression management in Chapter 5). Look for predictors of failure in previous positions, like changing jobs frequently. Ask questions that may reveal selfish tendencies, such as blaming others for previous failures and claiming all the credit for success. Use personality instruments to identify narcissistic and Machiavellian personality traits. (You may also want to complete these instruments yourself to determine if you have these characteristics.)

We can curb the selfish tendencies of current leaders—in others or in ourselves—by building in checks and balances on the use of power and by making leaders accountable for their actions. Performance reviews should be designed to reveal potential trouble spots like employee mistreatment and defensiveness. Those working for selfish leaders should carefully document abuses and form coalitions with others to confront them. Encourage employee development and succession planning. (Self-centered leaders are not likely to want to develop or promote others, because they are threatened by competent coworkers and fear the loss of power.) Create a culture that emphasizes honesty and collaboration over competition and self-promotion.

Stepping Out of the Shadows: Normative Leadership Theories

Normative leadership theories tell leaders how to act. They are designed to help us manage our ethical duties when we take on leadership roles and can help us avoid the shadow side of leadership. Each encourages selfless behavior—to focus on the needs of followers, avoid manipulative behaviors and so on. Two normative theories, in particular, have drawn widespread attention from leadership scholars and practitioners: servant leadership and authentic leadership.

Servant Leadership

The servant leadership model is based on the premise that leaders should put the needs of followers before their own needs. This approach has its roots in both Eastern and Western thought. Taoist philosophers encouraged leaders to act like children and humble valleys instead of mountains.[19] Jesus told his disciples, "Whoever wants to become great among you must be your servant, and whoever wants to be first must be slave of all."[20]

Current interest in leaders as servants can be traced back to management expert Robert Greenleaf. He coined the term *servant leader* in 1970 to describe those whose primary concern is the growth and development of their followers.[21] Greenleaf later founded a nonprofit organization to promote servant leadership. A number of businesses (Toro Company, TD Industries, The Container Store, Synovus), nonprofit groups, and community leadership programs have adopted this approach. Other notable advocates of servant leadership include James Autry, Margaret Wheatley, Max DePree, and Peter Block. (Case Study 7.1 describes a group of leaders who failed to act as servants.)

Much of the early support for the theory of servant leadership was anecdotal, consisting of examples of servant-leaders and lists of servant characteristics. More recently, scholars have subjected servant leadership to empirical testing. They developed servant leadership questionnaires like the one in Self-Assessment 7.1 and then used these tools to determine how servant leadership influences followers, organizational culture, and organizational performance in a variety of societies.[22] They discovered that servant leadership has global appeal and is practiced in Ghana, India, Australia, Indonesia, the United States, and elsewhere. While the specific attributes of servant leaders vary among studies, there are some common themes. First, servant leadership is person centered or altruistic. Servant leaders are genuinely concerned about their followers as well as their organizations and communities (reflecting an ethic of care). They measure their success based on what happens in the lives of their followers, not on what they themselves have accomplished. Concern for followers, organizational stakeholders, and society comes before concern for self. Putting the needs of others first discourages shadowy behavior. Other-centered leaders are less likely to accumulate power and privilege for themselves, to lie to followers, to take advantage of them, or to act inconsistently or irresponsibly.

Second, servant leadership promotes equity or justice. Servant leaders distribute power by delegating authority to carry out important tasks, sharing information, engaging in collaborative decision making, and encouraging constituents to develop and exercise their talents. Servant leaders are also concerned with distributing rewards fairly. When the company as a whole does well, for example, both employees and executives receive bonuses.

Third, servant leadership rests on ethical character. Servant leaders possess such virtues as empathy, integrity, honesty, and wisdom. They set a high moral example for the rest of the organization through their consistent ethical behavior.

Fourth, servant leadership incorporates stewardship. Servant leaders work on behalf of others—employees, shareholders, communities. They recognize that their positions and organizations are entrusted to them. Practicing servant leadership has a positive influence on followers as well as on collective performance.[23] Subordinates working under servant leaders are more likely to engage in organizational citizenship behaviors, to have a greater sense of self-efficacy, to believe their needs are being met, to report higher job satisfaction, and to say they will stay with their organizations. They also spend more time building relationships with customers and responding to consumer needs. Employees who work for servant leaders believe that they are being treated fairly, which encourages them to work hard. In sum, servant leadership can help us become more ethical and effective leaders. Putting others first helps us meet the ethical challenges of leadership while avoiding destructive leadership behaviors. At the same time, our organizations benefit.

SELF-ASSESSMENT 7.1

Servant Leadership Questionnaire

Respond to each of the following items on a scale of 1 to 5 (1 = strongly disagree, 5 = strongly agree). The scale asks you to evaluate a department manager, but you can substitute another type of leader instead (CEO, instructor, team leader). Total scores can range from 14 to 70. The higher the score, the more this leader demonstrates servant leader behaviors and attributes.

1. My department manager spends the time to form quality relationships with department employees.
2. My department manager creates a sense of community among department employees.
3. My department manager's decisions are influenced by department employees' input.
4. My department manager tries to reach consensus among department employees on important decisions.
5. My department manager is sensitive to department employees' responsibilities outside the workplace.
6. My department manager makes the personal development of department employees a priority.
7. My department manager holds department employees to high ethical standards.
8. My department manager does what she or he promises to do.
9. My department manager balances concern for day-to-day details with projections for the future.
10. My department manager displays wide-ranging knowledge and interests in finding solutions to work problems.
11. My department manager makes me feel like I work with him/her, not for him/her.
12. My department manager works hard at finding ways to help others be the best they can be.
13. My department manager encourages department employees to be involved in community service and volunteer activities outside of work.
14. My department manager emphasizes the importance of giving back to the community.

Source: Ehrhart (2004), p. 93. Used by permission.

Authentic Leadership

Authentic leadership theory (ALT) is an offshoot of positive psychology and positive organizational scholarship. Positive psychologists, as we saw in Chapter 2, believe in developing people's strengths instead of trying to fix their weaknesses; positive organizational scholars try to bring out the collective best in organizations. Fred Luthans, Bruce Avolio, and their colleagues assert that this positive approach is also a more productive way to develop leaders.[24] Traditional development programs address deficiencies in a leader's skills, knowledge, and motivations. Failure and other negative events are seen as critical to leader development. ALT proponents argue, instead, that we ought to build on the strengths of individuals and look for positive moments that foster their growth as leaders.

To Luthans, Avolio, and others, authenticity is the "root construct," or principle, underlying all forms of positive leadership. Authentic leaders know themselves well, and they behave in ways that are consistent with their beliefs. (In other words, they "walk their talk.") Self-awareness, balanced processing, internalized moral perspective, and relational transparency all play an important role in authentic leadership.[25] *Self-awareness* means being conscious of, and trusting in, motives, desires, feelings, and self-concept. Self-aware people know their strengths and weaknesses, personal traits, and emotional patterns, and they are able to use this knowledge when interacting with others and their environments. *Balanced processing* denotes remaining objective when receiving information. Inauthentic responses involve denying, distorting, or ignoring negative feedback. Authentic leaders accept their blind spots and failings and try to address them. *Internalized moral perspective* refers to regulating behavior according to internal standards and values, not according to what others say. Authentic leaders act in harmony with what they believe and do not change their behavior to please others or to earn rewards or avoid punishment. *Relational transparency* is presenting the authentic self to others, openly expressing true thoughts and feelings appropriate for the situation.

Authentic leadership has a strong moral component.[26] Not only has authenticity been seen as a virtue since ancient Greece and Rome, but ALT theorists define authentic leaders as "those who are deeply aware of how they think and behave and are perceived by others as being aware of their own and others' values/moral perspectives, knowledge, and strengths; aware of the context in which they operate; and who are confident, hopeful, optimistic, resilient, and of high moral character."[27] Such leaders acknowledge the ethical responsibilities of their roles, can recognize and evaluate ethical issues, and take moral actions that are thoroughly grounded in their beliefs and values. Proponents of authentic leadership argue that it is impossible to achieve a high level of authenticity without reaching an advanced level of moral development and holding to high ethical standards.[28]

Critical incidents called *trigger events* play an important role in the development of the moral component of authentic leadership.[29] These events can be positive or negative and promote introspection and reflection. Trigger experiences are often dramatic (facing racial hatred, visiting a third world village). However, authentic leadership theorists posit that, more often than not, these experiences are more mundane—for example, reading an important book, seeing a powerful film, serving under an authentic leader. Sometimes a series of small events, such as several minor successes or failures, can have a cumulative effect, triggering significant thought. Leaders develop a clearer sense of who they are, including their standards of right and wrong, through these experiences. They build a store of moral knowledge that they can draw on to make better choices when facing future ethical dilemmas.

Authentic leadership produces a number of positive effects in followers, beginning with increased commitment and performance.[30] Followers are also likely to emulate the example of authentic leaders who set a high ethical standard. They feel empowered to make ethical choices on their own without the input of the leader and demonstrate moral courage. They align themselves with the values of the organization and become authentic moral agents themselves. (I'll have more to say about authentic followership in the next section of the chapter.) Leader authenticity fosters feelings of self-efficacy (competence), hope, optimism, and resilience in followers, what positive psychologists refer to as *psychological capital*. Followers who believe in their abilities are more likely to take initiative and to achieve more, even in the face of difficult circumstances. Feelings of hope and optimism foster their willpower. Resiliency enables followers to recover more quickly from setbacks.

Authenticity also pays dividends for leaders. Followers provide feedback that increases the leaders' self-knowledge. They reward authentic leaders by giving them more latitude to make difficult, unpopular choices and by getting more done. (Followers are also more productive because they have to waste less time and energy figuring out what their leaders will do next.) In addition, authentic leaders engender more trust; and trust, in turn, has been linked to higher organizational productivity and performance. Those who work in a trusting environment are more productive because they have high job satisfaction, enjoy better relationships, stay focused on their tasks, feel committed to the group, sacrifice for the greater organizational good, and are willing to go beyond their job descriptions to help out fellow employees.[31]

The benefits of authenticity demonstrate the truth of the familiar adages "Know thyself" and "To thine own self be true." Avolio and Luthans encourage you to look to the past, present, and future in order to build your self-awareness, which, in turn, will promote your development as an authentic leader.[32] First, reflect on your past experiences—both good and bad—to see what you can learn from them, and then develop ways to improve. For example, if you successfully managed a conflict with a roommate, consider what that experience can teach you about handling a conflict at work, and put those insights into practice. Next, actively monitor how you currently think and feel and how your actions influence others. Build your self-confidence or self-efficacy through visualization and by observing positive role models; hold high positive expectations for yourself (employ the Galatea effect; see Chapter 5). Finally, focus on the future, identifying emerging trends that may impact you and your organizations. You are more likely to spot such developments if you read outside of your field of study, attend seminars, and develop social networks. (In Chapter 11 we'll talk about more about issues management.)

ETHICAL FOLLOWERSHIP

The Ethical Challenges of Followership

Like leaders, followers face a special set of demands or challenges based on the nature of the role they play. Followers, who have less power and status, are charged with carrying out the work and implementing the directives of leaders. In light of these realities, here are important moral challenges confronted by followers.

The Challenge of Obligation

All followers have obligations to their leaders as well as to the institutions that provide them with paychecks, retirement plans, friendships, prestige, training, fulfilling work, and other benefits. Obligations don't end at the organizational door, however. Followers must frequently fulfill duties to external stakeholders. For instance, government employees "owe" it to taxpayers to use their money wisely by working hard and spending carefully. Members of a law firm owe their clients the best possible representation as well as accurate billing.

Determining minimal responsibilities is easier than deciding how far follower obligations should extend. At the very least, employees shouldn't rip off their employers by showing up late (or not at all), doing nothing, and stealing property. Yet some workers are asked to sacrifice too much for their organizations. Consider the case of technology and consulting firms that demand that employees travel constantly, work nights and weekends, and attend meetings instead of their kids' school events. Giving in to the excessive demands of workaholic organizations generates stress and burnout, endangering mental health, marriages, and relationships with children. Volunteers must also determine what they owe their leaders and groups. Religious cults are criticized for demanding that followers devote long hours to the cause, turn over their paychecks to leaders, and cut off their connections to families and friends.

Every situation is different, so followers have to determine if they are meeting their ethical obligations or giving too little or too much. However, the questions below can serve as a guide to sorting out the obligations we owe as followers.

- Am I doing all I reasonably can to carry out my tasks and further the mission of my organization? What more could I do?
- Am I earning the salary and benefits I receive?
- Can I fulfill my organizational obligations and, at the same time, maintain a healthy personal life and productive relationships?
- If not, what can I do to bring my work and personal life into balance?

The Challenge of Obedience

Followers must routinely obey orders and directives, even the ones they don't like. Deciding when to disobey is the challenge. There's no doubt that following authority can drive followers to engage in illegal and immoral activities in which they would never participate on their own. This point was driven home in experiments carried out by Stanley Milgram in the 1970s.[33] Students playing the role of teacher were asked to administer shocks to a learner, hidden behind a partition, when the learner answered incorrectly. Subjects continued to ramp up the voltage of the shocks at the request of the experimenter, even though the learner (really an actor who received no shock at all) expressed more and more discomfort. Two thirds of the students obeyed the experimenter despite the pleas and screams of the learner.

Milgram's findings only confirm what has been repeated time and again in real life. Philippine police who execute drug suspects without trials claim to be following orders, as did members of Rwandan death squads, and Saddam Hussein's torturers. However, following orders is no excuse. This is called the Nuremberg principle.[34] At the Nuremberg war crime trials following World War II, the tribunal rejected claims that atrocities were justified because German defendants were obeying authority. Based on this principle, the U.S. Army punishes those who follow illegal orders.

Every follower has to consider such factors as these: (1) Does this order appear to call for unethical behavior? (2) Would I engage in this course of action if I weren't ordered to? (3) What are the potential consequences for others if these directions are followed? For myself? (4) Does obedience threaten the mission and health of the organization as a whole? (5) What steps should I take if I decide to disobey? (Contemporary Issues in Organizational Ethics 7.1 describes government followers who decide to deliberately disobey their leaders.)

The term "intelligent disobedience" is useful for determining when and how to disobey.[35] The concept comes from guide dog training. Guide dogs for the blind normally follow the orders of their owners. However, they must also know when to disobey commands that would put both the dog and the human in harm's way, such as an order to cross the street when a car is coming. Practicing intelligent disobedience is a four step process: (1) understand the mission, values and goals for of the group or organization; (2) pause and examine any order that seems inconsistent with the mission, values and goals; (3) make a conscious choice to comply or to resist the order, providing an alternative when possible; and (4) assume personal accountability for your choice to obey or disobey. When faced with an unethical order, gather your thoughts. Ask relevant questions while pointing out that the order isn't in the best interest of the leader or the organization. Refuse to participate and be prepared to accept the consequences. One example of intelligent disobedience was provided by a solider asked to waterboard "high-value" prisoners in Iraq. He believed that this technique—which involves pouring water down the throats of victims who gag and convulse—was a form of torture that violated the rules of the Geneva convention. He replied, "I will need that order in writing before executing it." He was never asked to waterboard again.

CONTEMPORARY ISSUES IN ORGANIZATIONAL ETHICS 7.1

GUERRILLA BUREAUCRATS

Public administration professor Rosemary O'Leary uses the term "guerrilla government" to describe the activities of career public sector managers who decide to work secretly, behind the scenes, to thwart the wishes of their leaders. Examples of guerrilla bureaucrats include:

- Chiune Sugihara, a Japanese diplomat stationed in Nazi Lithuania, who secretly signed 10,000 visas to save Jewish refugees in World War II.

- Mark Felt, deputy director of the FBI, who, under the code name "Deep Throat," provided reporters with information that led to the resignation of Richard Nixon.

- A state transportation employee, who repaired a train gate near where children were playing despite the objections of his superior. He did so "because it was the right thing to do."

- Forest Service ranger Claude Ferguson, who joined an environmentalist lawsuit against his own agency when it allowed off-road vehicles in the Hoosier National Forest.
- U.S. Bureau of Reclamation scientist Dave Wegner, who successfully led efforts to protect the Grand Canyon even as his bosses tried to fire him.

Guerrilla actions are often sparked when a political appointee takes over an established agency. Conflicts arise when the new manager who is appointed by a governor, the president, or another official has different values and priorities than the career public servants who run the agency. Environmental Protection Agency officials leaked internal memos to the press after President Trump appointed Scott Pruitt to be the agency's director. Before being appointed to this post, Pruitt filed a number of lawsuits against the EPA as Oklahoma's attorney general. EPA employees accused their new leader of trying to undo environmental regulations, discarding the findings of agency scientists, and forbidding employees from talking to outsiders. They believed that he was trying to seriously weaken the EPA with the blessing of the president.

Sorting through the ethics of guerrilla government is not easy. Disobedient bureaucrats often appear to be heroes (when they protect children's safety or national security, for instance). Yet, by circumventing the rules, they threaten to undermine their agencies. Guerrilla managers may argue that they are serving the public. But at the same time these officials appear to thwarting the will of the electorate who, after all, elected the politicians to put new policies in place. Then, too, the determination of what constitutes ethical or unethical guerrilla government depends on who is making this judgment. Some applaud EPA staffers for leaking memos and opposing their boss in order to protect the environment. Others, who feel hamstrung by EPA regulations, condemn these actions. When it comes to judging government guerrillas, "to some they are brilliant entrepreneurs. To others they are deviant insubordinates."[1]

In light of the difficulty of determining the morality of guerrilla actions, Professor O'Leary says that potential guerrillas should ask themselves the following questions before engaging in silent disobedience.

- Am I correct? More than a sincere belief is needed.
- Is the feared damage immediate, permanent, and irreversible? Are safety and health issues involved? Or is there time for a longer view and a more open strategy?
- Am I adhering to the rule of law?
- Is there a legitimate conflict of laws?
- Is this an area that is purely and legitimately discretionary?
- Were all reasonable alternative avenues pursued?
- Would it be more ethical to promote transparency rather than work clandestinely?
- Would it be more ethical to work with sympathetic legislators before turning to media and outside groups?
- Is whistle-blowing a preferable route?

While guerrilla activity will likely always be around, managers can take advantage of the underlying dissent that triggers such actions to create healthier agencies. They need to (1) create an organizational culture that encourages questions, dialogue, and debate; (2) listen to hear and then to evaluate the dissent to determine if it is viable;

(Continued)

(Continued)

(3) understand the informal organization where dissent often originates; (4) focus on the merits of the message even if is delivered the wrong way (separate the people from the problem); (5) create multiple channels for expressing dissent (conversations, memos, suggestion boxes); and (6) put boundaries on dissent (decide when the time for dissent is over.)

Note

1. O'Leary (2014), p. 14.

Sources: O' Leary (2009, 2010, 2014).

The Challenge of Cynicism

It's easy for followers to become cynical. They don't have much power, and they are frequently left out of the information loop and important decisions. Often, the choices and actions of their leaders appear arbitrary if not stupid. Surveys reveal that 43% to 48% of American employees are cynical about their workplaces.[36] Skepticism can be justified (just look at what happened to thousands of loyal, hardworking employees at Washington Mutual Savings and Loan, Enron, WorldCom, Countrywide Financial, and elsewhere). Then, too, cynical employees often have a more realistic perspective on the problems facing their organizations and are more resistant to leaders who want them to engage in unethical behavior. Nevertheless, cynicism acts like acid, reducing commitment levels, destroying trust, lowering job satisfaction, increasing resistance to change, generating negative feelings, and lowering both individual and organizational performance.[37] Few of us give our best effort when we are skeptical about the organizations we've committed ourselves to. The more cynical we become, the more energy we put into critiquing and complaining and the less we devote to the task at hand. Followers must walk a fine line between healthy skepticism, which prevents them from being exploited and alerts them to unethical behavior, and unhealthy cynicism, which undermines their efforts and those of the group as a whole.

Scholars report that dissatisfied employees choose among four possible responses: exit, loyalty, voice, and neglect (ELVN).[38] Workers either *exit* (leave) the organization, demonstrate *loyalty* by waiting patiently for things to get better, give *voice* to their concerns, or *neglect* their jobs by spending less time at work and withdrawing from relationships. Cynics generally don't express their concerns or remain loyal (the most constructive options). Instead they opt to neglect their responsibilities or to leave the organization.

The Challenge of Dissent

Followers frequently take issue with policies, procedures, orders, working conditions, pay, benefits, values, and other factors. They can't make the changes themselves, so they must express their disagreement to those who can. At this point, followers must make a number of strategic decisions. To begin with, they have to determine when to speak up and when to keep silent. There may be several points of contention, but generally followers have to "pick their battles." Raising too many issues may turn leaders off and can label the follower as a whiner. On the other hand, silence can be immoral, as in the case of the engineer who discovers his company is shipping defective airplane parts but decides to keep this information to himself. (See Case Study 7.2, "Challenging the Chancellor," to learn more about how one group of followers successfully brought about change.)

Once the decision to protest has been made, followers must then determine the following:

- How to express dissent (when, what to say, through what channels)
- Whom to contact with their concerns (immediate supervisor, professional supervisor, etc.)
- How to respond if their opinions are rejected
- When to go outside the organization with concerns and complaints

Arizona State University Professor Jeffrey Kassing reports that workers employ five strategies to express dissent to their leaders.[39] *Direct-factual appeals* are based on physical evidence, organizational policies and procedures, and personal experience. *Solution presentations* offer ideas for resolving the issue either in addition to, or instead of, presenting the facts. *Repetition* describes consistent attempts to draw attention to a topic over a period of time. *Circumvention* means taking dissent to someone above an immediate supervisor. *Threatening resignation* is vowing to quit in order to get supervisors and management to respond.

Employees rate direct-factual appeals and solution presentations (prosocial strategies) as most effective, in part because these strategies are less threatening to the image or "face" of leaders. Circumvention and repetition pose more face threat and thus are riskier, frequently damaging the subordinate–supervisor relationship. Threatening resignation is the riskiest tactic, and supervisors and organizational members rate this strategy as least competent. With this in mind, start with prosocial strategies when expressing upward dissent. Gather evidence and propose solutions. Meet first with your supervisor before approaching senior leaders. If you must repeatedly raise your concern, continue to offer evidence and solutions. Threaten to quit only as a last resort.

The Challenge of Bad News

Few of us have a problem with telling our superiors what they want to hear. For example, we've reached our goals, sales are up, the project is under budget, and the software implementation will be done on time. Delivering bad news is much riskier. Telling our bosses what they don't want to hear can incur their wrath, bring penalties, and seriously damage our standing in the organization. The risk is highest when we are directly at fault. No wonder that researchers report that subordinates routinely keep negative information from their superiors, including feedback about leader behaviors that could be undermining the group's success.[40]

Organizations can pay a high price when followers hide or cover up bad news, deny responsibility, or shift blame. Leaders can't take corrective steps if they don't know a problem exists. Their failure to address serious deficiencies, like safety hazards and accounting fraud, can destroy an organization. Further, leaders who don't get feedback about their ineffective habits can't change these patterns. Teachers who use lots of "ums" and "ahs" in their lectures, for example, need feedback about their speech behaviors from students if they are to eliminate these language features. Finally, denying accountability and shifting blame undermines trust and focuses people on defending themselves instead of on solving the problem.

Declaring that ethical followers should faithfully deliver bad news and accept responsibility for their actions is easier than doing so ourselves. Being the bearer of bad tidings takes courage, as we'll see later in the chapter. The challenge is not so much in determining what to do but in following through. As in delivering all messages, selecting the right time, place, and channel is critical. Significant problems should be brought to light as soon as possible, when the receiver is most receptive, and delivered face to face, not through email or other less personal channels.

William J. LeMessurier is an excellent example of someone who didn't hesitate to deliver bad news that revealed his errors. LeMessurier was the lead structural engineer for the Citicorp tower in New York City, which was completed in 1979. After the building was finished, he discovered that the structure's design and braces made it susceptible to wind damage. The building would likely collapse in a violent storm, which might occur every 16 years. LeMessurier could have kept silent. Instead, he put his professional reputation on the line and admitted his mistakes to the architect and to top Citicorp officers. Working together, LeMessurier and company officials developed a plan to fix the brace problem. In three months, the mistake was fixed. The project manager for the project described the incident and LeMessurier this way: "It started with a guy who stood up and said, 'I got a problem, I made the problem, let's fix the problem.'"[41]

MEETING THE MORAL DEMANDS OF FOLLOWERSHIP: PRINCIPLES AND STRATEGIES

Now that we've identified the ethical duties of the followership role, we'll look at key concepts and tactics designed to help you master these challenges. To be an ethical, effective follower, you will need to redefine what it means to be a follower, overcome unhealthy motivations, and determine when to bring organizational misconduct to the attention of outsiders.

Redefining the Follower Role

Many people equate followership with passivity. To them, being a good follower means taking a subordinate position and deferring to the leader. They focus on carrying out the orders of their superiors. Others take a proactive approach to the follower role. They see themselves as coproducers or partners with leaders, working with them to reach important organizational objectives. Proactive followers are more likely to take the initiative, not only offering feedback and advice to their leaders but also challenging them. Melissa Carsten and Mary Uhl-Bien found that there is a relationship between coproduction beliefs and willingness to engage in unethical behavior.[42] Followers who see themselves as active partners with leaders (possess strong coproduction beliefs) are less likely to obey the unethical directives of their superiors. They are more likely to offer constructive resistance by supplying alternatives or reasons for noncompliance. Followers who view themselves as passive and dependent (hold weak coproduction beliefs) are more likely to submit to unlawful and unethical requests, to engage in "crimes of obedience." They shift or displace responsibility for their actions to their leaders. (Complete Self-Assessment 7.2 to determine your coproduction beliefs.) Carsten and Uhl-Bien's findings suggest that how we define followership has a lot to do with our ethical or unethical behavior as followers. In order to stand up to leaders, we need to consider ourselves as their partners, which may mean that we need to shift our thinking. We share responsibility for the ethical success or failure of the group whether we serve in a leader or follower position. According to the researchers, as followers we can strengthen our ability to remain ethical even when our bosses are not. We can reduce our dependence on our leaders by becoming more marketable (so we can move to other jobs if needed), by becoming more valuable to the organization, and by being willing to do what's right no matter what the consequences. We can build our personal power through building relationships and establishing our competence and reputations. We can become more effective at exerting upward influence through honing our communication skills and developing news ways to approach problems.

Taking a proactive approach to followership not only increases resistance to unethical leader influence, but it also opens the way for followers "lead their leaders" by improving their—the leaders'—moral performance.[43] Followers influence leader ethicality along two dimensions: affiliative/challenging and promotive/prohibitive. *Affiliative* behaviors sustain or strengthen the follower–leader relationship while *challenging* activities can weaken this connection. *Promotive* behaviors encourage something to occur while *prohibitive* behaviors try to stop activities and practices. These two dimensions, in turn, combine into four types of ethical influence tactics which we can use to help shape how our leaders respond to moral dilemmas:

1. *Modeling* (affiliative/promotive). Leaders often look up to followers who model high moral standards and are willing to sacrifice and take responsibility. Such followers encourage leaders to be optimistic about being able to behave ethically. By demonstrating commitment, they encourage leaders to do so as well. Followers thus "teach" leaders how to act ethically and that ethical behavior can be practical and successful.

2. *Eliciting* (challenging/promotive). Eliciting behaviors encourage leaders to "recognize and to act on his/her own values, beliefs, and capabilities." Eliciting followers highlight moral issues, tie these issues to leaders' values, and "sell" issues (get them on the organizational agenda). They use moral language to activate moral schemas and make connections to what leaders believe to be important. For example, a male executive might become more sensitive to sexual harassment if followers point out that his daughter could be the victim of such behavior. Eliciting followers try to promote action by triggering leaders' moral emotions like anger and compassion. They may also point to extreme exemplars to make their arguments. They might ask: "You don't want to become the next Bernie Ebbers (of WorldCom), do you?" Or, conversely: "This sustainability program will put our firm in the same category as Patagonia or Whole Foods Market."

3. *Guiding* (affiliative/prohibitive). Guiding behaviors steer leaders away from bad ethical choices by narrowing their options. This can occur by highlighting particular moral guidelines, increasing the moral intensity of issues, facilitating the discussion of the implications of ethical choices, and highlighting the leader's moral identity (and when the course of action contradicts this identity). Having an ethical culture and climate in place—see Chapter 9—limits the leader's opportunity to engage in immoral activities.

4. *Sensemaking* (challenging/prohibitive) Followers help leaders structure and interpret (make sense of) moral situations. They provide explanations, point out the ethical implications of courses of actions, highlight ethical guidelines and procedures to apply to the decision, point out errors, and tell stories that explain why organizational policies and procedures are in place.

SELF-ASSESSMENT 7.2

Followership Role Orientation Scale

Instructions

In the questions below, think about your beliefs about followers' roles in relation to leaders in an organizational setting. "Follower" refers to an employee who is working with leaders to achieve outcomes. In answering the following questions, please think generally about followers and their interactions with leaders or "higher-ups" in organizations. Please indicate the extent to which you agree with the following statements.

1	2	3	4	5	6
Strongly Disagree	Disagree	Somewhat Disagree	Somewhat Agree	Agree	Strongly Agree

1. Followers should be on the lookout for suggestions they can offer to superiors.
2. Followers should proactively identify problems that could affect the organization.
3. As part of their role, followers must be willing to challenge superiors' assumptions.
4. Followers should be proactive in thinking about things that could go wrong.
5. Followers should communicate their opinions, even when they know leaders may disagree.

Scoring

Add up your score (range 5–30). The higher your score, the more you believe that followers should act as partners with their leaders.

Source: Carsten and Uhl-Bien (2010). Used by permission of Melissa Carsten.

Overcoming Unhealthy Motivations

All too often, followers seek leaders for the wrong reasons. These unhealthy motivations encourage subordinates to tolerate and support the bad leaders described in the last chapter. Toxic followership makes toxic leadership possible. Meeting the ethical challenges of followership, then, begins with avoiding these motivational traps. Professor Lipman-Blumen argues that there are a number of factors that "seduce" us into toxic followership:[44]

- Our need for authority (parentlike) figures
- Our need for security and certainty, which prompts us to abandon our freedom
- Our need to feel chosen or special, which we meet by following a leader apparently engaged in a greater cause
- Our need to be part of a community
- Our fear of being ostracized and isolated from the group
- Our fear that we are powerless to challenge a bad leader
- Our anxiety about life and death, which makes us vulnerable to the illusion that heroic, godlike leaders can protect us
- Our need to be at the center of the action in order to feel alive, meaningful, and in control
- Our desire to identify with a noble vision (which may turn out to be toxic)
- Our feelings of anxiety, caused by uncertainty, change, and crisis, that drive us to leaders for protection
- Our worship of achievement, which makes us admire gifted individuals who may have serious flaws
- Our need for self-esteem, which we meet by aligning ourselves with successful leaders (even when they have toxic qualities)

Lipman-Blumen offers five strategies that can keep us from becoming dependent on toxic leaders while helping us become self-reliant instead. One, recognize that anxiety is a fact of life. Any serious change sparks fear and uncertainty, but we need to step out and take risks despite our fears. Two, learn to act independently—develop the leader within. Become proactive rather than reactive. Work with others to develop democratic organizations where many individuals share leadership responsibilities. Three, demand leaders who tell the truth, no matter how unpleasant that truth might be. Such leaders disillusion us and force us to take our follower duties seriously. Four, beware of leaders with grandiose visions who divide the world into us versus them (see the discussion of moral exclusion in Chapter 8). Five, don't let a few individuals self-select for top positions. View leadership as responsibility to be shared by a variety of group members. Draft worthy candidates for leadership roles based on their character, and limit their terms of service; rotate individuals in and out of leadership positions.

Christian Thoroughgood and his colleagues argue that certain types of individuals are more susceptible to destructive leaders.[45] They identify two categories of vulnerable followers: *conformers* and *colluders*. Conformers are driven by obedience. Passive, these subordinates engage in unethical and illegal activities only when directed to do so by their toxic leaders. Colluders, on the other hand, are actively engaged in supporting the leader's unhealthy goals. They willingly engage in destructive acts. The three conformer subtypes and two colluder subtypes are described below.

1. *Conformers: lost souls.* Lost souls are particularly needy, seeking affection, safety, certainty, or a sense of purpose. These individuals also have an unclear self-concept (which is easily influenced) and suffer from low self-esteem. Lost souls identify with their leaders and obey out of loyalty, hoping to gain their leaders' approval.

2. *Conformers: authoritarians.* Authoritarians believe that leaders have a right to exercise power and they obey orders—including unethical ones—without question. Authoritarians are generally intolerant of outsiders, prefer order and structure, and believe that the world is fair and just. In this fair and just world, victims deserve to suffer or fail because of their behavior or character.

3. *Conformers: bystanders.* Bystanders are more passive than lost souls or authoritarians. They are motivated by fear, believing they will be punished if they don't conform to the leader's wishes. Bystanders have low self-evaluations but are skilled at monitoring their behavior to conform to the wishes of the leader and the group. They tend to be introverts and lack the courage to confront unethical leaders.

4. *Colluders: opportunists.* Opportunists are ambitious and willingly follow destructive leaders to gain money, power, prestige, or status. Like unethical leaders, opportunists are often greedy, manipulative, and narcissistic. They lack self-control as well.

5. *Colluders: acolytes.* Acolytes are "true believers" who share the values and goals of their toxic leaders. They have a clear sense of themselves and behave in a way that is consistent with their identities. Acolytes don't seek rewards like opportunists. Instead, they eagerly participate in unethical and illegal activities because they support the group's destructive mission.

Organizations can take steps to protect themselves from destructive leadership by reducing the susceptibility of followers. Allow followers to challenge their leaders and hold those leaders accountable for unethical behavior. Avoid micromanagement, authoritarian leadership styles, rigid bureaucracies, top-down decision making, and large status and power differentials. Screen out job applicants that demonstrate authoritarian, Machiavellian, and narcissistic tendencies.

Courageous Followership

Government and business consultant Ira Chaleff believes that followership requires courage.[46] He defines courage as accepting a higher level of risk. It's risky for a camp counselor to confront a camp director who is demeaning children, for a shift supervisor to oppose new work rules developed by the plant manager, or for a member of the cabinet to challenge the decision of the president of the United States. Acting courageously is easier if followers recognize that their ultimate allegiance is to the purpose and values of the organization and not to the leader. Chaleff identifies five types of follower courage.

1. *The courage to assume responsibility.* The first dimension of courageous followership specifically addresses the challenge of obligation. Courageous followers assume responsibility for themselves and the organization as a whole. They assess their own performance, elicit feedback from others, seek opportunities for personal growth, manage their tasks, and maintain a healthy personal life. At the same time, they are passionate about the work of the organization as a whole, taking initiative to challenge the status quo by modifying the culture, challenging rules and mind-sets, and improving processes.

2. *The courage to serve.* Courageous followers actively support their leaders, often by working behind the scenes. This service takes the following forms:

   - Helping leaders conserve their energies by focusing their attention on the most important tasks
   - Organizing communication flow from and to the leader
   - Controlling and allowing access to the leader
   - Screening out unsubstantiated criticism of the leader and defending the leader from unjust criticism
   - Relaying a leader's messages in an accurate, effective manner
   - Acting on behalf of the leader when appropriate
   - Shaping a leader's public image
   - Focusing the creative leader on the most fruitful ideas
   - Presenting options during decision making
   - Encouraging the leader to develop healthy peer relationships
   - Preparing for and preventing crises
   - Helping the leader and the group cope with the leader's illness
   - Mediating conflicts between leaders
   - Promoting performance reviews for leaders

3. *The courage to challenge.* Inappropriate behavior threatens the leader–follower relationship and the entire organization. Leaders may engage in petty theft, scream at or use demeaning language with employees, display an arrogant attitude, and engage in sexual harassment. Such behavior needs to be confronted immediately, before it becomes a habit. In some instances, a

gentle, indirect approach will do, as in questioning the wisdom of a policy or focusing attention on the idea or program rather than on the personal shortcomings of the leader. In more extreme cases, followers will need to directly challenge or disobey orders.

4. *The courage to participate in transformation.* Left unchecked, negative behavior patterns can lead to a leader's destruction. But changing ingrained habits is a long, difficult process. Leaders often deny the need to change or justify their behavior. They may claim that anger is an effective management tool or that misleading investors boosts company profits. To modify their behavior, leaders must admit they have a problem, accept responsibility, and desire to change. They are more likely to persist in the change process if they can visualize positive outcomes, like more productive employees, better health, restored relationships, and higher self-esteem. Followers play a critical role in the transformation process by (1) drawing attention to what needs to be changed (and not reinforcing dysfunctional behavior), (2) providing honest feedback, (3) suggesting resources and outside facilitators, (4) creating a supportive climate, (5) modeling openness to change and empathy, (6) helping contain abusive behavior, and (7) providing positive reinforcement when the leader adapts effective new patterns.

5. *The courage to leave.* There are lots of reasons to leave an organization. A new setting may offer more opportunities for personal growth, leaving may help the group as a whole, and followers may be experiencing exhaustion and burnout. However, leaving for principled reasons takes the most courage because it may mean the loss of a job, career, or reputation. Followers should resign when they have failed to fulfill the organization's purpose or have violated an important trust. They may also withdraw their support when those in authority continue their abuse, violate their professed values, serve their own agendas, and ask followers to engage in unethical and illegal behavior.

Chaleff is quick to point out that courageous followership involves more than challenge; it also involves support for the leader. The best followers serve as *partners* with leaders, providing high challenge and high support. Other types of followers fall short on one or both of these dimensions. *Individualistic* followers will speak up when others don't but are seen as unsupportive and thus may be ignored. *Resource* followers don't provide much support or challenge, doing just enough to get by. *Implementer* followers are very supportive but rarely challenge their leaders. Leaders often like followers who use this style. Nevertheless, implementers put their leaders at risk because they don't warn them about problems.

According to Chaleff, identifying your follower style is the first step in developing your courage.[47] Determine whether you function as a partner with your leaders or as an individualist, resource, or implementer instead. Be willing to support your leader, and practice the skills you need to act courageously by role-playing confrontation scenarios like the ones in Application Project 10. When preparing to challenge a leader, try to identify any misperceptions or blind spots you might have as a follower by asking yourself the following questions:

Does what I want from the leader seem reasonable?

Do I need to build or repair trust by giving my leader more or better support?

Is a better strategy needed for raising the issue with the leader?

Do I need to conduct more research or gather more documentation to present my case effectively?

What options should I develop for the leader to consider?

Do I need to change anything about my behavior if I want the leader to transform her or his behavior?

Do I need to do something to reinforce changes already agreed to in earlier conversations?

Are there any other observations or suggestions that I should keep in mind?

Blowing the Whistle

Whistle-blowers are organizational members who decide to remain in the organization but take their concerns about abuses (e.g., bid rigging, bribery, unsafe products, substandard working conditions) to outsiders in the hope of correcting the problem.[48] They often begin by expressing their dissent through organizational channels but end up making problems public when their concerns are ignored. Whistle-blowing is worthy of special attention because whistle-blowers play a critical role in uncovering organizational wrongdoing. They are credited with revealing nearly one out of five fraud cases in large U.S. corporations in one eight-year period.[49] Whistle-blowers triggered high-profile scandals at the Veterans Administration, Abu Ghraib prison, the New York police department, WorldCom, UN peacekeeping forces, and the National Security Agency (NSA). Billionaire investor Warren Buffet acknowledged the importance of whistle-blowing when he declared that his investment firm would have been more successful if it had acted earlier to install a complaint hotline: "Berkshire would be more valuable today if I had put in a whistleblower line decades ago. The issues raised are usually not of a type discovered by audit, but relate instead to personnel and business practices."[50] Several U.S. federal laws are designed to protect whistle-blowers. The 1989 Whistleblower Protection Act forbids retaliation against government employees and was extended in 2007 to cover many government contractors. The Sarbanes-Oxley Act (2002) protects the employees of publicly held companies, and the Dodd-Frank Act of 2010 added additional protections, including financial incentives for coming forward.[51]

Whistle-blowers can pay a steep price for speaking up. Edward Snowden fled to Russia to avoid arrest after revealing that the NSA was spying on United States citizens. In one whistle-blower support group, all had lost their high-paying jobs and careers and most had lost their homes and their families. The researcher studying the group concluded, "An average fate is for a nuclear engineer to end up selling computers at Radio Shack."[52] Those who blew the whistle on wrongdoing in collegiate sports report being labeled as "crazy," subject to increased scrutiny, the victims of physical violence such as tire slashing and shoving, and recipients of death threats.[53] After conducting a national survey of past whistle-blowers, Terrence Miethe concludes, "Exposing organizational misconduct is a low-reward and high-risk activity."[54]

Not all whistle-blowers experience retaliation, but dissenters should be prepared to be attacked instead of supported. They may be abandoned by coworkers, criticized or humiliated by superiors, attacked by supporters of the organization, denied promotions, relegated to meaningless positions, cut off from neighbors, and on and on. (See Case Study 7.3 for an example of what happened to one young whistle-blower.) And federal regulations have been of little help. Whistle-blowers won only 4 out of the first 10,000 cases brought under the 1989 statute. During one month, 499 out of 677 complaints filed under Sarbanes-Oxley were dismissed, and 95 out of the remaining complaints were withdrawn.[55] It costs somewhere between $50,000 and $100,000 to pursue a case through the federal court system. No wonder that of employees who witness unethical conduct, many (37%) do not report the misconduct to the proper authorities.[56] Students are also reluctant to blow the whistle. Only half of 2,000 doctoral students surveyed would report that faculty members falsified research data, used university resources for private consulting, discriminated against students, or engaged in other forms of misconduct.[57]

In light of the risks, blowing the whistle on organizational wrongdoing takes a great deal of courage. Yet courage by itself is not enough. Whistle-blowers must also engage in careful ethical reasoning. They have to determine where their ultimate loyalty should rest and whether the disruption they will cause is justified. When the whistle blows, everyone in the organization suffers. Workers lose their jobs, the credibility of the organization is damaged, stock prices decline, and so forth.

Ethicist Sissela Bok divides the act of whistle-blowing into three parts to help ethical decision makers weigh the moral implications of exposing misbehavior to outsiders.[58] Each element of the process raises ethical questions, which are summarized by R. A. Johnson in Ethical Checkpoint 7.1. *Dissent* addresses the relative benefits of going public. Most whistle-blowers believe that their actions will benefit society as a whole. Before going forward, they need to determine if this is indeed the case. Whistle-blowers break their *loyalty* to fellow members and to the group as a whole. Therefore, whistle-blowing should be used only as a last resort, when time is limited and internal channels aren't an option. Doing so may be the only way to serve the organization's mission, values, and goals, however. Whistle-blowers bring serious charges against individuals in public. *Accusation* highlights the fact that dissenters are ethically obligated to consider such issues as fairness, the public's right to know, anonymity, and their personal motives.

ETHICAL CHECKPOINT 7.1

The Whistle-Blower Checklist

Dissent: When whistle-blowers claim their dissent will achieve a public good, they must ask

- What is the nature of the promised benefit?
- How accurate are the facts?
- How serious is the impropriety?
- How imminent is the threat?
- How closely linked to the wrongdoing are those accused?

Loyalty: When whistle-blowers breach loyalty to their organization, they must ask

- Is whistle-blowing the last and only alternative?
- Is there no time to use routine channels?
- Are internal channels corrupted?
- Are there no internal channels?

Accusation: When whistle-blowers are publicly accusing others, they must ask

- Are the accusations fair?
- Does the public have a right to know?
- Is the whistle-blower *not* anonymous?
- Are the motives *not* self-serving?

Source: From Whistleblowing: When It Works—And Why by Roberta Ann Johnson. Copyright © 2002 by Lynne Rienner Publishers, Inc. Used with permission of the publisher.

As managers, we can take steps to encourage employees to blow the whistle internally so corrective actions can be taken without incurring the costs of going public.[59] These steps are both preventive and responsive. Preventive actions are designed to reduce the likelihood that wrongdoing will occur in the first place. Responsive actions address whistle-blower complaints. Create tough antiretaliation policies, and disseminate those policies throughout the organization. Identify types of unethical behavior, and spell out what employees should do if they observe such actions. When an employee makes a complaint, concentrate on the wrongdoing and not on the whistle-blower. Thoroughly investigate all reports, and take quick action when justified. Publicize corrective actions, and monitor to make sure retaliation doesn't occur.

CHAPTER TAKEAWAYS

- Both leaders and followers determine the ethical performance of organizations.

- The ethical challenges of leaders and followers are a product of their complementary roles. As a leader, you will have power, broader authority, and more responsibility for the overall direction of the group. As a follower, you are accountable for implementing plans and carrying out the work.

- The six moral demands you'll face as a leader include (1) the challenge of power, (2) the challenge of privilege, (3) the challenge of information management, (4) the challenge of consistency, (5) the challenge of loyalty, and (6) the challenge of responsibility.

- Failure to meet the ethical challenges of the leadership role leads to a variety of misbehaviors that constitute the dark, or shadow, side of leadership. Understanding this side of leadership can keep you from casting shadows.

- Shadow leaders have been described as bad (ineffective and/or unethical), toxic (engaging in antisocial behaviors and demonstrating dysfunctional characteristics), and selfish (impulsive, narcissistic, Machiavellian).

- We can keep from casting shadows by sharing power, remaining accountable, and being alert to signs of toxicity and selfishness in ourselves.

- Servant leaders avoid the ethical pitfalls of the leadership role by putting the needs of followers first. They are person centered (altruistic), promote justice, demonstrate ethical character, and practice stewardship.

- Authentic leaders reflect a high level of self-understanding, and their actions are consistent with their core values. They demonstrate self-awareness, balanced processing (they can remain objective when receiving information), and an internalized moral perspective based on internal standards and relational transparency. You can develop authenticity by developing your ethical skills and knowledge and by increasing your level of self-awareness. You can become more self-aware by drawing lessons from past events, building your current level of self-efficacy, and identifying emerging trends that will shape you and your organization in the future.

- The moral demands you'll face as a follower are the challenge of obligation, the challenge of obedience, the challenge of cynicism, the challenge of dissent, and the challenge of delivering bad news.

- If you see yourself as an active partner with your leaders, you will be less likely to obey unethical directives and can help improve the moral performance of your supervisors.

- Beware of fear, anxiety, the need to belong, and other forces that can make you dependent on toxic leaders. Learn to live with anxiety, and don't be afraid to act independently. Demand leaders who tell the truth; avoid those with grandiose visions. Don't let a few selfish individuals select themselves as leaders, but draft a large number of organizational members to take on leadership responsibilities. Screen out susceptible followers who are tempted to conform to or collude with destructive leaders.

- You will need to demonstrate courage if you are to fulfill your ethical duties as a follower. Dimensions of courage include the courage to assume responsibility, the courage to serve, the courage to challenge, the courage to participate in transformation, and the courage to leave. Develop your courage by seeking to serve as a partner with your leader, practicing the skills you need to act courageously and identifying possible misperceptions or blind spots you have as a follower.

- Whistle-blowing is bringing wrongdoing to the attention of outsiders. The possibility of retaliation means you will need courage to be a whistle-blower. You'll also have to engage in careful moral reasoning, weighing the relative benefits of going public, breaking loyalties, and publicly accusing others. Take steps to encourage others to blow the whistle by setting tough antiretaliation policies and by taking quick corrective action when complaints surface.

APPLICATION PROJECTS

1. In a group, identify additional ethical demands on leaders and followers that you would add to those in the chapter.

2. Create a case study that illustrates how a leader or follower responded to one of the ethical challenges.

3. Which ethical challenge is the most difficult to resolve? Write up your conclusions.

4. Debate the following propositions.
   - The power of followers is growing.
   - Studying the dark side of leadership can help us become more ethical leaders.
   - Authenticity is the most important characteristic a leader can have.
   - Incompetent leaders are unethical leaders.

- It is impossible to practice servant leadership in certain situations.
- Narcissistic individuals can be effective leaders.

5. Share your score from the Servant Leadership Questionnaire (Self-Assessment 7.1) with a partner. Explain why you rated this individual the way you did and how she/he might improve. How do you think you would rate if others evaluated you?

6. If you have a leadership role, spend a week trying to function as a servant leader. Summarize your experience, paying particular attention to how acting as a servant may have changed your attitudes and behaviors.

7. Describe toxic followership. Explain how toxic followership and toxic leadership are related.

8. Develop a strategy for improving the ethical performance of one of your leaders.

9. Have you had to display any of the dimensions of courageous followership? Share your story in a small group.

10. Role-play these confrontation scenarios:

    You are the vice president for product development at a large manufacturing firm. Your division is ready to begin work on a major new product line. Due to the investment required to develop the new products, the board of directors has to give its approval. Your boss, the company CEO, has enthusiastically supported the project. That's why his behavior at last night's board meeting was so disappointing. When several board members began to express opposition to your plans after your presentation, the CEO agreed with them and stated that the new product line was "not well thought out." You are scheduled to meet with the CEO this morning to debrief the board session.

    You are the director of an MBA program at a private university. On more than one occasion, the president of your school has exaggerated the number of students in your program when making presentations to donors. He continues to overstate enrollments, even though you have provided him with the correct figures. You have an appointment with him to discuss other items but want to address this issue as well.

    You are a junior accountant at a small accounting firm. You notice that your supervisor, who generates the most income for your business, appears to be advising clients to claim unauthorized deductions on their tax forms. She denies that she is doing anything illegal and asserts that she is trying to save money for her hard-working clients. You, however, are unconvinced by her arguments and set up a meeting to confront her about the deductions.

11. Analyze the actions of a whistle-blower using Bok's checklist. Was this person justified in coming forward?

CASE STUDY 7.1

Failing to Serve Those Who Served

The mission of the Veterans Affairs health care system is to meet the medical needs of armed forces personnel. To fulfill this mission, the VA operates the largest medical organization in the United States, with 9 million enrollees receiving treatment at 150 medical centers

(Continued)

(Continued)

and 800 outpatient clinics. The VA also provides annual disability payments to 4 million veterans.

Demand for VA medical services has skyrocketed as Vietnam vets age and as service personnel from Iraq and Afghanistan (many with traumatic brain injuries and post-traumatic stress disorder) return from their deployments to the Middle East. At the same time, the agency has trouble recruiting and retaining medical personnel. The number of outpatient visits grew by 26% in a recent five-year period while the number of doctors and nurses went up by only 18%. As a result, veterans have trouble getting appointments for care and are placed on wait lists.

To shorten the waiting time for treatment, former VA director Eric Shinseki mandated that new patients be seen within two weeks of contacting a medical center or clinic. Middle- and senior-level managers were given bonuses and promotions for meeting this objective. Unfortunately, Shinseki's mandate didn't solve the access problem but drove it underground. Managers "gamed the system" by falsifying patient access records. They created secret waiting lists that contained the actual number of veterans seeking treatment. At the same time they created another set of shorter lists to present to VA administrators. According to these "official" lists, facilities were meeting the guidelines, which meant that managers received their bonuses. In other cases officials kept wait times down by failing to record new patients, marking the first available appointment as the one requested by the veteran, or by canceling previously scheduled appointments.

The sham wait lists came to light after a doctor at the Phoenix VA medical center complained. An audit by the Veterans Administration inspector general discovered that the deceptive practices extended well beyond the Phoenix facility, revealing what Secretary Shinseki called "a systemic, totally unacceptable lack of integrity."[1] Two thirds of Veterans' facilities manipulated data in at least one instance in order to conceal the true extent of the access problem. An estimated 100,000 veterans (1,700 in Phoenix) were kept off official waiting lists and, in some cases, were not scheduled for the appointments they requested. The average wait time for Phoenix veterans was 115 days, and 18 to 40 patients died while waiting for care, though it is not clear if the deaths were caused by the delay in treatment. (Some on the list were terminally ill and requested end-of-life care.)

The VA inspector general put much of the blame on VA leadership for creating an "overarching environment and culture that allowed this state of practice to take root."[2] The audit called for a complete overhaul of the VA's performance management system. A White House report said that the VA medical system had a "corrosive culture" that "encourages discontent and backlash against employees."[3]

Americans were outraged at the reports of the falsified records and lengthy wait times. Military personnel risk their lives for their country, and citizens honor their loyalty and devotion by pledging to meet their needs during and after active service. Lengthy wait times break what former president Barack Obama called the "sacred trust" between the country and those who serve in uniform.

VA director Shinseki was forced to resign under pressure from congressional representatives. The new director eliminated the 14-day scheduling goal, froze all executive bonuses, vowed to change the reward system to discourage hiding the truth, and promised to fire those engaged in deceptive practices. The agency contacted those who were on the secret lists to initiate treatment. With bipartisan support, Congress passed legislation that allows veterans to seek treatment at private clinics (called Veterans Choice) when they can't promptly schedule VA appointments or live more than 40 miles away from a veterans facility. Congress also approved $10 billion for hiring more staff and building more hospitals.

Problems continued despite the changes. Managers at some facilities still falsified wait times. The director of the Shreveport, Louisiana, VA hospital was fired after a report that patients went without sheets, pajamas, and toiletries while the facility spent millions on televisions, solar panels, and furniture. The VA inspector general warned that patients at the VA Medical Center in Washington, DC, were in danger because the hospital ran out of surgical supplies and tools. The Veterans Choice program actually increased wait times. Not only is Veterans Choice complicated and confusing, but it requires that patients apply for (and wait for) the waiver to see private doctors. Private physicians and hospitals complain that it takes up to a year for them to be reimbursed for veteran treatment.

David Shulkin, the newest director of the Veterans Administration, vows to continue efforts to better serve patients He wants to simplify and expand Veterans Choice, speed up provider reimbursements, track service quality, reduce overhead, and modernize facilities. He points out that the agency has retrained schedulers and updated software and plans to roll out a program that allows vets to book their own appointments. Evening and weekend hours have been added to the schedule along with 14,000 new medical providers.

Discussion Probes

1. Have you or has someone you know been treated by the VA health system? What type of experience did you or this other person have?

2. What leadership challenges did VA managers fail to meet?

3. What steps can the VA take to encourage managers to act as servant leaders?

4. How does the size of the VA medical system complicate efforts to improve the organization's culture and service to patients?

5. What, if any, additional steps should the VA take to address the patient access problem and to improve treatment quality?

Notes

1. Shear and Joachim (2014).
2. Daley (2014).
3. Zoroya (2014).

Sources: Carter (2014). Goodnough (2014). Kaplan (2014). Lawrence, Whitney, and Tomsic (2016). Ogrysko (2017). Perez (2014). Richards (2017). Shear and Oppel (2014). Slack (2016, 2017). Tritten (2014). Wagner (2014).

CASE STUDY 7.2

Challenging the Chancellor

The shooting death of unarmed black teen Michael Brown in Ferguson, Missouri, heightened awareness of racial issues on college campuses around the country. At the University of Missouri–Columbia campus, only 120 miles from Ferguson, a series of racial incidents sparked

(Continued)

(Continued)

tensions. On Facebook, African American student government president Payton Head reported being the victim of racial slurs yelled from the back of passing pickup truck. Head posted:

> I really just want to know why my simple existence is such a threat to society. For those of you who wonder why I'm always talking about the importance of inclusion and respect, it's because I've experienced moments like this multiple times at THIS university, making me not feel included here.[1]

Later in the same semester a drunken white student interrupted an African American student group preparing for homecoming and responded with a racial epithet when asked to leave. In another incident someone used feces to draw a swastika on the wall of a residence hall.

Angered by the slow response of administrators to Head's complaint and the other incidents, protestors (including some faculty) held "Racism Lives Here" rallies. Demonstrators locked hands to block the car of Missouri University system chancellor Timothy Wolfe during a homecoming parade. Wolfe didn't acknowledge the demonstrators and his car bumped one of the protestors. Head wrote that the chancellor "smiled and laughed" during the demonstration.

Shortly after homecoming, a student group named Concerned Student 1950 (named for the year African American students were first admitted to the university) issued a list of demands, the most important being that Wolfe resign as chancellor. Graduate student Jonathan Butler launched a hunger strike after the chancellor met with Concerned Student 1950 members but refused to meet their conditions. Butler was motivated in part by his participation in the Ferguson protests and by the university's decision to eliminate health insurance for graduate student employees. He refused to eat until Wolfe left his post.

Students at 80 other colleges expressed their solidarity with protestors at the University of Missouri. Thirty black players on the Missouri football team, with the support of Coach Gary Pinkel, a number of white players, and the athletic department, announced they wouldn't practice or play until Butler ended his fast. This boycott put the university at risk of forfeiting a game and having to pay a $1 million penalty to the Southeastern Athletic Conference. The next day Chancellor Wolfe resigned, saying later that he "had no choice" due to worries about violence on campus.

The chancellor's resignation didn't end racism on campus. Tensions continue as black students, largely from Kansas City and St. Louis, interact with white students largely from rural areas. The two groups generally remain segregated. In one incident a year later, white men yelled racial slurs and insults at a two black coeds walking in front of a fraternity house. The response of campus leaders was much quicker than in the past, however. Campus police immediately identified the offending students and administrators met with the victims of the abuse, offering counseling and other support. Mizzou continues to make progress toward Concerned Student 1950's demands, including an increase in black faculty and minority counselors at the Student Counseling Center and a long-term plan to improve the retention rates of marginalized students.

Discussion Probes

1. What risks did students (and some faculty) take in participating in the protests?
2. Would the protest have succeeded without the participation of the football team? Why or why not?

3. What did the football team, coach, and athletic department stand to lose in supporting the hunger strike? What did they stand to lose if they didn't support the protests?

4. How should campus leaders—staff and students—prevent and respond to racially charged incidents?

5. Can you think of other cases where students have been able to bring about significant changes in campus administration? What strategies did they use?

6. What do you learn about expressing dissent from this case?

Note

1. Serven (2015).

Sources: Eligon (2015). Eligon and Perez-Pena (2015). Lecci (2016). Nadkarni (2015). "One Year After" (2016). Pearce (2015). M. Pearson (2015). Svriuga (2016). M. Tracy and Southall (2015).

CASE STUDY 7.3

Putting Fraud Before Family

Stanford graduate Tyler Shultz probably thought he had landed the perfect job. After interning at Theranos labs, he was hired on full time. He started as a member of the team that verified the accuracy of blood tests and later moved to the company's production area. Tyler wasn't the only family member connected with Theranos. His grandfather George Shultz, who had served in the cabinets of Richard Nixon and Ronald Reagan, sat on the Theranos board of directors. In fact, Tyler first met Theranos founder Elizabeth Holmes at his grandfather's house and was inspired by her vision for the company.

A college dropout, Holmes started Theranos (the name is a combination the words of "therapy" and "diagnosis") at age 19. She claimed that her company had a new, less painful and less intrusive way to conduct blood tests. Instead of using a needle to draw blood from the arm, Holmes touted the fact that Theranos's Edison machine could analyze a drop of blood taken from a finger prick. She told investors and the public that this new technology could save lives and "change the world." Holmes raised $680 million for the company (at one time valued at $9 billion) and partnered with Walgreens to establish wellness centers in a number of its stores. She was featured on the covers of *Fortune*, *Forbes*, *Inc.*, and other publications and was inducted into the Harvard Medical School Board of Fellows.

Holmes liked to think of herself as a "female Steve Jobs," dressing like her hero in black turtlenecks, never taking a vacation, sitting in his favorite type of office chair, and becoming a vegan like him. Most importantly, she adopted Jobs's obsession with secrecy. Employees were strictly forbidden to share information about their projects with each other, and the company prevented outside scientists from writing peer-reviewed papers on its Edison device. Theranos was quick to threaten to sue employees to prevent them from speaking to the media. When a company scientist committed suicide,

(Continued)

(Continued)

a Theranos representative called his widow—not to offer condolences, but to demand that she return any confidential company property. Holmes herself was always vague about how her technology worked, saying at one point, "A chemistry is performed so that a chemical reaction occurs and generates a signal from the chemical interaction with the sample, which is translated into a result, which is then reviewed by certified laboratory personnel."[1]

Shortly after taking his new position, Tyler Shultz discovered that the company's touted Edison blood testing technology produced wildly varying results from the same blood sample. The company discarded some findings and made inflated claims about how accurate the tests were. For example, Theranos claimed that the Edison machine could detect sexual transmitted diseases 95% of the time even though the tests were only 65% to 85% accurate. Shultz also discovered that blood-testing machines failed quality controls. Alarmed, he emailed CEO Holmes with his concerns. Holmes then turned his message over to company president Sunny Balwani. Balwani responded by belittling Shultz for not understanding basic math or laboratory science. "The only reason I have taken so much time away from work to address this personally is because you are Mr. Shultz's grandson," Balwani said dismissively. "Had this email come from anyone else in the company, I would have already held them accountable for the arrogant and patronizing tone and reckless comments."[2]

George Shultz came to the defense of Theranos, not his grandson. (Tyler claims that he spoke out in part to protect the reputation of his grandfather.) When Holmes told George that his grandson was being "unreasonable" and would "lose" if he continued to challenge the company, he called Tyler's parents. They phoned Tyler with a frantic message the day he quit the firm, asking him to stop "whatever you're about to do." On one of Tyler's visits to his grandfather, the elder Shultz ushered in two attorneys, who served Tyler with a temporary restraining order, a notice to appear in court, and a letter alleging he had leaked company trade secrets. (George Shultz later said he thought that the lawyers were going to present a confidentiality agreement for Tyler to sign.) Tyler resisted the legal pressure, asserting, "Fraud is not a trade secret."[3]

Tyler took his concerns to New York regulators and writer John Carreyrou at *The Wall Street Journal*, who produced a series of articles exposing the fraud. Holmes and Theranos were initially defiant. Holmes went on CNBC's *Mad Money*, defending herself with a variation of a line from Steve Jobs: "This is what happens when you work to change things. First they think you're crazy, then they fight you, and then, all of a sudden, you change the world."[4] At a company pep rally, Holmes vented her anger at the *Journal*, claiming it had a vendetta against the company. Employees starting chanting "F*** you, Carrey-rou!"

Ultimately, Holmes was forced to admit that Theranos outsourced nearly all of its tests to other labs, and the company invalidated all in-house results for 2014 and 2015. Federal regulators shut down the company's California lab after finding problems that posed "immediate jeopardy" to patient safety. Holmes and Balwani were banned from running laboratories for two years. The CEO's net worth went from $4 billion to nearly nothing. Theranos laid off 40% of its workforce and no longer does blood testing, focusing instead on manufacturing medical equipment for clinics.

Fallout from the fraud continues. The company is being investigated by the U.S. attorney's office, the FBI, and the Securities and Exchange Commission. It faces lawsuits from investors as well as patients. Walgreens filed a $140 million suit alleging that Holmes and Balwani had broken their promises and made false statements. Theranos assured Walgreens that its Edison machine had been validated by the 10 largest pharmaceutical companies and was widely used by research institutions, governments, and military organizations. Neither statement was true.

For Tyler Shultz, vindication has not reduced the financial and relational costs of whistle-blowing. His parents may have to refinance their house to pay for $400,000 in legal bills generated by his court battles against Theranos. His family remains split. A spokesman for George Shultz says he is proud of Tyler, but the two communicate only through lawyers. Tyler didn't attend the elder Shultz's 95th birthday party (though Holmes did).

Discussion Probes

1. Were there signs that Theranos was engaged in fraud before the scandal broke?
2. What shadows did CEO Holmes cast?
3. Do you fault investors for not doing enough investigation into Theranos before investing? Do you fault Walgreens for partnering with Theranos?
4. Why do you think George Shultz sided with the company instead of his grandson?
5. Should Theranos be forced to pay Tyler Shultz's legal bills?
6. What qualities does Tyler Shultz share with other whistle-blowers?

Notes

1. Mole (2016b).
2. Bilton (2016).
3. Stockton (2016).
4. Mole (2016b).

Sources: Durden (2016a, 2016b). Farr (2016). Masnick (2016). Mole (2016a). Wilkinson (2016).

CHAPTER EIGHT

IMPROVING GROUP ETHICAL PERFORMANCE

Chapter Preview

Acting as a Morally Responsible Team Member
    Adopting a Cooperative Orientation
    Doing Your Fair Share (Not Loafing)
    Displaying Openness and Supportiveness
    Being Willing to Stand Alone

Responding to Ethical Danger Signs
    Groupthink
    Polythink
    Mismanaged Agreement
    Escalating Commitment
    Excessive Control
    Moral Exclusion

Chapter Takeaways
Application Projects

Groups play a larger role than ever in the workplace. Most significant projects—creating a video game or film, building an apartment complex, opening a new market, raising money for a nonprofit—require the efforts of teams of people. Self-directed work groups are now charged with everything from organizing the assembly line to hiring and firing. Teams, not individuals, generally make important organizational decisions.

Groups tend to bring out the moral best and worst in us. If you're like me, some of your proudest moments are associated with small groups. Your team may have completed a service project for your local community or determined how to fairly distribute student fees to campus organizations. (See Case Study 8.1 for an example of outstanding group moral performance.) At the same time, some of your most regrettable moments (like mine) may also relate to group experiences. Your team may have made poor moral choices and convinced you to engage in unethical activities.

Transforming our teams so that they spur us to higher, not lower, moral performance is the goal of this chapter. Achieving that end requires that we act as morally responsible group members and help our teams steer clear of ethical dangers.

ACTING AS A MORALLY RESPONSIBLE TEAM MEMBER

Group membership does not excuse us from our individual ethical responsibilities. Quite the contrary; in small groups, our behaviors can have a significant impact on the team's ethical success or failure.[1] We have a duty to apply the concepts and skills discussed in earlier chapters—ethical theories, character, moral reasoning, and ethical communication competencies—to the team setting. In addition, we need to adopt a cooperative orientation, do our fair share of the work, be open and supportive, and offer dissent.

Adopting a Cooperative Orientation

In Chapter 4, we noted that the outcome of interpersonal communication is dependent on the attitude we bring to our conversations. The same is true for our group interactions. Groups committed to cooperation can accomplish great things. Conversely, if we lack this commitment to working together, our performance, as well as that of the team as a whole, is likely to suffer.

A cooperative orientation is based on the realization that an individual's success is dependent on the success of other team members.[2] To reach shared goals, everyone must do her or his part. This perspective stands in sharp contrast to individualistic and competitive points of view. Individualistic members rely on their own efforts to achieve their private agendas. For example, an individualist assigned to a class project group puts personal goals (developing a romantic relationship with someone else on the team, earning an A in another class) ahead of the collective goal of producing an excellent presentation. Competitive group members achieve their objectives at the expense of others. They want to earn the highest grade in the class, for instance, or get promoted ahead of other employees. In order to succeed, they may withhold information or claim too much credit for the group's success.

Individualism and competition are celebrated in Western culture but are counterproductive in small groups. In an analysis of the results of over 100 studies, brothers David and Roger Johnson and their colleagues found that in the vast majority of cases, cooperative groups had higher levels of achievement and productivity.[3] No matter what the subject matter (math, psychology, physical education), task (problem solving, retention and memory, categorization), and age group (elementary school through adult), cooperative groups are more successful. That's because cooperative team members are more likely to do these things:[4]

- Help one another
- Put forth more effort and invest more time in completing the task
- Support (reinforce) the identities of other group members
- Are open to influence from others

- Detect and correct errors in reasoning
- Generate more new ideas, strategies, and solutions
- Think clearly because they feel relaxed
- Engage in healthy conflict that refines solutions
- Develop positive relationships with other group members
- Understand the perspectives of other team members
- Share accurate messages and accurately interpret messages from others
- Provide positive feedback to other members, which builds self-esteem
- Value and accept differences
- Demonstrate a positive attitude toward the task
- Act in trustworthy ways
- Enjoy better psychological health
- Share resources

In light of this evidence, we have an ethical duty to behave in a cooperative manner while encouraging others to do the same. We need to ask ourselves if we are committed to the success of the group and can put aside our desire to pursue personal agendas and to best others. If we can't answer in the affirmative, a change in attitude or withdrawal from the group is in order. As group members, we should avoid playing these selfish group roles: (1) *the aggressor* who attacks the ideas, opinions, values and beliefs of others; employs aggressive humor; and makes personal judgments; (2) *the blocker* who resists the input of others and brings up "dead" proposals after the team has rejected them; (3) *the recognition-seeker* who claims to be more expert and knowledgeable on almost every topic; (4) *the player* who doesn't care or is cynical and jokes around at the wrong times; or (5) *the dominator* who demonstrates lack of respect, engages in disconfirmation and frequently interrupts.[5]

To foster cooperation, engage in such communication behaviors as proposing compromises or concessions, carrying through on promises, pointing out the need to cooperate, asking for help, and accurately paraphrasing others' points of view.[6] The group as a whole needs to make sure that the team pursues a joint product, which fosters interdependence, and not a series of individual products, which encourages individualistic or competitive behavior. Collectively, members should divide the work fairly, hold individuals responsible for their assignments, reward the team as whole (not individual members), involve everyone in decision making, engage in constructive conflict (see Chapter 6), and emphasize shared values, like a commitment to service or quality.

Fostering cooperation is key to project management. Project managers direct teams that build bridges, develop new products, manage software installations, and carry out other major initiatives. We can adopt the strategies they use to encourage collaboration in our class project teams and other groups. Successful project managers engage in collaborative decision making, helping team members define their goals, logistics, schedules, subtasks, and deliverables as the group launches. They require documentation of individual and collective work through traditional (memos, project logs, reports) and electronic (blogs, online discussion) means. Such documentation keeps members informed about the activities of others and can help the team work together more effectively. Project leaders also encourage ongoing assessment and reflection. This allows members to adjust roles and assignments as needed to better coordinate their efforts.[7]

Cooperation between groups can be as important as cooperation within groups. The success of any organization depends in large part on the coordinated efforts of teams and units. Product designers, production staff, shippers, and marketers must work together to roll out a new athletic shoe; nurses, doctors, pharmacists, housekeeping staff, and dieticians coordinate their efforts to meet the needs of hospital patients; employees of newly merged companies have to integrate their products, production facilities, offices, and payroll.

Promoting intergroup cooperation—collaboration between organizational subgroups—can be challenging.[8] Often the units being asked to work together have been competing with one another for organizational resources like money, staff, and facilities. They may differ in status as well, as in the case of a business acquisition. Employees of the newly acquired firm have less power and may feel alienated as the dominant group tries to impose its values and culture on them. Group identities are the most significant barrier to intergroup coordination, however. Most of us define ourselves according to our group memberships, referring to ourselves as business students, engineers, salespeople, or lawyers. These group identities favor the in-group over the out-group. In addition, we prefer leaders who put the interests of our group over those of outside groups. If you are called upon to lead more than one team, you can promote intergroup collaboration by doing the following:[9]

1. *Encouraging interaction between units*. Provide opportunities for members of different teams to interact informally through meals, social activities, and shared hobbies. Emphasize the need to achieve a shared goal like rolling out a new product or overseeing a change initiative. Promote universal values like equality and respect for others.

2. *Creating an intergroup relational identity*. Encourage members to develop a dual identity, where they see themselves as members of the larger organization as well as members of their subgroups. Create dual identities by developing a shared vision and by emphasizing the importance of coordination. Remind units that collaboration helps each subgroup maintain its own unique goals and values.

3. *Boundary spanning*. Bridge or span groups by having frequent contact with members of every team. Develop quality relationships with individuals from all groups and be careful not to favor one unit over the other. Embody intergroup relational identity by leading both groups. Act as a role model for cooperation.

Doing Your Fair Share (Not Loafing)

Many attempts to create a cooperative climate falter because participants fail to do their fair share of the work. Scholars use the term *social loafing* to describe the tendency of individuals to reduce their efforts when working in a group. Interest in this phenomenon can be traced back to the 1880s. In one of the first experimental studies in social psychology, a researcher asked male volunteers to pull on a rope.[10] He discovered that as the size of the group increased, each man exerted less force. Modern investigators have determined that social loafing is common on all kinds of teams, though individuals differ in their tendency to slack off. Women and people from Eastern cultures are less likely to reduce their efforts, for example. Those who enjoy thinking maintain their efforts when engaged in intellectually demanding group activities. Conscientious individuals and those motivated by a high need for achievement continue to work as hard in a group as they do on their own.[11] (Complete Self-Assessment 8.1 to determine how much social loafing took place in your group and to determine what impact this behavior had on your team.)

SELF-ASSESSMENT 8.1

Class Project Social Loafing Scale

Instructions

To identify the behaviors associated with their impact on team performance, respond to the following questions based on your recent experiences with *one* social loafer in a class project team.

1. **What Did the Social Loafer Do?**

   1 = Does NOT describe AT ALL
   2 = Describes the LEAST
   3 = Does not describe much
   4 = Describes SOMEWHAT
   5 = Describes the MOST

   - Member had *trouble attending* team meetings
   - Member had *trouble paying attention* to what was going on in the team
   - Member was *mostly silent* during the team meetings
   - Member *engaged in side conversations* a lot while the team was working
   - Member came *poorly prepared* to the team meetings
   - Member *contributed poorly* to the team discussions when present
   - Member had trouble *completing team-related homework*
   - Member *mostly declined to take on any work for the team*
   - Member did *a poor job* of the work she or he was assigned
   - Member did *poor quality* work
   - Member *mostly distracted* from the team's focus on its goals and objectives
   - Member *did not fully participate* in the team's formal presentation

2. **What Was the Impact of the Social Loafer on Your Team?**

   Indicate the extent to which you agree or disagree with the following statements about the IMPACT the SOCIAL LOAFER had on your team (1 = *strongly disagree*; 2 = *disagree*; 3 = *neither agree nor disagree*; 4 = *agree*; 5 = *strongly agree*)

As a result of the SOCIAL LOAFING . . .

- The team took *longer than anticipated* to complete its tasks
- The team meetings *lasted longer* than expected
- The team had *fewer good ideas* than other teams

- Team members had to *waste their time* explaining things to the social loafer
- Other team members *had to do more* than their share of work
- Other team members were *frustrated and angry*
- There was a higher level of *stress* on the team
- Other team members had to *redo or revise* the work done by the social loafer
- The work had to be *reassigned* to other members of the team
- The team's final *presentation* was not as high quality as that of other teams
- The team *missed* deadlines

Source: Adapted from Jassawalla, Malshe, and Sashittal (2008). Used by permission.

Social psychologists Steven Karau and Kipling Williams developed the collective effort model (CEM) to identify the causes of social loafing.[12] They theorize that the motivation of group members depends on three factors: (1) *expectancy:* how much an individual expects that his or her effort will lead to high group performance; (2) *instrumentality:* the strength of the perceived relationship between personal and group effort and group achievement; and (3) *valence:* how desirable the outcome is for individual group members. (Ethical Checkpoint 8.1 describes how these factors also operate in the online environment.)

Motivation drops when any of these factors is low. Individuals are more likely to slack off in collectives because the group can still succeed even if they do less (low expectancy). Participants may also believe that the group won't succeed—win a majority of its games, secure a contract—no matter how hard they and their fellow group members try (low instrumentality). Or participants may not value the group's goal or outcome (low valence). Karau, Williams, and other investigators treat social loafing as undesirable, unethical behavior that undermines cooperation, encourages others to slack off for fear of being seen as "suckers," and diminishes the productivity of the group as a whole. They've identified ways to reduce or eliminate this phenomenon through the strategies outlined below. Each set of tactics is designed to address one of the three elements of motivation.[13]

Strategies for Increasing Expectancy

Take these steps to reinforce the tie between individual efforts and successful group performance:

- Select members carefully and match them to tasks.
- Provide training in needed skills.
- Set challenging yet realistic goals.
- Supply needed resources and support.
- Build feelings of self-efficacy.
- Raise the visibility of individual tasks.
- Monitor individual efforts.

Strategies for Increasing Instrumentality

Use the following to link individual performance to group performance:

- Make sure tasks are not too demanding.
- Reduce the size of the group so that members don't feel that their efforts are redundant.
- Point out that each member is making a unique, valuable contribution.
- Clarify how individual efforts relate to the team's final product.

Link group performance and outcomes this way:

- Recognize group work.
- Evaluate team products.
- Create norms that emphasize high performance standards.

Outcomes

Use these methods to increase the positive value of the group's collective product to members:

- Offer meaningful, interesting work that becomes intrinsically motivating.
- Provide tangible incentives like raises and bonuses.
- Encourage members to identify with the group.
- Strengthen the social bonds between members.
- Create norms that foster a sense of group pride and mutual obligation.

Displaying Openness and Supportiveness

Ethical team members are both open and supportive.[14] *Openness* refers to an individual's willingness to surface issues and talk about problems while, at the same time, enabling others to do the same. *Supportiveness* denotes the desire to help others succeed. Supportive group members encourage and defend others, help teammates overcome obstacles, and put the goals of the group first. These two characteristics work together. Openness by itself could pave the way for brutal honesty, insults, and sarcasm, so ethical issues must be discussed in a supportive manner. Otherwise, participants feel threatened and divert their attention from understanding and problem solving to defending themselves. Poorer ethical choices result.

Psychologist Jack Gibb identified six pairs of behaviors that promote either a defensive or a supportive group climate.[15] Our moral duty as group members is to engage in supportive communication that contributes to a positive emotional climate and accurate understanding. At the same time, we need to draw attention to the comments of others that spark defensive reactions.

ETHICAL CHECKPOINT 8.1

Social Loafing in Virtual Teams

Virtual teams are geographically scattered groups that collaborate primarily though technology. Such teams can draw upon the expertise of individuals from different locations around the world. They have low operating costs, since members don't have to travel to a central location. Instead, they communicate through email, videoconferencing, bulletin boards, and other electronic means. Large corporations—like Hewlett-Packard, IBM, Intel, NCR, and Microsoft—rely on virtual teams to carry out a variety of functions, including project engineering, customer service, consulting, and marketing.

Initial indications are that social loafing is more common in virtual teams than in face-to-face groups. Two factors apparently account for the prevalence of social loafing in technology-supported groups. One, virtual teams are often large. In bigger groups, members feel as though their contributions aren't as important to the team's success, and therefore they are less motivated to contribute. Also, it is harder to identify who contributes and who doesn't. Two, members of virtual teams are widely dispersed. In face-to-face groups, members know instantly what others are doing, a fact that can encourage them to keep working. Feedback in virtual teams, on the other hand, can be delayed for hours or days. Virtual team members also have less contact with each other, which can reduce cohesion.

Researchers Omar Alnuaimi, Lionel Robert, and Likoebe Maruping tested the effects of team size and dispersion in an experiment using 32 groups of students. They assigned approximately half of the groups to work on a brainstorming task with their teammates in the same room, while members of the rest of the teams worked in separate locations and interacted online. Group size ranged from 3 to 10 members. The investigators recorded the number of ideas produced by each group and surveyed the attitudes of team members. Dispersed and larger teams generated fewer ideas. Members of these groups felt less responsible for the group's final product and less connected to other members. At the same time, they were more likely to blame others for the fact that they were loafing. They saw themselves as victims who were justified in reducing their efforts.

Based on their findings, Alnuaimi and his colleagues urge managers to change how they structure and coordinate virtual teams. Keep teams as small as possible. Emphasize that each team member has responsibility for accomplishing the group's task. Implement an evaluation system that identifies each individual's contribution (or lack of contribution). Remind participants that they are dealing with other people, not computers. Use richer communication channels (videoconferencing, for example) that are better at fostering personal connections.

Sources: Alnuaimi, Robert, and Maruping (2010). Blaskovich (2008). Bryant, Albring, and Murthy (2009). Chidambaram and Tung (2005). Zhang, Chen, and Latimer (2011).

Evaluation Versus Description

Evaluative messages are judgmental. They can be sent through statements ("What a jerk!") or through such nonverbal cues as using a sarcastic tone of voice or rolling one's eyes. Those being evaluated put up their guard. Insecure group members are likely to respond by assigning blame ("You messed up"), by making judgments of their own ("At least my proposal didn't go over budget"), and by questioning the motives of the speaker. Descriptive messages, such as asking for information and reporting data and feelings, create a more positive environment.

Control Versus Problem Orientation

Controlling messages imply that the recipient is inadequate—uninformed, immature, stubborn, overly emotional—and needs to change. Control, like evaluation, can be communicated through both verbal (issuing orders, threats) and nonverbal (stares, threatening body posture) means. Problem-centered messages ("What will be your next step?") reflect a willingness to collaborate in defining and solving problems. They demonstrate that the sender has no predetermined solution and give the receiver permission to set his or her own direction.

Strategy Versus Spontaneity

Strategic communicators are seen as manipulators who try to hide their true motivations. They appear to be playing games, withholding data, or developing special sources of information. Worse yet, strategic communicators engage in "false spontaneity" by using gimmicks to disguise their intentions. Some supervisors solicit the input of employees in order to appear open-minded, for instance, when they have already made the decision. In contrast, behavior that is truly spontaneous (unplanned) and honest reduces defensiveness.

Neutrality Versus Empathy

Neutral messages, like "Don't worry" and "Don't take it personally," communicate little warmth or caring. These low-affect messages may be meant as supportive, but listeners come away feeling disconfirmed. Empathetic statements, such as "I can see why you would be worried" and "No wonder you were offended by the boss's comment," communicate reassurance and acceptance.

Superiority Versus Equality

Attempts at "one-upmanship," like claiming to be smarter or more knowledgeable, generally provoke such defensive responses as ignoring the message, competition, and jealousy. Those claiming superiority communicate that they don't want help or need feedback and may try to reduce the social standing of receivers. Status and power differences are less disruptive if participants indicate that they want to work with others on an equal basis. Supportive communicators treat others as partners worthy of respect and trust.

Certainty Versus Provisionalism

Dogmatic, inflexible individuals claim to have all the answers and are unwilling to change or to consider other points of view. They have little patience with those they consider wrong. As a consequence, they appear more interested in being right than in solving the problem and maintaining group relationships. Gibb found that listeners often perceive the certainty of dogmatic individuals as a mask hiding their feelings of inferiority. Conversely, provisional individuals are willing to experiment and explore. They want to investigate issues instead of taking sides or controlling outcomes. These communicators gladly accept help from others as they seek information and answers.

Psychological safety is an important by-product of open, supportive communication. Psychological safety refers to the shared belief that individuals can speak up without fear of being embarrassed or rejected. Members trust and respect each other and know that they can challenge the leader's decisions if necessary.[16] Lack of psychological safety played an important role in the 1996 climbing disaster on Mt. Everest.[17] That year, the leaders of two climbing groups and several of their clients died after getting caught in a storm. The climbers perished because they continued to the summit long after they should have turned back. Both clients and guides were reluctant to challenge the decision to continue on because they didn't feel safe doing so. Clients were strangers who didn't trust one another and feared being embarrassed if they expressed an unpopular opinion. Group leaders also made it clear that they weren't open to discussing issues or problems. One told his group that his word was "absolute law" and that he would tolerate no dissension during the climb.

Being Willing to Stand Alone

This final responsibility may be the toughest to assume. Being in the minority is never easy, because it runs contrary to our strong desire to be liked and accepted by others. Nevertheless, the difficulty of standing alone should not be an excuse for keeping quiet instead of speaking up. As we'll see in the second half of the chapter, team members' willingness to take issue with the prevailing group opinion is essential if the team is to avoid moral failure. Further, minority dissent can significantly improve group performance. Teams with minority members generally come up with better solutions even if the group doesn't change its collective mind.[18] Group members focus on one solution when there is no minority. They have little incentive to explore the problem in depth. As a result, they disregard novel solutions and converge on one position. Minorities cast doubt on group consensus, stimulating more thought about the dilemma. Members exert more effort because they must resolve the clash between the majority and minority solutions. They pay closer attention to all aspects of the issue, consider more viewpoints, and use a wider variety of problem-solving strategies. Such divergent thinking leads to more creative, higher-quality solutions. Responding to the dissenting views of minorities also encourages team members to resist conformity in other settings.[19]

In some cases, minorities are successful in persuading the rest of the group to their point of view. Often, this influence is slow and indirect. Majorities initially reject dissenters and their ideas but, over time, forget the source of the arguments and focus instead on the merits of their proposals. This can gradually convert them to the minority viewpoint.[20] However, minorities can have an immediate, powerful impact on group opinion under certain conditions.[21] Minorities are more likely to convince the rest of the group when members are still formulating their attitudes about an issue. Well-respected dissenters who consistently advocate for their positions are generally more persuasive.

Recognizing the importance of minority opinion should increase our motivation to play this role. We'll also need to exercise courage in order to accept the consequences for doing so. Teams can do their part to spark dissent by making sure that members come from significantly different backgrounds and perspectives and by protecting rather than attacking those who disagree.

RESPONDING TO ETHICAL DANGER SIGNS

Accepting our moral responsibilities is a good start to improving group ethical performance. However, we also need to be alert to moral pitfalls that arise during team interaction. These traps account for the ethical failure of a great many groups and their members. In this section, I'll identify six signs that indicate that a team is in ethical danger—groupthink, polythink, mismanaged agreement, escalating commitment, excessive control, and moral exclusion—and provide some suggestions for responding to the risks posed by each.

Groupthink

Earlier, I noted that adopting a cooperative orientation is critical to group success. However, there is significant danger in making team unity the group's primary goal. Social psychologist Irving Janis popularized the term *groupthink*, which describes teams that put unanimous agreement ahead of reasoned problem solving.[22] Janis first noted faulty thinking in small groups of ordinary citizens. For example, he observed one group of heavy smokers meeting to kick the habit who decided that quitting was impossible. One member had stopped, but the rest of the group pressured him back into smoking two packs a day.

The term *groupthink* became part of the national vocabulary largely based on Janis's analysis of major U.S. policy disasters, like the failure to anticipate the attack on Pearl Harbor, the invasion of North Korea, the Bay of Pigs fiasco, and the escalation of the Vietnam War. In each of these incidents, some of the brightest (and presumably most ethically minded) political and military leaders in our nation's history made terrible choices. More recent examples of groupthink include the *Challenger* and *Columbia* space shuttle disasters; the choice to invade Iraq; the decision to storm the Branch Davidian compound in Waco, Texas; the accounting fraud at WorldCom; and the collapse of Britain's HBOS Bank.[23] (Case Study 8.2, "Groupthink in the Sweat Lodge," describes another instance of the powerful impact of group conformity.)

Groups are more likely to fall victim to this syndrome when they (1) are highly cohesive, (2) find themselves insulated or isolated from other groups, (3) lack decision-making formats like those described in Chapter 3, (4) have highly directive leaders and members who push for a particular solution, (5) close themselves off from outside information or use such information to reinforce their biases, and (6) are under stress with little hope of coming up with alternatives to the ideas offered by their leaders. These forces exert pressure on members to agree and produce the following symptoms, which I'll illustrate through examples taken from Janis's analysis of major policy disasters. The greater the number of these characteristics displayed by a group, the greater the likelihood that members have made cohesiveness their top priority.[24]

Signs of Overconfidence

1. *The illusion of invulnerability.* Members think they can do no wrong. They are overly optimistic and prone to take extraordinary risks. President Lyndon Johnson and his advisers kept escalating the war in Vietnam because they thought the North Vietnamese would back down. One policy maker later remarked, "We thought we had the golden touch."

2. *Belief in the inherent morality of the group.* Participants do not question the inherent morality of the group and therefore ignore the ethical consequences of their actions and decisions. In discussions of the Cuban Bay of Pigs operation (which resulted in the death or capture of all the invading troops), President Kennedy's policy group barely noted the ethical implications of attacking a small neighboring country or of lying to the American public about the invasion. Later, during the deliberations that safely ended the Cuban missile crisis, many of the same group members debated at length the morality of a surprise air attack. The team decided that this option was not in the best, moral American tradition.

Signs of Closed-Mindedness

1. *Collective rationalization.* Group members invent rationalizations to protect themselves from any feedback that would challenge their operating assumptions. In 1941, U.S. naval officers rationalized that any enemy carriers headed for Hawaii would be detected before attack. Warships anchored in Pearl Harbor would be safe from torpedo bombs because the water was too shallow.

2. *Stereotypes of outside groups.* Decision makers underestimate the capabilities of other groups (armies, citizens, teams), thinking that people in these groups are weak or stupid. President Truman and his advisers fell victim to the belief that the Chinese wouldn't be able to respond to an invasion of North Korea by the United States. As a result of this miscalculation, China entered the Korean conflict, and the war ended in a stalemate.

Signs of Group Pressure

1. *Pressure on dissenters.* Majority members coerce dissenters to go along with the prevailing opinion in the group. Former presidential adviser Bill Moyers felt the power of this pressure after taking issue with the escalation of the Vietnam War. When he arrived at one strategy discussion, President Johnson greeted him by saying, "Well, here comes Mr. Stop-the-Bombing."

2. *Self-censorship.* Individuals keep their doubts about group decisions to themselves. Perhaps because of being labeled as "Mr. Stop-the-Bombing," Moyers became a "domesticated dissenter" who expressed reservations only about a few details of the plan to ratchet up the war in Vietnam.

3. *The illusion of unanimity.* Since members keep quiet, the group mistakenly assumes that everyone agrees on a course of action. Historian Arthur

Schlesinger, a participant in the Bay of Pigs planning sessions, had serious doubts about the project, but he and others remained silent because they assumed the group had consensus.

4. *Self-appointed mind-guards.* Certain members take it upon themselves to protect the leader and others from dissenting opinions that might disrupt the group's consensus. President Kennedy's brother Robert took this role during the Bay of Pigs decision. He told Schlesinger, "You may be right or you may be wrong, but the President has made his mind up. Don't push it any further. Now is the time for everyone to help him all they can."[25]

The symptoms of groupthink seriously disrupt the decision-making process. Members fail to consider all the alternatives, outline objectives, or gather additional information. They follow preconceived notions, are less likely to reexamine a course of action when it's not working, don't carefully weigh risks, or work out contingency plans. While groupthink undermines all types of decisions, it is particularly destructive to ethical reasoning. This helps explain why, in the 1980s, Beech-Nut employees decided to sell adulterated apple juice, and E. F. Hutton officials defrauded financial institutions by writing checks before they had deposited the funds to cover them. Nearly everyone (including employees of these two firms) would agree that selling "phony" apple juice and bouncing checks are wrong. However, groupthink banished any moral considerations.[26]

Interest in the causes and prevention of groupthink remains high decades after Janis first offered his theory.[27] Contemporary researchers have discovered that social cohesion is dangerous, while task cohesion—agreement about how to complete the group's work—is not. Investigators note that self-directed teams, which incorporate an estimated 40% of the workforce, are particularly vulnerable to groupthink. Members work under strict time limits and are often isolated and undertrained. They may fail at first, and the need to function as a cohesive unit may blind them to ethical dilemmas.[28]

Janis and his successors offer the following suggestions for preventing groupthink:

- As a leader, don't express a preference for a particular solution; solicit ideas instead.
- Utilize a decision-making format.
- Divide the group regularly into subgroups, and then bring the entire group back together to negotiate differences.
- Construct and then debate counterproposals.
- Bring in outsiders—experts or colleagues—to challenge the group's ideas.
- Appoint individuals to act as devil's advocates at each session to air doubts and objections.
- Realistically assess dangers and anticipate possible setbacks.
- Train members to speak up.
- Encourage dissenting points of view.
- Think through the ethical implications of options.

- Adopt an optimistic frame of mind, viewing obstacles as opportunities and envisioning success.

- Develop group norms that encourage critical thinking about reasoning, assumptions, and alternatives.

- Avoid isolation; keep the group in contact with other groups.

- Initiate role play of the reactions of other groups and organizations to reduce the effects of stereotyping and rationalization.

- Once a decision has been made, give group members one last chance to express any remaining doubts about the decision.

Polythink

While groupthink is marked by excessive conformity, polythink is marked by extreme disunity. The term "polythink" comes from the word "poly," which means "many." In fragmented groups, members bring many different viewpoints, goals, and perspectives to the decision-making process. They find it difficult and often impossible to agree on how to define the problem and how to solve it.

Like Irving Janus, polythink theorists Alex Mintz and Carly Wayne focus their attention on high-level decision-making bodies, mostly U.S. presidential advisory groups involved in setting antiterrorism and Middle Eastern policies. They identify the following as symptoms of polythink based on their analyses.[29]

Greater likelihood for intragroup conflict. In Washington DC, the CIA, the FBI, the military and other groups protect their turf, fighting over how to combat terror.

Greater likelihood of leaks. Driven by competing perspectives, decision makers are more likely to leak information to undermine other members. For example, General Stanley McChrystal derided Vice President Joe Biden, Special Afghan adviser Richard Holbrooke, and President Obama in a *Rolling Stone* interview.

Confusion and lack of communication. Group members intentionally or unintentionally withhold information or send out mixed messages. Before the 9/11 attacks, for instance, "somewhere in CIA there was information that two known al Qaeda terrorists had come into the United States . . . Somewhere in FBI there was information that strange things had been going on at flight schools in the United States."[30] Nobody pulled this information together to identify the threat.

Greater likelihood of framing effects. Competing factions frame their preferences in the most favorable light at the expense of the other parties. (See Chapter 5 for a closer look at framing.) Close political aides to President Obama, who opposed further involvement in the Syrian civil war, highlighted the costs of intervening to arm the Syrian rebels. In contrast, CIA director David Petreaus, who supported greater involvement, framed his argument in terms of loss. If the U.S. didn't intervene, he argued, any gains from the Iraq/Afghanistan war would be lost as extremists entered the fight.

Adoption of positions with the lowest common denominator. Finding it difficult to reach agreement, members compromise to create a proposal that can garner majority support. President Obama campaigned on a 16-month pledge to draw down troops in Iraq, but military commanders pushed for 23 months. He and his advisers settled for 19 months as a compromise position, though it might not have been the best option.

Decision paralysis. Sometimes groups can't reach agreement even when seeking the lowest common denominator. In this case they fail to act or revert to previous options. During his first term, Obama's advisers were unable to come up with new options to deal with Iran's nuclear threat. It wasn't until his second term that the president and his advisers were able to initiate a new strategy of negotiation.

Limited review of options. Debate becomes unwieldy in groups suffering from polythink. Leaders of these groups quickly eliminate some ideas from consideration to limit the discussion.

No room for reappraisal of previously rejected policy options. Polythink keeps groups from revisiting proposals because members don't want to reopen earlier topics, which can lead to rehashing prior disagreements.

Polythink, like groupthink, leads to defective and often unethical choices. Disunity helped keep law enforcement and intelligence agencies from preventing the 9/11 attacks. Confusion about how to intervene in Syria has helped create a humanitarian crisis, with 5 million refugees fleeing to other countries. Mintz and his colleagues attribute the collapse of the 2000 Israeli–Palestinian Camp David peace negotiations largely to polythink on the part of the Israeli delegation.[31] Failure of the talks sparked a Palestinian uprising, which left thousands dead and wounded on both sides, led to high unemployment and poverty in the Gaza Strip and West Bank, and undermined Israel's economy.

Polythink does have some advantages over groupthink. Team members are less likely to lock in to choices, for example, or to ignore information or to be overconfident. However, to be beneficial, polythink must be channeled. Leaders need to focus members on the overall objectives of the group and identify desired outcomes. Team leaders can take advantage of diverse opinions to brainstorm ideas and to identify options. They can also ask subgroups to tackle different parts of the problem—which makes the discussion more manageable—and then come back together. Mintz and Wayne conclude that groups generally make better decisions when they strike a balance between uniformity and disunity, both converging and diverging. The theorists visualize groupthink and polythink as opposite ends of a continuum. The most effective (and most ethical) groups operate in the middle of the continuum.

Mismanaged Agreement

Groups frequently run into trouble when members publicly express their support for decisions that they oppose in private. Teams continue to pour time and money into new products that no one believes will succeed, for example, or engage in illegal activities that everyone in the group is uneasy about. George Washington University management professor Jerry Harvey refers to this phenomenon as *mismanaged agreement*, or the Abilene paradox.[32] He describes a time when his family decided to drive (without air-conditioning) 100 miles across the Texas desert one hot July afternoon, from their home in Coleman to Abilene, so they could eat a bad meal at a rundown cafeteria. After returning home, family members discovered that no one had really wanted to make the trip. Each had agreed to go to Abilene on the assumption that everyone else in the group was enthusiastic about eating out.

Harvey believes that failure to manage agreement, not failure to manage conflict, is the biggest problem facing organizations. Like his family, teams also take needless "trips":

> I now call the tendency for groups to embark on excursions that no group member wants "the Abilene Paradox." Stated simply, when organizations blunder into the Abilene Paradox, they take actions in contradiction to what they really want to do and therefore defeat the very purposes they are trying to achieve.[33]

Members of groups caught in the Abilene paradox agree in private about the nature of the problem and what ought to be done about it. However, they fail to communicate their desires and beliefs, misleading others into believing that consensus exists. Based on faulty assumptions, members act in counterproductive ways that undermine their purposes. These actions generate lots of anger and irritation, and participants blame each other for the group's failures. The cycle of miscommunication and misunderstanding continues unless confronted.

Why do members publicly support decisions they privately oppose? Harvey offers the following five psychological factors to account for the paradox:

1. *Action anxiety.* Group members know what should be done but are too anxious to follow through on their beliefs. They choose to endure the negative consequences of going along—professional and economic failure—instead of speaking up.

2. *Negative fantasies.* Action anxiety is driven in part by the negative fantasies members have about what will happen if they voice their opinions. These fantasies ("I'll be shunned or branded as disloyal") serve as an excuse for not attacking the problem, absolving the individual (in his or her own eyes) of any responsibility.

3. *Real risk.* There are risks to expressing dissent: getting fired, lost income, damaged relationships. However, most of the time the danger is not as great as we think.

4. *Fear of separation.* Separation, alienation, and loneliness constitute the most powerful force behind the paradox. Ostracism is strong punishment. Group members fear being cut off or separated from others. To escape this fate, they cheat, lie, take bribes, use accounting tricks to boost earnings, and so forth.

5. *Psychological reversal of risk and certainty.* In the Abilene paradox, participants let their negative fantasies drive them into real dangers. Fearing that something bad may happen, decision makers act in a way that fulfills the fantasy. For instance, group members may support a project with no chance of success because they are afraid they will be fired or demoted if they don't. Ironically, they are likely to be fired or demoted anyway when the flawed project fails.

Harvey takes issue with proponents of groupthink who blame moral failure on group pressure. He contends that as long as we can blame our peers, we don't have to accept personal responsibility. In reality, we always have a choice as to how we respond. He uses the *Gunsmoke* myth to drive home this point. In this myth, the lone Western sheriff (Matt Dillon in the radio and television series *Gunsmoke*) stands down a mob of armed townsfolk out to lynch his prisoner. If group tyranny is really at work, Harvey argues, Dillon stands no chance. After all, he is outnumbered 500 to 1 and could be felled with a single bullet from one rioter. The mob disbands because its members really didn't want to lynch the prisoner in the first place.

Breaking out of the paradox begins with diagnosing its symptoms in your group or organization. Important indicators of mismanaged agreement include frustration and blaming, contradictions between privately and publicly expressed opinions, and the inability to solve problems. If you believe that the group is on its way to its own Abilene, call a meeting where you own up to your true feelings and invite feedback. The team may immediately come up with a better approach, or it may engage in extended conflict that generates a more creative solution. You might suffer for your honesty, but you could be rewarded for saying what everyone else was thinking. In any case, you'll feel better about yourself for speaking up.

Escalating Commitment

As we've seen, one of the products of mismanaged agreement is continuation along a failed course of action. Social psychologists refer to this phenomenon as the *escalation of commitment*.[34] Instead of cutting their losses, groups redouble their efforts, pouring in more resources. Costs continue to multiply, until the moment when the team finally admits defeat. Escalating commitment helps explain why bankers continue to loan money to problem borrowers (see Case Study 8.3), why managers maintain support for failing employees, why nations continue to pour resources into hosting the Olympics (the average games go over budget by 156%), and why investors put more money into declining stocks. Well-publicized cases of this phenomenon include creation of the automated baggage system at the Denver International Airport (which delayed the opening of the airport and never worked), the decision to introduce the New Coke, and the failed Shoreham Nuclear Power Plant. Costs for the Shoreham project on New York's Long Island ballooned from $75 million to over $5 billion over a 23-year period. The installation failed to produce a single kilowatt of electric power. Escalation of commitment also played a role in the Everest tragedy in 1996 as well as in a similar disaster on K-2 in 2008. Clients paid $60,000 to $70,000 to summit these mountains. Once they were near the top, it was very difficult to convince some of them to turn around after they had invested so much time, money, and effort. Instead, they fell victim to "summit fever" and put themselves in grave (and sometimes fatal) danger.

Teams may stay the course to justify their earlier choices, to remain consistent, and to retain their credibility. (In some cases, the larger organization pressures them to continue.) Group members may have a personal stake in continuing the project because their jobs and reputations are at stake. They often hope to recoup their "sunk costs" (previous investments). Setbacks are viewed as temporary; success is seen as just around the corner. Groups have a tendency to take more risks than individuals (a phenomenon referred to as *risky shift*), which can encourage members to contribute more resources than they would on their own. Teams also fall victim to cognitive biases that encourage escalation. They may (1) ignore negative feedback or interpret evidence so it supports their point of view (selective perception), (2) believe that they have more control over outcomes than they actually do (illusion of control), (3) blame those who bring bad news, and (4) become overconfident based on past successes.[35]

Group members have a moral obligation to avoid escalation of commitment. Continuing to invest in doomed projects wastes resources that could go to better uses and puts the organization at risk. Often, maintaining a failing course of action involves unethical behaviors, like overstating potential benefits or hiding safety problems. (See Contemporary Issues in Organizational Ethics 8.1 for more information about the risks of quitting too soon.) We can take a number of steps to deescalate commitment to destructive courses of action.[36] First, don't ignore negative feedback or external pressure. Combat the tendency to be overly optimistic by being alert to red flags like missed deadlines, cost overruns, and pressure from outsiders who take issue with the project. Second, bring new group members or leaders into the group who are less invested in the program. Third, hire an outside auditor to provide a "fresh set of eyes" to assess the severity of the problem and to suggest alternative courses of action. Fourth, don't be afraid to withhold further funding until more information can be gathered. Fifth, look for opportunities to deinstitutionalize the project by separating it from the key goals of the organization or by isolating it physically. Corporations frequently spin off troubled units, for example, and risky projects can be redefined as "experiments."

CONTEMPORARY ISSUES IN ORGANIZATIONAL ETHICS 8.1

PREMATURE ABANDONMENT

Prematurely abandoning projects poses its own set of dangers. Organizations lose their investments and possible benefits to employees, clients, investors, communities, and other stakeholders. Liverpool, England, professor Helga Drummond points to a number of cases where organizations quit too soon. Both Microsoft and Hewlett-Packard developed and then abandoned tablet computers before Apple came out with its wildly successful iPad, for instance. U.S. firms routinely divest themselves of foreign operations that still generate a profit. Drummond also cites examples of successes that came when teams persisted despite time and cost overruns: BP's discovery of oil in Libya, the renovation of London's Savoy Hotel and Australia's Sydney Opera House, and the construction of the Amsterdam subway.

A number of factors push managers into prematurely ending projects. They are averse to loss, can't tolerate failure, feel locked into previous time limits and budgets, are new to the project, and so on. The danger of erroneous abandonment is greatest in the middle of the project, when completion and anticipated benefits—higher revenue, better transportation, nicer facilities—seem far away.

There is no magic formula for determining when to persist or to let go. However, Drummond suggests keeping the project on track to prevent doubts from taking hold. (The scale of the project may need to be cut back.) Don't create a self-fulfilling prophecy by expecting failure. Weigh the hidden benefits of persistence. (Even failure can generate useful information that can be used in future projects.) Consider the options that will be lost if the program is abandoned. Answer the following questions: "What is one good reason to persist with this project?" "What is one good reason to pursue an alternative?" If other similar projects have succeeded elsewhere, then be reluctant to abandon this effort.

Source: Drummond (2014).

Excessive Control

Members of newly formed self-directed work teams frequently find that the group exerts more control over their behavior than their former managers ever did. One team member at a small manufacturing company complained, for example, that his group had stricter rules about tardiness than his old boss and that he was more closely observed than before:

> [Now] I don't have to sit there and look for the boss to be around; [before] if the boss is not around, I can sit there and talk to my neighbor or do what I want. Now the whole team is around me and the whole team is observing what I'm doing.[37]

The experience of this employee illustrates the power of *concertive control*. Concertive control has replaced the traditional rules-based bureaucracy in many organizations.[38] Members of these companies and nonprofits identify with the organization, putting its needs above their own. In these settings, groups empowered to direct their own behaviors exert control by agreeing on a common set of values, engaging in high levels of coordination, and creating their own enforcement mechanisms. Concertive control—sometimes referred to as *unobtrusive control*—is subtler than its bureaucratic predecessor and often goes unrecognized. This combination of high power and low visibility makes concertive influence, while necessary, particularly dangerous. Members can unwittingly exert excessive, unhealthy influence over one another.

Organizational communication expert James Barker describes how self-directed work teams transition from freeing to imprisoning their members.[39] In the first phase, newly formed groups develop their vision and values statements. These values then become the basis for making ethical decisions in the group. Members commit themselves to reaching shared goals and develop norms for putting their values into action. A group might implement its concern for customer service, for instance, by adopting the norm that it will do whatever it takes to ship products on time.

In the second phase, members turn their norms into specific behavioral rules, like "You must stay late in order to meet shipping schedules." These rules are then used to regulate the behavior of new members. In the third phase, the rules are formalized. They are written down and used for evaluation. A member may be removed from the team if he or she doesn't work overtime to help ship products, for example. These rules can be stricter than those operating in a bureaucracy. Group members are thus imprisoned in an "iron cage" of regulations of their own making.

Barker is concerned that "concertive control is the next step on our long march toward totally organized lives."[40] Members pay a high price for remaining in good standing with the team, including burnout and the sacrifice of family and personal time. Teams can make sure that concertive control is put to constructive use by continually criticizing their own actions, according to Barker. They need to set aside regular times (perhaps an hour a month) to talk about their moral reasoning and the positive and negative effects of their practices. Some values and rules will be reaffirmed, while others will be modified. In such discussions, it is critical that everyone be heard and that members engage in dialogue, working through their differences. This ongoing group analysis is the best way to ensure that a team creates a fair and reasonable system of norms and regulations to guide its members. The instrument in Self-Assessment 8.2 can be used as part of these discussions.

SELF-ASSESSMENT 8.2

Concertive Control Scale

Respond to each item on a scale of 1 to 5.

1 = To a very little extent

3 = To some extent

5 = To a very great extent

1. Does your team have team rules/policies, etc.?
2. Does your team have its own system of determining when people can take leave or roster days off, etc.?
3. Is there a "way of doing things" in your team?
4. Does your team make sure everyone in the team "pulls their weight"?
5. Do you need everyone's agreement in the team to change the way you do your job?
6. Do you usually check with other team members before doing something that might affect them?

Scoring

The scale is designed to give a "picture" of how much control the team has over the activities of its members. Some teams—like those engaged in highly coordinated projects—will need more control than other teams. Scores on individual items can indicate trouble spots, where members feel that the team has too much or too little control.

Source: Wright and Barker (2000), p. 352. Used by permission.

Moral Exclusion

The worst examples of group behavior arise out of the process of moral exclusion. In moral exclusion, group and societal members set a psychological boundary around justice.[41] Those inside the boundary treat each other fairly, are willing to sacrifice for one another, and share collective resources. However, insiders treat outsiders much differently. Fairness is no longer a consideration. Those beyond the scope of justice (often members of low-status groups) are seen as unimportant and expendable. Insiders don't feel remorse when outsiders are harmed but believe that the mistreatment is morally justified.

Mild forms of exclusion are part of everyday life and include, for example, acting in a patronizing manner, applying double standards to judge the behavior of different groups, and making unflattering comparisons to appear superior to others. An example of ordinary exclusion would be a work team that mocks other groups while excusing its own failings. Milder forms of exclusion are common in conflicts over environmental issues, where opposing sides claim the moral high ground and are quick to label their opponents as "ecofreaks," or "foot-dragging big businesses."[42] Extreme forms of exclusion produce human rights violations, torture, genocide, and other atrocities. For instance, Japanese soldiers in World War II viewed the Chinese with contempt. Murdering them was no more troubling than "squashing a bug or butchering a hog."[43]

Driven by this belief, they were willing to rape, torture, and slaughter civilians in the Chinese city of Nanking, killing approximately 300,000 residents. Similar exclusionary reasoning has been used to justify genocide in Serbia and Guatemala, attacks on villages in the Darfur region of Sudan, the execution of captured Iraqi soldiers by ISIS militia members, and the abuse of prisoners at Abu Ghraib prison. A list of the symptoms of moral exclusion is given in Table 8.1.

Table 8.1 Symptoms of Moral Exclusion

Symptom	Description
Double standards	Having different norms for different groups
Concealing effects of harmful outcomes	Disregarding, ignoring, distorting, or minimizing injurious outcomes that others experience
Reducing moral standards	Asserting that one's harmful behavior is proper while denying one's lesser concern for others
Utilizing euphemisms	Sanitizing harmful behavior and outcomes
Biased evaluation of groups comparisons	Making unflattering between-group comparisons that bolster one's own group at the expense of others
Condescension and derogation	Regarding others with disdain
Dehumanization	Denying others' rights, entitlements, humanity, and dignity
Fear of contamination	Perceiving contact or alliances with other stakeholders as posing a threat to oneself
Normalization and glorification of violence	Glorifying and normalizing violence; viewing violence as an effective, legitimate, or even sublime form of human behavior while denying the potential of violence to damage people, the environment, relationships, and constructive conflict resolution processes
Victim blaming	Placing blame on those who are hated
Deindividuation	Believing that one's contribution to social problems is undetectable
Diffusing responsibility	Denying personal responsibility for harms by seeing them as the result of collective rather than individual decisions and actions
Displacing responsibility	Identifying others, such as subordinates or supervisors, as responsible for harms inflicted on victims

Source: Opotow, Gerson, and Woodside (2005), p. 307. Used by permission.

Dispute resolution expert Susan Opotow believes that moral exclusion progresses through five stages or elements, which can reinforce one another. The presence of one or more of these elements serves as a warning that this danger is present.[44]

1. *Conflicts of interest are salient.* Moral exclusion is more likely to occur during conflicts where one group wins at the expense of the other. As tensions increase, members separate themselves from their opponents, focusing on differences based on religion, education, ethnic background, social status, skin color, job functions, and other factors.

2. *Group categorizations are salient.* The characteristics of members of the opposing group are given negative labels, dividing the world into those who deserve empathy and help and those who don't. These derogatory labels excuse unfair treatment and negative outcomes. Romanians and Hungarians, for example, reinforce negative stereotypes of Gypsies or Romanies by describing them as "dirty," "thieves," and "lazy."[45]

3. *Moral justifications are prominent.* Damaging behavior is justified and even celebrated as a way to strike a blow against a corrupt foe. Such exclusionary moral claims are self-serving, excuse wrongdoing, and set boundaries by denigrating outsiders. For instance, Hutu leaders in Rwanda whipped their followers into a murderous rage by playing on their resentments toward their higher-status Tutsi neighbors.

4. *Unjust procedures are described as expedient.* Harm is often disguised through policies and procedures, what some observers label "administrative evil."[46] In administrative evil, ordinary people commit heinous crimes while carrying out their daily tasks as "good" professionals. The Holocaust demonstrates administrative evil in action. Extermination camps would not have been possible without the cooperation of thousands of civil servants who identified "undesirables" and seized their assets, managed the ghettos, built concentration camp latrines, and shipped prisoners to their deaths. Procedures can be identified as unjust when they fail to serve the interests of those they are supposed to benefit. For example, government bureaucrats in the United States and Australia claimed to be helping Native peoples even as they stole their lands and tried to eradicate their cultures. Military officials in Japan believed that committing atrocities would ultimately benefit the Chinese because, once subjugated, they would prosper under Japanese rule.

5. *Harmful outcomes occur.* The negative products of exclusion are both physical and psychological. Members of excluded groups may suffer physical harm and, at the same time, suffer from a loss of self-esteem and identity as they internalize the negative judgments of the dominant group. Perpetrators also pay a high price. They have to expend significant energy and resources to deal with conflicts, excuse their conduct, and maintain exclusionary systems. The harm they cause overshadows any good that they do.

Opotow argues that adopting a pluralistic perspective—one that acknowledges the legitimacy of a variety of groups—can help us deter moral exclusion at each stage of its development.[47] This approach sees conflicts as opportunities to integrate the interests of all parties, not as win-lose battles. Members of pluralistic groups enlarge the definition of moral community by including people of all categories and try to understand their perspectives. Participants engage in critical analysis of moral justifications, calling into question suspect claims at the same time they develop equitable procedures for distributing resources. They also support dissenters.

CHAPTER TAKEAWAYS

- Your behavior will have a significant impact on your team's ethical success or failure.

- Recognize that your success in a group is dependent on the efforts of others. Adopt a cooperative orientation, not an individualistic or competitive perspective, and encourage others to do the same.

- Do your fair share. Combat the tendency to engage in social loafing by strengthening connections between individual effort and group performance as well as between group performance and group success. Increase the positive value of the team's collective product to members.

- Be open and supportive. Talk about issues and help others to succeed. Promote a supportive climate by engaging in communication that is descriptive, problem oriented, spontaneous, empathetic, egalitarian, and provisional. Create an atmosphere in which members feel safe to discuss problems and challenge leaders.

- Have the courage to stand alone. Expressing a minority opinion is key to avoiding moral failure and increases group decision-making effectiveness even when the majority does not adopt the dissenters' point of view. In some cases, you might convert the rest of the group to your way of thinking.

- Signs of groupthink—putting unanimity ahead of careful problem solving—include overconfidence (the illusion of invulnerability and belief in the inherent morality of the group), closed-mindedness (collective rationalization and stereotypes of outside groups), and group pressure (pressure on dissenters, self-censorship, the illusion of unanimity, and self-appointed mind-guards).

- Reduce the likelihood of groupthink by (1) withholding your initial opinion, (2) dividing the group into subgroups, (3) bringing in outsiders, (4) keeping the group in contact with other groups, (5) role playing the reactions of other teams, and (6) revisiting the decision.

- Polythink is the product of disunity. Symptoms of polythink include: (1) greater likelihood for intragroup conflict, (2) greater likelihood of leaks, (3) confusion and lack of communication, (4) greater likelihood of framing effects, (5) adoption of positions with the lowest common denominator, (6) decision paralysis, (7) limited review of options, and (8) no room for reappraisal of previously rejected polity options. Channel polythink to strike a balance between convergence and divergence during deliberations.

- Mismanaged agreement—the Abilene paradox—occurs when members publicly express support for decisions that they oppose in private. The group then acts in counterproductive ways that undermine its goals. Owning up to your doubts can stop the team from taking unwanted "trips."

- Groups trapped in escalating commitment pursue failed courses of action, continuing to pour in additional resources when they should go in another direction instead. Deescalate the situation by noting warning signs, bringing in new members

- or outside auditors, withholding funding, and deinstitutionalizing the project—making it less central to group goals and physically isolating it.

- Be aware of the power of concertive control, in which teams manage the behavior of members by agreeing on a common set of values, engaging in high levels of coordination, and creating their own enforcement mechanisms. Put this form of group influence to constructive use by encouraging your team to regularly examine, criticize, and modify its values and rules.

- Resist the temptation to engage in moral exclusion—placing members of other groups outside the scope of justice where the rules of fairness do not apply. The five stages or elements of moral exclusion are these: (1) Conflicts of interest are salient. (2) Group categorizations are salient. (3) Moral justifications are prominent. (4) Unjust procedures are described as expedient. (5) Harmful outcomes occur. Deter moral exclusion by adopting a pluralistic perspective that respects the rights of all groups.

APPLICATION PROJECTS

1. What was your best small-group experience? Your worst? What accounts for the differences between these two experiences? How would you rate the moral behavior of each group?

2. Interview a project manager. What strategies does this individual use to foster collaboration and individual and team accountability? Report your findings to the rest of the class.

3. Record a group discussion, and then identify and categorize the defensive and supportive comments made by team members. What do you conclude about the communication climate of the group? Report your conclusions to the team you observe.

4. Rate your performance as a morally responsible group member. What behaviors do you demonstrate? Need to develop? What steps can you take to improve?

5. Find a partner and discuss your responses to Self-Assessment 8.1. What similarities do you note between the behaviors and the impact of the social loafers both of you rated? How did you respond to them? How would you respond differently to them in the future?

6. If you are part of an ongoing team, meet together to discuss members' tendencies to loaf and how the group exercises control over its members. Develop an action plan to address these issues. As an alternative, complete Self-Assessment 8.2 as a group and then discuss your results as a team. Address those areas where members feel that the team has too much or too little control.

7. How can groups strike a balance between convergence and divergence? To operate between groupthink and polythink? Write up your conclusions.

8. Create a case study based on a group that fell victim to escalation of commitment. Why did the group stay the course? Was it able to deescalate? What was the end result? What do you learn from the case? As an alternative, write a case study based on a group that quit too soon, that prematurely abandoned a project or idea.

9. Examine a significant conflict between groups that produced negative outcomes. Analyze the role played by moral exclusion in this situation. Provide examples of the five elements of exclusion in action. Write up your findings.

10. Which of the dangers described in the chapter does the most damage to the ethical performance of groups? Defend your choice.

CASE STUDY 8.1

Team Denial

Emory University Holocaust studies professor Deborah Lipstadt faced an uphill battle when she was sued by British amateur historian David Irving in 1995. Irving was the world's best known Holocaust denier. He claimed that Hitler didn't order the killing of Jews. Instead, the Führer's subordinates acted on their own, without his knowledge. Irving's most audacious assertion was that no Jews and other victims were gassed at the Auschwitz concentration camp. He denied that there were gas chambers. Instead, deaths were caused by typhus and other illnesses, not murder. Speaking before neo-Nazi groups, Irving declared that more people died in the back of Senator Edward Kennedy's car (one young woman) than were deliberately killed at Auschwitz.

In her book *Denying the Holocaust: The Growing Assault on Truth and Memory*, professor Lipstadt called Irving "a Hitler partisan wearing blinkers" who distorted historical evidence to "reach historically untenable conclusions."[1] Irving then threatened to sue unless she retracted her comments. He likely thought she would settle out of court. Not Lipstadt. Surrender would give deniers a victory, meaning a "second death" to the victims of Auschwitz and other Jews who perished under the Nazis. But Irving had the upper hand. Under British law, Lipstadt had to defend herself from the allegations. (In the United States, accusers have to prove that they have been libeled and defamed.) The lengthy court case would cost over a million dollars to fight and would be held in London, thousands of miles from Atlanta, where Lipstadt taught.

Fortunately for Dr. Lipstadt, others rallied to her cause. Emory gave her financial support and paid leave while hiring adjuncts to teach her classes. (School officials believed that canceling Holocaust courses would be a victory for Irving.) Penguin, her publisher, provided legal and financial support and Jewish groups raised money for her defense. Most important, she gained the support of a top-notch legal team who believed in her cause. This team included (1) those who prepared her case—a team of researchers who gathered information and the attorneys who assembled court documents; and (2) a pair of barristers who argued in front of the judge. (In Britain, one set of attorneys prepares the case while a different set of attorneys presents the case in court.) Lipstadt needed all the help she could get. Preparation for the trial took five years. Researchers had to sift through thousands of documents checking footnotes as well as hundreds of Irving's personal diaries. They generated an eight-foot-tall stack of trial notebooks.

The legal team decided to put Irving on trial, demonstrating how he systematically altered historical evidence to support his anti-Semitic views. That meant that Deborah wouldn't testify, turning her into a spectator at her own trial. Lipstadt, a skilled public speaker, objected to these restrictions but eventually gave in. She said, "Being quiet for me is an unnatural act. But I had legal and historical experts second to none."[2] To prepare for the trial, Lipstadt and barrister Richard Rampton—the attorney who would present the defense case in court—traveled to Auschwitz to collect data. Rampton called the visit a "forensic tour" and gathered information about the size of the camp, the location of the crematoria, and other details. Lipstadt, who treated the camp as a sacred memorial, was offended by the attorney's aggressive questioning.

The trial took five weeks before a judge with Irving representing himself. Because Irving could cross-examine witnesses as his own lawyer, concentration camp survivors (some of whom attended the trial and were eager to speak) were not called upon to testify for fear that Irving would humiliate them. Earlier he had ridiculed a camp survivor on an Australian radio show by asking her, "How much money have you made out of that tattoo since 1945?"[3]

The defense team argued that the amateur historian systematically misreported, altered, and distorted historical documents and photographs to support his racist views. The reason for attorney Rampton's behavior during the team's visit to Auschwitz became clear during the trial. When Irving asserted that the gas chambers were bomb shelters, the barrister was able to demonstrate that the chambers were too far away for the SS guards to take shelter there.

In a 355-page ruling, the trial judge ruled in favor of Lipstadt. He rejected Irving's claims that he had made inadvertent mistakes while doing research. Instead, the judge concluded, "He has deliberately skewed the evidence to bring it in line with his political beliefs."[4] He declared Irving to be "an active Holocaust denier; that he is anti-Semitic and racist, and that he associates with right-wing extremists who promote neo-Nazism."[5] Irving's subsequent appeals of the verdict were denied.

Professor Lipstadt credits her victory to her legal team. She acknowledges that her advisers were right to suppress her desire to testify. (They also forbid her from saying anything to the press outside the courtroom during the proceedings.) Her researchers not only identified deliberate misstatements but were able to produce the needed documents at critical moments during the trial, often catching Irving in contradictory claims. Trial attorney Rampton mastered the historical details of the Holocaust and demonstrated that Irving systematically altered the truth and had ties to radical right-wing groups.

Members of Deborah's team viewed their participation in her defense as a watershed moment in their lives. Rampton said that working on the case was "a privilege," and now that the trial was over, he missed the daily contact with other team members who had become friends. His young assistant felt "enormous pride" that "I have done something that is so important to many others. I made a difference."[6] One of the law partners who prepared the case noted that this was the rare legal confrontation where no accommodation could be made with the other side: "Here there was an absolute difference between right and wrong. We could wholeheartedly be on the side of the angels."[7]

Discussion Probes

1. What risks did Lipstadt take in deciding to go forward with her case? What if she had lost?

2. Why was the denial defense team successful? How did the mission of the team and the values of its members contribute to its success?

3. How do you determine when to follow or when to reject the advice of the group?

4. Have you ever been on a team that performed at a high level? What similarities do you note between your experience and that of the denial defense team?

Notes

1. Lipstadt (2005), p. xx.
2. Muslea (2006).
3. Lipstadt (2005), p. 33.
4. Ibid., p. 275.
5. Joseph (2016).
6. Lipstadt (2005), p. 287.
7. Ibid., p. 288.

Sources: Foster, Krasnoff, and Jackson (2016). Friend (2016).

CASE STUDY 8.2

Groupthink in the Sweat Lodge

In October 2009, a group of spiritual seekers paid from $9,000 to $10,000 each to attend a five-day Spiritual Warrior Retreat near Sedona, Arizona, led by self-help expert and New Age guru James Arthur Ray. Ray is the author of the best-selling book *Harmonic Wealth: The Secret of Attracting the Life You Want* and is featured in the video *The Secret*. His company, James Ray International, took in over $9 million in 2008.

The Spiritual Warrior Retreat, which participants were told "will push you beyond your perceived limits," included seminars, spiritual cleansing exercises, and other activities.[1] The week culminated in a 36-hour vision quest without food or water in the desert, followed by a meal and a closing sweat lodge ceremony. The ceremony was designed as an intense "rebirthing" experience to help participants make significant life changes. Held in a 415-square-foot enclosure built of blankets and plastic sheeting surrounding a fire pit, the lodge could comfortably handle 20 to 25 people but was packed with 55 seekers that day. Heated rocks were placed in the fire pit every round and doused with water. Sandalwood (believed to be toxic when burned) was added to produce incense. Participants sat in darkness, while Ray, standing near the tent door, exhorted them to continue despite their extreme discomfort. He told the group, "Play full on, you have to go through this barrier,"[2] and "You will have to get to a point where you surrender and it's O.K. to die."[3]

The sweat lodge soon became what one reporter called "a human cooking pot," searing the lungs of retreat-goers and baking their internal organs.[4] Not only was the sweat lodge overcrowded, but also the plastic sheeting didn't let the steam escape, further increasing the temperature in the enclosure. Three people died, and 19 more received emergency medical treatment for dehydration, burns, breathing problems, organ failure, and elevated body temperature. Those who were in the lodge report that Ray ignored signs that something was terribly amiss. When people started vomiting, he declared that vomiting "was good for you, that you are purging what your body doesn't want, what it doesn't need."[5] When told that a woman had fainted just after he closed the enclosure door between rounds of the ceremony, Ray continued on, noting, "We will deal with that after the next round."[6]

Police and other observers wonder why participants didn't leave the tent even when they literally began to cook to death. (It should be noted that some might have been overcome before they could save themselves.) Escalation of commitment might be partially to blame. Retreat-goers spent thousands of dollars and invested several days in the event and wanted to continue to the end, hoping for a final spiritual breakthrough. However, groupthink appears to be a more significant contributing factor. The retreat experience put a good deal of pressure on participants to conform. They were isolated, under the direction of a powerful authority figure, and subjected to significant physical stress even before entering the sweat lodge. Thus, it is not surprising that followers displayed symptoms of groupthink. Ray allegedly pressured possible dissenters. He discouraged members from leaving the tent by his presence at the door and by telling those tempted to exit, "You can do better than this."[7] Individuals apparently engaged in self-censorship, keeping their doubts about the safety of the lodge to themselves. One client, for example, was troubled about a game played earlier in the week in which Ray (dressed in white robes) played God and ordered some participants to commit mock suicide. However, she didn't leave then because she didn't want to ruin the experience for others. There was also the illusion of unanimity. Some members of the group may have concluded that if the rest of the participants thought conditions in the lodge were tolerable, then it must be safe to stay. The darkness may have hidden the fact that others were in serious trouble.

Ray claimed that what happened in the lodge was a tragic accident, not a crime, and that he didn't know anyone was in distress. He and his attorneys and supporters argued that the participants were warned of the dangers of the experience (they signed waivers indicating that death could result). A nurse was on duty outside the lodge, and drinks were available. People were free to leave the lodge when they wished.

Ray was acquitted of manslaughter charges (which could have led to a sentence of 30 years) in 2011. He was convicted of three counts of negligent homicide instead, spent two years in prison, and was released in 2013. Since his release, Ray has mounted a comeback, declaring that self-help is "exactly where I should be, and absolutely must be."[8] He currently coaches entrepreneurs and has plans for a book and an online platform. Ray successfully petitioned a judge to restore his right to vote and to hold public office, though the judge refused to set aside his three convictions.

Members of the victims' families feel that the New Age guru should have gotten a much longer sentence and are angry that he is filing motions to get his rights back "while the rest of us [victims' families] are all still living with the pain."[9] They don't think Ray has taken full responsibility for the tragedy and is motivated to return to the self-help business by money, not to help others.[10]

Discussion Probes

1. What other symptoms of groupthink (if any) do you see in this case?
2. Is groupthink a greater danger for spiritual groups than other types of groups? Why or why not?
3. What other ethical danger signs do you see in the sweat lodge tragedy?
4. What steps could retreat participants have taken to protect themselves and others?
5. Was Ray's sentence too harsh or too light? Should his rights be restored and convictions set aside?
6. What do you learn from this case that you can apply as a group member? As a spiritual seeker?

Notes

1. Archibold and Berger (2010).
2. Dougherty (2009c).
3. Lacey (2011).
4. Gumbel (2009).
5. Dougherty (2009b).
6. Dougherty (2009c).
7. Dougherty (2009b).
8. Kravarik and Sidner (2016).
9. Ibid.
10. Other sources for this section are: Archibold (2010). Dougherty (2009a). Lirbyson (2009). O'Neill (2013). Ortega (2011). M. Jacobs (2016). Woods (2017).

CASE STUDY 8.3

To Loan or Not to Loan?

Harry Edwards is the loan officer at High Plains Bank, a small bank located in a town of 3,000 people in rural Oklahoma. High Plains, like many other small financial institutions, makes most of its loans to small businesses and engages in relational banking. In relational banking, bank officials focus on establishing close relationships with customers. Relational banking allows loan officers to get to know their customers better to determine if they are good credit risks. (Small businesses are not required to have audited financial statements.) Customers benefit because the trusting relationships they develop with their bankers allows them more flexibility in negotiating their loan terms. The community benefits as the flow of capital keeps businesses open. However, relational banking can pose a risk to small institutions because it encourages bank officers to make bad loans to those they have befriended.

Edwards is scheduled to meet with the bank president and vice president to evaluate the High Plains loan portfolio, which has not performed well lately. The Highway Market loan will be the main topic of discussion. Highway Market borrowed $500,000 to upgrade its store, replacing the flooring and roof, adding a new bakery and deli department, replacing freezers, creating wider aisles, and so on. However, market owners Bert and Samantha Smith have fallen behind in their loan payments and need another $150,000 to finish the renovation project. They have asked High Plains for the additional amount.

The Smiths are longtime customers of the bank and have never fallen behind in their payments before. Edwards, the bank president, and vice president all serve on community nonprofit boards with the Smiths. In paperwork submitted to High Plains, the Smiths blame their delinquent loan payments on the fact that the disruption caused by the remodel has reduced traffic to their store. They are convinced that the renovation will more than pay for itself in higher sales when completed. While Highway Market is the only grocery store in town (and badly needs the upgrade), Harry knows that a new Walmart superstore featuring low prices is coming to another small community 15 miles away. He anticipates that residents of his town will spend some of their grocery budgets at Walmart after it opens in two months.

Should Harry Edwards recommend that the bank loan another $150,000 to Highway Market? Why or why not?

Source: Background information on relationship banking at small financial institutions is taken from Kang, Zardkoohi, Paetzold, and Fraser (2011).

PART FOUR

PRACTICING ETHICS IN ORGANIZATIONAL SYSTEMS

CHAPTER NINE

BUILDING AN ETHICAL ORGANIZATION

Chapter Preview

Making Ethics Matter
Components of Ethical Culture
   Formal Elements
   Informal Elements
Cultural Change Efforts
Ethical Drivers
Chapter Takeaways
Application Projects

MAKING ETHICS MATTER

As we've seen throughout this text, fallen organizations pay a high price for their moral shortcomings in the form of damaged reputations; declining revenues, earnings, donations, and stock prices; downsizing and bankruptcy; increased regulation; and civil lawsuits and criminal charges. Unfortunately, managers and employees looking to integrate moral values into their work structures and processes often settle for superficial measures that have little influence on day-to-day operations. They focus on complying with legal requirements through official policies; ethical issues are rarely discussed, and decisions are typically made without reference to core values or moral standards. In other words, their ethical efforts are easily disconnected or "decoupled" from the most important organizational activities.[1]

The poor track record of contemporary organizations is proof that the decoupled approach to ethics doesn't work. Our task, then, is to make sure that ethics matter, (1) by ensuring that members recognize the moral dimension of every aspect of organizational life and (2) by encouraging improvement in collective ethical performance. Investigators use a variety of terms to describe such an ethics-based approach, including *integrated, integrity focused, purpose driven*, and *values centered*.[2] However, *transformational* is a more inclusive descriptor. This broader label incorporates integration, integrity, purpose, and values. To transform something means to alter its very nature or essence for the better, producing fundamental, long-lasting, positive change.[3] When applied to ethics, transformation goes beyond lip service to moral values or grudging compliance with legal requirements. Transformation places ethics at the center of the workplace, significantly altering attitudes, thinking, communication, behavior, culture, and systems. Key values drive individual decisions, interpersonal relationships, group interaction, and organizational goals.

Table 9.1 contrasts the qualities of ethically decoupled and ethically transformed organizations. The objective of this chapter is to help you move your organization from the disconnected column to the transformed column or to help it maintain its transformed status. To reach this goal, you will need to understand the components of ethical culture and engage in successful cultural change efforts.

Table 9.1 Characteristics of Ethically Decoupled and Ethically Transformed Organizations

Ethically Decoupled Organizations	Ethically Transformed Organizations
See ethics as a means to an end (profit, better public image)	See ethics as an end in itself
Comply with legal requirements	Exceed legal requirements
Exhibit organizational behavior inconsistent with stated values	Take actions that reflect collective values; the transformed organization "walks its talk"
Are insensitive to potential moral issues	Are highly sensitive to moral dilemmas
Emphasize rules and penalties	Emphasize adherence to shared values
Have a low awareness of ethical duties	Have a high awareness of individual and collective ethical responsibilities
Engage in dysfunctional conflict	Engage in functional conflict
Tolerate misbehavior	Swiftly punish misbehavior
Rarely discuss ethics; rarely use moral vocabulary	Routinely discuss ethics using moral vocabulary
Omit ethics from daily decisions and operations	Make ethics part of every decision and operation
Are driven by practical or pragmatic considerations (the bottom line)	Are driven by mission and values
React to destructive behaviors	Prevent destructive behaviors
Have ethically inconsistent reward structures	Have reward systems that promote moral behavior
Show a high concern for self	Show a high concern for others

(Continued)

Table 9.1 (Continued)

Ethically Decoupled Organizations	Ethically Transformed Organizations
Sacrifice individual rights for organizational good	Honor and protect individual rights
Engage in self-centered communication (monologue)	Engage in other-centered communication (dialogue)
Have low to moderate trust and commitment levels	Have high trust and commitment levels
Have teams that routinely fall victim to unethical group processes	Have teams that are rarely victimized by unethical group processes
Show high concern for the organization	Show high concern for stakeholders, society, and the global environment
Hold and build power bases	Give power away
Exhibit low-level moral reasoning	Base reasoning on universal ethical principles
Prevent members from making moral choices	Equip members to make moral choices
Respond to changes in the ethical environment	Anticipate changes in the ethical environment
Invest little in building a positive ethical climate	Invest significantly in creating and maintaining an ethical workplace (i.e., training, socialization, leader involvement)
Are at significant risk of ethical misbehavior and scandal	Are at low risk of ethical misbehavior and scandal

COMPONENTS OF ETHICAL CULTURE

Scholars from a variety of fields borrow the concept of culture from the field of anthropology to describe how organizations create shared meanings. As members meet and interact, they develop common beliefs, values, and assumptions, which are expressed through architecture, ceremonies, rituals, dress, and other visible artifacts. Culture binds the organization together and, at the same time, greatly influences the behavior of individuals. What members wear and drive to work, the way they carry out their tasks and organize their time, and with whom they socialize at lunch are all products of shared culture. Ethicists are particularly interested in how cultural elements, both formal and informal, promote or discourage moral action. Formal cultural components include core values, mission statements, codes of ethics, structure, boards of directors, reward and evaluation systems, reporting and communication systems, and ethics officers. They are officially acknowledged and recorded. Informal components include language, norms, rituals, and stories.[4] These features are not part of the organization's official record. In this section, I'll describe each of these elements and its relationship to ethical behavior. I will also outline ways you can use each component to contribute to the formation of an ethical environment.

Formal Elements

1. Core Values

Core values serve as enduring, guiding principles. Most organizations have between three and five such values, which are central to their collective identities.[5] Leaders at the Sealed Air Corporation (the makers of bubble wrap) consider their "bedrock values" to be personal accountability, respect for the individual, truth, and fair dealing. They take these values seriously. Concern for truth and fair dealing, for example, prevents company salespeople from slamming the competition. Independent energy producer AES incorporated the following values in the prospectus for its initial public offering: (1) integrity (wholeness, honoring commitments, adhering to the truth, consistency); (2) fairness to all stakeholders and just rewards; (3) fun (creating an enjoyable work atmosphere); and (4) social responsibility (doing a good job of fulfilling the company's purpose and doing something extra for society).[6]

Organizations run into trouble when they either fail to identify and communicate their core values or fail to live up to them. (Case Study 9.1, "Winning at All Costs at Uber," describes a company suffering from its poor values.) Some groups have never taken the time and effort to isolate those principles that set them apart; others have clearly defined values but don't put enough effort into publicizing them. To shape behavior, values must be continually reinforced through training, public meetings, annual reports, corporate videos, brochures, and other means. In addition, leaders must "walk the talk," living out the values through their performance.

Implementation Guidelines. There is no universal set of correct organizational core values. Instead, the key is to determine what members find intrinsically valuable in your work group, regardless of what outsiders think. Ask individuals to identify their own core values. Then bring members from around the organization together to share their personal values and to consider such questions as these: "If we were penalized for holding this core value, would we still hold on to it?" "Would we want to keep this value no matter how the world around us changes in the next 10 years?" "What are the very best attributes of our organization?"[7] Once they have been selected, incorporate these values into decision-making processes and evaluation systems; continually communicate them. Hold your leaders as well as followers to these standards.

2. Mission (Purpose) Statement

A mission statement identifies an organization's reason for being, which reflects the ideals of its members. This statement combines with core values to form what management experts James Collins and Jerry Porras refer to as *core ideology*.[8] Core ideology is the central identity or character of an organization. Collins and Porras found that the character of the outstanding companies they studied remained constant, even as those firms continued to learn and adapt. Examples of purpose statements from the United States, Canada, Great Britain, and Australia are found in Ethical Checkpoint 9.1.

ETHICAL CHECKPOINT 9.1

Sample Mission Statements

Provide children facing adversity with strong and enduring, professionally supported one-to-one relationships that change their lives for the better, forever. (Big Brothers/Big Sisters)

To solve unsolved problems innovatively. (3M)

Seeking to put God's love into action, Habitat for Humanity brings people together to build homes, communities and hope. (Habitat for Humanity International)

To be Australia's finest financial services organization through excelling in customer service. (Commonwealth Bank)

To organize the world's information and make it universally accessible and useful. (Google)

To nourish and delight everyone we serve. (Darden Restaurants)

To develop people to work together to create value for the Company's shareholders by doing it right with fun and integrity. (Canadian Natural Resources)

To bring inspiration and innovation to every athlete in the world. (Nike)

To improve patients' lives by delivering innovative products and services that drive quality and efficiency in pharmaceutical care. (AmerisourceBergen)

To champion every client's goals with passion and integrity. (Charles Schwab)

To provide reliable supplies of energy across the continent, safely and responsibility. (TransCanada)

Dedication to the highest quality of Customer Service delivered with a sense of warmth, friendliness, individual pride, and Company Spirit. (Southwest Airlines)

To create a world class diversified property group. (Stockland—Australia)

To provide products, services and solutions of the highest quality and deliver more value to our customers that earns their respect and loyalty. (Hewlett-Packard)

To create value for customers to earn their lifetime loyalty. (Tesco-Great Britain)

Provide America's taxpayers top quality service by helping them understand and meet their tax responsibilities and by applying the tax law with integrity and fairness to all. (Internal Revenue Service)

We will deliver an ever-improving quality shopping experience for our customers with great products at fair prices. (J. Sainsbury—Great Britain)

To earn money for shareholders and increase the value of their investment. (Cooper Tire & Rubber)

To make Dreyer's Grand Ice Cream, Inc. the leading premium ice cream company in America. (Dreyer's Grand Ice Cream)

To be earth's most customer centric company. (Amazon)

We fulfill dreams through the experience of motorcycles . . . (Harley Davidson)

To unlock the potential of nature to improve the quality of life. (ADM)

Committed to gathering and disseminating the information people need to work, live and govern themselves in a free society. (*Times Mirror*)

To constantly improve what is essential to human progress by mastering science and technology. (Dow Chemical)

Sources: King, Case, and Premo (2011). Corporate websites.

Many mission statements fail to guide and inspire or promote moral conduct. "Maximize shareholder wealth" is a purpose that provides minimal guidance or inspiration to members. Not only does it fail to distinguish a company from its competitors, but few people get excited about increasing earnings per share. Pursuing this objective may promote such unethical activities as overstating revenue, hiding expenses, lying to investors, and shipping shoddy products. In contrast, pursuing such goals as "to bring inspiration and innovation to every athlete in the world" (Nike) and "to improve patients' lives" (AmerisourceBergen) is likely to inspire employees and encourage them to produce quality goods and services that benefit others.

Like core values, mission statements must be continually communicated and reinforced. They, too, can be undermined by inconsistent behavior. Lofty official goals do little to promote morality when leaders and followers ignore them in order to pursue their personal agendas.

Implementation Guidelines. To create your organizational mission statement, try to identify what members of your organization are passionate about, and capture this passion in your document. In the case of a business, ask what purpose would keep employees working for the group even if they had enough money to retire. Evaluate the mission statement on how well it guides, inspires, and promotes moral behavior.

3. Codes of Ethics

Codes of ethics are among the most common ethics tools. Nearly all major corporations have them, along with a great many government departments, professional associations, social service agencies, and schools.[9] Under Securities and Exchange Commission (SEC) guidelines, all publicly traded companies must have codes and enforcement procedures that apply to top-level financial and other managers. The New York Stock Exchange (NYSE), the American Stock Exchange (AMEX), and the NASDAQ Stock Market all require listed companies to adopt ethics codes and disclose their content to the public.[10] Codes must include provisions that describe how the code will be enforced and how the company will respond to violations. The Ethics Resource Center suggests the following outline for structuring codes.[11]

I. Memorable Title
II. Leadership Letter
III. Table of Contents
IV. Introduction—Prologue
V. Core Values of the Organization
VI. Code Provisions—Substantive Matters
VII. Information and Resources

Codes typically address these six areas:[12]

- *Conflicts of interest.* Conflict provisions deal with cases in which employees benefit at the expense of the organization or in which an individual's judgment might be compromised. Cases of conflict of interest include accepting gifts from suppliers or diverting contracts to relatives. Federal guidelines dictate that any waiver of conflict of interest provisions must be promptly reported to shareholders. (We'll take a closer look at financial conflicts of interest in the next chapter.)

- *Records, funds, and assets.* All chartered and tax-exempt organizations must keep accurate financial records. Publicly traded firms must follow SEC regulations as well as state and local laws and their own bylaws.

- *Information.* For-profit organizations try to keep information from competitors. Revealing such data—even to family members—can result in legal action. Public sector organizations, on the other hand, may have codes that encourage compliance with "sunshine laws" that require the release of information.

- *Outside relationships.* Relationships with suppliers, competitors, government agencies, and others have legal and ethical ramifications. Members must avoid behaviors ranging from collusion, price-fixing, and insider trading to gossiping about the competition.

- *Employment practices.* Employment provisions deal with discrimination, drug use, sexual harassment, aggression, and related issues.

- *Other practices.* This category incorporates statements about employee health and safety, the use of technology, treatment of the environment, political activities, overseas conduct, and other topics. One provision found in many codes forbids the use of organizational assets for personal benefit. According to Coca-Cola's code of ethics, such assets include work time, work products, equipment, vehicles, computers, and software, as well as the company's information, trademarks, and name.[13] (Contemporary Issues in Organizational Ethics 9.1 describes how employees use organizational technology for personal use and how firms should respond.)

Despite their popularity, formal ethics statements are controversial. Skeptics argue that they are vague public relations documents designed to improve an organization's image. Few employees know what the codes say, and their provisions are rarely enforced. Worse yet, critics say, codes are ineffectual. These statements do nothing to improve ethical behavior.

Defenders of ethical codes point out that such documents describe an organization's ethical position to insiders as well as outsiders. They are particularly important to newcomers who are learning about the work group's ethical standards and potential moral problems they may face. Referring to a code can encourage members both new and old to resist unethical group and organizational pressures. In the case of wrongdoing, an organization can point to the code as evidence that the immoral behavior is not official policy.

Most important, ethics codes can have a direct, positive influence on ethical behavior.[14] Students who sign honor codes, for instance, are significantly less likely to plagiarize and cheat on tests.[15] Codes influence ethical perceptions even when organizational members don't remember exactly what is in them. Those in organizations with codes judge themselves and their coworkers as more ethical than those in organizations without codes. They believe that their organizations are more supportive of ethical behavior, and they are more satisfied with their group's moral decisions. These employees feel freer to act ethically and are more committed to their organizations.[16]

Researcher Mark Schwartz identified eight metaphors that can help explain how codes influence ethical behavior. These metaphors and their impact on the actions of organizational members are described below.[17]

Rule book: The code clarifies what behavior is expected of employees. Outcome: Members read the code and follow its provisions.

Signpost: The code encourages members to consult with others or organizational policies to determine if an action is ethical. Outcome: Members speak with a manager or an ethics officer and follow the advice they receive.

Mirror: The code confirms whether or not a behavior is acceptable. Outcome: Greater compliance with required behaviors.

Magnifying glass: The code cautions members to exercise care before moving forward. Outcome: Reduces the likelihood of unintentional violation of rules.

Shield: The code equips members to challenge unethical behavior and helps them resist the pressure to engage in unethical activities. Outcome: Increased resistance to unethical requests.

Smoke detector: The code empowers individuals to warn others about inappropriate activities and to convince them to stop. Outcome: Members are more likely to end their unethical behavior.

Fire alarm: The code causes members to contact the appropriate people or offices to report violations. Outcome: The organization intervenes to stop unethical behavior; members are deterred from engaging in immoral activities.

Club: The code is used to force members to comply with its provisions. Outcome: Members modify their behavior due to the threat of discipline.

Implementation Guidelines. While adopting a code doesn't guarantee moral improvement, the evidence cited above demonstrates that codes can play an important role in fostering an ethical environment. You need to encourage your organization to develop a formal set of ethical guidelines, using the input of a variety of organizational members. Make sure that the language of the code is understandable and that employees can meet its expectations. Distribute the document to everyone in the organization. Provide training so workers know how the code provisions apply; provide opportunities to ask questions. Standards will have most impact when senior executives make them a priority and follow their provisions while at the same time rewarding followers who do the same. Back up your code with enforcement. Create procedures for interpreting the code and applying sanctions. Set up systems for reporting problems, investigating charges, and reaching conclusions that are fair and impartial.[18] Listen carefully to determine which metaphors are used to describe the code of ethics in your organization, and adjust these perceptions if necessary. For example, if employees at your firm see the code as a club used to punish unethical behavior, you may want to encourage them to take a more positive perspective, viewing the code as a signpost instead.

CONTEMPORARY ISSUES IN ORGANIZATIONAL ETHICS 9.1

CYBERLOAFING

Internet access has created a new way to procrastinate at work called *cyberloafing* or *cyberslacking*. In cyberloafing, employees use organizational computers, tablets, and smartphones for nonproductive activities like surfing the Web for personal information, playing games, posting Facebook messages, watching cat videos and other videos, managing finances, job hunting, or shopping and chatting online. Estimates of how much time employees spend cyberloafing vary but, according to one survey, American employees spend up to a quarter of their time cyberslacking (10 hours per week). Even conscientious employees routinely engage in cyberslacking, and men are more likely to cyberloaf than women.

Many observers consider cyberloafing unethical because it diverts time and attention from organizational tasks and lowers productivity. However, some researchers suggest that cyberslacking can have positive effects. Non-job-related Internet use reduces stress, provides practice with computer skills, can stimulate creativity, enhances employees' sense of well-being, and helps workers manage their lives so that they can spend more time at work. For example, instead of leaving the office to meet with their children or to run errands, employees can email their kids and conduct banking and other tasks online. Then, too, many employees work online when they are at home, more than making up for any time they spend cyberloafing at the office.

Rather than try to outlaw cyberloafing, organizations can regulate and monitor it instead. (Employees resent close computer monitoring, feeling that "Big Brother" is watching.) Some companies create technology use (TU) codes of conduct that spell out organizational policies and guidelines for Internet use. Some TU codes urge employees to use the Internet and email responsibly, stating that personal use should not interfere with work productivity. Others contain specific provisions that limit the amount of time spent on non-work-related business or specify times when such activity is forbidden. Then, too, as employees we can regulate our own Internet use by setting a schedule for taking online breaks, installing site blockers that limit access or set time limits, and using common sense (turning down the volume, avoiding pornographic and gambling sites).

Sources: D'Abate (2005). Garrett and Danziger (2008). Griffiths (2010). Henle and Blanchard (2008). Grave (2013). Lavoie and Pychyl (2001). Lim and Chen (2012). McGill and Baetz (2011). Sampat and Basu (2017). Trian (2015).

4. Structure

Structure influences moral behavior through the creation of authority relationships, delineation of lines of accountability, and allocation of decision-making rights.[19] As we saw in Chapter 7, leaders are granted a great deal of power over the lives of followers. Their power is enhanced by the fact that people appear "programmed" to obey authority.[20] The greater the demand for obedience, the higher the likelihood that employees will engage in unethical activities and keep silent about the ethical violations they observe.[21]

Lines of accountability are blurred in many large, complex organizations, diffusing responsibility for choices and actions. The result can be an increase in immoral behavior. Managers may deliberately keep themselves in the dark about illegal activities so that they can maintain "plausible deniability" if the wrongdoing ever comes to light. Division of labor and compartmentalization can distance employees from the consequences of their choices.[22] One department can develop a drug, for example, and expect that another department will test it for side effects. At the same time, another unit will market the drug, assuming that the medication is safe. However, the testing group may fail to communicate that there is no way to accurately determine side effects. A harmful drug (like thalidomide, which caused serious birth defects) is released as a result.[23] Individuals may also shift ethical responsibilities from themselves to their roles. They use their jobs as cover by claiming that they had no choice but to engage in unethical behavior or that there was little that they could do to stop immoral or illegal activities.

Allocation of decision-making rights is another important structural determinant of moral behavior. Empowered employees are more likely to make better ethical choices (see Chapter 5). Those closest to the problem are best equipped to solve it and are more likely to be sensitive to ethical issues. Denying decision-making authority to such knowledgeable workers can be costly. This was vividly illustrated in the *Challenger* and *Columbia* space shuttle disasters. In both cases, managers overruled lower-level engineers who had safety concerns.

Implementation Guidelines. Try to modify structural defects that contribute to immoral behavior. As a leader, encourage others to challenge orders and at times disobey them. Help your employees to recognize how their activities relate to the organization's overall direction and to consider how their actions affect others. Ensure that those closest to the ethical dilemma have significant input into how it is resolved.

5. Boards of Directors

Boards of directors sit at the top of the organizational structure. Boards act as the link between those who own the corporation or support the nonprofit and the managers who run the organization. Their role is to see that the organization's business is conducted in the best interests of the stockholders or supporters.[24] They select and oversee top managers who, in turn, set the ethical tone of the organization. Corporate board members have two legal duties—the duty of loyalty and the duty of care. *Duty of loyalty* means that a director must be always loyal to shareholders. For example, an individual can't sit on the boards of two companies (like McDonalds and Wendy's) that compete against each other. *Duty of care* requires that a director make a diligent effort when making decisions, discovering as much information as possible and considering all the alternatives. If a board member meets both of these responsibilities, then the courts generally won't challenge the director's decision, deferring to her/his business judgment.

According to the Business Roundtable, an association of chief executive officers, boards of directors should follow these nine ethical principles.[25]

1. Select the CEO and oversee the CEO and senior management to make sure they operate in a competent and ethical manner.

2. Ensure that top leadership establishes a culture that emphasizes integrity and legal compliance. The goal should be to create long-term value for shareholders through ethical operations. Neither the directors nor management should put personal interests ahead of the interests of the corporation.

3. Help management develop and implement strategic plans. Directors must understand the risks in the company's corporate strategy and help managers prepare for them.

4. Produce accurate financial statements that reflect the true state of the company; disclose information that would impact stock value in a timely manner.

5. Hire an independent accounting firm to audit financial statements prepared by management.

6. Determine the makeup of the board and assess the skills and experience of board members. This includes developing a plan for board succession.

7. Implement compensation policies for top management that are aligned with the firm's strategy. Compensation ought to be tied to corporate performance and compensation policies should be communicated to shareholders.

8. Engage with long-term shareholders about their issues and concerns.

9. Deal with employees, customers, suppliers, and others in a fair manner, according to "the highest standards of corporate citizenship."

Directors are in a difficult spot. They oversee managers, but the managers determine what information directors receive.[26] The CEO is often a very powerful figure who can sway the group's opinion. When the CEO is the chairman of the board, that individual may end up evaluating her or his own performance. Boards have limited time to learn about the day-to-day operations of organizations that in some cases employ hundreds of thousands of people. Some directors serve on multiple boards, which further reduces the time and energy they can devote to their duties. If these challenges weren't enough, directors on some boards are beholden to top management. They might be friends with the CEO, do business with the company, or receive donations from the firm. CEOs may sit on one another's boards. This creates a "you scratch my back and I'll scratch yours" mentality. A CEO is likely to approve a generous pay package for a fellow CEO in hopes that the other CEO will return the favor. Directors who disagree with the CEO or fellow board members' opinions are often the victims of groupthink. They may be asked to leave the board because they threaten the group's cohesion.

Given these factors, it is not surprising that many of the major ethical failures of the past 40 to 50 years can be blamed in large part on corporate and nonprofit boards. The years 2000–2002 marked a watershed period for unethical corporate governance. Directors at Adelphia, Tyco, K-Mart, WorldCom, Global Crossing, and other firms failed both their legal and ethical duties. They did little to stop top managers from making risky investments, diverting funds for personal use, engaging in accounting fraud, lying to investors, and so on. The collapse of Enron, in particular, created a crisis of confidence in corporate boards. Directors at Enron gave their approval to off-the-books financial arrangements that hid corporate debt and benefitted managers at the expense of shareholders. They approved unethical accounting methods and misguided investments that put the company in danger. The firm, once the fifth largest corporation in the United States with a value of $100 billion, collapsed. Investors lost millions; employees lost their jobs and retirement savings. In response to the Enron debacle and other corporate scandals, Congress passed the Sarbanes-Oxley Act. Under its provisions, CEOs must personally attest to the accuracy of financial statements under the threat of imprisonment; board audit committees must have at least one member with financial expertise. In addition, the New York Stock Exchange now requires that member firms have boards consisting of a majority of independent directors who meet regularly without management.

Implementation Guidelines. Future boards will likely fail to carry out their duties, thus helping to sustain unethical organizational cultures. But corporate governance experts suggest that such failure is much less likely if companies follow several guidelines.[27] First, separate the roles of board chair and CEO, designating an independent director as chair. Second, ensure that the company is living up to the requirements of the Sarbanes-Oxley Act. Third, ask managers to present options for decisions, not reports. Fourth, make sure that directors make a concerted effort to gather the information they need, talking to lower-level managers, visiting company or nonprofit locations, and so forth. Home Depot, for example, asks its directors to spend one day a month at one of its stores and to visit 8 to 10 outlets a quarter. Fifth, prevent top officers from serving on the boards of other companies or nonprofits. Sixth, don't allow a director to serve on more than two boards. Seventh, be sure that boards put their responsibilities ahead of group cohesion, welcoming dissent instead of repressing it. (Ethical Checkpoint 9.2 describes an approach to corporate governance specifically designed to foster healthy ethical climates.)

ETHICAL CHECKPOINT 9.2

Integrity-Based Governance

Corporate governance expert Jerry Goodstein argues that businesses ought to restore public trust by demonstrating that they are serious about integrity. They can do so through integrity-based governance. Rather than seeking to serve the interests of just investors (shareholders) or of all

(Continued)

(Continued)

stakeholders (anyone with an interest or stake in the business), they should, instead, be guided by what the company stands for. According to Goodstein: "Governing boards must ask not only what is the bottom line, but how did we get there? In particular, how well did the corporation fulfill the commitments inherent in the corporate values?" (p. 169)

Under the integrity-based model, governing boards would ensure that company strategy reflects its core ideology—its mission and values. For example, a company that values treating workers with respect and dignity would reject a merger with a firm that has a reputation for mistreating employees. CEO performance evaluation and compensation would be tied to how well the executive team achieves the company's long-term mission and creates the necessary systems and processes to support important values. To foster integrity, CEOs would be responsible for continually communicating the company's ideology to shareholders and other stakeholders. Board members would also bring integrity to bear on their deliberations, making decision-making processes accountable to company ideology. This might mean creating integrity board committees or using values to measure company performance. Some healthcare organizations, for instance, use "mission discernment" to apply purpose and values to critical strategic decisions. They discuss how a proposal meets the needs of stakeholders as part of the decision-making process.

Goodstein acknowledges that some investors might object to this new governance model. However, he points out that a board's fiduciary duty is broader than just acting in the stockholders' interest. Boards and top leaders are obligated to act in the best interests of the company. They might decide to take actions that lower the stock price in the short term, for instance, but improve the long-term financial health of the organization. Integrity driven boards would be equipped to prioritize the demands of stakeholder groups, determining whose interests should come first. They would reject the claims of individuals or groups that want to undermine the company's mission and values.

Source: Goodstein (2004).

6. Reward and Performance Evaluation Systems

Organizational members determine what actions are measured and rewarded. They then engage in those activities, moral or otherwise. That fact makes reward systems a powerful determinant of ethical or unethical behavior. Unfortunately, ethical behavior often goes unnoticed and unrewarded. (Who gets praised for *not* padding expense accounts or *not* inflating earnings?)[28] Organizations often reward immoral behavior instead, as in the case of Washington Mutual Savings. Loan officers approved unsuitable and fraudulent mortgages because they were rewarded for doing so. The lender collapsed when losses from these bad loans mounted, causing the largest bank failure in the history of the United States.[29] (Case Study 9.2, "Getting the Ethics You Pay For," describes another bank that rewarded the wrong behavior.)

Focusing on ends to the exclusion of means is another problem with many reward and performance appraisal systems. Consumed with the bottom line, leaders set demanding performance goals but intentionally or unintentionally ignore how these objectives are to be reached. They pressure employees to produce sales and profits by whatever means possible. Followers then feel powerless and alienated, becoming estranged from the rest of the group. Sociologists use the term *anomie* to refer to this sense of normlessness and unease that results when rules lose their force.[30] Anomie increases the likelihood that group members will engage in illegal activities, and it reduces their resistance to demands from authority figures who want them to break the law. Loss of confidence in the organization encourages alienated employees to retaliate against coworkers and the group as a whole.

Implementation Guidelines. Use the following strategies to help ensure that reward and performance systems in your organization reinforce rather than undermine ethical behavior:

- *Catch people doing good (reward moral behavior that might otherwise go unappreciated).* Publicly acknowledge workers who offer outstanding customer service, government departments that spend taxpayer money wisely, and so on.

- *Evaluate current and proposed reward and performance systems to ensure that they are not reinforcing undesirable behavior.* In particular, take note of possible unintended consequences. Consider the case of teacher performance standards based on student test scores. Such standards are supposed to improve learning but can encourage teachers and administrators to cheat (provide too much assistance to pupils, change answers) in order to boost test results. That was the case in Atlanta, where 35 educators, including principals, teachers, test coordinators, and the former district superintendent, were charged with altering test answers.[31]

- *Avoid a bottom-line mentality.* Financial returns (profits, donations) are critical to business and nonprofits alike. Yet focusing solely on the bottom line blinds decision makers to other important responsibilities, like supporting workers and the community. Develop other measures of performance, such as civic involvement and work-family balance. (We'll take an in-depth look at alternative performance scorecards in Chapter 11.)

- *Evaluate based on processes as well as on results.* Measuring how individuals achieve their goals should be part of any performance review process. Provide incentives for moral behavior and disincentives for unethical actions. Punish salespeople who lie about delivery times or exaggerate the features of products, for instance. Resist the temptation to forgive organizational "stars" who generate great results while bending the rules. To reinforce the importance of ethical process, the U.S. Army's chief recruiting officer held a day-long "values stand-down." He took this action after recruiters were accused of making their enlistment quotas by helping unqualified applicants cheat (pass drug tests, hide criminal records). During the stand-down, recruiters viewed a video on Army values, reviewed their oaths of office and correct procedures, and discussed current recruiting challenges.[32]

7. Reporting and Communication Systems

SEC guidelines require publicly held companies to have systems in place for reporting ethical violations. Amendments to the 2004 Federal Sentencing Guidelines require that these mechanisms ensure "anonymous or confidential reporting."[33] Ethics hotlines are the most common reporting tool. Employees use the hotlines, many of which operate 24 hours a day, 365 days a year, to ask for advice and to report ethical problems. One hotline provider studied 200,000 calls and found that two-thirds were made without first talking to management. Nearly two-thirds of reports sparked investigations with nearly half resulting in some action being taken.[34] Members should also be able to contact ethics staff in person for advice and to report problems. To be effective, a reporting system must have the support of top management, protect whistle-blowers, and promptly follow up on allegations of wrongdoing.

Organizations also need systems for communicating ethics messages. Managers should use a wide variety of channels (e.g., email, newsletters, bulletin boards, video conferencing, speeches, meetings) to send messages about corporate values, the provisions of ethics codes, disciplinary actions, and so on. Constant communication is essential to reinforce the importance or salience of ethics. Nevertheless, ethics communication systems need to allow for reflection and feedback. Managers and employees ought to have regular opportunities to discuss ethical issues and values, to analyze past mistakes, and to admit and rectify errors.[35]

Implementation Guidelines. Get the buy-in of top leaders for any reporting system. Provide adequate funding to staff the ethics office and hotlines. Ensure that all reports are confidential and that whistle-blowers are shielded from retribution. If most of your hotline users seek information, take that as a good sign that the system is working. Employees seeking advice are likely trying to prevent problems before they develop. Use every channel possible to continually communicate ethics messages. Create an atmosphere where members feel free to discuss ethical issues. Set aside time for ethical reflection and feedback; engage in active listening.

8. Ethics Officers

Ethics officers (EOs) are charged with making sure that their organizations comply with the law and engage in ethical conduct. They "provide strategic and operational leadership to the ethics and compliance program."[36] The number of ethics officers at large corporations has skyrocketed in recent years. Much of the increase in the number of ethics officers, as well as in budgets and staff, is undoubtedly due to the fact that having a chief ethics officer signals to regulators that the company is serious about compliance. When firms with ethics officers violate the law, they generally receive lower fines. However, organizations are increasingly recognizing the importance of the position. In the past, ethics officers used to hold other titles, like general counsel or human resource director. Now, more chief ethics officers focus exclusively on their ethics and compliance duties.

Two factors are key to the success of chief ethics officers. First, they must have sufficient power and status to command the respect of organizational members and enforce ethical standards.[37] In ethical turnaround situations like the ones at Computer Associates and KPMG, for example, former judges and prosecutors were given wide-ranging power to root out unethical behavior. At Tyco, once notorious for corporate excess and scandal, Eric Pillmore was hired as vice president of corporate governance to oversee the company's ethical transformation. He spearheaded the development of a new corporate code of conduct and then visited sites around the world to introduce the new standards. Pillmore instituted performance evaluations that were based in part on how well employees demonstrated the values of integrity, excellence, accountability, and teamwork.[38]

Second, EOs must have the necessary independence to function effectively. Some experts argue that the EO (as was the case at Tyco) should report directly to the board of directors, not to senior management. Those who report to the CEO may be hesitant to challenge his or her behavior for fear of being fired. That was the case at Strong Capital Management. Tom Hooker, the chief compliance officer, knew that company chairman Richard Strong was engaged in irregular trading practices that favored some shareholders (including Strong himself) while hurting others. Yet, Hooker didn't try to stop Strong. The Securities and Exchange Commission not only punished Strong but also fined Hooker $50,000 and banished him from the investment industry for aiding and abetting the former CEO.

Common duties of ethics officers include these:

- Advising top management and the board of directors
- Ensuring that the company makes the necessary regulatory filings
- Resolving discrimination and sexual harassment cases
- Creating ethics training
- Instituting ethics reforms
- Developing and revising ethics codes
- Monitoring ethical performance
- Ensuring continual ethical improvement
- Overseeing complaint systems
- Chairing ethics committees
- Creating ethics policies
- Communicating ethics concerns and policies to employees
- Enforcing the discipline process
- Representing the interests of shareholders and stakeholders

Implementation Guidelines. Make the ethics officer role a full-time position, and have the board of directors make a strong statement of support for the position. Give the EO the power to interview, challenge, and discipline anyone in the organization. Be sure the office gets adequate funding and that the CEO consults regularly with this person. Have the EO report directly to the board of directors.

Informal Elements

1. Language

Informal language is the type of talk used in daily organizational conversations. Such talk reflects underlying attitudes and values. Language at Goldman Sachs changed as the ethical climate deteriorated, according to former executive Greg Smith.[39] When he joined the financial firm, the focus was on putting the customer first, even if doing so meant less profit for the company. Employees used the term "rabbis" to describe those who mentored new employees and "culture carriers" to refer to those who upheld the values of the firm. Later on cultural values shifted to maximizing profit, even at the expense of clients. The term "quants" was used to describe employees who generated complex mathematical formulas to maximize returns. Employees were encouraged to "hunt elephants" by pursuing trades that generated a minimum of $1 million in profit. Traders began taking advantage of customers, using the term "muppets" to label clients they thought were dumb or stupid.

Language can also blind members to the ethical implications of their actions. Ethics officers report that the word *ethical* is "charged" and "emotional" for some workers.[40] These employees become defensive if their decisions are challenged. They're more comfortable using words like *shared values, mission,* and *integrity* instead. The fact that many employees are uneasy with ethical terminology, coupled with the fact that many managers are morally mute (see Chapter 3), makes it less likely that members will identify the ethical implications of their choices. They decide based on efficiency, profitability, convenience, or other criteria instead of on moral principles. Unethical choices are more likely to result.

Not only do organizational members avoid ethical terminology, but they sometimes invent euphemisms to avoid thinking about the true ethical implications of their choices. It is easier to send troops on a military "mission" than into a full-fledged war, for example, or to "counsel someone out of an organization" instead of firing this individual.

Implementation Guidelines. Be alert to what your organization's vocabulary says about its values and challenge inappropriate labels. You and your colleagues need to become comfortable with moral terminology to encourage ethical behavior. Employ such vocabulary when discussing routine decisions and behaviors. Reject terms that hide the moral dimension of activities.

2. Norms

Norms are widely accepted standards of behavior that reveal how an organization "really works."[41] Some norms ("Deal honestly with suppliers"; "Pitch in to help team members") support ethical conduct. Others ("Do whatever it takes to get the lowest price"; "Do as little as you can") encourage immoral behavior instead. One way to determine what norms are operating is to ask how others would respond to certain behaviors. Would they approve or disapprove of taking office supplies home for personal use or taking long lunches? Approval signals that these behaviors are unofficially sanctioned; disapproval signals that these actions violate norms. Norms generally exert more influence over individual behavior than formal rules and policies do, which helps explain why some codes of ethics are ineffectual. Members will generally do what is expected and accepted even if it is officially forbidden. For instance, while universities officially condemn plagiarism, students continue to copy the work of others when their classmates accept such behavior. Case Study 9.3 describes how one norm kept employees at General Motors from accepting responsibility for a serious safety problem.

Implementation Guidelines. Your organization's norms should be aligned with its ethical codes and policies. Identify important informal standards, and then determine if these norms support your organization's stated rules, mission, and values. If they don't, consider how they might be modified. (See Application Project 5 at the end of the chapter.)

3. Rituals

Rituals are organizational dramas that are repeated at regular intervals. They capture our attention, evoke an emotional response, and help shape our beliefs.[42] Actors follow carefully planned scripts in front of selected audiences; costumes and props may be involved. Take the retirement party, for instance. In this common ritual, workers and managers step away from their usual routines to acknowledge the departing employee. These events typically include food, speeches, and presentations of parting gifts.

Rituals serve many functions, some more visible than others. The manifest function of the retirement party is to honor the retiree while marking an official change in this individual's relationship to the group. Latent or hidden functions of this rite include reinforcing the values and expectations of the organization, demonstrating respect for individuals, cementing the bonds between employees, and signaling that the organization will continue even as it loses valuable members.

Harrison Trice and Janice Beyer provide the most popular typology of organizational rites based on their functions. These six rituals include the following:[43]

- *Rites of passage.* These dramas mark important changes in roles and statuses. One of the most dramatic rites of passage is military boot camp. New recruits are stripped of their civilian identities and converted into soldiers, with new haircuts, uniforms, and prescribed ways of speaking, standing, and walking. Rites of passage impart important values and enforce behaviors. In military boot camps, recruits learn the importance of obeying authority. In company boot camps in Japan, new employees develop loyalty to their firms.

- *Rites of degradation.* Degradation rituals lower the status of organizational members, as when an officer is stripped of rank or when a player is kicked off the team. These routines identify punishable behaviors and signal the organization's willingness to stand behind its values.

- *Rites of enhancement.* In contrast to rites of degradation, rites of enhancement raise the standing of organizational members. Giving vacation trips to top salespeople, announcing the university's teacher of the year, and identifying the team's most valuable player are examples of this type of ritual. Recipients become positive role models, illustrating how members can get ahead in the organization.

- *Rites of renewal.* These rituals strengthen and improve the current system. Examples include team-building exercises, Six Sigma quality processes, and organizational development (OD) programs. The manifest function of such rituals is to bring about improvement. However, they also have hidden consequences, like reassuring members that the organization is dealing with problems and focusing attention toward some issues and away from others.

- *Rites of conflict reduction.* Organizations develop rituals for releasing tension and managing conflicts. Common conflict resolution rituals are collective bargaining sessions and committee meetings. In collective bargaining, union and management representatives engage in such ritualistic behavior as presenting demands and proposals, talking long hours, and threatening to walk out. In committees, members try to resolve differences between competing interests and cooperate to solve problems. The formation of a task force or committee signals that organizational leaders are serious about addressing issues.

- *Rites of integration.* Integration dramas tie members into larger systems, reinforcing feelings of commitment and belonging. Companies hold holiday parties and picnics where members of all ranks mix informally. Integration ceremonies also bind individuals to regional, national, and international associations. Annual conventions and conferences connect professors, lawyers, and doctors to larger professional communities.

Rites of passage, degradation, and enhancement have manifest ethical functions. They reinforce important values, provide role models, and identify desirable and undesirable behaviors. In contrast, rites of renewal, conflict reduction, and integration have latent moral effects. One of the latent ethical effects of renewal rites is the highlighting of important organizational priorities. For example, a company may focus on cost cutting while ignoring diversity issues. Rites of conflict reduction send indirect yet important messages about how an organization values its people. Most airlines are locked into hostile relationships with their unions, for instance. Not so at Southwest Airlines. It treats unions as partners, thus reinforcing the firm's emphasis on building high-quality relationships.[44] Integration rituals, which are designed to increase feelings of belonging, also have the latent effect of tying members to the values and codes of conduct of larger groups.

Implementation Guidelines. Since every ritual has an impact on ethical behavior, direct or indirect, you will need to carefully analyze each one. Some questions to consider include these: What values and behaviors are being reinforced? What priorities are being communicated? Are these values, behaviors, and priorities desirable and ethical? Are important ethical issues being ignored? What might be the unintended ethical consequences of this ritual? (See Application Project 6.)

Trice and Beyer suggest modifying rituals rather than eliminating them. Discontinuing rituals can be risky, since they are important events in the life of the organization. Instead, change current rites and add new ones. Open your firm's books to union personnel during negotiations instead of shutting them out, for instance. Introduce an ethics award to your company's annual gathering, or reward teams of salespeople rather than individuals.

4. Stories

One way to determine an organization's ethical stance is to examine its stories. Narratives, as noted in Chapter 2, provide meaning, impart values, and promote desired behavior.

A tale qualifies as an organizational story when (1) many people know it, not just a few individuals, (2) the narrative focuses on one sequence of events rather than an extended history of a person or organization, (3) central characters are organization members, and (4) the story is supposedly true.

Joanne Martin of Stanford University divides organizational stories into two parts: the narrative itself and the interpretations or morals of the story that follow.[45] Both the narrative and its meaning vary depending on the storyteller, audience, and organizational context. Martin provides three examples of a common story that illustrate how the same basic narrative pattern can send different ethical messages. In the first version of the story, a security guard refused to let IBM chair Thomas Watson enter a restricted area without the proper badge. Instead of firing her, Watson sent someone off to get his badge. In the second version, an assembly-line worker ordered the president of another company to leave the work area and return with his safety glasses. He apologized and obeyed, impressed with the fact that the employee was not intimidated by his organizational rank.

These two accounts demonstrate the importance of upholding the rules regardless of status. In both cases, the high-ranking official complied, thus reinforcing the behavior of the employee. The third variation of the story is quite different and paints a much more negative picture of corporate values. At the Revlon Company, everyone was to sign in when they arrived in the morning. One morning, company founder Charles Revson arrived and picked up the sign-in sheet. The receptionist, who was new, refused to let him take the sheet because she was under "strict orders that no one is to remove the list." Revson then asked her, "Do you know who I am?" She replied that she did not. "Well," Revson said, "when you pick up your final paycheck this afternoon, ask 'em to tell ya."[46]

Heroes play a particularly important role in organizational narratives. They embody organizational values while modeling desirable behaviors. IBM's Thomas Watson was one such figure. Watson's response to the lowly security guard demonstrated how important it was to obey the rules and to treat others with respect. Stories about Watson are still told at IBM and continue to guide behavior. Another enduring corporate legend is that of the 1950s-era Motorola senior executive who negotiated a large sale that would have increased company profits by 25% for that year. However, he walked away from negotiations when the other party demanded a $1 million bribe. Motorola CEO Robert Galvin publicly backed the executive's action and made him an example by telling and retelling his story. Of course, heroes aren't always executives. Walmart's website told the story of a local employee, Norman Price, who returned $11,000 he discovered in a shopping cart.

Not all those cast as heroes truly deserve that label. Enron's Jeffrey Skilling and top trader Lou Pai created a fictional trading floor to impress financial analysts during a 1998 meeting. Visitors were escorted into what was called the Enron Energy Services war room. During their 10-minute tour, they "beheld the very picture of a sophisticated, booming business: a big open room bustling with people, all busily working the telephones and hunched over computer terminals, seemingly cutting deals and trading energy."[47] In reality, it was all a ruse. The room was filled with secretaries and other employees who were brought in for the demonstration and coached to look busy. One administrative assistant reports that she was told to bring her personal pictures to make it look as if she worked at the desk where she sat. The analysts (who were charged with evaluating the financial health of the firm) were completely fooled. Skilling and his accomplices were seen as heroes, which helped foster the climate of deception that led to the firm's collapse.

Implementation Guidelines. Tell stories that reinforce important cultural values. Strive to find heroes who embody these values and provide positive role models; tell their stories at every opportunity. However, your most pressing task may be to reduce the damage done by stories currently being told in your work or volunteer group. Take the case of a tale of an abusive executive, for instance. This narrative, which illustrates how poorly the company treats its employees, can be reframed. If you fire the abuser, the tale serves as an example of how the organization has changed. Lay the groundwork for more positive stories by modeling moral behavior, which can become the basis for future tales.

CULTURAL CHANGE EFFORTS

Every component of culture contributes to the formation of an ethical organizational environment. However, by focusing on each element, it is easy to lose sight of the reality that cultures function as interrelated systems. If you want to change an organization's ethical culture, you must simultaneously address all the components described in the previous section. In fact, introducing piecemeal changes can backfire. Members can become more entrenched in their current behavior patterns when, for instance, managers create a new values statement without also changing the way employees are rewarded and evaluated. Disillusioned workers conclude that management isn't really serious about moral behavior. They greet future ethics initiatives with skepticism.

Highly ethical organizations make sure that cultural components align or support one another.[48] (See our earlier discussion of ethically transformed organizations.) Ethical codes are backed by norms, stories reflect core values, structure supports individual initiative, and so forth. These collectives also demonstrate ethical consistency. All units and organizational levels share a commitment to high moral standards. Ethical values are factored into every organizational activity, be it planning and goal setting, spending, gathering and sharing of information, or marketing. Further, constituents are encouraged and equipped to make ethical choices following core principles.

Ethical Drivers

Ethical drivers are factors that play a particularly significant role in promoting or driving systematic ethical change. Without them, any change effort is likely to fail. These drivers include ethical diagnosis, engaged leadership, targeted socialization processes, ethics training, and continuous ethical improvement.

Driver 1: Ethical Diagnosis

Determining the organization's current ethical condition should be the first step in any systematic change initiative. Diagnosis surfaces moral strengths and weaknesses, areas of misalignment, the criteria for making ethical choices, and shared perceptions of the organization's moral health. These data should then drive the rest of the change effort. For example, the American Hospital Association (AHA) created a six-part organizational assessment tool that focuses on ethics documents, ethics training, organizational structure, organizational character, specific ethical challenges facing the organization, and employee assessment of the organization's ethical performance. Follow-up to the AHA assessment includes developing detailed plans to address problem areas, establishing new policies, redesigning orientation and training programs, and creating a casebook on ethical dilemmas.[49]

Auditing the cultural components described earlier is one way to diagnose your workplace's current ethical condition. The ethical culture audit probes both formal and informal systems, using the questions listed in Self-Assessment 9.1. When conducting the audit, use surveys, interviews, observation, and analysis to gather information. You could also ask these questions when you apply for jobs, to assess the ethical status of prospective employers.

A growing number of firms are also conducting risk assessments.[50] These assessments are designed to identify the organization's vulnerability to fraud and misbehavior. And the risks may be higher than you think. According to the Association of Certified Fraud Examiners, most frauds last 18 months before they are exposed and the average loss is $2.7 million. Organizations lose an estimated 5% of their annual revenues to false financial statements, stolen assets, skimming, check tampering and other forms of fraud.[51] Risk assessments try to develop a comprehensive picture of the group's risk profile by asking: What is the likelihood of fraud and who is most likely to commit fraud and how? What controls are in place to prevent fraud risks? Are there any controls that are inadequate and how should we deal with risks that remain?

SELF-ASSESSMENT 9.1

Ethics Audit Questions

Use the following set of questions to evaluate the ethical culture of your current organization or one that you would like to join.

Selected Questions for Auditing the Formal System

1. Do organizational leaders send a clear ethics message? Is ethics part of their "leadership" agenda? Are managers trained to be ethical leaders?

2. Does the organization incorporate ethics into its selection procedures? Is integrity emphasized in orienting new employees and training existing ones?

3. Does a formal code of ethics and/or values exist? Is it distributed? How widely? Is it used? Is it reinforced in other formal systems, such as performance management and decision-making systems?

4. Does the performance management system support ethical conduct? Are only people of integrity promoted? Are ethical means as well as ends important in performance management systems?

5. Is misconduct disciplined swiftly and justly in the organization, no matter what the organizational level?

6. Are workers at all levels encouraged to take responsibility for the consequences of their behavior? To question authority when they are asked to do something they consider to be wrong? How?

(Continued)

(Continued)

7. Are employees encouraged to report problems, and are formal channels available for them to make their concerns known confidentially?
8. Are ethical concerns incorporated into formal decision-making processes? How? Or are only financial concerns taken into account?
9. Are employees and managers oriented to the values of the organization in orientation programs? Are they trained in ethical decision making?
10. Are ethical considerations a routine part of planning and policy meetings, new venture reports? Is the language of ethics taught and used? Does a formal committee exist high in the organization for considering ethical issues?

Selected Questions for Auditing the Informal System

1. Identify the organization's role models and heroes. What values do they represent? What advice do mentors give?
2. What informal socialization processes exist, and what norms for ethical or unethical behavior do they promote? Are these different for different organizational subgroups?
3. What are some important organizational rituals? How do they encourage or discourage ethical behavior? Who gets the awards—people of integrity who are successful or individuals who use unethical methods to attain success?
4. What are the messages sent by organizational stories and myths? Do they reveal individuals who stand up for what's right despite pressure, or is conformity the valued characteristic? Do people get fired or promoted in these stories?
5. Does acceptable language exist for discussing ethical concerns? Is "ethics talk" part of the daily conversation?

Conclusion

What is your overall evaluation of this organization's ethical culture? What are its areas of strength and weakness?

Source: Trevino and Nelson (2014), pp. 192–193. Reprinted by permission of John Wiley & Sons, Inc.

Climate analysis is another way to measure moral performance. Ethical climate refers to the "shared perceptions of what is ethically correct behavior and how ethical issues should be handled in the organization." Bart Victor and John Cullen's Ethical Climate Questionnaire (ECQ) is by far the most popular measure of shared ethical perceptions.[52] The ECQ classifies moral climates according to (1) the ethical principles that members use to make moral choices and (2) the groups that members refer to when making ethical determinations. Members out to maximize their self-interest are guided by egoism. Individuals may also seek to benefit others (benevolence) or act according to universal standards (principle). To determine what is ethically correct, they may rely on their own judgments, refer to local organizational standards, or look to outside groups for help.

Victor and Cullen identify five climate types. *Instrumental* climates encourage self-serving (egoistic) behavior, which is often economically driven. *Caring* climates emphasize concern for others and the organization as a whole, even at the cost of meeting individual needs. *Rules* climates are governed by the policies, rules, and procedures (principles) developed within the organization. *Law and code* climates turn to external criteria or principles, like professional codes of conduct or state laws, for guidance. *Independence* climates are also principled but encourage individuals to make choices based on their personal values and ethics.

Victor and Cullen suggest that an organization's ethical orientation might make it more susceptible to some forms of unethical behavior and shape its response to change efforts. For instance, members of caring organizations may break laws in order to help others. A written code of ethics is likely to receive a better reception in a rules or law and code climate than in a caring or independence environment.

When it comes to the relationship between climate types and ethical behavior, researchers have discovered the following:[53]

- Ethical climates often vary between departments and locations within an organization.

- Rates of immoral behavior are highest in instrumental climates.

- Organizational commitment and positive feelings toward the organization are greatest in caring climates and lowest in instrumental climates.

- For-profit climates are more likely to be driven by self-interest, while nonprofit climates are more likely to be founded on benevolence.

- An emphasis on obeying the law and adhering to professional codes reduces unethical behavior, particularly when internalized within the organization.

- Employees are more satisfied when they work for organizations with ethical climates that reflect their personal preferences.

- Professionals prefer to work for organizations with rule or law and code climates.

- Authoritarian leadership is positively related to egoistic climates and negatively related to benevolent climates.

- Climate has a similar impact on ethical and unethical behavior in a variety of cultural settings, including North America, Africa, and Asia.

According to these findings, self-interest poses the greatest threat to ethical performance, and you need to confront this attitude, whether at the unit level or organization wide. Creating a more caring environment in your work group can pay off in higher trust and commitment levels; referring to rules and codes can decrease immoral behavior. Finally, match the person (yourself or potential hires) with the climate. Employees are more satisfied and are less likely to leave if their personal ethical preferences match those of the organization.

Driver 2: Engaged Leadership

Significant cultural change is extremely difficult without the buy-in of top leadership.[54] We've already noted how leaders are largely responsible for shaping organizations, play a key role in curbing or promoting destructive behaviors, reinforce or undermine values and standards, and so on.

Organizational psychologist Edgar Schein outlines six primary mechanisms that you can use in a leadership role to establish, maintain, and change ethical culture.[55]

1. *Attention.* Followers will pick up on your priorities through what you pay attention to, measure, and control. Ethics won't be taken seriously unless you consistently talk about the importance of ethical behavior, act ethically, measure moral performance, and punish those who fall short of standards. Systematically and persistently emphasize core values and mission.

2. *Reactions to critical incidents.* The way you respond to stressful events sends important messages about underlying organizational values. Some firms that value efficiency, for example, handle financial setbacks through layoffs. Others, valuing cooperation, cut costs by asking everyone to work fewer hours. Major crises quickly reveal the true ethical character of a leader and his or her organization. Johnson & Johnson CEO James Burke is a case in point. He earned widespread praise for his response to the Tylenol product-tampering crisis. Under his leadership, the company cooperated with authorities, voluntarily recalled the product, admitted when it released faulty information, and developed new packaging. In contrast, the leaders of Toyota waited months after learning of sudden acceleration problems before issuing a recall in the United States; the delay put the lives of thousands of drivers at risk. Executives at BP grossly understated the amount of oil gushing into the Gulf of Mexico following an oil rig explosion.[56]

3. *Resource allocation.* How an organization spends its money is a key indicator of its values and priorities. What types of projects get supported? How much money is devoted to ethics programs and training? Does the organization invest in the health and well-being of its employees? Does it support their personal development? The budgeting process also reveals underlying moral assumptions. The greater the organization's commitment to empowering its members, the more likely it is to involve people from all levels of the organization in setting financial targets. Because resource allocation and budgeting send strong cultural signals, think carefully about what you want to communicate when deciding how to create the departmental or organizational spending plan.

4. *Role modeling.* Acting as a role model is more than setting an example; it also means developing others. Become a coach and teacher to others, particularly to those who report directly to you. Help them identify and manage ethical issues and develop their ethical problem-solving skills.

5. *Rewards.* Rewards, discussed earlier in the chapter as an element of performance and evaluation systems, also go hand in hand with attention mechanisms. Use them to draw attention to important goals, shared values, and desirable and undesirable behaviors.

6. *Selection.* Organizations tend to perpetuate current cultural components by hiring people who fit into the current system. If you want to reform the culture, recruit members who share the new ethical standards rather than the old ones. Include ethics in the recruiting process by highlighting corporate values and looking closely at the character of the candidate. Ask applicants such questions as "What ethics coursework did you take in college?" and "Would you accept a free gift from a supplier?"[57] One outstanding candidate for a pharmaceutical position was asked if he had ever been asked to do anything illegal in business. The candidate was happy to report that he had falsified billing records so that he and a previous supervisor could make their revenue goals. (He didn't get the job.) When selecting individuals for promotion, advance those who support the group's mission values and, if necessary, remove those who don't.

Driver 3: Targeted Socialization Processes

Socialization describes the process of becoming a group member. To make this transition, individuals have to learn how to perform their individual roles and, at the same time, absorb information about the organization's culture.[58] There are several reasons why socialization can play a key role in driving ethical change. First, new members are most susceptible to influence and open to instruction about ethical behavior. Their values and perceptions are being formed, and they are eager to learn how to behave in a new environment. Second, discussion of ethics can be incorporated into existing socialization programs. Third, the values learned during the socialization process will shape an employee's behavior throughout her or his career with the organization. Fourth, when newcomers become ethical veterans, they then communicate and model important values to new generations of members.

Socialization begins even before a member joins a profession or new organization or organizational unit. For instance, some would-be accountants begin adopting the attitudes and beliefs of the accounting profession before they enroll in their first accounting course.[59] Job applicants typically form impressions about the prospective organization gathered from recruitment brochures, websites, and other channels. The employment interview plays a particularly significant role in shaping these expectations. Applicants come away with an image of what the organization is like, which may be unrealistic. This can lead to dissatisfaction and a quick exit after they join.

Formal socialization mechanisms kick in when newcomers begin their membership. As they "learn the ropes," rookies participate in training and orientation sessions designed to integrate them into the organization. They also come under the influence of socializing agents. Important socializing agents include veteran coworkers who serve as day-to-day guides and sounding boards, respected senior peers who guide by example and impart organizational standards and values, supervisors who act as official guides to policies and procedures, and mentors and advisers who model core organizational values and philosophy. Mentoring relationships can play a particularly critical role in ethical socialization.[60] Mentors and mentees are accountable to one another and can discuss how to live out organizational values. They establish trusting relationships in which parties can reveal what they believe and why they hold those convictions. Close contact gives the mentor the opportunity to observe the character and behavior of the mentee in both normal and stressful situations.

Socialization concludes when newcomers become accepted members of the group. It should be noted that new members aren't merely sponges that soak up cultural information. They also help to shape the culture by introducing new values and practices. Those who disagree with important organizational goals and values are generally less productive and more likely to find employment elsewhere.[61] To determine how well you have been socialized into the goals and values of your organization, complete Self-Assessment 9.2.

Unfortunately, socialization processes may contribute to immoral behavior. New members can be corrupted through cooptation, incrementalism, and compromise.[62] In *cooptation*, the organization uses rewards to reduce newcomers' discomfort with unethical behaviors. Targets may not realize that these incentives are skewing their judgment, making it easier to rationalize poor behavior. For example, brokers who are rewarded for pushing certain stocks may convince themselves that these picks are outstanding investments. *Incrementalism* gradually introduces new members to unethical practices, leading them up the "ladder of corruption." Newcomers are first persuaded to engage in a practice that is only mildly unethical. They turn to the rationalizations offered by their peers ("Everybody does it"; "Nobody was really hurt"; "They deserved it") to relieve the cognitive dissonance produced by this act. After the first practice becomes normal, acceptable behavior, individuals are then encouraged to move on to increasingly more corrupt activities. In the end, they find themselves participating in acts that they would have rejected when they first joined the organization. *Compromise* "backs" members into corruption as they strive to solve dilemmas and conflicts. Politicians, for instance, enter into lots of compromises in order to keep and expand their power. Cutting deals and forming networks makes it harder for them to take ethical stands.

The danger of dysfunctional socialization is greatest when newcomers join a social cocoon. A *social cocoon* is a strong culture in which norms and values are very different from those in the rest of the organization or society. In cocoons, members highly prize their membership in the group and tend to compartmentalize their lives, holding one set of values outside work and another on the job. At a prestigious law firm, a cocoon may develop as new attorneys strive to become partners. Veterans of the firm (whom newcomers admire) may encourage rookies to overbill for services and to neglect their families by working extremely long hours. The recent law school graduates put aside their misgivings about these patterns, blaming themselves for their doubts rather than blaming the firm for encouraging unhealthy practices.

As a change agent, target the socialization process in your work group. Promote positive ethical change rather than reinforce corrupt behavior. Start with clearly describing your organization's values and ethical climate in the employment interview. Paint a truthful picture of conditions in your organization. Ask applicants about their ethical experiences and standards. Ensure that ethics is a top priority in orientation and training sessions. Communicate core values and mission statements, present the code of ethics, highlight potential ethical dilemmas, introduce ethics officers and procedures, and engage in ethics discussions. Then place newcomers with socializing agents, particularly mentors, who reinforce rather than undermine values and standards. Provide channels for new hires to express their concerns about ongoing practices. Puncture the social cocoon by training employees to think about the perspectives of outsiders and by bringing in external change agents (new leaders, consultants, speakers).

SELF-ASSESSMENT 9.2

Socialization Scale

This scale, adapted from a much longer instrument, measures how well you have learned/adopted the goals and values of your organization. Complete this scale for an organization of your choice (work, nonprofit, college or university).

1 = strongly disagree, 5 = strongly agree.

1. I would be a good representative of my organization.
2. The goals of my organization are also my goals.
3. I believe I fit in well with my organization.
4. I do not always believe in the values set by my organization.
5. I understand the goals of my organization.
6. I would be a good example of an employee (member) who represents my organization's values.
7. I support the goals that are set by my organization.

Scoring

Reverse your score on item 4 and add up your total. Scores can range from 7 to 35. The higher the score, the more complete your socialization process and organizational fit.

Source: Adapted from Chao, O'Leary-Kelly, Wolf, Klein, and Gardner (1994). Copyright © 2016 by the American Psychological Association. Reproduced with permission.

Driver 4: Ethics Training

Formal ethics training, as we've seen, should be part of the socialization process. However, the need for ethics education doesn't end when members are assimilated into the group. Ongoing training can play an important role in creating and maintaining ethical environments. Training sessions can increase moral sensitivity and moral judgment, make it easier to use moral vocabulary, reduce destructive behaviors, prevent scandals, reinforce mission and values, and integrate ethical considerations into the fabric of organizational life.

Of course, offering ethics training is not a panacea. There is no guarantee that those who attend will make better decisions or change their behaviors; poorly designed training programs can actually increase resistance to change. Nonetheless, effective ethics training can make a positive difference in your organization. Effective training does the following:[63]

1. *Focuses on your organization's unique ethical problems.* The most useful training addresses the dilemmas encountered by group members. Issues that professors face (grading, academic freedom, tenure decisions) will be different from

those encountered by physicians (managed care, patient privacy, malpractice), for instance. Help your organization's employees identify potential ethical issues that may be hidden at first. Introduce examples drawn directly from the organization, industry, and profession. Equip trainees with the tools they need to solve these dilemmas.

2. *Allows plenty of time for discussion and interaction.* Key concepts can be presented in lectures and handouts, but spend most of your class time in dyadic, small group– and large group–discussion. Introduce case studies, raise questions, and debate issues. Trainees can also interact about ethical issues outside of class via the Internet. However, be cautious about offering ethics training solely over the Internet. Web-based programs are not as conducive to in-depth discussion of complex ethical issues.

3. *Taps into the experiences of participants.* Ask your trainees to provide dilemmas and insights drawn from their own experiences. Participants then become the instructors, teaching one another. They also receive feedback that enables them to better handle their dilemmas.

4. *Is integrated into the entire curriculum.* The stand-alone ethics workshop or class promotes moral reasoning but is easily disconnected from the rest of the organization's activities. Whenever possible, you should integrate ethics discussion into other subjects, like sales skills, leadership development, conflict management, and supervision.

CHAPTER TAKEAWAYS

- Strive to create organizations that are ethically transformed rather than ethically decoupled. Transformed organizations are ethics driven; values and standards shape behaviors, decisions, and relationships.

- Both the formal and informal components of your organization's culture will influence the ethical behavior of employees. Address all of these elements to foster an ethical workplace.

- Core values serve as enduring, guiding principles that reflect what organizational members find intrinsically valuable.

- Create a powerful mission or purpose statement that reflects the ideals of members while inspiring and promoting ethical behavior.

- Codes of ethics can play a vital role in improving an ethical climate. Your organization's ethical guidelines need to address the specific ethical dilemmas faced by members and have the backing of senior managers who consistently enforce them.

- Structure shapes ethical behavior through the creation of authority relationships, delineation of lines of accountability, and the allocation of decision-making rights.

- Boards of directors are tasked with seeing that the organization's business is conducted in the best interests of the stockholders/supporters.

- Effective ethical boards maintain their independence from top management and take their duties seriously.

- To promote moral behavior, acknowledge ethical performance, reward desirable (not undesirable) activities, and make sure goals are reached through ethical means.

- Set up channels that members can use to report misbehavior and ask for information. Appoint ethics officers to oversee compliance and ethics programs. Ensure that they have the power and independence to carry out their duties.

- Monitor the organization's vocabulary to see if it reflects unhealthy attitudes and values. Use moral terminology even when making routine decisions, and avoid euphemisms, which hide the ethical implications of choices.

- Create norms—widely accepted standards of behavior—that support, not undermine, formal codes and policies.

- Analyze rituals to determine the behaviors, values, and priorities they promote. Modify those rites that poison the ethical climate.

- Tell and retell organizational stories that model desired behaviors; identify worthy heroes.

- Diagnosis should be the first step in any ethical change initiative. Conduct a risk assessment to identify potential dangers. Use an ethics audit to measure the relationship of cultural components and ethical behavior. Conduct an ethical climate analysis to determine how members perceive what is ethically correct behavior and how they believe the organization deals with ethical issues.

- As a leader, be actively engaged in creating, maintaining, and changing ethical culture through attention, your reaction to critical incidents, resource allocation, role modeling, rewards, and selection.

- Communicate positive moral values and standards to newcomers through recruitment materials, employment interviews, formal orientation programs, and socializing agents.

- Focus ongoing ethics training on your organization's unique ethical problems, allow plenty of time for trainees to discuss issues, tap into the experiences of participants, and integrate discussion of ethics into the entire curriculum.

APPLICATION PROJECTS

1. Brainstorm a list of ethically decoupled organizations and a list of ethically transformed organizations. How do these organizations differ?

2. List the core values of your organization. How well are they publicized? How well are they supported by the behavior of organizational leaders?

3. Evaluate the effectiveness of the mission statements in Ethical Checkpoint 9.1, or, as an alternative, collect and evaluate your own examples. How well do these statements guide, inspire, and promote ethical behavior? What characteristics separate the effective statements from their ineffective counterparts?

4. Partner with an organization to develop a code of ethics for its members. Determine the common ethical issues faced by the group. Follow the guidelines presented in the chapter to create the code provisions. Get feedback from the organization on the usefulness and effectiveness of your document.

5. With your fellow employees, volunteers, or students, identify a list of norms in your organization. Compare these norms with the group's formal code of ethics, core values, and mission statement. Do the norms support the formal cultural components? Brainstorm strategies for bringing them into alignment. Report your findings to a significant organizational decision maker.

6. Do an in-depth analysis of an important organizational ritual. Identify its manifest and latent ethical functions. Write up your findings. As an alternative, analyze an important organizational story to determine the messages it communicates.

7. Complete Self-Assessment 9.1 to analyze your organization's ethical culture. Record your answers to each question. Conclude with an overall evaluation of the group's moral condition and suggestions for improvement. If you can, distribute the ethics audit questions to others, and discuss your findings as a group.

8. Analyze your socialization experience from an ethical vantage point. How well did the organization communicate its values and standards? Was ethics incorporated into the job interview? How well were you socialized based on your answers to Self-Assessment 9.2? What could be done to improve the socialization process?

9. Attend an ethical training program, and evaluate its effectiveness using the guidelines in the chapter.

10. Interview an organizational ethics officer, basing your questions on material presented in the chapter. Report the results of your conversation to the rest of the class.

11. Create a case study based on an organization's attempt to change its ethical culture. Outline what can be learned from this group's experience.

CASE STUDY 9.1

Winning at All Costs at Uber

In early 2017, Uber, the world's leading ride-sharing service, had a very bad month. Within the span of 30 days, the $70 billion company suffered a series of blows:

- Former Uber engineer Susan Fowler blogged about her "slightly horrifying" time at the company.[1] She reported that male managers routinely engaged in sexual harassment (one propositioned her on her first official day at work). Human resource staff ignored her complaints, defending repeat harassers who were star performers by continually claiming they were "first time offenders."
- A *New York Times* report backed up Fowler's claims, finding widespread harassment (a manager was fired for groping multiple women) as well as evidence that employees snorted cocaine at a company retreat.
- The senior vice president of engineering was fired after it was revealed that, before coming to Uber, he had been fired from Google for sexual harassment.
- Several high-level executives quit, including company president Jeff Jones, who had been at the firm only six months. In his resignation statement, Jones criticized management, saying, "The beliefs and approach to leadership that have guided my career are inconsistent with what I saw and experienced at Uber."[2]
- A video surfaced of company founder and president Travis Kalanick berating an Uber driver.

- Google—a major investor in the company—sued Uber for stealing its self-driving-car technology.
- Uber blamed "human error" when one of its self-driving cars was involved in an accident when, in fact, the car's system failed to recognize a red light at an intersection.
- The #DeleteUber hashtag movement encouraged users to boycott the company, blaming it for trying to make extra profits off of an anti-immigration ban protest at New York City's Kennedy airport.
- News stories revealed that for years Uber used a secret software program to evade authorities in Las Vegas; Portland, Oregon; Boston; Australia; China; Italy; and other cities and countries where it was banned or closely regulated.

The tsunami of bad news was the product of a corporate culture that has been called "toxic," "aggressive," and "unrestrained." Uber's culture, in turn, is a reflection of founder Travis Kalanick. Since Kalanick and a partner started their firm in 2009 after failing to land a cab ride in Paris, Uber has been focused on growth at seemingly any cost. Kalanick is combative, willing to take on taxi companies, government officials, and anyone else who might stand in his way. He doesn't let government edicts slow him down, operating in cities that have outlawed the service. The company seemingly battles everyone, being the subject of more lawsuits than any other comparable startup. Many of these suits involve the classification of drivers as contractors instead of employees. Others address labor laws violations, passenger safety, lax driver background checks, and lack of access for disabled riders.

The company's winner-take-all approach to the marketplace carries over to employee relationships within the company. Uber uses a stack ranking system that pits employees against one another. Their fate depends on the ratings of their direct managers. Those rated highly receive stock bonuses; those receiving low ratings on a bell curve are disciplined. Susan Fowler described a "game-of-thrones political war" among upper management. Managers boasted that they were out to undermine their supervisors so they could take their jobs, withholding critical information and currying favor with other executives.

Rapid expansion and decentralized management helped foster the infighting. General managers in charge of city ride markets operate autonomously. They have wide latitude to make decisions without supervision if they achieve their growth and revenue targets. Geographic regions compete with one another. Company meetings usually begin with highlighting the ride volume in different markets. One former employee compared the system to how the Empire operates in the *Star Wars* films.

> Imagine you're in charge of the outpost and you've got to build this planetary annihilation system, and your boss is back at HQ. In that universe, of course you're going to be aggressive and competitive, because it's your numbers that are going up on the board.[3]

It wasn't until six years after Uber started that CEO Kalanick unveiled the company's official values, called "Uber competencies." These include many traditional values, like vision, obsession with customers' innovation, and communication, but also values like "make magic" (seek major, long-lasting breakthroughs) "super pumpedness" (high energy and enthusiasm), "toe-stepping" (don't sacrifice good ideas

(Continued)

(Continued)

for social cohesion), and "champion's mind-set" (put everything you have on the line for the company to help it succeed.)

Kalanick vowed to change the corporate culture. In an email to employees, the CEO declared his determination to create a better organization, one "where a deep sense of justice underpins everything we do."[4] The firm hired former U.S. attorney general Eric Holder to investigate its corporate culture. The Holder report recommended the company rewrite its cultural values to remove items like "always be hustling" and "principled confrontation" that were used to excuse bad behavior. Holder's group also recommended finding a chief operating officer, changing the firm's party culture (instituting limits on alcohol at company events and in the office), making diversity a priority, and increasing the independence of the board. The Uber board unanimously agreed to adopt all of the report's recommendations, and Kalanick announced he was taking a leave of absence. Soon after, five major investors forced him to resign as CEO, though he remains on the board of directors.

Discussion Probes

1. What has been your experience with Uber? Why do you use the service? Will you continue to use the service? Why or why not?
2. Would Uber be as successful if it focused less on growth?
3. What mistakes did Kalanick make in creating his company? What did he do right?
4. Should Kalanick have been replaced as CEO?
5. Do you think that Uber will succeed in improving the company's ethical culture? What advice would you offer?

Notes

1. Fowler (2017).
2. Newcomer (2017).
3. Isaac (2017b).
4. B. Solomon (2017).

Sources: K. Brown (2016). B. Carson (2017a, 2017b). Dawson (2017). Durden (2017). Griswold (2017). Isaac (2017a, 2017c). Lamm (2017). Marinova (2017). Shontell (2014). B. Smith (2017). Yohn (2017).

CASE STUDY 9.2

Wells Fargo: Getting the Ethics You Pay For

Wells Fargo was the only large U.S. bank to come through the financial crisis largely unscathed. For the most part, Wells Fargo avoided the fines and penalties issued to its competitors. Wells Fargo also acquired Wachovia Bank during the economic downturn, helping it become the world's most valuable bank and the country's largest home lender. CEO John Stumpf earned the nickname "the Mister Clean" of the banking industry. In 2015, he was honored as

Morningstar's CEO of the Year for "shunning activities that put profits above customers."[1]

The sterling reputation of the bank and its CEO took a serious hit when Los Angeles prosecutors revealed that Wells Fargo employees had created 1.5 to 2 million accounts without the knowledge of bank customers. Bank officials used the personal information and funds of their existing customers to open new checking, savings, and other accounts in their names. In some cases, clients were charged fees on accounts they didn't know they had. To hide the fact that they were opening bogus debit cards, employees had the cards sent to bank branches rather than to home addresses. Customers could pay higher loan rates because insufficient funds or overdraft fees charged to phantom accounts lowered their credit scores.

Employees and regulators blame the scandal on Wells Fargo's aggressive cross-selling program. Cross-selling is convincing customers with existing accounts to sign up for other banking services, as in the case of a checking customer who then takes out a home and auto loan. Cross-selling is highly lucrative because the practice generates more revenue from the same customers, often moving them into more profitable products. Wells Fargo is the leading cross-seller in the banking industry, averaging over six accounts per customer. However, the bank wanted to raise the number to eight. Stumpf rallied employees with the slogan "Eight is great!" Loan officers and other employees were faced with losing their jobs if they fell short of sales quotas but received bonuses if they reached sales targets. Fake accounts allowed them to meet sales objectives while being rewarded for doing so.

Leaders at Wells Fargo were slow to address the bogus account scandal, which ended up costing the bank $185 million in fines and penalties while shrinking its valuation. Employees complained about the pressure to cross-sell as early as 2005, but those who spoke up or refused to use unethical tactics say they were fired or demoted. The *Los Angeles Times* revealed the scam in 2013 and the board learned of the problem in 2014. But the bank waited until 2015 to hire consultants to determine the extent of the scam. Shortly thereafter, 5,300 employees were fired. Stumpf was forced to resign. Later the Wells Fargo board took steps to "claw back" much of his compensation as well that of the former head of the community banking division.

According to Mark Pastin, CEO of the Council of Ethical Organizations, what happened at Wells Fargo illustrates the importance of rewarding the right (not the wrong) behavior.

> The Wells Fargo mess teaches a clear lesson which is that you get what you pay for. Specifically, you can talk yourself blue in the face about ethics, as many Wells Fargo managers did, but you cannot send employees a clearer signal than their paycheck ... Organizations signal what they really care about through their reward systems. Remember that the one corporate document every employee reads is their paycheck.[2]

Discussion Probes

1. If you were a customer (or if you are currently a customer) of Wells Fargo, would you change banks?

2. What steps should the bank take to restore the trust of those who might withdraw their accounts and those who plan to stay?

3. Can you think of other organizations that have rewarded the wrong behaviors? What happened as a result?

(Continued)

(Continued)

4. Who deserves the most blame for the scandal? The leaders who pushed cross-selling or the employees who created the fake accounts?

5. When it comes to ethics, do you "get what you pay for"? Why or why not?

Notes

1. Eagan, Wattles, and Alesci (2016).
2. Pastin (2017).

Sources: Cowley and Kingson (2017). A. Davidson (2016). Faux, Keller, and Surane (2016). Fox (2016). Hiltzik (2016a). Mount (2016). Shen (2016).

CASE STUDY 9.3

GM's Deadly Ignition Switch

There is an unwritten "safety contract" between car buyers and automobile manufacturers. In return for purchasing their cars, drivers assume that auto manufacturers will do everything they can to ensure that the cars they make are safe. General Motors, one of the "Big Three" domestic automakers, broke this safety contract. In 2001, GM first learned of problems with the ignition switch on its Chevy Cobalt, Saturn Ion, and other small cars. The switch would turn to the accessory position or to the off position if accidently jostled or if pulled down by the weight of a key chain. When this happened, the engine, power steering, and power brakes would shut down. The airbags were also disabled. One hundred twenty-four deaths are attributed to crashes involving the faulty switch, and a number of survivors suffered injuries resulting in paralysis, amputation, permanent brain damage, and serious burns.

In 2002, Delphi, the switch manufacturer, told GM officials that the part did not meet specifications. In 2006, two engineers ordered a replacement for the original switch. However, they didn't change the part number, which disguised the defect. (The cost of the replacement part was less than $1.00.) In May 2009, a group of company engineers met and concluded, based on data taken from wrecked vehicles, that the switch was at fault. But GM did not issue a recall, choosing instead to issue service bulletins. These bulletins go directly to dealers and are much less expensive than recalls. However, they are not designed to address serious safety problems. During the same period, company representatives told customers that there wasn't enough evidence to establish that the switch was defective. GM lawyers threatened some victims' families who wanted to bring lawsuits. They reached settlements with other families that forced claimants to keep quiet about the switch problem.

It wasn't until December 2013 that a management committee decided to issue a recall for the potentially fatal switch. The recall wasn't announced until eight weeks later, after Mary

Barra became CEO. Initially, 778,000 vehicles were recalled. Eleven days later, the recall was expanded to nearly twice the number of vehicles, followed by a later recall of 1.55 million vans, sport utility vehicles, and sedans. The National Highway Traffic Safety Administration fined GM a record $35 million for failing to promptly notify the agency of problems with the switch, and the company paid 1.7 billion to cover the cost of the recall and $625 million to cover victim claims.

An internal investigation carried out by attorney Anton Valukas (who also investigated the collapse of Lehman Brothers) cleared the top management of wrongdoing in the safety failure and put the blame instead on lower level executives and employees. According to Barra, the Valukas report reveals a pattern of "incompetence and neglect." "Repeatedly," said Barra, "individuals failed to disclose critical pieces of information that could have fundamentally changed the lives of those impacted by a faulty ignition switch."[1] She pointed to "The GM Nod" as evidence of a lack of employee initiative. This term describes how GM managers at meetings nod in agreement about what needs to be done but then leave the room and do nothing. The authors of the Valukas report described a similar phenomenon called "The GM Salute." In the GM Salute, employees sit in meetings with their arms folded, pointing outward at others. This communicates that the responsibility lies with the persons sitting next to them, not with the employee.

Hundreds if not thousands of employees share the blame for GM's failure to recall the faulty switch for over a decade. Staff in several different departments knew about the defective switch but failed to share information across organizational "silos." Company lawyers received word of lawsuits, accident reports, and insurance data, but customer complaints and warranty claims went to the sales and service division. Each of these divisions reports to a different executive, and these executives may not have communicated about the Cobalt model. In one case, GM officials did not know about a fatal 2005 Cobalt crash even though the legal department had a two-year-old open case file on the wreck. Engineers opened and closed four different Cobalt investigations between 2004 and 2009 without widely disclosing the results. There is no indication that the group of engineers who determined that the switch was defective ever spoke to their supervisors or to company executives. In addition, the two engineers who switched the part without changing the part number made it harder for company safety officials and federal investigators to identify the problem. Company attorneys (who likely had suspicions about the switch) stonewalled victims' families. Customer service representatives and communication staff may have unwittingly done their part to carry out the coverup by denying problems and drafting safety bulletins instead of issuing recalls.

GM has taken a number of steps to reshape a culture that failed to take safety seriously, where, in the words of CEO Barra, "there was no demonstrated sense of urgency, right to the end" for addressing the deadly switch problem.[2] Fifteen employees were fired and five disciplined. Safety issues are now a concern of senior management, a department was created to oversee overall safety, new safety investigators have been hired, and an employee safety hotline has been set up.

Discussion Probes

1. What formal cultural factors contributed to the defective switch scandal?

2. What informal cultural factors contributed to the scandal?

(Continued)

(Continued)

3. Have you been in organizations that practice their versions of the "GM Nod" and "GM Salute"? How do members try to shift responsibility?

4. How can General Motors and other large bureaucratic organizations break down organizational silos that keep information from being shared between divisions and departments?

5. What can organizations do to help followers speak up when they identify problems?

6. Should GM employees face criminal prosecution for their role in the cover up?

7. How much blame should go to top leadership for overseeing a culture that failed to correct the defective switch?

Notes

1. Maynard (2014).
2. Heineman (2014).

Sources: Dickerson (2014). Healy (2014). Korosec (2015). (2014). Lauener (2014). Liberto (2014). Muller (2014). Priddle and Bomey (2014). Stout, Vlasic, Ivory, and Ruiz (2014). Vlasic (2014). Vlasic and Stout (2014). Vlasic and Wald (2014). M. L. Wald (2014).

CHAPTER TEN

ETHICAL MARKETING, FINANCE, ACCOUNTING, AND HUMAN RESOURCE MANAGEMENT

Chapter Preview

Ethical Marketing
    Ethical Issues in Marketing
    Ethical Principles and
        Strategies
Ethical Finance and Accounting
    Ethical Issues in Finance and
        Accounting
    Ethical Principles and
        Strategies

Ethical Human Resource
    Management
    Ethical Issues in Human
        Resource Management
    Ethical Principles and
        Strategies
Chapter Takeaways
Application Projects

Forest firefighting crews provide summer employment for college students, particularly for those studying in the western United States. An important part of the forest firefighter's job is managing hot spots so they don't flare up and become major blazes. Hotshot crews parachute in to put out small fires caused by lightning strikes, and when a major fire is contained, firefighters are careful not to leave areas that could reignite.

While forest fire crews have to be alert for physical hot spots, organizational leaders and followers have to recognize ethical "hot spots." These are organizational activities or functions that frequently put the group at risk. Three common ethical hot spots are marketing, finance/accounting, and human resources. Failure to manage these moral danger zones is behind many of the organizational scandals described in previous chapters, including, for example, the Veterans Administration, Fox News, the Port of Portland, Wells Fargo, and Uber. Not only do marketing, financial, and human relations practices offer lots of opportunity to engage in unethical behavior, they are essential to all types of organizations. Every organization must deal with customers, must track and invest financial resources, and must meet the needs of its members.

In this chapter, I'll introduce principles and strategies specifically designed to help you and your organization manage the ethical dangers posed by marketing, financial operations, and human resource management. We can never completely eliminate these hot spots, but we can help prevent them from exploding into ethical fires. In this chapter, I'll describe some of the ethical issues that arise in the practice of each function and then introduce guidelines for responding to these challenges.

ETHICAL MARKETING

Ethical Issues in Marketing

All types of organizations have to manage relationships with customers, including businesses selling products and services, government agencies encouraging citizens to take advantage of their programs, universities trying to lower binge drinking among students, and nonprofits soliciting donors. However, marketing involves far more than the transaction between buyer and seller. Instead, this function "involves all aspects of creating a product or service and bringing it to market where an exchange can take place."[1] These aspects include product, price, promotion, and place. Product describes *what* is being marketed. Price refers to the *cost*, which is determined by the parties in an exchange. Promotion deals with *how* products and services are marketed. Placement is concerned with *where* a product or service gets placed in the marketplace.

Ethical dilemmas arise throughout the marketing process. Important ethical issues include:

1. *Ethical issues related to product:* Product safety, product quality, product design, packaging, labeling, and ethical products.

2. *Ethical issues related to price*: Price fairness, price fixing, price discrimination, price gouging, and misleading pricing. (Turn to Case Study 10.1 to take a closer look at a major pricing controversy.)

3. *Ethical issues related to place:* Exclusive distribution rights, channel control, and slotting allowances.

4. *Ethical issues related to promotion:* Advertising, ethics, product placement, direct marketing, and sales promotion.

5. *Ethical issues related to sales:* Ethical conflicts of salespeople, ethical values and behavior of salespeople.

6. *Corporate ethical decision making:* Corporate ethical decision making, ethical values and ethical behavior of managers, corporate social responsibility (CSR), and marketing.

7. *Codes and norms:* Marketing ethics theory, ethical norms, and codes of ethics.

8. *Ethical issues related to consumers:* Consumer ethical decision making, ethical values, and ethical perceptions of consumers.

9. *Ethical issues related to vulnerable consumers:* Ethical aspects of marketing decisions regarding children, the elderly, and poor people.

10. *International/cross-cultural marketing ethics:* Unethical conduct of multinational corporations, cross-national comparisons of various topics, such as corporate ethical decision making and consumer ethical decision making.

11. *Ethical issues related to marketing research:* Ethical responsibility and conduct of marketing research enterprises and their customers, such as embellishing results, privacy issues, and so on.

12. *Ethical issues related to marketing education:* Integration of ethical questions in marketing education.

13. *Ethical issues related to social marketing:* Concept and definition of social marketing, ethical dimensions of social marketing, social responsibility of marketing managers, and cause-related marketing.

14. *Ethical issues related to green marketing:* Social responsibility and costs of green marketing.

15. *Ethical issues related to law:* Relationship between law and ethics within the marketing field.

16. *Ethical issues related to the Internet:* Web privacy, identity theft, phishing, and online auctions.

17. *Ethical issues related to religion:* Impact of religion and religious values on marketing ethics.

Source: Schlegelmilch and Oberseder (2010), pp. 2–3. Used with kind permission from Springer Science & Business Media.

Ethical Principles and Strategies

As you can see, ethical issues in marketing vary greatly. Fortunately, researchers and practitioners offer guidelines that can help us deal with these issues no matter what form they take. Five such sets of ethical marketing guidelines are the ABCs of marketing ethics, the American Marketing Association's norms and values, the mutuality principle, ethical marketing standards, and marketing virtues.

The ABCs of Marketing Ethics

Marketing professor Patrick Murphy and his colleagues provide some simple rules of thumb to guide marketing managers facing moral choices.[2] To make their guidelines easy to remember, they created short words and phrases beginning with the first three letters of the alphabet.

Applied. Marketing professionals, like professionals in other fields (e.g., medicine, the law, architecture), draw upon ethical theories and values and apply them to the specific problems they face.

Above the law. Ethical marketers go beyond what is required by the law, which sets the baseline expectations of society. Many marketing techniques, while not illegal, still raise ethical concerns. Take the case of "ambush marketing." Creating an ad campaign similar to a competitor's special event promotion is not forbidden by law, but it is widely perceived as unfair.

Aspirational. Marketing executives should always aspire to do their ethical best. They may not always reach their lofty goals but should learn from their mistakes and seek continual improvement.

Beneficial. Ethical marketing benefits the firm or nonprofit over the long run. Unethical marketing can cost the organization market share and bring legal penalties. For instance, the Federal Trade Commission fined Lumosity $2 million for unfounded claims that its brain training program would help users perform better at school and on the job as well as reduce cognitive impairment related to age and health problems.[3]

Beyond the bottom line. Ethical marketers think beyond financial results. They consider the environmental, social, and safety impact of their decisions. For example, ad campaigns for all-terrain vehicles have boosted sales but at a significant cost in deaths and injuries, particularly to children. Advertisers have an ethical duty to communicate safety messages that reduce the risk to riders.

Breaking new ground. Moral imagination, as we saw in Chapter 1, is critical to coming up with solutions to problems that have no easy answers. In response to health concerns and slipping sales, soft drink companies are developing and promoting lower calorie drinks.[4]

Compliance. Marketing managers must comply with federal and state guidelines as well as the codes of ethics of their organizations.

Consequences. Possible negative consequences need to be a consideration in every marketing decision. What might be the negative impact of selling sugary breakfast cereals to children, for instance? Or offering unneeded product warranties?

Contributions. Ethical marketing executives (as well as other ethical leaders) want to make contributions to their customers and to society. They seek to save customers money, provide shoppers with an enjoyable buying experience, create more jobs, stimulate the economy, and so on.

American Marketing Association Statement of Ethics

The American Marketing Association urges practitioners, academics, and students to follow the "highest professional ethical norms" as well as the values that come from serving stakeholders like customers, employees, regulators, investors, peers, and communities. Key components of the AMA's code of ethics include the following:[5]

1. *Do no harm.* Consciously avoid harmful actions or omissions of fact; follow all laws and regulations when making choices.

2. *Foster trust in the marketing system.* Act in good faith and deal fairly with others, which ensures that exchanges are done efficiently. Avoid deception in every aspect of marketing—product design, distribution, pricing, and advertising.

3. *Embrace ethical values.* Build relationships and consumer confidence in marketing by embracing these core values:

   - Honesty—being forthright in dealings with customers and other stakeholders. For instance: tell the truth, stand behind products, honor commitments and promises.

   - Responsibility—accepting the consequences of marketing decisions and strategies. For example: avoid coercion, protect vulnerable market segments, practice environmental stewardship.

   - Fairness—balancing the needs and interests of buyer and seller. For example: avoid deception and false misleading advertising, reject manipulation, refuse to engage in price fixing or predatory pricing, protect the private information of customers.

   - Respect—recognizing the human dignity of all stakeholders. For example: avoid ethnic stereotypes of customers, listen to consumers, treat people from all cultures with respect.

   - Transparency—creating a climate of openness in all marketing operations. For example: communicate clearly, accept criticism, disclose pricing and financing information.

   - Citizenship—fulfilling economic, legal, philanthropic, and societal responsibilities to serve stakeholders. For example: protect the environment, give back to the community through contributions of time and money, treat producers in developing countries fairly.

The Mutuality Principle

Nigerian business professor Juan Manuel Elegido believes that reciprocity should underlie all relationships between companies and their customers.[6] Marketing should create mutually beneficial exchanges between buyers and sellers. Rather than favoring the interest of one party or the other, the interests of both should be kept in mind through win-win transactions.

Elegido outlines four requirements of the mutuality principle which balance the interests of both buyers and sellers.

1. Firms should strive to make their products safe and functional, effectively performing the tasks for which they are purchased. However, the firm doesn't always have to provide the highest quality and service.

2. When pricing products, companies won't charge as much as they could but will match the price with the value supplied to the consumer. On the other hand, firms aren't obligated to offer the lowest possible price.

3. Companies shouldn't undermine the autonomy of consumers by denying them information that will help them benefit from sales transactions. They should also refrain from encouraging buyers to abuse products (alcohol, prescription drugs, etc.). But firms aren't the agents of customers so they don't have to provide all the information that customers might want, like product formulas or manufacturing costs.

4. Sellers should refrain from subverting the interests of buyers by, for instance, trying to increase sales by promoting materialistic messages that can lower self-esteem and increase the risk of anxiety and depression.

Mutuality doesn't eliminate profit but shifts the focus to providing goods and services that are of value to customers while ensuring a fair return to sellers. Under this principle high profits are possible. According Elegido, "There is nothing in this principle that precludes sellers from making large profits; all it requires is that they make their profits by creating very high value for their buyers and then insisting on receiving commensurate benefits from those buyers."[7] Apple products are an example of high-value/high-profit relationships. Consumers are willing to pay high prices for the company's iPhones, iPads, and other devices because they believe they are receiving high value in return. High profit margins and sales have made the company one of the most valuable in the world.

Ethical Marketing Standards

One way to improve ethical performance of marketers is by outlining aspirational standards for them to strive for.[8] These core or essential principles paint a picture of what marketing organizations can and should be. Marketers who want to "operate on a high moral plane" will try to live up to five guidelines. The *principle of nonmalfeasance* is based on the notion that marketers, like doctors, should do no major harm to consumers. Products should be backed by warranties and marketers shouldn't promote products that endanger customers. Under this principle, promoting many weight loss programs and herbal health supplements (which can have serious side effects) would be unethical. The *principle of nondeception* states that marketers should never intentionally mislead or manipulate consumers. Those who exaggerate the benefits of products, promise unrealistic delivery dates or spread lies to undermine political opponents are in violation of this principle. Such practices undermine the audience's normal decision-making process.[9] The *principle of protecting vulnerable market segments* encourages marketers to take "extraordinary care" when selling to children, the elderly, the poor and those with mental challenges. This principle protects the disadvantaged and maintains their dignity. Violators of this precept include rent-to-own furniture outlets and payday loan companies that charge high interest rates.

The *principle of distributive justice* highlights the obligation marketers have to make sure that their practices are fair to all market segments. These practices shouldn't further disadvantage groups that have less information, money and access to products. A supermarket chain that offers better meat and produce in high income neighborhoods than in poor areas falls short on this guideline. However, the distributive justice principle goes beyond the actions of individual marketers to address their shared responsibilities as a profession. An individual company might behave justly but larger marketing trends may be unfair. For example, the "digital divide" means that low-income consumers have less access to computers and the Internet and can't take advantage of additional products and online discounts found on the Web. Collectively, companies who rely heavily on e-marketing have a greater duty to consider and mitigate these effects.

The *principle of stewardship* highlights the social duties of marketers, urging them to serve the common good. Specifically they should not impose additional costs on society or on the environment through their internal marketing programs and activities. For instance, paying substandard wages to marketing employees lowers costs for the company but increases the burden on society if they are forced to go on welfare. The clutter of billboards and electronic signs are a form of aesthetic pollution that puts an added burden on the environment. Stewardship oriented marketers and businesses use sustainable products, buy from local growers, support fair trade polices and so on. (I'll have more to say about sustainability and corporate citizenship in the next chapter.)

Marketing Virtues. Dissatisfaction with the current state of marketing has prompted some experts to argue for significant reform.[10] Not only are many marketing programs wasteful and ineffective (most industries spend half of their resources on the marketing function), but also a great number are unethical, exploiting consumers. Marketers prey on the needs and fears of buyers, deceive them, and pressure the people they trust (doctors, pharmacists) into giving them bad advice. Aggressive, combative marketing mind-sets and tactics need to be replaced by a "kinder, gentler" approach that puts a premium on treating consumers with respect and fostering two-way communication. Ethical reform will require that marketing professionals and their organizations demonstrate high character (see Chapter 2). Here is a list of the virtues that foster positive relationships with customers:

Truth. Restore marketing credibility by being objective and truthful.

Integrity. Maintain high standards with customers.

Authenticity. Don't try to fool customers by "personalizing" impersonal messages.

Trust. Develop mutual trust to build relationships with customers.

Respect. Don't treat customers like idiots.

Reciprocal empathy and vulnerability. Employ empathy with customers and allow marketers and customers to open up to one another.

Dialogue. Listen to consumers instead of always speaking at them.

Manners. Use marketing messages that are polite and deferential instead of loud and insensitive.

Forgiveness. Ask for forgiveness for past abuses.

Courage and patience. Recognize that changing past marketing practices takes courage and time.

Gratitude and recognition. Recognize and honor customers, and help customers recognize outstanding employees.

Humility. Shed the pride and excessive self-confidence of many marketers and organizations.

Perspective. Seek to be a positive force in the lives of consumers, not a nuisance.

ETHICAL FINANCE AND ACCOUNTING

Ethical Issues in Finance and Accounting

Finance and accounting are closely related functions that support the ongoing operations of the organization.[11] *Finance* is concerned with "the generation, allocation, and management of monetary resources for any purpose."[12] The field of finance includes personal finance (how individuals invest and spend); corporate finance (raising and spending capital); public finance (government taxation, borrowing, and spending); financial markets where stocks, bonds, and other financial instruments are traded; and financial intermediaries, such as banks and other lenders that make financial transactions. Ethical issues in finance generally coalesce around these themes:[13]

1. *Financial markets.* Fairness is the key to ethical behavior in financial markets. Securities must be priced fairly, and buyers must be able to determine the true value of a stock or bond. Unfair trading practices include making false statements about the true value of the company, omitting important information from financial reports (e.g., the company is facing a major lawsuit, the CEO is retiring), or bidding up a stock price in hopes of selling at a peak price to other, unwary investors. Unfair trading conditions exist when some people have access to more information. Insider trading—investing in stocks based on information not available to the general public—is illegal. In one major case of insider trading, the former CEO of Dean Foods pled guilty to passing along information on company earnings and expansion plans that enabled a friend to make profits and avoid losses on his $40 million in Dean Foods stock. Unfair financial contracts (home mortgages and futures options, for instance) are vague and deceptive.

2. *Financial services.* The financial services industry includes banks, investment firms, insurance companies, financial planners, and mutual fund and pension firms that generally act as intermediaries between buyers and financial providers. (In some cases, they may market their own financial products directly to consumers.) Acting as an intermediary or as an agent on behalf of someone else brings fiduciary duties or responsibilities. Conflicts of interest—where the interests of the agent interfere with acting in the best interest of the client— are common ethical problems for those in fiduciary roles. (See the discussion of conflicts of interest in negotiation in Chapter 6.) Brokers may sell inferior in-house mutual funds to clients because they generate higher commissions. They might profit from engaging in excessive trading in a client's account, a practice called "churning." Or they may use confidential information from clients to enrich themselves by copying or "piggybacking" on the moves of

successful investors. Analysts might recommend that clients buy the same stocks they are trying to unload from their personal accounts.

Financial sales practices also raise ethical concerns. Agents all too often peddle investment products that are unsuitable for clients or lie about fees and rates of return. Loan officers may encourage homeowners to continually refinance their homes in order to generate fees and bonuses. Insurance agents can "twist" clients by convincing them to replace existing policies with ones that are no better in order to secure additional commissions. Finally, those who manage portfolios for mutual funds, pension funds, and endowments must determine where to put their money. Should they invest in mining companies with operations in war-torn Congo? Buy stock in tobacco makers?

3. *Financial management.* Financial managers make decisions about how to allocate organizational resources. They, too, have fiduciary duties, in this case to their employers. Financial managers are obligated to use organizational assets wisely and not for personal gain. Insider trading violates these duties, as do excessive compensation and benefits. Balancing competing interests raises additional ethical concerns. Financial managers make decisions that impact a variety of stakeholders both inside and outside the organization. They have an obligation to consider the claims of competing groups. Closing a plant may reduce costs, producing higher returns for company investors. However, this determination should not be made without considering the impact on laid-off employees, suppliers, and the local community.

4. *Financial professionals.* Financial employees must make a variety of individual ethical choices that typically challenge their integrity. They may be pressured to overstate earnings or the likely financial return on a project. Or they might be encouraged to make an undeserved stock "buy" recommendation for a company that is a client of the firm. Or they must decide whether or not to accept underwriting business that was secured through a bribe. Employees at giant insurance broker Marsh USA failed to act with integrity when they accepted undisclosed payments from insurance companies for recommending them to clients.

Accounting, as the name suggests, tracks or accounts for the operations of the organization. Accountants provide a picture or report of the organization's health or status. Ethical issues arise in each of the four major functions of accounting:[14]

1. *Auditing.* Maintaining independence is a constant challenge for those who audit organizations. Outside (external) auditors worry that they will lose valuable clients if they point out financial irregularities. Before the Sarbanes-Oxley Act of 2002, many major accounting firms earned much more from consulting than from auditing. Auditors and their supervisors signed off on many questionable accounting practices for fear of losing lucrative consulting contracts with the same firms they were monitoring. Internal auditors often find their independence compromised by their bosses who want them to certify misleading income statements, questionable expenditures, and other forms of financial

fraud. (Turn to Ethical Checkpoint 10.1 for a closer a look at why organizational members commit fraud.)

2. *Management accounting.* Managerial accountants prepare financial statements for managers and, in some cases, for those outside the organization. Their obligation is to create a truthful picture of the firm's financial situation, even if it hurts the company or organization. There are plenty of pressures to be less than candid. Executive bonuses may depend on painting a rosy picture of fourth-quarter earnings; banks are more willing to lend funds if they believe that the organization is in good financial condition. Then, too, accountants have a good deal of discretion in interpreting rules. They may decide to use "aggressive" accounting procedures that, while legal, may disguise the true state of the company.

3. *Tax accounting.* Tax accountants determine what their clients owe the government. They have a responsibility both to the client and to the public through the government. After all, without revenue the government cannot operate, and society suffers. Tax returns should be truthful, and by signing a tax form the preparer is attesting to its accuracy. Common unethical practices include promoting dubious tax shelters, taking advantage of unintended tax loopholes, and signing off on fraudulent returns.

4. *Consulting.* Those who work in accounting firms offer their accounting and consulting (training, financial) services to organizations. As noted above, this has made it difficult for accountants to maintain their objectivity, leading to a number of audit failures. Focusing strictly on profit tempts accountants to ignore the needs of society and to engage in dishonest, deceptive practices.

ETHICAL CHECKPOINT 10.1

The Geometry of Financial Fraud

Auditors often employ a tool called the fraud triangle to estimate the likelihood of financial fraud. Motivation or need is the first side of the triangle. Financial troubles, gambling debts, drug addiction, fear of failure, pressure from employers, and other forces can make employees vulnerable to committing fraud. They then begin to look for ways to meet their needs. Opportunity is the second side of the triangle. Motivated employees cannot commit fraud unless they have the opportunity to do so. Lax financial controls, access to assets, remote locations, high management turnover, and other factors make it easier to engage in illegal activity. Justification (rationalization) is the third side of the triangle. Fraudsters excuse their actions by, for example, promising themselves that they will return the money later. They may claim that the fraud is justified because the company has cut their salaries or benefits.

Fraud experts David Wolfe and Dana Hermanson argue that the fraud triangle should be converted into the fraud diamond by adding a fourth element—capability. They note that major frauds take "the right person with the right capabilities." Wolfe and Hermanson identify six capacities that contribute to the success of fraudsters.

1. *Position or function.* Wrongdoers must have the position, power, or role to carry out the fraud. This helps to explain why corporate CEOS are involved in 70% of illegal public company accounting schemes. Those who oversee functions like setting up vendor accounts or reconciling bank balances are also in a good position to commit fraud.

2. *High intelligence.* It takes knowledgeable, experienced, creative, smart individuals to understand organizational weaknesses and then determine how to exploit those vulnerabilities.

3. *Strong ego and high self-confidence.* Fraudsters often believe they won't get caught or can talk themselves out of trouble if they are. They are often driven to succeed at whatever the cost. Often narcissistic, wrongdoers may take pleasure in both in the crime as well as in demonstrating their superiority by fooling others.

4. *Coercion/persuasion skills.* Successful frauds often take the cooperation of colleagues and followers. Effective fraudsters can convince others to participate in their crimes or to ignore them. They are often bullies who demand that coworkers and subordinates help them carry out their illegal activities.

5. *Skilled liars.* Successful fraudsters are excellent liars, which enables them to escape detection. They can look others in the eye and convince them that they are innocent. Further, fraudsters can remember and manage their lies in order to keep their stories straight.

6. *Immunity from stress.* Perpetuating a fraud over a long period of time is highly stressful. Those who succeed are able to deal with the risk of being detected, the continual need to conceal the fraud, the need to maintain appearances, and so on.

Wolfe and Hermanson go on to suggest that organizations can prevent fraud by paying close attention to capability. Be alert to job candidates who may be tempted to cut corners or who demonstrate authoritarian or bullying tendencies. Impose additional controls on individuals who present a significant risk, such as the aggressive sales vice president focused solely on meeting monthly sales quotas. Rotate functions among staff members to keep any one person from gaining too much knowledge or control. Identify those situations that might pose a risk to the employee with the right capabilities. Continually reassess capabilities and situations to determine if individuals have gained the necessary skills and opportunities to commit fraud.

Sources: Cressy (1950). Lister (2007). Murdock (2008). Wolfe and Hermanson (2004).

Ethical Principles and Strategies

The past few decades have not been kind to the accounting and finance professions. Between 1997 and 2000, 700 firms were forced by the Securities and Exchange Commission to restate their earnings.[15] Then came massive accounting scandals at WorldCom, Enron, Freddie Mac, Global Crossing, K-Mart, and Parmalat. Fraud and mismanagement in the financial services industry led to the near collapse of the U.S. and world economies near the end of the first decade of the millennium. All too often, financial experts violated ethical standards and lost the trust of their fellow citizens, prompting some to describe accounting as "a profession in crisis."[16] To add insult to injury, researchers have discovered that the moral reasoning level of accounting students is lower than that of students in other majors. There is also evidence to suggest that the moral judgment of accounting graduates declines still further after they enter the workforce and later become supervisors and partners in accounting firms![17]

All this bad news has sparked a good deal of soul searching among financial educators and practitioners. What is it, they wonder, about accounting and finance that makes students and professionals susceptible to moral failure? What can be done to encourage the ethical practice of finance and accounting? I will highlight three responses to these questions: (1) recognize the ethical foundations of these fields, (2) follow widely held professional principles, and (3) adopt the right guiding values.

Recognize the Ethical Foundations of Accounting and Finance

Many financial experts consider their work to be value neutral. They view people as rational decision makers driven solely by economic values.[18] These professionals have lost sight of the fact that economic values are not always most important. Financial considerations need to be balanced against concern for others, care for the environment, and other priorities. Focusing only on the bottom line has also made financial experts susceptible to the pressure to "make the numbers" by any means possible. Trained to believe that they serve only their immediate client or organization, they deny their responsibility to other groups, the environment, and their professions. They are reluctant to blow the whistle when they see financial wrongdoing. On the other hand, accountants and other financial workers find it all too easy to view people as numbers or assets, which makes it easier to treat them cruelly.[19] Moving production to another state may save labor and shipping costs, for example, but it uproots families.

Any attempt to improve the ethical performance of financial professionals, then, needs to address the mind-set of practitioners. Recognizing the ethical implications of accounting and finance is a good place to start. These are not ethically neutral activities. In reality, "Virtually all aspects of their [accountants'] work have an ethical dimension."[20] The origins of financial reporting demonstrate that fact. In Jewish tradition, the earliest financial records were kept to ensure that precious metals donated to the tabernacle weren't stolen or misused.[21] In the Middle Ages, double-entry bookkeeping was created to keep track of what was owed to individuals and organizations.[22] In modern times, the work of accountants has a significant impact both inside and outside the organization. As we've seen, corporate leaders use financial reports to make budgets and allocate resources. Investors also depend on the financial description of firms.

Boston University professor Sandra Waddock summarizes the ethical core of accounting this way:

> The accounting profession seems to have failed to acknowledge that accounting is fundamentally an ethical, rather than a technical, discourse. Accountability inescapably assumes the fulfilling of some dutiful

requirements.... Accountants have positions that are inherently value-laden and imbued with ethical responsibilities. Their decisions affect other people, organizations, communities and the natural environment.[23]

Waddock goes on to suggest that as an accountant you are more likely to take your ethical duties seriously and to better serve society if you take a more holistic approach to your preparation. First, develop a sense of balance. The marketplace is *not* all important. Acknowledge the significance of other values, like love, community, spirituality, the desire for meaning, and nature. The needs of business have to be balanced against these other priorities. Second, strive for the integration of body, mind, and heart. Study a variety of disciplines to develop a unified perspective on the organization and its role in society. Look beyond corporate stakeholders to consider how auditing and accounting practices influence the community and the environment.

Third, seek holistic understanding. Recognize the fact that we live in a world of limited resources and that technology has made the world more interdependent. Economic choices have a significant impact on the environment, on societies, and on individuals. Fourth, respect diversity. Honor other cultures, and recognize that accounting is done differently in other countries. Develop the ability to synthesize these differences when making decisions. Fifth, develop a grasp of complex change. Technology, renewed nationalism, immigration, the rise of Islam, and other forces are reshaping the world. Financial professionals will need to develop conflict resolution and collaboration skills at the same time they are transparent and accountable.

Adopt a Different Set of Guiding Values

Accounting professors Michael Shaub and Dann Fisher believe that the ethical performance of the accounting profession will improve if graduates take a different set of values with them into the workforce. They urge accounting students to adopt the following three guiding values:[24]

1. *Don't be stupid.* This principle takes aim at the self-interest or egocentrism that lies at the heart of many accounting scandals. Those who fall victim to moral failure are generally interested only in serving themselves. Shaub and Fisher identify leadership fallacies that warp the reasoning of financial professionals.[25]

   Enron's CFO Andy Fastow fell victim to the *fallacy of omnipotence*, convinced that he was all powerful and could pretty much do whatever he wanted. He believed that he was so skilled at creating ways to hide company debt that he could divert profits to himself and a few others without being discovered. Fastow and CEO Jeffrey Skilling thought they were smarter than anyone else and could keep the special accounting schemes from failing while, at the same time, propping up Enron's stock price (the *fallacy of omniscience*). Former AIG CEO Hank Greenberg, at one time one of the most important leaders in the insurance industry, fell victim to the *fallacy of invulnerability*, believing that he could survive as CEO despite a series of accounting misstatements. (He was wrong.) Ordinary auditors can become convinced of their invulnerability as well, tending to be overconfident about their knowledge and that of their subordinates. As a result, they may rely on outdated procedures and assign tasks to employees that the followers cannot handle. Executives at the KPMG Personal Financial Planning division fell victim to the *fallacy of unrealistic optimism* when they advised clients that the aggressive tax strategies they recommended would survive any challenge from the IRS. Instead, the company had to pay a $456 million fine to avoid prosecution for advocating these tactics.

2. *Tell the truth.* There are three duties to truth telling: integrity, objectivity, and transparency. *Integrity* refers to being honest and candid with other financial experts as well as with the public. Client confidentiality should not keep you, as an auditor, from revealing that a firm has violated widely held accounting or auditing standards. *Objectivity* refers to being impartial and avoiding conflicts of interest. *Transparency* is the duty to make sure that generally accepted accounting principles are carefully applied and that information is openly shared with the public.

3. *Find fraud and expose liars.* Auditors need to be sensitive to the possibility of fraud and to develop creative new ways of uncovering wrongdoing. For example, some colleges and universities are introducing forensic accounting and fraud examination coursework into their curricula. Unfortunately, many accounting programs promote conformity instead of creativity, turning out graduates who are good fits for existing accounting firms. They are ill prepared to dissent when the situation calls for it. These newly minted accountants lack professional skepticism. Professional skepticism refers to being alert to the possibility that financial statements may be inaccurate and to deferring judgment until there is sufficient evidence to draw a conclusion.[26] Characteristics of professional skepticism include a questioning mind-set, the tendency to withhold judgment, curiosity, understanding the motivation and integrity of others, deciding for oneself (autonomy), and self-esteem—belief in one's abilities and the confidence to challenge others. To determine if you demonstrate these traits, complete Self-Assessment 10.1.

SELF-ASSESSMENT 10.1

Skepticism Scale

Statements that people use to describe themselves are given below. Please circle the response that indicates how you generally feel. There are no right or wrong answers. Do not spend too much time on any one statement.

Strongly disagree					Strongly agree
1	2	3	4	5	6

1. I often accept other people's explanations without further thought.
2. I feel good about myself.
3. I wait to decide on issues until I can get more information.
4. The prospect of learning excites me.

5. I am interested in what causes people to behave the way that they do.
6. I am confident of my abilities.
7. I often reject statements unless I have proof that they are true.
8. Discovering new information is fun.
9. I take my time when making decisions.
10. I tend to immediately accept what other people tell me.
11. Other people's behavior does not interest me.
12. I am self-assured.
13. My friends tell me that I usually question things that I see or hear.
14. I like to understand the reason for other people's behavior.
15. I think that learning is exciting.
16. I usually accept things I see, read, or hear at face value.
17. I do not feel sure of myself.
18. I usually notice inconsistencies in explanations.
19. Most often I agree with what the others in my group think.
20. I dislike having to make decisions quickly.
21. I have confidence in myself.
22. I do not like to decide until I've looked at all the readily available information.
23. I like searching for knowledge.
24. I frequently question things that I see or hear.
25. It is easy for other people to convince me.
26. I seldom consider why people behave in a certain way.
27. I like to ensure that I've considered most available information before making a decision.
28. I enjoy trying to determine if what I read or hear is true.
29. I relish learning.
30. The actions people take and the reasons for those actions are fascinating.

Scoring

Items 1, 10, 11, 16, 17, 19, 25, and 26 are reverse-scored (1 = 6; 6 = 1). Then add up the total for all 30 items. Total scores can range from 30 to 180. The higher the score, the greater your tendency to be skeptical.

Source: Hurtt (2010). Used by permission.

Follow Professional Principles

Codes of ethics have long played an important role in regulating ethics in the financial field. Of course, as all the accounting and financial scandals demonstrate, these codes have not always been effective. Professional codes of ethics suffer from all the shortcomings of organizational codes described in the last chapter, including a lack of specifics and enforcement.[27] They do not solve all the ethical dilemmas that arise in accounting and finance. Nevertheless, the principles outlined in these codes are useful. If you are a financial professional, they identify your ethical duties and set a high standard for your behavior.

Those of us who are not involved in financial operations can use these guidelines to evaluate the behavior of those who are. (Test the usefulness of these standards by applying them to the scenarios in Case Study 10.2.)

The Chartered Financial Analyst (CFA) Code of Ethics and Standards of Professional Conduct is an important ethical statement for the finance profession. The CFA code was drafted by the CFA Institute, which is made up of over 100,000 licensed financial analysts and professionals. The CFA code begins by identifying a set of important ethical standards, which are described below:[28]

- Act with integrity, competence, diligence, respect, and in an ethical manner with the public, clients, prospective clients, employers, employees, colleagues in the investment profession, and other participants in the global capital markets.
- Place the integrity of the investment profession and the interests of clients above [one's] own personal interests.
- Use reasonable care and exercise independent professional judgment when conducting investment analysis, making investment recommendations, taking investment actions, and engaging in other professional activities.
- Practice and encourage others to practice in a professional and ethical manner that will reflect credit on themselves and the profession.
- Promote the integrity of and uphold the rules governing capital markets.
- Maintain and improve [one's] professional competence and strive to maintain and improve the competence of other investment professionals.

The Association of Independent Certified Public Accountants (AICPA) Code of Professional Conduct is based on the premise that accounting professionals share a set of moral standards. Here are the six principles or professional standards:[29]

1. *Principle I. Responsibilities:* In carrying out their responsibilities as professionals, members should exercise sensitive professional and moral judgments in all their activities. This principle highlights the moral dimension of accounting. Professional behavior is ethical behavior.[30] Sensitive moral judgment involves consideration of possible harm and benefit, fairness, respect for persons, and concern for others.

2. *Principle II. Serve the public interest:* Members should accept the obligation to act in a way that will serve the public interest, honor the public trust, and demonstrate commitment to professionalism. Accounting serves a social purpose, which is to facilitate commerce. Public interest is defined as the "collective well-being of the community of people and institutions the profession serves." Serving the public also best serves the interests of clients and employers.

3. *Principle III. Integrity:* To maintain and broaden public confidence, members should perform all professional responsibilities with the highest sense of integrity. Integrity means being honest and candid and putting service above

personal interests. When specific rules and standards are not available, the financial professional should ask "Am I doing what a person of integrity would do?" This principle also requires practitioners to follow "the spirit of technical and ethical standards." Hiding liabilities in off-the-books accounts violates this principle, as does trying to circumvent the intent of tax legislation.

4. *Principle IV. Objectivity and independence:* A member should maintain objectivity and be free of conflicts of interest in discharging professional responsibilities. A member in public practice should be independent in fact and appearance when providing auditing and other attestation services. Accountants are to be impartial (removing personal feelings and interests from judgments or recommendations), intellectually honest, and free of conflicts of interest. Members of the profession should avoid even the appearance of a conflict of interest.

5. *Principle V. Due care:* A member should observe the profession's technical and ethical standards, strive continually to improve competence and the quality of services, and discharge professional responsibility to the best of the member's ability. Due care means the accountant should strive for excellence, and continually improve his or her knowledge and skills. The accountant should never accept duties that he or she is not competent to fulfill. Due care also means doing prompt, careful work.

6. *Principle VI. Scope and nature of services:* A member in public practice should observe the Principles of the Code of Professional Conduct in determining the scope and nature of services to be provided. Professional accountants are obligated to follow the AICPA principles in all activities. This means practicing in firms with good quality control systems, avoiding situations where providing consulting services would conflict with auditing functions, and determining whether an activity would be inconsistent with what a true professional would do.

ETHICAL HUMAN RESOURCE MANAGEMENT

Ethical Issues in Human Resource Management

Human resource management (HRM) addresses the human, or "people," side of the organization. It has been defined as "the process of acquiring, training, appraising, and compensating employees, and of attending to their labor relations, health and safety, and fairness concerns."[31] All managers carry out some human relations functions, like determining personnel needs and conducting performance reviews, but HR managers focus exclusively on these duties.[32] Important human resource management activities include the following:

Conducting job analyses

Determining staffing needs

Hiring

Conducting new employee orientation

Designing compensation systems

Providing benefits

Holding performance reviews

Enforcing disciplinary procedures

Training and development

Implementing workforce reductions

Each of these activities, in turn, is an ethical hot spot that can flare up, generating lawsuits and unfavorable publicity while undermining morale and productivity. Ethical issues in human resource management include the following:[33]

Bogus job requirements

Employment discrimination

Lack of workforce diversity

Favoritism in hiring and promotion

Invalid job placement tests

Inconsistent interviewing procedures

Overselling the benefits of working for an organization

Invasion of applicant and employee privacy

Intrusive monitoring of employee activities

Unfair compensation systems

Excessive executive compensation

Biased performance appraisal systems

Conflicts of interest in selecting HR consultants

Indoctrinating employees in a particular religion

Morally objectionable training

Inadequate safety training

Unsafe working conditions

Pressuring employees for charitable contributions or forcing them to engage in volunteer activities

Requiring employees to work long hours

Failure to discipline unethical or illegal behavior

Treating dismissed employees disrespectfully

Contract negotiation disputes

Violations of employee rights

Providing inadequate notification of layoffs

In a market economy, there are three moral hazards or dangers that frequently lead to unethical human resource management behaviors. The first is "regarding employees as mere commodities."[34] Commodifying people means treating them like inanimate objects or impersonal goods. Even the term "human resources" is problematic because it suggests that people are just another resource or commodity like raw materials, money, or land. When people are seen as commodities, it is easy to lose sight of their humanness and to use them to get what we want. Corporations then see their workforces as tools to generate profits, tools that can be downsized or jettisoned altogether if the economy sours. Any notion that people are intrinsically valuable is lost. Former Carl's Jr. fast food CEO Andy Puzder, who was nominated but failed to become U.S. labor secretary, seemed to view his employees as commodities. He told an interviewer that restaurant automation had advantages over people because machines are "always polite, they always upsell, they never take a vacation, they never show up late, there's never a slip-and-fall, or an age, sex, or race discrimination case."[35]

The doctrine of *employment at will* (EAW) encourages managers to treat people as tools.[36] In the United States, employers are generally allowed to fire individuals without providing specific reasons, unless there are employment contracts spelling out grounds for dismissal. This stands in contrast to Europe, where employees can be let go only with justification—the *just cause doctrine*. While employment at will provides a lot of freedom to employees, who can also leave for any reason, this approach clearly favors employers. As long as they don't violate laws against discrimination or certain state statutes, organizations can fire workers as they see fit. Online activities like posting unfavorable comments about the boss on Facebook or a blog are now serving as grounds for dismissal.

Exploitation is the second moral hazard of human resources. Organizations focused solely on profits or reducing expenses are tempted to exploit their members by cutting their wages, forcing them to work more hours, reducing their benefits, and so on. Layoffs become an exercise in cost cutting; human costs are overlooked. Profit is a legitimate goal, but other objectives are also important, like meeting the needs of employees and serving stakeholders. The growth of the contingent workforce has resulted in greater exploitation of workers. Uber, Lyft, TaskRabbit and other companies in the "gig economy," for instance, don't hire employees but treat service providers as independent contractors. As a result, they don't have to pay minimum wage or overtime or provide health insurance or retirement benefits. Even in traditional organizations more workers are finding themselves on the periphery.[37] A small, skilled core of workers hold permanent jobs and receive traditional human resource benefits. The rest of the workforce is made up of temporary contract workers hired at lower rates. These peripheral workers receive little opportunity for training or for promotion and can be let go at any time. A great many universities operate under this model, hiring large numbers of adjuncts to supplement a small core of tenured faculty. As a result, more than half of college faculty are part-time adjuncts with another 19% working full time on temporary contracts.[38]

Defining people in economic terms is the third moral hazard. Like their colleagues in finance, HR managers are tempted to view people only in economic terms. Taking a utilitarian approach, one that bases personnel decisions solely on financial grounds, ignores the human component of human resources. People have intrinsic value and should be able to develop their competencies at work. In addition, they have the right to engage in significant labor.[39]

Ethical Principles and Strategies

All four of the ethical approaches in this final portion of the chapter address the moral hazards described above. Taking a Kantian approach, acting justly, following professional guidelines, and recognizing the potential harm caused by human resource decisions will help us to recognize the dignity of employees, keep us from exploiting them, and encourage us to treat others as people, not as economic resources.

A Kantian Approach to Human Resource Management

Kant, as noted in Chapter 1, urges us to treat humanity as an end. In other words, we need to recognize that persons have inherent dignity. University of Minnesota professor Norman Bowie argues that applying Kantian principles would encourage managers to look beyond shareholders and profit when making human resource decisions.[40] For example, downsizing might reduce costs, but that doesn't mean it should be put into effect. Work hours for all employees could be reduced instead. Retirees and pension holders would also continue to receive their promised benefits despite economic downturns. In addition, companies would no longer coerce or deceive their employees but would be transparent by opening their financial books to workers. Further, everyone coming into contact with the organization—customers, vendors, neighbors—would be treated with respect.

A Kantian perspective on human resources treats businesses and other organizations as moral communities in which members have a significant voice in the rules and policies that govern them. Kantian organizations operate more like democracies, and members are organizational citizens with both rights and duties.[41] These organizational citizens enjoy free speech and privacy rights and receive information on the future of the group. Leaders persuade rather than impose, helping groups make well-reasoned choices.

Providing meaningful work is another way to treat people as ends and to promote their autonomy. From a Kantian perspective, meaningful work supports the right of workers to make decisions, provides a living wage, enables employees to develop their reasoning abilities, does not interfere with moral decision making and reasoning, and lets workers decide what makes them happy. This approach differs sharply from the scientific management tradition that emphasizes division of labor and requires workers to carry out specialized—and often repetitive and boring—tasks in the name of efficiency.

Current human resource practices at a number of corporations clearly violate Kantian principles. Some companies, including clothing retailers and food producers, do not appear to be paying a living wage, leading to a growing number of "working poor" who are forced to rely on various government subsidies. At the same time that many of these corporations claim they can't pay workers better, they reward top executives with lucrative pay packages. Other organizations deny the autonomy of employees by trying to regulate what employees do on their own time. (Turn to Case Study 10.3, "Regulating Love at the Office," for a closer look at human resource policies that may limit the autonomy of workers.)

Acting Justly

Many of the ethical issues in human resource management described earlier—employment discrimination, favoritism in hiring and promotion, biased performance and appraisal systems—involve violations of fairness or justice. Researchers report that there are three types of organizational justice.[42] *Distributive justice* refers to how resources and benefits are allocated. Perceptions of injustice arise, for example, when applicants and employees perceive that jobs and promotions go to less-qualified candidates. As we saw in Chapter 1, John Rawls specifically addresses this type of justice, advocating that we protect the rights of individuals but also encourage the more equal distribution of benefits. That means providing a minimum level of benefits, such as health insurance and a living wage, while lowering the difference in compensation between the bottom and top layers of an organization. At the same time, employees are rewarded based on their contributions.

Procedural justice describes how allocation decisions are made. We may not like the outcome of a decision, but we are generally more willing to accept the determination if it was made using fair procedures. Judgments of procedural justice are based on (1) consistency—everyone is treated the same; (2) lack of bias—no person or group receives unfair treatment; (3) accuracy—determinations are based on accurate information; (4) representation—all relevant stakeholders have input into the decision; (5) correction—there is a process for fixing mistakes; and (6) ethics—professional standards of conduct are not violated.[43]

Interactional justice describes how individuals perceive their treatment by authority figures. Managers are seen as more just if they treat members with dignity and share relevant information with them. (Complete the Organizational Justice Scale in Self-Assessment 10.2 to determine the level of justice in your organization.)

Employees care a great deal about organizational justice. They want to be assured that they will be treated well over the long term; fair treatment signals that they have status and worth in the group. Further, people see fairness as a virtue in and of itself. Treating others fairly is the right thing to do because it protects their value as humans.[44] It's not surprising, then, that investigators have found a strong link between justice perceptions and organizational behavior. If employees believe their organizations are fair, they perform better, are more likely to help one another out, are more satisfied with their jobs, and are more committed to their organizations. This, in turn, boosts the performance of entire organizational units. At the same time, those treated justly are less likely to engage in unethical behavior. Conversely, when organizational members feel unjustly treated, they are more apt to be absent, withdraw, quit, and engage in destructive behavior.[45]

There are a number of ways to foster perceptions of justice when carrying out human resource functions.[46] When it comes to selecting candidates, procedural justice is key. Make sure that questions and criteria are related to the job, and give candidates enough opportunity to make a case for themselves. For instance, set aside adequate interview time, and allow for retaking standardized tests. Interactional justice also plays a role in the selection process. Be considerate of applicants, and provide timely feedback. When it comes to rewards, distributive justice is important, but procedural justice is also a consideration. Being denied a raise is less damaging if the system for making salary determinations is perceived as fair. When it comes to performance appraisal, due process is important. Provide adequate notice of the review—when it will occur and the criteria to be used. Also, involve workers in setting performance standards. Provide a just hearing setting that focuses on the "evidence" of worker performance (not on personal attack); allow employees to provide their own interpretations and to disagree.

SELF-ASSESSMENT 10.2

Organizational Justice Scale

Evaluate your employer or another organization of your choice on the following items. Respond to each of the statements on a scale of 1 (strongly disagree) to 5 (strongly agree).

Strongly disagree				Strongly agree
1	2	3	4	5

1. In general, this company (organization) treats its employees (members) fairly.
2. Generally employees (members) think of this company (organization) as fair.
3. Rewards are allocated fairly in this firm (organization).
4. Employees (members) in this firm (organization) are rewarded fairly.
5. In this firm (organization), people get the reward or punishment they deserve.
6. Supervisors (leaders) in this company (organization) treat employees (members) with dignity and respect.
7. Employees (members) can count on being treated with courtesy and respect in this firm (organization).

Scoring

Scores can range from 7 to 35. The higher the score, the more just you believe your organization to be. You may want to give this instrument to other organizational members to determine if their perceptions are similar to your own.

Source: Adapted from Trevino and Weaver (2001). Used by permission.

SHRM Code of Ethics

The Society for Human Resource Management (SHRM), the largest association of HR practitioners, offers a set of core principles that address the ethical responsibilities members have to their organizations, to themselves, and to employees and stakeholders. These core principles incorporate elements of the Kantian and justice approaches described earlier. A summary of the SHRM Code of Ethics, including some sample guidelines for implementing each provision, is provided below.[47]

Professional responsibility. Add value to the organization and contribute to its ethical success; accept responsibility for individual decisions; engage in activities that enhance the credibility of the HR profession. Guidelines:

Comply with the law, advocate for the "appropriate use and appreciation of human beings as employees."

Professional development. Strive to meet high competence standards; continually strengthen personal competencies. Guidelines: Pursue education, commit to continuous learning, share knowledge to help the profession and other individuals.

Ethical leadership. Act as a role model of the highest ethical standards. Guidelines: Behave ethically in every professional encounter, question the ethics of proposed actions, promote the development of other ethical leaders.

Fairness and justice. Promote fairness and justice for all employees. Guidelines: Respect the intrinsic worth of every employee, treat people with dignity and respect, ensure that everyone has the opportunity to develop their skills, develop and administer just policies.

Conflicts of interest. Protect the interests of stakeholders and personal integrity. Guidelines: Adhere to organizational conflict of interest policies, don't use HR positions for personal gain, don't seek advantage from human resource polices and processes.

Use of information. Protect the rights of individuals when acquiring and disseminating information; ensure truthful communication; facilitate informed decision-making. Guidelines: Ethically gather and use information, maintain current, accurate HR data, safeguard confidential information.

Three Ethical Standards for Dealing With Harm

Many HR management decisions cause harm to at least some organizational members. Some applicants are hired, but the vast majority of job seekers are turned away. When one employee receives a salary increase, others may not. Achieving organizational objectives also comes at a cost to people working in the organization. Layoffs, for example, are often justified as serving the greater good (saving the organization, keeping the majority of members employed) but are extremely costly to those dismissed. This final set of ethical principles is specifically designed to address the reality that many human resource decisions hurt human beings.[48]

Standard 1: Advance the organization's objective. All HR activities need to be aligned with particular goals they are supposed to advance. As a manager, you need to make sure that the practice really does serve the objective. For example, forced-ranking appraisals like the one used at Uber (see the case in Chapter 9) inflict harm on those who rate lowest, even if their performance has been good. Perhaps there is another, less painful way to accomplish the same objective, which is to improve the performance of the work unit. Having a sense of direction makes it easier to carry through on difficult duties and to see that these activities serve a larger purpose. Remember that advancing the organization's objectives does serve employees, owners, suppliers, and clients despite any unpleasant outcomes.

Standard 2: Enhance the dignity of those harmed by the action. Fair procedures, as noted previously, must be followed when making harmful choices. In addition, you must help those who are hurt function effectively *after* the damage has been done. Significant numbers of people undergo suffering as profits and nonprofits alike participate in "cycles of destruction" involving restructuring and downsizing. Others are victimized when they lose out on promotions and pay raises. In these cases, as a human resource specialist, you need to see yourself as more than a messenger bringing bad news; you need to view yourself as a helper who can assist victims as they deal with the consequences of decisions. The goal is to help members recover from the blow and move forward. (Contemporary Issues in Organizational Ethics 10.1 describes how some managers deal with harms done to followers, with mixed results.)

Unfortunately, all too often when the news is bad, organizations, managers, and HR specialists further reduce the dignity of victims. Radio Shack laid off employees via email, for example, and Dell summoned employees to a hotel, where a "firing squad" following a script dismissed employees in eight minutes. Unsuccessful job candidates often receive the same treatment, receiving form letters or brief calls with no justification for why they weren't selected.[49] Organizations adopt such tactics to avoid lawsuits. Managers use refusals and distancing in response to the social awkwardness caused when one person in the interaction has been harmed. *Refusal* describes spending less time explaining how and why the decision was made, which reduces managers' exposure to the threatening situation. They may not know what to say—want to protect their reputations as ethical persons or fear making a bad situation worse. However, victims are upset by such behaviors. *Distancing* refers to reducing or avoiding contact with victims. While such tactics reduce the threat to superiors, they are seen as inconsiderate and insensitive by those harmed. Researchers report that refusal and distancing strategies backfire. Failing to provide explanations is seen as unfair. Recipients of the bad news are less willing to cooperate, and they withdraw or retaliate instead. Ironically, organizations are more, not less, likely to be sued if they fail to provide explanations for their actions. However, explanations need be adequate—reasonable, clear, detailed—in order to be effective. Inadequate explanations like those used by Dell ("The economy is bad"; "We can't afford to keep you") may be worse than not offering explanations at all.

Standard 3: Sustain the moral sensibility of those executing morally ambiguous tasks. This standard focuses on those doing the work of human resource management. As a manager or human resource professional, you must live with the reality that a bonus may go to the wrong person, outsourcing did not significantly reduce costs, or an individual suffered greatly from an unfair performance review. This dissonance can tempt you to ignore unpleasant tasks or to rationalize your behaviors. If you can't deal with the negative emotions that come with making harmful decisions, then you will not consider the dignity of those negatively impacted by those choices. Instead of reducing your dissonance or being overcome with guilt, learn to live with these feelings. Doing so will make you more sensitive to the needs of others, encourage you to address inequities, and help you carry out your responsibilities.

CONTEMPORARY ISSUES IN ORGANIZATIONAL ETHICS 10.1

THE ROBIN HOOD EFFECT

Employing remedial strategies is one way to address harm in the workplace. When organizational policies or high-level executives have treated employees unjustly, middle managers sometimes engage in corrective justice through *invisible remedies*. Managers using invisible remedies offer something extra to wronged employees, for example, an extra day off, a one-time bonus, permission to take tools home, or time to work on personal projects at work. Such remedies are invisible because they are generally hidden from higher-level managers and other employees.

The *Robin Hood Effect* describes the impact these remedial actions have on recipients as well as on their coworkers. According to French business professor Thierry Nadisic, the Robin Hood Effect produces mixed results. Invisible remedies meet three needs of victims: instrumental (the need for material benefits), relational (the need to have their standing in the group acknowledged), and moral (the need to see a wrong corrected). Recipients of invisible remedies generally have positive feelings toward their managers. Yet, their bad feelings toward their companies remain. Coworkers who discover that extra benefits have been offered to a colleague often feel unfairly treated themselves.

Because the Robin Hood Effect describes both positive and negative consequences, Nadisic is hesitant to recommend that organizations encourage the use of invisible remedies. Such tactics appear to offer a convenient, flexible, and effective means to address injustice without having to go through formal procedures. The manager and the immediate work team benefit because the wronged employee is less likely to retaliate or to withdraw. On the other hand, the organization sees little benefit because the victim still has a negative attitude toward the source of the injustice—upper management and the company. Then, too, invisible remedies appear to undermine procedural and distributive justice. The process is secretive and favors some employees over others. Distributing rewards to correct prior injustices may create new inequities.

Source: Nadisic (2008).

CHAPTER TAKEAWAYS

- Marketing, finance/accounting, and human resources are three important organizational activities or functions that put organizations at risk. Manage these ethical hot spots in order to reduce the likelihood that they will damage your group.

- Marketing includes every aspect of generating a product or service and then bringing it to market for an exchange with buyers, including product, price, placement, and performance. Each of these elements, in turn, raises significant ethical issues.

- When engaging in marketing activities, make sure that consumers are capable, avoid deception, and embrace ethical values and virtues that foster positive relationships with consumers. Strive for mutual benefit when interacting with buyers.

- Finance is concerned with the generation and use of funds; accounting tracks the operations of an organization. Remember that both activities have an ethical dimension. Financial priorities need to be balanced with other significant values like the community and the environment. Be careful not to overestimate your abilities; tell the truth; be alert to fraud and deception in others.

- Accounting and finance codes of ethics outline the moral obligations of finance professionals. While not the final word on financial ethics, they can be a useful reminder of the importance of serving the public and maintaining high moral standards.

- Accountants who adopt these values will boost the ethical performance of the profession: Seek to serve others, not the self; tell the truth through integrity, objectivity, and transparency; develop heightened sensitivity to the possibility of fraud.

- Human resource management is concerned with the "people," or human, side of the organization and involves such functions as hiring, training, compensation and benefits, performance appraisal, discipline, and downsizing. The moral hazards you will face as a manager or as an HRM specialist include treating members as commodities, exploitation, and viewing people in economic terms.

- One way to avoid the moral hazards of human resource management is by adopting Kantian principles. This means treating people with dignity and respect while creating moral communities where members have a significant voice.

- Many ethical issues in human resources come from perceptions of unfairness and injustice. Organizational justice is distributive, procedural, and interactional. Distribute benefits as equitably as possible. At the same time, make sure that the procedures for allocating goods are fair, and treat members with courtesy and respect. Follow professional guidelines that recognize the value of individuals and promote justice.

- HRM decisions often cause harm to some organizational members. Mitigate such harm by making sure that (1) your actions advance organizational objectives, (2) you enhance the dignity of those harmed by an action, and (3) you grapple with the moral tensions that come from making decisions that have negative impacts.

APPLICATION PROJECTS

1. Analyze a contemporary marketing campaign using the ethical marketing guidelines presented in the chapter. How ethical is the campaign based on your analysis?

2. Create your own set of ethical guidelines for marketers. Provide examples for each provision.

3. Debate the following:

    Certain products should never be marketed.

    Advertising should never target young children.

    Credit card companies should not be allowed to advertise on college campuses.

    Accounting majors are not as ethical as other majors.

    Finance and accounting are fundamentally ethical activities.

    Professional skepticism is the most important guiding value for accountants.

    Employees should be terminated only for just cause.

    The term "human resources" is exploitative.

    Sellers are justified in limiting the amount of information they provide buyers.

    Marketers are under no obligation to always provide the lowest price and best service.

4. Apply the AICPA and CFA code principles to a case study involving finance and accounting that

was presented in an earlier chapter of this text. What conclusions do you draw and why?

5. Do a research project on what it means to be a professional. What are the hallmarks of a profession? What is the relationship between professionalism and ethics? Write up your findings.

6. Identify other professional codes of ethics, and compare them to the codes described in the chapter. What similarities do you note? Differences? How useful are such codes in promoting ethical behavior?

7. Organizational justice analysis: Analyze your response to Self-Assessment 10.2. What factors contributed to your perceptions of justice or injustice? Based on material from the chapter, what can the organization do to be perceived as more just? Expand your analysis by having others in the organization take the instrument. Interview them to find out why they responded as they did and what they think needs to be done to make the organization more just. Write up your findings.

8. Reflect on a time when you were harmed by an organizational decision. How was this message delivered? Was an explanation provided and was it adequate? Did the bearer of the message engage in refusal and distancing behaviors? Did you feel that you were treated with dignity? What is your perception of the justice climate of the organization?

9. Profession ethical analysis: Determine the ethical challenges you are likely to face if you enter the professions of marketing, finance, accounting, or human resource management. Collect information online and through press reports and written materials. Interview a professional and a professor who teaches in that field. Identify potential ethical issues and what your interviews and research reveal about how to best prepare for these ethical challenges.

CASE STUDY 10.1

Boosting the Cost of the EpiPen: Price Gouging or Good Business?

Soaring drug prices play a major role in driving up the cost of health care. Drug prices increased 20% between 2013 and 2015 and now account for 17% of all health care costs in the United States. Americans pay over twice as much for medications ($858) than citizens in 19 other industrialized nations (who pay an average of $400). An administrator at the Cleveland Clinic compared containing drug costs to "playing whack-a-mole."

Many drug companies acquire existing medications and then jack up the prices of these products to boost profits. Turing Pharmaceuticals bought the rights of an HIV drug and raised the price by 5,000%. Valeant Pharmaceuticals boosted the cost of two heart drugs by hundreds of percentage points, and Jazz Pharmaceuticals increased the price of the sleep disorder drug Xyrem by 29% a year. These firms (particularly Turing) have come under fire for price gouging. However, Mylan Pharmaceuticals has been singled out for quintupling the cost of the EpiPen after purchasing it and other generic drugs from Merck. Between 2007 and 2015, Mylan raised the price of the injector two-pack from $100 to $600. EpiPen currently has no generic equivalent. The device must be replaced every 12 months, and some states require schools to have them on hand in case of emergency.

The EpiPen likely became the focus of the drug pricing controversy because it is widely used and saves lives. Injection of epinephrine immediately counteracts severe allergic reactions like those triggered by bee stings or eating peanut products. The dramatic price increase made the company appear heartless to many. According to one financial analyst: "No one's expecting Mylan to give away their products. But empathy is the most human emotion. And when you raise price year after year—by a lot—for a drug that's lifesaving, it shows a complete lack of empathy."[1] Mylan CEO Heather Bresch (who called the EpiPen "her baby") defended the price increases when appearing before Congress and at a health care summit, blaming the complex health system, the Affordable Care Act, and high insurance deductibles for the drug's increased costs. She claimed that the company had improved the design of the device and offered generous assistance to low-income patients who need the product. When pressed, she admitted the firm makes $100 on each packet sold. But, according to Bresch, few consumers end up paying the full price because of insurance. She also announced that Mylan would roll out a generic version of the drug costing $300.

To some observers, Mylan and Bresch symbolize corporate greed. Representative Stephen Lynch of Massachusetts called the price hikes "disgraceful" and "disgusting." Congressman Elijah Cummings of Maryland accused Mylan of trying "to get filthy rich at the expense of our constituents."[2] Critics point out that Bresch's compensation went up as fast as the price of the EpiPen, rising 600%. She received the second-highest pay package in the drug industry over a five-year period, $18.9 million in 2015 alone. To other observers, Mylan is fulfilling its responsibility to stockholders by maximizing profits. From their perspective, Bresch is a savvy businesswoman doing what she is paid to do, which is to help her company make money. Her pay and that of other executives at Mylan soared because the company's stock price soared under her leadership. According to one of her defenders, "It would have been managerial malpractice had CEO Bresch not tried to maximize Mylan's market position or respond to unfavorable changes in health insurance."[3]

Discussion Probes

1. Do you or someone you know carry an EpiPen? When would you or this other person have to use it?
2. Should the price of some items, like lifesaving drugs, be controlled?
3. What guidelines should we use to determine if an item has a "fair" price? Is the $100 profit on each EpiPen too great based on these standards?
4. Is the dramatic price increase for the EpiPen ethical based on the principles presented in the chapter? Why or why not?
5. Are Mylan and CEO Heather Bresch symbols of corporate greed, or do they demonstrate smart business practices?
6. Would it have been "managerial malpractice" for Bresch *not* to have hiked the price of the EpiPen?

Notes

1. Egan (2016).
2. Bomey (2016).
3. Allison (2016).

Sources: Garde (2016). Ramsey (2016). Silverman (2016). Tuttle (2016). Weintraub (2015).

CASE STUDY 10.2

Accounting/Finance Ethics Scenarios

Scenario 1

Tom Waterman is a young management accountant at a large, diversified company. After some experience in accounting at headquarters, he has been transferred to one of the company's recently acquired divisions run by its previous owner and president, Howard Heller. Howard has been retained as vice president of the new division, and Tom is his accountant. With a marketing background and a practice of calling his own shots, Howard seems to play by a different set of rules than those to which Tom is accustomed. So far, it is working; earnings are up and sales projections are high.

The main area of concern to Tom is Howard's expense reports. Howard's boss, the division president, approves the expense reports without review and expects Tom to check the details and work out any discrepancies with Howard. After a series of large and questionable expense reports, Tom challenges Howard directly about charges to the company for word processing that Howard's wife did at home. Although company policy prohibits such charges, Howard's boss again signed off on the expense. Tom feels uncomfortable with this and tells Howard that he is considering taking the matter to the board audit committee for review. Howard reacts sharply, reminding Tom that "the board will back me anyway" and that Tom's position would be in jeopardy.

ACTION: Tom decides not to report the expense charge to the board audit committee.

Evaluate Tom's action based on the AICPA and CFA codes of conduct.

Scenario 2

Anne Devereaux, company comptroller, is told by the chief financial officer that, in an executive committee meeting, the CEO told them that the company "has to meet its earning forecast, is in need of working capital, and that's final." Unfortunately, Anne does not see how additional working capital can be raised even through increased borrowing, since income is well below the forecast sent to the bank. The CFO suggests that Anne review bad debt expense for possible reduction and holding sales open longer at the end of the month.

At home on the weekend, Anne discusses the situation with her husband, Larry, senior manager of another company in town. "They're asking me to manipulate the books," she says. "On the one hand," she complains, "I'm supposed to be the conscience of the company, and on the other, I am supposed to be absolutely loyal." Larry tells her that companies do this all the time and that when business picks up, then she will be covered. He reminds her how important her salary is to maintaining their comfortable lifestyle and that she should not do anything drastic that might cause her to lose her job.

ACTION: Anne decides to go along with the suggestions proposed by her boss.

Evaluate Anne's decision based on the AICPA and CFA codes of conduct.

(Continued)

(Continued)

Scenario 3

Drew Isler, the plant's chief accountant, is having a friendly conversation with Leo Sullivan, operations manager and old college buddy, and Fred LaPlante, the sales manager. Leo tells Drew that the plant needs a computer system to increase operating efficiency. Fred adds that with the increased efficiency and decreased late deliveries, their plant will be the top plant next year.

However, Leo wants to bypass the company policy that requires the purchase of items costing more than $20,000 to receive prior board approval and to be capitalized. Leo would prefer to generate orders for each component part of the system, each of which is under the $20,000 limit, and thereby avoid the approval "hassle." Drew knows that this is clearly wrong from a company standpoint as well as an accounting and financial standpoint, and he says so. Nevertheless, he eventually says that he will go along.

Six months later, the new computer system has not lived up to its expectations. Drew indicates to Fred that he is really worried about the problems with the computer system and that the auditors will discover how the purchase was handled in their upcoming visit. Fred acknowledges the situation by saying that production and sales are down, and his sales representatives are also upset. Leo wants to correct the problems by upgrading the system (and increasing the expenses) and urges Drew to "hang in there."

ACTION: Feeling certain that the system will fail without the upgrade, Drew agrees to approve the additional expense.

Evaluate Drew's decision to invest the additional funds based on the AICPA and CFA codes of conduct.

Source: Sweeney and Costello (2009), pp. 92–94. Reprinted by permission of the publisher (Taylor & Francis Group, http://www.informaworld.com).

CASE STUDY 10.3

Regulating Love at the Office

The office has become a hotbed of romance. In one survey, 60% of employees surveyed reported that they had participated in an office romance during their careers and 64% said they would do so again. And the percentage of workplace romances is likely to climb as younger workers (ages 25 to 34) put in more hours at work. As one human resource writer notes:

> Traditional places like church, family events, and leisure time don't present the same pool of candidates as they did in earlier times. The workplace provides a preselected pool of people who share at least one important area of common ground. People who work together also tend to live within a reasonable dating distance, and they see each other on a daily basis.[1]

Office romances can pose a number of problems, including a loss of productivity, public displays of affection, gossip, damage to the professional image of the organization, charges of favoritism, and affairs in cases where romantic partners already have spouses or significant others. Serious issues arise when superiors and subordinates date and then break up. The subordinate (often a young female assistant) may claim that she was sexually harassed because she was pressured into having sex to keep her job or that her supervisor (often an older male executive) retaliated when the relationship ended.

The nation was reminded of the dangers of superior–subordinate relationships when former late-night talk show host David Letterman admitted that he'd had a series of sexual relationships with female writers and staffers at his production company. Letterman went public with his affairs after a CBS producer who dated his long-term girlfriend, Stephanie Birkett, tried to extort money from the entertainer in return for keeping silent about his sexual activities. While Letterman's relationships were consensual, it appeared as if the women he dated received special benefits. For example, Birkitt was featured in broadcast segments even though she did not seem to be particularly talented.

Human resource departments are taking note of the dangers of office romances. The number of companies developing written policies to address office romances rose from 20% to 42% over an eight-year period, according to the Society of Human Resource Management. And the policies grew stricter. Almost all the firms surveyed by SHRM forbid romantic relationships between superiors and subordinates; one-third forbid relationships between those reporting to the same supervisor or with a client or customer; 10% don't allow romances between their employees and employees of competitors. Punishments range from minimal (relationship counseling and department transfers) to severe (suspension and termination). Executives at the American Red Cross, the World Bank, Walmart, Boeing, and the *Harvard Business Review* lost their jobs for having relationships with subordinates.

Not everyone is convinced that restrictions on dating are justified or ethical. Canadian business professor Colin Boyd believes these policies invade employee privacy and restrict their right to associate with others. The costs to employees outweigh any benefits to the company. He points out that the number of romance-related sexual harassment claims (14,200 in one recent year) is small compared with the total number of work relationships. Conflict-of-interest policies can deal with those issues that do arise when a few couples misbehave. Further, workplace romances benefit participants, with 44% leading to marriage and 23% to long-term relationships. (Michelle and Barack Obama met at work, for instance, and she was his supervisor.) This high relational success rate may be due in part to the fact that parties get to know each other gradually over a period of years. In addition, Boyd notes that spouses who work together are much less likely to divorce. Because office romances are low risk/high reward, Boyd urges organizations to promote rather than restrict romance. He points to Southwest Airlines, AT&T, and Ben & Jerry's as examples of successful companies that actively encourage employee marriage and long term relationships.

Discussion Probes

1. What has been your experience as an observer of workplace romances? What impact have they had on other employees and the organization?

2. Should all romantic relationships between supervisors and subordinates be banned? Should romantic partners be able to report to the same supervisor?

3. If you were asked to develop an office romance policy, what would you include in it?

(Continued)

(Continued)

4. Do strict romance policies violate employee privacy, autonomy and the right to associate with others? Are they unfair?

5. Do the benefits of restricting office romances outweigh the costs?

6. Should office romances be promoted instead of restricted?

Note

1. Heathfield (2016).

Sources: American Management Association (2003). J. Baird (2009). Boyd (2010). Dowd (2009). Greenwald (2009). Wilker (2013).

CHAPTER ELEVEN

PROMOTING ORGANIZATIONAL CITIZENSHIP

Chapter Preview

The Organization as Citizen
    Components of Organizational Citizenship
    Corporate Social Responsibility
    Corporate/CEO Activism
    Sustainability
    The Stages of Corporate Citizenship

Promoting Organizational Citizenship
    Adopting a Stewardship Mind-Set
    Measuring Social Performance
Chapter Takeaways
Application Projects

In this chapter, we'll look beyond the borders of our organizations to focus on the role that they should play in local and national communities. Our individual responsibility is to equip our groups to act as socially responsible citizens. The first section of the chapter describes what it means for an organization to act as a citizen. Section two outlines strategies for encouraging our organizations to play this role.

THE ORGANIZATION AS CITIZEN

"From those to whom much has been given, much will be required." That saying encapsulates the relationship between organizations and Western society over the past several decades. Organizations wield more power than ever before. The decline of the extended family, urbanization, industrialization, and other factors have increased our reliance on corporations, governments, schools, nonprofit agencies, and other institutions. At the same time, societal expectations of organizations have greatly expanded. We now demand that organizations, even for-profit entities, behave responsibly. As evidence of that fact, consider the following:[1]

- 79% of Americans believe that businesses should support social causes; 90% say companies should operate in ways that benefit society and environment; three quarters of business leaders say that the public should expect good citizenship from corporations.

- Nearly nine out of 10 millennials (those born between 1982 and 2004) from around the world believe "the success of a business should be measured in terms of more than just its financial performance."

- A Nielsen survey of survey of 30,000 citizens in 60 countries found that 60% were willing to pay more for sustainable brands, up from 50% two years before. Commitment to sustainable products and services crossed all income levels and was highest in Latin America, Asia, the Middle East, and Africa.

- Organic foods, once sold only in specialty markets, are now carried by Walmart, Safeway, and other major food chains.

- $6.57 trillion in U.S. assets (1 out of every 6 dollars under professional management) is held in funds that invest only in companies that meet high environmental, social, and corporate governance standards.

- America's Most Admired Companies earn that label in part because they are concerned about the community and the environment.

- Watchdog groups regularly monitor the financial status and effectiveness of charities.

- Labor activists, disability advocates, environmentalists, and other groups are quick to bring suit against governments and businesses that don't fulfill their social duties.

The term *organizational citizenship* best describes what society expects from businesses, governments, and nonprofits. Good citizens acknowledge their obligations to their communities. They use their influence to improve society.[2] Sandra Waddock offers this definition of outstanding corporate citizenship:

> Leading corporate citizens are companies that live up to clear constructive visions and core values consistent with those of the broader societies within which they operate, respect the natural environment, and treat well the entire range of stakeholders who risk capital in, have an interest in, or are linked to the firm through primary and secondary impacts . . . They recognize they are responsible for their impacts and are willing to be held accountable for them.[3]

Four components or elements are key to the practice organizational citizenship: (1) a stakeholder focus, (2) corporate social responsibility (CSR), (3) corporate advocacy, and (4) sustainability.

Components of Organizational Citizenship

Stakeholder Focus

To function as citizens, organizations must first recognize that they have obligations to a variety of groups who have an interest or "stake" in their operations. The stakeholder framework first developed as an alternative way to define the relationship between large businesses and society but since has been extended to organizations of all types—partnerships, small businesses, governments, and nonprofits.[4] Traditionally, corporate executives were viewed as agents who acted on behalf of the company's owners. According to this perspective (called *agency theory*), the manager's primary ethical obligation is to promote the interests of stockholders. Companies that operate efficiently and profitably benefit the community through the creation of jobs and wealth as well as through higher tax revenues.

Stakeholder theorists challenge the notion that a manager's sole moral duty is to company owners.[5] They note that the pursuit of corporate wealth doesn't benefit everyone. When a major retailer like Walmart forces its suppliers to cut costs, for example, lots of groups suffer. Employees manufacturing the goods see their wages and benefits cut, and jobs are lost; local businesses and economies decline. Also, shareholders aren't the only groups with an interest or stake in what the company does. Governments charter corporations based in part on the expectation that they will provide benefits to society. Governments invest in businesses by supplying them with cheap land, building access roads, and offering tax breaks.

Advocates of stakeholder theory argue that organizations of all kinds have an ethical obligation to "heed the needs, interests, and influence of those affected by their policies and operations."[6] Drawing from Kant's categorical imperative, some proponents believe that all stakeholders have intrinsic value.[7] It is wrong to use any group of people as a means to organizational ends. The interests of diverse stakeholder groups are valid and worthy of respect. Other supporters of this approach draw upon justice-as-fairness theory to emphasize that outside groups and individuals need to be treated fairly by the organization.[8] Still others believe that the stakeholder framework best reflects the feminist commitment to relationships. Feminists see corporations as webs of relationships with stakeholders, not as independent entities.[9] One final group adopts a communitarian perspective, which emphasizes the importance of serving the common good. They point out that serving stakeholders, not just stockholders, is more likely to promote cooperation and the development of networks that advance the overall good of society.[10] Recognizing the concerns of multiple stakeholders has strategic as well as ethical implications. Identifying the needs of stakeholders should be part of any major decision, like entering additional markets, establishing a new social service program, or changing an investment strategy. You will want to engage in stakeholder management in order to improve organizational performance at the same time that you respond to your moral responsibilities. Stakeholder management means answering five key questions:[11]

1. *Who are our stakeholders?* Categorizing stakeholders can make it easier to answer this question. Those with an interest in the organization can be classified as primary or secondary stakeholders. Primary stakeholders—customers, investors, employees, suppliers—have a direct stake in the organization's success or failure and thus exert significant influence. Their interests generally are given priority. Secondary stakeholders—social pressure groups, media, trade bodies—have an indirect stake in the organization. Accountability to these groups is therefore less.

2. *What are our stakeholders' stakes?* Stakeholder groups have different interests, concerns, and demands. Some of these stakes are more legitimate than others. Owners, for example, have a legal interest in a corporation, while suppliers do not. Further, some groups have more power than others. The board of trustees of a university system typically wields more power than the faculty or students.

3. *What opportunities and challenges do our stakeholders present?* Opportunities allow organizations to build cooperative, productive relationships with stakeholder groups. An inner-city church, for instance, might view other religious groups, local merchants, civic associations, and government agencies as potential allies in combating neighborhood blight. Challenges take the form of demands from groups who believe that the organization is at fault. These must be handled carefully, or they may result in significant damage. Home Depot faced such a challenge from the Rainforest Action Network. The retailer pulled old-growth lumber from the shelves after the environmental group threatened to picket if it did not.

4. *What responsibilities does the firm have to its stakeholders?* These include, for example, economic, legal, ethical, and environmental duties

5. *What strategies or actions should management take to best handle stakeholder challenges and opportunities?* Organizations can take the offensive or go on the defensive when dealing with stakeholders, decide to accommodate or negotiate, use one strategy or a combination of several, and so on. One consideration is the potential for cooperation or threat posed by a particular group. Typically, the best strategy is to become involved with groups that are currently supportive or could be cooperative in the future and to defend against those who pose a significant threat.

University of Virginia business professor Edward Freeman and his colleagues urge organizations to focus on creating value for all stakeholders.[12] Freeman believes that it is possible to simultaneously meet the needs of a variety of groups. For instance, companies are more likely to survive over the long term if they generate profits for owners and at the same time treat employees well, deal fairly with suppliers, and serve the community. Trade-offs—meeting the needs of one group at the expense of another—are inevitable but should not become standard operating procedure. Freeman is also convinced that businesses should take the initiative to engage all stakeholders in dialogue, including those who could be seen as a threat. It is not always possible to satisfy every critic, but opponents provide an alternative point of view. Understanding their concerns can open up new opportunities to generate value (e.g., enter new markets, reduce costs). Engaging with both primary and secondary stakeholders also provides information that can be used to better meet their needs.

In addition to managing ongoing relationships with stakeholders, organizations also need to identify and respond to changing social and ethical conditions. This process is called *issues management*. Ethical sensitivities and moral customs continually evolve. Smoking, which once was allowed nearly everywhere in this country, is now banned from many indoor public spaces, for instance. Same-sex marriages, which used to be banned, are now legal.

Issues management is a function of public relations departments at a number of major corporations, though it can also be housed in other departments like legal, government relations, or quality assurance. SC Johnson credits its issues management program for the firm's decision to eliminate fluorocarbons from aerosol sprays three years before federal regulations took effect. Coke and other beverage companies are marketing lower calorie drinks as concerns about obesity grow.[13] It would be wrong to make issues management solely the responsibility of public relations or another department, however. Companies skilled at issues management place individuals from a variety of functional areas on their issues management teams.[14] Then, too, all employees have a responsibility to be on the lookout for future trends through scanning and monitoring. In this context, *scanning* refers to surveying the environment to identify potential issues that might impact your organization. Surf the Web; monitor tweets, Facebook, blogs, and YouTube; read a wide variety of issues-oriented print and online publications (*The Nation*, *Huffington Post*, *The Standard*, for example); track news sources and talk shows; and interact with stakeholder groups.

One model of the stages of issue development is shown in Self-Assessment 11.1. You can monitor the progress of any issue using this format. Take the issue of global warming, for example. At first, only a few environmental groups were aware of this problem, and evidence of its existence was scarce. Next, the issue began to grab political and media attention, and some businesses began to take note. Currently, this concern appears to be moving from the consolidating to the institutionalized stage with increasing recognition of the ethical dimension of the problem. A number of nations have passed measures aimed at reducing greenhouse emissions, and businesses around the world have joined in the effort to combat global warming.

SELF-ASSESSMENT 11.1

The Four Stages of Issue Maturity Scale

Pharmaceutical company Novo Nordisk created a scale to measure the maturity of societal issues and the public's expectations surrounding the issues. An adaptation of the scale appears here.

Stage	Characteristics
Latent	Activist communities and NGOs (nongovernmental organizations) are aware of the societal issue. There is weak scientific or other hard evidence. The issue is largely ignored or dismissed by the business community.
Emerging	There is political and media awareness of the societal issue. There is an emerging body of research, but data are still weak. Leading businesses experiment with approaches to dealing with the issue.
Consolidating	There is an emerging body of business practices around the societal issue. Sectorwide and issue-based voluntary initiatives are established. There is litigation and an increasing view of the need for legislation. Voluntary standards are developed, and collective action occurs.
Institutionalized	Legislation or business norms are established. The embedded practices become a normal part of a business-excellence model.

Brainstorm three or four ethical issues that could pose a challenge to your college or university or your employer. Track each issue's stage of development using the issue maturity scale. Determine how your school or employer should respond to each issue.

Source: Zadek (2004), p. 128. Used by permission.

Once an issue has been identified, determine its significance and its likely impact. Evaluate the issue according to magnitude and probability.[15] Some issues have low probability and magnitude. They are not likely to affect the organization and, if they do, their effects will likely be minimal. These developments should be given low priority. Focus instead on issues with higher probability and magnitude. Create a list of these high-priority issues and develop strategies for responding to them. Failure to prepare can have disastrous effects. Beef producers underestimated how concerned U.S. residents are about food—and particularly meat—safety. When media reports surfaced that "pink slime" (officially known as "lean finely textured beef" made from meat scraps) was being used in hamburger, the meat industry stood by instead of promoting the safety of its products. (Lean finely textured beef has been tested over 7,000 times for the school lunch program and has never been linked to food-borne illness.) Activists then succeeded in getting fast food chains and supermarkets to pull meat with pink slime from menus and shelves and several midwestern meat-processing plants closed as a result.[16] (Case Study 11.1, "Why the Circus No Longer Comes to Town," describes two companies that failed to respond effectively to the same issue.)

Corporate Social Responsibility

Corporate social responsibility (CSR) describes the efforts of companies and other organizations to actively improve the welfare of society. Not everyone is supportive of such activities. Some follow the lead of economist Milton Friedman, who argued that business should focus solely on making profits.[17] Managers who give to philanthropic causes are not only deciding how to spend the money of stockholders without their consent, but they also lack the skills to effectively address social concerns. Dealing with social problems is best left to the government. Disciples of Friedman worry that if businesses are distracted from their primary goal, they will generate less economic activity, which will mean fewer jobs and lower tax revenues. In other words, society benefits more if business sticks to business. Others take issue with claims that CSR adds to the bottom line, noting that while some companies see higher profits from CSR activities, many others do not. Skeptics note that CSR can be used as a public relations "smokescreen," enabling firms to burnish their images while still behaving unethically. Encouraging corporations to become more active in meeting social problems appears to further increase the influence of business, which already wields tremendous economic and political power.[18]

CSR critics make some valid points. There is no guarantee that citizenship will lead to higher profits. Some firms employ CSR activities for public relations purposes only. We should be concerned about the amount of power wielded by multinational corporations (see Chapter 12). But the objections of CSR detractors fall short. Friedman seems to equate CSR with philanthropy. As we'll see, CSR activities extend well beyond corporate giving, and many organizations (Timberland, Interface, Tom's Shoes) build CSR into their corporate DNA. Governments, by themselves, have not always been able to effectively deal with social problems. While not every company benefits financially from being socially responsible, many do.[19] Participating in CSR activities can pay significant dividends. Studies reveal that engaging in social responsibility efforts improves a firm's reputation while increasing customer loyalty and ratings of its products. Employees who work for socially responsible firms are more likely to identify with their employers, while getting along better with fellow workers. They perform better, stay with the company longer, and engage in more organizational citizenship behaviors. CSR also makes a company more attractive as a prospective employer.[20]

From an ethical perspective, being a corporate citizen appears to be the right thing to do. CSR behaviors are altruistic, contribute to the common good, treat others with dignity, are just, and so on. Finally, as we noted at the beginning of the chapter, society expects more from its organizations than ever before. Corporations must be good citizens or risk being punished by investors and consumers alike.

CSR efforts can take many different forms. To demonstrate the wide scope of CSR activities, I'll describe three different typologies. The first typology is the CSR pyramid developed by Archie Carroll.[21] *Economic responsibilities* form the base of Carroll's CSR Pyramid. Businesses have a duty to be profitable so they can provide goods and services, pay employees, and reward investors. If they go bankrupt, they cannot carry out the duties to follow. *Legal responsibilities* make up the next level of the CSR pyramid. Corporations and small businesses must obey employment laws, follow environmental regulations, honor contracts, make good on warranties and guarantees, and so on. However, the law only outlines minimum acceptable behavior. Legal regulations don't cover all situations and what is legal is not always moral. As a result, corporations should move to the next stage of the pyramid—*ethical responsibilities*. They must live up to the ethical values and standards of society, which include being fair and just and doing the right thing. *Philanthropic responsibilities* are at the top of the CSR pyramid. At this level businesses voluntarily give back to the community through making contributions, donating goods and services, employee volunteerism, partnering with nonprofits and other means.

A second classification system divides CSR activities according to the domain or area they are designed to impact.[22] According to this typology, CSR efforts address four domains:

Human resources: The development of protection of people. For example: providing a safe work environment, fairly compensating workers, offering training opportunities, refusing to support organizations that engage in child labor or slavery.

Community, cultural, and societal involvement and philanthropy. For example: respecting the culture and rights of indigenous people, obeying laws and regulations, giving back to the community through donations, foundations, and volunteerism.

Environmental protection, waste reduction, and sustainability. For example: restoring biodiversity, eliminating waste, treating animals humanely, recycling, reducing energy and water use.

Product, consumer, and service contributions and protections. For example: protecting consumers, using renewable materials in manufacturing, providing truthful information about the environmental impacts of products, buying in a socially responsible manner from minority, indigenous, and women-owned businesses.

A third approach ties CSR strategies to the particular stakeholder groups.[23] See Ethical Checkpoint 11.1 for a list of CSR actions aimed at important stakeholder groups.

ETHICAL CHECKPOINT 11.1
Stakeholder Approach to CSR

Stakeholder	Actions
Employees	Provides a family friendly work environment
	Engages in responsible human resource management
	Provides an equitable reward and wage system for employees
	Engages in open and flexible communication with employees
	Invests in employee development
	Encourages freedom of speech and promotes employees' rights to speak up and report their concerns at work
	Provides child care support/paternity/maternity leave in addition to what is expected by law
	Engages in employment diversity in hiring and promoting women, ethnic minorities, and those with physical disabilities
	Promotes dignified and fair treatment of all employees
Consumers	Respects the rights of consumers
	Offers quality products and services
	Provides information that is truthful, honest, and useful
	Products and services provided are safe and fit with their intended use
	Avoids false and misleading advertising
	Discloses all substantial risks associated with products or service
	Avoids sales promotions that are deceptive/manipulative
	Avoids manipulating the availability of a product for purpose of exploitation
	Avoids engagement in price fixing
Community	Fosters reciprocal relationships between the corporation and community
	Invests in communities in which the corporation operates
	Launches community development activities
	Encourages employee participation in community projects

Stakeholder	Actions
Investors	Strives for a competitive return on investment
	Engages in fair and honest business practices in relationships with shareholders
Suppliers	Engages in fair trading transactions with suppliers
Environment	Demonstrates a commitment to sustainable development
	Demonstrates a commitment to the environment

Source: Jamili (2008). Used by permission.

Corporate/CEO Activism

In recent years corporate activism, also known as "CEO activism" and "corporate social advocacy," has emerged as a new component of organizational citizenship. Companies engaged in corporate activism take moral stances on social-political issues like gay marriage, race relations, immigration bans and LGBT freedoms.[24] Corporations have traditionally taken positions related to their business interests, such as when an oil company pushes the federal government to open up new areas for off-shore drilling. In corporate social advocacy, however, firms take public positions on issues that are not directly related to their operations. In the past CEOS were reluctant to speak out about social issues for fear of alienating customers, believing "it is better to be seen than heard." They followed the lead of basketball star and athletic shoe promoter Michael Jordan. Jordan refused to support a Democratic North Carolina Senate candidate, noting "Republicans wear shoes too." Now CEOs are speaking out. One group of business leaders signed a letter protesting President Trump's ban on Muslim immigrants and others signed a letter asking him not to withdraw from the Paris climate accord. PayPal, Deutsche Bank, the National Basketball Association, and other companies retaliated against North Carolina after the state passed a law (later modified) requiring transgender individuals to use the bathrooms that match the sex listed on their birth certificates. CEOs at Angie's List, Anthem, Eli Lilly, and Salesforce led efforts to repeal a similar law in Indiana. However, corporate activism isn't limited to one side of the political spectrum. Chick-Fil-A CEO Don Cathy stated his opposition to gay marriage, and Hobby Lobby fought efforts to require coverage of birth control under the Affordable Care Act.

Several factors appear to be driving CEO/corporate advocacy.[25] First, for some firms like Starbucks, political stances appear to be a natural outgrowth of their commitment to social responsibility. Starbucks has taken positions on everything from addressing unemployment to helping impoverished communities. The public increasingly expects companies to speak out on societal issues, particularly those firms that tout themselves as socially conscious. Second, it makes sense for companies who have invested millions in fostering diverse workforces to support diversity in society. Failure to do so would undercut their credibility with employees. Third, in the age of social media CEOs can speak directly to consumers. Four, many employees, particularly millennials, want their leaders to speak out. They may change companies if their CEOs do not. This is a particular concern for high tech companies who face a shortage of qualified workers. Finally, some CEOs believe that they have an ethical/moral duty to take stances. That's the motivation for Marc Benioff, CEO and founder of SalesForce:

> I think that CEOs today and business leaders are as important as political leaders and that they have a role like political leaders, which is that they have to stand for something. When things happen in the world that you don't agree with, as a CEO, you have a responsibility to come forward and say, "hey, I don't agree with that because it doesn't support my employees, or it doesn't support my customers."[26]

Corporate advocacy can have an impact. The "bathroom bills" in Indiana and North Carolina were repealed or modified in response to business pressure. Corporate pressure also kept Georgia from adopting such a law. In one research project, respondents were less likely to support Indiana's bathroom bill when they read a message from Apple CEO Tim Cook opposing the legislation. Those who agreed with Cook's stance on gender discrimination were more likely to buy Apple products than those who disagreed with him.[27] An online survey by Weber Shandwick found that 38% of consumers think CEOs should address controversial social issues. Only 20% were favorable to CEOS speaking out on issues not directly tied to a firm's business, however. Many were skeptical of the CEOs' motivation, with one-third believing that corporate leaders taking political stands did so to get media attention.[28]

Companies taking social positions run the risk of reflecting the political divisions of the country, being seen as red (Republican) or blue (Democrat). Every social stance seems to generate a counter stance. When Starbucks said it would hire 10,000 immigrants, for instance, it was the target of a boycott. (See Contemporary Issues in Organizational Ethics 11.1 for more examples of counter activism.) Companies might alienate employees who don't support their positions. Politicians sometimes resent business pressure, as in the case of former Louisiana Governor Bobby Jindal, who accused pro–LGBT rights companies of "bullying" elected officials. Despite the risks, expect more CEOS to speak out. Corporate activism seems to be following the pattern of CSR, which went from voluntary to a "public expectation."[29] Remaining silent also sends a message. According to Harvard Business School professor Michael Toffel, "I think silence is also political. I think people are starting to interpret that."[30]

CONTEMPORARY ISSUES IN ORGANIZATIONAL ETHICS 11.1

THE RISE OF CONSUMER BOYCOTTS

Consumers are increasingly voicing their frustrations through boycotts of products and organizations. Uber was the subject of a #DeleteUber boycott for appearing to undercut a New York City Muslim immigration ban protest; #GrabYourWallet urges shoppers to avoid L.L. Bean, Bloomingdales, Macy's, and other retailers selling Trump goods. Evangelical Christians targeted Target and Wells Fargo over their support for marriage equality.

Consumer boycotts are not always as effective as their proponents hope. Often a boycott from the left or right sparks a counterresponse from the other side. Liberals boycotted Chick-Fil-A after its CEO condemned homosexuality. Shortly thereafter, conservative commentator Mike Huckabee launched a "Support Chick-Fil-A Day," which prompted 125,000 customers to flock to the chain's outlets. Then, too, other factors come into play when making buying decisions. Consumers may not think that the issue is that serious, may be confused about the sheer number of boycotts, might not have many other options (Walmart may be the only major store in a rural area, for instance), could be attracted by the features and prices of a company's products, and so on. Take the case of the eight-year Disney boycott, launched by Southern Baptists in 1996 to protest Disney's support for gay rights. This action did not change Disney's position. As one observer noted, "It turns out that too few parents had the heart to deny their children Disney products to make a boycott effectve."[1]

The most successful boycotts are those focused on a single company over a single issue, such as the boycott of Nike for its labor practices in the 1990s or the boycott of college bookstores selling garments manufactured in sweatshops. In the words of Arcadia professor Eric McInnis: "Strangling one company into bankruptcy sends a much more frightening message than lowering the weekly sales of a dozen retailers."[2]

Advertiser boycotts appear to bring about greater change than consumer boycotts. Fox News fired both Glenn Beck and Bill O'Reilly after BMW and other companies pulled their ads. A number of major corporations in the UK and U.S.—Amazon, Verizon, AT&T, Microsoft—withdrew their advertising from Google after their ads appeared in websites and YouTube videos containing hate speech and other objectionable material. These firms vowed not to return to these platforms until Google did a better job of policing them. Google immediately pledged to institute better filtering tools.

Notes

1. J. Davis (2017).
2. McInnis (2017).

Sources: Klein, Smith, and John (2004). Levick (2015). Statt (2017).

Sustainability

As we saw in the previous section, treating the environment well is an important social responsibility. In fact, environmental care or *sustainability* serves as the primary standard or guideline for corporate citizenship in Europe and other parts of the world. Sustainability means preserving the natural environment while at the same time creating long-lasting economic and social value. Sustainable organizations want to meet their current needs, but they want to do so in a way that doesn't reduce the ability of future generations to meet their needs.[31] They adopt a long-term perspective, hoping to create conditions that foster decades of economic health and social responsibility and ensure the well-being of future generations. Corporate citizens reduce greenhouse gases and waste, develop environmentally friendly products, and so on. (One list of sustainable practices is found in Ethical Checkpoint 11.2.)

ETHICAL CHECKPOINT 11.2

CERES Principles

CERES, a nonprofit organization dedicated to sustainability, published the following corporate environmental conduct principles right after the 1989 crash of the Exxon Valdez oil tanker that caused significant environmental damage in Alaska's Prince William Sound. Companies that pledge to adhere to these principles also commit themselves to publicly reporting on their performance.

Protection of the Biosphere

We will reduce and make continual progress toward eliminating the release of any substance that may cause environmental damage to the air, water, or the earth and its inhabitants. We will safeguard all habitats affected by our operations and will protect open spaces and wilderness, while preserving biodiversity.

Sustainable Use of Natural Resources

We will make sustainable use of renewable natural resources, such as water, soils, and forests. We will conserve non-renewable natural resources through efficient use and careful planning.

Reduction and Disposal of Wastes

We will reduce and where possible eliminate waste through source reduction and recycling. All waste will be handled and disposed of through safe and responsible methods.

Energy Conservation

We will conserve energy and improve the energy efficiency of our internal operations and of the goods and services we sell. We will make every effort to use environmentally safe and sustainable energy sources.

Risk Reduction

We will strive to minimize the environmental, health and safety risks to our employees and the communities in which we operate through safe technologies, facilities and operating procedures, and by being prepared for emergencies.

Safe Products and Services

We will reduce and where possible eliminate the use, manufacture or sale of products and services that cause environmental damage or health or safety hazards. We will inform our customers of the environmental impacts of our products or services and try to correct unsafe use.

Environmental Restoration

We will promptly and responsibly correct conditions we have caused that endanger health, safety or the environment. To the extent feasible, we will redress injuries we have caused to persons or damage we have caused to the environment and will restore the environment.

Informing the Public

We will inform in a timely manner everyone who may be affected by conditions caused by our company that might endanger health, safety or the environment. We will regularly seek advice and counsel through dialogue with persons in communities near our facilities. We will not take any action against employees for reporting dangerous incidents or conditions to management or to appropriate authorities.

Management Commitment

We will implement these Principles and sustain a process that ensures the Board of Directors and Chief Executive Officer are fully informed about pertinent environmental issues and are fully responsible for environmental policy. In selecting our Board of Directors, we will consider demonstrated environmental commitment as a factor.

Audits and Reports

We will conduct an annual self-evaluation of our progress in implementing these Principles. We will support the timely creation of generally accepted environmental audit procedures. We will annually complete the Ceres Report, which will be made available to the public.

Source: CERES. Retrieved from http://www.ceres.org/about-us/our-history/ceres-principles. Used by permission.

The need for sustainable business practices is great because the natural world is under assault, largely because of population growth. The world's population is expected to grow from over 7.3 billion in 2016 to around 9.7 billion by 2050.[32] (Africa will account for half of this population increase.) More people means more air and water pollution, deforestation, flooding, climate change, water shortages, soil erosion, and species loss. (A quarter of all mammals and a third of all amphibians face extinction within the next 30 years.) Affluence also stresses the environment. As families around the world reach the middle class, they buy more consumer products and often change their diets. There are now an estimated 1.2 billion cars on the road and millions of Asian consumers are developing a taste for meat. A pound of beef takes 16 pounds of grain to produce; meat production demands lots of water, energy, and fertilizers while producing tons of animal waste.

Sustainability is a high standard that demands constant improvement. For instance, manufacturers seeking to boost their environmental records generally begin by transitioning from pollution control to pollution prevention.[33] Instead of cleaning up messes after they occur, they try to prevent them from happening in the first place by reducing smokestack emissions and waste. Such tactics can greatly reduce the costs of disposing of toxic substances. However, if manufacturers want to continue to improve, they shift their focus from minimizing pollution to considering all the possible environmental impacts over the life cycle of a product. They create goods that are easier to recover, recycle, or reuse. Xerox took this approach by taking parts from leased copiers and reconditioning them for use in new machines. If environmentally conscious organizations want to progress still further, they must invest in clean technology that is environmentally sustainable. Hybrid gas and electric cars are a step in this direction. So are BMW automobiles, which are built to be easier to disassemble when they leave the road for good.

While sustainability efforts can be expensive, more often than not they boost profits. Throwing away less translates into lower raw materials costs and disposal fees. Spanish stone company Cosentino uses 95% of all the material it extracts from its mines, a much higher percentage than its competitors.[34] Recycling parts, as in the case of Xerox, reduces costs yet further. Sustainable firms greatly reduce the risk of being sued or fined for environmental infractions like polluting rivers or producing toxic emissions. They enjoy better relationships with activists, local communities, and other stakeholder groups. Their corporate reputations or "brands" get a boost. Consumers and investors reward companies with good environmental records through purchases and investment. Those working for such firms are more committed to their organizations and more willing to put forth effort. Higher employee engagement, in turn, produces higher productivity and revenue.

Sustainability increased employee engagement and profit at one large restaurant chain.[35] While the chain's customers weren't too concerned about the environment, employees at this chain were. Company leaders created green teams of frontline employees and charged them with addressing the results of an environmental audit. Auditors found widespread waste. Some stores left their lights and appliances on 24 hours a day, many used excessive amounts of water, few had recycling or composting programs, and waste disposal costs were not tracked. The green teams reduced these wasteful practices, saving each restaurant $10,000 a year while heightening the level of employee engagement.

Individuals can play an important role in promoting sustainability initiatives. Take the case of Sweden's Per Carstedt, for example.[36] Due in large part to his efforts, Sweden is one of the world leaders in reducing dependence on fossil fuels. Carstedt, who owned a Ford dealership, convinced the Ford Motor Company to provide him with vehicles that burned ethanol. Then he and colleagues from a biofuels institute persuaded 500 municipalities, companies, and individuals to buy flexi-fuel vehicles and talked filling stations into selling ethanol fuel. Later Carstedt and his allies moved toward other energy sources, such as forestry industry waste, that don't come from food crops and generate lower greenhouse emissions. His next project was to build the world's "most environmentally friendly car dealership." To reach this goal, he built a block of interconnected businesses called a Green Zone which reduced overall energy consumption by 80%. Excess heat from the kitchen of a McDonalds, for example, was used to warm a gas station and the car dealership. The Green Zone became the inspiration of a larger BioFuel Region focused on developing renewable energy supplies.

The Stages of Corporate Citizenship

Becoming an outstanding citizen doesn't happen overnight. Scholars at Boston College's Center for Corporate Leadership believe that organizational citizenship follows a developmental path.[37] At each stage, corporate citizenship efforts become more aligned, integrated and institutionalized. Alignment means tying corporate citizenship to business objectives and developing a coherent citizenship framework and strategy. Integration describes embedding corporate citizenship principles and practices throughout the organization and creating systems that cross departmental and functional boundaries. Institutionalization refers to ensuring that corporate citizenship is sustained by making it part of the standard way of doing business. For example: incorporating citizenship into mission and values and embedding it into the group's culture.

Knowing your company's stage of development can help you identify the challenges the group faces and set goals for going forward.

Stage 1: Elementary. This is the lowest developmental stage. Companies at this stage don't understand corporate citizenship. They are interested only in complying with laws and industry standards. Department heads make sure the company obeys the law to prevent harm to the group's reputation. Nike was in this phase when it was first accused of abusive labor practices in the 1990s and claimed that it had no responsibility for the actions of its overseas contractors. Credibility is the primary challenge for elementary-level firms. Their reputations are particularly vulnerable to crises, such as when outside groups challenge their employment practices or treatment of the environment.

Stage 2: Engaged. These organizations have "awakened" to the need for social responsibility. DuPont's leaders, for example, determined that the company would move from complying with environmental regulations to actively seeking to win the public's trust. Engaged companies adopt policies to lower the risk of lawsuits and reputational damage. These policies generally call for exceeding legal requirements for safety, environmental health, and employment. Engaged firms enter into two-way communication with stakeholders like community groups and NGOs. Corporate units begin to participate in CSR efforts. Developing capacity is the biggest challenge in this phase. The group must develop its ability to address a variety of needs, which can seem overwhelming. As Case Study 11.2 suggests, Facebook appears to be in this stage of development.

Stage 3: Innovative. Organizations in the innovative stage implement creative ways to improve and measure social performance. In this stage, leaders become even more involved in CSR, engage in dialogue with a greater variety of stakeholders, and develop new citizenship initiatives. In 2000, for example, Ford Motor Company developed a set of CSR principles after hosting a forum with company executives and citizenship experts, followed by discussions with employees. As an outcome of these conversations, the firm converted one of its aging plants into a highly efficient, environmentally friendly facility. Data collection is another important component of this phase. Innovative organizations monitor their social and environmental activities and may report the results to the public. (We'll take a closer look at social audits in the next section of the chapter.) Creating coherence is the primary challenge for Stage 3 organizations. Managers typically work independently on citizenship initiatives, and these efforts are not tied to corporate strategy and culture. While innovative organizations compile data, they don't make effective use of the information.

Stage 4: Integrated. In this stage, organizations take a more unified approach to citizenship than their counterparts in Stage 3. They try to incorporate citizenship concerns throughout every level and unit of the firm, making CSR part of the business plan. Leaders set citizenship goals, create performance indicators, and then monitor how well they do. They report the findings of all social and environmental audits, even when they are not favorable. Integrated organizations—Henkel, Interface, Groupe Diageo, Danone—often have committees made up of senior executives or board members to oversee these efforts. Deepening commitment is the primary challenge in Stage 4. Maintaining and strengthening commitment to citizenship is difficult when tackling significant problems like neighborhood blight and poverty.

Stage 5: Transformative. Companies like Tom's Shoes and Patagonia make citizenship central to their missions and reputations. Consumers buy their products in part because of their citizenship activities. Transformative organizations hope to create new markets by merging their social commitment with their business strategies. They are willing to lose money in the short term if there is the possibility of a significant social and economic payoff in the long term. Stage 5 organizations often have visionary leaders who, troubled by the world's problems, are out to make it a better place. Firms in the transformative stage often partner with nonprofits, other businesses, and community groups to address these problems. Hewlett-Packard demonstrates how organizations can simultaneously meet social and financial goals. HP worked with other groups and organizations in India, South Africa, and Brazil to provide communication technology infrastructure that enables underserved residents to access the Web. This effort not only improved the lives of poor citizens in these areas but also gave HP an advantage in these markets. The challenge for transformative companies is to learn how to develop alliances with other organizations and to balance stockholder interests with social concerns. (See Case Study 11.3 for a closer look at a new kind of corporation that addresses the tension between profit and social responsibility.)

While Center for Corporate Citizenship researchers emphasize that top leaders are critical to the development of organizational citizenship, they also cite examples where lower-level leaders and followers led the way. At AMD, Petro-Canada, and Agilant, mid-level managers from a variety of departments—community affairs, corporate communication, environmental management—joined together to convince senior management of the importance of citizenship and to form coordinating committees. Unilever's Asian food business employees encouraged the company to address nutritional needs in the region. As a result, the company launched a children's nutrition program and implemented the campaign in conjunction with UNICEF and Indian nonprofit groups.[38]

Corporate citizenship investigators use the term "catalytic approach" to describe leading citizenship from the middle or lower levels of the organization. In this non programmed, organic strategy, employees take advantage of opportunities that arise, take small steps, and recognize that change can flow from many different sources. These experts suggest that if you want to be a corporate citizenship catalyst, recognize the importance of small wins or changes. Demonstrate the value of citizenship through modest success before moving on. Re-use structures already in place. For instance, add citizenship measures to existing performance evaluations and introduce citizenship into training programs. Be prepared to work over time to balance the needs of stakeholders, weigh benefits against costs and so on. Finally, be a "passionate practitioner." A single person can make a difference through sustained commitment to citizenship.[39]

PROMOTING ORGANIZATIONAL CITIZENSHIP

To move our organizations to a higher stage or level of citizenship development, two factors are critical: (1) taking on a stewardship mentality and (2) adopting strategies for measuring citizenship. We'll conclude this chapter by taking a closer look at each of these elements.

Adopting a Stewardship Mind-Set

Organizational citizenship is founded in large part on a commitment to stewardship. Stewardship, as we noted in our discussion of servant leadership in Chapter 7, means acting on behalf of others. Stewards seek to serve the interests of the organization and followers rather than pursue selfish concerns. On an organizational level, stewardship theory operates on the premise that virtuous managers will meet the needs of internal and external groups and society as a whole.[40] By pursuing long-term organizational benefits or goals instead of short-term gain, stewards are better able to serve the needs of all stakeholders and the common good. They also keep in mind the interests of future generations by, for example, spending more on production now to reduce pollution.

Several characteristics set organizational stewards apart from their organizational colleagues. First, they are intrinsically motivated. They seek such intangible rewards as personal growth, affiliation, achievement, and self-actualization rather than tangible rewards like bonuses and company cars. Second, stewards identify themselves with the goals, mission, and vision of their organizations. They take credit for the group's success and shoulder the blame for its failure when it falls short. Third, stewards rely on personal power instead of on positional forms of power (see Chapter 5) to achieve their goals. Fourth, stewards demonstrate a high level of concern not only for the performance of the organization but also for employees, customers, and the disadvantaged.

Covenantal relationships are critical to organizational stewardship.[41] Unlike traditional transactional contracts, which are based on exchanges between parties (labor for money, money for products), covenantal relationships are based on the commitment of parties to each other and on loyalty to shared values. The relational partners realize that they may not benefit from every decision but remain committed to the relationship. Covenants are directly tied to social responsibility. Covenantal relationships between workers and employers are more likely to develop in organizations that invest in social welfare. Employees are more likely to buy into the ideology of groups that promote community interests. Of course, establishing covenantal relationships can be difficult, particularly with those outside the organization. Nonetheless, if you place collective interests over selfish concerns, you are less tempted to engage in such ethical abuses as excessive executive compensation and lying to boost short-term profits. By acting as a steward, you are more likely to be a committed, productive organizational member who reaches out to help your colleagues and outsiders. You can promote stewardship in your organization as a whole through

- Sharing leadership responsibilities
- Building collaborative relationships
- Emphasizing shared values and a collective purpose
- Empowering workers
- Promoting a long-term orientation that benefits the next generation
- Helping members see their work as a calling
- Emphasizing collective interests
- Modeling other-focused behaviors
- Investing in employee development
- Promoting a sense of employee ownership[42]

To determine if your employer has made efforts to develop a covenantal relationship with its workers, complete Self-Assessment 11.2.

SELF-ASSESSMENT 11.2

Covenantal Relationship Questionnaire

Part 1. Organizational Relationship With Employees

Rate each of the following items on the following scale.

1 = Strongly disagree, 2 = Disagree, 3 = Neither agree nor disagree, 4 = Agree, 5 = Strongly agree

My superior gives personal attention to subordinates who seem neglected.

My superior delegates responsibilities to me to provide me with training opportunities.

My superior treats each subordinate as an individual.

My superior spends a lot of time coaching each individual subordinate who needs it.

My superior gives newcomers lots of help.

Part 2. Company Identification

Rate each of the following items:

I think [your organization's name] considers employees: 1 = much less important than sales and profits, 2 = less important than sales and profits, 3 = neither less nor more important than sales and profits, 4 = more important than sales and profits, 5 = much more important than sales and profits

How do you describe [your organization's name] as a company to work for? poor (1), just another place to work (2), fairly good (3), very good (4), couldn't be much better (5)

From my experience, I feel [your organization's name] probably treats its employees: poorly (1), somewhat poorly (2), fairly well (3), quite well (4), extremely well (5)

Scoring

Possible scores range from 8 to 40. The higher your score, the more you believe that you have a covenantal relationship with your employer. You can also compare your scores on both parts of the instrument to determine, for instance, if you have a strong sense of identification with your employer even though your superior doesn't make an effort to build a strong relationship with you and other workers.

Source: Van Dyne, Graham, and Dienesch (1994). Used by permission.

Measuring Social Performance

When it comes to organizational citizenship, "you get what you measure."[43] As we noted in Chapter 9, organizational members engage in those activities, in this case citizenship initiatives, that are measured and rewarded. The same is true of organizations as a whole. Companies recognized for their CSR activities or sustainability practices try to maintain those accolades. Survey results also reveal whether organizations are reaching their goals and lay the groundwork for improvement. This data is critical not only to members but to stakeholder groups like socially conscious customers and investors who use this information when making buying and investment choices.

Financial statements don't provide an accurate (total) picture of an organization's performance because they ignore the group's social impact and environmental performance. Proponents of CSR and sustainability argue that corporations need to be judged by a *triple bottom line*.[44] In addition to providing traditional financial data, companies should supply information on how well they are meeting their three social and environmental responsibilities: profit, people, and planet. The triple bottom line is measured in a variety of ways. A number of companies sponsor self-audits. Starbucks' annual "Global Responsibility Report" is one such example. This document addresses such topics as ethical sourcing, environmental impact, energy and water conservation, recycling, and community service. Self-audits are particularly prone to abuse, however. Firms may use them as public relations tools, limiting the analysis to just a few areas of strength or reporting only favorable findings. To be credible, such audits need to be complete and should be conducted and certified by an outside group, such as an accounting firm.

Standardized audits are gaining in popularity. Social Accountability 8000 is designed to measure labor practices at overseas suppliers. A firm must meet measurable, verifiable performance standards in nine areas to be certified. These standards forbid child labor, forced labor, coercion, discrimination, unlimited overtime, and substandard wages.[45] The

Global Reporting Initiative, which has been adopted by such organizations as Baxter International, Canon, Deutsche Bank, and Ford Motor Company, is another popular measure.[46] This instrument examines three sets of performance indicators. Economic indicators look at an organization's direct and indirect impacts on stakeholders and on local, national, and global economic systems. These include such elements as wages, pensions and benefits, payments to suppliers, taxes, and subsidies received. Environmental indicators reveal an organization's impacts on natural systems. They cover energy, material and water use, greenhouse gases and waste generation, hazardous materials, recycling, pollution, and fines and penalties for environmental violations. Social indicators concern an organization's influence on social systems and cluster around labor practices (diversity, health, and safety), human rights (child labor, for example), and other social issues (bribery and corruption, community relations).

Social or responsibility auditing has become a "mainstream business practice," according to accounting firm KPMG, which regularly surveys corporate social responsibility reporting.[47] Over 90% of the largest 250 firms it surveyed provide such information, with the highest reporting rates in the Asia Pacific region. Nonetheless, social measurement still is plagued with a number of problems.[48] Standardized social performance instruments aren't as universally accepted as financial audits. There are questions about who is qualified to conduct social audits, what they should cover, how data should be collected, who should have access to the results, and how to draw comparisons between organizations. Determining social and environmental impact is more difficult than determining profits and losses. According to KPMG, there is "room for improvement"; the average reporting quality score is only 57 out of 100. The accounting firm says that the best CR (corporate reporting) reporting practices include the following:

Stakeholder engagement. Identify stakeholders, how the company engages with stakeholders, and how the company has responded to their feedback.

Materiality. Demonstrate an ongoing process to identify the social/environmental issues that have the greatest potential impact on a firm and its stakeholders.

Risk, opportunity, and strategy. Include a careful assessment of the CSR risks and opportunities the business faces and what it is doing to respond to these factors.

Targets and indicators. Use measurable targets and indicators (and specify time frames) to measure progress and report on performance.

Transparency and balance. Provide information on challenges as well as achievements.

Suppliers and the value chain. Explain the social and environmental impacts of the firm's suppliers, products, and services.

Corporate responsibility governance. Spell out who is responsible for CR and how CR performance is linked to pay.

Outside groups often conduct their own audits of an organization's social performance. To make the *Forbes* list of the companies with the best CSR reputations, consumers must rate firms highly on such items as "_____ is a good corporate citizen—it supports good causes and protects the environment"; "_____ is a responsibly run company—it behaves ethically and is open and transparent in its business dealings"; and "_____ is an appealing place to work—it treats its employees well." (Google, Microsoft, and Walt Disney, took the top three spots in 2016.)[49]

Socially conscious mutual funds and other institutional investors rely on the Dow Jones Sustainability Index and other, similar indices when deciding whether or not companies meet their investment criteria. The Dow Jones Sustainability Index (DWSI) evaluates companies in various regions and industries according to such factors as corporate governance, climate change mitigation, labor practices, and risk management; evaluators reject firms that don't operate in an ethical, responsible manner. Charities are also subject to external evaluation. Charity Navigator rates the performance of nonprofits based on these categories: (1) program expenses, (2) administration expenses, (3) fund-raising expenses, (4) fund-raising efficiency (the percentage of the budget spent on raising money), (5) primary revenue growth (the ability to sustain income over time), (6) program expenses growth (the ability to expand programs), (7) working capital (the ability to survive a short downturn in revenue), (8) accountability (willingness to explain actions to the public), and (9) transparency (willingness to share critical data with outsiders).[50]

Third-party evaluations, like self-audits, are far from perfect. Oil producer BP qualified for the DWSI before it caused the massive oil spill in the Gulf of Mexico. The firm was quickly removed from the index. Volkswagen dropped out of the *Forbes* top 10 most socially responsible companies after it was caught bypassing pollution controls on its diesel cars.

CHAPTER TAKEAWAYS

- In today's society, organizations are expected to act as citizens who promote the welfare of society.

- Your organization has a moral obligation to respond to groups affected by its policies and operations. Engage in stakeholder management by responding to five questions: (1) Who are our stakeholders? (2) What are our stakeholders' stakes? (3) What opportunities and challenges do our stakeholders present? (4) What responsibilities does the firm have to its stakeholders? (5) What strategies or actions should management take to best handle stakeholder challenges and opportunities?

- Whenever possible, seek to create value for all stakeholders, engaging in dialogue with supporters and critics alike. Track the progress of moral issues that might impact your organization. Develop strategies for addressing those trends with highest probability and magnitude.

- Corporate social responsibility (CSR) describes a corporation's efforts to better society. These activities can be classified (1) according to levels of responsibility (economic, legal, ethical, philanthropic), (2) according to areas of impact (human resources; community, cultural, societal, philanthropic; environmental protection, waste reduction, and sustainability; product, consumer, and service contributions and protections), and (3) according to important stakeholder groups.

- In corporate activism or corporate social advocacy, CEOs take positions on sociopolitical issues not related to their businesses. They do so in response to employee and societal pressure and personal moral conviction. However, firms taking social stances run the risk of alienating some consumers and other stakeholder groups.

- Sustainability is doing business in a way that preserves the natural environment while creating long-lasting economic and social value. Sustainability is a standard that demands constant improvement, but sustainability efforts can reduce costs, build better relationships with stakeholders, enhance the corporate reputation, and foster employee engagement.

- Determining your organization's stage of citizenship development can help you identify challenges and set objectives. Elementary organizations, which are at the lowest stage of development, don't understand corporate citizenship. Engaged organizations adopt social responsibility policies. Innovative organizations develop creative ways to improve and measure social performance. Integrated organizations incorporate citizenship into every operation. Transformative companies make citizenship central to their missions and reputations.

- Citizenship efforts can be spearheaded by front-line employees and middle managers as well as by top-level executives. To act as a catalyst for change, take small steps, repurpose existing structures to support citizenship, balance the needs of stakeholders, and demonstrate sustained commitment to citizenship over time.

- Organizational citizenship rests largely on a commitment to stewardship. As an employee or manager, seek to meet the interests of the organization, followers, and external groups rather than your own needs. Seek to build covenantal relationships based on mutual commitments and shared values.

- Focus attention on organizational citizenship by auditing social and environmental performance in addition to financial performance (the triple bottom line). You can create your own audit or use a standardized one.

APPLICATION PROJECTS

1. In a group, identify the important stakeholders of your college or university. What ethical responsibilities does your institution have to each group?

2. Identify the ethical issue that could pose the greatest challenge to your college or university or employer based on Self-Assessment 11.1. Share your conclusions in a small group. Then, together, generate a strategy for the issue that has the greatest likelihood and greatest magnitude for your organization.

3. Evaluate the sustainability efforts of your college or university. How well does your institution live up to the CERES Principles found in Ethical Checkpoint 11.1? Write up your findings.

4. Create a list of sustainability practices you can adopt as an individual both at work (or school) and at home.

5. As a class, debate the following propositions:

    *Business should stick to business.

    *The risks of taking positions on controversial political/social issues outweigh the benefits.

    *Consumer boycotts are a waste of time and effort.

    *Most companies who engage in CSR do so primarily to improve their public image.

6. Discuss your scores on Self-Assessment 11.2 with a partner. Why do you think you do or do not have a covenantal relationship with your employer or organization? How can you encourage your organization to adopt a stewardship mind-set?

7. Compare and contrast two corporate social audits reports available online. What do you

learn from examining these materials? Do they meet the standards set out in the chapter?

8. Create a case study based on an organization that you identify as a leading citizen. How is its citizenship reflected in its stakeholder focus, corporate social responsibility activities, and sustainability efforts? How does it report on its social and environmental activities? How is it rated by external agencies and why? As an alternate, select an organization and determine its stage of corporate citizenship development.

9. What can you do to help your organization become a better corporate citizen? Outline a strategy.

CASE STUDY 11.1

Why the Circus No Longer Comes to Town

For 146 years, the Ringling Brothers and Barnum & Bailey Circus traveled the United States by train, putting on shows featuring acrobats, trapeze artists, clowns, and exotic animals. In 2017, the circus held its last performances after a significant decline in attendance and revenue due to changing public tastes. Shorter attention spans also contributed to its demise. The final blow to the circus came from its decision to eliminate elephant acts. According to a press release from Feld Entertainment, the company that owned the circus, this move led to a "greater than could have been anticipated" decline in ticket sales.[1]

For decades the American Humane Society, PETA (People for the Ethical Treatment of Animals), and other animal rights groups tried to ban elephant acts in Ringling Brothers performances. Protesters regularly picketed the circus, and for 14 years animal rights groups fought Ringling Brothers in court. Activists claimed that elephant acts were cruel and pointed out that these highly intelligent animals were chained up much of their lives. In 2011, Feld Entertainment was fined $270,000 for violations of the Animal Welfare Act. However, Feld Entertainment successfully fended off the lawsuits, winning a $24 million judgment against the animal rights groups in 2014. Nonetheless, Ringling Brothers agreed to retire all traveling elephants to its Center for Elephant Conservation in Florida that same year. (During this same period, Los Angeles, Oakland, and Asheville, North Carolina, restricted animal acts.)

Animal rights groups cheered the closing of the circus. According to PETA's president, "PETA heralds the end of what has been the saddest show on earth for wild animals, and asks all other animal circuses to follow suit, as this is a sign of changing times."[2] The CEO of the United States Humane Society said, "I applaud their decision to move away from an institution grounded on inherently inhumane wild animal acts."[3] CEO Kenneth Feld acknowledged that the negative publicity generated by the lawsuits took its toll: "We prevailed in court 100% [but] obviously, in the court of public opinion we didn't win."[4]

Ringling Brothers/Feld Entertainment isn't the only company that has had to deal with changing societal attitudes toward animals. For decades killer whales were the major attraction at SeaWorld parks in San Diego, Orlando, and San Antonio. However, the death of trainer Dawn Brancheau, who was dragged into the water and drowned by Sea World's largest breeding male, Tilikum ("Tilly"), galvanized opposition to

(Continued)

(Continued)

captive orca programs. The film *Blackfish* documented the death of Brancheau and whale mistreatment. Matt Damon, Harry Styles, Willie Nelson, and other celebrities joined the protest. Animal activists noted that orcas (which are really large dolphins) never kill humans in the wild. In captivity, young killer whales are separated from their families and are forced to live their lives in small steel or concrete enclosures with little stimulation. Captive orcas display a variety of unhealthy behaviors like banging against pool walls, biting on metal gates and attacking other whales.

SeaWorld vigorously fought attempts to ban its orca program, spending $15 million on an advertising campaign that emphasized the company's conservation efforts while attacking the truthfulness of *Blackfish*, calling it "emotionally manipulative." Despite the campaign, SeaWorld lost half of its stock value and attendance dropped dramatically. Congressman Adam Schiff of California threatened to introduce legislation banning captive orca programs, and the California coastal commission refused to let SeaWorld double the size of its killer whale tanks unless it stopped breeding orcas.

In 2016, SeaWorld agreed to end its breeding program, though the killer whale shows continued. In 2017 it announced that it was discontinuing the theatrical orca programs in its San Diego park, which has seen the largest decline in attendance. SeaWorld CEO Joel Manby said the company listened to customers who no longer wanted to see whales perform at the commands of trainers, and would provide "an all new orca experience focused on the natural environment [of the whales]." He told investors that the company would change its focus from entertainment to conservation, noting: "People love companies that have a purpose, even for-profit companies."[5]

Activists aren't done pushing for animal rights, which may mean additional changes in public attitudes that could threaten the business models of other organizations. Zoos, for example, are coming under increasing pressure to improve living conditions for their animals or shut down.

Discussion Probes

1. Was the circus the "saddest show on earth" because of the way it treated its elephants and other animals?
2. Could the circus have been saved if Ringling Brothers had taken a different approach to its critics?
3. Do you agree with Sea World's decision to end its captive orca breeding program and theatrical orca performances? Why or why not?
4. Why was SeaWorld unable to resist the pressure to end its orca-breeding program?
5. Based on the issue maturity scale, what is the stage of development of the issue of animal rights?
6. Are zoos in danger? What steps should they take to respond to animal rights activists?

Notes

1. Feld Entertainment (2017).
2. Hayden (2017).
3. Lang (2016).
4. Neuhaus (2017).
5. Neate (2015).

Sources: Fuggetta (2012). Karimi (2016). Solis (2017).

CASE STUDY 11.2

Facebook Takes on Fake News

In the run-up to the 2016 U.S. Presidential election, Facebook, Google, and Instagram were flooded with fake news stories. These bogus stories had such headlines as: "Hillary Clinton's Discarded BlackBerry Turns Up in Goodwill Thrift Store"; "Yoko Ono: 'I Had an Affair With Hillary Clinton in the '70s'"; "Pope Francis Shocks World, Endorses Donald Trump for President"; and "Donald Trump Is a Member of the Illuminati." These false news items were widely circulated and believed. Researchers at BuzzFeed found that fake news stories generated more interest than legitimate news stories. Following the election, 75% of Americans who remembered a fake news headline believed that it was true. One North Carolina man drove to Washington, DC, to "self-investigate" online rumors of a pedophile ring being run out of a pizza restaurant by Hillary Clinton and other important Democrats. He walked into the restaurant—filled with employees and families—carrying an AR-15 assault rifle and a revolver and fired one shot into a door. Fake news isn't limited to the United States, however. Hundreds of bogus stories were also posted during election campaigns in France and Germany.

Russia is behind many political fake news stories but profit, not politics, appears to be the motivation behind others. Researcher Craig Silverman of BuzzFeed found that there were a hundred false news websites located in the town of Veles in central Macedonia. During the 2016 election, writers (mainly young people) received a portion of the ad revenue generated through Google AdSense each time someone clicked on their sites. They would entice visitors through catchy headlines and domain names that closely resembled those of reputable news outlets. Early in the campaign they discovered that pro-Trump material produced much greater interest than anti-Trump content. Often readers would first go to Facebook and then click on a link that connected to the false news story on Google. To encourage visits from Facebook, the Macedonians would create or buy fake accounts and then introduce their stories to pro-Trump Facebook groups. According to Silverman:

> Facebook doesn't really earn them [fake news creators] a lot of money but the key thing about Facebook—and this is true whether you're running a politics site in Macedonia or whether you run a very large website in the US—Facebook is the biggest driver of traffic to news websites in the world now. 1.8 billion people log into Facebook every month.[1]

Both Facebook and Google are under pressure in the United States and Europe to reduce the spread of fake news on their sites. One group of Facebook shareholders proposed a resolution warning that the company could face government regulation and a loss of reputation (and users) because of fake news. They demanded a report on the company's efforts to deal with the problem. Germany approved a plan to fine social media companies for as much as $53 million if they didn't quickly take down posts that break German law. Britain's Parliament began an investigation of fake news. The chair of the committee launching the British probe claimed that the false news trend was "a threat to democracy and undermines

(Continued)

(Continued)

confidence in the media in general."[2] He went on to say that Parliament might make it illegal for tech companies not to act if they learn of false or inappropriate content. This would be a "massive incentive" for tech companies to "get their house in order."[3] (In one embarrassing case of fake news, Google Home repeated a bogus story that British prime minister Theresa May is secretly a lizard.)

Facebook CEO Mark Zuckerberg first denied that his firm had any responsibility for influencing votes, saying, "Personally, I think the idea that fake news on Facebook—of which it's a small amount of content—influenced the election in any way is a pretty crazy idea."[4] Later he changed course, declaring that the company had "much more work to do" when it came to false news content. Facebook users can now click a box to indicate if they think a story is a hoax. If identified as false, it is tagged with an alert message indicating that it has been "disputed by 3rd party fact-checkers" (outside groups hired to check stories). Any flagged story will be banned from being promoted as an ad. The trending feature, which used to be based on how many people shared a single story, has been changed to indicate, instead, how many people are accessing related stories on the same topic. For its part, Google banned 200 publishers from its AdSense network. Company engineers are developing better algorithms for identifying fake news sources. A previous algorithm failed when Google featured a bogus story claiming Donald Trump won the popular vote. He did not, garnering 2.8 million fewer votes than Hillary Clinton.

So far efforts by Facebook and Google to combat fake news have failed to silence critics. The *New York Times* declared in its own catchy headline, "In Race Against Fake News, Google and Facebook Stroll to the Starting Line."[5] *Times* technology writers consider Facebook's efforts to be small experiments and note that Google's publisher bans "were a drop in the bucket" when compared with the nearly two million publishers who use the AdSense program. One supporter of the fake news resolution at Facebook cautioned that the company could interfere with free speech and engage in censorship. Altering the algorithm might introduce "systematic bias." Conservatives who view Facebook as a liberal organization worry that the company will suppress other points of view.

Discussion Probes

1. Do you think that fake news had a significant impact on the 2016 U.S. presidential election?

2. Why do you think fake news is so believable? How can you tell if a news story item is bogus?

3. Do you agree that fake news poses "a threat to democracy?" Why or why not?

4. What responsibility do Internet platforms have for the content that appears on their sites?

5. Have Facebook and Google done enough to curb fake news? What additional steps could they take?

6. Is it fair for governments to fine Google and Facebook for not doing more to stop fake news content?

7. Do you worry that Facebook and Google will engage in censorship? How can the companies ensure that some perspectives aren't unfairly suppressed?

Notes

1. "Fake News Expert" (2016). NPR.
2. Lake and Flynn (2017).
3. Ibid.
4. Kottasova (2017).
5. Wakabayashi and Isaac (2017).

Sources: Slotkin (2017). Sterne (2017).

CASE STUDY 11.3

The Public Benefit Corporation and Profit-With-Purpose Businesses

Corporate officers, as we saw in Chapter 10, serve the financial interests of stockholders. This fiduciary duty can come into conflict with other goals, like helping to improve the local school system or restoring the environment. Shareholders may argue that companies should focus less on corporate responsibility and more on the bottom line. For example, Costco, which pays it employees well and provides them with health insurance, is under constant pressure from Wall Street to pay workers less in order to increase profits and raise the stock price.

In recognition of the fact that many companies have other goals besides profit, 30 states have passed laws creating a new category of corporation called the public benefit corporation. Public benefit corporations (BCs) are for-profit entities that "create a material positive impact on society and the environment."[1] Their social purposes are written into their corporate charters, which enables them to pursue social as well as financial objectives. To maintain their standing, BCs must file yearly reports on how well they are reaching their social or environmental goals according to a third-party standard, and their directors must consider interests beyond shareholder profit.

Alter Eco, Plum Organics, Method, Kickstarter, and New Leaf Paper are some of the firms that have registered as public benefit corporations Yves Chouinard, founder of the Patagonia outdoor clothing company, was the first corporate leader to file under California's public benefit corporation law. Patagonia is known for its strong environmental emphasis, giving 1% of sales to environmental causes, manufacturing recyclable clothing, funding a national park in Chile, and encouraging consumers to purchase their products only if they really need to do so. Chouinard registered the company as a BC because he feared that when he died, his successors might set aside the sustainability values and practices of the company in favor of higher financial returns.

Benefit corporations aren't for everyone. The vast majority of companies will continue to focus on the bottom line and investors will continue to demand high returns. (Delaware law requires that existing publicly held corporations receive 90% stockholder approval before changing to BC status.) And there are concerns about how well this new model will work. The statutes provide little guidance to directors to help them determine how to balance the needs of shareholders against the needs of other stakeholders. Some worry that managers will use the BC designation as cover for poor business decisions. Other observers are leery of the annual reporting requirement, arguing that measuring social progress is much more complex than tracking financial objectives. It may take years to demonstrate progress on social goals, and there is no "one size fits all" standard that applies to all types of public benefits. Then, too, it is not clear what happens to companies that fail to meet their social objectives in a given year.

Interest in social enterprises extends well beyond the United States. Other countries in the Group of 7 (which includes Canada, United Kingdom, France, Germany, Italy, and Japan) use the term "profit-with-purpose businesses" (PPBs) to describe companies that seek both profits and social benefits. Like benefit corporations, PPBs have to pursue the common good, keep the social purpose of their organizations in mind when making decisions, and report on their progress toward meeting their social objectives. The

(Continued)

(Continued)

Canadian province of British Columbia passed legislation setting up structures for PPBs. France and the UK provide tax benefits for such companies and those who invest in them.

Since benefit corporations and profit-with-purpose businesses are recent developments, it remains to be seen how effective they will be in attracting investment and fulfilling their stated purposes. Nevertheless, proponents are optimistic, saying that BCs and PPBs are the latest developments in corporate social responsibility and should be attractive to the millennial generation, many of whom are social entrepreneurs who start businesses to meet social needs like housing the homeless and training unskilled workers.

Discussion Probes

1. What advantages or disadvantages do you see in public benefit corporations and profit-with-purpose businesses?

2. Would you be more likely to purchase goods and services from public benefit corporations and PPBs than traditional corporations? Why or why not?

3. Would you invest in a public benefit corporation or profit-with-purpose business even if it meant that you would earn significantly less? Would you invest in a mutual fund that held only socially responsible companies?

4. Are there certain companies or types of businesses you would never invest in? Why?

5. Do you think that annual reports will be enough to guarantee that benefit corporations fulfill their objective to create a "positive material impact on society and the environment?"

Note

1. H. Martin (2012).

Sources: R. Burke and Bragg (2014). B. Cummings (2012). K. Gilbert (2013). Herdt (2012). Hiller (2013). Loewenstein (2013). Markell (2013). Orrick, Herrington & Sutcliffe LLP (2016). E. A. Peterson and Patel (2016). Social Impact Investment Taskforce (2014). Solnik (2012). Thorelli (2017). M. Wright (2011). S. B. Young (2014).

CHAPTER TWELVE

ETHICS IN A GLOBAL SOCIETY

Chapter Preview

The Dangers of Globalization and the Challenges of Ethical Diversity
Developing Cross-Cultural Ethical Competence
    Coming to Grips With Ethnocentrism
    Becoming a World Citizen
Understanding Ethical Diversity
Finding Moral Common Ground
Resolving Ethical Cross-Cultural Conflicts
Chapter Takeaways
Application Projects

Globalization is having a dramatic impact on life in the 21st century. We inhabit a global society knit together by free trade, international travel, immigration, satellite communication systems, and the Internet. In this interconnected world, ethical responsibilities extend beyond national boundaries. Decisions about raw materials, manufacturing, outsourcing, farm subsidies, investments, marketing strategies, suppliers, safety standards, and energy use made in one country have ramifications for residents of other parts of the world. Organizational citizenship is now played out on a global stage. Businesses, in particular, are being urged to take on a larger role in solving the world's social problems.

To act as ethical global citizens, organizations must confront and master the dangers of globalization and the dilemmas of ethical diversity. In this section, I'll describe these obstacles and offer tactics for overcoming them.

THE DANGERS OF GLOBALIZATION AND THE CHALLENGES OF ETHICAL DIVERSITY

The benefits of living in a global economy are obvious: lower labor costs, higher sales and profits, cheaper goods and services, instant communication to anywhere on Earth, increased information flow, and cross-cultural contact. What's often hidden is the downside of globalization. Of particular concern is the growing divide between the haves and the have-nots. The richest 10% of the global population controls 89% of the world's assets and income. The eight richest men on Earth have as much wealth as half of the world's population. Governments of wealthy nations appear more interested in promoting the sale of their goods (including agricultural products) than in opening up their markets to poor countries.[1] Lumber, minerals, and oil are extracted from poor regions and consumed in privileged areas, leaving environmental damage behind.[2] The pain of globalization isn't limited to developing economies, however. Millions in industrialized nations have seen their jobs outsourced to China, the Philippines, Vietnam, and other nations with lower labor costs. These job losses helped fuel renewed nationalism in the United States and Great Britain, which elected to leave the European Union.

Critics note that global capitalism frequently promotes greed rather than concern for others. Ethical and spiritual values have been shunted aside in favor of the profit motive. Few industrialized countries give even the suggested minimum of .07% of gross national product (70 cents of every $100 produced by the economy) to alleviate global poverty. The United States doesn't crack the top 10 list of most generous nations, which is led by Sweden (1.41%), the United Arab Emirates (1.09%) and Norway (1.05%).[3] Local cultural traditions are being destroyed in the name of economic progress. As burgers, fries, pizza, and other popular American foods replace local fare, people around the world can expect to suffer the same kinds of chronic health problems as U.S. residents do—type II diabetes, obesity, and heart failure.

The big winners in globalization are multinational corporations. According to one estimate, 69 of the world's 100 largest economies are corporations. The combined revenue of the top 10 companies is greater than the 180 poorest nations combined, a list which includes South Africa, Israel, Ireland, Iran, and Greece.[4] Some multinationals have pursued free trade at the cost of human rights and the environment. They have employed sweatshop and slave labor, stood by as repressive regimes tortured their citizens, and plundered local resources.

Along with the potential moral pitfalls of globalization, organizations also face the challenges of ethical diversity.[5] Nations, tribes, ethnic groups, and religions approach moral dilemmas differently. What members of one group accept as right may raise serious ethical concerns for another. For example, in Germany contracts are highly detailed and strictly enforced. In Egypt, contracts spell out guidelines for business deals rather than specific requirements. Egyptians expect to renegotiate and revise contracts, and there is no moral stigma attached to violating a signed agreement. In Mexico, honoring a contract is based on the signer's personal ethics. There is little legal recourse if a contract is violated.

Bribery offers another instance of conflicting moral standards. In South American countries, it is nearly impossible to move goods through customs without making small payments to cut through red tape. At the other extreme, Malaysia executes corporate officials who offer and accept bribes. U.S. corporations and foreign firms listed on a U.S. stock exchange are prevented from exchanging money or goods for favors or services under the Foreign Corrupt Practices Act of 1977. However, in recognition of the fact that petty bribery is common in some parts of the world, small payments to facilitate travel and business are permitted under the statute. Cultures also clash over intellectual property rights (which are strictly enforced in the West but not protected in parts of Southeast Asia) and deception (Americans lie to protect their privacy, whereas Mexicans are more likely to lie to protect the group or family). Another clash of moral standards is described in Case Study 12.1.

The challenges posed by globalization and ethical diversity can undermine ethical decision making. For some organizations, it is business as usual. Interested only in making a profit or expanding their influence, they fail to weigh the possible negative consequences of their choices in the global environment. Leaders faced with ethical diversity sometimes behave as ethical imperialists by imposing their personal moral standards on members of other cultures. Or they may opt for cultural relativism by always following local customs ("When in Rome, do as the Romans do"). Nevertheless, being in a new culture or working with a diverse group of followers doesn't excuse managers from careful ethical deliberation. Standards from one culture can't be blindly forced upon another; conversely, just because a culture has adopted a practice doesn't make it right. For example, trafficking in humans takes place in some parts of the world, but most societies condemn this practice.

Fortunately, you can develop your cross-cultural ethical competence and help your organizations to do the same. To achieve this goal, you must first wrestle with ethnocentrism and consider becoming a world citizen. Next, you have to recognize the value orientations of cultural groups and how these patterns influence ethical decision making. Then, you need to adopt universal moral principles that should govern behavior in every cultural setting and employ guidelines for sorting through conflicts between competing ethical norms.

DEVELOPING CROSS-CULTURAL ETHICAL COMPETENCE

Coming to Grips With Ethnocentrism

Overcoming the challenges of globalization and ethical diversity is impossible if we fall victim to ethnocentrism. *Ethnocentrism* is viewing the world from our cultural group's point of view, which makes our customs and values the standard by which the rest of the world is judged. Our ways are "right," while their ways fall short. A certain degree of ethnocentrism is probably inevitable; it can help a group band together and survive in the face of outside threats. Nevertheless, high levels of ethnocentrism can lead to reduced contact with outsiders, racial slurs, insensitivity to strangers, pressure on other groups to conform, justification for violence and war, and other negative outcomes.[6] (Contemporary Issues in Organizational Ethics 12.1 describes the controversy surrounding one form of ethnocentric behavior.)

A number of the ethical communication competencies introduced earlier in the text can be used to confront ethnocentrism. Pursue dialogue in cross-cultural conversations by treating members of other cultures as equal partners and by trying to understand their points of view. Mindfulness is particularly important in diverse cultural settings because the scripts we follow in our own groups don't work when we find ourselves in other cultures. Adopt a pluralistic perspective that acknowledges the legitimacy of other groups and customs in order to avoid moral exclusion. (See the next section for more information on an ethical approach that greatly expands the circle of moral inclusion.)

Personal virtues can help undermine ethnocentric attitudes and at the same time lay the groundwork for meeting the challenges of globalization and ethical diversity. Philosopher and theologian Michael Novak identified four cardinal or hinge virtues essential to encouraging global cooperation: cultural humility, truth, dignity, and solidarity.[7]

Cultural humility means acknowledging the shortcomings of our own cultures as well as our personal biases. A commitment to truth allows for reasoned argument based on evidence and logic. Recognition of human dignity forbids using others as a means to an end. Solidarity is being aware that each individual lives in communion with others and has responsibility for their welfare.

CONTEMPORARY ISSUES IN ORGANIZATIONAL ETHICS 12.1

CULTURAL APPROPRIATION: WHEN DOES BORROWING BECOME EXPLOITATION?

The term "cultural appropriation" describes the unauthorized use of ideas, dress, medicine, food, music, symbols, and other elements taken from another culture. Recently, accusations of cultural appropriation have been levied against

—the Boston Museum of Fine Arts for sponsoring "Kimono Wednesdays," where visitors were invited to try on the kimono Claude Monet's wife wore for the impressionist painting *La Japonnaise*.

—the two white, middle-class owners of Kooks Burritos food cart in Portland, Oregon, for "stealing recipes" during a visit to Mexico to start their own business.

—curators of the Whitney Museum for displaying the painting *Open Casket* by white artist Dana Schutz that depicts the body of Emmett Till, a black lynching victim. (Till's murder helped spark the civil rights movement.)

—Victoria's Secret for featuring a Caucasian runway underwear model wearing a "sexy Indian" costume made up of a fringed suede bikini, feathered headdress, and turquoise jewelry.

Cultural appropriation as exploitation has its origins in colonialism. Rich white nations would steal or appropriate the artworks and other cultural elements of oppressed peoples to assert domination and/or to eradicate the local culture. Cultural appropriation often benefits the borrower at the expense of the culture of origin. For example, white entertainers made millions from performing in a "black" music style at the same time African American vocalists faced segregation and discrimination. Then, too, use of some cultural symbols like blackface and Indian headdresses reinforce demeaning stereotypes. Nonetheless, cultures have always borrowed from one another. According to columnist Cathy Young:

> Peoples have borrowed, adopted, taken, infiltrated and reinvented from time immemorial. The medieval Japanese absorbed major elements of Chinese and Korean civilizations while the cultural practice of modern-day Japan includes such Western borrowings as a secularized and reinvented Christmas. Russian culture with its Slavic roots is also the product of Greek, Nordic, Tatar and Mongol influences—and the rapid Westernization of the elites in the 18th century. America is the ultimate blended culture.[1]

Since cultures constantly take from one another, the question then becomes When does borrowing become unauthorized stealing or exploitation? Making this determination is not always easy. While Victoria's Secret crossed into exploitation, many observers believe that the Boston Art Museum did not. The kimonos for the museum exhibit were created in Japan with the support of Japanese museums. (The Japanese don't appear bothered when people from other cultures wear the garment.) Those protesting Kimono Wednesdays were met by counterprotesters holding signs saying, "I am Japanese. I am not offended." The Kooks Burrito owners, who closed their business after receiving death threats, didn't actually steal their recipe but developed it after returning home from their vacation. (When a group of ethnic restaurateurs in Portland were interviewed, they noted that they often "borrow" food items from other regions and see no problem with the practice.) Whitney artist Dana Schutz said that while she isn't black, she is a mother and could relate to the suffering of Emmett Till's mother. She based her painting on photographs of Emmett released by his mother to spur outrage.

Arguments over what constitutes cultural appropriation will continue. These disputes raise further questions. Should some elements of culture, like sacred symbols, be off limits to those of other cultures? Is someone from one culture automatically disqualified from writing about, speaking about, or otherwise communicating about the experiences of another culture? How can we share cultural symbols in a way that benefits the originating culture while giving proper credit? Can members of one ethnic group wear the clothing and styles of another group? (Whites have been criticized for wearing dreadlocks and Africans have criticized African Americans for wearing African dress and tribal symbols.) Can they sell the food of another culture? How should we in the West respond to significant works of art and music, like those created by Picasso, Matisse, and Puccini, that were inspired by Africa or the Far East?

Note

1. C. Young (2015).

Sources: Arewa (n.d.). Avins (2015). Friedersdorf (2017). Korthage (2017). Malik (2017). Moreno (2017). Valk (2015).

Becoming a World Citizen

A number of scholars argue that *cosmopolitanism* is the best way to meet the ethical challenges of globalization while avoiding ethnocentrism. Since we live in a global society, they argue, we should consider ourselves citizens of the world (cosmopolitans) rather than of one particular nation-state. This approach acts as an "ethics of strangers" in a world where we increasingly interact with those outside our cultural group.[8]

Cosmopolitanism has a long history in Western philosophy, stretching back to the ancient Greek Stoic philosophers who believed that our responsibilities extend to strangers as well to acquaintances. Immanuel Kant proposed the creation of an international legal authority to regulate relations between nations. He encouraged hospitality toward foreigners.[9] Modern cosmopolitans take a humanistic approach to globalization based on the fundamental premise that every human being has dignity and value, regardless of their location, status, or background. They have a strong sense of global justice and work to ensure human rights. Their sense of care or empathy for the needs of others extends well beyond their immediate group to helping the "distant needy"—the less privileged who are often found in the world's developing nations. Cosmopolitans believe that they have a moral obligation or duty to act on that concern by providing assistance to others around the world. In particular, cosmopolitans argue that affluent businesses and nations are responsible to give to less fortunate people and nations.[10] Some other values and norms underlying ethical cosmopolitanism include the following:[11]

1. Limitations on patriotism and the sovereignty of countries
2. Opposition to nationalism
3. Commitment to aid those suffering from natural or human-made disaster, which includes extreme poverty
4. Liberalization of immigration and refugee policies
5. Quest for lasting world peace
6. Prosecution of crimes against humanity
7. Submission to the rule of international law
8. Religious and cultural tolerance
9. Dialogue and communication across cultural and national boundaries
10. Viewing the world as single polity and community

Acting as a global citizen takes certain attitudes and skills, what British political and social theorist William Smith calls cosmopolitan "worldliness."[12] Worldliness means, first off, being self-reflexive. To be self-reflexive, we need to step back from (create distance from) our relationships and culture in order to offer criticism and reform. Next, worldliness involves compassion for the world's people and working to create institutions and laws that will protect the less fortunate. Worldliness does not mean feeling pity for others, however, but having a sense of solidarity with them. Third, worldly individuals have the necessary skills to bring about change through setting strategy, persuading others, working with governments and nonprofits to promote global initiatives, and so forth.

Being totally cosmopolitan may be impossible given the fact that, as we noted earlier, humans naturally band together in local groups. And you might take issue with some of the tenets of cosmopolitanism, such as its rejection of patriotism and promotion of a world government. Nevertheless, cosmopolitans offer an attractive normative framework for living ethically in a global society. They encourage us to be altruistic, becoming compassionate citizens of the world who keep the dignity of all human beings in mind. We do need to be able to step back from, and then critique, our cultural norms and values. If we fail to distance ourselves, we blindly follow our cultural programming no matter how unethical our culture's practices.

Understanding Ethical Diversity

Ethical decisions and practices are shaped by widely held cultural values. Every culture has its own set of ethical priorities; however, researchers have discovered that ethnic groups and nations hold values in common. As a result, cultures can be grouped according to their value orientations. Understanding these orientations helps explain ethical differences and enables us to better predict how members of other societies will respond to moral dilemmas. Four widely used cultural classification systems include Hofstede's programmed value patterns, the GLOBE studies, universal values dilemmas, and moral foundations theory.

1. Programmed Value Patterns

Geert Hofstede of the Netherlands argues that important values are "programmed" into members of every culture. To uncover these value dimensions, he conducted the first extensive international investigation of cultural value patterns, surveying more than 100,000 IBM employees in 50 countries and three multicountry regions.[13] He then checked his findings against those of other researchers who studied the same countries. Four value orientations emerged:

Power distance. The first category concerns how societies deal with human inequality. While status and power differences are universal, cultures treat them differently. In high–power distance cultures (Malaysia, Guatemala), inequality is accepted as part of the natural order. Leaders are set apart and enjoy special privileges and make no attempt to reduce power differentials. Low–power distance cultures (Israel, Austria), on the other hand, are uneasy with large gaps in wealth, power, privilege, and status. Superiors tend to downplay status and power differentials, and such societies stress equal rights.

Individualism versus collectivism. This category divides cultures according to their preference for either the individual or the group. Individualistic cultures (the United States, Australia, Great Britain) put the needs and goals of the person and her or his immediate family first. Members of these cultures see themselves as independent actors and believe that everyone should take care of themselves and their nuclear family. In contrast, collectivistic cultures give top priority to the desires of the larger group—extended family, tribe, community. Members of these societies (Guatemala, Ecuador, Panama) think in terms of "we," not "I." They want to fit into the collective, not stand out. (You can determine your level of individualism and collectivism by completing Self-Assessment 12.1.)

Masculinity versus femininity. The third dimension reflects attitudes toward the roles of men and women. Highly masculine cultures (Japan, Austria, Saudi Arabia) maintain clearly defined sex roles. Men are expected to be tough and focus on performance; women are to be tender and focus on relationships. Men should be ambitious and assertive, while women are expected to care for the weak. Feminine cultures (Sweden, Norway, Netherlands) blur the differences between the sexes. Both men and women can be competitive and caring, assertive and nurturing. These cultures are more likely to stress cooperation, quality of life, and concern for others.

SELF-ASSESSMENT 12.1

Individualism/Collectivism Scale

Instructions

This questionnaire will help you assess your individualistic and collectivistic tendencies. Respond by indicating the degree to which the values reflected in each phrase are important to you: "Opposed to My Values" (answer 1), "Not Important to Me" (answer 2), "Somewhat Important to Me" (answer 3), "Important to Me" (answer 4), or "Very Important to Me" (answer 5).

_____ 1. Obtaining pleasure or sensuous gratification

_____ 2. Preserving the welfare of others

_____ 3. Being successful by demonstrating my individual competency

_____ 4. Restraining my behavior if it is going to harm others

_____ 5. Being independent in thought and action

_____ 6. Having safety and stability of people with whom I identify

_____ 7. Obtaining status and prestige

_____ 8. Having harmony in my relations with others

_____ 9. Having an exciting and challenging life

_____ 10. Accepting cultural and religious traditions

_____ 11. Being recognized for my individual work

_____ 12. Avoiding the violation of social norms

_____ 13. Leading a comfortable life

_____ 14. Living in a stable society

_____ 15. Being logical in my approach to work

_____ 16. Being polite to others

_____ 17. Being ambitious

_____ 18. Being self-controlled

_____ 19. Being able to choose what I do

_____ 20. Enhancing the welfare of others

Scoring

To find your individualism score, add your responses to the *odd-numbered* items. To find your collectivism score, add your responses to the *even-numbered* items. Both scores will range from 10 to 50. The higher your scores, the more individualistic or collectivistic you are.

Source: Gudykunst (2004). Used by permission.

Uncertainty avoidance. This dimension describes the way in which cultures respond to uncertainty about the future. Members of high–uncertainty avoidance societies (Greece, Portugal, Uruguay) feel anxious about uncertainty and view it as a threat. They are less likely to break the rules; they value loyalty to the company, accept directives from those in authority, and view outsiders and change as threats. In addition, they are reluctant to change jobs or to express dissatisfaction with their current employers. People who live in low–uncertainty avoidance cultures (Sweden, Denmark, Jamaica) are more comfortable with uncertainty, viewing ambiguity as a fact of life. They experience lower stress and are more likely to pursue their ambitions by, for example, starting a new company or accepting a new job in another part of the country. These people tend to trust their own judgments instead of obeying authority figures. As a result, they are more likely to break rules and regulations.

Hofstede argues that the value patterns he identifies have a significant influence on ethical behavior.[14] For instance, countries characterized by masculinity, high power distance, and high uncertainty avoidance are generally more corrupt. Masculine European countries give little to international development programs but invest heavily in weapons. Feminine European nations do just the opposite. High–uncertainty avoidance cultures are prone to ethnocentrism and prejudice because they follow the credo "What is different is dangerous." Low–uncertainty avoidance cultures follow the credo "What is different is curious" and are more tolerant of strangers and new ideas.

Other researchers have also linked Hofstede's value patterns to ethical attitudes and behavior.[15] They have discovered that members of feminine cultures are more sensitive to the presence of moral issues. Consumers from societies characterized by low power distance and low uncertainty avoidance generally punish socially irresponsible firms. Corporate governance is better in individualist societies as compared to masculine, high uncertainty societies. Accounting organizations from high individualism/high uncertainty avoidance cultures are less likely to adopt global codes of ethics because they don't want to submit to the authority of outside, international organizations. Individualistic countries prefer universal ethical standards such as Kant's categorical imperative. Collectivistic societies take a more utilitarian approach, seeking to generate the greatest good for in-group members.

Individualistic and collectivist societies have different communication patterns, which also shape the ethical behavior of citizens.[16] Individualists use low-context communication in which most of the information in the message is embedded in the message itself. In nations like Germany and Switzerland, communicators directly express their thoughts and feelings as clearly as possible and rely heavily on carefully crafted written messages like contracts. To them, conflict should be faced head on. Collectivists engage in high context communication where most of the information is contained in the situation or context where the message is delivered. Speakers in Japan and other high-context cultures communicate indirectly, rarely expressing direct disagreement, for instance. They are more interested in maintaining harmony in the group than in expressing their true thoughts and feelings and often avoid direct confrontation. As a consequence, followers are much less likely to confront unethical superiors or coworkers or to blow the whistle on corporate misbehavior.[17] They are more willing to sacrifice the truth to save "face" and to protect their group.

Additional examples of how individualism and collectivism affect ethical decisions are presented in Table 12.1.

Table 12.1

Issue	Individualistic	Collectivistic
Bribery	Seen as a form of corruption	A way to meet community obligations, more common
False information	Lie to protect privacy	Lie to protect the group or family
Expressing disagreement	Direct	Indirect; save face
Intellectual property	Protected by copyright laws	Knowledge is to be shared
Gender equality	Promote equal opportunity	Women seen as an out-group; need to protect status quo
Nepotism	Hire based on qualifications	Hire based on connections (family and friends)
Privacy	Right to privacy	Public interests take priority over privacy
Wealth	Wealth distributed more equally	Large differences in wealth
Human rights	High human rights ratings	Low human rights ratings
Laws	The same for all	Vary according to tradition and status

Source: S. J. Carroll and Gannon (1997). Copyright © 1996, SAGE Publications, Inc. Used by permission.

2. Project GLOBE

Project GLOBE (Global Leadership and Organizational Behavior Effectiveness) is an ongoing international effort. To date, 200 researchers from around the world have gathered data from more than 17,000 managers in 62 countries. The goal of the project is to identify the relationship between cultural values and effective leadership behaviors. This information can help managers become more successful in cross-cultural settings. The GLOBE researchers incorporate into their study Hofstede's dimensions of power distance, uncertainty avoidance, gender differentiation (masculinity and femininity), and individualism versus collectivism. However, they also extend Hofstede's list by identifying four additional values patterns:[18]

> *Performance orientation.* This is the "extent to which a community encourages and rewards innovation, high standards, and performance improvement."[19] Places such as Hong Kong, Singapore, and the United States are results focused. Citizens value competition and materialism and want to be rewarded for individual achievement. In countries such as Russia, Italy, and

Argentina, people put loyalty and belonging ahead of performance. They are uncomfortable with competition and merit pay and put more weight on someone's seniority, family, and background than on his or her performance.

Future orientation. This is the extent to which a society fosters and reinforces such future-oriented activities as planning and investing (Singapore, Switzerland, the Netherlands) rather than immediate rewards (Russia, Argentina, Poland).

Assertiveness. Assertiveness is defined as the extent to which a culture encourages individuals to be tough, confrontational, and competitive, as opposed to modest and tender. Spain and the United States rate high on this dimension; Sweden and New Zealand rate low. Those in highly assertive societies have a take-charge, can-do attitude and value competition. They admire the strong and assertive and are not particularly sympathetic to the weak and less fortunate. Members of less assertive cultures place more value on empathy, loyalty, and solidarity. They have empathy for the weak and want to live in harmony with the environment rather than control it.

Humane orientation. Humane orientation refers to the extent to which a culture encourages and honors people for being altruistic, caring, kind, fair, and generous. Support for the weak and vulnerable is particularly high in such countries as Malaysia, Ireland, and the Philippines. Members of society care for one another and rely much less on the government. In contrast, power and material possessions are more likely to motivate people in the former West Germany, Spain, and France; self-enhancement takes precedence. Individuals are to solve their own problems, and the state provides more support for the less fortunate.

The GLOBE values dimensions have also been linked to ethical diversity. People oriented toward the future save and invest. They will condemn those who live in the moment and spend all they earn. Future-oriented organizations are also more likely to engage in practices that benefit society. Competition, direct communication, power, and personal advancement are applauded in assertive, performance-oriented, less humane groups. These elements are undesirable to people who put more value on harmony, cooperation, family, and concern for others. Those living in assertive, performance-oriented cultures are tempted to engage in unethical activities in order to succeed. The businesses they create are more likely to be focused on shareholders, profits, and results instead of on stakeholders and social responsibility (including care for the environment).[20] Countries high in uncertainty avoidance and future orientation are more likely to protect intellectual property than cultures high in humane orientation and in-group collectivism.[21]

3. Universal Dilemmas

Cross-cultural experts Fons Trompenaars and Charles Hampden-Turner are convinced that humans the world over face the same set of values choices they call universal dilemmas. Cultures differ in how they respond to these dilemmas, which accounts for cultural diversity. Trompenaars and Hampden-Turner identify the following six dimensions of cultural diversity based on their surveys of 50,000 managers from over 40 countries.[22]

Universalism (focus on rules, codes, laws, and generalizations across situations) or *particularism* (focus on exceptions, special circumstances, and unique relations between individuals and groups). Universalist societies: Norway, Switzerland, Finland, Austria. Particularist societies: Yugoslavia, South Korea, Russia, Nepal.

Individualism (emphasis on personal freedom, human rights and competitiveness) or *communitarianism* (emphasis on social responsibility, harmonious relationships, and cooperation). Individualist societies: Czech Republic, Canada, United States, Denmark. Communitarian societies: Egypt, Nepal, Mexico, India.

Specificity (reality is viewed through a atomistic, reductive, objective lens) or *diffusion* (reality is viewed through a holistic, elaborative, relational lens). Specificity societies: United States, United Kingdom, Netherlands, Australia. Diffuse societies: Venezuela, Japan, South Korea, Philippines.

Achieved status (social standing is based on what you've done—your track record) or *ascribed status* (social standing is based on who you are, your potential and connection to others). Achieved status societies: United States, Canada, Great Britain, Australia. Ascribed status societies: South Korea, Japan, France, Singapore.

Inner direction (virtue is found within; in conscience, will, core beliefs, principles) or *outer direction* (virtue comes from outside through natural rhythms, beauty, nature and relationships). Inner-directed societies: Canada, United States, Germany, Australia. Outer-directed societies: China, Indonesia, Singapore, Japan.

Sequential time (time is viewed as a race along a set course) or *synchronous time* (time is seen as a involving ongoing coordination. Sequential time societies: Turkey, India, United States, Brazil. Synchronous time societies: Israel, South Korea, Sweden, China.

Trompenaars and Hampden-Turner urge us to view the ends of each dimension as part of the same circle, not as not as opposites. That's because we need elements of both no matter what culture we live in. For example, completing a project like a major term paper takes both specificity (breaking the paper into parts and researching subtopics) and diffusion (developing an overall structure for the paper that puts the sections in a logical order). Each end of the continuum has its strengths, but focusing on one value to the exclusion of the other not only reduces an organization's chances of success but also encourages unethical behavior. For example:

—Universalist cultures strive to treat everyone equally and welcome diversity. However, universalists are tempted to treat people as objects. Particularistic cultures highlight the uniqueness of individuals and relationships but are often hostile to human rights and engage in favoritism and moral exclusion.

—Individualism promotes dissent and individual freedom but, at the same time, encourages greed and over consumption. Communitarianism promotes cooperation and leaves a legacy for future generations. Taken too far, though, communitarianism leads to collusion and can undermine attempts at self-improvement.

—Achieved status promotes excellence and persistence but can lead to a "winner take all" society. Ascribed status fosters trust and encourages those of high status to give back to the community but inhibits personal achievement and can produce dictatorships.

—Inner directness fosters courage and moral identity. Yet inner directedness also produces driven individuals. Inner directed cultures like the United States too often honor "tough," inner directed bosses who do it their way without concern for others. Outer directedness fosters care for the environment and recognition of others. Nevertheless, outward focus can lead to pessimism and a willingness to give in and go along with immoral behavior.

Since there are ethical dangers at both extremes, Trompenaars and Hampden-Turner urge us to strive for reconciliation, integrating elements of each value perspective.[23] They use the example of a California oil company to illustrate this process. The firm (operating in a culture that honors achieved status) employed ascribed status to improve safety. Managers wanted unionized truck drivers to drive more carefully and to report "unsafe acts," near accidents or unsafe conditions that could lead to accidents. Such a procedure greatly reduces the chances of mishaps as steps are taken to eliminate the danger. And safety was a major concern given that each company truck carried enough gasoline to incinerate cars three hundred yards away as well as entire neighborhoods. However, teamster truck drivers, who viewed themselves macho "Cowboys," resisted the safety push, refusing to "snitch" on their union colleagues. Management decided to help the drivers redefine themselves as "Knights of the Road" who provide a public service to the community. Instead of using their CB radios to warn other truckers about speed traps, they were encouraged to warn other drivers of rock slides, ice, and other road hazards. Drivers also pointed out poorly designed entrance ramps and areas prone to black ice. Once a year they made a presentation to the California Highway Authority about how to improve hazardous highways. In the first twelve months of the program, accidents were cut in half and fleet insurance rates dropped.

4. Moral Foundations Theory

Hofstede, the GLOBE researchers, and Trompenaars and Hampden-Turner treat ethical diversity as just one of the outcomes of cultural diversity. In contrast, moral foundations theory was developed specifically to account for the ethical differences between cultures. University of Virginia moral psychologist Jonathan Haidt and others believe that to understand ethical diversity we first need to understand the psychological systems or foundations of morality. These mental foundations, which are part of our genetic makeup, enable humans to successfully live together in groups. Cultures shape how these systems are used, emphasizing one or more values over the others. Haidt compares these moral systems to taste buds. Nearly everyone is born with the same set of taste receptors, but each culture develops its own cuisine, which highlights different tastes.

Haidt identifies five foundations for our moral intuitions.[24] They include the following:

Harm/care. All species are sensitive to suffering in their own offspring, but for primates and humans, sensitivity to suffering extends beyond the family.

We can also feel compassion for outsiders. Attuned to cruelty and harm, we generally approve of those who prevent or alleviate suffering. Kindness and compassion are therefore important human virtues. However, the other moral foundations described below temper the amount of compassion that individuals in different cultures display.

Fairness/reciprocity. Reciprocity—paying back others—is essential for the formation of alliances between individuals who are not related to each other. As a result, all cultures have virtues related to justice and fairness. Individual rights and equality are highly prized in the West. However, many traditional societies put little value on personal autonomy or equal treatment.

In-group/loyalty. Trust and cooperation have been critical to human survival. Individuals need to work effectively with others in their group while being wary of outsiders. As a result, they value those who sacrifice on behalf of the in-group while despising members who don't come to their aid in times of conflict. They are disturbed when fellow citizens challenge symbols of group unity, like the pledge of allegiance to the national flag.

Authority/respect. Hierarchy is fact of life in primate as well as human groups. Dominant individuals get special perks but are expected to provide services (e.g., protection, food) in return. Primates rely on brute strength to assert their authority; people use such factors as prestige and deference. Followers in many cultures feel respect, awe, and admiration for leaders and expect them to act like wise parents. Many of these same societies make virtues out of duty, obedience, respect, and other subordinate behaviors.

Purity/sanctity. Only humans appear to feel disgust, which helps to protect the body against the transmission of disease through corpses, feces, vomit, and other possible contaminants. Disgust has a social dimension as well, becoming associated with those who are diseased or deformed or with certain occupations (gravediggers and those who dispose of excrement, for example). Members of most cultural groups admire those who are spiritually minded or pure and disapprove of individuals who seem to be ruled by lust, gluttony, greed, and uncontrolled anger. For instance, in the United States, one of the most materialistic societies in the world, most citizens still look down on those who regularly "shop until they drop."

The United States and many other Western nations largely focus on reducing harm and promoting autonomy. But as Haidt points out, that is not the case in much of the rest of the world. In Brazil, morality is based on loyalty, family, respect, and purity in addition to care. Confucian and Hindu value systems emphasize authority and stability. Muslim societies place a high priority on purity, which is reflected in the segregation of men and women and separation from infidels. Haidt urges us to keep all five moral systems in mind when dealing with diverse groups. Purity and authority may not be important to us, but they are to a great proportion of the world's population. Our ethical appeals will be most effective if they speak to loyalty, authority, and purity in addition to care and fairness. (Complete Self-Assessment 12.2 to determine which moral intuitions are most important to you.)

SELF-ASSESSMENT 12.2

Moral Foundations Questionnaire

Part I. Moral Relevance

When you decide whether something is right or wrong, to what extent are the following considerations relevant to your thinking? Please rate each statement using this scale:

0 = not at all relevant, 1 = not very relevant, 2 = slightly relevant, 3 = somewhat relevant, 4 = very relevant, 5 = extremely relevant

1. Whether or not someone suffered emotionally.
2. Whether or not someone cared for someone weak or vulnerable.
3. Whether or not some people were treated differently from others.
4. Whether or not someone acted unfairly.
5. Whether or not someone's action showed love for his or her country.
6. Whether or not someone did something to betray his or her group.
7. Whether or not someone showed a lack of respect for authority.
8. Whether or not someone conformed to the traditions of society.
9. Whether or not someone violated standards of purity and decency.
10. Whether or not someone did something disgusting.

Part II. Moral Judgments

Please read the following sentences and indicate your agreement or disagreement.

0 = strongly disagree, 1 = moderately disagree, 2 = slightly disagree, 3 = slightly agree, 4 = moderately agree, 5 = strongly agree

11. Compassion for those who are suffering is the most crucial virtue.
12. One of the worst things a person could do is hurt a defenseless animal.
13. When the government makes laws, the number one principle should be ensuring that everyone is treated fairly.
14. Justice is the most important requirement for a society.
15. I am proud of my country's history.
16. People should be loyal to their family members, even when they have done something wrong.
17. Respect for authority is something all children need to learn.
18. Men and women each have different roles to play in society.
19. People should not do things that are disgusting, even if no one is harmed.
20. I would call some acts wrong on the grounds that they are unnatural.

Scoring

Add up the scores on each moral foundation (range 0–20). The higher the score, the more important that foundation is to you.

Harm: Items 1, 2, 11, 12 _____

Fairness: Items 3, 4, 13, 14 _____

Ingroup/Loyalty: Items 5, 6, 15, 16 _____

Authority: Items 7, 8, 17, 18 _____

Purity: Items 9, 10, 19, 20 _____

Source: J. Graham et al. (2011). Copyright © 2016 by the American Psychological Association. Reproduced with permission.

Professor Haidt developed his theory to explain moral differences between cultures, but he soon discovered that moral foundations explain the differences between liberals and conservatives in the United States.[25] Contrasts between these political philosophies further demonstrate how the moral foundations shape ethical attitudes. Haidt believes that the purity/sanctity dimension is the best predictor of positions on abortion, for example. American liberals who value autonomy want to preserve the woman's right to choose, and conservatives want to preserve the sanctity of the fetus. Authority predicts competing attitudes toward gay marriage. Liberals believe that individuals have a right to do as they choose if they don't hurt anyone else. In their minds, opposition to gay marriage is homophobic. Conservatives, on the other hand, see gay marriage as a threat to the family, which serves as the foundation of society. Those on the political left and right are also divided by their attitudes toward loyalty. Liberals believe that citizens can protest against a war while at the same time supporting the soldiers fighting in the conflict. This argument offends conservatives, who believe it is unpatriotic to protest when the country is at war.

Finding Moral Common Ground

Some organizations and their members respond to ethical diversity by practicing ethical relativism, which is conformity to local customs. Ethical relativism avoids the problem of ethnocentrism while simplifying the decision-making process. We never have to pass judgment and can concentrate on fitting in with the prevailing culture. However, this approach is fraught with difficulties. Without shared standards, there is little hope that people of the world can come together to tackle global problems. There is no basis upon which to condemn the actions of governments, such as Sudan and Myanmar, that are engaged in genocide and torture or to criticize businesses that exploit their employees and the environment. Cultural relativism obligates us to follow (or as least not to protest against) abhorrent local practices like female genital mutilation. Without universal rights and wrongs, we have no grounds for contesting such practices.

There appears to be a growing consensus that ethical common ground can be found. In fact, the existence of common moral standards has enabled the world community to punish crimes against humanity in Germany, Serbia, and Rwanda. Responsible multinational corporations like Starbucks, The Body Shop, and Proctor & Gamble adhere to widely held moral principles as they do business in a variety of cultural settings. Activist groups use these same guidelines to condemn irresponsible firms.

One group of researchers used the "trolley problem" to determine if there are similarities in cross-cultural reasoning.[26] In the trolley problem, an out-of-control trolley threatens to kill five people unless immediate action is taken. In one case, the trolley operator is incapacitated, and a passenger has to decide whether or not to throw a switch that will divert the vehicle to safety on a side track (and save the five passengers) but will kill a pedestrian who happens to be standing on the rails. In the other case, someone standing by the tracks must decide whether or not to directly intervene by throwing another bystander into the path of the trolley to slow it down and save the five passengers.

Responses to the trolley problem from 30,000 subjects in 120 countries revealed widespread agreement across all groups, regardless of nationality, educational level, or religion. By a significant margin, participants said it was justified to throw the switch to save the trolley passengers but not to throw someone onto the tracks to accomplish the same goal. Respondents reported that throwing a switch is an impersonal act, and they saw the death of the pedestrian as an unfortunate consequence. On the other hand, throwing a bystander onto the track is a deliberate, highly personal act that makes the victim a means to an end.

The hypothetical trolley problem has parallels in real life. For example, most of us would allow terminally ill patients to refuse treatment and thus die sooner than they would have with the additional care. (This approach is similar to throwing the trolley switch.) However, it is illegal in most states to give a drug overdose to hasten a terminally ill patient's death (which raises the same concerns as throwing a bystander onto the trolley track).

Universal standards provide additional evidence that members of diverse societies can find moral common ground. Such global standards have enabled members of the world community to punish crimes against humanity and to create the United Nations. I'll describe three different approaches to universal ethics, any one of which could serve as a worldwide standard. You'll note a number of similarities between the lists. Decide for yourself which approach or combination of approaches best captures the foundational values of humankind. (See Application Project 4 at the end of the chapter). Apply one or more of the standards to evaluate the actions of Goldman Sachs and other financial institutions in Case Study 12.2.

The United Nations Universal Declaration of Human Rights

Human rights are granted to individuals based solely on their status as persons. Such rights protect the inherent dignity of every individual regardless of background. Rights violations are unethical because they deny human value and potential.[27]

The most influential list of basic human rights was adopted by the United Nations immediately following World War II, a conflict fought in large part to protect human freedoms. Among the key rights spelled out in the universal declaration are the following:[28]

Article 4. No one shall be held in slavery or servitude; slavery and the slave trade shall be prohibited in all their forms.

Article 5. No one shall be subjected to torture or to cruel, inhuman, or degrading treatment or punishment.

Article 9. No one shall be subjected to arbitrary arrest, detention, or exile.

Article 13. Everyone has the right to freedom of movement and residence.

Article 17. Everyone has the right to own property alone as well as in association with others.

Article 19. Everyone has the right to freedom of thought, conscience, and religion.

Article 25. Everyone has the right to a standard of living adequate for the health and well-being of him[her]self and of his [her] family, including food, clothing, housing and medical care and necessary social services.

Article 26. Everyone has the right to education.

In 2000, the United Nations launched a program called the Global Compact (GC) to encourage multinational corporations to honor human rights, labor rights, and the environment. Members agree to the principles outlined in Ethical Checkpoint 12.1 and specify how they are complying with these guidelines. Nonprofit watchdog groups meet regularly with corporate representatives to talk about their firms' performance. Membership in the Global Compact has grown rapidly. It is now the largest voluntary corporate citizen group in the world. Nonetheless, there is considerable debate about the effectiveness of this organization. Critics argue that the UN leaders have weakened the Compact's standards in order to attract new members and they claim that there is little evidence that the GC has improved the conduct of member firms. GC staff and supporters argue, on the other hand, that the Global Compact has contributed to growing consensus about moral norms for global business. They point to the contrasting responses of Nike and Apple to mistreatment of overseas workers as evidence of that fact. It took Nike 20 years to take responsibility for the behavior of subcontractors after initial criticism in the 1970s. Apple responded immediately in 2012 to reports that Foxconn, a major contract supplier in China, was forcing employees to work long hours for low wages in unsafe conditions, all while living in overcrowded dormitories. The Global Compact has also sponsored initiatives to reduce bribery in India, Brazil, Nigeria, Egypt, and South Africa.[29]

ETHICAL CHECKPOINT 12.1

United Nations Global Compact: The Ten Principles

Human Rights

Principle 1: Businesses should support and respect the protection of international human rights within their sphere of influence; and

Principle 2: make sure that they are not complicit in human rights abuses.

Labour

Principle 3: Businesses should uphold the freedom of association and the effective recognition of the right to collective bargaining;

Principle 4: the elimination of all forms of forced and compulsory labour;

Principle 5: the effective abolition of child labour; and

Principle 6: the elimination of discrimination in respect of employment and occupation.

Environment

Principle 7: Businesses should support a precautionary approach to environmental challenges;

Principle 8: undertake initiatives to promote greater environmental responsibility; and

Principle 9: encourage the development and diffusion of environmentally friendly technologies.

Anti-Corruption

Principle 10: Businesses should work against corruption in all its forms, including extortion and bribery.

Source: United Nations Global Compact: The ten principles. Retrieved from http://unglobalcompact.org.

The Global Business Standards Codex

Harvard business professor Lynn Paine and her colleagues argue that outstanding ("world-class") corporations base their codes of ethics on a set of eight universal, overarching moral principles.[30] Paine's group came to this conclusion after surveying a variety of global and corporate codes of conduct and government regulations. They offer the following Global Business Standards Codex as a benchmark for those who want to conform to universal standards of corporate conduct.

I. *Fiduciary principle*. Act on behalf of the company and its investors. Be diligent and loyal in carrying out the firm's business. As a trustee, be candid (open and honest).

II. *Property principle*. Respect and protect property and the rights of its owners. Don't steal or misuse company assets, including information, funds, and equipment. Avoid waste and take care of property entrusted to you.

III. *Reliability principle*. Honor all commitments. Keep promises and follow through on agreements even when they are not in the form of legally binding contracts.

IV. *Transparency principle*. Do business in a truthful manner. Avoid deceptive acts and practices and keep accurate records. Release information that should be shared in a timely fashion but maintain confidentiality and privacy as necessary.

V. *Dignity principle*. Respect the dignity of all who come in contact with the corporation, including employees, suppliers, customers, and the public. Protect their health, privacy, and rights. Avoid coercion. Promote human development instead by providing learning and development opportunities.

VI. *Fairness principle*. Deal fairly with everyone. Engage in fair competition, provide just compensation to employees, and be evenhanded in dealings with suppliers and corporate partners. Practice nondiscrimination in both employment and contracting.

VII. *Citizenship principle*. Act as a responsible member of the community by (a) obeying the law, (b) protecting the public good (not engaging in corruption, protecting the environment), (c) cooperating with public authorities, (d) avoiding improper involvement in politics, and (e) contributing to the community (e.g., economic and social development, giving to charitable causes).

VIII. *Responsiveness principle*. Engage with groups (neighborhood groups, activists, customers) that may have concerns about the company's activities. Work with other groups to better society while not usurping the government's role in protecting the public interest.

The Caux Principles

The Caux Round Table is made up of corporate executives from the United States, Japan, and Europe who meet every year in Caux, Switzerland. Round Table members believe that businesses should improve economic, social, and environmental conditions and hope to set a world standard by which to judge business behavior. Their principles are based on twin ethical ideals. The first is the Japanese concept of *kyosei*, which refers to living and working together for the common good. The second is the Western notion of human dignity, the sacredness and value of each person as an end rather than as a means to someone else's end.[31] The Caux Principles for Business, perhaps because they were written by corporate executives from around the world, have gained widespread support. Business schools in Latin America, Asia, Europe, and the United States have endorsed them, and a number of international firms have used them as a guide when developing their own mission statements and ethics codes.

> *Principle 1. Respect stakeholders beyond shareholders.* Businesses should have goals that extend beyond economic survival. Corporations have a responsibility to improve the lives of everyone they come in contact with, starting with employees, customers, shareholders, and suppliers, and then reaching out to local, national, regional, and global communities.
>
> *Principle 2. Contribute to economic, social, and environmental development.* Companies operating in foreign countries not only should create jobs and wealth but should also foster human rights, better education, and social welfare. Multinational corporations have an obligation to enrich the world community through the wise use of resources, fair competition, and innovation.
>
> *Principle 3. Build trust by going beyond the letter of the law.* Businesses ought to promote honesty, transparency, integrity, and keeping promises. These behaviors make it easier to conduct international business and to support a global economy.
>
> *Principle 4. Respect rules and conventions.* Leaders of international firms must respect both international and local laws in order to reduce trade wars, to ensure fair competition, and to promote the free flow of goods and services. They also need to recognize that some behaviors may be legal but still have damaging consequences.
>
> *Principle 5. Support responsible globalization.* Firms should support international trading systems and agreements and eliminate domestic measures that undermine free trade.
>
> *Principle 6. Respect the environment.* Corporations ought to protect and, if possible, improve the physical environment through sustainable development and by cutting back on the wasteful use of natural resources.
>
> *Principle 7. Avoid illicit activities.* Global business managers must ensure that their organizations aren't involved in such forbidden activities as bribery, money laundering, supporting terrorism, and drug and arms trafficking.[32]

After spelling out general principles, the Caux accord applies them to important stakeholder groups. Corporations following these standards seek to (1) treat customers and employees with dignity, (2) honor the trust of owners and investors, (3) create relationships with suppliers based on mutual respect, (4) interact fairly with competitors, and (5) work for reform and human rights in host communities. The Caux Round Table has also developed principles for moral governments and nongovernmental organizations (NGOs). Integrity is the fundamental principle for NGOs, which must serve the common good while remaining true to their mission. NGO staff members should not abuse the public trust or use their positions for personal gain. Grounded in integrity, NGOs need to retain their independence, respect international and local laws, take care to be truthful when advocating positions while recognizing the potential impact on governments and corporations, and be accountable by regularly reporting on their activities and finances.[33]

Resolving Ethical Cross-Cultural Conflicts

So far, we've established that (1) there are significant differences between cultures in how they respond to ethical issues, and (2) there are universal moral principles that apply across cultural boundaries. Reconciling these two facts when making ethical decisions is not easy. How do we respect ethical diversity while remaining true to global moral principles, for example? What do we do when two competing ethical perspectives appear to be equally valid? What set of standards should have top priority—those of the host nation or those of the international organization? Business ethicists Thomas Donaldson and Thomas Dunfee developed the integrated social contracts theory (ISCT) to help us answer questions like these.[34]

ISCT is based on the notion of social contracts, which are agreements that spell out the obligations or duties of institutions, communities, and societies. The model is integrative because it incorporates two kinds of contracts. The first kind of contract (*macrosocial*) sets the groundwork or standards for social interaction. Examples of ideal contracts include the requirement that governments respect the rights of people and help the poor. The second type of contract (*microsocial*) governs the relationships between members of particular communities—nations, regions, towns, professions, industries. These contracts are revealed by the norms of the group. Community contracts are considered authentic or binding if (1) members of the group have a voice in the creation of the norms, (2) members can exit the group if they disagree with prevailing norms, and (3) the norms are widely recognized and practiced by group members.

According to ISCT, universal principles (called *hypernorms*) act as the ultimate ethical standard in making choices. Communities have a great deal of latitude, or *moral free space*, to create their own rules, however, as long as these local norms do not conflict with hypernorms. Victim compensation provides one example of norms arising out of moral free space. In Japan (where the victim compensation system is unreliable), airline officials go in person to offer compensation to victims' families after an accident. In the United States (where the compensation system is more reliable), payments are determined through court decisions.

Dunfee and Donaldson offer a number of guidelines for determining which norms should take priority. Three of these rules of thumb are particularly important. One, determine if the local practice is authentic (widely shared) and legitimate (in harmony with hypernorms). If it's not, it should be rejected. Second, follow the legitimate local customs of the host community whenever possible. To return to our earlier compensation example, a U.S. airline official stationed in Japan should distribute compensation directly to crash victims' families instead of relying on the Japanese court system. Third, give more weight to norms generated by larger communities. A norm embraced by a nation as a whole, for instance, should generally take precedence over the norm of a region. The U.S. government followed this guideline in overturning laws promoting racial discrimination in the South. A similar argument can be made for choosing the norm of gender equality—which has broad international acceptance—over the norms of a particular nation that discriminates against women. (You can test the ISCT model and the one that follows by applying them to one or more of the scenarios in Case Study 12.3 at the end of the chapter.)

University of Louisiana professors J. Brooke Hamilton, Stephen B. Knouse, and Vanessa Hill offer an alternative strategy for resolving cross-cultural ethical conflicts, one specifically designed for use in multinational enterprises (MNEs).[35] They provide six questions (the HKH model) to guide managers in determining whether to follow the values of their firms or to adopt the practices of the host country instead. Decision makers don't have to completely answer one question before moving on to the next. Instead, they can move ahead, returning to reconsider earlier questions as needed in order to clarify the final course of action.

1. *What is the questionable practice (QP) in this situation?* The first question identifies the nature of the problem, which may or may not have an ethical component. To qualify as an ethical conflict, the norms and values of the host country and the business must clash. A firm then has to determine whether to comply with local customs or to follow its own standards, which may mean leaving the host country.

2. *Does the QP violate any laws that are enforced?* Managers need to determine if the contested practice violates either the laws of their home country or the country where they are doing business. For example, as noted earlier, the Foreign Corrupt Practices Act prevents U.S. firms from offering bribes anywhere in the world. Chinese law requires that Internet companies support government censorship.

3. *Is the QP simply a cultural difference, or is it also a potential ethics problem?* A questionable practice qualifies as an ethical issue if it seems to cause harm or violates widely accepted ethical principles like justice or human rights. For example, offering small gifts to show respect is standard business procedure in much of Asia. Gift giving doesn't become an ethical issue unless significant sums are offered to bribe recipients at the expense of other parties.

4. *Does the QP violate the firm's core values or code of conduct, an industrywide or international code to which the firm subscribes, or a firmly established hypernorm?* The answer to this question may differ based on whether a company is interested only in complying with the law or is also interested in living up to its values. For a compliance-only company, an action is ethical as long as it is legal. Managers are interested only in avoiding punishment or harm to the company. Corporations seeking both to comply with the law and to live out their values (compliance/integrity firms) follow a higher standard. They recognize that the law doesn't condemn all forms of unethical behavior, and at the same time they

empower their employees to base their decisions on core values. For instance, workers at Motorola are encouraged to follow the firm's guidelines, called "Uncompromising Integrity and Constant Respect for People." Organizational decision makers can also base their choices on the widely accepted moral standards described earlier in the chapter.

5. *Does the firm have leverage (something of value to offer) in the host country that allows the firm to follow its own practices rather than the QP?* Companies with leverage have greater freedom to follow their own standards or to adapt their practices in a way that doesn't violate their central principles. Leverage comes from contributing to the local economy, offering jobs, supplying currency that can be used for international trade, providing training, purchasing local goods and services, transferring technology to the regional economy, and having an ethical reputation. McDonald's used its leverage to operate in Moscow without engaging in bribery and other forms of corruption endemic to the Russian economy. Of course, compliance-only companies don't have to worry about using leverage, since they automatically follow local regulations.

6. *Will market practices in the host country improve if the firm follows its own practices rather than the QP in the host country marketplace?* This question should be considered only after determining the amount of leverage held by the firm. If the company has significant leverage, it has a responsibility to try to change prevailing practices by refusing to engage in the questionable practice. Improving the way business is done (by not offering bribes, for example) may encourage local firms to follow suit, and local residents will benefit as a result.

CHAPTER TAKEAWAYS

- In addition to providing significant benefits, globalization poses a number of ethical dangers, including increasing the gap between the haves and have-nots and promoting greed and corporate power at the expense of individuals.

- Overcome ethnocentrism—the tendency to see the world from your cultural group's point of view—through dialogue, mindfulness, adoption of a pluralistic perspective, and the practice of personal virtues that promote global cooperation.

- Seeking to be a citizen of the world is one way to address the dangers of globalization while combating ethnocentrism. Cosmopolitanism encourages compassion for those outside our nations, extending aid to the less fortunate no matter how distant from us.

- Understanding the values that ethnic groups and nations hold in common helps explain ethical differences and better equips you to predict how members of other societies will respond to moral dilemmas. Common values orientations include power distance, individualism versus collectivism, masculinity versus femininity, uncertainty avoidance, performance orientation, future orientation, assertiveness, and humane orientation.

- Cultures differ in their responses to universal dilemmas, which produces contrasting values dimensions. Societies take different positions on universalism/particularism, individualism/communitarianism, specificity/diffusion, achieved status/ascribed status, inner/outer direction, and sequential/synchronous time. Focusing on one value to the exclusion of the other dimension encourages unethical behavior. Instead, integrate or reconcile elements from each end of the continuum.

- Ethical differences between cultures can also be explained by the emphasis that various groups place on one or more of the following: harm/care, fairness/reciprocity, in-group/loyalty, authority/respect, purity/sanctity.

- Resist the temptation to practice cultural relativism. Instead, look for ethical common ground, found in such universal principles as the UN Universal Declaration of Human Rights, the Global Business Standards Codex, and the Caux Principles for Business.

- When making ethical decisions in global settings, balance universal principles with the need to honor local laws and values. Keep three key decision-making guidelines in mind: local customs must (1) conform to global standards or hypernorms; (2) give priority to the authentic, legitimate norms of the host country; and (3) whenever possible, give more weight to norms generated by larger communities. In cases involving conflicts between your company's norms and those of the host country (questionable practices), empower employees to decide based on corporate values, and look for ways to leverage your firm's influence to change local business practices.

APPLICATION PROJECTS

1. Do you think the benefits of globalization outweigh its costs? Defend your position.

2. What do you think it means to be a "citizen of the world"? Should you strive to be a cosmopolitan? Why or why not? What would be some of the implications of living as a world citizen? Write up your response.

3. Select a culture, and write an analysis using the Hofstede and GLOBE dimensions. Determine how the culture rates on each dimension, and determine how this cultural profile shapes the ethical attitudes and behaviors of citizens. Write up your findings. As an alternative, select a culture and analyze it based on the six universal dilemmas.

4. Is there a common morality that peoples of all nations can share? Which of the global codes described in the chapter best reflects these shared standards and values? If you were to create your own declaration of global ethics, what would you put in it?

5. What do your scores on Self-Assessment 12.1 and Self-Assessment 12.2 reveal about how your culture has shaped your values and ethical decision making?

6. Develop a case study based on the conflict between the ethical norms of different countries. Identify the values patterns that are contributing to this dilemma. Resolve the conflict using the guidelines provided by integrated social contracts theory or the HKH (questionable practices) model.

7. Create a case study based on a company or other organization that you believe is a good example of a global citizen.

8. Select one of the diversity scenarios in Case Study 12.3, and reach a conclusion based on concepts presented in the chapter.

CASE STUDY 12.1

The Right to Be Forgotten

Individual privacy is a fundamental right in both the United States and Europe. However, the two regions define this right very differently. In the United States, privacy is "the right to be left alone," and this right is often superseded by free press and free speech rights.[1] This view of privacy was illustrated by a California Supreme Court ruling that journalists could publicize the sexual orientation of a gay man who stopped an assassination attempt on former President Gerald Ford. The hero repeatedly asked the press not to reveal this information, which was hidden from his family, but the court ruled that helping to protect the president had made him a public figure. In Europe, dignity underlies privacy concerns. According to Zurich law professor Rolf Weber, Europeans consider "dignity, honor and the right to private life" the most fundamental rights. There is the "right for the [moral and legal] integrity of a person not to be infringed and for a sphere of privacy to be maintained and distinguished."[2] The European Court of Human Rights ruled, for example, that German papers had violated Princess Caroline of Monaco's privacy rights by publishing photographs of her and her family. The tribunal noted that the pictures were taken in "a climate of continual harassment" and involved "a very strong sense of intrusion into their private life."[3]

The European Court of Justice applied the European conception of privacy to the Internet when it ruled that its citizens have the "right to be forgotten." A Spaniard petitioned the court to force Google to remove information about the auction sale of his repossessed home. He argued that this reference was irrelevant because the matter had been resolved years earlier. He asked Google to remove the pages and to ensure that news of the auction no longer appeared in search results. The Court of Justice agreed, declaring that individuals have a limited right to ask search engines to remove links with personal information if the information is "inaccurate, inadequate, irrelevant or excessive."[4] This judgment applies to all current or future Internet providers operating in Europe. Opponents of the decision believe that the right to be forgotten is a form of censorship, comparable to allowing librarians to destroy books they don't like. Media outlets worry that prominent people and corporations will use the system to delete unfavorable information about them.

In response to the EU ruling, Google, which handles an estimated 85% of Europe's Web traffic, set up a system to handle data removal requests. Applicants fill out an online form that is submitted to a team within Google's legal department, which weighs the request against the public interest. If the request is approved, the search engine then checks with the publisher, who may argue that the link be retained. Country data-protection regulators decide in cases where individuals dispute Google's decision. The company received 431,000 applications to remove 1.5 million links from search results and granted approximately 43% of the requests in the first year after the EU judgment. To illustrate the kinds of requests it accepts and rejects, a company official said Google removed a five-year-old story about an individual cleared in a child pornography case but refused to remove a news article about someone recently convicted of child abuse.

Initially, removal applied to the 28 nations of the European Union as well as to Iceland, Norway, Switzerland, and Liechtenstein. The

(Continued)

(Continued)

deleted links were still available on Google.com and other search engines. French regulators then ruled that Google must remove the links on all of its databases, thus extending the right to be forgotten beyond Europe. This judgment appeared to violate a basic principle of international law that regulations drafted in one nation apply only to that territory. David Price, senior product counsel for Google, complained, "One country shouldn't get to make the rules for what happens in another country."[5] Google appealed the French decision to the EU but then decided to comply. Now delisting requests made in any European country apply regardless of the search engine domain.

Efforts are under way to extend the right to be forgotten to the United States and Canada. Two New York state legislators proposed a law similar to the EU statute. The California Minor Eraser Law allows state residents under 18 to petition to have information they posted online removed. Many states have laws prohibiting "revenge porn"—sexually explicit pictures posted without the permission of the other party. The Canadian courts and Office of Privacy are beginning to address Internet privacy cases.

Discussion Probes

1. What does the right to privacy mean to you? The right to be left alone or the right to maintain your dignity?
2. What should take precedence—the right of privacy or the right of free speech?
3. What do you think constitutes "inaccurate, inadequate, irrelevant or excessive" information on the Internet? Can you think of any examples?
4. Should American and Canadian citizens "have the right to be forgotten"?
5. What information should never be deleted from the Internet?
6. Should the regulations of one nation or region apply to the global Internet?

Notes

1. Chow (2013).
2. Ibid.
3. Ibid.
4. European Commission (2014).
5. Bradshaw (2016).

Sources: Gibbs (2016). "Google Restores Links" (2014). Manjoo (2015). M. Scott (2014a, 2014b). Shackford (2017). Spanier (2014). Toobin (2014).

CASE STUDY 12.2

Goldman Sachs and Hunger Bonds

Life in Venezuela is tough. The country has the world's highest inflation rate (800%) and suffers from shortages of medicine and, more importantly, food. When oil prices were high, domestic food production dropped as the country imported foodstuffs using oil revenue. When oil prices dipped, less money was available to pay for food imports. The country's president, Nicolás Maduro, compounded the problem by refusing food shipments from humanitarian organizations and turning over control of the food supply to the corrupt military. The average citizen is 19 pounds lighter due to the food shortage, and some have been forced to eat kernels of corn and rice that fall off food trucks.

Venezuelans have taken to the streets to demonstrate against Maduro's regime. So far the embattled president has maintained power through repression, murder, and control of the military. According to one estimate, during 60 days of citizen protests, the regime killed 60 people, injured 13,000, and prosecuted nearly 2,000 in military courts.

Desperately short of foreign currency to stay financially afloat, Venezuelan officials offered deeply discounted national oil company bonds. New York investment bank Goldman Sachs purchased $2.8 billion of these bonds from the national oil company of Venezuela for $890 million, a 30% discount. Goldman's purchase set off a firestorm of criticism from Venezuelan opposition leaders and others who accused the bank of propping up a murderous dictator. They described these instruments as "blood" or "hunger bonds." They pointed out that Venezuelan authorities pay creditors first, before the needs of the people. Thus, money that could have gone toward feeding the population would go to Goldman Sachs and other bondholders. Julio Borges, the head of Venezuela's opposition-controlled congress, sent a letter to Goldman CEO Lloyd Blankfein accusing the bank of making "a quick buck off of the suffering of the Venezuelan people."[1] He vowed not to pay the debt should he come to power.

Goldman defended the bond purchase, stating, "We believe that the situation in the country must improve over time."[2] Bank officials were careful to point out that Goldman was investing on behalf of clients and didn't deal directly with the Venezuelan government. Instead, the purchase was made on the open market through an intermediary. In a statement, bank officials also pointed out that other banks and hedge funds are invested in Venezuelan securities. Reports are that BlackRock, T. Rowe Price, Fidelity, and other companies hold these oil company bonds. Venezuela bonds are attractive given that their interest rate is much higher than for most other international bonds. Deep discounts mean that firms can make money even if the country eventually defaults on the debt.

Borges dismissed Goldman's claims that it hadn't dealt directly with the Maduro regime as "putting lipstick on this pig of a deal."[3] Protestors gathered outside Goldman headquarters holding signs reading "Don't Support Venezuela's Hunger Bonds" and "Goldman Sachs Profits Off the Killing of Venezuelans by Maduro$ Regime." Said a Venezuelan college student: "By giving $900 million to a dictatorship they are funding a systematic human rights violator, they are funding immorality and for Maduro to stay in power while he keeps killing people."[4]

Discussion Probes

1. Is Goldman "making money off of the suffering of the Venezuelan people?" Are other bondholders doing the same?
2. Does the fact that Goldman didn't deal directly with the Venezuelan government make any difference in how you evaluate its bond purchase? Why or why not?
3. Is Goldman being unfairly targeted for criticism given that other financial institutions also hold these bonds?
4. Which, if any, of the universal ethical standards outlined in the chapter are foreign Venezuelan bondholders violating?
5. If you were an investment officer, would you recommend that your fund buy Venezuelan bonds? Or, if your fund held these bonds, would you recommend getting rid of them? What do you base your decision on?

Notes

1. Gillespie (2017).
2. Ibid.
3. "Nomura Admits Part" (2017).
4. Ellsworth and Scigliuzzo (2017).

Sources: V. Hernandez (2016). Neumann (2017). The Takeaway (2017). L. Thomas (2017). E. R. Wald (2017). Wigglesworth and Long (2017).

CASE STUDY 12.3

Scenarios for Analysis

The Branch Manager

You have been appointed as manager of your British manufacturing company's operations in Columbia. The previous manager, also an expatriate, followed local customs when it came to staffing and leadership style. In keeping with the widespread belief in Latin America that "only family can be trusted," the branch hired relatives of current employees. In addition, the previous branch manager acted as "the grand patron," which met cultural expectations of how a leader should behave. As the grand patron, he dispensed cash, time off, and other benefits that ensured the loyalty of an inner circle of subordinates. Columbian operations consistently meet production targets, but you are bothered by the inefficiencies you see. Some family members lack the qualifications to carry out their duties. You don't believe that as a leader you should be dispensing resources that belong to the organization. The home office will give you the freedom to lead as you see fit, though headquarters bases hiring on merit, and "treating all employees fairly" is enshrined in the company's values statement.

Should you follow the example of the previous manager or follow the practice of the home office?

Note: This scenario is loosely based on a real-life example found in Osland, Franco, and Osland (2000).

Real Estate Guanxi

You are a licensed realtor who recently helped a family from Hong Kong find a new home in the San Francisco, California, area. Fortunately for you, locating a suitable property for your clients wasn't hard and didn't require much effort on your part. (It can be difficult to find reasonably priced housing in the Bay Area, which is one of the most expensive regions of the United States.) In two weeks, your clients made an offer that was accepted by the seller. At the home closing, after the papers were signed, the father of the family took you aside and gave you $2,000 in cash as a thank you gift. This money is an addition to your commission, which is a percentage of the home's sale value. You know that gifts are frequently used to cement business relationships in China, part of the practice known as *guanxi*. However, you don't believe that your effort on behalf of these clients merits any special consideration and worry that this "gift" could be seen as a "bribe."

Will you accept the $2,000?

Note: For more information on the practice of *guanxi*, see Langenberg (2013).

The Warlord Tax

You are the CEO of a small international relief agency. Your group's policy is never to pay bribes in any of the countries in which you operate, no matter how corrupt. The policy has not seriously hampered your operations until now. Severe famine has struck in the Horn of Africa, in an area controlled by armed warlords. For food to reach the 100,000 starving residents of the region, you must pay a "tax" to the local military commander in the form of money or foodstuffs. This "tax" is clearly a form of extortion and violates your antibribery policy and possibly U.S. law. Other international relief agencies pay the tax, so you know that food shipments won't be completely cut off if your organization decides to pull out of the area. On the other hand, stopping shipments would significantly reduce food supplies to the region and could contribute to malnutrition and starvation.

Will you pay the warlord tax and continue the food shipments?

Note: This scenario is loosely based on actual events.

Shutting Down the Internet

You are in charge of Far East operations for a multinational Internet and cell phone company. Your firm recently became the largest provider for a small country in your region. Over the past month, thousands of citizens have taken to the street to overthrow this nation's repressive regime. Antigovernment forces rely heavily on email, Facebook, Twitter, and phone calls to rally their supporters and to pressure government leaders to step down. To cripple the protest movement, the head of the nation's security forces has demanded that your company shut down all service for a week. You believe the government has the authority to make this request and, if you don't comply, will cut off service on its own and imprison your local employees. However, shutting off service puts you on the side of an authoritarian government and violates your company's mission, which is to promote the free flow of information. Based on the response to a similar shutdown during antigovernment protests in Egypt, you expect heavy criticism from international human rights groups if you go along with the current government's request.

Will you shut down Internet and cell phone service for a week?

Note: Thanks to Jonathan Cooley, Portland, Oregon, for bringing my attention to the issues raised in this case.

Sources: Beam (2011). Garside (2011).

NOTES

INTRODUCTION

1. Edelman (2017).
2. Barbara Toffler provides an in-depth look at what went wrong at Arthur Andersen in Toffler and Reingold (2003).
3. Paine (1996b), p. 477.
4. Narvaez and Vaydich (2008).
5. Kohlberg (1984). Rest (1993).
6. Ethics Resource Center (2013).
7. Foote, Gaffney, and Evans (2010). Byus, Deis, and Ouryang (2010).

CHAPTER 1

1. Narvaez (2006).
2. Sean Hannah and his colleagues use the term *moral maturation* to describe the abilities needed to make better ethical choices. See: Hannah, Avolio, and May (2011).
3. Narvaez and Lapsley (2005), p. 151.
4. Menzel (2010). T. L. Cooper and Menzel (2013).
5. Petrick (2008, 2011).
6. Cheney, Christensen, Zorn, and Ganesh (2011).
7. Jaska and Pritchard (1994), p. 3.
8. W. H. Shaw (2011), p. 7.
9. Trevino and Nelson (2014), p. 18.
10. Johannesen, Valde, and Whedbee (2008), p. 1.
11. R. R. Sims (1994), p. 5.
12. A. B. Carroll and Buchholtz (2012), p. 23.
13. Stanwick and Stanwick (2009), p. 2.
14. Day (2003). Jarrett (1991).
15. Material for this summary of utilitarian theory is drawn from the following sources: Barry (1978). Bentham (1948). De George (1995), Chap. 3. Driver (2011). Troyer (2003). Velasquez (1992), Chap. 2. West (2004).
16. Are biotech foods safe to eat? (2014). Kantor (2013).
17. Barry (1978). DesJardins (2011). Hartman (1996), Chap. 2. Velasquez (1992).
18. Fink (2013).
19. Gillett (2017).
20. Christians, Rotzell, and Fackler (1990). Kant (1964). Leslie (2000). Sullivan (1994). Uleman (2010). Velasquez (1992).
21. G. Graham (2004), Chap. 6.
22. W. H. Shaw (2011).
23. Material on Rawls's theory of justice and its critics is taken from the following sources: Rawls (1971, 1993a, 1993b, 2001). Blocker and Smith (1980). Mulhall and Swift (1992). Velasquez (1992).
24. Rawls (2001), p. 42.
25. Gladwell (2005).
26. Barnes (1982).
27. Material on Aristotelian ethics is taken from the following sources: Ackerill (1981). Aristotle (1984). Barnes (1995). Bragues (2006). Kenny (2004). Shields (2011). Vella (2008).
28. Aristotle (1984), p. 1751.
29. Aristotle (1962), Book II, p. 1.
30. Solomon (1992).
31. Johannesen et al. (2008).
32. Cleary (1992). Wusun (2010).
33. Weber (2009).
34. See, for example: G. K. Y. Chan (2008). Confucius (2007). Romar (2002, 2004).
35. For more information on the parallels between the ethical tenets of Confucius and Aristotle, see Sim (2007) and Provis (2010).
36. Lau (1970).
37. Lau (1979).
38. Ip (2009).
39. Ihara (2004).
40. Batson, Van Lange, Ahmad, and Lishner (2003). Post, Underwood, Schloss, and Hurlbut (2002).
41. Batson et al. (2003). Post (2002).
42. Piliavin and Charng (1990).
43. Batson et al. (2003), p. 279.
44. Kung (1998).
45. Kanungo and Conger (1993). Organ (1988).
46. Gilligan (1982). Larrabee (1993). Noddings (2003). Held (2006).
47. Jaffee and Shibley Hyde (2000).
48. Held (2004).
49. Tronto (1993).
50. Held (2006).
51. Kracher and Wells (1998).
52. Kann (2017).
53. Sorokin (1954).
54. J. A. Kottler (2000).

CHAPTER 2

1. Rayburn (1997).
2. Duffy and Sedlacek (2007, 2010).
3. Bunderson and Thompson (2009). Duffy and Autin (2013). Isaksen (2000). Wrzesniewski, McCauley, Rozin, and Schwartz (1997).
4. See, for example: Dik and Duffy (2009). Dik, Duffy, and Eldridge (2009). Stairs and Galpin (2010).
5. Bunderson and Thompson (2009). Wrzesiniewski et al. (1997).
6. Gouws (1995). Super (1990).
7. Buechner (1973), p. 95.
8. L. Hardy (1990).
9. Mahan (2002).
10. Levoy (1997).
11. Wrzesniewski and Dutton (2001).
12. S. H. Schwartz and Sagiv (1995), p. 93.
13. Crace and Brown (1992).
14. D. Brown (1995).
15. Coldwell, Billsberry, van Meurs, and Marsh (2008). De Clercq, Fontaine, and Anseel (2008). A. L. Kristof (1996). Kristof-Brown, Zimmerman, and Johnson (2005). Posner (2010).
16. Kasser (2002). Kasser and Ahuvia (2002). Kasser, Vansteenkiste, and Deckop (2006).
17. Johannesen, Valde, and Whedbee (2008), p. 10.
18. D. K. Hart (1994).
19. N. Park and Peterson (2003).
20. C. Peterson, Stephens, Park, Lee, and Seligman (2010). Seligman (2002).
21. Damon (2002). Lockwood (2009). Salls (2007).
22. Narvaez (2009). Narvaez and Lapsley (2005).
23. Brandenberger (2005).
24. See, for example: Burke and Koyuncu (2010). Carver and Scheier (2005). Emmons and McCullough (2003). Luthans, Youssef, and Avolio (2006). Morris, Brothridge, and Urbanski (2005). Tangney (2005).
25. Covey (1989). See also Covey (2004).
26. T. L. Cooper and Wright (1992).
27. D. K. Hart (1992).
28. Gregory (2009). Kirkpatrick (1992).
29. MacIntyre (1984), p. 216. See also Hauerwas (1981).
30. O'Connor (1997).
31. Ellenwood (2007), pp. 22–23.
32. Oatley (2008).
33. Gottschall (2012).
34. Dotlich, Noel, and Walker (2004, 2005). See also: Bennis and Thomas (2002). Moxley (2004).
35. Blasi (1984, 2005). S. A. Hardy and Carlo (2005). Lapsley (2008).
36. Colby and Damon (1992, 1995).
37. Colby and Damon (1995), p. 364.
38. Aquino and Freeman (2009). S. J. Reynolds and Ceranic (2007). Shao, Aquino, and Freeman (2008).
39. Information on the benefits of workplace spirituality is taken from the following: Craigie (1999). Fairholm (1996). Garcia-Zamor (2003). Giacalone and Jurkiewicz (2010). Jurkiewicz and Giacalone (2004). Karakas (2009). Mirvis (1997). Rego and Pina e Cunha (2008). Tejeda (2015).
40. Ashmos and Duchon (2000), p. 137. See also: Duchon and Plowman (2005).
41. Oman (2013). Zinnbauer and Pargament (2005).
42. T. Moore (1992, 1995).
43. Fisher, Francis, and Johnson (2000). Gomez and Fisher (2003).

CHAPTER 3

1. Rest (1986, 1994).
2. Gaudine and Thorne (2001).
3. Werhane (1999). See also: Whitaker and Godwin (2013).
4. Bird (1996).
5. Trevino and Nelson (2004).
6. T. M. Jones (1991).
7. Ibid., p. 375.
8. See, for example: Butterfield, Trevino, and Weaver (2000). Carlson, Kacmar, and Wadsworth (2009). Frey (2000). May and Pauli (2002). McMahon and Harvey (2006). M. Singer, Mitchell, and Turner (1998).
9. Kohlberg (1984, 1986).
10. Rest, Narvaez, Bebeau, and Thoma (1999). Trevino and Weaver (2003), Chap. 7.
11. Rest et al. (1999).
12. See, for example: Rest (1979). Rest and Narvaez (1991). Trevino and Weaver (2003).
13. Not all studies reveal a relationship between education and moral reasoning. See: Loe, Ferrell, and Mansfield (2000).
14. Gergen (2000).
15. Callahan (2004).
16. Aubrey (2014).
17. Sternberg (2002).
18. Nash (1990), p. 166.
19. Gaudine and Thorne (2001).
20. Nutt (2002).
21. "Why Your Negotiating Behavior" (2008).

22. Epley and Dunning (2000). Tenbrunsel, Diekman, Wade-Benzoni, and Bazerman (2009).
23. Bandura (1999).
24. Shu, Gino, and Bazerman (2009).
25. Gino, Moore, and Bazerman (2008).
26. Banaji, Bazerman, and Chugh (2003). Bazerman, Chugh, and Banaji (2005).
27. Banaji et al. (2003).
28. Gino et al. (2009).
29. Batson, Collins, and Powell (2006). Batson and Thompson (2001). Batson, Thompson, and Chen (2002). Batson, Thompson, Seuferling, Whitney, and Strongman (1999). Lammers, Stapel, and Galinsky (2010).
30. James (2000).
31. Haidt (2002). Moll, de Oliveira-Souza, Zahn, and Grafman (2008). Prinz and Nichols (2010).
32. Herzog and Golden (2009).
33. Hannah, Jennings, Bluhm, Peng, and Schaubroeck (2014).
34. Trevino and Weaver (2003), Chap. 7.
35. Coles (2001).
36. Hannah and Avolio (2010).
37. Gentile (2010).
38. Lonergan (1973).
39. C. A. Baird (2003).
40. Ibid., p. 138.
41. Paine (2003).
42. Goldman (2008).
43. Badaracco (2016).

CHAPTER 4

1. Arnett and Arneson (1999). Biemann (2002). Buber (1970). Johannesen, Valde, and Whedbee (2008). Mayhall and Mayhall (2004).
2. Stewart (2008).
3. Arnett (1986). Czubaroff (2000).
4. Cissna and Anderson (1994).
5. C. T. Brown and Keller (1994).
6. Hulsheger, Alberts, Feinholdt, and Lang (2013).
7. K. W. Brown (2007). K. W. Brown and Ryan (2003). Ruedy and Schweitzer (2010).
8. Langer and Burgoon (1995).
9. K. W. Brown (2007). K. W. Brown and Ryan (2003). Burgoon, Berger, and Waldron (2000).
10. Langer (2014). Sternberg (2000).
11. Wolf (2014).
12. Marainetti and Passmore (2010).
13. Brownell (2002, 2003).
14. Nichols (2014).
15. Barker and Watson (2000). Chesebro (1999). Imhof (2004). Villaume and Bodie (2007). Watson, Barker, and Weaver (1995).
16. D. W. Johnson (2012).
17. Rosh and Offermann (2013).
18. D. W. Johnson (2012). Offermann and Rush (2012).
19. Buber (1965).
20. Cissna and Sieburg (1990). Laing (1994).
21. Ellis (2000, 2004b).
22. Frymier and Houser (2000).
23. Ellis (2004a).
24. Bucker and Frisby (2015). Ellis (2000, 2004a). Goodboy and Myers (2008). Schrodt, Turman, and Soliz (2006). Sidelinger and Booth-Butterfield (2010). Turman and Schrodt (2006).
25. J. D. Mayer, Salovey, and Caruso (2008), p. 503.
26. Caruso and Salovey (2004). See also: J. D. Mayer, Caruso, and Salovey (2000). J. D. Mayer and Salovey (1993, 1995, 1997). J. D. Mayer, Salovey, and Caruso (2004).
27. Ekman (2003).
28. Gaudine and Thorne (2001).
29. Caruso, Bien, and Kornaci (2006). J. D. Mayer et al. (2004). Salovey and Grewal (2005).
30. Caruso et al. (2006). Lopes, Cote, and Salovey (2006). Mayer, Salovey, and Caruso (2004). Salovey and Grewal (2005).
31. "Emotional Competence Training" (n.d.). Lennick (2007).
32. Examples of the effects of trust and its qualities are drawn from the following sources: Brockner, Siegel, Daly, Tyler, and Martin (1997). Dirks (1999). Dirks and Ferrin (2002). R. C. Mayer and Davis (1995). McAllister (1995). Mishra (1996). R. B. Shaw (1997). Zand (1972).
33. Bruhn (2001), p. 82.
34. M. A. Cohen and Dienhart (2013). Hosmer (1995). See also: Michalos (1995), Chap. 6.
35. Reina and Reina (2006). See also Lewicki and Bunker (1996).
36. Reina and Reina (2006).
37. Finlayson (2000, 2005). Habermas (1970, 1990).
38. Meisenbach (2006).
39. Inch and Warnick (2002). Infante (1988).

CHAPTER 5

1. French and Raven (1959).
2. Yukl (2006).
3. C. E. Johnson and Hackman (2018).
4. Carney (2005). K. Smith (2014).

5. Bilton (2016).
6. Fiske (1993). S. A. Goodwin (2003).
7. Kipnis, Schmidt, Swaffin-Smith, and Wilkinson (1984).
8. Yukl (2006).
9. Bennett (1998). Kanter (1977), Chap. 7. Smith, Jostmann, Galinsky, and van Dijk (2008).
10. Hocker and Wilmot (2014).
11. Champoux (2003). Drory and Romm (1990).
12. Miller, Rutherford, and Kolodinsky (2008).
13. Fedor, Maslyn, Farmer, and Bettenhausen (2008). Perrewe, Ferris, Stoner, and Brouer (2007).
14. Valle (2006).
15. Kurchner-Hawkins and Miller (2006).
16. Ferris et al. (2005). Valle (2006).
17. See, for example: Kirkman and Rosen (1999). Seibert, Silver, and Randolph (2004). Spreitzer, Kizilos, and Nason (1997). Tuuli and Rowlinson (2009). Ugboro and Obeng (2000).
18. Bass (1990).
19. Spreitzer (1995, 1996). Spreitzer et al. (1997). K. W. Thomas and Velthouse (1990).
20. Bandura (1977).
21. Kanter (1979).
22. Example taken from Forrester (2000).
23. Randolph (2000).
24. Lincoln, Travers, Ackers, and Wilkinson (2002).
25. Fairhurst (2011).
26. MacLean (2007).
27. Fairhust and Sarr (1996).
28. Edmondson (2003).
29. Fairhurst (2011).
30. Ibid.
31. Yukl (2013). Yukl, Chavez, and Seifert (2008).
32. Hunter and Boster (1987). S. R. Wilson (2002).
33. Goffman (1959). Schlenker (1980). Leary and Kowalski (1990).
34. Rosenfeld, Giacalone, and Riordan (1995).
35. Bratton and Kacmar (2004). W. L. Gardner (1992). Guadagno and Cialdini (2007). Seabright and Moberg (1998). Singh, Kumra, and Vinnicombe (2002). C. K. Stevens and Kristof (1995).
36. Brooks (2012). Kidwell (2004). Lupica (2014). M. R. Williams (2017).
37. Rosenfeld et al. (1995).
38. Turnley, Klotz, and Bolino (2013).
39. Offermann (2004).
40. Provis (2004).
41. Aquino (1998). Grover (1993, 1997). W. T. Ross and Robertson (2000). R. L. Sims (2000).
42. R. C. Solomon (1993).
43. Grover (1997). Cialdini, Petrova, and Goldstein (2004). Not everyone is convinced that organizational lies are harmful. See, for example: Shulman (2007).
44. Bok (1978, 1989).
45. T. Carson (2001).
46. Duke, Goodman, Treadway, and Breland (2009).
47. Hochschild (1983). Leidner (1991, 1993). S. J. Tracy (2000). S. J. Tracy and Tracy (1998). Van Maanen (1991).
48. Sutton (1991). Yanay and Sharar (1998).
49. Fulmer and Barry (2009).
50. Fineman (1995).
51. Hulsheger and Schewe (2011). Sutton and Rafaeli (1988). Waldron (1994). Zapf and Holz (2006).
52. P. Smith and Lorentzon (2005).
53. Steinberg and Figart (1999).
54. Rafaeli and Sutton (1989).
55. See, for example: Collins, Hari, and Rocco (2009). Eden (1984, 1990, 1993). Eden and Shami (1982). Inamori and Analoui (2010). D. Reynolds (2007). Rosenthal and Jacobson (1968).
56. White and Locke (2000). McNatt (2000). Divir, Eden, and Banjo (1995).
57. Oz and Eden (1994).
58. Rosenthal (1993).
59. Good and Brophy (1980).
60. White and Locke (2000).

CHAPTER 6

1. Isenhart and Spangle (2000), Chap. 2. Runde and Flanagan (2007).
2. De Dreu and Gelfand (2008).
3. Hocker and Wilmot (2014).
4. Amason (1996). J. Folger, Poole, and Stutman (1993). Scileppi (2005), Chap. 10.
5. See, for example: De Dreu and Weingart (2003). Jehn (1995). S. P. Robins and Judge (2011).
6. Rahim (2011).
7. Runde and Flanagan (2008).
8. Shapiro (2016).
9. Rahim (1983). K. W. Thomas and Kilmann (1977).
10. Rahim, Garrett, and Buntzman (1992).
11. Isenhart and Spangle (2000).
12. Rahim, Buntzman, and White (1999).
13. Shockley-Zalabak (2015).
14. Hocker and Wilmot (2014). Sillars (1986). For another list of collaborative tactics, see: Canary and Lakey (2013), Chap. 2.
15. Kador (2009). Krell (2013).
16. C. E. Johnson and Shelton (2014).
17. Dennis (2017). Kresge and Rauwald (2016).

18. Lazare (2004).
19. Enright, Freedman, and Rique (1998).
20. Spangle and Isenhart (2003). R. R. Sims (2002).
21. Lax and Sebenius (2004).
22. Ibid., p. 7.
23. Bok (1978). See also: Lewicki, Sanders, and Barry (2015), Chap. 5.
24. J. R. Cohen (2004).
25. Lax and Sebenius (2004).
26. Crampton and Dees (1993).
27. M. Wheeler (2004).
28. "Why Your Negotiating Behavior" (2008).
29. Fisher, Ury, and Patton (2011).
30. Ibid., p. 42.
31. Buss (1961).
32. Information on the frequency of workplace violence and aggression is taken from: Depre and Barling (2003). Glomb and Hui (2003). Neuman (2004). Schat, Frone, and Kelloway (2006).
33. "Commission: 'Going Postal'" (n.d.). "The Origin of the Term" (2011).
34. Kassing and Waldron (2014). Pearson and Porath (2004, 2005).
35. Einarsen, Hoel, Zapf, and Cooper (2011). Keashly and Jagatic (2011).
36. Waldron and Kassing (2011), Chap. 6.
37. Barling (1996). Glomb, Steel, and Arvey (2002). Salin (2013).
38. Barling (1996). Baron (2004). Douglas and Martinko (2001). R. Folger and Baron (1996). Hershcovis et al. (2007). Neuman and Baron (1997). O'Leary-Kelly, Griffin, and Glew (1996).
39. Lutgen-Sandvik (2006).
40. O'Reilly and Aquino (2011).
41. Tomlinson, Thompson Heames, and Bockanic (2014).
42. Hershcovis and Barling (2008).
43. Feder (2010). McDonald (2012).
44. K. C. Woods and Buchanan (2008).
45. U.S. Equal Employment Opportunity Commission (n.d.).
46. Arens Bates, Bowes-Sperry, and O'Leary-Kelly (2008). Levy and Paludi (2002).
47. Boehlert (2016). Reuters (2016). Sommerfeldt (2017). Steel and Schmidt (2017). Stelter (2016).
48. Ilies, Hauserman, Schwochau, and Stibal (2003).
49. Associated Press (2014). Fitzgerald (1993).
50. "Victim Speaks Out" (2017).
51. Fitzgerald (1993). Levy and Paludi (2002).
52. See, for example: Fitzgerald, Drasgow, Hulin, Gelfand, and Magley (1997). Offermann and Malamut (2002). O'Leary-Kelly, Paetzold, and Griffin (2000). Wiener and Gutek (1999). F. Wilson and Thompson (2001).
53. Bowes-Sperry and O'Leary-Kelly (2005). Bowes-Sperry and Powell (1996). O'Leary-Kelly (2001).

CHAPTER 7

1. Kellerman (2015), p. 272.
2. Yukl (2013), Chap. 1.
3. Hornstein (1996). Porath (2014).
4. Whicker (1996).
5. Sellers (2005).
6. Sternberg (2002).
7. Che (2015). "Gini in the Bottle" (2013). N. Kristof (2010). Shadi (2016). Sommeiller and Price (2014).
8. Matthews (2016). J. P. Wright, Cullen, and Blankenship (2002).
9. Wright, Cullen, and Blankenship (2002). Matthews (2016). Portions of this chapter are adapted from C. E. Johnson (2018).
10. Kellerman (2004).
11. Ibid., p. xvi.
12. Lipman-Blumen (2005).
13. Keltner, Langner, and Allison (2006).
14. Higgs (2009). Lubit (2002). McFarlin and Sweeney (2010). Padilla, Hogan, and Kaiser (2007).
15. McFarlin and Sweeney (2000).
16. Christie and Geis (1970).
17. Becker and O'Hair (2007). Paulus and Williams (2002).
18. Keltner, Langner, and Alison (2006). McFarlin and Sweeney (2010).
19. C. E. Johnson (2000).
20. Matthew 20:26 in *The Holy Bible: New International Version* (1973). Grand Rapids, MI: Zondervan.
21. Greenleaf (1977). Ruschman (2002).
22. Hale and Fields (2007). Mehta and Pillay (2011). Pekerti and Sendjaya (2010).
23. See Jaramillo, Grisaffe, Chonko, and Roberts (2009a, 2009b). D. M. Mayer, Bardes, and Piccolo (2008). McCuddy and Cavin (2008). Parris and Peachey (2013). Walumbwa, Hartnell, and Oke (2010).
24. Luthans and Avolio (2009).
25. Avolio and Gardner (2005). A. Chan, Hannah, and Gardner (2005). Kernis (2003). Walumbwa, Avolio, Gardner, Wernsing, and Peterson (2008).

26. Hannah, Lester, and Vogelgesang (2005). May, Chan, Hodges, and Avolio (2003).
27. Avolio and Gardner (2005), p. 321.
28. A. Chan et al. (2005).
29. Gardner, Avolio, and Walumbwa (2005). Gardner, Avolio, Luthans, May, and Walumbwa (2005). May et al. (2003).
30. Avolio, Gardner, Walumbwa, Luthans, and May (2004). Clapp-Smith, Vogelgesang, and Avey (2009). Gardner et al. (2005). Hannah, Avolio, and Walumbwa (2011). Harvey, Martinko, and Gardner (2006). Ilies, Morgeson, and Nahrgang (2005). Leroy, Palanski, and Simons (2012). Zhu, May, and Avolio (2004). Walumbwa, Luthans, Avery, and Oke (2011).
31. See, for example: Bruhn (2001), p. 82; Shockley-Zalabak, Ellis, and Winograd (2000).
32. Avolio and Luthans (2006).
33. Milgram (1974).
34. Chaleff (2003).
35. Chaleff (2015).
36. Watt and Piotrowski (2008).
37. Andersson and Bateman (1997). Bedian (2007). M. Brown and Cregan (2008). Cutler (2000). Dean, Brandes, and Dharwadkar (1998).
38. Hirschman (1970). Withey and Cooper (1989).
39. Kassing (2002, 2005, 2007, 2009, 2011).
40. Roloff and Paulson (2001).
41. Susskind and Field (1996), p. 223.
42. Carsten and Uhl-Bien (2013). Carsten, Uhl-Bien, West, Patera, and McGregor (2010). Uhl-Bien and Carsten (2007).
43. Hernandez and Sitkin (2012).
44. Lipman-Blumen (2005, 2008).
45. Thoroughgood, Padilla, Hunter, and Tate (2012). See also: Barbuto (2000). Padilla, Hogan, and Kaiser (2007).
46. Chaleff (2003).
47. Chaleff (2008).
48. R. A. Johnson (2003).
49. MacGregor and Stuebs (2014).
50. Slovin, D. (2006), p. 43.
51. "Whistleblower Protection History" (n.d.). Sipe, Metrejean, and Pearson (2014).
52. Alford (2001), p. 403.
53. Richardson and McGlynn (2011).
54. Miethe (1999), p. 209.
55. Alford (1999). Dasgupta and Kesharwani (2010).
56. Ibid.
57. Anderson, Seashore Louis, and Earle (1994).
58. Bok (1980).
59. Miceli, Near, and Dworkin (2008, 2009).

CHAPTER 8

1. Locke et al. (2001).
2. Rothwell (1998).
3. D. W. Johnson, Maruyama, Johnson, Nelson, and Skon (1981).
4. D. W. Johnson and Johnson (1974, 2006). Milton and Westphal (2005). Tjosvold (1984, 1986).
5. Benne and Sheats (1948).
6. D. W. Johnson (1974). D. W. Johnson and Johnson (2005). Rubin and Brown (1975).
7. Ding and Ding (2008).
8. C. E. Johnson and Hackman (2018).
9. Duck and Fielding (2003). Ernst and Yip (2009). Hogg, Van Knippenberg, and Rast (2012). Pittinsky (2010).
10. K. D. Williams, Harkins, and Karau (2003).
11. Amichai-Hamburger (2003). Schippers (2014). B. N. Smith, Kerr, Markus, and Stasson (2001).
12. Karau and Williams (1993, 2001).
13. Karau and Williams (2001). Sheppard (1993, 2001).
14. LaFasto and Larson (2001).
15. Gibb (1961).
16. Edmundson (1999), p. 354.
17. Roberto (2002).
18. For summaries of research on minority influence process, see: Crano and Seyranian (2009). Levine and Prislin (2012). Mass and Clark (1984). Moscovici, Mucchi-Faina, and Mass (1994). Moscovici, Mugny, and Van Avermaet (1985). Wood, Lundgren, Ouellette, Busceme, and Blackstone (1994).
19. Nemeth (1985). Nemeth and Chiles (1986).
20. Mugny and Perez (1991).
21. Crano and Seyranian (2009). De Dreu and Beersma (2001).
22. Janis (1971, 1982, 1989).
23. For additional examples of groupthink in action, see: Schafer and Crichlow (2010). `t Hart (1990).
24. Portions of this material were adapted from C. E. Johnson and Hackman (1995), Chap. 5.
25. Janis (1982), p. 40.
26. R. R. Sims (1992).
27. See, for example: Bernthal and Insko (1993). Chen, Lawson, Gordon, and McIntosh (1996). Esser (1998). Flippen (1999). Packer (2009). W. W. Park (2000). Postmes, Spears, and Cihangir (2001). Schafer and Crichlow (2010). Street (1997). `t Hart (1990).

28. Manz and Neck (1995). Moorhead, Neck, and West (1998).
29. Mintz and Wayne (2016a, 2016b).
30. Clarke (2004), p. 236.
31. Mintz, Mishal, and Mora (2003).
32. J. Harvey (1988, 2001). Kanter (2001).
33. J. Harvey (2001), p. 15.
34. See, for example: Bobocel and Meyer (1994). McNamara, Moon, and Bromiley (2002). J. Ross and Staw (1993). Staw (1981).
35. Drummond (1996, 2001). P. E. Jones and Roelofsma (2000). Whyte (1991).
36. Drummond (2001). Huan and Chang (2010). Keil, Depledge, and Rai (2007). Keil and Montealegre (2000). J. Ross and Staw (1993).
37. J. R. Barker (1993).
38. Bullis (1991). Tompkins and Cheney (1985). Tompkins, Montoya, and Candrian (2014).
39. J. R. Barker (1993, 1999).
40. J. R. Barker (1999), p. 177.
41. Opotow (1990b). Opotow and Weiss (2000).
42. Opotow (2005).
43. Chang (1997), p. 218.
44. Opotow (1990b).
45. Tileaga (2006).
46. G. B. Adams and Balfour (2015).
47. Opotow (1990a, 1995).

CHAPTER 9

1. Weaver, Trevino, and Cochran (1999a, 1999c).
2. See, for example: Paine (1996a, 2003). G. Pearson (1995). Schminke (1998).
3. Burns (2003), p. 24.
4. Trevino (1990). Trevino and Nelson (2004).
5. J. C. Collins and Porras (1996).
6. Paine (2003).
7. J. C. Collins and Porras (1996).
8. J. C. Collins and Porras (1994).
9. Adams, Tashchian, and Shore (2001).
10. Brasswell, Foster, and Poe (2009).
11. Ethics Resource Center (2013).
12. Boudreaux and Steiner (2005). Hoppen (2002).
13. Barth (2003).
14. B. Stevens (2007).
15. McCabe and Trevino (1993).
16. Adams et al. (2001). Valentine and Barnett (2003).
17. M. S. Schwartz (2001).
18. Brandl and Maguire (2002). Johannesen, Valde, and Whedbee (2008), Chap. 10. M. S. Schwartz (2002).
19. S. J. Harvey (2000).
20. Cialdini (2009).
21. Trevino, Weaver, Gibson, and Toffler (1999).
22. Zyglidopoulos and Fleming (2007).
23. Darley (1996).
24. Monks and Minow (2004).
25. Business Roundtable (2012).
26. MacAvoy and Millstein (2003). Rezaee (2009).
27. Ibid. Monks and Minnow (2004).
28. Trevino (1990).
29. Goodman and Morgenson (2008). Grind (2012).
30. D. V. Cohen (1993).
31. "Former Atlanta Schools" (2013).
32. Lumpkin (2005).
33. Weber and Wasieleski (2013).
34. "Ethics: Phoning" (2007).
35. B. Stevens (2007).
36. Hoffman and Rowe (2007), p. 556.
37. Hoffman, Neill, and Stovall (2007). Hoffman and Rowe (2007). Liopis, Gonzalez, and Gasco (2007). Weber (2008).
38. Pillmore (2003). Staczek (2008).
39. G. Smith (2012).
40. Trevino and Nelson (2004).
41. Ibid.
42. A. C. T. Smith and Stewart (2011). See also: Rossano (2012).
43. Beyer and Trice (1987). Trice and Beyer (1984).
44. Gittell (2003).
45. J. Martin (2002).
46. Tobias (1976), pp. 98–99.
47. McLean and Elkind (2003).
48. Paine (1996a). Tenbrunsel, Smith-Crowe, and Umphress (2003). Trevino and Nelson (2004). Unruh (2008).
49. Hofmann (2006), pp. 44–45.
50. Brewer (2008). A. B. Carroll and Buchholtz (2012). Whitehouse (2010).
51. Association of Certified Fraud Examiners (2016).
52. B. Victor and Cullun (1988, 1990).
53. See, for example: Brower and Shrader (2000). Cullen, Parboteeah, and Victor (2003). Fritzche (2000). K. D. Martin and Cullen (2006). Parboteeah, Martin, and Cullen (2011). D. K. Peterson (2002). R. L. Sims and Keon (1997). Trevino, Butterfield, and McCabe (1998). B. Victor, Cullen, and Boynton (1993). Wimbush, Shepard, and Markham (1997). Wu and Tsai (2012).
54. Andreoli and Lefkowitz (2008). Gellerman (1989). Longnecker (1985). Trevino, Hartman, and Brown (2000). Weaver, Trevino, and Cochran (1999b, 1999c).
55. Schein (1992).
56. Bunkley and Maynard (2010). Gillis and Fountain (2010).

57. Unruh (2008).
58. Albrecht and Bach (1997).
59. Elias (2006).
60. Staczek (2008).
61. Kraimer (1997).
62. Anand, Ashforth, and Joshi (2004).
63. Hartog and Frame (2004). Heames and Service (2003). Mintzberg (2004). Piper, Gentile, and Parks (1993). Rest (1994). Rice and Dreilinger (1990). Swanson and Fisher (2008). Sekerka (2009).

CHAPTER 10

1. DesJardins (2011).
2. Taylor, K. (2016).
3. Elegido (2016).
4. Taylor, K. (2016). Murphy, Laczniak, Bowie, and Klein (2005).
5. American Marketing Association (2007).
6. Elegido (2016).
7. Ibid., p. 72.
8. Laczniak & Murphy (2006).
9. Sher (2011).
10. Sheth and Sisodia (2006). Lucadamo (2010).
11. Wicks, Freeman, Werhane, and Martin (2010).
12. Boatright (2008), p. 5.
13. Boatright (1999, 2008, 2010).
14. Duska and Duska (2003).
15. Flanagan and Clarke (2007).
16. Duska and Duska (2003).
17. See, for example: Abdolmohammadi, Read, and Scarbrough (2003). Ponemon (1990, 1992). Trevino and Weaver (2003).
18. Kolb (2010). Ryan, Buchholtz, and Kolb (2010).
19. McPhail (2001).
20. Flanagan and Clarke (2007), p. 488.

21. Gellis, Giladi, and Friedman (2002).
22. Dolfsma (2006).
23. Waddock (2005), p. 147.
24. Shaub and Fisher (2008).
25. Sternberg (2002).
26. Hurtt (2010). Nelson (2009). Shaub and Lawrence (1996).
27. Beets (2006).
28. CFA Institute (2010).
29. The provisions of the AICPA code and material on code provisions come from Duska and Duska (2003).
30. Flanagan and Clarke (2007).
31. Dessler (2008), p. 2.
32. Scarpello (2008).
33. E. D. Scott (2005). W. H. Shaw (2011).
34. Walsh (2007), p. 103.
35. Hiltzik (2016b).
36. McCall (2003). Radin and Werhane (2003).
37. Mellahi & Wood (2003).
38. Edmonds (2015).
39. Radin and Werhane (2003). See also: Ciulla (2010). Pfeffer (1998).
40. Bowie (2005).
41. Radin and Werhane (2003).
42. Fortin (2008).
43. Cropanzano, Bowen, and Gilliland (2007).
44. Cropanzano and Stein (2009).
45. Y. Cohen-Charash and Spector (2001). Trevino and Weaver (2001). Viswesvaran and Ones (2002). Whitman, Caleo, Caprent, Horner, & Bernerth (2012).
46. Cropanzano et al. (2007).
47. Society of Human Resource Management (2007).
48. Margolis, Grant, and Molinsky (2007).
49. Lavelle, Folger, & Manegold (2016). J. S. Shaw, Wild, & Colquitt (2003).

CHAPTER 11

1. A. B. Carroll and Buchholtz (2012). Deloitte (2017). Fullerton (2017). "Global Consumers Are Willing" (2014). USSIF Foundation (2014).
2. Crane, Matten, and Moon (2008).
3. Waddock (2008), p. 63.
4. Phillips (2003).
5. See, for example: Agle et al. (2008). Freeman (1984, 1994, 1995). Laplume, Sonpar, and Litz (2008). R. R. Sims (2003).
6. Frederick (1992), p. 5.
7. S. Cooper (2004). Donaldson and Preston (1995). Gibson (2000). Goodpaster (1991).
8. Freeman (1994). Phillips (2003).
9. Buchholz and Rosenthal (2005).
10. Argandona (1998).
11. A. B. Carroll and Buchholtz (2012).
12. Freeman, Harrison, and Wicks (2007).
13. A. B. Carroll and Buchholtz (2009). "Coca-Cola and the Balance Calories Initiative" (2017).
14. Coombs and Holladay (2013). Doorley and Garcia (2007). Heath (2009).
15. Doorley and Garcia (2007).
16. Hsu and Lopez (2012).
17. Friedman (1970).
18. A. B. Carroll and Buchholz (2012). Ihlen, Bartlett, and May (2011).
19. Byus, Deis, and Ouryang (2010). Foote, Gaffney, and Evans (2010).
20. Aquinas and Glavas (2013).
21. A. B. Carroll (1979).
22. Hatcher (2002).

23. Jamili (2008).
24. J. Davis (2016a). Dodd (2016). Dodd and Supa (2014). Price (2017).
25. J. Davis (2016a, 2016b). Korschun (2016). McGregor and Dwoskin (2017).
26. Soergel (2016).
27. Chatterji and Toffel (2016, 2017).
28. "The Dawn of CEO Activism" (n.d.).
29. Dodd (2016).
30. Soergel (2016).
31. D. Wheeler, Colbert, and Freeman (2003).
32. Savitz (2013). Robertson (2014). United Nations Department of Economic and Social Affairs (2015). Voelcker (2014).
33. S. L. Hart (1997).
34. Saracco (2016).
35. Savitz (2013).
36. Senge, Smith, Kruschwitz, Lauer, and Schley (2008).
37. Mirvis and Googins (2006). Mirvis and Manga (2010).
38. Mirvis and Googins (2006).
39. Googins, Mirvis, and Rochlin (2007). Mirvis and Manga (2010).
40. J. H. Davis, Schoorman, and Donaldson (1997). Yankelovich (2006).
41. Barnett and Schubert (2002). Caldwell, Bishchoff, and Karri (2002). Caldwell and Karri (2005).
42. M. Hernandez (2008, 2012).
43. Waddock (2002), p. 229.
44. R. Robins (2006). Savitz (2006).
45. Social Accountability International (2014).
46. Global Reporting Initiative (2014).
47. King and Bartels (2015).
48. C. A. Adams and Evans (2004). H. H. Johnson (2001).
49. J. Smith (2013). Strauss (2016).
50. Charity Navigator (www.charitynavigator.org).

CHAPTER 12

1. "Harvesting Poverty" (2003). Lacey (2003). Muzaffar (2002). Reuters (2017). P. Singer (2002). Taylor (2014).
2. Newton (2005).
3. Myers (2016).
4. "10 Biggest Corporations" (2016).
5. Examples of ethical diversity are taken from: S. J. Carroll and Gannon (1997). Mitchell (2003).
6. Gudykunst and Kim (1997).
7. Novak (2003).
8. Appaiah (2006). Fine and Boon (2007).
9. Fine and Boon (2007). Van Hooft (2009).
10. Maak (2009). Maak and Pless (2009).
11. Delanty (2012).
12. W. Smith (2007).
13. Hofstede (1984, 1991).
14. Hofstede (2001).
15. A. W. H. Chan and Cheung (2012). Clements, Neill, and Stovall (2009). Davis and Ruhe (2003). Franke and Nadler (2007). Husted (1999). Vitell, Nwachukwu, and Barnes (1993). Williams and Zinkin (2008).
16. Hall (1976). Gudykunst and Kim (1997). Rogers and Steinfatt (1999).
17. Brody, Coulter, and Mihalek (1998).
18. House, Hanges, Javidan, Dorfman, and Gupta (2004). Javidan and House (2001).
19. House et al. (2004), p. 239.
20. Quigley, Sully de Luque, and House (2005).
21. Budde-Sung (2013).
22. Hampden-Turner and Trompenaars (2000). Kleiner (2001). Trompenaars (1994). Trompenaars and Wooliams (2011).
23. Hampden-Turner and Trompenaars (2000).
24. Haidt (2012). Haidt and Bjorklund (2008). Haidt and Graham (2007).
25. J. Graham, Haidt, and Nosek (2009). T. Jacobs (2009).
26. Hauser (2006). Hauser, Young, and Cushman (2008).
27. Donnelly (1989). Humphrey (1989).
28. Mares (2004), pp. 2–7.
29. Sethi and Schepers (2011). O. F. Williams (2014).
30. Paine, Deshpande, Margolis, and Bettcher (2005).
31. Caux Round Table (2000, 2004).
32. Caux Round Table (2000, 2010).
33. Caux Round Table (2006).
34. Donaldson and Dunfee (1994, 1999). Dunfee and Donaldson (1999).
35. Hamilton and Knouse (2001). Hamilton, Knouse, and Hill (2009).

REFERENCES

Abdolmohammadi, M. J., Read, W. J., & Scarbrough, D. P. (2003). Does selection-socialization help to explain accountants' weak ethical reasoning? *Business Ethics, 42,* 71–81.

Accreditation group gives "warning" to Baylor University. (2016, December 11). *Associated Press.*

Ackerill, J. L. (1981). *Aristotle the philosopher.* Oxford, UK: Oxford University Press.

Adams, C. A., & Evans, R. (2004). Accountability, completeness, credibility and the audit expectations gap. *Journal of Corporate Citizenship, 14,* 97–115.

Adams, G. B., & Balfour, D. L. (2015). *Unmasking administrative evil* (4th ed.). Armonk, NY: M. E. Sharpe.

Adams, J. S., Tashchian, A., & Shore, T. H. (2001). Codes of ethics as signals for ethical behavior. *Journal of Business Ethics, 29,* 199–211.

Adams, W. L. (2010, May 10). Postcard: Halden. A look inside the world's most humane prison. *Time,* p. 14.

Agle, B. R., Donaldson, T., Freeman, R. E., Jensen, M. C., Mitchell, R. K., & Wood, D. J. (2008). Dialogue: Toward superior stakeholder theory. *Business Ethics Quarterly, 18,* 153–190.

Albom, M. (1997). *Tuesdays with Morrie: An old man, a young man, and life's greatest lesson.* New York, NY: Doubleday.

Albrecht, T. L., & Bach, B. W. (1997). *Communication in complex organizations: A relational approach.* Fort Worth, TX: Harcourt Brace.

Alford, C. F. (1999). Whistleblowers: How much we can learn from them depends on how much we can give up. *American Behavioral Scientist, 43,* 264–277.

Alford, C. F. (2001). Whistleblowers and the narrative of ethics. *Journal of Social Philosophy, 32,* 402–418.

Allison, C. (2016, October 16). In defense of Heather Bresch. (2016, October 8). *Pittsburgh Post-Gazette.*

Alnuaimi, O. A., Robert, L. P., & Maruping, L. M. (2010). Team size, dispersion, and social loafing in technology-supported teams: A perspective on the theory of moral disengagement. *Journal of Management Information Systems, 27*(10), 203–230.

Amason, A. C. (1996). Distinguishing the effects of functional and dysfunctional conflict on strategic decision-making: Resolving a paradox for top management teams. *Academy of Management Journal, 39*(1), 123–148.

American Management Association. (2003, February 10). Workplace dating survey: 2003.

American Marketing Association (2007). Statement of ethics.

Amichai-Hamburger, Y. (2003). Understanding social loafing. In A. Sagie, S. Stashevsky, & M. Koslowsky (Eds.), *Misbehaviour and dysfunctional attitudes in organizations* (pp. 79–102). New York, NY: Palgrave Macmillan.

Anand, V., Ashforth, B. E., & Joshi, M. (2004). Business as usual: The acceptance and perpetuation of corruption in organizations. *Academy of Management Executive, 18,* 39–53.

Anderson, M. S., Seashore Louis, K., & Earle, J. (1994, May-June). Disciplinary and departmental effects on observations of faculty and graduate student misconduct. *Journal of Higher Education, 65,* 331–350.

Andersson, L. M., & Bateman, T. S. (1997). Cynicism in the workplace: Some causes and effects. *Journal of Organizational Behavior, 18,* 449–469.

Andreoli, N., & Lefkowitz, J. (2008). Individual and organizational antecedents of misconduct in organizations. *Journal of Business Ethics, 85,* 309–332.

Antonio Ynoa, JetBlue passenger, arrested at Kennedy airport for assaulting flight attendant. (November 27, 2011). *Huffington Post.*

Appaiah, K. A. (2006). *Cosmopolitanism: Ethics in a world of strangers.* New York, NY: Norton.

Aquinas, H., & Glavas, A. (2013). What we know and don't know about corporate social responsibility: A review and research agenda. *Journal of Management, 38*, 932–968.

Aquino, K. (1998). The effects of ethical climate and the availability of alternatives on the use of deception during negotiation. *International Journal of Conflict Management, 9*, 195–217.

Aquino, K., & Freeman, D. (2009). Moral identity in business situations: A social-cognitive framework for understanding moral functioning. In D. Narvaez & D. S. Lapsley (Eds.), *Personality, identity and character: Explorations in moral psychology* (pp. 375–395). Cambridge, UK: Cambridge University Press.

Archibold, R. C. (2010, January 14). Sweat lodge deaths not criminal, Guru's lawyer says. *New York Times*, p. A22.

Archibold, R. C., & Berger, J. (2010, February 5). Sweat lodge leader is indicted in deaths. *New York Times*.

Are biotech foods safe to eat? (2014, February 6). WebMD.

Arens Bates, C., Bowes-Sperry, L., & O'Leary-Kelly, A. M. (2008). Sexual harassment in the workplace: A look back and a look ahead. In E. K. Kelloway, J. Barling, & J. J. Hurrell (Eds.), *Handbook of workplace violence* (pp. 381–415). Thousand Oaks, CA: SAGE.

Arewa, O. (n. d.). Cultural appropriation: When "borrowing" becomes exploitation. *HuffPost*.

Argandona, A. (1998). The stakeholder theory and the common good. *Journal of Business Ethics, 17*, 1093–1102.

Aristotle. (1962). *Nicomachean ethics* (Martin Ostwald, Trans.).
Indianapolis, IN: Bobbs Merrill. (Original work published 350 B.C.E.)

Aristotle. (1984). *The complete works of Aristotle* (Vol. 2, M. Barnes, Ed.). Princeton, NJ: Princeton University Press.

Arnett, R. C. (1986). *Communication and community: Implications of Martin Buber's dialogue*. Carbondale: Southern Illinois University Press.

Arnett, R. C., & Arneson, P. (1999). *Dialogic civility in a cynical age: Community, hope, and interpersonal relationships*. Albany: State University of New York Press.

Art Briles denies covering up sexual assaults in Baylor scandal. (2017, March 2). *USA Today Sports*.

Ashmos, D. P., & Duchon, D. (2000). Spirituality at work: A conceptualization and measure. *Journal of Management Inquiry, 9*, 134–145.

Associated Press (2014, September 14). As freshmen enter "red zone," colleges re-think sexual assault policies. *USA Today*.

Associated Press. (2017a, March 3). Baylor's Kim Mulkey apologizes for remarks about assault scandal. *Chicago Tribune*.

Associated Press. (2017b, May 19). New Orleans removes its final Confederate-era statue. *The Guardian*.

Association of Certified Fraud Examiners. (2016). 2016 report to the nations.

Aubrey, A. (2014, April 25). Fast-food CEOs earn supersize salaries; workers earn small potatoes. *NPR*.

Avins, J. (2015, October 20). The dos and don'ts of cultural appropriation. *The Atlantic*.
Avolio, B. J., & Gardner, W. L. (2005). Authentic leadership development: Getting to the root of positive forms of leadership. *Leadership Quarterly, 16*, 315–340.

Avolio, B. J., Gardner, W. L., Walumbwa, F. O., Luthans, F., & May, D. R. (2004). Unlocking the mask: A look at the process by which authentic leaders impact follower attitudes and behaviors. *Leadership Quarterly, 15*, 801–823.

Avolio, B. J., & Luthans, F. (2006). *The high impact leader: Moments matter in accelerating authentic leadership development*. New York, NY: McGraw-Hill.

Axon, R. (2016, October 28). Baylor regents reveal shocking information surrounding sexual assault scandal. *USA Today Sports*.

Badaracco, J. L. (2016). *Managing in the gray: 5 timeless questions for resolving your toughest problems at work*. Boston, MA: Harvard Business School Press.

Baird, C. A. (2003). *Everyday ethics: Making hard choices in a complex world*. Denver, CO: CB Resources.

Baird, J. (2009, October 19). We are all getting lucky: But we are not all the boss. *Newsweek*, p. 26.

Banaji, M. R., Bazerman, M. H., & Chugh, D. (2003, December). How (un)ethical are you? *Harvard Business Review*, pp. 56–64.

Bandura, A. (1977). Self-efficacy: Toward a unifying theory of behavioral change. *Psychological Review, 84*, 191–215.

Bandura, A. (1999). Moral disengagement in the perpetration of inhumanities. *Personality and Social Psychology Review, 3*, 193–209.

Barbuto, J. E. (2000). Influence triggers: A framework for understanding follower compliance. *Leadership Quarterly, 11*, 365–387.

Barker, J. R. (1993). Tightening the iron cage: Concertive control in self-managing teams. *Administrative Science Quarterly, 38*, 408–437.

Barker, J. R. (1999). *The discipline of teamwork: Participation and concertive control*. Thousand Oaks, CA: SAGE.

Barker, L., & Watson, K. (2000). *Listen up: How to improve relationships, reduce stress, and be more productive by using the power of listening*. New York, NY: St. Martin's Press.

Barling, J. (1996). The prediction, experience, and consequences of workplace violence. In G. R. VandenBos & E. Q. Bulato (Eds.), *Violence on the job: Identifying risks and developing solutions* (pp. 29–49). Washington, DC: American Psychological Association.

Barnes, J. (1982). *Aristotle*. Oxford, UK: Oxford University Press.

Barnes, J. (1995). *The Cambridge companion to Aristotle*. Cambridge, UK: Cambridge University Press.

Barnett, T., & Schubert, E. (2002). Perceptions of the ethical work climate and covenantal relationships. *Journal of Business Ethics, 36*, 279–290.

Baron, R. A. (2004). Workplace aggression and violence: Insights from basic research. In R. W. Griffin & A. M. O'Leary-Kelly (Eds.), *The dark side of organizational behavior* (pp. 23–61). San Francisco, CA: Jossey-Bass.

Barry, V. (1978). *Personal and social ethics: Moral problems with integrated theory*. Belmont, CA: Wadsworth.

Barth, S. R. (2003). *Corporate ethics: The business code of conduct for ethical employees*. Boston, MA: Aspatore Books.

Bass, B. M. (1990). *Bass and Stogdill's handbook of leadership* (3rd ed.). New York, NY: Free Press.

Batson, C. D., Collins, E., & Powell, A. A. (2006). Doing business after the fall: The virtue of moral hypocrisy. *Journal of Business Ethics, 66*, 321–335.

Batson, C. D., & Thompson, E. R. (2001). Why don't people act morally: Motivational considerations. *Current Directions in Psychological Science, 10*, 54–57.

Batson, C. D., Thompson, E. R., & Chen, H. (2002). Moral hypocrisy: Addressing some alternatives. *Journal of Personality and Social Psychology, 83*, 330–339.

Batson, C. D., Thompson, E. R., Seuferling, G., Whitney, H., & Strongman, J. A. (1999). Moral hypocrisy: Appearing moral to oneself without being so. *Journal of Personality and Social Psychology, 77*(3), 525–537.

Batson, C. D., Van Lange, P. A. M., Ahmad, N., & Lishner, D. A. (2003). Altruism and helping behavior. In M. A. Hogg & J. Cooper (Eds.), *The Sage handbook of social psychology* (pp. 279–295). London, UK: SAGE.

Baylor fans line up for t-shirts supporting Art Briles. (2016, November 5). *USA Today Sports*.

Bazerman, M. H., Chugh, D., & Banaji, M. R. (2005, October). When good people (seem to) negotiate in bad faith. *Negotiation, 8*, 3–5.

Beam, C. (2011, January 28). Block like an Egyptian. *Slate*.

Becker, J. A. H., & O'Hair, H. D. (2007). Machiavellians' motives in organizational citizenship behavior. *Journal of Applied Communication Research, 35*, 246–267.

Bedian, A. G. (2007). "Even if the tower is 'ivory,' it isn't white": Understanding the consequences of faculty cynicism. *Academy of Management Learning and Education, 6*, 9–32.

Beets, S. D. (2006). The vanishing AICPA code: Past, present, and future significance. In J. E. Ketz (Ed.), *Accounting ethics: Critical perspectives on business and management* (Vol. 1, pp. 270–306). London, UK: Routledge.

Benne, K. D., & Sheats, P. (1948). Functional roles of group members. *Journal of Social Issues, 4*, 41–49.

Bennett, R. J. (1998). Perceived powerlessness as a cause of employee deviance. In R. W. Griffin, A. O'Leary-Kelly, & J. M. Collins (Eds.), *Dysfunctional behavior in organizations: Violent and deviant behavior* (pp. 221–239). Stamford, CT: JAI.

Bennis, W. G., & Thomas, R. J. (2002). *Geeks and geezers: How era, values and defining moments shape leaders*. Boston, MA: Harvard Business School Press.

Bentham, J. (1948). *An introduction to the principles of morals and legislation*. New York, NY: Hafner.

Berlinger, J., & Smith-Spark, L. (2017, June 29). Top adviser to Pope charged with sexual assault offenses. *CNN.com*.

Bernstein, E., Bunch, J., Canner, N., & Lee, M. (2016, July/August).

Beyond the holocracy hype. *Harvard Business Review*.

Bernthal, P. R., & Insko, C. A. (1993). Cohesiveness without groupthink: The interactive effects of social and task cohesion. *Group and Organizational Management, 18*, 66–87.

Beyer, J. M., & Trice, H. M. (1987). How an organization's rites reveal its culture. *Organizational Dynamics, 15*, 5–24.

Biemann, A. D. (Ed.). (2002). *The Martin Buber reader: Essential writings*. New York, NY: Palgrave Macmillan.

Bilton, N. (2016, October). How Elizabeth Holmes's house of cards came tumbling down. *Vanity Fair*.

Bird, F. B. (1996). *The muted conscience: Moral silence and the practice of ethics in business*. Westport, CT: Quorum Books.

Bishop, G. (2012, February 27). No longer defined by futility and tragedy. *New York Times*, p. D1.

Blasi, A. (1984). Moral identity: Its role in moral functioning. In W. M. Kurtnes & J. L. Gerwirtz (Eds.), *Morality, moral behavior, and moral development* (pp. 128–139). New York, NY: Wiley.

Blasi, A. (2005). Moral character: A psychological approach. In D. K. Lapsley & F. C. Power (Eds.), *Character psychology and character education* (pp. 67–100). Notre Dame, IN: University of Notre Dame Press.

Blaskovich, J. L. (2008). Exploring the effect of distance: An experimental investigation of virtual collaboration, social loafing, and group decisions. *Journal of Information Systems, 22*(1), 27–46.

Blocker, H. G., & Smith, E. H. (Eds.). (1980). *John Rawls' theory of justice: An introduction*. Athens: Ohio University Press.

Boatright, J. R. (1999). Finance ethics. In R. E. Frederick (Ed.), *A companion to business ethics* (pp. 153–163). Malden, MA: Blackwell.

Boatright, J. R. (2008). *Ethics in finance* (2nd ed.). Malden, MA: Blackwell.

Boatright, J. R. (2010). Ethics in finance. In J. R. Boatright (Ed.), *Finance ethics: Critical issues in theory and practice* (pp. 3–19). Hoboken, NJ: Wiley.

Bobocel, D. R., & Meyer, J. P. (1994). Escalating commitment to a failing course of action: Separating the roles of choice and justification. *Journal of Applied Psychology, 79*, 360–363.

Boehlert, E. (2016, December 23). The year Fox News flushed Roger Ailes and his sexual harassment scandal down the memory hole. *Media Matters*.

Boje (2008). Critical theory approaches to spirituality in business. In J. Biberman & L. Tischler (Eds.), *Spirituality in business: Theory, practice, and future directions* (pp. 160–187). New York, NY: Palgrave Macmillan.

Bok, S. (1978). *Lying: Moral choice in public and private life*. New York, NY: Pantheon Books.

Bok, S. (1980). Whistleblowing and professional responsibilities. In D. Callahan & S. Bok (Eds.), *Ethics teaching in higher education* (pp. 277–295). New York, NY: Plenum Press.

Bok, S. (1989). *Secrets: On the ethics of concealment and revelation*. New York, NY: Random House.

Boksem, M. A. S., & de Cremer, D. (2009). The neural basis of morality. In D. de Cremer (Ed.), *Psychological perspectives on ethical behavior and decision-making* (pp. 153–166). Charlotte, NC: Information Age.

Bomey, N. (2016, September 22). 5 things we learned from EpiPen price hike hearing. *USA Today*.

Boudreaux, G., & Steiner, T. (2005, Spring). Developing a code of ethics. *Management Quarterly*, pp. 2–19.

Bowes-Sperry, L., & O'Leary-Kelly, A. M. (2005). To act or not to act: The dilemma faced by sexual harassment observers. *Academy of Management Review, 30*, 288–306.

Bowes-Sperry, L., & Powell, G. N. (1996). Sexual harassment as a moral issue: An ethical decision-making perspective. In M. S. Stockdale (Ed.), *Sexual harassment in the workplace: Perspectives, frontiers, and response strategies* (Vol. 5, pp. 105–124). Thousand Oaks, CA: SAGE.

Bowie, N. E. (2005). Kantian ethical thought. In J. W. Budd & J. G. Scoville (Eds.), *The ethics of human resources and industrial relations* (pp. 61–87). Champaign, IL: Labor Relations and Employment Association.

Boyd, C. (2010). The debate over the prohibition of romance in the workplace. *Journal of Business Ethics, 97*, 325–338.

Bradshaw, J. (2016, May 23). Google ruling puts Europe's "right to be forgotten" law back in focus. *Globe and Mail*.

Bragues, G. (2006). Seek the good life, not money: The Aristotelian approach to business ethics. *Journal of Business Ethics, 67*, 341–357.

Brandenberger, J. W. (2005). College, character, and social responsibility: Moral learning through experience. In D. K. Lapsley & F. C. Power (Eds.), *Character psychology and character education* (pp. 305–334). Notre Dame, IN: University of Notre Dame Press.

Brandl, P., & Maguire, M. (2002, Winter). Codes of ethics: A primer on their purpose, development and use. *Journal for Quality and Participation, 25,* 9–12.

Brasswell, M. K., Foster, C. M., & Poe, S. L. (2009, Summer). A new generation of corporate codes of ethics. *Southern Business Review,* pp. 1–10.

Bratton, V. K., & Kacmar, K. M. (2004). Extreme careerism: The dark side of impression management. In W. Griffin & K. O'Reilly (Eds.), *The dark side of organizational behavior* (pp. 291–308). San Francisco, CA: Jossey-Bass.

Breaking down the Baylor cases. (n.d.). *Houston Chronicle.*

Brennfleck, K., & Brennfleck, K. M. (2005). *Live your calling: A practical guide to finding and fulfilling your mission in life.* San Francisco, CA: Jossey-Bass.

Brewer, L. (2008, December). Fraud's house of cards. *Financial Executive,* pp. 39–43.

Brockner, J., Siegel, P. A., Daly, J. P., Tyler, T., & Martin, C. (1997). When trust matters: The moderating effect of outcome favorability. *Administrative Science Quarterly, 42,* 558–583.

Brody, R. G., Coulter, J. M., & Mihalek, P. H. (1998, June). Whistle-blowing: A cross-cultural comparison of ethical perceptions of U.S. and Japanese accounting students. *American Business Review,* pp. 14–21.

Brooks, C. (2012, May 15). Yahoo CEO not alone: 7 execs busted for resume lies. *Business News Daily.*

Brower, H. H., & Shrader, C. B. (2000). Moral reasoning and ethical climate: Not-for-profit vs. for-profit boards of directors. *Journal of Business Ethics, 26,* 147–167.

Brown, C. T., & Keller, P. W. (1994). Ethics. In R. Anderson, K. N. Cissna, & R. C. Arnett (Eds.), *The reach of dialogue: Confirmation, voice, and community* (pp. 284–290). Cresskill, NJ: Hampton Press.

Brown, D. (1995). A values-based approach to facilitating career transitions. *Career Development Quarterly, 44,* 4–10.

Brown, K. (2016, June 16). Here's what's going on with all of those Uber lawsuits. *Fusion.net.*

Brown, K. W. (2007). Mindfulness: Theoretical foundations and evidence for its salutary effects. *Psychological Inquiry, 18*(4), 211–237.

Brown, K. W., & Ryan, R. M. (2003). The benefits of being present: Mindfulness and its role in psychological well-being. *Journal of Personality and Social Psychology, 84*(4), 822–848.

Brown, M., & Cregan, C. (2008). Organizational change cynicism: The role of employee involvement. *Human Resource Management, 47,* 667–686.

Brownell, J. (2002). *Listening: Attitudes, principles, and skills* (2nd ed.). Boston, MA: Allyn & Bacon.

Brownell, J. (2003, November 22). *The skills of listening-centered communication.* Paper presented at the National Communication Association convention, Miami, FL.

Bruhn, J. G. (2001). *Trust and the health of organizations.* New York, NY: Kluwer/Plenum.

Bryant, S. M., Albring, S. M., & Murthy, U. (2009). The effects of reward structure, media richness and gender on virtual teams. *International Journal of Accounting Information Systems, 10,* 190–213.

Buber, M. (1965). *The knowledge of man: Selected essays* (M. Friedman, Ed.). New York, NY: Harper & Row, pp. 67–68.

Buber, M. (1970). *I and thou* (R. G. Smith, Trans.). New York, NY: Scribner's.

Buchanen, L. (2013, April 2013). One company's audacious org. chart: 400 leaders, 0 bosses. *Inc.com.*

Buchholz, R. A., & Rosenthal, S. B. (2005). Toward a conceptual framework for stakeholder theory. *Journal of Business Ethics, 58,* 137–148.

Bucker, M., & Frisby, B. N. (2015). Feeling valued matters: An examination of instructor confirmation and instructional dissent. *Communication Studies, 66,* 398–413.

Budde-Sung, A. (2013). The invisible meets the intangible: Culture's impact on intellectual property protection. *Journal of Business Ethics, 117,* 345–359.

Buechner, F. (1973). *Wishful thinking: A theological ABC.* New York, NY: Harper & Row.

Bullis, C. (1991). Communication practices as unobtrusive control: An observational study. *Communication Studies, 42*(3), 254–271.

Bunderson, J. S., & Thompson, J. A. (2009). The call of the wild: Zookeepers, callings, and the dual edges of deeply meaningful work. *Administrative Science Quarterly, 54,* 32–57.

Bunkley, N., & Maynard, M. (2010, April 19). Toyota is expected to pay $16.4 million fine sought by U.S. over recall of sticking pedals. *New York Times*, p. B3.

Burgoon, J. K., Berger, C. R., & Waldron, V. R. (2000). Mindfulness and interpersonal communication. *Journal of Social Issues,* 56(1), 105–127.

Burke, D. (2015, April 16). Journalist gets unexpected phone call from Pope. *CNN.*

Burke, R., & Bragg, S. P. (2014, Winter). Sustainability in the boardroom: Reconsidering fiduciary duty under Revlon in the wake of public benefit corporation legislation. *Virginia Law & Business Review*, p. 8.

Burke, R. J., & Koyuncu, M. (2010). Developing virtues and virtuous behavior at workplace. *The IUP Journal of Soft Skills, 4*(3), 39–48.

Burns, J. M. (2003). *Transforming leadership: A new pursuit of happiness.* New York, NY: Atlantic Monthly Press.

Business Roundtable. (2012, March 27). *2012 principles of corporate governance.*

Buss, A. H. (1961). *The psychology of aggression.* New York, NY: Wiley.

Butterfield, K. D., Trevino, L. K., & Weaver, G. R. (2000). Moral awareness in business organizations: Influences of issue-related and social context factors. *Human Relations, 53,* 981–1018.

Byus, K., Deis, D., & Ouryang, B. (2010). Doing well by doing good: Corporate social responsibility and profitability. *SAM Advanced Management Journal,* 75(1), 44–55.

Caldwell, C., Bishchoff, S. J., & Karri, R. (2002). The four umpires: A paradigm for ethical leadership. *Journal of Business Ethics, 36,* 153–163.

Caldwell, C., & Karri, R. (2005). Organizational governance and ethical systems: A covenantal approach to building trust. *Journal of Business Ethics, 58,* 249–259.

Callahan, D. (2004). *The cheating culture.* Orlando, FL: Harcourt.

Canary, D. J., & Lakey, S. (2013). *Strategic conflict.* New York: Routledge, Chap. 2.

Carlson, D. S., Kacmar, K. M., & Wadsworth, L. L. (2009). The impact of moral intensity dimensions on ethical decision-making: Assessing the relevance of orientation. *Journal of Managerial Issues, 21,* 534–551.

Carney, J. (2005, May 2). Temper, temper, temper. *Time,* pp. 55–57.

Carroll, A. B. (1979). A three-dimensional conceptual model of corporate performance. *Academy of Management Review, 4,* 497–508.

Carroll, A. B., & Buchholtz, A. K. (2009). *Business and society: Ethics and stakeholder management* (7th ed.). Mason, OH: South-Western Cengage Learning.

Carroll, A. B., & Buchholtz, A. K. (2012). *Business & society: Ethics, sustainability, and stakeholder management* (8th ed.). Mason, OH: South-Western Cengage Learning.

Carroll, S. J., & Gannon, M. J. (1997). *Ethical dimensions of international management.* Thousand Oaks, CA: SAGE.

Carson, B. (2017a, March 4). Uber's unraveling: The stunning 2 week string of blows that has upended the world's most valuable startup. *Business Insider.*

Carson, B. (2017b, June 13). Here's the full 13-page report that's rocking Uber's culture to the core. *Business Insider.*

Carson, T. (2001). Deception and withholding information in sales. *Business Ethics Quarterly, 11,* 275–306.

Carsten, M. K., & Uhl-Bien, M. (2010). Follower beliefs in the co-production of leadership: Examining upward communication and the moderating role of context. *Journal of Psychology/Zeitschrift fur Psychologie, 220,* 210–220.

Carsten, M. K., & Uhl-Bien, M. (2013). Ethical followership: An examination of followership beliefs and crimes of obedience. *Journal of Leadership and Organizational Studies, 20,* 49–61.

Carsten, M. K., Uhl-Bien, M. West, B. J., Patera, J. L., & McGregor, R. (2010). Exploring social constructions of followership: A qualitative study. *Leadership Quarterly, 21,* 543–562.

Carter, C. J. (2014, May 30). Report: 1,700 vets not on Phoenix wait list, at risk of being "lost or forgotten." *CNN.*

Caruso, D. R., Bien, B., & Kornacki, S. A. (2006). Emotional intelligence in the workplace. In *Emotional intelligence in everyday life*

(2nd ed., pp. 187–205). New York, NY: Psychology Press.

Caruso, D. R., & Salovey, P. (2004). *The emotionally intelligent manager: How to develop and use the four key emotional skills of leadership*. San Francisco, CA: Jossey-Bass.

Carver, C. S., & Scheier, M. F. (2005). Optimism. In C. R. Snyder & S. J. Lopez (Eds.), *Handbook of positive psychology* (pp. 231–243). Oxford, UK: Oxford University Press.

Casebeer, W. D. (2003). Moral cognition and its neural constituents. *Neuroscience, 4*, 841–846.

Casperson, D. (2015). *Changing the conversation: The 17 principles of conflict resolution*. New York, NY: Penguin Books.

Caux Round Table. (2000). Appendix 26: The Caux Principles. In O. F. Williams, *Global codes of conduct: An idea whose time has come* (pp. 384–388). Notre Dame, IN: Notre Dame University Press.

Caux Round Table. (2004). The Caux Round Table principles for business, 1994. In R. Mares (Ed.), *Business and human rights: A compilation of documents* (pp. 288–292). Leiden, Netherlands: Brill.

Caux Round Table. (2006). Principles for non-governmental organizations.

Caux Round Table. (2010). Principles for business.

CFA Institute. (2010, June). Codes, standards and position papers. Vol. 2010, No. 14.

Chaleff, I. (2003). *The courageous follower: Standing up to and for our leaders* (2nd ed.). San Francisco, CA: Berrett-Koehler.

Chaleff, I. (2008). Creating new ways of following. In R. E. Riggio, I. Chaleff, & J. Lipman-Blumen (Eds.), *The art of followership: How great followers create great leaders and organizations* (pp. 67–92). San Francisco, CA: Jossey-Bass.

Chaleff, I. (2015). *Intelligent disobedience: Doing right when what you're told to do is wrong*. Oakland, CA: Berrett-Koehler.

Champoux, J. E. (2003). *Organizational behavior: Essential tenets* (2nd ed.). Mason, OH: South-Western Cengage Learning.

Chan, A., Hannah, S. T., & Gardner, W. L. (2005). Veritable authentic leadership: Emergence, functioning, and impacts. In W. L. Gardner, B. J. Avolio, & F. O. Walumbwa (Eds.), *Authentic leadership theory and practice: Origins, effects and development* (pp. 3–41). Amsterdam, Netherlands: Elsevier.

Chan, A. W. H., & Cheung, H. Y. (2012). Cultural dimensions, ethical sensitivity, and corporate governance. *Journal of Business Ethics, 110*, 45–59.

Chan, G. K. Y. (2008). The relevance and value of Confucianism in contemporary business ethics. *Journal of Business Ethics, 77*, 347–360.

Chang, I. (1997). *The rape of Nanking: The forgotten holocaust of World War II*. New York, NY: Basic Books.

Chao, G. T., O'Leary-Kelly, A. M., Wolf, S., Klein, H. J., & Gardner, P. D. (1994). Organizational socialization: Its content and consequences. *Journal of Applied Psychology, 79*, 730–743.

Chatterji, A. K., & Toffel, M. W. (2016, April 1). The power of C.E.O. activism. *New York Times*, p. SR10.

Chatterji, A. K., & Toffel, M. W. (2017). Can CEO activism spark sustainability transitions? Evidence from a field experiment. Harvard Business School Working Paper 16–100.

Che, J. (2015, August 27). Here's how outrageous the pay gap between CEOs and their workers is. 200 highest-paid CEOs 2016. *New York Times*.

Chen, A., Lawson, R. B., Gordon, L. R., & McIntosh, B. (1996). Groupthink: Deciding with the leader and the devil. *Psychological Record, 46*, 581–590.

Cheney, G., Christensen, L., Zorn, T. E., & Ganesh, S. (2011). *Organizational communication in an age of globalization: Issues, reflections, practices*. Long Grove, IL: Waveland Press.

Chesebro, J. L. (1999). The relationship between listening styles and conversational sensitivity. *Communication Research Reports, 16*(3), 233–238.

Chidambaram, L., & Tung, L. L. (2005). Is out of sight, out of mind? An empirical study of social loafing in technology-supported groups. *Information Systems Research, 16*(2), 149–168.

Chotiner, I. (2017, May 9). How should we remember the confederacy? *Slate*.

Chow, E. (2013, September 9). Learning from Europe's "right to be forgotten." *Huffington Post*.

Christians, C. G., Rotzell, K. B., & Fackler, M. (1990). *Media ethics* (3rd ed.). New York, NY: Longman.

Christie, R., & Geis, F. L. (1970). *Studies in Machiavellianism.* New York, NY: Academic Press.

Cialdini, R. B. (2009). *Influence: Science and practice* (5th ed.). Boston, MA: Allyn & Bacon.

Cialdini, R. B., Petrova, P. K., & Goldstein, N. J. (2004, Spring). The hidden costs of organizational dishonesty. *MIT Sloan Management Review*, pp. 67–73.

Cissna, K. N., & Anderson, R. (1994). Communication and the ground of dialogue. In R. Anderson, K. N. Cissna, & R. C. Arnett (Eds.), *The reach of dialogue: Confirmation, voice, and community* (pp. 9–30). Cresskill, NJ: Hampton Press.

Cissna, K. N., & Sieburg, E. (1990). Patterns of interactional confirmation and disconfirmation. In J. Stewart (Ed.), *Bridges not walls: A book about interpersonal communication* (5th ed., pp. 237–246). New York, NY: McGraw-Hill.

Ciulla, J. (2000). *The working life.* New York, NY: Times Books.

Clapp-Smith, R., Vogelgesang, G. R., & Avey, J. B. (2009). Authentic leadership and positive psychological capital: The mediating role of trust at the group level of analysis. *Journal of Leadership and Organizational Studies, 15*(3), 227–240.

Clarke, R. A. (2004). *Against all enemies: Inside America's war on terror.* New York, NY: Free Press.

Cleary, T. (1992). *The essential Confucius: The heart of Confucius' teachings in authentic I Ching order.* San Francisco, CA: HarperSanFrancisco.

Clements, C. E., Neill, J. D., & Stovall, O. S. (2009). The impact of cultural differences on the convergence of international accounting codes of ethics. *Journal of Business Ethics, 90*, 383–391.

Coca-Cola and the Balance Calories Initiative to reduce sugar from beverages nationally. (2017, April 4). *Coca-Cola Journey.*

Cohen, D. V. (1993). Creating and maintaining ethical work climates: Anomie in the workplace and implications for managing change. *Business Ethics Quarterly, 3*, 343–358.

Cohen, J. R. (2004). The ethics of respect in negotiation. In C. Menkel-Meadow & M. Wheeler (Eds.), *What's fair: Ethics for negotiators* (pp. 257–263). San Francisco, CA: Jossey-Bass.

Cohen, M. A., & Dienhart, J. (2013). Moral and amoral conceptions of trust, with an application in organizational ethics. *Journal of Business Ethics, 112*, 1–13.

Cohen-Charash, Y., & Spector, P. E. (2001). The role of justice in organizations: A meta-analysis. *Organizational Behavior and Human Decision Processes, 86*(2), 278–321.

Colby, A., & Damon, W. (1992). *Some do care: Contemporary lives of moral commitment.* New York, NY: Free Press.

Colby, A., & Damon, W. (1995). The development of extraordinary moral commitment. In M. Killen & D. Hart (Eds.), *Morality in everyday life: Developmental perspectives* (pp. 342–369). Cambridge, UK: Cambridge University Press.

Coldwell, D. A., Billsberry, J., van Meurs, N., & Marsh, P. J. G. (2008). The effects of person-organization ethical fit on employee attraction and retention: Towards a testable explanatory model. *Journal of Business Ethics, 78*, 611–622.

Coles, R. (2001). *Lives of moral leadership.* New York, NY: Random House.

Collins, J. C., & Porras, J. I. (1994). *Built to last: Successful habits of visionary companies.* New York, NY: HarperBusiness.

Collins, J. C., & Porras, J. I. (1996, September/October). Building your company's vision. *Harvard Business Review*, pp. 65–77.

Collins, M. H., Hari, J. F., & Rocco, T. S. (2009). The older-worker-younger-supervisor dyad. A test of the reverse Pygmalion effect. *Human Resource Development Quarterly, 20*(1), 21–41.

Commission: "Going postal" is just a myth. (n.d.) *ABC News.*

Confucius. (2007). *The analects of Confucius* (B. Watson, Trans.). New York, NY: Columbia University Press.

Coombs, W. T., & Holladay, S. J. (2013). *It's not just PR: Public relations in society* (2nd ed.). Hoboken, NJ: Wiley.

Cooper, S. (2004). *Corporate social performance: A stakeholder approach.* Burlington, VT: Ashgate.

Cooper, T. L., & Menzel, D. C. (2013). In pursuit of ethical competence. In T. L. Cooper & D. C. Menzel (Eds.), *Achieving ethical competence for public service leadership* (pp. 2–23). Armonk, NY: Sharpe.

Cooper, T. L., & Wright, N. D. (1992). *Exemplary public administrators: Character and leadership in government.* San Francisco, CA: Jossey-Bass.

Covey, S. R. (1989). *The seven habits of highly effective people.* New York, NY: Simon & Schuster.

Covey, S. R. (2004). *The 8th habit: From effectiveness to greatness.* New York, NY: Free Press.

Cowley, S., & Kingson, J. A. (2017, April 10). Wells Fargo to claw back $75 million from 2 former executives. *New York Times*, p. A1.

Crace, R. K., & Brown, D. (1992). *The life values inventory.* Minneapolis, MN: National Computer Systems.

Craigie, F. C. (1999). The spirit and work: Observations about spirituality and organizational life. *Journal of Psychology and Christianity, 18*, 43–53.

Crampton, P. C., & Dees, J. G. (1993). Promoting honesty in negotiation: An exercise in practical ethics. *Business Ethics Quarterly, 3*, 359–394.

Crane, A., Matten, D., & Moon, J. (2008). The emergence of corporate citizenship: Historical development and alternative perspectives. In A. G. Scherer & G. Palazzo (Eds.), *Handbook of research on global corporate citizenship* (pp. 25–49). Cheltenham, UK: Edward Elgar.

Crano, W. D., & Seyranian, V. (2009). How minorities prevail: The context/comparison-lenience contract model. *Journal of Social Issues, 65*(2), 335–363.

Creech, J. D. (2016, August 12). Baylor sexual assault victims met with skepticism, little assistance from the university. *Houston Chronicle*.

Cressy, D. R. (1950). The criminal violation of financial trust. *American Sociological Review, 15*(6), 738–743.

Crooks, H. (2011, July 30). He could be out before he is 53. *Weekend Post* (South Africa).

Cropanzano, R., Bowen, D. E., & Gilliland, S. W. (2007). The management of organizational justice. *Journal of Management Perspectives, 21*(4), 34–48.

Cropanzano, R., & Stein, J. H. (2009). Organizational justice and behavioral ethics: Promises and prospects. *Business Ethics Quarterly, 19*(2), 193–233.

Cullen, J. B., Parboteeah, K. P., & Victor, B. (2003). The effects of ethical climates on organizational commitment: A two-study analysis. *Journal of Business Ethics, 46*, 127–141.

Cummings, B. (2012). Benefit corporations: How to encourage a mandate to promote the public interest. *Columbia Law Review, 112*, 578–627.

Cutler, I. (2000). The cynical manager. *Management Learning, 31*, 295–312.

Cyberbullying in the workplace. (2016, August 4). *Workplace Ethics Advice*.

Czubaroff, J. (2000). Dialogic rhetoric: An application of Martin Buber's philosophy of dialogue. *Quarterly Journal of Speech, 2*, 168–189.

D'Abate, C. P. (2005). Working hard or hardly working: A study of individuals engaging in personal business on the job. *Human Relations, 58*, 1009–1032.

Daley, M. (2014, June 10). Audit says 57,000 await first VA appointment. *Boston Globe*.

Damon, W. (Ed.). (2002). *Bringing in a new era in character education.* Stanford, CA: Hoover Institution Press.

Darley, J. M. (1996). How organizations socialize individuals into evildoing. In D. M. Messick & A. E. Tenbrunsel (Eds.), *Codes of conduct: Behavioral research into business ethics* (pp. 13–43). New York, NY: Russell Sage Foundation.

Dasgupta, S., & Kesharwani, A. (2010). Whistle-blowing: A survey of the literature. *IUP Journal of Corporate Governance, IX*, 57–70.

Davidson, A. (2016, September 12). How regulation failed with Wells Fargo. *New Yorker*.

Davidson, J. D. (2017, April 25). New Orleans is wrong to remove its Confederate monuments. *The Federalist.com*.

Davis, J. (2016a, September 27). What's driving corporate activism? *New Republic*.

Davis, J. (2016b, September 27). When did Che Guevara become CEO? The roots of the new corporate activism. *The Conversation*.

Davis, J. (2017, August 30). Why corporate America is entering social justice fray. *UPI*.

Davis, J. H., & Ruhe, J. A. (2003). Perceptions of country corruption: Antecedents and outcomes. *Journal of Business Ethics, 43*, 275–288.

Davis, J. H., Schoorman, F. D., & Donaldson, L. (1997). Toward a stewardship theory of management. *Academy of Management Review, 22*, 20–47.

The dawn of CEO activism. (n.d.). *Weber Shandwick*.

Dawson, J. (2017, March 2). Travis Kalanick has no one but himself to blame for Uber's toxic company culture. *Recode*.

Day, L. A. (2003). *Ethics in media communications: Cases and controversies* (4th ed.). Belmont, CA: Thomson/Wadsworth.

Dean, J. W., Brandes, P., & Dharwadkar, R. (1998). Organizational cynicism. *Academy of Management Review, 23*, 341–352.

De Clercq, S., Fontaine, J. R. J., & Anseel, F. (2008). In search of a comprehensive value model for assessing supplementary person–organization fit. *Journal of Psychology, 142*(3), 277–302.

De Dreu, C. K. W., & Beersma, B. (2001). Minority influence in organizations: Its origins and implications for learning and group performance. In C. K. W. De Dreu & N. K. DeVries (Eds.), *Group consensus and minority influence: Implications for innovation* (pp. 258–283). Oxford, UK: Blackwell.

De Dreu, C. K. W., & Gelfand, J. J. (2008). Conflict in the workplace: Sources, functions, and dynamics across multiple levels of analysis. In C. K. W. De Dreu & M. J. Gelfand (Eds.), *The psychology of conflict and conflict management in organizations* (pp. 3–54). New York, NY: Lawrence Erlbaum.

De Dreu, C. K. W., & Weingart, L. R. (2003). Task versus relationship conflict, team performance, and team member satisfaction: A meta-analysis. *Journal of Applied Psychology, 88*(4), 741–749.

De George, R. T. (1995). *Business ethics* (4th ed.). Englewood Cliffs, NJ: Prentice Hall.

Delanty, G. (2012). The emerging field of cosmopolitism studies. In G. Delanty (Ed.), *Routledge international handbook of cosmopolitan studies* (pp. 1–8). Hoboken, NJ: Routledge.

Deloitte. (2017). *The 2016 Deloitte millennial survey: Winning over the next generation of leaders.*

Dennis, B. (2017, February 28). Flint residents must start paying for water they still can't drink without a filter. *Washington Post.*

Department of Defense, Office of General Counsel, Standards of Conduct Office. (2011, August). *Encyclopedia of ethical failure.* Retrieved from http://www.samhouston.army.mil.

Depre, K. E., & Barling, J. (2003). Workplace aggression. In A. Sagie, S. Stashevsky, & M. Koslowsky (Eds.), *Misbehaviour and dysfunctional attitudes in organizations* (pp. 13–32). Hampshire, UK: Palgrave Macmillan.

DesJardins, J. (2011). *An introduction to business ethics* (4th ed.). New York, NY: McGraw-Hill.

Dessler, G. (2008). *Human resource management.* Upper Saddle River, NJ: Pearson.

Dickerson, B. (2014, April 17). Bankruptcy shield can't restore moral solvency. *Detroit Free Press.*

Dik, B. J., & Duffy, R. D. (2009). Calling and vocation at work: Definitions and prospects for research and practice. *Counseling Psychologist, 37*, 424–450.

Dik, B. J., Duffy, R. D., & Eldridge, B. M. (2009). Calling and vocation in career counseling: Recommendations for promoting meaningful work. *Professional Psychology: Research and Practice, 40*, 625–632.

Ding, H., & Ding, X. (2008). Project management, critical praxis, and process-oriented approach to teamwork. *Business Communication Quarterly, 71*(4), 456–471.

Dirks, K. T. (1999). The effects of interpersonal trust on work group performance. *Journal of Applied Psychology, 84*, 445–455.

Dirks, K. T., & Ferrin, D. L. (2002). Trust in leadership: Meta-analytic findings and implications for research and practice. *Journal of Applied Psychology, 87*, 611–628.

Divir, T., Eden, D., & Banjo, M. L. (1995). Self-fulfilling prophecy and gender: Can women be Pygmalion and Galatea? *Journal of Applied Psychology, 80*, 253–270.

Dodd, M. D. (2016, April 18). Corporate activism: The new challenge for an age-old question. Institute for Public Relations.

Dodd, M. D. & Supa, D. W. (2014). Conceptualizing and measuring "corporate social advocacy" communication: Examining the impact of corporate financial performance. *Public Relations, 8*, 1–22.

Dolfsma, W. (2006). Accounting as applied ethics: Teaching a discipline. *Journal of Business Ethics, 63*, 209–215.

Donadio, R. (2013, May 26). Francis' humility and emphasis on the poor strike a new tone at the Vatican. *New York Times*, p. A4.

Donadio, R., & Yardley, J. (2013, March 19). Vatican's bureaucracy tests even the infallible. *New York Times*, p. A1.

Donaldson, T., & Dunfee, T. W. (1994). Toward a unified conception of business ethics: Integrative social contracts theory. *Academy of Management Review, 19*, 252–284.

Donaldson, T., & Dunfee, T. W. (1999). *Ties that bind: A social contracts approach to business ethics*. Boston, MA: Harvard Business School Press.

Donaldson, T., & Preston, L. E. (1995). The stakeholder theory of the corporation: Concepts, evidence, and implications. *Academy of Management Review, 20*, 65–91.

Donnelly, J. (1989). *Universal human rights in theory and practice*. Ithaca, NY: Cornell University Press.

Doorley, J., & Garcia, H. F. (2007). *Reputation management: The key to successful public relations and corporate communication*. New York, NY: Routledge.

Dotlich, D. L., Noel, J. L., & Walker, N. (2004). *Leadership passages: The personal and professional transitions that make or break a leader*. San Francisco, CA: Jossey-Bass.

Dotlich, D. L., Noel, J. L., & Walker, N. (2005, Autumn). Leadership passages: Being part of an acquisition or merger. *Journal of Organizational Excellence*, pp. 23–29

Dougherty, J. (2009a, October 12). Sweat lodge deaths: Bring soul-searching to area deep in seekers. *New York Times*, p. A13.

Dougherty, J. (2009b, October 22). A witness recalls a grim end to a quest for spiritual rebirth. *New York Times*, p. A1.

Dougherty, J. (2009c, October 23). New Age vibes strike tragic chord. *International Herald Tribune*, p. 2.

Douglas, S. C., & Martinko, M. J. (2001). Exploring the role of individual differences in the prediction of workplace aggression. *Journal of Applied Psychology, 86*, 547–559.

Dowd, M. (2009, October 7). Men behaving badly. *New York Times*, p. A29.

Driver, J. (2011). *Consequentialism*. Hoboken, NJ: Taylor and Francis.

Drory, A., & Romm, T. (1990). The definition of organizational politics: A review. *Human Relations, 43*(11), 1133–1154.

Drummond, H. (1996). *Escalation in decision-making: The tragedy of Taurus*. New York, NY: Oxford University Press.

Drummond, H. (2001). *The art of decision-making: Mirrors of imagination, masks of fate*. Chichester, UK: Wiley.

Drummond, H. (2014). Escalation of commitment: When to stay the course? *Academy of Management Perspectives, 28*, 430–446.

Duchon, D., & Plowman, D. A. (2005). Nurturing the spirit at work: Impact on work unit performance. *The Leadership Quarterly, 16*, 807–833.

Duck, J. M., & Fielding, K. S. (2003). Leaders and their treatment of subgroups: Implications for evaluations of the leader and the superordinate group. *European Journal of Social Psychology, 33*, 387–401.

Duffy, R. D., & Autin, K. L. (2013). Disentangling the link between perceiving a calling and living a calling. *Journal of Counseling Psychology, 60*, 219–227.

Duffy, R. D., & Sedlacek, W. E. (2007). The presence of and search for a calling: Connections to career development. *Journal of Vocational Behavior, 70*, 590–601.

Duffy, R. D., & Sedlacek, W. E. (2010). The salience of a career calling among college students: Exploring group differences and links to religiousness, life meaning, and life satisfaction. *Career Development Quarterly, 59*, 27–40.

Dufresne, R. L., & Offstein, E. H. (2012). Holistic and intentional student character development process: Learning from West Point. *Academy of Management Learning & Education, 11*, 570–590.

Duke, A. B., Goodman, J. M., Treadway, D. C., & Breland, J. W. (2009). Perceived organizational support as a moderator of emotional labor/outcomes relationships. *Journal of Applied Social Psychology, 39*(5), 1013–1034.

Dunfee, T. W., & Donaldson, T. (1999). Social contract approaches to business ethics: Bridging the "is-ought" gap. In R. E. Frederick (Ed.), *A companion to business ethics* (pp. 38–52). Malden, MA: Blackwell.

Durden, T. (2016a, May 19). Elizabeth Holmes admits Theranos "technology is a fraud": Restates, voids years of test results. *ZeroHedge*.

Durden, T. (2016b, November 17). Theranos whistleblower tells all on intimidation and coercion tactics employed to silence him. *ZeroHedge*.

Durden, T. (2017, March 3). Uber used "secret" Greyball tool to deceive authorities. *ZeroHedge*.

Duska, R. F., & Duska, B. S. (2003). *Accounting ethics*. Malden, MA: Blackwell.

Eagan, M., Wattles, J., & Alesci, C. (2016, October 12). Wells Fargo CEO John Stumpf is out. *CNNMoney*.

Edelman. (2017) Edelman Trust Barometer executive summary.

Eden, D. (1984). Self-fulfilling prophecy as a management tool: Harnessing Pygmalion. *Academy of Management Review, 9*, 64–73.

Eden, D. (1990). *Pygmalion in management.* Lexington, MA: Lexington Books/D.C. Heath.

Eden, D. (1993). Interpersonal expectations in organizations. In P. D. Blanck (Ed.), *Interpersonal expectations: Theory, research, and applications* (pp. 154–178). Cambridge, UK: Cambridge University Press.

Eden, D., & Shami, A. B. (1982). Pygmalion goes to boot camp: Expectancy, leadership, and trainee performance. *Journal of Applied Psychology, 67*, 194–199.

Edmonds, D. (2015, May 28). More than half of college faculty are adjuncts: Should you care? *Forbes.*

Edmondson, A. (2003, Winter). Framing for learning: Lessons in successful technology implementation. *California Management Review, 45*, 34–54.

Edmundson, A. (1999). Psychological safety and learning behavior in work teams. *Administrative Science Quarterly, 44*, 350–383.

Egan, M. (2016, August 29). How the EpiPen came to symbolize corporate greed. *The Buzz.*

Ehrhart, M. G. (2004). Leadership and procedural justice climate as antecedents of unit-level organizational citizenship behavior. *Personnel Psychology, 57*(1), 61–94.

The 8 biggest recent revelations in Baylor's sexual assault scandal. (2017, May 24). *SportsDay DallasNews.com.*

Einarsen, S., Hoel, H., & Notelears, G. (2009). Measuring exposure to bullying and harassment at work: Validity, factor structure and psychometric properties of the Negative Acts Questionnaire-Revised. *Work and Stress, 23* (1), 24–44.

Einarsen, S., Hoel, H., Zapf, D., & Cooper, C. C. (Eds.). (2011). *Bullying and harassment in the workplace: Developments in theory, research and practice.* Boca Raton, FL: CRC Press.

Eisenberg, E. M., & Goodall, H. L. (2001). *Organizational communication: Balancing creativity and constraint* (3rd ed.). Boston, MA: Bedford/St. Martin's.

Ekman, P. (2003). *Emotions revealed: Recognizing faces and feelings to improve communication and emotional life.* New York, NY: Times Books.

Elegido, J. M. (2016). Mutuality: A root principle for marketing ethics. *African Journal of Business Ethics, 10*, 67–96.

Elias, R. Z. (2006). The impact of professional commitment and anticipatory socialization on accounting students' ethical orientation. *Journal of Business Ethics, 68*, 83–90.

Eligon, J. (2015, November 11). At University of Missouri, black students see a campus riven by race. *New York Times*, p. A1.

Eligon, J. & Perez-Pena, R. (2015, November 9). University of Missouri protests spur day of change. *New York Times.*

Ellenwood, S. (2007). Revisiting character education: From McGuffey to narratives. *Journal of Education, 187*(3), 21–43.

Ellis, K. (2000). Perceived teacher confirmation: The development of validation of an instrument and two studies of the relationship to cognitive and affective learning. *Human Communication Research, 26*, 264–291.

Ellis, K. (2004a). The impact of perceived teacher confirmation on receiver apprehension, motivation, and learning. *Communication Education, 53*, 1–20.

Ellis, K. (2004b). Perceived parental confirmation: Development and validation of an instrument. *Southern Communication Journal, 67*, 319–334.

Ellsworth, B., & Scigliuzzo, D. (2017, May 31). Venezuelan opposition condemns Goldman for $2.8 billion bond deal. *Reuters.*

Emmons, R. A., & McCullough, M. E. (2003). Counting blessings versus burdens: An experimental investigation of gratitude and subjective well-being in daily life. *Journal of Personality and Social Psychology, 84*(2), 377–389.

Emotional competence training— American Express financial advisors. (n.d.). Consortium for Research on Emotional Intelligence in Organizations.

Engle Bromwich, J. (2017, April 16). United Airlines staff will no longer take seats of boarded passengers. *New York Times.*

Enright, R. D., Freedman, S., & Rique, J. (1998). The psychology of forgiveness. In R. D. Enright & J. North (Eds.), *Exploring forgiveness* (pp. 46–62). Madison: University of Wisconsin Press.

Epley, N., & Dunning, D. (2000). Feeling "holier than thou": Are self-serving assessments produced by errors in self- or social prediction? *Journal of Personality and Social Psychology, 79*, 861–875.

Ernst, C., & Yip, J. (2009). Boundary-spanning leadership: Tactics to bridge social identity groups in organizations. In T. L. Pittinsky (Ed.), *Crossing the divide: Intergroup leadership in a world of difference*. Boston, MA: Harvard Business Press.

Esser, J. K. (1998). Alive and well after 25 years: A review of groupthink research. *Organizational Behavior and Human Decision Processes, 73*, 116–141.

Ethics: Phoning it in. (2007, February). *CFO*, p. 21.

Ethics Resource Center. (2013). *National Business Ethics Survey*.

European Commission. (2014, May 13). Factsheet on the "Right to be Forgotten" ruling. Retrieved from http://ec.europa.eu/justice/data-protection/files/factsheets/factsheet_data_protection_en.pdf

Fairholm, G. W. (1996). Spiritual leadership: Fulfilling whole-self needs at work. *Leadership & Organization Development Journal, 17*(5), 11–17.

Fairhurst, G. (2011). *The power of framing: Creating the language of leadership*. San Francisco, CA: Jossey-Bass.

Fairhust, G., & Sarr, R. A. (1996). *The art of framing: Managing the language of leadership*. San Francisco: Jossey-Bass.

Fake news expert on how false stories spread and why people believe them. (2016, December 14). *NPR*.

Farr, C. (2016, May 10). The Theranos scandal is just the beginning. *Fast Company*.

Faux, Z., Keller, L, J., & Surane, J. (2016, October 12). Wells Fargo CEO Stumpf quits in fallout from fake accounts. *Bloomberg*.

Feder, J. (2010). Sexual harassment: Developments in Federal law [1]. In K. C. Wong (Ed.), *Sexual harassment around the globe* (pp. 85–120). New York, NY: Nova Science.

Fedor, D., Maslyn, J., Farmer, S., & Bettenhausen, K. (2008). The contribution of positive politics to the prediction of employee reactions. *Journal of Applied Social Psychology, 38*, 76–96.

Feld Entertainment. (2017, January 14). Feld entertainment announces final performances of Ringling Bros. and Barnum & Bailey circus in May 2017 [Press release].

Ferris, G. R., Treadway, D. C., Kolodinsky, R. W., Hochwarter, W. A., Kacmar, C. J., Douglas, C., & Frink D. D. (2005). Development and validation of the Political Skill Inventory. *Journal of Management, 31*, 149–150.

Fine, R., & Boon, V. (2007). Cosmopolitanism: Between past and future. *European Journal of Social Theory, 10*, 5–16.

Fineman, S. (1995). Stress, emotion and intervention. In T. Newton (Ed.), *Managing stress: Emotion and power at work* (pp. 120–136). London, UK: Sage.

Fink, S. (2013). *Five days at Memorial: Life and death in a storm-ravaged hospital*. New York, NY: Crown.

Finlayson, J. G. (2000). Modernity and morality in Habermas's discourse ethics. *Inquiry, 43*, 319–340.

Finlayson, J. G. (2005). *Habermas: A very short introduction*. Oxford, UK: Oxford University Press.

Fisher, J. W., Francis, L. J., & Johnson, P. (2000). Assessing spiritual health via four domains of spiritual wellbeing: The SH5DI. *Pastoral Psychology, 49*, 133–145.

Fisher, R., Ury, W., & Patton, B. (2011). *Getting to yes: Negotiating agreement without giving in* (Rev. ed.). New York, NY: Bantam Books.

Fiske, S. T. (1993, June). Controlling other people: The impact of power on stereotyping. *American Psychologist, 48*, 621–628.

Fitzgerald, L. F. (1993). Sexual harassment: Violence against women in the workplace. *American Psychologist, 48*, 1070–1076.

Fitzgerald, L. F., Drasgow, F., Hulin, C. L., Gelfand, M. J., & Magley, V. (1997). Antecedents and consequences of sexual harassment in organizations: A test of an integrated model. *Journal of Applied Psychology, 82*, 578–589.

Flanagan, J., & Clarke, K. (2007). Beyond a code of professional ethics: A holistic model of ethical decision-making for accountants. *Abacus, 43*, 488–518.

Flippen, A. R. (1999). Understanding groupthink from a self-regulatory perspective. *Small Group Research, 30*, 139–165.

Folger, J., Poole, M., & Stutman, R. (1993). *Working through conflict*. New York, NY: HarperCollins.

Folger, R., & Baron, R. A. (1996). Violence and hostility at work: A model of reactions to perceived injustice. In G. R. VandenBos & E. Q. Bulato (Eds.), *Violence on the job: Identifying risks and developing solutions* (pp. 51–85). Washington, DC: American Psychological Association.

Foote, J., Gaffney, N., & Evans, J. R. (2010). Corporate social responsibility: Implications for performance excellence. *Total Quality Management, 21*(8), 799–812.

Former Atlanta schools superintendent reports to jail in cheating scandal. (2013, April 4). *CNN*.

Forrester, R. (2000). Empowerment: Rejuvenating a potent idea. *Academy of Management Executive, 14,* 67–80.

Fortin, M. (2008). Perspectives on organizational justice: Concept clarification, social context, integration, time and links with morality. *International Journal of Management Reviews, 10*(2), 93–126.

Foster G., & Krasnoff, R. (Producers) & Jackson, M. (Director). (2016). *Denial* [Motion picture]. United Kingdom: Bleeker Street.

Fouche, G. (2009, October 19). Where convicts lead the good life. *Globalpost*.

Fowler, S. J. (2017, February 19). Reflecting on one very, very strange year at Uber [Blog post].

Fox, T. (2016, December). Wells Fargo: The lessons of an ethics failure. *National Defense*.

Franke, G. P., & Nadler, S. S. (2007). Culture, economic development, and national ethical attitudes. *Journal of Business Research, 61,* 254–264.

Frederick, W. C. (1992). *Social issues in management: Coming of age or prematurely gray?* Paper presented at the Academy of Management annual meeting, Las Vegas, NV.

Freeman, R. E. (1984). *Strategic management.* Marshfield, MA: Pitman.

Freeman, R. E. (1994). The politics of stakeholder theory: Some future directions. *Business Ethics Quarterly, 4,* 409–421.

Freeman, R. E. (1995). Stakeholder thinking: The state of the art. In J. Nasi (Ed.), *Understanding stakeholder thinking* (pp. 35–73). Helsinki, Finland: LSR-Julkaisut Oy.

Freeman, R. E., Harrison, J. S., & Wicks, A. C. (2007). *Managing for stakeholders: Survival, reputation, and success.* New Haven, CT: Yale University Press.

French, R. P., & Raven, B. (1959). The bases of social power. In D. Cartwright (Ed.), *Studies in social power* (pp. 150–167). Ann Arbor: University of Michigan, Institute for Social Research.

Frey, B. F. (2000). The impact of moral intensity on decision making in a business context. *Journal of Business Ethics, 26,* 181–195.

Friedersdorf, C. (2017, April 3). What does "cultural appropriation" actually mean? *The Atlantic*.

Friedman, M. (1970, September 13). The social responsibility of business is to increase its profits. *New York Times Magazine,* p. 18.

Friend, T. (2016, October 3). Rachel Weiz and Deborah Lipstadt. *New Yorker*.

Fritzche, D. J. (2000). Ethical climates and the ethical dimension of decision making. *Journal of Business Ethics, 24,* 125–140.

Frymier, A. B., & Houser, M. L. (2000). The teacher–student relationship as an interpersonal relationship. *Communication Education, 49*(3), 207–219.

Fuggetta, E. (2012, July 2). Activists protest elephant captivity at Oregon Zoo. *The Oregonian*.

Fullerton, L. (2017, May 17). Expectations of corporate social responsibility means Americans looking to businesses to drive change. *The Drum*.

Fulmer, I. S., & Barry, B. (2009). Managed hearts and wallets: Ethical issues in emotional influence by and within organizations. *Business Ethics Quarterly, 12,* 155–191.

Fussell, S. (January 18, 2017) New American Airlines fare doesn't let you bring overhead baggage. *Gizmodo*.

Garcia-Zamor, J. C. (2003). Workplace spirituality and organizational performance. *Public Administration Review, 63,* 355–363.

Garde, D. (2016, August 24). The EpiPen was her "baby." Now this pharma CEO is in the hot seat over price hikes. *STAT*.

Gardner, H. (2010, September 10). Stem cell financing ban ends, for now. *New York Times,* p. 14.

Gardner, W. L. (1992). Lessons in organizational dramaturgy: The art of impression management. *Organizational Dynamics, 21,* 33–47.

Gardner, W. L., Avolio, B. J., Luthans, F., May, D. R., & Walumbwa, F. O. (2005). "Can you see the real me?" A self-based model of authentic leader and follower development. *Leadership Quarterly, 16,* 343–372.

Gardner, W. L., Avolio, B. J., & Walumbwa, F. O. (2005). Authentic leadership development: Emergent themes and future directions. In W. L. Gardner, B. J. Avolio, &

F. O. Walumbwa (Eds.), *Authentic leadership theory and practice: Origins, effects and development* (pp. 387–406). Amsterdam, Netherlands: Elsevier.

Garrett, R. K., & Danziger, J. N. (2008). On cyberslacking: Workplace status and personal Internet use at work. *CyberPsychology & Behavior, 11*, 287–292.

Garside, J. (2011, July 26). Vodaphone under fire for bowing to Egyptian pressure. *The Guardian*.

Gaudine, A., & Thorne, L. (2001). Emotion and ethical decision-making in organizations. *Journal of Business Ethics, 31*, 175–187.

Gellerman, S. W. (1989, Winter). Managing ethics from the top down. *Sloan Management Review*, pp. 73–79.

Gellis, H., Giladi, K., & Friedman, H. H. (2002). Biblical and Talmudic basis of accounting ethics. *CPA Journal, 72*(9), 11–13.

Gentile, M. C. (2010). *Giving voice to values: How to speak your mind when you know what's right*. New Haven, CT: Yale University Press.

Gentlemen, A. (2012, June 1). A prison with humanity. *Guardian Weekly*, p. 25.

Gergen, D. (2000). *Eyewitness to power: The essence of leadership*. New York, NY: Simon & Schuster.

Giacalone, R. A., & Jurkiewicz, C. L. (2010). The science of workplace spirituality. In R. A. Giacalone & C. L. Jurkiewicz (Eds.), *The Handbook of workplace spirituality and organizational performance* (2nd. ed., pp. 3–26). Armonk, NY: Sharpe.

Gibb, J. R. (1961). Defensive communication. *Journal of Communication, 11–12*, 141–148.

Gibbs, S. (2016, February 16). Google to extend "right to be forgotten" to all its domains accessed in EU. *The Guardian*.

Gibson, K. (2000). The moral basis of stakeholder theory. *Journal of Business Ethics, 26*, 245–257.

Gilbert, K. (2013, May 23). Delaware overcomes its qualms and advances B corps law. *Institutional Investor*.

Gillespie, P. (2017, May 31). Venezuelans are outraged at Goldman Sachs. *CNNMoney*.

Gillett, R. (2017, June 20. "I just don't call in sick anymore at all." *Business Insider*.

Gilligan, C. (1982). *In a different voice: Psychological theory and women's development*. Cambridge, MA: Harvard University Press.

Gillis, J., & Fountain, H. (2010, June 7). Rate of oil leak, still not clear, puts doubt on BP. *New York Times*, p. A1.

Gini in the bottle: Inequality in America. (2013, November 26). *The Economist*.

Gino, F., Moore, D. A., & Bazerman, M. H. (2008, January). See no evil: When we overlook other people's unethical behavior. *Harvard Business School Working Paper No. 08–045*.

Gino, F., Moore, D. A., & Bazerman, M. H. (2009). No harm, no foul: The outcome bias in ethical judgments. Harvard Business School Working Paper No. 08-080.

Gittell, J. H. (2003). *The Southwest Airlines way*. New York, NY: McGraw-Hill.

Gladwell, M. (2005). *Blink: The power of thinking without thinking*. New York, NY: Little, Brown.

Global consumers are willing to put their money where their heart is. (2014, July 17). *Nielsen*.

Global Reporting Initiative. (2014). G4 Guidelines.

Glomb, T. M., & Hui, L. (2003). Interpersonal aggression in work groups: Social influence, reciprocal, and individual effects. *Academy of Management Journal, 46*, 486–496.

Glomb, T. M., Steel, P. D. G., & Arvey, R. D. (2002). Office sneers, snipes, and stab wounds: Antecedents, consequences, and implications of workplace violence and aggression. In R. G. Lord, R. J. Klimoski, & R. Kanfer (Eds.), *Emotions in the workplace* (pp. 227–259). San Francisco, CA: Jossey-Bass.

Goffman, E. (1959). *The presentation of self in everyday life*. Garden City, NY: Doubleday.

Goldman, S. (2008). *Temptations in the office: Ethical choices and legal obligations*. Westport, CT: Praeger.

Goleman, D. (1998). *Working with emotional intelligence*. New York, NY: Bantam Books.

Goleman, D. (2001). An EI-based theory of performance. In C. Cherniss & D. Goleman (Eds.), *The emotionally intelligent workplace: How to select for, measure, and improve emotional intelligence in individuals, groups, and organizations* (pp. 27–44). San Francisco, CA: Jossey-Bass.

Gomez, R., & Fisher, J W. (2003). Domains of spiritual well-being and development and validation of the Spiritual Well-Being Questionnaire. *Personality and Individual Differences, 35*, 1975–1991.

Good, T., & Brophy, J. (1980). *Educational psychology: A realistic approach.* New York, NY: Holt, Rinehart & Winston.

Goodboy, A. K., & Myers, S. A. (2008). The effect of teacher confirmation on student communication and learning outcomes. *Communication Education, 57*(2), 153–179.

Goodman, P. S., & Morgenson, G. (2008, December 28). Saying yes to anyone, WaMu built empire on shaky loans. *New York Times*, p. A1.

Goodnough, A. (2014, June 1). Many veterans praise care, but all hate the wait. *New York Times*, p. A1.

Goodpaster, K. E. (1991). Business ethics and stakeholder analysis. *Business Ethics Quarterly, 1*, 53–72.

Goodstein, J. (2004). Integrity based governance: Responding to the call for corporate governance reform. In R. J. Burke & C. L. Cooper (Eds.), *Leading in turbulent times* (pp. 167–181). Malden, MA: Blackwell.

Goodstein, L. (2013, September 20). Pope calls church a "home for all." *The Oregonian*, p. A1.

Goodwin, D. (2017, May 17). Fearing Shadow Brokers leak, NSA reported critical flaw to Microsoft. *Ars Technica*.

Goodwin, S. A. (2003). Power and prejudice: A social-cognitive perspective on power and leadership. In D. van Knippenberg & M. A. Hogg (Eds.), *Leadership and power: Identity processes in groups and organizations* (pp. 138–152). London, UK: Sage.

Googins, B. K., Mirvis, P. H., & Rochlin, S. A. (2007). *Beyond good company: Next generation corporate citizenship.* New York, NY: Palgrave MacMillan.

Google restores links to some news articles after outcry. (2014, July 3). *Reuters*.

Gordon, S. (2016, August 31). 11 ways to deal with a workplace cyberbully. *Verywell*.

Gottschall, J. (2012). *The storytelling animal: How stories make us human.* New York, NY: Mariner Books.

Gouws, D. J. (1995). The role concept in career development. In D. E. Super & B. Sverko (Eds.), *Life roles, values and careers: International findings of the Work Importance Study* (pp. 22–53). San Francisco, CA: Jossey-Bass.

Graham, G. (2004). *Eight theories of ethics.* London, UK: Routledge.

Graham, J., Haidt, J., & Nosek, B. A. (2009). Liberals and conservatives rely on different sets of moral foundations. *Journal of Personality and Social Psychology, 96*, 1029–1046.

Graham, J., Nosek, B. A., Haidt, J., Iyer, R., Koleva, S. & Ditto, P. H. (2011). Mapping the moral domain. *Journal of Personality and Social Psychology, 101*, 366–385.

Grant, A. (2013, November 13). Seven sneaky influence tactics you never saw coming. *Psychology Today*.

Grave, J. A. (2013, March 21). The top cyberloafing activities of a distracted office worker. *US News and World Report*.

Greene, J. (2005). Cognitive neuroscience and the structure of the moral mind. In P. Carruthers, S. Laurence, & S. Stich (Eds.), *The innate mind: Structure and content* (pp. 338–352). Oxford, UK: Oxford University Press.

Greenleaf, R. K. (1977). *Servant leadership.* New York, NY: Paulist Press.

Greenwald, J. (2009, November 2). Scandals put spotlight on workplace romance: Task for employers is finding balance of protection, privacy. *Business Insurance News*, p. 3.

Gregory, M. (2009). *Shaped by stories: The ethical power of narratives.* Notre Dame, IN: Notre Dame Press.

Griffiths, M. (2010). Internet abuse and internet addiction in the workplace. *Journal of Workplace Learning, 22*, 463–472.

Grind, K. (2012). *The lost bank: The story of Washington Mutual—the biggest bank failure in American history.* New York, NY: Simon & Schuster.

Griswold, A. (2017, February 27). Uber is designed so that for one employee to get ahead, another must fail. *Quartz*.

Grover, S. (1993). Lying, deceit, and subterfuge: A model of dishonesty in the workplace. *Organization Science, 4*, 478–494.

Grover, S. L. (1997). Lying in organizations: Theory, research, and future directions. In R. A. Giacalone & J. Greenberg (Eds.), *Antisocial behavior in organizations* (pp. 68–84). Thousand Oaks, CA: Sage.

Guadagno, R. E., & Cialdini, R. B. (2007). Gender differences in impression management in organizations: A qualitative review. *Sex Roles, 56*, 483–494.

Gudykunst, W. B. (2004). *Bridging differences: Effective intergroup communication* (4th ed.). Thousand Oaks, CA: Sage.

Gudykunst, W. B., & Kim, Y. Y. (1997). *Communicating with strangers: An approach to intercultural communication* (3rd ed.). New York, NY: McGraw-Hill.

Gumbel, A. (2009, October 22). Death in Arizona. *The Guardian*, Features, p. 5.

Guth, D. W., & Marsh, C. (2006). *Public relations: A values-driven approach* (3rd ed.). Boston, MA: Pearson.

Habermas, J. (1970). Towards a theory of communicative competence. *Inquiry, 13*, 360–375.

Habermas, J. (1990). *Moral consciousness and communicative action* (C. Lenhardt & S. Weber Nicholsen, Trans.). Cambridge, MA: MIT Press.

Hackman, M. Z., & Johnson, C. E. (2013). *Leadership: A communication perspective* (6th ed.). Prospect Heights, IL: Waveland Press.

Haidt, J. (2001). The emotional dog and its rational tail: A social intuitionist approach to moral judgment. *Psychological Review, 108*, 814–834.

Haidt, J. (2002). The moral emotions. In R. J. Davidson, K. R. Scherer, & H. H. Goldsmith (Eds.), *Handbook of affective sciences* (pp. 852–870). Oxford, UK: Oxford University Press.

Haidt, J. (2012). *The righteous mind: Why good people are divided by politics and religion.* New York, NY: Pantheon Books.

Haidt, J., & Bjorklund, F. (2008). Social intuitionists answer six questions about moral psychology. In W. Sinnott-Armstrong (Ed.), *Moral psychology: Vol. 2. The cognitive science of morality: Intuition and diversity* (pp. 182–217). Cambridge, MA: MIT Press.

Haidt, J., & Graham, J. (2007). When morality opposes justice: Conservatives have moral intuitions that liberals may not recognize. *Social Justice Research, 20*, 98–116.

Hale, J. R., & Fields, D. L. (2007). Exploring servant leadership across cultures: A study of followers in Ghana and the USA. *Leadership, 3*, 397–417.

Hall, E. T. (1976). *Beyond culture.* New York, NY: Random House.

Hamel, G. (2011, December). First, let's fire all the managers. *Harvard Business Review*.

Hamilton, J. B., & Knouse, S. B. (2001). Multinational enterprise decision principles for dealing with cross cultural ethical conflicts. *Journal of Business Ethics, 31*, 77–94.

Hamilton, J. B., Knouse, S. B., & Hill, V. (2009). Google in China: A manager-friendly heuristic model for resolving cross-cultural ethical conflicts. *Journal of Business Ethics, 86*, 143–157.

Hampden-Turner, C. M., & Trompenaars, F. (2000). *Building cross-cultural competence: How to create wealth from conflicting values.* New Haven, CT: Yale University Press;

Hannah, S. T., & Avolio, B. J. (2010). Moral potency: Building the capacity for character-based leadership. *Consulting Psychology Journal: Practice and Research, 62*, 291–310.

Hannah, S. T., Avolio, B J., & May, D. R. (2011). Moral maturation and moral conation: A capacity approach to explaining moral thought and action. *Academy of Management Review, 36*, 663–685.

Hannah, S. T., Avolio, B. J., & Walumbwa, F. O. (2011). Relationships between authentic leadership, moral courage, and ethical and pro-social behaviors. *Business Ethics Quarterly, 21*, 555–578.

Hannah, S. T., Jennings, P. L., Bluhm, D., Peng, A. C., & Schaubroeck, J. M. (2014). *Organizational Behavior and Human Decision Processes, 123*, 220–238.

Hannah, S. T., Lester, P. B., & Vogelgesang, G. R. (2005). Moral leadership: Explicating the moral component of authentic leadership. In W. L. Gardner, B. J. Avolio, & F. O. Walumbwa (Eds.), *Authentic leadership theory and practice: Origins, effects and development* (pp. 43–81). Amsterdam, Netherlands: Elsevier.

Harbarger, M. (2015a, February 13). What the heck is going on at the Port of Portland: A beginner's guide to longshore, Hanjin, more. *The Oregonian/OregonLive*.

Harbarger, M. (2015b, February 24). Port of Portland, longshore union still trading blame, barbs as rest of West Coast goes back to work. *The Oregonian/OregonLive*.

Hardy, L. (1990). *The fabric of this world: Inquiries into calling, career choice, and the design of human work.* Grand Rapids, MI: Eerdmans.

Hardy, S. A., & Carlo, G. (2005). Identity as a source of moral motivation. *Human Development, 48*, 232–256.

Hart, D. K. (1992). The moral exemplar in an organizational society. In T. L. Cooper & N. D. Wright (Eds.), *Exemplary public administrators: Character and leadership in government* (pp. 9–29). San Francisco, CA: Jossey-Bass.

Hart, D. K. (1994). Administration and the ethics of virtue. In T. C. Cooper (Ed.), *The handbook of administrative ethics* (pp. 107–123). New York, NY: Marcel Dekker.

Hart, S. L. (1997, January/February). Beyond greening; Strategies for a sustainable world. *Harvard Business Review*, pp. 66–76.

Hartman, E. (1996). *Organizational ethics and the good life*. New York, NY: Oxford University Press.

Hartog, M., & Frame, P. (2004). Business ethics in the curriculum: Integrating ethics through work experience. *Journal of Business Ethics, 54*, 399–409.

Harvesting poverty: Inching toward trade fairness. (2003, August 15). *New York Times*, p. A28.

Harvey, J. (1988). *The Abilene Paradox and other meditations on management*. Lexington, MA: Lexington Books.

Harvey, J. (2001). The Abilene Paradox: The management of agreement. *Organizational Dynamics, 33*, 17–34.

Harvey, P., Martinko, M. J., & Gardner, W. L. (2006). Promoting authentic behavior in organizations: An attributional perspective. *Journal of Leadership and Organizational Studies, 12*, 1–11.

Harvey, S. J., Jr. (2000). Reinforcing ethical decision making through organizational structure. *Journal of Business Ethics, 28*, 43–58.

Hatcher, T. (2002). *Ethics and HRD: A new approach to leading responsible organizations*. Cambridge, MA: Perseus.

Hauerwas, S. (1981). *A community of character*. Notre Dame, IN: University of Notre Dame Press.

Hauser, M. D. (2006). *Moral minds: How nature designed our universal sense of right and wrong*. New York, NY: HarperCollins.

Hauser, M. D., Young, L., & Cushman, F. (2008). Reviving Rawls's linguistic analogy: Operative principles and the causal structure of moral actions. In W. Sinnott-Armstrong (Ed.), *Moral psychology: Vol. 2: The cognitive science of morality: Intuition and diversity*. Cambridge, MA: MIT Press.

Hayden, M. E. (2017, January 16). Ringling Bros. says circus closing "not a win" for animal rights groups. *ABC News*.

Healy, J. R. (2014, April 1). GM's Barra apologizes to families in testimony. *USA Today*.

Heames, J. T., & Service, R. W. (2003). Dichotomies in teaching, application, and ethics. *Journal of Education for Business, 79*, 118–122.

Heath, R. L. (2009). *Strategic issues management: Organizations and public policy challenges* (2nd ed.). Thousand Oaks, CA: Sage.

Heathfield, S. M. (2016, August 17). Tips about dating, sex and romance at work. *The Balance*.

Heineman, B. (2014 June 6). GC and CEO responsibility for GM's dysfunctional culture. *Belfer Center for Science and International Affairs*.

Held, V. (2004). Taking care: Care as practice and value. In C. Calhoun (Ed.), *Setting the moral compass: Essays by women philosophers* (pp. 59–71). Oxford, UK: Oxford University Press.

Held, V. (2006). The ethics of care. In D. Copp (Ed.), *The Oxford handbook of ethical theory* (pp. 537–566). Oxford, UK: Oxford University Press.

Henle, C. A., & Blanchard, A. L. (2008). The interaction of work stressors and organizational sanctions on cyberloafing. *Journal of Managerial Issues, 20*, 383–400.

Herdt, T. (2012, January 4). Patagonia first in line to register as a "benefit corporation." *Ventura County Star*.

Hernandez, M. (2008). Promoting stewardship behavior in organizations: A leadership model. *Journal of Business Ethics, 20*, 121–128.

Hernandez, M. (2012). Toward an understanding of the psychology of stewardship. *Academy of Management Review, 37*, 172–193.

Hernandez, M., & Sitkin, S. B. (2012). Who is leading the leader? Follower influence on leader ethicality. In D. De Cremer & A. E. Tenbrunsel (Eds.), *Behavioral business ethics: Shaping an emerging field* (pp. 81–102). New York: Taylor & Francis.

Hernandez, V. (2016, July 29). Going hungry in Venezuela. *BBC*.

Herper, M., & Langreth, R. (2006, September 4). Anti-ban billionaires. *Forbes*, pp. 124–130.

Hershcovis, M. S., & Barling, J. (2008). Preventing insider-initiated workplace violence. In E. K. Kelloway, J. Barling, & J. J. Hurrell (Eds.), *Handbook of workplace violence* (pp. 607–632). Thousand Oaks, CA: SAGE.

Hershcovis, M. S., Turner, N., Barling, J., Arnold, K. A., Dupre, K. E., Inness, M., & Sivanathan, N. (2007). Predicting workplace aggression: A meta-analysis. *Journal of Applied Psychology, 92*, 228–238.

Herzog, H. A., & Golden, L. L. (2009). Moral emotions and social activism: The case of animal rights. *Journal of Social Issues, 65*, 485–498.

Hesse, M. (2016, May 8). The South's confederate-monument problem is not going away. *Washington Post*.

Higgs, M. (2009). The good, the bad and the ugly: Leadership and narcissism. *Journal of Change Management, 9*, 165–178.

Hiller, J. S. (2013). The benefit corporation and corporate social responsibility. *Journal of Business Ethics, 118*, 287–301.

Hiltzik, M. (2016a, September 20). Wells Fargo CEO John Stumpf offers a clinic in how to weasel out of real accountability. *Los Angeles Times*.

Hiltzik, M. (2016b, December 8). Andy Puzder, Trump's choice for Labor secretary, is a good spokesman for fast-food restaurant owners. For their employees, not so much. *Los Angeles Times*.

Hinken, T. R., & Schreisheim, C. A. (1989). Development and application of new scales to measure the French and Raven (1959) Bases of Social Power. *Journal of Applied Psychology, 74*, 561–567.

Hirschman, A. O. (1970). *Exit, voice, and loyalty: Responses to decline in firms, organizations, and states*. Cambridge, MA: Harvard University Press.

Hochschild, A. R. (1983). *The managed heart: Commercialization of human feeling*. Berkeley: University of California Press.

Hocker, J. L., & Wilmot, W. (2014). *Interpersonal conflict* (9th ed). New York, NY: McGraw-Hill.

Hoffman, W. M., Neill, J. D., & Stovall, O. S. (2007). An investigation of ethics officer independence. *Journal of Business Ethics, 78*, 87–95.

Hoffman, W. M., & Rowe, M. (2007). The ethics officer as agent of the board: Leveraging ethical governance capability in the post-Enron corporation. *Business and Society Review, 112*(4), 553–572, 556.

Hofmann, P. B. (2006, March/April). The value of an ethics audit. *Healthcare Executive*, pp. 44–45.

Hofstede, G. (1984). *Culture's consequences*. Beverly Hills, CA: SAGE.

Hofstede, G. (1991). *Cultures and organizations: Software of the mind*. London, UK: McGraw-Hill.

Hofstede, G. (2001). Difference and danger: Cultural profiles of nations and limits to tolerance. In M. H. Albrecht (Ed.), *International HRM: Managing diversity in the workplace* (pp. 9–23). Oxford, UK: Blackwell.

Hogg, M. A., Van Knippenberg, E., & Rast, D. E. (2012). Intergroup leadership in organizations: Leading across group and organizational boundaries. *Academy of Management Review, 37*, 232–255.

Hoppen, D. (2002, Winter). Guiding corporate behavior: A leadership obligation, not a choice. *Journal for Quality and Participation, 25*, 15–19.

Hornstein, H. (1996). *Brutal bosses and their prey*. New York, NY: Riverhead.

Hosmer, L. T. (1995). Trust: The connecting link between organizational theory and philosophical ethics. *Academy of Management Review, 20*, 279–403.

House, R. J., Hanges, P. J., Javidan, M., Dorfman, P. W., & Gupta, V. (Eds.). (2004). *Culture, leadership, and organizations: The GLOBE study of 62 societies*. Thousand Oaks, CA: SAGE.

Hsu, R., & Lopez, R. (2012, May 3). Beef industry grapples with PR. *Los Angeles Times*, p. B1.

Huan, C-L., & Chang, B-G. (2010). The effects of manager's moral philosophy on project decision under agency problem conditions. *Journal of Business Ethics, 94*, 595–611.

Hulsheger, U. R., Alberts, H. J. E. M., Feinholdt, A., & Lang, J. W. B. (2013). Benefits of mindfulness at work: The role of mindfulness in emotional regulation, emotional exhaustion, and job satisfaction. *Journal of Applied Psychology, 98*, 310–325.

Hulsheger, U. R., & Schewe, A. F. (2011). On the costs and benefits of emotional labor: A meta-analysis of three decades of research. *Journal of Occupational Health Psychology, 16*, 361–389.

Humphrey, J. (1989). No distant millennium: The international law of human rights. Paris, France: UNESCO.

Hunter, J. E., & Boster, F. (1987). A model of compliance-gaining message selection. *Communication Monographs, 54*, 63–84.

Hurtt, R. K. (2010). Development of a scale to measure professional skepticism. *Auditing: A Journal of Practice and Theory, 29*, 167–168.

Husted, B. W. (1999). Wealth, culture and corruption. *Journal of International Business Studies, 30*, 339–359.

Ihara, C. K. (2004). Are individual rights necessary? A Confucian perspective. In K.-L. Shun & D. B. Wong (Eds.), *Confucian ethics: A comparative study of self, autonomy, and community* (pp. 11–30). Cambridge, UK: Cambridge University Press.

Ihlen, O., Bartlett, J. L., & May, S. (2011). Corporate social responsibility and communication. In O. Ihlen, J. L. Bartlett, & S. May (Eds.), *The handbook of communication and corporate social responsibility* (pp. 3–22). Malden, MA: Wiley-Blackwell.

Ilies, R., Hauserman, N., Schwochau, S., & Stibal, J. (2003). Reported incidence rates of work-related sexual harassment in the United States: Using meta-analysis to explain reported rate disparities. *Personnel Psychology, 56*, 607–651.

Ilies, R., Morgeson, F. P., & Nahrgang, J. D. (2005). Authentic leadership and eudemonic well-being: Understanding leader–follower outcomes. *Leadership Quarterly, 16*, 373–394.

Imhof, M. (2004). Who are we as we listen? Individual listening profiles in varying contexts. *The International Journal of Listening, 18*, 36–45.

Inamori, T., & Analoui, F. (2010). Beyond Pygmalion effect: The role of managerial perception. *Journal of Management Development, 29*(4), 306–321.

Inch, E. S., & Warnick, B. (2002). *Critical thinking and communication: The use of reason in argument* (4th ed.). Boston, MA: Allyn & Bacon.

Infante, D. A. (1988). *Arguing constructively*. Long Grove, IL: Waveland Press.

Ip, P. K. (2009). Is Confucianism good for business ethics in China? *Journal of Business Ethics, 88*, 463–476.

Isaac, M. (2017a, January 31). What you need to know about #DeleteUber. *New York Times*.

Isaac, M. (2017b, February 22). Inside Uber's aggressive, unrestrained workplace culture. *New York Times*, p. A1.

Isaac, M. (2017c, June 21). Uber founder Travis Kalanick resigns as C.E.O. *New York Times*.

Isaksen, J. (2000). Constructing meaning despite the drudgery of repetitive work. *Journal of Humanistic Psychology, 40*, 84–197.

Isenhart, M. W., & Spangle, M. (2000). *Collaborative approaches to resolving conflict*. Thousand Oaks, CA: SAGE.

Isidor, C. (2015, March 12). West Coast port goes back to work. *CNN Money*.

Jacobs, M. (2016, April 29). James Arthur Ray, disgraced self-help guru, still hopes to "enlighten us." *Huffington Post*.

Jacobs, T. (2009, May). Morals authority. *Miller-McCune*, pp. 47–55.

Jaffee, S., & Shibley Hyde, J. (2000). Gender differences in moral orientation: A meta-analysis. *Psychological Bulletin, 126*, 703–726.

James, H. S. (2000). Reinforcing ethical decision making through organizational structure. *Journal of Business Ethics, 28*, 43–58.

Jamili, D. (2008). A stakeholder approach to corporate social responsibility: A fresh perspective into theory and practice. *Journal of Business Ethics, 82*, 213–231.

Janis, I. (1971, November). Groupthink: The problems of conformity. *Psychology Today*, pp. 271–279.

Janis, I. (1982). *Groupthink* (2nd ed.). Boston, MA: Houghton Mifflin.

Janis, I. (1989). *Crucial decisions: Leadership in policymaking and crisis management*. New York, NY: Free Press.

Jaramillo, F., Grisaffe, D. B., Chonko, L. B., & Roberts, J. A. (2009a). Examining the impact of servant leadership on sales force performance. *Journal of Personal Selling and Sales Management, 29*, 257–275.

Jaramillo, F., Grisaffe, D. B., Chonko, L. B., & Roberts, J. A. (2009b). Examining the impact of servant leadership on salesperson's turnover intention. *Journal of Personal Selling and Sales Management, 29*, 351–365.

Jarrett, J. L. (1991). *The teaching of values: Caring and appreciation*. London, UK: Routledge.

Jaska, J. A., & Pritchard, M. S. (1994). *Communication ethics: Methods of analysis*. Belmont, CA: Wadsworth.

Jassawalla, A. R., Malshe, A., & Sashittal, H. (2008). Student perceptions of social loafing in undergraduate business classroom teams. *Decision Sciences Journal of Innovative Education, 6*, 423–424.

Javidan, M., & House, R. J. (2001). Cultural acumen for the global manager: Lessons from Project GLOBE. *Organizational Dynamics, 29*, 289–305.

Jehn, K. A. (1995). A multimethod examination of the benefits and detriments of intragroup conflict. *Administrative Science Quarterly, 40*, 256–282.

Johannesen, R. L., Valde, K. S., & Whedbee, K. E. (2008). *Ethics in human communication* (6th ed.). Long Grove, IL: Waveland Press.

Johnson, C. E. (2000). Taoist leadership ethics. *Journal of Leadership Studies, 7*, 82–91.

Johnson, C. E. (2018). *Meeting the ethical challenges of leadership: Casting light or shadow* (6th ed.). Thousand Oaks, CA: SAGE.

Johnson, C. E., & Hackman, M. Z. (1995). *Creative communication: Principles and applications.* Prospect Heights, IL: Waveland Press.

Johnson, C. E., & Hackman, M. Z. (2018). *Leadership: A communication perspective* (7th ed.). Prospect Heights, IL: Waveland Press.

Johnson, C. E., & Shelton, P. (2014). Ethical leadership in the Age of Apology. *International Leadership Journal, 6*(3), 7–29.

Johnson, D. W. (1974). Communication and the inducement of cooperative behavior in conflicts: A critical review. *Speech Monographs, 41*, 64–78.

Johnson, D. W. (2012). Being open with and to other people. In J. Stewart (Ed.), *Bridges not walls: A book about interpersonal communication* (11th ed., pp. 209–218). New York, NY: McGraw-Hill.

Johnson, D. W., & Johnson, R. T. (1974). Instructional goal structure: Cooperative, competitive, or individualistic. *Review of Educational Research, 44*, 212–239.

Johnson, D. W., & Johnson, R. T. (2005). Training for cooperative group work. In M. A. West, D. Tjosvold, & K. G. Smith (Eds.), *The essentials of teamworking: International perspectives* (pp. 131–147). West Sussex, UK: Wiley.

Johnson, D. W., & Johnson, R. T. (2006). *Joining together: Group theory and group skills* (9th ed.). Boston, MA: Pearson.

Johnson, D. W., Maruyama, G., Johnson, R., Nelson, D., & Skon, L. (1981). Effects of cooperative, competitive, and individualistic goal structures on achievement: A meta-analysis. *Psychological Bulletin, 82*, 47–62.

Johnson, H. H. (2001). Corporate social audits—this time around. *Business Horizons, 44*, 29–37.

Johnson, R. A. (2002). *Whistleblowing: When it works—and why.* Boulder, CO: Lynne Rienner.

Jones, P. E., & Roelofsma, P. H. M. P. (2000). The potential for social contextual and group biases in team decision-making: Biases, conditions and psychological mechanisms. *Ergonomics, 43*, 1129–1152.

Jones, T. M. (1991). Ethical decision making by individuals in organizations: An issue-contingent model. *Academy of Management Review, 16*, 366–395.

Jose Serrano, American Eagle flight attendant, yells at passengers on intercom. (2012, June 29). *Huffington Post*.

Joseph, A. (2016, September 29). Amid *Denial*'s Hollywood fanfare, Deborah Lipstadt stays focused on spreading truth. *Times of Israel*.

Jurkiewicz, C. L., & Giacalone, R. A. (2004). A values framework for measuring the impact of workplace spirituality on organizational performance. *Journal of Business Ethics, 49*, 129–142.

Kador, J. (2009). *Effective apology: Mending fences, building bridges, and restoring trust*. Williston, VT: Berrett-Koehler.

Kang, E., Zardkoohi, A., Paetzold, R. L., & Fraser, D. (2011). Relationship banking and escalating commitments to bad loans. *Small Business Economics, 40*, 899–910.

Kann, D. (2017, April 18). Meet the top 10 CNN heroes of 2016. *CNN*.

Kant, I. (1964). *Groundwork of the metaphysics of morals* (H. J. Ryan, Trans.). New York, NY: Harper & Row.

Kanter, R. M. (1977). *Men and women of the corporation*. New York, NY: Basic Books.

Kanter, R. M. (1979, July–August). Power failure in management circuits. *Harvard Business Review*, pp. 65–75.

Kanter, R. M. (2001). An Abilene defense: Commentary one. *Organizational Dynamics, 33*, 37–40.

Kantor, K. (2013, April 16). GMO's: Pros and cons. *CNN*.

Kanungo, R. N., & Conger, J. A. (1993). Promoting altruism as a corporate goal. *Academy of Management Executive, 7*, 37–49.

Kaplan, R. (2014, May 21). Under pressure to respond, Obama addresses VA hospital scandal. *CBS News*.

Karakas, F. (2009). Spirituality and performance in organizations: A literature review. *Journal of Business Ethics, 94*, 89–106.

Karau, S. J., & Williams, K. D. (1993). Social loafing: A meta-analytic review and theoretical integration. *Journal of Personality and Social Psychology, 65*, 681–706.

Karau, S. J., & Williams, K. D. (2001). Understanding individual motivation in groups: The collective effort model. In M. Turner (Ed.), *Groups at Work: Theory and Research* (pp. 113–141). London, UK: Psychology Press.

Karimi, F. (2016, May 2). Ringling Bros. circus elephants perform last show. *CNN.com*.

Kasser, T. (2002). *The high price of materialism*. Cambridge, MA: Bradford/MIT Press.

Kasser, T., & Ahuvia, A. (2002). Materialist values and well-being in business students. *European Journal of Social Psychology, 32*, 137–146.

Kasser, T., Vansteenkiste, & Deckop, J. H. (2006). The ethical problems of a materialistic value orientation for businesses. In J. H. Deckop (Ed.), *Human resource management ethics* (pp. 283–303). Charlotte, NC: Information Age.

Kassing, J. W. (2002). Speaking up: Identifying employees' upward dissent strategies. *Management Communication Quarterly, 16*, 187–209.

Kassing, J. W. (2005). Speaking up competently: A comparison of perceived competence in upward dissent strategies. *Communication Research Reports, 22*, 227–234.

Kassing, J. W. (2007). Going around the boss: Exploring the consequences of circumvention. *Management Communication Quarterly, 21*, 55–74.

Kassing, J. W. (2009). "In case you didn't hear me the first time": An examination of repetitious upward dissent. *Management Communication Quarterly, 22*, 416–436.

Kassing, J. W. (2011). *Dissent in organizations*. Cambridge, UK: Polity Press.

Kassing, J., & Waldron, V. R. (2014). Incivility, destructive workplace behavior, and bullying. In L. L. Putnam & D. K Mumby (Eds.), *The SAGE handbook of organizational communication: Advances in theory, research, and methods* (3rd ed., pp. 643–664). Thousand Oaks, CA: SAGE.

Kaye, K. (2010, December 17). Why we freak out in the sky. *The Leader-Post* (Regina, Canada), p. C10.

Keashly, L., & Jagatic, K. (2011). North American perspectives on hostile behaviors and bullying at work. In S. Einarsen, H. Hoel, D. Zapf, & C. C. Cooper (Eds.), *Bullying and harassment in the workplace: Developments in theory, research and practice* (pp. 41–71). Boca Raton, FL: CRC Press.

Keil, M., Depledge, G., & Rai, A. (2007). Escalation: The role of problem recognition and cognitive bias. *Decision Science, 38*(3), 391–417.

Keil, M., & Montealegre, R. (2000, Spring). Cutting your losses: Extricating your organization when a big project goes awry. *Sloan Management Review*, pp. 55–58.

Kellerman, B. (2004). *Bad leadership: What it is, how it happens, why it matters*. Boston, MA: Harvard Business School Press.

Kellerman, B. (2015). *Hard times: Leadership in America*. Stanford, CA: Stanford University Press.

Keltner, D., Langner, C. A., & Allison, M. L. (2006). Power and moral leadership. In D. L. Rohde (Ed.), *Moral leadership: The theory and practice of power, judgment, and policy* (pp. 177–194). San Francisco, CA: Jossey-Bass.

Kenny, A. (2004). *Ancient philosophy* (Vol. 1). Oxford, UK: Clarenton Press.

Kernis, M. H. (2003). Toward a conceptualization of optimal self-esteem. *Psychological Inquiry, 14*, 1–26.

Kidwell, R. E. (2004). "Small" lies, big trouble: The unfortunate consequences of résumé padding, from Janet Cooke to George O'Leary. *Journal of Business Ethics, 51*, 175–184.

Kilpatrick, R. (2017, April 25). Pope Francis calls for humility and togetherness in surprise TED talk. *Time.com*.

King, A., & Bartels, W. (2015). Currents of change: The KPMG survey of corporate responsibility reporting 2015. *KPMG*.

King, D. L., Case, C. J., & Premo, K. M. (2011). A mission statement analysis comparing the United States and three other English speaking countries. *Academy of Strategic Management Journal, 10*, 21–45.

Kipnis, D., Schmidt, S. M., Swaffin-Smith, C., & Wilkinson, I. (1984). Patterns of managerial influence: Shotgun managers, tacticians, and bystanders. *Organizational Dynamics, 12*, 58–76.

Kirkman, B. L., & Rosen, B. (1999). Beyond self-management: Antecedents and consequences of team empowerment. *Academy of Management Journal, 42*, 58–74.

Kirkpatrick, W. K. (1992). Moral character: Story-telling and virtue. In R. T. Knowles & G. F. McLean (Eds.), *Psychological foundations of moral education and character development: An integrated theory of moral development* (pp. 169–184). Washington, DC: Council for Research in Values and Philosophy.

Klein, J. G., Smith, N. C., & John, A. (2004). Why we boycott: Consumer motivations for boycott participation. *Journal of Marketing, 68*, 92–109.

Kleiner, A. (2001, April). The dilemma doctors. *Strategy and Business.*

Kohlberg, L. A. (1984). *The psychology of moral development: The nature and validity of moral stages* (Vol. 2). New York, NY: Harper & Row.

Kohlberg, L. A. (1986). A current statement on some theoretical issues. In S. Modgil & C. Modgil (Eds.), *Lawrence Kohlberg: Consensus and controversy* (pp. 485–546). Philadelphia, PA: Falmer Press.

Kolb, R. W. (2010). Ethical implications of finance. In J. R. Boatright (Ed.), *Finance ethics: Critical issues in theory and practice* (pp. 23–43). Hoboken, NJ: Wiley.

Korosec, K. (2015, August 24). Ten times more deaths linked to faulty switch than GM first reported. *Fortune.com.*

Korschun, D. (2016, June 26). Corporate political activism: Why corporations are taking political stands more than ever. *Drexel University News Blog.*

Korthage, M. (2017, June 6). The battle over Kooks Burritos led to death threats and international outrage. We invited Portland chefs to weigh in. *Willamette Week.*

Kottasova, I. (2017, April 21). Facebook targets 30,000 fake accounts in France. *CNN.*

Kottler, J. A. (2000). *Doing good: Passion and commitment for helping others.* Philadelphia, PA: Brunner-Routledge.

Kottler, P., & Lee, N. (2005). *Corporate social responsibility.* Hoboken, NJ: Wiley.

Kracher, B., & Wells, D. L. (1998). Employee selection and the ethic of care. In M. Schminke (Ed.), *Managerial ethics: Management of people and processes* (pp. 81–97). Mahwah, NJ: Lawrence Erlbaum.

Kraimer, M. L. (1997). Organizational goals and values: A socialization mode. *Human Resource Management Review, 7*, 425–447.

Kravarik, J., & Sidner, S. (2016, December 8). Sweat lodge guru's attempted comeback angers victims. *CNN.com.*

Krell, E. (2013). Learning how to say "I'm sorry." *Baylor Business Review.*

Kresge, N. & Rauwald, C. (2016, January 12). VW CEO flubs interview with apology tour off to rocky start. *Bloomberg.*

Krisher, T. (2014, May 17). Why GM's $35 million fine is just the beginning. *Huffington Post.*

Kristof, A. L. (1996). Person-organization fit: An integrative review of its conceptualization, measurement, and implications. *Personnel Psychology, 49*(1), 1–49.

Kristof, N. (2010, November 19). Becoming our own version of a banana republic. *The Oregonian*, p. B7.

Kristof-Brown, A. L., Zimmerman, R. D., & Johnson, E. C. (2005). Consequences of individuals' fit at work: A meta-analysis of person-job, person-organization, person-group, and person-supervisor fit. *Personnel Psychology, 58*, 281–343.

Kung, H. (1998). *A global ethic for global politics and economics.* New York, NY: Oxford University Press.

Kurchner-Hawkins, R., & Miller, R. (2006). Organizational politics: Building positive political strategies in turbulent times. In E. Vigoda-Gadot & A. Drory (Eds.), *Handbook of organizational politics* (pp. 328–351). Cheltenham, UK: Edward Elgar.

Lacey, M. (2003, September 10). Africans' burden: West's farm subsidies. *New York Times*, p. A9.

Lacey, M. (2011, June 23). New age guru guilty in sweat lodge deaths. *New York Times*, p. 16.

Laczniak, G. R., & Murphy, P. E. (2006). Normative perspectives for ethical and socially responsible marketing. *Journal of Macromarketing, 26*, 154–177.

LaFasto, F., & Larson, C. (2001). *When teams work best.* Thousand Oaks, CA: SAGE.

Laing, R. D. (1994). Confirmation and disconfirmation. In R. Anderson, K. N. Cissna, & R. C. Arnett (Eds.), *The reach of dialogue: Confirmation, voice, and community* (pp. 73–78). Cresskill, NJ: Hampton Press.

Lake, E., & Flynn, E. (2017, April 13). You couldn't make it up. *The Sun* (UK).

Lamm, B. (2017, March 9). Scandal-plagued Uber is still dominating app stores. *The Atlantic.*

Lammers, J., Stapel, D. A., & Galinsky, A. D. (2010). Power increases hypocrisy: Moralizing in reasoning, immorality in behavior. *Psychological Science, 21*(5), 737–745.

Lang, K. E. (2016, May/June. Big changes at SeaWorld. *All Animals* (Humane Society of the United States).

Langenberg, E. A. (2013). Chinese guanxi and business ethics. In

C. Luetge (Ed.), *Handbook of the philosophical foundations of business ethics* (pp. 955–981). New York, NY: Springer.

Langer E. J. (2014). *Mindfulness* (25th Anniversary Edition). Boston, MA: De Capo Press.

Langer, E. J., & Burgoon, J. K. (1995). Language, fallacies, and mindlessness-mindfulness in social interaction. In B. Burleson (Ed.), *Communication yearbook 18* (pp. 83–104). Thousand Oaks, CA: SAGE.

Laplume, A. O., Sonpar, K., & Litz, R. A. (2008). Stakeholder theory: Reviewing a theory that moves us. *Journal of Management, 34*(6), 1152–1189.

Lapsley, D. K. (2008). Moral self-identity as the aim of education. In L. P. Nucci & D. Narvaez (Eds.), *Handbook of moral and character education* (pp. 30–52). New York, NY: Routledge.

Lapsley, D. K., & Hill, P. L. (2008). On dual processing and heuristic approaches to moral cognition. *Journal of Moral Education, 37*, 313–332.

Larrabee, M. J. (Ed.). (1993). *An ethic of care: Feminist and interdisciplinary perspectives*. New York, NY: Routledge.

Lau, D. C. (Trans.) (1970). *Mencius*. New York, NY: Penguin Books.

Lau, D. C. (Trans.) (1979). *The Analects*. New York, NY: Penguin Books.

Lauener, P. (2014, April 2). GM saved only a dollar per car by avoiding defective switch redesign. *RT*.

Lavelle, J. J., Folger, R., & Manegold, J.G. (2016). Delivering bad news: How procedural unfairness affects messengers' distancing and refusals. *Journal of Business Ethics, 136*, 43–55.

Lavoie, J. A. A., & Pychyl, T. A. (2001). Cyberslacking and the procrastination superhighway: A web-based survey of online procrastination, attitudes and emotion. *Social Science Computer Review, 12*, 431–444.

Lawrence, F., & Lidstone, J. (2016, January 24). Cyberbullying widespread amongst public servants. *The Conversation*.

Lawrence, Q., Whitney, E., & Tomsic, M. (2016, May 16). Despite $10B "fix," veterans are waiting even longer to see doctors. *NPR*.

Lax, D. A., & Sebenius, J. K. (2004). Three ethical issues in negotiation. In C. Menkel-Meadow & M. Wheeler (Eds.), *What's fair: Ethics for negotiators* (pp. 5–14). San Francisco, CA: Jossey-Bass.

Lazare, A. (2004). *On apology*. Oxford, UK: Oxford University Press.

Leary, M. R., & Kowalski, R. M. (1990). Impression management: A literature review and two-component model. *Psychological Bulletin, 107*, 34–47.

Lecci, S. (2016, September 28). Racial slurs force Mizzou to address continuing problems, a year after protests. *St. Louis Public Radio*.

Lee, K., & Allen, N. J. (2002). Organizational citizenship behavior and workplace deviance: The role of affect and cognitions. *Journal of Applied Psychology, 87*, 131–142.

Leidner, R. (1991). Selling hamburgers and selling insurance: Gender, work, and identity in interactive service jobs. *Gender and Society, 5*, 154–177.

Leidner, R. (1993). *Fast food, fast talk: Service work and the routinization of everyday life*. Berkeley: University of California Press.

Lennick, D. (2007). Emotional competence development and the bottom line: Lessons from American Express Financial Advisors. In R. Bar-On, J. G. Maree, & M. J. Elisa (Eds.) *Educating people to be emotionally intelligent* (pp. 199–210). Westport, CT: Praeger.

Leroy, H., Palanski, M. E., & Simons, T. (2012). Authentic leadership and behavioral integrity as drivers of follower commitment and performance. *Journal of Business Ethics, 107*, 255–264.

Leslie, L. Z. (2000). *Mass communication ethics: Decision-making in postmodern culture*. Boston, MA: Houghton Mifflin.

Levick, R. (2015, December 5). The "Trump Effect": Consumer boycotts could become pervasive on both sides. *Forbes*.

Levine, J. M., & Prislin, R. (2012). Majority and minority influence. In J. M. Levine (Ed.), *Group processes* (pp. 135–163). Hoboken, NJ: Taylor and Francis.

Levoy, G. (1997). *Callings: Finding and following an authentic life*. New York, NY: Three Rivers Press.

Levy, A. C., & Paludi, M. A. (2002). *Workplace sexual harassment* (2nd ed.). Upper Saddle River, NJ: Prentice Hall.

Lewicki, R. J., & Bunker, B. B. (1996). Developing and maintaining trust in work relationships. In

R. M. Kramer & T. R. Tyler (Eds.), *Trust in organizations: Frontiers of theory and research* (pp. 114–139). Thousand Oaks, CA: Sage.

Lewicki, R., Sanders, D. M. & Barry B. (2015). *Negotiation* (7th ed.). New York McGraw-Hill.

Lewis, M., & Lyall, S. (2013, August 24). Norway mass killer gets the maximum: 21 years. *New York Times*.

Li, Q. (2007). Bullying in the new playground: Research into cyberbullying and cyber victimization. *Australasian Journal of Education Technology, 23*, 435–454.

Liberto, J. (2014, April 1). Barra's recall apology not enough, families say. *CNN*.

Lim, V. K. G., & Chen, D. J. Q. (2012). Cyberloafing at the workplace: Gain or drain on work? *Behavior and Information Technology, 31*, 343–353.

Lincoln, N. D., Travers, C., Ackers, P., & Wilkinson, A. (2002). The meaning of empowerment: The interdisciplinary etymology of a new management concept. *International Journal of Management Reviews, 4*, 271–290.

Liopis, J., Gonzalez, M. R., & Gasco, J. L. (2007). Corporate governance and organizational culture: The role of ethics officers. *International Journal of Disclosure and Governance, 4*(2), 96–105.

Lipman-Blumen, J. (2005). *The allure of toxic leaders: Why we follow destructive bosses and corrupt politicians—And how we can survive them*. Oxford, UK: Oxford University Press.

Lipman-Blumen, J. (2008). Following toxic leaders: In search of posthumous praise. In R. E. Riggio, I. Chaleff, & J. Lipman-Blumen (Eds.), *The art of followership: How great followers create great leaders and organizations* (pp. 181–194). San Francisco, CA: Jossey-Bass.

Lipstadt, D. E. (2005). *History on trial: My day in court with a Holocaust denier*. New York, NY: Harper Perennial.

Lirbyson, F. (2009, October 24). Police probe deaths at "sweat lodge." *National Post*, p. A7.

Lister, L. M. (2007, December). A practical approach to fraud risk. *Internal Auditor*, pp. 61–65.

Liu, Y., Ferris, G. R., Xu, J., Weitz, B. A., & Perrewe, P. L. (2014). When ingratiation backfires: The role of political skill in the ingratiation-internship performance relationships. *Academy of Management Learning and Education, 13*, 569–586.

Locke, E. A., Tirnauer, D., Roberson, Q., Goldman, B., Lathan, M. E., & Weldon, E. (2001). The importance of the individual in an age of groupism. In M. E. Turner (Ed.), *Groups at work: Theory and research* (pp. 501–528). Mahwah, NJ: Lawrence Erlbaum.

Lockwood, A. L. (2009). *The case for character education: A developmental approach*. New York, NY: Teachers College Press.

Loe, T. W., Ferrell, L., & Mansfield, P. (2000). A review of empirical studies assessing ethical decision making in business. *Journal of Business Ethics, 25*, 185–204.

Loewenstein, J. J. (2013). Benefit corporations: A challenge in corporate governance. *Business Lawyer, 68*.

Lonergan, B. (1973). *Method in theology*. Toronto, Canada: University of Toronto Press.

Longnecker, J. G. (1985). Management priorities and management ethics. *Journal of Business Ethics, 4*, 65–70.

Lopes, P. N., Cote, S., & Salovey, P. (2006). An ability model of emotional intelligence: Implications for assessment and training. In V. J. Druskat, F. Sala, & G. Mount (Eds.), *Linking emotional intelligence and performance at work: Current research evidence with individuals and groups* (pp. 53–80). Mahwah, NJ: Lawrence Erlbaum.

Lowe, K. (2012, April 15). Last year he killed 77 people; now it's room service, his own suite and Japanese meditation. *London Mail*.

Lubit, R. (2002). The long-term organizational impact of destructively narcissistic managers. *Academy of Management Executive, 18*, 127–183.

Lumpkin, J. L. (2005, May 11). One-day halt called in Army recruiting. *My Plain View.com*.

Lupica, M. (2014, March 28). Steve Masiello, in limbo at Manhattan, latest coach to lie. *New York Daily News*.

Lutgen-Sandvik, P. (2006). Take this job and . . . : Quitting and other form of resistance to workplace bullying. *Communication Monographs, 73*, 406–433.

Luthans, F., & Avolio, B. J. (2009). The "point" of positive organizational behavior. *Journal of Organizational Behavior, 30*, 291–307.

Luthans, F., Youssef, C. M., & Avolio, B. J. (2006). *Psychological capital: Developing the human competitive edge.* Cary, NC: Oxford University Press.

Maak, T. (2009). The cosmopolitical corporation. *Journal of Business Ethics, 84,* 361–372.

Maak, T., & Pless, N. M. (2009). Business leaders as citizens of the world: Advancing humanism on a global scale. *Journal of Business Ethics, 88,* 537–550.

MacAvoy, P. W., & Millstein, I. M. (2003). *The current crisis in corporate governance.* New York, NY: Palgrave Macmillan.

MacFarquhar, L. (2015). *Strangers drowning: Grappling with impossible idealism, drastic choices, and the overpowering urge to help.* New York, NY: Penguin.

MacGregor, J., & Stuebs, M. (2014). The Silent Samaritan Syndrome: Why the whistle remains unblown. *Journal of Business Ethics, 120,* 149–164.

MacIntyre, A. (1984). *After virtue: A study in moral theory* (2nd ed.). Notre Dame, IN: University of Notre Dame Press.

MacLean, T. L. (2007). Framing and organizational misconduct: A symbolic interactionist study. *Journal of Business Ethics, 27,* 3–16.

Mahan, B. J. (2002). *Forgetting ourselves on purpose: Vocation and the ethics of ambition.* San Francisco, CA: Jossey-Bass.

Malhotra, D. (2004, May). Some alternatives to lying in negotiation. *Negotiation, 7*(5), 3–5.

Malik, K. (2017, June 14). In defense of cultural appropriation. *New York Times.*

Manjoo, F. (2015, August 5). "Right to be forgotten" online could spread. *New York Times.*

Manz, C. C., & Neck, C. P. (1995). Teamthink: Beyond the groupthink syndrome in self-managing work teams. *Journal of Managerial Psychology, 10,* 7–15.

Marainetti, O., & Passmore, J. (2010). Mindfulness at work: Paying attention to enhance well-being and performance. In P. A. Lineley, S. Harrington, & N. Garcea (Eds.), *Oxford handbook of positive psychology at work* (pp. 189–200). Oxford, UK: Oxford University Press.

Mares, R. (Ed.). (2004). *Business and human rights: A compilation of documents.* Leiden, Netherlands: Martinus Nijhoff.

Margolis, J. D., Grant, A. M., & Molinsky, A. L. (2007). Expanding the ethical standards of HRM: Necessary evils and the multiple dimensions of impact. In A. H. Pinnington, R. Macklin, & T. Campbell (Eds.), *Human resource management: Ethics and employment* (pp. 237–251). Oxford, UK: Oxford University Press.

Marinova, P. (2017 March 20). Here are all the executives who have left Uber in the last month. *Fortune.com.*

Markell, J. (2013, July 22). A new kind of corporation to harness the power of private enterprise for public benefit. *Huffington Post.*

Martin, H. (2012, May 25). Clothier's products all come in green. *Los Angeles Times,* p. B1.

Martin, J. (2002). *Organizational culture: Mapping the terrain.* Thousand Oaks, CA: SAGE.

Martin, K. D., & Cullen, J. B. (2006). Continuities and extensions of ethical climate theory: A meta-analytic review. *Journal of Business Ethics, 69,* 175–194.

Masnick, M. (2016, November 21). Theranos's insane campaign to punish whistleblower, who happened to be famous boardmember's grandson. *Techdirt.*

Mass, A., & Clark, R. D. (1984). Hidden impact of minorities: Fifteen years of minority influence research. *Psychological Bulletin, 95,* 428–450.

Matthews, C. (2016, December 28). The 5 biggest corporate scandals of 2016. *Fortune.com.*

May, D. R., Chan, A. Y. L., Hodges, T. D., & Avolio, B. J. (2003). Developing the moral component of authentic leadership. *Organizational Dynamics, 32,* 247–260.

May, D. R., & Pauli, K. P. (2002). The role of moral intensity in ethical decision-making: A review and investigation of moral recognition, evaluation and intention. *Business and Society, 41,* 84–117.

Mayer, D. M., Bardes, M., & Piccolo, R. F. (2008). Do servant-leaders help satisfy follower needs? An organizational justice perspective. *European Journal of Work and Organizational Psychology, 17*(2), 180–197.

Mayer, J. D., Caruso, D. R., & Salovey, P. (2000). Emotional intelligence meets traditional standards for an intelligence. *Intelligence, 27,* 267–298.

Mayer, J. D., & Salovey, P. (1993). The intelligence of emotional intelligence. *Intelligence, 17,* 433–442.

Mayer, J. D., & Salovey, P. (1995). Emotional intelligence and the construction and regulation of feelings. *Applied and Preventive Psychology, 4,* 197–208.

Mayer, J. D., & Salovey, P. (1997). What is emotional intelligence? In P. Salovey & D. J. Sluyter (Eds.), *Emotional development and emotional intelligence: Educational implications* (pp. 3–31). New York, NY: Basic Books.

Mayer, J. D., Salovey, P., & Caruso, D. R. (2004). Emotional intelligence: Theory, findings, and implications. *Psychological Inquiry, 15*(3), 197–215.

Mayer, J. D., Salovey, P., & Caruso, D. R. (2008). Emotional intelligence: New ability or eclectic traits? *American Psychologist, 63*(6), 503–517.

Mayer, R. C., & Davis, J. H. (1995). An integrative model of organizational trust. *Academy of Management Review, 29,* 709–734.

Mayhall, C. W., & Mayhall, T. B. (2004). *On Buber.* Belmont, CA: Wadsworth-Thomson Learning.

Maynard, M. (2014, June 5). "The GM Nod" and other cultural flaws exposed by the ignition defect report. *Forbes.*

McAllister, D. J. (1995). Affect- and cognition-based trust as foundations for interpersonal cooperation in organizations. *Academy of Management Journal, 38,* 24–61.

McCabe, D., & Trevino, L. K. (1993). Academic dishonesty: Honor codes and other contextual influences. *Journal of Higher Education, 64,* 522–569.

McCall, J. J. (2003). A defense of just cause dismissal rules. *Business Ethics Quarterly, 13*(2), 151–175.

McCuddy, M. K., & Cavin, M. C. (2008). Fundamental moral orientations, servant leadership, and leadership effectiveness: An empirical test. *Review of Business Research, 8*(4), 107–117.

McDonald, P. (2012). Workplace sexual harassment 30 years on: A review of the literature. *International Journal of Management Reviews, 14,* 1–17.

McFarlin, D. B., & Sweeney, P. D. (2000). *Where egos dare.* London, UK: Kogan Page.

McFarlin, D. B., & Sweeney, P. D. (2010). The corporate reflecting pool: Antecedents and consequences of narcissism in executives. In B. Schyns & T. Hansbrough (Eds.), *When leadership goes wrong: Destructive leadership, mistakes, and ethical failures* (pp. 247–283). Charlotte, NC: Information Age.

McGill, S., & Baetz, M. (2011). Technology use codes of conduct: Is it a choice between shaping the organizational culture and effective legal enforcement? *Employee Rights and Employment Policy Journal, 15,* 379–410.

McGregor, J. & Dwoskin, E. (2017, February 17). The cost of silence: Why more CEOs are speaking out in the Trump era. *Washington Post.*

McInnis, E. (2017, February 20). Voting with your dollar. *StudyBreaks.*

McKay, B. (2014). Facebook etiquette: 11 dos and don'ts. The list was reprinted at the following site: http://information-of-technology.blogspot.com/2011/06/facebook-etiquette-11-dos-and-don.html

McLean, B., & Elkind, P. (2003). *The smartest guys in the room: The amazing rise and fall of Enron.* New York, NY: Portfolio.

McMahon, J. M., & Harvey, R. J. (2006). An analysis of the factor structure of Jones' moral intensity construct. *Journal of Business Ethics, 64,* 381–404.

McNamara, G., Moon, H., & Bromiley, P. (2002). Banking on commitment: Intended and unintended consequences of an organization's attempt to attenuate escalation of commitment. *Academy of Management Journal, 45,* 443–452.

McNatt, D. B. (2000). Ancient Pygmalion joins contemporary management: A meta-analysis of the result. *Journal of Applied Psychology, 85,* 314–322.

McPhail, K. (2001). The other objective of ethics education: Re-humanising the accounting profession: A study of ethics education in law, engineering, medicine and accountancy. *Journal of Business Ethics, 34,* 279–298.

Mehta, S., & Pillay, R. (2011). Revisiting servant leadership: An empirical study in Indian context, *The Journal of Contemporary Management Research, 5,* 24–41.

Meisenbach, R. J. (2006). Habermas's discourse ethics and principle of universalization as a moral framework for organizational communication. *Management Communication Quarterly, 20*(1), 39–62.

Mellahi, K., & Wood, G. (2003). *The ethical business: Challenges and controversies.* New York, NY: Palgrave Macmillan.

Menzel, D. C. (2010). *Ethics moments in government: Cases and controversies.* Boca Raton, FL: CRC Press.

Miceli, M. P., Near, J. P., & Dworkin, T. M. (2008). *Whistle-blowing in organizations.* New York, NY: Routledge.

Miceli, M. P., Near, J. P., & Dworkin, T. M. (2009). A word to the wise: How managers and policy-makers can encourage employees to report wrongdoing. *Journal of Business Ethics, 86*, 379–396.

Michalos, A. C. (1995). *A pragmatic approach to business ethics.* Thousand Oaks, CA: SAGE.

Miethe, T. D. (1999). *Whistleblowing at work: Tough choices in exposing fraud, waste, and abuse on the job.* Boulder, CO: Westview Press.

Milgram, S. (1974). *Obedience to authority.* New York, NY: Harper & Row.

Miller, B. K., Rutherford, M. A., & Kolodinsky, R. W. (2008). Perceptions of organizational politics: A meta-analysis. *Journal of Business Psychology, 22*, 209–222.

Milton, L. P., & Westphal, J. D. (2005). Identity confirmation networks and cooperation in work groups. *Academy of Management Journal, 48*, 191–212.

Mintz, A., Mishal, S., & Mora, N. (2003). Evidence for polythink? The Israeli delegation at Camp David 2000. Illinois State University.

Mintz, A., & Wayne, C. (2016a). The polythink syndrome and elite group decision-making. *Advances in Political Psychology, 37*, 3–21.

Mintz, A., & Wayne, C. (2016b). *The polythink syndrome: U.S. foreign policy decisions on 9/11, Afghanistan, Iraq, Iran, Syria, and ISIS.* Stanford, CA: Stanford University Press.

Mintzberg, H. (2004). *Managers, not MBAs.* San Francisco, CA: Berrett-Koehler.

Mirvis, P., & Manga, J. (2010). Integrating corporate citizenship: Leading from them middle. In N. C. Smith, C.B. Bhattacharya, D. Vogel & D. I. Levine (eds.), *Global challenges in responsible business* (pp. 78–105). Cambridge UK: Cambridge University Press.

Mirvis, P. H. (1997). "Soul work" in organizations. *Organization Science, 8*, 193–206.

Mirvis, P. H., & Googins, B. (2006). Stages of corporate citizenship. *California Management Review, 48*, 104–126.

Mishra, A. K. (1996). Organizational responses to crisis: The centrality of trust. In R. M. Kramer & T. R. Tyler (Eds.), *Trust in organizations: Frontiers of theory and research* (pp. 261–287). Thousand Oaks, CA: SAGE.

Mitchell, C. (2003). *A short course in international business ethics: Combining ethics and profits in global business.* Novato, CA: World Trade Press.

Mole, B. (2016a, November 15). In searing $140M lawsuit, Walgreens alleges that Theranos broke every promise. *Ars Technica.*

Mole, B. (2016b, November 23). Beyond business: Disgraced Theranos bloodied family, friends, neighbors. *Ars Technica.*

Moll, J., de Oliveira-Souza, R., Zahn, R., & Grafman, J. (2008). The cognitive neuroscience of moral emotions. In W. Sinnott-Armstrong (Ed.), *Moral psychology: Vol. 3. The neuroscience of morality: Emotion, brain disorders, and development* (pp. 1–18). Cambridge, MA: MIT Press.

Monin, B., Pizarro, D. A., & Beer, J. S. (2007a). Deciding versus reacting: Conceptions of moral judgment and the reason-affect debate. *Review of General Psychology, 11*, 99–111.

Monin, B., Pizarro, D. A., & Beer, J. S. (2007b). Reason and emotion in moral judgment: Different prototypes lead to different theories. In K. D. Vohs, R. F. Baumeister, & G. Lowenstein (Eds.), *Do emotions help or hurt decision making? A hedgefoxian perspective* (pp. 219–244). New York, NY: Russell Sage Foundation.

Monks, R. A. G., & Minow, N. (2004). *Corporate governance* (3rd ed.). Malden, MA: Blackwell.

Moore, D. (2017, February 17). When does renaming a building make sense? *The Nation.com.*

Moore, T. (1992). *Care of the soul: A guide to cultivating depth and sacredness in everyday life.* New York, NY: HarperCollins.

Moore, T. (1995). Caring for the soul in business. In B. Defoore & J. Renesch (Eds.), *Rediscovering the soul of business: A renaissance of values* (pp. 341–356). San Francisco, CA: Sterling & Stone.

Moorhead, G., Neck, C. P., & West, M. S. (1998). The tendency toward defective decision making within self-managing teams: The relevance of groupthink for the 21st century. *Organizational Behavior and Human Decision Processes, 73*, 327–351.

Moreno, C. (2017, May 25). Portland burrito cart closes after owners of cultural appropriation. *HuffPost.*

Morris, J. A., Brothridge, C. M., & Urbanski, J. C. (2005). Bringing humility to leadership: Antecedents and consequences of leader humility. *Human Relations, 58*(10), 1323–1350.

Moscovici, S., Mucchi-Faina, A., & Mass, A. (1994). *Minority influence.* Chicago, IL: Nelson-Hall.

Moscovici, S., Mugny, G., & Van Avermaet, D. (Eds.). (1985). *Perspectives on minority influence.* Cambridge, UK: Cambridge University Press.

Moskovitz, D. (2015, August 17). The Baylor football sexual assault trial you haven't heard about. *DeadSpin.*

Mount, I. (2016, October 12). Wells Fargo's fake accounts may go back to 2005. *Fortune.com.*

Moxley, R. S. (2004). Hardships. In C. D. McCauley, R. S. Moxley, & E. Van Velsor (Eds.), *Handbook of leadership development* (2nd ed., pp. 183–204). San Francisco, CA: Jossey-Bass.

Moyn, S. (2015, November 5). The beauty and the costs of extreme altruism. *The Nation.*

Mugny, G., & Perez, J. A. (1991). *The social psychology of minority influence* (V. W. Lamongie, Trans.). Cambridge, UK: Cambridge University Press.

Mulhall, S., & Swift, A. (1992). *Liberals and communitarians.* Oxford, UK: Blackwell.

Muller, J. (2014, June 17). CEO Mary Barra: "It's past time" to fix GM's problems. *Forbes.*

Munrol, N. (2002). Patient-lobbyists divided over cloning. *National Journal, 34,* 1490–1491.

Murdock, H. (2008, August). The three dimensions of fraud. *Internal Auditor,* pp. 81, 83.

Murphy, P. E., Laczniak, G. R., Bowie, N. E., & Klein, T. A. (2005). *Ethical marketing.* Upper Saddle River, NJ: Pearson Education.

Muslea, R. (2006, August/September). Profile: Deborah Lipstadt. *Hadassah.*

Muzaffar, C. (2002). Conclusion. In P. F. Knitter & C. Muzaffar (Eds.), *Subverting greed: Religious perspectives on the global economy* (pp. 154–172). Maryknoll, NY: Orbis Books.

Myers, J. (2016, August 19). Foreign aid: These countries are the most generous. World Economic Forum. Retrieved from https://www.weforum.org/agenda/2016/08/foreign-aid-these-countries-are-the-most-generous/

Nadisic, T. (2008). The Robin Hood effect: Antecedents and consequences of managers using invisible remedies to correct workplace injustice. In S. W. Gilliland, D. D. Steiner, & D. P. Skarlicki (Eds.), *Justice, morality, and social responsibility* (pp. 125–153). Charlotte, NC: Information Age Publishing.

Nadkarni, R. (2015, November 9). Why Missouri's football team joined a protest against school administration. *SI.com.*

Narvaez, D. (2006). Integrative ethical education. In M. Killen & J. G. Smetana (Eds.), *Handbook of moral development* (pp. 703–733). Mahwah, NJ: Lawrence Erlbaum.

Narvaez, D. (2009). *Ethical action: Nurturing character in the classroom.* Notre Dame: IN: Alliance for Catholic Education Press.

Narvaez, D., & Lapsley, D. K. (2005). The psychological foundations of morality and moral expertise. In D. K. Lapsley & F. C. Power (Eds.), *Character psychology and character education* (pp. 140–165). Notre Dame, IN: University of Notre Dame Press.

Narvaez, D., & Vaydich, J. L. (2008). Moral development and behaviour under the spotlight of the neurobiological sciences. *Journal of Moral Education, 37*(2), 289–312.

Nash, L. (1990). *Good intentions aside: A manager's guide to resolving ethical problems.* Boston, MA: Harvard Business School Press.

Neate, R. (2015, November 9). SeaWorld to end killer whale shows in wake of mounting protests. *The Guardian.*

Nelson, M. W. (2009). A model and literature review of professional skepticism in auditing. *Auditing: A Journal of Practice & Theory, 28,* 1–34.

Nemeth, C. (1985). Dissent, group process and creativity: The contribution of minority influence research. In E. Lawler (Ed.), *Advances in group processes* (Vol. 2, pp. 57–75). Greenwich, CT: JAI.

Nemeth, C., & Chiles, C. (1986). Modeling courage: The role of dissent in fostering independence. *European Journal of Social Psychology, 18,* 275–280.

Neuhaus, L. (2017, January 16). Without elephants, the circus couldn't go on, Ringling Bros. officials say. *Los Angeles Times.*

Neuman, J. H. (2004). Injustice, stress, and aggression in organizations. In R. W. Griffin & A. M. O'Leary-Kelly (Eds.), *The dark side of organizational behavior* (pp. 62–102). San Francisco, CA: Jossey-Bass.

Neuman, J. H., & Baron, R. A. (1997). Aggression in the workplace.

In R. A. Giacalone & J. Greenberg (Eds.), *Antisocial behavior in organizations* (pp. 37–67). Thousand Oaks, CA: SAGE.

Neumann, V. (2017, May 31). How Goldman Sachs is ruining my Venezuela. *Daily Beast*.

New Orleans Confederate statues' removal ends a long-running battle. (2017, May 20). *NPR*.

Newcomer, E. (2017, March 21). Uber's messy breakup complicates search for COO. *Bloomberg*.

Newsome, M. (2017, April 25). Is removing confederate monuments like erasing history? *NBC News*.

Newton, L. H. (2005). *Business ethics and the natural environment*. Malden, MA: Blackwell.

Nichols, M. (2014). *The lost art of listening*. New York, NY: Guilford Press.

Njus, E. (2012, July 26). At trial, longshore union blames Port of Portland, terminal operator for driving away business. *The Oregonian/OregonLive*.

Njus, E. (2017, February 28). Port of Portland to split with ICTSI, seek new life for idled shipping terminal. *The Oregonian/Oregon Live*.

Nixey, C. (2012, April 16). We don't talk much about revenge. *The Times* (London), pp. T4–T5.

Noddings, N. (2003). *Caring: A feminine approach to ethics and moral education*. Berkeley: University of California Press.

Nomura admits part in Goldman Venezuelan bond deal. (2017, June 1). *BBC*.

Novak, M. (2003). A universal culture of human rights and freedom's habits: Caritapolis. In J. H. Dunning (Ed.), *Making globalization good: The moral challenges of global capitalism* (pp. 253–279). Oxford, UK: Oxford University Press.

Nutt, P. (2002). *Why decisions fail*. San Francisco, CA: Berrett-Koehler.

Oatley, K. (2008). The mind's flight simulator. *Psychologist, 21*, 1030–1032.

O'Boyle, E. H., Humphrey, R. H., Pollack, J. M., Hawver, T. H., & Story, P. A. (2011). The relation between emotional intelligence and job performance: A meta-analysis. *Journal of Organizational Behavior, 32*, 788–818.

O'Connor, E. S. (1997). Compelling stories: Narrative and the production of the organizational self. In O. F. Williams (Ed.), *The moral imagination: How literature and films can stimulate ethical reflection in the business world* (pp. 185–202). Notre Dame, IN: University of Notre Dame Press.

Offermann, L. R. (2004, January). When followers become toxic. *Harvard Business Review*, pp. 55–60.

Offermann, L. R., & Malamut, A. B. (2002). When leaders harass: The impact of target perceptions of organizational leadership and climate on harassment reporting and outcomes. *Journal of Applied Psychology, 87*, 885–893.

Offermann L, & Rosh, L. (2012, June 13). Building trust through skillful self-disclosure. *Harvard Business Review*.

O'Leary, R. (2009, January/February). When a career public servant sues the agency he loves: Claude Ferguson, the forest Service, and off-road vehicles in the Hoosier National Forest. *Public Administration Review*, pp. 1068–1076.

O'Leary, R. (2010, January/February). Guerrilla employees: Should managers nurture, tolerate, or terminate them? *Public Administration Review*, pp. 8–19.

O'Leary, R. (2014). *The ethics of dissent: Managing guerrilla government*. Washington, DC: CQ Press.

O'Leary-Kelly, A. M. (2001). Sexual harassment as unethical behavior: The role of moral intensity. *Human Resource Management Review, 11*, 73–92.

O'Leary-Kelly, A. M., Griffin, R. W., & Glew, D. J. (1996). Organization-motivated aggression: A research framework. *Academy of Management Review, 21*, 225–253.

O'Leary-Kelly, A. M., Paetzold, R. L., & Griffin, L. W. (2000). Sexual harassment as aggressive behavior: An actor-based perspective. *Academy of Management Review, 25*, 372–388.

Oman, D. (2013). Defining religion and spirituality. In R. F. Paloutzian & C. L. Park (Eds.), *Handbook of the psychology of religion and spirituality* (2nd ed., pp. 23–47). New York, NY: Guilford Press.

One year after protest rocked Missouri, the effects on the football team and university remain tangible. (2016, November 8). *SI.com*.

O'Neill, A. (2013, July 13). They're watching as guru in sweat lodge case goes free. *CNN*.

Opotow, S. (1990a). Deterring moral exclusion. *Journal of Social Issues, 46*, 173–182.

Opotow, S. (1990b). Moral exclusion and injustice: An introduction. *Journal of Social Issues, 46*, 1–20.

Opotow, S. (1995). Drawing the line: Social categorization, moral exclusion, and the scope of justice. In B. B. Bunker & J. Z. Rubin (Eds.), *Conflict, cooperation, and justice: Essays inspired by the work of Morton Deutsch* (pp. 347–369). San Francisco, CA: Jossey-Bass.

Opotow, S. (2005). Hate, conflict, and moral exclusion. In R. J. Sternberg (Ed.), *The psychology of hate* (pp. 121–154). Washington, DC: American Psychological Association.

Opotow, S., Gerson, J., & Woodside, S. (2005). From moral exclusion to moral inclusion: Theory for teaching peace. *Theory into Practice, 44*(4), 303–318.

Opotow, S., & Weiss, L. (2000). Denial and the process of moral exclusion in environmental conflict. *Journal of Social Issues, 56*(3), 475–490.

O'Reilly, J., & Aquino, K. (2011). A model of third parties' morally motivated responses to mistreatment in organizations. *Academy of Management Review, 36,* 526–543

Organ, D. W. (1988). *Organizational citizenship behavior: The good soldier syndrome*. Lexington, MA: Lexington Books.

Ogrysko, N. (2017, May 31). Shulkin details 13 areas of improvement in his diagnosis of VA. *FederalNewsRadio.com*.

The origin of the term "going postal." (2011, September 19). *Today I Found Out*.

Orrick, Herrington & Sutcliffe LLP. (2016, June). Balancing purpose and profit: Legal mechanisms to lock in social mission for "profit with purpose businesses across the G8: Addendum: Review of legal and policy developments since 2014.

Ortega, B. (2011, November 19). James Arthur Ray gets prison time in sweat-lodge deaths. *The Arizona Republic*.

Osland, J. S., Franco, S de, & Osland, A. (2000). Organizational implications of Latin American culture: Lessons for the expatriate manager. *Journal of Management Inquiry, 8,* 219–234.

Oz, S., & Eden, D. (1994). Restraining the Golem: Boosting performance by changing the interpretation of low scores. *Journal of Applied Psychology, 79,* 744–754.

Packer, D. J. (2009). Avoiding groupthink: Whereas weakly identified members remain silent, strongly identified members dissent about collective problems. *Psychological Science, 20*(5), 546–548.

Padilla, A., Hogan, R., & Kaiser, R. B. (2007). The toxic triangle: Destructive leaders, susceptible followers, and conducive environments. *Leadership Quarterly, 18,* 176–194.

Paine, L. S. (1996a, March–April). Managing for organizational integrity. *Harvard Business Review*, pp. 106–117.

Paine, L. S. (1996b). Moral thinking in management: An essential capability. *Business Ethics Quarterly, 6*(4), 477–492, 477.

Paine, L. S. (2003). *Value shift: Why companies must merge social and financial imperatives to achieve superior performance*. New York, NY: McGraw-Hill.

Paine, L. S., Deshpande, R., Margolis, J. D., & Bettcher, K. E. (2005, December). Up to code. *Harvard Business Review*, pp. 122–133.

Parboteeah, K. P., Martin, K. D., & Cullen, J. B. (2011). An international perspective on ethical climate. In N. M. Ashkanasy, C. P. M. Wilderon, & M. F. Peterson (Eds.), *The handbook of organizational culture and climate* (2nd ed., pp. 600–616). Thousand Oaks, CA: SAGE.

Park, N., & Peterson, C. M. (2003). Virtues and organizations. In K. S. Cameron, J. E. Dutton, & R. E. Quinn (Eds.), *Positive organizational scholarship: Foundations of a new discipline* (pp. 33–47). San Francisco, CA: Berrett-Koehler.

Park, W. W. (2000). A comprehensive empirical investigation of the relationships among variables of the groupthink model. *Journal of Organizational Behavior, 21,* 873–887.

Parris, D. L., & Peachey, J. W. (2013). A systematic literature review of servant leadership theory in organizational contexts. *Journal of Business Ethics, 113,* 377–393.

Pastin, M. (2017, January 20). The surprise ethics lesson of Wells Fargo. *Huffington Post*.

Paulus, D. L., & Williams, K. M. (2002). The dark triad of personality: Narcissism, Machiavellianism, and psychopathy. *Journal of Research in Personality, 36,* 556–563.

Pearce, M. (2015, October 11). Hunger striker gives credit to fellow activists fighting racism at University of Missouri. *Los Angeles Times*.

Pearson, C. M., & Porath, C. L. (2004). On incivility, its impact, and directions for future research. In R. W. Griffin & A. M. O'Leary-Kelly (Eds.), *The dark side of organizational behavior* (pp. 23–61). San Francisco, CA: Jossey-Bass.

Pearson, C. M., & Porath, C. L. (2005). On the nature, consequences and remedies of workplace incivility: No time for "nice"? Think again. *Academy of Management Executive, 19*, 7–18.

Pearson, G. (1995). *Integrity in organizations: An alternative business ethic*. London, UK: McGraw-Hill.

Pearson, M. (2015, November 10). Top officials resign at University of Missouri. *CNN.com*.

Pekerti, A. A., & Sendjaya, S. (2010). Exploring servant leadership across cultures: Comparative study in Australia and Indonesia. *International Journal of Human Resource Management, 21*, 754–780.

Perez, E. (2014, June 11). FBI launches criminal probe of VA. *CNN*.

Perloth, N., & Sanger, D. E. (2017, June 29). Hacks raise fear of N.S.A. control. *New York Times*.

Perrewe, P. L., Ferris, G. R., Stoner, J. S., & Brouer, R. L. (2007). The positive role of political skill in organizations. In D. Nelson & C. L. Cooper (Eds.), *Positive organizational behavior* (pp. 117–128). London, UK: SAGE.

Peterson, C., & Pakr, N. (2009). Classifying and measuring strengths of character. In S. J. Lopez & C. R. Snyder (Eds.), *Oxford handbook of positive psychology* (2nd ed., pp. 25–33). New York, NY: Oxford University Press.

Peterson, C., Stephens, J. P., Park, N., Lee, F., & Seligman, M. E. P. (2010). Strengths of character and work. In P. A. Linley, S. Harrington, & N. Garcea (Eds.), *Oxford handbook of positive psychology and work*

(pp. 221–231). Oxford, UK: Oxford University Press.

Peterson, D. K. (2002). The relationship between unethical behavior and the dimensions of the Ethical Climate Questionnaire. *Journal of Business Ethics, 41*, 313–326.

Peterson, E. A., & Patel, D. S. (2016). Benefit corporations: Fostering socially conscious corporate leadership. *Southern Journal of Business and Ethics, 48*, 92–197.

Petrick, J. A. (2008). Using the business integrity capacity model to advance business ethics education. In D. L. Swanson & D. G. Fisher (Eds.), *Advancing business ethics education* (pp. 103–124). Charlotte, NC: Information Age.

Petrick, J. A. (2011). The measured impact of the transtheoretical model of educational change on advancing business ethics education. In D. L. Swanson & D. G. Fisher (Eds.), *Toward assessing business ethics education* (pp. 335–360). Charlotte, NC: Information Age.

Pew Research Center. (2017, July 11). Online harassment 2017.

Pfeffer, J. (1998). *The human equation: Building profits by putting people first*. Boston, MA: Harvard Business School Press.

Phillips, R. (2003). *Stakeholder theory and organizational ethics*. San Francisco, CA: Berrett-Koehler.

Piliavin, J. A., & Charng, H.-W. (1990). Altruism: A review of recent theory and research. *American Sociological Review, 16*, 27–65.

Pillmore, E. M. (2003, December). How we're fixing up Tyco. *Harvard Business Review*, pp. 96–97.

Piper, T. R., Gentile, M. C., & Parks, S. D. (1993). *Can ethics be taught? Perspectives, challenges, and approaches at Harvard Business School*. Boston, MA: Harvard Business School Press.

Pittinsky, T. L. (2010, April). A two-dimensional model of intergroup leadership: The case of national diversity. *American Psychologist*, pp. 194–200.

Ponemon, L. A. (1990). Ethical judgments in accounting: A cognitive-developmental perspective. *Critical Perspectives on Accounting, 1*, 191–215.

Ponemon, L. A. (1992). Ethical reasoning and selection-socialization in accounting. *Accounting, Organizations and Society, 17*(3/4), 239–258.

Porath, C. (2014). Half of employees don't feel respected by their bosses. *Harvard Business Review*.

Posner, B. Z. (2010). Another look at the impact of personal and organizational values congruency. *Journal of Business Ethics, 97*, 535–541.

Post, S. G. (2002). The tradition of agape. In S. G. Post, L. G. Underwood, J. P. Schloss, & W. B. Hurlbut (Eds.), *Altruism and altruistic love: Science, philosophy, and religion in dialogue* (pp. 51–64). Oxford, UK: Oxford University Press.

Post, S. G., Underwood, L. G., Schloss, J. P., & Hurlbut, W. B. (2002). General introduction. In S. G. Post, L. G. Underwood, J. P. Schloss, & W. B. Hurlbut (Eds.), *Altruism and altruistic love: Science, philosophy, and religion in dialogue* (pp. 3–12). Oxford, UK: Oxford University Press.

Postmes, T., Spears, R., & Cihangir, S. (2001). Quality of decision-making and group norms. *Journal of Personality and Social Psychology, 80*, 918–930.

Povoledo, E., & Bilefsky, D. (2013, September 9). The pope gets on the line, and everyone is talking. *New York Times*.

Powell, M. (2016, December 4). All sins forgiven on the altar of football. *New York Times*, p. SP1.

Preble, J. F., & Reichel, A. (1988). Attitudes towards business ethics of future managers in the U.S. and Israel. *Journal of Business Ethics, 7*, 941–949.

Prehn, K., & Heekeren, H. R. (2009). Moral judgment and the brain: A functional approach to the question of emotion and cognition in moral judgment integrating psychology, neuroscience and evolutionary biology. In J. Verplatetse, J. Schrijver, S. Vanneste, & J. Braeckman (Eds.), *The moral brain: Essays on the evolutionary and neuroscientific aspects of morality* (pp. 129–154). London, UK: Springer.

Preston, B. (2013, September 12). Wheelies: The papal beater car edition. *New York Times Blog*.

Price, S. (2017, February 8). What CEOs need to know as we enter a new era of corporate activism. *Forbes*.

Priddle, A., & Bomey, N. (2014, April 22). GM restructures engineering team to better respond to safety problems. *Detroit Free Press*.

Prinz, J. J., & Nichols, S. (2010). Moral emotions. In J. M. Doris (Ed.), *The moral psychology handbook* (pp. 111–146). New York, NY: Oxford University Press.

Social Impact Investment Taskforce. (2014, September). Profit-with-purpose businesses.

Provis, C. (2004). *Ethical organisational politics*. Cheltenham, UK: Edward Elgar.

Provis, C. (2010). Virtuous decision making for business ethics. *Journal of Business Ethics, 91*, 3–16.

Quigley, N. R., Sully de Luque, M., & House, R. J. (2005). Responsible leadership and governance in a global context: Insights from the GLOBE study. In J. P. Doh & S. A. Stumpf (Eds.), *Handbook on responsible leadership and governance in global business* (pp. 352–379). Cheltenham, UK: Edward Elgar.

Radin, T. J., & Werhane, P. H. (2003). Employment-at-will, employee rights, and future directions for employment. *Business Ethics Quarterly, 13*(2), 113–130.

Rafaeli, A., & Sutton, R. I. (1989). The expression of emotion in organizational life. In L. L. Cummings & B. M. Staw (Eds.), *Research in organizational behavior* (Vol. 2, pp. 1–42). Greenwich, CT: JAI.

Rahim, M. A. (1983). A measure of styles of handling interpersonal conflict. *Academy of Management Journal, 26*, 368–376.

Rahim, M. A. (2011). *Managing conflict in organizations* (4th ed.). New Brunswick, NJ: Transaction.

Rahim, M. A., Buntzman, G. F., & White, D. (1999). An empirical study of the stages of moral development and conflict management styles. *International Journal of Conflict Management, 10*, 154–171.

Rahim, M. A., Garrett, J. E., & Buntzman, G. F. (1992). Ethics of managing interpersonal conflict in organizations. *Journal of Business Ethics, 11*, 423–432.

Rahim, M. A., & Magner, N. R. (1995). Confirmatory factor analysis of the styles of handling interpersonal conflict: First-order factor model and its invariance across groups. *Journal of Applied Psychology, 80*(1), 122–132.

Ramsey, L. (2016, September 20). The EpiPen pricing scandal just got even more complicated for the CEO and her family at the heart of it. *Business Insider*.

Randolph, W. A. (2000). Re-thinking empowerment: Why is it so hard to achieve? *Organizational Dynamics, 29*, 94–107.

Rawls, J. (1971). *A theory of justice*. Cambridge, MA: Belknap Press.

Rawls, J. (1993a). Distributive justice. In T. Donaldson & P. H. Werhane (Eds.), *Ethical issues in business: A philosophical approach* (4th ed., pp. 274–285). Englewood Cliffs, NJ: Prentice Hall.

Rawls, J. (1993b). *Political liberalism*. New York, NY: Columbia University Press.

Rawls, J. (2001). *Justice as fairness: A restatement* (E. Kelly, Ed.). Cambridge, MA: Belknap Press.

Rayburn, C. A. (1997). Vocation as calling. In D. P. Bloch & L. J. Richmond (Eds.), *Connections between spirit and work in career development* (pp. 162–183). Palo Alto, CA: Davies-Black.

Rego, A., & Pina e Cunha, M. (2008). Workplace spirituality and organizational commitment: An empirical study. *Journal of Organizational Change Management, 21*(1), 53–75.

Reina, D. S., & Reina, M. L. (2006). *Trust and betrayal in the workplace.* San Francisco, CA: Berrett-Koehler.

Reinghold, J. (2016, March 4). Management changes at Medium. *Fortune.com.*

Rest, J. R. (1979). *Development in judging moral issues.* Minneapolis: University of Minnesota Press.

Rest, J. R. (1986). *Moral development: Advances in research and theory.* New York, NY: Praeger.

Rest, J. R. (1994). Background: Theory and research. In J. R. Rest & D. Narvaez (Eds.), *Moral development in the professions: Psychology and applied ethics* (pp. 1–25). Hillsdale, NJ: Lawrence Erlbaum.

Rest, J. R., & Narvaez, D. (1991). The college experience and moral development. In W. M. Kurtines & J. L. Gewirtz (Eds.), *Handbook of moral behavior and development. Vol. 2: Research* (pp. 229–245). Hillsdale, NJ: Lawrence Erlbaum.

Rest, J. R., Narvaez, D., Bebeau, M. J., & Thoma, S. J. (1999). *Postconventional moral thinking: A neo-Kohlbergian approach.* Mahwah, NJ: Lawrence Erlbaum.

Reuters (2016, December 13). Former Fox News chief Roger Ailes faces new sexual harassment allegations. *Fortune.com.*

Reuters. (2017, January 16). The world's 8 richest men are now as wealthy as half the world's population. *Fortune.com.*

Reynolds, D. (2007). Restraining Golem and harnessing Pygmalion in the classroom: A laboratory study of managerial expectations and task design. *Academy of Management Learning & Education, 6*(4), 475–483.

Reynolds, S. J. (2006a). A neurocognitive model of the ethical decision-making process: Implications for study and practice. *Journal of Applied Psychology, 91,* 737–748.

Reynolds, S. J. (2006b). Moral awareness and ethical predispositions: Investigating the role of individual differences in the recognition of moral issues. *Journal of Applied Psychology, 91,* 233–245.

Reynolds, S. J., & Ceranic, T. L. (2007). The effects of moral judgment and moral identity on moral behavior: An empirical examination of the moral individual. *Journal of Applied Psychology, 92*(6), 1610–1624.

Rezaee, A. (2009). *Corporate governance and ethics.* Hoboken, NJ: Wiley.

Rice, D., & Dreilinger, C. (1990, May). Rights and wrongs of ethics training. *Training and Development Journal,* pp. 103–108.

Richards, T. (2017, May 2). VA fires embattled Louisiana director amid scandal, secret wait lists. *Fox News.*

Richardson, B. K., & McGlynn, J. (2011). Rabid fans, death threats, and dysfunctional stakeholders: The influence of organizational and industry contexts on whistle-blowing cases. *Management Communication Quarterly, 25,* 121–150.

Roberto, M. A. (2002). Lessons from Everest: The interaction of cognitive bias, psychological safety, and system complexity. *California Management Review, 45*(1), 136–158.

Robertson, M. (2014). *Sustainability: Principles and practice.* Hoboken, NJ: Taylor and Francis.

Robins, R. (2006). The challenge of TBL: A responsibility to whom? *Business and Society Review, 111,* 1–14.

Robins, S. P., & Judge, T. A. (2011). *Organizational behavior* (14th ed.). Boston, MA: Prentice Hall.

Rogers, E. M., & Steinfatt, T. M. (1999). *Intercultural communication.* Long Grove, IL: Waveland Press.

Roloff, M. E., & Paulson, G. D. (2001). Confronting organizational transgressions. In J. M. Darley, D. M. Messick, & T. R. Tyler (Eds.), *Social influences on ethical behavior in organizations* (pp. 53–68). Mahwah, NJ: Lawrence Erlbaum.

Romar, E. J. (2002). Virtue is good business: Confucianism as a practical business ethics. *Journal of Business Ethics, 38,* 119–131.

Romar, E. J. (2004). Globalization, ethics, and opportunism: A Confucian view of business relationships. *Business Ethics Quarterly, 14,* 663–678.

Romero, S., & Neuman, W. (2013, March 18). Starting a papacy, amid echoes of a 'Dirty War.' *New York Times,* p. A1.

Rosenfeld, P., Giacalone, R. A., & Riordan, C. A. (1995). *Impression management in organizations: Theory, measurement, practice.* London, UK: Routledge.

Rosenthal, R. (1993). Interpersonal expectations: Some antecedents and some consequences. In P. D. Blanck (Ed.), *Interpersonal expectations: Theory, research, and applications* (pp. 3–24). Cambridge, UK: Cambridge University Press.

Rosenthal, R., & Jacobson, L. (1968). *Pygmalion in the classroom.* New York, NY: Holt, Rinehart & Winston.

Rosh, L., & Offermann, L. (2013, October). Be yourself, but carefully. *Harvard Business Review*.

Ross, J., & Staw, B. M. (1993). Organizational escalation and exit: Lessons from the Shoreham Nuclear Plant. *Academy of Management Journal, 36*, 701–732.

Ross, W. T., & Robertson, D. C. (2000). Lying: The impact of decision context. *Business Ethics Quarterly, 10*, 409–440.

Rossano, M. J. (2012). The essential role of ritual in the transmission and reinforcement of social norms. *Psychological Bulletin, 138*, 529–549.

Rothwell, J. D. (1998). *In mixed company: Small group communication* (3rd ed.). Fort Worth, TX: Harcourt Brace.

Rubin, J. Z., & Brown, B. R. (1975). *The social psychology of bargaining and negotiation*. New York, NY: Academic Press.

Ruedy, N. E., & Schweitzer, M. E. (2010). In the moment: The effect of mindfulness on ethical decision-making. *Journal of Business Ethics, 95*, 73–87.

Runde, C. E., & Flanagan, T. A. (2007). *Becoming a conflict competent leader*. San Francisco, CA: Jossey-Bass.

Runde, C. E., & Flanagan, T. A. (2008, Winter). Conflict competent leadership. *Leader to Leader*, pp. 46–51.

Ruschman, N. L. (2002). Servant-leadership and the best companies to work for in America. In L. C. Spears & M. Lawrence (Eds.), *Focus on leadership: Servant-leadership for the twenty-first century* (pp. 123–139). New York, NY: Wiley.

Ryan, L. V., Buchholtz, A. K., & Kolb, R. W. (2010). New directions in corporate governance and finance: Implications for business ethics research. *Business Ethics Quarterly, 20*(4), 673–694.

Salin, D. (2013). Bullying and well-being. In R. A. Giacalone & M. D. Promiso (Eds.), *Handbook of unethical work behavior: Implications for individual well-being* (pp. 73–88). Armonk, NY: M. E. Sharpe.

Salls, H. (2007). *Character education: Transforming values into virtue*. Lanham, MD: University Press of America.

Salovey, P., & Grewal, D. (2005). The science of emotional intelligence. *Current Directions in Psychological Science, 14*(6), 281–285.

Salvador, R., & Folger, R. G. (2009). Business ethics and the brain. *Business Ethics Quarterly, 19*(1), 1–31.

Sampat, B., & Basu, P. A. (2017). Cyberloafing: The di(sguised) gital way of loafing on the job. *IUP Journal of Organizational Behavior, XVI*, 19–37.

Saracco, C. (2016). Conversations etched in stone. In S. Horlings & N. Ind (Eds.), *Brands with conscience: How to build a successful and responsible brand*. London: KaganPage.

Savitz, A. W. (2006). *The triple bottom line*. San Francisco, CA: Jossey-Bass.

Savitz, A. W. (2013). *Talent, transformation, and the triple bottom line: How corporations can leverage human resources to achieve sustainable growth*. Hoboken, NJ: Wiley.

Scarpello, V. G. (2008). Parallel approaches to development of the HRM field and HRM education. In V. G. Scarpello (Ed.), *The handbook of human resource management education: Promoting an effective and efficient curriculum* (pp. 3–37). Thousand Oaks, CA: SAGE.

Schafer, M., & Crichlow, S. (2010). *Groupthink versus high-quality decision making in international relations*. New York, NY: Columbia University Press.

Schat, A. C. H., Frone, M. R., & Kelloway, E. K. (2006). Prevalence of workplace aggression in the U.S. workforce: Findings from a national study. In E. K. Kelloway, J. Barling, & J. J. Hurrell (Eds.), *Handbook of workplace violence* (pp. 47–89). Thousand Oaks, CA: SAGE.

Schein, E. H. (1992). *Organizational culture and leadership* (2nd ed.). San Francisco, CA: Jossey-Bass.

Schimmel, K., & Nicholls, J. (2014). Workplace cyber bullying: A research agenda. In J. Lipinski & L. M. Crothers (Eds.), *Bullying in the workplace: Causes, symptoms, and remedies* (pp. 223–236). New York, NY: Routledge.

Schippers, M. C. (2014). Social loafing tendencies and team performance: The compensating effect of agreeableness and conscientiousness. *Academy of Management Learning & Education, 13*, 62–81.

Schlegelmilch, B. B., & Oberseder, M. (2010). Half a century of marketing ethics: Shifting perspectives and emerging trends. *Journal of Business Ethics, 93*, 2–3.

Schlenker, B. R. (1980). *Impression management: The self-concept, social identity, and interpersonal relations*. Monterey, CA: Brooks/Cole.

Schminke, M. (Ed.). (1998). *Managerial ethics: Moral management of people and processes*. Mahwah, NJ: Lawrence Erlbaum.

Schrodt, P., Turman, P. D., & Soliz, J. (2006). Perceived understanding as a mediator of perceived teacher confirmation and students' rating of instruction. *Communication Education, 55*(4), 370–388.

Schwartz, M. S. (2001). The nature of the relationship between corporate codes of ethics and behaviour. *Journal of Business Ethics, 32*, 247–262.

Schwartz, M. S. (2002). A code of ethics for corporate code of ethics. *Journal of Business Ethics, 41*, 27–43.

Schwartz, S. H., & Sagiv, L. (1995). Identifying culture-specifics in the content and structure of values. *Journal of Cross-Cultural Psychology, 26*, 92–116.

Scileppi, P. A. (2005). *Values for interpersonal communication: How then shall we live?* Belmont, CA: Star.

Scott, E. D. (2005). The ethics of human resource management. In J. W. Budd & J. G. Scoville (Eds.), *The ethics of human resources and industrial relations* (pp. 173–201). Champaign, IL: Labor Relations and Employment Association.

Scott, M. (2014a, June 18). Google ready to comply with "right to be forgotten" rules in Europe. *New York Times Blog*.

Scott, M. (2014b, July 5). Adapting to privacy ruling, Google chooses to hit "undo." *New York Times*, p. B3.

Seabright, M. A., & Moberg, D. J. (1998). Interpersonal manipulation: Its nature and moral limits. In M. Schminke (Ed.), *Managerial ethics: Moral management of people and processes* (pp. 153–175). Mahwah, NJ: Lawrence Erlbaum.

Seibert, S. E., Silver, S. R., & Randolph, W. A. (2004). Taking empowerment to the next level: A multiple-level model of empowerment, performance, and satisfaction. *Academy of Management Journal, 47*, 332–349.

Sekerka, L. E. (2009). Organizational ethics education and training: A review of best practices and their application. *International Journal of Training and Development, 13*, 77–95.

Seligman, M. E. P. (2002). *Authentic happiness: Using the positive psychology to realize your potential for lasting fulfillment*. New York, NY: Free Press.

Sellers, P. (2005, August 22). Retire? No way! *Fortune*, p. 18.

Senge, P., Smith, B., Kruschwitz, N., Lauer, J., & Schley, S. (2008). *The necessary revolutions: How individuals and organizations are working together to create a sustainable world*. New York, NY: Doubleday.

Serven, R. (2015, September 14). MSA president speaks out about racist incident. *Columbian Missourian*.

Sethi, S. P., & Schepers, D. H. (2011). United Nations Global Compact: An assessment of ten years of progress, achievements, and shortfall. In S. P. Sehi (Ed.), *Globalization and self-regulation: The crucial role that corporate codes of conduct play in global business* (pp. 249–275). New York, NY: Palgrave Macmillan.

Shackford, S. (2017, March 15). "Right to be forgotten" legislation attempts foothold in New York. *Reason.com*.

Shadi, J. (2016, August 18). The richest 10% hold 76% of the wealth. *CNN Money*.

Shadow Brokers group leaks stolen National Security Agency hacking tools. (2017, June 29). *National Public Radio*.

Shao, R., Aquino, K., & Freeman, D. (2008). Beyond moral reasoning: A review of moral identity research and its implications for business ethics. *Business Ethics Quarterly, 18*(4), 513–540.

Shapiro, D. (2016). *Negotiating the nonnegotiable: How to resolve your most emotionally charged conflicts*. New York, NY: Penguin.

Shaub, M. K., & Fisher, D. G. (2008). Beyond agency theory: Common values for accounting. In D. L. Swanson & D. G. Fisher (Eds.), *Advancing business ethics education* (pp. 305–328). Charlotte, NC: Information Age.

Shaub, M. K., & Lawrence, J. E. (1996). Ethics, experience and professional skepticism: A situational analysis. *Behavioral Research in Accounting, 8*, 124–157.

Shaw, J. C., Wild, E., & Colquitt, J. S. (2003). To justify or excuse? A meta-analytic review of the effects of explanations. *Journal of Applied Psychology, 88*, 44–458.

Shaw, R. B. (1997). *Trust in the balance: Building successful organizations on results, integrity and concern*. San Francisco, CA: Jossey-Bass.

Shaw, W. H. (2011). *Business ethics: A textbook with cases* (7th ed.). Boston, MA: Wadsworth.

Shear, M. D., & Joachim, D. S. (2014, May 31). Shinseki apologizes for misconduct at V.A. hospitals. *New York Times*.

Shear, M. D., & Oppel, R. A. (2014, May 31). V.A. chief resigns in face of furor on delayed care. *New York Times*, p. A1.

Shearman, S. (2017, March 30). Cyberbullying in the workplace: "I became paranoid." *The Guardian*.

Shen, L. (2016, October 13). Wells Fargo CEO John Stump is leaving the bank with a big payday. *Fortune.com*.

Sheppard, J. A. (1993). Productivity loss in performance groups: A motivation analysis. *Psychological Bulletin, 113*, 67–81.

Sheppard, J. A. (2001). Social loafing and expectancy-value theory. In S. G. Harkins (Ed.), *Multiple perspectives on the effects of evaluation on performance: Toward an integration* (pp. 1–24). Boston, MA: Kluwer.

Sher, S. (2011). A framework for assessing immorally manipulative marketing tactics. *Journal of Business Ethics, 102*, 97–118.

Sheth, J. N., & Sisodia, R. S. (2006). Introduction: Does marketing need reform? In J. H. Sheth and R. S. Sisodia (Eds.), *Does marketing need reform? Fresh perspectives on the future* (pp. 2–12). Armonk, NY: M. E. Sharpe.

Sheth, S. (2017, June 27). "The ultimate cyberweapon for espionage": The "Petya" cyberattack is exploiting a powerful NSA tool. *Business Insider*.

Shields, C. (2011). *Ancient philosophy: A contemporary introduction*. Hoboken, NJ: Taylor and Francis.

Shockley-Zalabak, P. S. (2015). *Fundamentals of organizational communication: Knowledge, sensitivity, skills, values* (9th ed.). Boston, MA: Pearson.

Shockley-Zalabak, P. S., Ellis, K., & Winograd, G. (2000). Organizational trust: What it means, why it matters. *Organizational Development Journal, 18*, 35–47.

Shontell, A. (2014, November 19). A leaked internal Uber presentation shows what the company really values in its employees. *Business Insider*.

Shu, L. L., Gino, F., & Bazerman, M. H. (2009). Dishonest deed, clear conscience: Self-preservation through moral disengagement and motivated forgetting. Harvard Business School Working Paper No. 09-078. Cambridge, MA: Harvard Business School.

Shulman, D. (2007). *From hire to liar: The role of deception in the workplace*. Ithaca, NY: Cornell University Press.

Sidelinger, R. J., & Booth-Butterfield, M. (2010). Co-constructing student involvement: An examination of teacher confirmation and student-to-student connectedness in the college classroom. *Communication Education, 59*, 165–184.

Sillars, A. L. (1986). *Procedures for coding interpersonal conflict* (rev.). Missoula, MT: University of Montana: Department of Communication Studies.

Silverman, E. (2016, August 23). Congress scolds pharmaceutical company's price hike on EpiPens. *PBS NewsHour*.

Sim, M. (2007). *Remastering morals with Aristotle and Confucius*. Cambridge, UK: Cambridge University Press.

Sims, R. L. (2000). The relationship between employee attitudes and conflicting expectations for lying behavior. *Journal of Psychology, 134*, 619–633.

Sims, R. L., & Keon, T. L. (1997). Ethical work climate as a factor in the development of person-organization fit. *Journal of Business Ethics, 16*, 1095–1105.

Sims, R. R. (1992). Linking groupthink to unethical behavior in organizations. *Journal of Business Ethics, 11*, 651–662.

Sims, R. R. (1994). *Ethics and organizational decision making: A call for renewal*. Westport, CT: Quorum Books.

Sims, R. R. (2002). *Managing organizational behavior*. Westport, CT: Quorum Books.

Sims, R. R. (2003). *Ethics and corporate social responsibility: Why giants fall*. Westport, CT: Praeger.

Singer, M., Mitchell, S., & Turner, J. (1998). Consideration of moral intensity in ethicality judgments: Its relationship with whistle-blowing and need-for-cognition. *Journal of Business Ethics 17*, 527–541.

Singer. P. (1971). Famine, affluence, and morality. *Philosophy and Public Affairs, 1*, 229–243.

Singer, P. (2002). *One world: The ethics of globalization*. New Haven, CT: Yale University Press.

Singer, P. (2017, June 6). Extreme altruism. *Project Syndicate*.

Singh, V., Kumra, S., & Vinnicombe, S. (2002). Gender and impression management: Playing the promotion game. *Journal of Business Ethics, 37*, 77–89.

Sipe, S. R., Metrejean, C. T., & Pearson, T. A. (2014). The SEC, the courts and whistleblowers: An examination into the strength of the anti-retaliation provisions of the Dodd-Frank Act as defined by recent federal court decisions. *Journal of Legal Studies in Business, 19,* 1–19.

Slack, D. (2016, April 7). VA bosses in 7 states falsified vets' wait times for care. *USA Today.*

Slack, D. (2017, April 12). Veteran patients in imminent danger at VA hospital in D.C. investigation finds. *USA Today.*

Slotkin, J. (2017, March 24). "Pizzagate" gunman pleads guilty to charges. *NPR.*

Slovin, D. (2006). Blowing the whistle. *Internal Auditor, 63,* 45–49.

Smith, A. C. T., & Stewart, B. (2011). Organizational rituals: Features, functions and mechanisms. *International Journal of Management Reviews, 13,* 113–133.

Smith, B. (2017). *The upstarts: How Uber, Airbnb, and the killer companies of the new Silicon Valley are changing the world.* New York: Little, Brown.

Smith, B. N., Kerr, N. A., Markus, M. J., & Stasson, M. F. (2001). Individual differences in social loafing: Need for cognition as a motivator in collective performance. *Group Dynamics: Theory, Research, and Practice, 5*(2), 150–158.

Smith, G. (2012). *Why I left Goldman Sachs: A Wall Street story.* New York, NY: Grand Central.

Smith, J. (2013, October 2). The companies with the best CSR reputations. *Forbes.*

Smith, K. (2014, November 28). The 8 worst bosses of all time. *New York Post.*

Smith, P., & Lorentzon, M. (2005). Is emotional labour ethical? *Nursing Ethics, 12,* 638–642.

Smith, P. K., Jostmann, N. B., Galinsky, A. D., & van Dijk, W. W. (2008). Lacking power impairs executive function. *Psychological Science, 19,* 441–447.

Smith, W. (2007). Cosmopolitan citizenship: Virtue, irony and worldliness. *European Journal of Social Theory, 10,* 37–52.

Smithers, G. D. (2015, July 27). Smithers: A historian's plea for the removal of confederate statues. *Richmond.com.*

Soares, C. (2007, September 4). Norwegian prisoners do organic porridge in world's first "green jail." *Belfast Telegraph.*

Social Accountability International. (2014). *Overview of SA8000: 2014.*

Society of Human Resource Management. (2007). SHRM Code of Ethics.

Soergel, A. (2016, April 8). Corporate activism and the rise of the outspoken CEO. *US News and World Report.*

Solis, S. (2017, January 14). Ringling Bros. Circus closing after 146 years. *USA Today.*

Solnik, C. (2012, June 14). New York B corps look past profit on the bottom line. *Long Island Business News.*

Solomon, B. (2017, February 20). Uber scrambles to investigate shocking sexual harassment claim. *Forbes.*

Solomon, R. C. (1992). *Ethics and excellence: Cooperation and integrity in business.* New York, NY: Oxford University Press.

Solomon, R. C. (1993). What a tangled web: Deception and self-deception in philosophy. In M. Lewis & C. Saarni (Eds.), *Lying and deception in everyday life* (pp. 30–58). New York, NY: Guilford Press.

Soltes, E. (2016). *Why they do it: Inside the mind of the white-collar criminal.* New York, NY: Public Affairs.

Sommeiller, E., & Price, M. (2014, February 14). The increasing unequal states of America. Economic Policy Institute.

Sommerfeldt, C. (2017, January 10). Fox News settles in Bill O'Reilly sexual harassment lawsuit. *New York Daily News.*

Sorokin, P. A. (1954). *The ways and power of love: Types, factors, and techniques of moral transformation.* Boston, MA: Beacon Press.

Spangle, M. L., & Isenhart, M. W. (2003). *Negotiation: Communication for diverse settings.* Thousand Oaks, CA: SAGE.

Spanier, G. (2014, May 30). Google forced to launch "right to be forgotten" form. *London Evening Standard,* p. 155.

Speciale, A., & Gibson, D. (2013, September 6). Pope Francis, the "cold call pope," reaches out and touches a lot of people. *Washington Post.*

Spreitzer, G. M. (1995). Psychological empowerment in the workplace: Dimensions, measurement, and validation. *Academy of Management Journal, 38,* 1442–1485.

Spreitzer, G. M. (1996). Social structural characteristics of psychological empowerment. *Academy of Management Journal, 39*, 483–504.

Spreitzer, G. M., Kizilos, M. A., & Nason, S. W. (1997). A dimensional analysis of the relationship between psychological empowerment and effectiveness, satisfaction, and strain. *Journal of Management, 23*, 679–705.

Staczek, J. J. (2008). An interview with Eric M. Pillmore: Hitting the CSR bull's-eye in a shifting corporate environment. *Thunderbird International Business Review, 50*, 295–301.

Stairs, M., & Galpin, M. (2010). Positive engagement: From employee engagement to workplace happiness. In P. A. Linley, S. Harrington, & N. Garcea (Eds.), *Oxford handbook of positive psychology and work* (pp. 155–172). New York, NY: Oxford University Press.

Stanwick, P. A., & Stanwick, S. D. (2009). *Understanding business ethics*. Upper Saddle River, NJ: Pearson Education.

Statt N. (2017, March 24). YouTube is facing a full-scale advertising boycott over hate speech. *The Verge*.

Staw, B. M. (1981). The escalation of commitment to a course of action. *Academy of Management Review, 6*, 577–587.

Steel, E., & Schmidt, M. S. (January 10, 2017). Fox News settled sexual harassment allegations against Bill O'Reilly, documents show. *New York Times*, p. A1.

Steinberg, R. J., & Figart, D. M. (1999). Emotional labor since The Managed Heart. *Annals of the American Academy of Political and Social Sciences, 561*, 10–26.

Stelter, B. (2016, September 6). Fox News settles with Gretchen Carlson, "handful" of other women. *CNN Media*.

Sterling, K. W. (2015, July 27). Sterling: Let's start a new conversation on Confederate symbols. *Richmond.com*.

Stern, A. (2012, April 4). Flight attendant rants about crashing. *Huffington Post*.

Sternberg, R. J. (2000). Images of mindfulness. *Journal of Social Issues, 56*(1), 11–26.

Sternberg, R. J. (2002). Smart people are not stupid, but they sure can be foolish: The imbalance theory of foolishness. In R. J. Sternberg (Ed.), *Why smart people can be so stupid* (pp. 232–242). New Haven, CT: Yale University Press.

Sterne, P. (2017, February 2). Facebook investors ask company to deal with "fake news." *Politico*.

Stevens, B. (2007). Corporate ethical codes: Effective instruments for influencing behavior. *Journal of Business Ethics, 78*, 601–609.

Stevens, C. K., & Kristof, A. L. (1995). Making the right impression: A field study of applicant impression management during job interviews. *Journal of Applied Psychology, 80*, 587–606.

Stewart, J. (2008). Cosmopolitan communication ethics understanding and action: Religion and dialogue. In K. Glenister Roberts & R. C. Arnett (Eds.), *Communication ethics: Between cosmopolitanism and provinciality* (pp. 105–119). New York, NY: Peter Lang.

Stockton. N. (2016, May 4). Everything you need to know about the Theranos saga so far. *Wired*.

Stoller, K. (2011, July 19). Fliers say they see more rude travelers. *USA Today*, p. 5B.

Stout, H., Vlasic, B., Ivory, D., & Ruiz, R. R. (2014, March 25). Carmaker misled grieving families on a lethal flaw. *New York Times*, p. A1.

Strauss, K. (2016, September 15). The companies with the best CSR reputations in the world in 2016. *Forbes*.

Street, M. D. (1997). Groupthink: An examination of theoretical issues, implications, and future research suggestions. *Small Group Research, 28*, 72–93.

Sullivan, R. J. (1994). *An introduction to Kant's ethics*. Cambridge, UK: Cambridge University Press.

Super, D. E. (1990). A life-span, life-space approach to career development. In D. Brown, L. Brooks, & Associates (Eds.), *Career choice and development: Applying contemporary theories to practice* (2nd ed.). San Francisco, CA: Jossey-Bass.

Susskind, L., & Field, P. (1996). *Dealing with an angry public: The mutual gains approach to resolving disputes*. New York, NY: Free Press.

Sutton, R. I. (1991). Maintaining norms about expressed emotions: The case of bill collectors. *Administrative Science Quarterly, 36*, 245–268.

Sutton, R. I., & Rafaeli, A. (1988). Untangling the relationship between displayed emotions and organizational sales: The case of convenience stores. *Academy of Management Journal, 31*, 461–487.

Swanson, D. L., & Fisher, D. G. (Eds.). (2008). *Advancing business ethics education*. Charlotte, NC: Information Age.

Sweeney, B., & Costello, F. (2009). Moral intensity and ethical decision-making: An empirical examination of undergraduate accounting and business students. *Accounting Education: An International Journal, 18*(1), 75–97.

Svriuga, S. (2016, September 28). "WE.ARE.SICK.OF.THIS!" Students respond after racial slurs are shouted at Mizzou. *Washington Post Grade Point.*

Szoldra, P. (2017, June 23). Obama reportedly directed the NSA to infect Russia with cyber weapons to cause "pain." *Business Insider.*

The Takeaway. (2017, January 6). Venezuela's military has turned its food crisis into a "racket." And it's profiting from people going hungry. *Public Radio International.*

Tangney, J. P. (2005). Humility. In C. R. Snyder & S. J. Lopez (Eds.), *Handbook of positive psychology* (pp. 411–419). Oxford, UK: Oxford University Press.

Taylor, K. (2016, January 2) The 4 biggest ways American beverage consumption will change in 2016. *Business Insider.*

Tejeda, M. J. (2015). Exploring the supportive effects of spiritual well-being on job satisfaction given adverse work conditions. *Journal of Business Ethics, 131,* 173–181.

10 biggest corporations make more money than most countries in the world combined. (2016, September 12). *Global Justice Now.*

Tenbrunsel, A. E., Diekman, K. A., Wade-Benzoni, K. A., & Bazerman, M. H. (2009). The ethical mirage: A temporal explanation as to why we aren't as ethical as we think we are. *Harvard Business School Working Paper* No. 08–012.

Tenbrunsel, A. E., Smith-Crowe, K., & Umphress, E. E. (2003). Building houses on rocks: The role of ethical infrastructure in organizations. *Social Justice Research, 16,* 285–307.

't Hart, P. (1990). *Groupthink in government: A study of small groups and policy failure.* Amsterdam, Netherlands: Swets & Zeitlinger.

Theen, A. (2017, January 25). UO will keep name of slavery supporter on oldest building, won't hide history. *The Oregonian/OregonLive.*

Thomas, K. W., & Kilmann, R. (1977). Developing a forced-choice measure of conflict-handling behavior: The MODE instrument. *Educational and Psychological Measurement, 37,* 390–395.

Thomas, K. W., & Velthouse, B. A. (1990). Cognitive elements of empowerment: An "interpretive" model of intrinsic task motivation. *Academy of Management Review, 15,* 666–681.

Thomas, L. (2017, May 30). Goldman buys $2.8 billion worth of Venezuelan bonds, and an uproar begins. *New York Times.*

Thorelli, R. (2017). Providing clarity for standard of conduct for directors within benefit corporations: Requiring priority of a specific public benefit. *Minnesota Law Review, 101,* 1749–1789.

Thoroughgood, C. N., Padilla, A., Hunter, S. T., & Tate, B. W. (2012). The susceptible circle: A taxonomy of followers associated with destructive leadership. *Leadership Quarterly, 23,* 899–917.

Tileaga, C. (2006). Representing the "other": A discursive analysis of prejudice and moral exclusion in talk about Romanies. *Journal of Community and Applied Social Psychology, 16,* 19–41.

Timeline: Baylor sexual assault controversy. (2017, March 3). *WacoTrib.com.*

Tjosvold, D. (1984). Cooperation theory and organizations. *Human Relations, 37,* 743–767.

Tjosvold, D. (1986). The dynamics of interdependence in organizations. *Human Relations, 39,* 517–540.

Tobias, A. (1976). *Fire and ice.* New York, NY: William Morrow.

Tomlinson, E. C., Thompson Heames, J., & Bockanic, W. N. (2014). Workplace bullying: Remedies for victims. In J. Lipinski & L. M. Crothers (Eds.), *Bullying in the workplace: Causes, symptoms, and remedies* (pp. 291–304). New York, NY: Routledge.

Tompkins, P. K., & Cheney, G. (1985). Communication and unobtrusive control in contemporary organizations. In R. D. McPhee & P. K. Tompkins (Eds.), *Organizational communication: Traditional themes and new directions* (pp. 179–210). Newbury Park, CA: SAGE.

Tompkins, P. K., Montoya, Y. J., & Candrian, C. B. (2014). Watch your neighbor watching you: Applying concertive control in changing organizational environments. In D. W. Stacks & M. B. Salwen (Eds.), *An integrated approach to communication theory and research.* Hoboken, NJ: Taylor and Francis.

Toobin, J. (2014, September 29). The solace of oblivion. *New Yorker.*

Tourish, D. (2013). *The dark side of transformational leadership: A critical perspective.* London, UK: Routledge.

Tracy, M. (2016, October 30). After scandal, Baylor and its problems roll on. *New York Times*, p. SP11.

Tracy, M., & Southall, A. (2015, November 8). Black football players lend heft to protests at Missouri. *New York Times*, p. A1.

Tracy, S. J. (2000). Becoming a character for commerce: Emotion labor, self-subordination, and discursive construction of identity in a total institution. *Management Communication Quarterly, 14*, 90–128.

Tracy, S. J., & Tracy, K. (1998). Emotional labor at 911. *Journal of Applied Communication Research, 26*, 390–411.

Trevino, L. K. (1990). A cultural perspective on changing and developing organizational ethics. In W. A. Pasmore & R. W. Woodman (Eds.), *Research in organizational change and development* (Vol. 4). Greenwich, CT: JAI.

Trevino, L. K., Butterfield, K. D., & McCabe, D. L. (1998). The ethical context in organizations: Influences on employee attitudes and behaviors. *Business Ethics Quarterly, 8*, 447–476.

Trevino, L. K., Hartman, L. P., & Brown, M. (2000). Moral person and moral manager: How executives develop a reputation for ethical leadership. *California Management Review, 42*, 128–142.

Trevino, L. K., & Nelson, K. A. (2004). *Managing business ethics: Straight talk about how to do it right* (3rd ed.). Hoboken, NJ: Wiley.

Trevino, L. K., & Nelson, K. A. (2014). *Managing business ethics: Straight talk about how to do it right* (6th ed.). Hoboken, NJ: John Wiley.

Trevino, L. K., & Weaver, G. R. (2001). Organizational justice and ethics program "follow-through": Influences on employees' harmful and helpful behavior. *Business Ethics Quarterly, 11*(4), 651–671.

Trevino, L. K., & Weaver, G. R. (2003). *Managing ethics in business organizations: Social scientific perspectives.* Stanford, CA: Stanford University Press.

Trevino, L. K., Weaver, G. R., Gibson, D. G., & Toffler, B. L. (1999). Managing ethics and legal compliance: What works and what hurts. *California Management Review, 41*, 131–151.

Trian, M. (2015, May 26). *How to reduce "cyberloafing" in the workplace.* University of Wisconsin School of Business.

Trice, H. M., & Beyer, J. M. (1984). Studying organizational cultures through rites and ceremonials. *Academy of Management Review, 9*, 653–699.

Tritten, T. J. (2014, June 5). Feds probing reports of VA whistleblowing reprisals. *Stars and Stripes.*

Trompenaars, F. (1994). *Riding the waves of culture: Understanding diversity in global business.* Burr Ridge, IL: Irwin.

Trompenaars, F., & Wooliams, P. (2011, April). Lost in translation. *Harvard Business Review.*

Tronto, J. C. (1993). *Moral boundaries: A political argument for an ethic of care.* New York, NY: Routledge.

Troyer, J. (Ed.). (2003). *The classical utilitarians: Bentham and Mill.* Indianapolis, IN: Hackett.

Turman, P. D., & Schrodt, P. (2006). Student perceptions of teacher power as a function of perceived teacher confirmation. *Communication Education, 55*(3), 265–279.

Turnley, W. H., Klotz, A. C., & Bolino, M. C. (2013). Crafting an image at another's expense: Understanding unethical impression management in organizations. In R. A. Giacalone & M. D. Promislo (Eds.), *Handbook of unethical work behavior: Implications for individual well-being* (pp. 123–139). Armonk, NY: M. E. Sharpe.

Tuttle, B. (2016, September 21). Why the EpiPen price Scandal sums up all we hate about big business & politics. *Money.*

Tuuli, M. M., & Rowlinson, S. (2009). Empowerment in project teams: A multilevel examination of the job performance implications. *Construction Management and Economics, 27*, 473–498.

Ugboro, I. O., & Obeng, K. (2000). Top management leadership, employee empowerment, job satisfaction, and customer satisfaction in TQM organizations: An empirical study. *Journal of Quality Management, 5*, 247–272.

Uhl-Bien, M., & Carsten M. K. (2007). Being ethical when the boss is not. *Organizational Dynamics, 36*, 187–201.

Uleman, J. K. (2010). *An introduction to Kant's moral philosophy.* Cambridge, UK: Cambridge University Press.

United Nations Department of Economic and Social Affairs. (2015, July 29). World population projected to reach 9.7 billion by 2050.

Unruh, G. (2008). Should you manage ethics or corruption?

Thunderbird International Business Review, 50, 287–293.

U.S. Equal Employment Opportunity Commission. (n.d.). What you should know about EEOC and the enforcement protections for LGBT workers.

USSIF Foundation. (2014). The impact of sustainable and responsible investment. Retrieved from www.ussif.org/files/Publications/USSIF_ImpactofSRI_FINAL

Valentine, S., & Barnett, T. (2003). Ethics code awareness, perceived ethical values, and organizational commitment. *Journal of Personal Selling & Sales Management, 23*, 359–367.

Valk, J. (2015). The "Kimono Wednesday' protests: Identity politics and how the Kimono became more than Japanese. *Asian Ethnology, 74*, 379–399.

Valle, M. (2006, May/June). The power of politics: Why leaders need to learn the art of influence. *Leadership in Action, 26*(2), 8–12.

Van Dyne, L., Graham, J. W., & Dienesch, R. M. (1994). Organizational citizenship behavior: Construct redefinition, measurement and validation. *Academy of Management Journal, 37*, 765–802.

Van Hooft, S. (2009). *Cosmopolitanism*. Durham, UK: Acumen.

Van Maanen, J. (1991). The smile factory: Work at Disneyland. In P. J. Frost, L. F. Moore, M. R. Louis, C. C. Lundberg, & J. Martin (Eds.), *Reframing organizational culture* (pp. 58–76). Newbury Park, CA: SAGE.

Velasquez, M. G. (1992). *Business ethics: Concepts and cases* (3rd ed.). Englewood Cliffs, NJ: Prentice Hall.

Vella, J. (2008). *Aristotle: A guide for the perplexed*. London, UK: Continuum International Publishing.

Victim speaks out after nude photo scandal rocks Marine Corps. (2017, March 17). *CBS News*.

Victor, B., & Cullen, J. B. (1988). The organizational bases of ethical work climates. *Administrative Science Quarterly, 33*, 101–125.

Victor, B., & Cullen, J. B. (1990). A theory and measure of ethical climate in organizations. In W. C. Frederic & L. E. Preston (Eds.), *Business ethics: Research issues and empirical studies* (pp. 77–97). Greenwich, CT: JAI.

Victor, B., Cullen, J. B., & Boynton, A. (1993). Toward a general framework of organizational meaning systems. In C. Conrad (Ed.), *Ethical nexus* (pp. 193–216). Norwood, NJ: Ablex.

Victor, D., & Stevens, M. (2017, April 10). United Airlines passenger is dragged from an overbooked flight. *New York Times*.

Villaume, W. A., & Bodie, G. D. (2007). Discovering the listener within us: The impact of trait-like personality variables and communicator styles on preferences for listening style. *International Journal of Listening, 21*(2), 102–123.

Viswesvaran, C., & Ones, D. S. (2002). Examining the construct of organizational justice: A meta-analytic evaluation of relations with work attitudes and behaviors. *Journal of Business Ethics, 38*, 193–203.

Vitell, S. J., Nwachukwu, S. L., & Barnes, J. H. (1993). *Journal of Business Ethics, 12*(10), 753–760.

Vlasic, B. (2014, April 16). G.M. chief cites new safety moves and says repairs are now underway. *New York Times*, p. B3.

Vlasic, B., & Stout, H. (2014, April 4). G.M. turns to a recall crisis expert. *New York Times*, p. B1.

Vlasic, B., & Wald, M. L. (2014, April 3). G.M. chief faces ire of senators in hearing. *New York Times*, p. B1.

Voelcker, J. (2014, July 29). 1.2 billion vehicles on world's roads now, 2 billion by 2035. *Green Car Reports*.

Vogel, G. (2001, March 3). Nobel laureates lobby for stem cells. *Science, 291*(5509), 1683–1684.

Waddock, S. (2002). *Leading corporate citizens: Vision, values, value added*. Boston, MA: McGraw-Hill Irwin.

Waddock, S. (2005). Hollow men and women at the helm . . . Hollow accounting ethics? *Issues in Accounting Education, 20*(2), 145–150.

Waddock, S. (2008). Corporate responsibility/corporate citizenship: The development of a construct. In A. G. Scherer & G. Palazzo (Eds.), *Handbook of research on global corporate citizenship* (pp. 50–73). Cheltenham, UK: Edward Elgar.

Wagner, D. (2014, June 9). VA scandal audit: 120,000 veterans experience long waits for care. *The Arizona Republic*.

Wakabayashi, D., & Isaac, M. (2017, January 25). In race against fake news, Google and Facebook stroll to the starting line. *New York Times*.

Wald, E. R. (2017, June 1). Why Goldman Sachs just made an embarrassing bet on Venezuela. *Forbes*.

Wald, M. L. (2014, April 1). Auto safety agency ready to point finger at G.M. in ignition flaw. *New York Times*, p. B1.

Waldron, V. R. (1994). Once more, with feeling: Reconsidering the role of emotion at work. In S. A. Deetz (Ed.), *Communication yearbook 17* (pp. 388–428). Thousand Oaks, CA: SAGE.

Waldron, V. R., & Kassing, J. W. (2011). *Managing risk in communication encounters*. Thousand Oaks, CA: SAGE.

Walsh, A. J. (2007). HRM and the ethics of commodified work in a market economy. In A. H. Pinnington, R. Macklin, & T. Campbell (Eds.), *Human resource management: Ethics and employment* (pp. 102–116). Oxford, UK: Oxford University Press.

Walter, F., Cole, M. S., & Humphrey, R. H. (2011). Emotional intelligence: Sine qua non of leadership or folderol? *Academy of Management Perspectives, 25*, 45–59.

Walumbwa, F. O., Avolio, B. J., Gardner, W. L., Wernsing, T. S., & Peterson, S. J. (2008). Authentic leadership: Development and validation of a theory-based measure. *Journal of Management, 34*(1), 89–126.

Walumbwa, F. O., Hartnell, C. A., & Oke, A. (2010). Servant leadership, procedural justice climate, service climate, and organizational citizenship behavior: A cross-level investigation. *Journal of Applied Psychology, 95*, 517–529.

Walumbwa, F. O., Luthans, F., Avery, J. B., & Oke, A. (2011). Authentically leading groups: The mediating role of collective psychological capital and trust. *Journal of Organizational Behavior, 32*, 4–24.

Watkins, M. (2015, August 25). Baylor may face legal fallout from rape case. *Texas Tribune*.

Watkins, M. (2016, October 19). Feds investigating Baylor University for handling of sexual assault. *Texas Tribune*.

Watson, K. W., Barker, L. L., & Weaver, J. B., III (1995). The Listening Styles Profile (LSP-16): Development and validation of an instrument to assess four listening styles. *International Journal of Listening, 9*, 1–13.

Watt, J. D., & Piotrowski, C. (2008). Organizational change cynicism: A review of the literature and intervention strategies. *Organization Development Journal, 26*, 23–31.

Weaver, G. R., Trevino, L. K., & Cochran, P. L. (1999a). Corporate ethics practices in the mid-1990s: An empirical study of the Fortune 1000. *Journal of Business Ethics, 18*, 283–294.

Weaver, G. R., Trevino, L. K., & Cochran, P. L. (1999b). Corporate ethics programs as control systems: Influence of executive commitment and environmental factors. *Academy of Management Journal, 42*, 41–57.

Weaver, G. R., Trevino, L. K., & Cochran, P. L. (1999c). Integrated and decoupled corporate social performance: Management commitments, external pressures, and corporate ethics practices. *Academy of Management Journal, 42*, 539–552.

Weber, J. (2008, February 13). The new ethics enforcers. *BusinessWeek*, pp. 76–77.

Weber, J. (2009). Using exemplary business practices to identify Buddhist and Confucian ethical value systems. *Business and Society Review, 114*(4), 511–540.

Weber, J., & Wasieleski, D. M. (2013). Corporate ethics and compliance programs: A report, analysis and critique. *Journal of Business Ethics, 112*, 609–626.

Weintraub, A. (2015, December 1). Mylan CEO Bresch admits "full responsibility" for EpiPen price hikes. *Forbes*.

Weise, E., & Woodyard, C. (2015, February 20). Deal reached in West Coast dockworkers dispute. *USA Today*.

Werhane, P. H. (1999). *Moral imagination and management decision-making*. New York, NY: Oxford University Press.

West, H. R. (2004). *An introduction to Mill's utilitarian ethics*. Cambridge, UK: Cambridge University Press.

Wheeler, D., Colbert, B., & Freeman, R. E. (2003). Focusing on value: Reconciling corporate social responsibility, sustainability and a stakeholder approach in a network world. *Journal of General Management, 28*, 1–28.

Wheeler, M. (2004, March). Fair enough: An ethical fitness quiz for negotiators. *Negotiation*, pp. 3–5.

Whicker, M. L. (1996). *Toxic leaders: When organizations go bad*. Westport, CT: Quorum Books.

Whistleblower protection history. (n.d.). Office of the Inspector General Social Security Administration.

Whitaker, B. G., & Godwin, L. N. (2013). The antecedents of moral imagination in the workplace: A social cognitive theory perspective. *Journal of Business Ethics, 114,* 61–73.

White, S. S., & Locke, E. A. (2000). Problems with the Pygmalion effect and some proposed solutions. *The Leadership Quarterly, 11,* 389–415.

Whitehouse, T. (2010, August). Measuring and explaining the ROI on compliance. *Compliance Week,* p. 49.

Whitman, D. S., Caleo, S., Caprent, N. C., Horner, M. T., & Bernerth, J. B. (2012). Fairness at the collective level: A meta-analytic examination of the consequences and boundary conditions of organizational justice climate. *Journal of Applied Psychology, 97,* 776–791.

Why your negotiating behavior may be ethically challenged—and how to fix it. (2008, April). *Negotiation,* pp. 1–5.

Whyte, G. (1991). Diffusion of responsibility: Effects on the escalation tendency. *Journal of Applied Psychology, 76,* 408–415.

Wicks, A. C., Freeman, R. E., Werhane, P. H., & Martin, K. E. (2010). *Business ethics: A managerial approach.* Boston, MA: Prentice-Hall.

Wiener, R. L., & Gutek, B. A. (1999). Advances in sexual harassment research, theory, and policy. *Psychology, Public Policy and Law, 5*(3), 507–518.

Wigglesworth, R., & Long, G. (2017, June 1). Why Goldman's Venezuela bond trade sparked controversy. *Financial Times* (London).

Wilker, D. (2013, September 24). Forbidden love: Workplace-romance policies now stricter. *Society for Human Resource Development.*

Wilkinson, J. (2016, November 16). Theranos whistleblower revealed as George Shultz's grandson Tyler. *DailyMail.com.*

Williams, G., & Zinkin, J. (2008). The effect of culture on consumers' willingness to punish irresponsible corporate behaviour: Applying Hofstede's typology to the punishment aspect of corporate social responsibility. *Business Ethics: A European Review, 17,* 210–226.

Williams, K. D., Harkins, S. G., & Karau, S. J. (2003). Social performance. In M. A. Hogg & J. Cooper (Eds.), *The SAGE handbook of social psychology* (pp. 333–346). London, UK: SAGE.

Williams, M. R. (2017, April 2). New Pittsburg, Kan, high school principal resigns after student journalists question her credentials. *Kansas City Star.*

Williams, O. F. (2014). The United Nations Global Compact: What did it promise? *Journal of Business Ethics, 122,* 241–251.

Wilmot, W. W., & Hocker, J. L. (2013). *Interpersonal conflict* (8th ed.). New York, NY: McGraw-Hill.

Wilson, F. (2015, November 10). *Strangers Drowning* by Larissa MacFarquhar: Review. *The Telegraph.*

Wilson, F., & Thompson, P. (2001). Sexual harassment as an exercise of power. *Gender, Work and Organization, 8,* 61–83.

Wilson, S. R. (2002). *Seeking and resisting compliance: Why people say what they do when trying to influence others.* Thousand Oaks, CA: SAGE.

Wimbush, J. C., Shepard, J. M., & Markham, S. E. (1997). An empirical examination of the relationship between ethical climate and ethical behavior from multiple levels of analysis. *Journal of Business Ethics, 16,* 1705–1716.

Withey, M. J., & Cooper, W. H. (1989). Predicting exit, voice, loyalty, and neglect. *Administrative Science Quarterly, 34,* 521–539.

Wolf, S. B. (2014). Emotion and mindfulness: Using emotion as information to raise collective performance. In N. M. Ashkanasy, W. J. Zerbe, & C. E. J. Hartel (Eds.), *Emotions and the organizational fabric* (pp. 367–395). UK: Emerald.

Wolfe, D. T., & Hermanson, D. R. (2004, December). The fraud diamond: Considering the four elements of fraud. *CPA Journal,* pp. 38–42.

Wood, W., Lundgren, S., Ouellette, J. A., Busceme, S., & Blackstone, T. (1994). Minority influence: A meta-analytic review of social influence processes. *Psychological Bulletin, 115,* 323–345.

Woods, A. (2017, January 31). Judge restores rights for self-help guru James Arthur Ray, but convictions in sweat-lodge deaths stand. *Arizona Republic.*

Woods, K. C., & Buchanan, N. T. (2008). Sexual harassment in the workplace. In M. Paludi (Ed.), *The psychology of women at work: Challenges and solutions for our female workforce* (Vol. 1, pp. 119–132). Westport, CT: Praeger.

Wright, B. M., & Barker, J. R. (2000). Assessing concertive control in the team environment. *Journal of Occupational and Organizational Psychology, 73,* 345–361.

Wright, J. P., Cullen, F. T., & Blankenship, M. B. (2002). Chained factory fire exits: Media coverage of a corporate crime that killed 25 workers. In M. D. Ermann & R. J. Lundman (Eds.), *Corporate and governmental deviance* (6th ed., pp. 262–276). New York, NY: Oxford University Press.

Wright, M. (2011, November 7). Success means telling people to buy less. *The Guardian*.

Wrzesniewski, A., & Dutton, J. E. (2001). Crafting a job: Revisioning employees as active crafters of their work. *Academy of Management Review, 26*, 179–201.

Wrzesniewski, A., McCauley, C., Rozin, P., & Schwartz, B. (1997). Jobs, careers, and callings: People's relations to their work. *Journal of Research in Personality, 31*, 21–33.

Wu, Y.-C., & Tsai, P. J. (2012). Multidimensional relationships between paternalistic leadership and perceptions of organizational ethical climates. *Psychology Reports: Human Resources and Marketing, 111*, 509–527.

Wusun, L. (2010). *Getting to know Confucius: A new translation of the Analects*. Beijing: Foreign.

Yanay, N., & Sharar, G. (1998). Professional feelings as emotional labor. *Journal of Contemporary Ethnography, 27*, 345–373.

Yancey, K. B. (2010a, February 26). Yikes on a plane with tykes in tow. *USA Today*, p. 11B.

Yancey, K. B. (2010b, September 3). The midair standoff: Crew vs. fliers. *USA Today*, p. 4D.

Yankelovich, D. (2006). *Profit with honor: The new stage of market capitalism*. New Haven, CT: Yale University Press.

Yglesias, M. (2013, March 12). How rich is the Catholic Church? No one knows. *Slate*.

Yoshino, K., & Blankstein, A. (2011, December 7). Alec Baldwin apologizes for airline incident. *Los Angeles Times*.

Yohn, D. L. (2017, March 25). Why did sexual harassment fell Uber? *Forbes*.

Young, C. (2015, August 21). To the new culture cops, everything is appropriation. *Washington Post*.

Young, S. B. (2014, March 12). Commentary: Public benefit corporations' time has come. *The Legal Ledger* (St. Paul, MN).

Yukl, G. (2006). *Leadership in organizations* (6th ed.). Upper Saddle River, NJ: Prentice Hall.

Yukl, G. (2013). *Leadership in organizations* (8th ed.). Upper Saddle River: Pearson.

Yukl, G., Chavez, C., & Seifert, C. F. (2008). Assessing the construct validity and utility of two new influence tactics. *Journal of Organizational Behavior, 26*, 705–725.

Zadek, S. (2004, December). The path to corporate responsibility. *Harvard Business Review, 82*(12), 125–132.

Zand, D. E. (1972). Trust and managerial problem solving. *Administrative Science Quarterly, 17*, 229–239.

Zapf, D., & Holz, M. (2006). On the positive and negative effects of emotion work in organizations. *European Journal of Work and Organizational Psychology, 15*(1), 1–28.

Zhang, L., Chen, F., & Latimer, J. (2011). Managing virtual team performance: An exploratory study of social loafing and social comparison. *Journal of International Technology and Information Management*, pp. 103–119.

Zhu, W., May, D. R., & Avolio, B. J. (2004). The impact of ethical leadership behavior on employee outcomes: The roles of psychological empowerment and authenticity. *Journal of Leadership and Organizational Studies, 11*, 16–26.

Zinnbauer, B. J., & Pargament, K. I. (2005). Religiousness and spirituality. In R. F. Paloutzian & C. L. Park (Eds.), *Handbook of the psychology of religion and spirituality* (pp. 21–42). New York, NY: Guilford Press.

Zoroya, G. (2014, June 28). Top officials describe 'corrosive culture' in VA system. *USA Today*.

Zyglidopoulos, S. C., & Fleming, P. J. (2007). Ethical distance in corrupt firms: How do innocent bystanders become guilty perpetrators? *Journal of Business Ethics, 78*, 265–274.

INDEX

ABCs marketing model, 297–298
Abilene paradox, 242–243
Accommodation in conflict resolution, 160
Accounting ethics. *See* Finance and accounting ethics
Acolyte followers, 214
Acquisitive impression management, 137–138
Action-oriented listener, 102
Adelphia, 269
ADM, 262
AES, 132, 261
Affective prebehavioral disposition, 5
Affiliative follower behavior, 211–212
Agency theory, 329
Aggression:
    in conflict management, 171–177
    in groups, 230
    personal aggression, 173–174
    situational aggression, 174–175
    social aggression, 174
Agilant, 342
AIG, 307–308
Ailes, Roger, 179, 190
Airline industry, 143, 153–154, 276
Al-Assad, Bashar, 196
Albom, Mitch, 117–118
Alter Eco, 353
Altruism, 20–25
Amazon, 262, 337
Ambush marketing, 298
AMD, 342
American Airlines, 153–154
American Eagle Airlines, 153
American Hospital Association (AHA), 278–279
American Humane Society, 349
American Marketing Association (AMA), 298–299
American Red Cross, 325
American Stock Exchange (AMEX), 263
Americans with Disabilities Act, 178
Ameriprise Financial, 109–110
AmerisourceBergen, 262, 263

Analects, The, 17
Angie's List, 335
Animal activism, 349–350
Anomie, 271
Anthem, 335
Apologizing in conflict resolution, 163–165
Apple, 245, 336
ARCA, 150
Aristotle, 14–16
Assertiveness, 365
Association of Independent Certified Public Accountants Code of Professional Conduct, 310–311
AT&T, 325, 337
Audits:
    in accounting ethics, 303–304
    for organizational citizenship, 345–347
    for organizational culture, 279–280
Authentic leadership theory (ALT), 203–204
Authoritarian followers, 214
Autry, James, 201
Avoidance in conflict resolution, 160

Balanced processing in leadership, 203
Baldwin, Alec, 153
Balwani, Sunny, 125, 226–227
Bank of Montreal, 48
Barra, Mary, 292–293
Barrett, Colleen, 190
Barry, Marion, Jr., 195
Baxter International, 345–346
Baylor University (Texas), 186–188
Beauregard, P. G. T., 55
Beck, Glenn, 337
Beech-Nut, 240
Benioff, Marc, 336
Ben & Jerry's, 325
Bentham, Jeremy, 8–10
Bergoglio, Jorge Mario, 56–58
Berkshire, 217

Betrayal, 113–114
Biden, Joe, 241
Bielski, Tuvia, 44
Bielski, Zus, 44
Big Brothers/Big Sisters, 262
Biogen, 84
BlackRock, 381
Blankfein, Lloyd, 381
Block, Peter, 201
Blockers in groups, 230
Bloomingdales, 336–337
BMW, 337, 340
Board of directors, 267–270
Body Shop, The, 370
Boeing Corporation, 325
Bolton, John, 125
Bonner, Dave, 118–119
Boston Museum of Fine Arts, 358, 359
Bradley, Omar, 127
Brancheau, Dawn, 349–350
Breivik, Anders Behring, 31
Bresch, Heather, 322
Bribery, 356
Briles, Art, 186–187
Brilliance Glass Manufacturing, 184–185
British Petroleum (BP), 196, 282, 347
Brown, Michael, 195, 223–224
Buffett, Warren, 217
Bullying, 172, 175–176, 191
Burke, James, 282
Butler, Jonathan, 224
Bystander followers, 214

Calhoun, John, 56
Callous leaders, 195–196
Cameron, James, 125
Canadian Natural Resources, 262
Canon, 345–346
Care ethic, 22–23
Caring climate, 281
Caring for the soul, 48–49
Carl's Jr., 313
Carlson, Gretchen, 179
Carstedt, Per, 340
Carter, Jimmy, 170
Categorical imperative, 10–11
Catholic Church, 56–58
Cathy, Don, 335

Caux Principles for Business, 373–375
CBS, 192
CEO activism, 335–336
CERES, 338–339
Challenging behavior of followers, 211–212
Character development, 39–46, 53–54
Charity Navigator, 347
Charles Schwab, 262
Chartered Financial Analyst Code of Ethics and
    Standards of Professional Conduct, 310
Chick-Fil-A, 335, 337
China:
    Confucianism, 16–19
    guanxi, 18–19
Chouinard, Yvon, 190
Churning, 302
Circumvention in followership, 209
Citicorp, 210
Clinton, Bill, 65–66
Closed-mindedness in groups, 239
CNN, 23
Coca-Cola, 214, 330
Code of ethics:
    American Marketing Association (AMA), 298–299
    Association of Independent Certified Public
        Accountants (AICPA), 310–311
    Chartered Financial Analyst (CFA), 310
    for organizational culture, 263–266
    Society for Human Resource Management
        (SHRM), 316–317
Coercive power, 122–125
Cognitive bias, 67–69, 70
Cognitive decision-making, 5
Cognitive dissonance, 67
Cognitive moral development, 64–65
Cognitive-process model, 79–81
Cole, Robert, 74–75
Collaboration in conflict resolution, 160
Collective effort model (CEM), 233
Collectivism, 361, 362, 363, 364*t*
Colluder followers, 214
Commonwealth Bank (Australia), 262
Competition in conflict resolution, 160
Compromising:
    in conflict resolution, 160
    in organizational culture, 284
Computer Associates, 272–273
Concertive control, 246–247

Confederate monuments, 55–56
Confirmation in interpersonal communication, 105–106
Conflict management:
  accommodation style, 160
  aggression, 171–177
  aggression reduction tactics, 176–177
  apologizing style, 163–165
  application projects, 182–183
  avoidance style, 160
  bullying, 172, 175–176
  case studies, 183–188
  chapter takeaway, 181–188
  collaborative style, 160
  collaborative tactics, 163
  competitive style, 160
  compromising style, 160
  conflict defined, 156
  conflict sources, 155–156
  conflict style, 160–162
  Conflict Style Inventory, 161–162
  contemporary issues, 175–176
  cyberbullying, 175–176
  deception in, 166–167
  destructive actions, 157
  distributive negotiation, 168, 169t
  emotional approach, 158–159
  ethical checkpoint, 157
  ethical managerial behaviors, 158–165
  functional *versus* dysfunctional conflict, 158
  gender harassment, 178
  in global society, 375–377
  guidelines, 162
  hostile work environment, 178–179
  incivility, 172
  integrative negotiation, 168–169
  labor unions, 183–184
  mobbing, 172
  Negative Acts Questionnaire, 172–173
  negotiation strategy, 165–170, 184–185
  personal aggression, 173–174
  principled negotiation, 169–170
  quid-pro-quo harassment, 178, 179
  self-assessment, 161–162, 172–173
  sexual assault, 186–188
  sexual coercion, 178
  sexual harassment, 177–181
  situational aggression, 174–175
  social aggression, 174
  unwanted sexual attention, 178
Conformer followers, 214
Confucianism, 16–19
Consequentialism, 8
Consistent leaders, 193–194
Consumer boycotts, 336–337
Container Store, 190, 201
Content-oriented listener, 102
Context management, 5
Cook, Tim, 336
Cooper Tire & Rubber, 262
Cooptation in organizational culture, 284
Core ideology, 261
Core values, 261
Corporate activism, 335–336
Corporate executive officer (CEO), 268–269, 282–283
Corporate social responsibility (CSR), 332–335
Corrupt leaders, 196
Cosentino, 340
Cosmopolitanism, 359–360
Countrywide Financial, 208
Courageous followers, 214–217
Covenantal relationship, 343–345
Covey, Stephen, 41–43
Cultural appropriation, 358–359
Cultural relativism, 357
Cummings, Elijah, 322
Cyberattacks, 29–30
Cyberbullying, 175–176
Cyberloafing, 266
Cynical followers, 208
Cypress Semiconductor, 134

Damon, Matt, 350
Danone, 342
Dao, David, 153
Darden Restaurants, 262
Dauman, Philippe, 192
Davis, Jefferson, 55
Dean Foods, 302
Deception:
  in conflict management, 166–167
  in influential ethics, 139, 141–143, 152
Decision making:
  application projects, 86–87
  case studies, 87–91
  chapter takeaway, 86–91

cognitive bias, 67–69, 70
cognitive dissonance, 67
cognitive moral development, 64–65
cognitive-process model, 79–81
contemporary issues, 72–73
Defining Issues Test (DIT), 65
destructive motivations, 65–67
duty orientation, 72
ego, 66, 67
ethical checkpoint, 70
ethical components, 59–78
five-"I" model, 85–86
five-questions model, 83–84
foursquare protocol, 82–83
in global society, 357
greed, 66
guidelines for, 78–86
implicit prejudice, 68
insecurity, 66
moral character, 74–78
moral compass, 81–82
moral courage, 75
moral disengagement, 67–68
moral efficacy, 75
moral emotion, 71–72
moral hypocrisy, 71
moral imagination, 60
moral intensity, 61–62
moral judgment, 64–71
moral motivation, 71–74
moral muteness, 61
moral potency, 75–77
moral sensitivity, 60–63
moral sensitivity scenarios, 63
motivated forgetting, 67–68
other-condemning emotion, 72
other-praising emotion, 72
other-suffering emotion, 71
perspective skills, 60
reason *versus* intuition, 72–73
reward system, 71
schemas, 64–65
self-assessment, 63, 77–78
self-conscious emotion, 72
Self-Knowledge Questions, 77–78
slippery slope, 68
stress, 67
white-collar crime, 87–89

Deep acting, 144
Default dialogue index, 95
Defining Issues Test (DIT), 65
Dell Computer, 318
Delphi, 292
Delta Airlines, 143
Denver International Airport, 244
Denying the Holocaust (Lipstadt), 252
DePree, Max, 201
Deutsche Bank, 335, 345–346
Dialogue, 95–96, 117–118
Difference principle, 13
Direct-factual appeal in followership, 209
Discourse ethics, 113–114
Disney, 191, 337, 347
Dissenting followers, 208–209
Distancing tactic, 318
Distributive justice:
　　in human resource management (HRM), 315
　　in marketing ethics, 300–301
Distributive negotiation, 168, 169*t*
Dodd-Frank Act (2010), 217
Dominators in groups, 230
Dow Chemical, 262
Dow Jones Sustainability Index, 347
Drexel Burnham Lambert, 197
Dreyer's Grand Ice Cream, 262
Dunlap, Al, 134, 197
DuPont, 341
Duty of care, 267–268
Duty of loyalty, 267–268
Duty orientation, 72

Edwards, Harry, 256
E.F. Hutton, 240
Ego, 66, 67
Eisenhower, Dwight, 127
Eisner, Michael, 191
Eliciting behavior of followers, 211
Eli Lilly, 335
Emotional intelligence, 106–111, 158–159
Emotional labor, 143–145, 153–154
Employment-at-will doctrine, 313
Empowerment, 130–133
Encyclopedia of Ethical Failure (U.S. Department of Defense), 27–29
Enron, 208, 269, 277, 306, 307
EpiPen, 321–322

Equal Employment Opportunity Commission (EEOC), 178
Equal liberty principle, 12
Equal opportunity principle, 12–13
Equal Pay Act, 178
Equifax, 81–82
Escalation of commitment, 244–245
EternalBlue program, 29–30
Ethical competencies:
   affective prebehavioral disposition, 5
   cognitive decision-making, 5
   context management, 5
   development of, 2–5
   in global society, 357–377
   for interpersonal communication, 96–115
Ethical diversity:
   global challenges, 356–357
   global characteristics, 360–370
Ethics defined, 7
Ethics officer (EO), 272–273
Ethics training, 285–286
Ethnocentrism, 357–359
Eudemonia, 15
Evil leaders, 196
Expedia, 192
Experiential learning, 41
Expert power, 122–125

Facebook:
   etiquette, 19
   fake news stories, 351–352
Fake news stories, 351–352
Fastow, Andy, 307
Federal Emergency Management Agency (FEMA), 195
Federal employees' ethics, 27–29
Feld Entertainment, 349–350
Felt, Mark, 206
Feminine cultures, 361, 363
Ferguson, Claude, 207
Fidelity, 381
Finance and accounting ethics:
   accounting defined, 303
   accounting issues, 303–304
   application projects, 320–321
   case study, 323–324
   chapter takeaway, 319–326
   churning, 302
   code of ethics, 309–311
   ethical checkpoint, 304–305
   ethical foundations, 306–307
   ethical issues, 302–305
   finance defined, 302
   finance issues, 302–303
   fraud triangle, 304–305
   guidelines for, 305–311
   guiding values, 307–308
   integrity, 308
   invulnerability fallacy, 307–308
   objectivity, 308
   omnipotence fallacy, 307
   omniscience fallacy, 307
   piggybacking, 302–303
   self-assessment, 308–309
   Skepticism Scale, 308–309
   transparency, 308
   unrealistic optimism fallacy, 308
Five-"I" model, 85–86
Five-questions model, 83–84
Followership ethics:
   acolytes, 214
   affiliative behavior, 211–212
   application projects, 220–221
   authoritarians, 214
   bad-news response, 209–210
   bystanders, 214
   case studies, 221–227
   challenges of, 204–210
   challenging behavior, 211–212
   chapter takeaway, 219–227
   colluders, 214
   conformers, 214
   contemporary issues, 206–208
   courageous followers, 214–217
   cynicism, 208
   dissent, 208–209
   eliciting behavior, 211
   follower role, 210–212
   Followership Role Orientation Scale, 212
   guerrilla bureaucrats, 206–208
   guiding behavior, 212
   implementers, 216
   individualists, 216
   intelligent disobedience, 206
   lost souls, 214
   modeling behavior, 211
   Nuremberg principle, 205–206

obedience, 205–206
obligation, 205
opportunists, 214
partner followers, 216
prohibitive behavior, 211, 212
promotive behavior, 211
resource followers, 216
self-assessment, 212
sensemaking behavior, 212
strategies for, 210–219
unhealthy motivations, 213–214
whistle-blower, 217–219
Whistle-Blower Checklist, 218–219
Forbes, 346–347
Ford Motor Company, 67, 340, 341, 345–346
Foreign Corrupt Practices Act (1977), 356
Foursquare protocol, 82–83
Fowler, Susan, 288
Fox News, 179, 190, 337
Framing strategy, 133–134
Francis, Pope, 56–58
Fraud triangle, 304–305
Freddie Mac, 306
Future-oriented cultures, 365

Galatea effect, 148
Galvin, Robert, 277
Ganda, Elvis, 184
Gandhi, Mohandas, 95
Gender harassment, 178
General Electric (GE), 132
General Motors (GM), 292–294
Gentile, Mary, 75–76
Geun-hye, Park, 190
Gig economy, 313
Giving Voice to Values, 75–76, 77–78
Global Business Standards Codex, 373
Global Compact (United Nations), 371–372
Global Crossing, 269, 306
Global Reporting Initiative, 345–346
Global society:
    application projects, 378
    assertiveness, 365
    bribery, 356
    case studies, 379–383
    Caux Principles for Business, 373–375
    chapter takeaway, 377–383
    collectivism, 361, 362, 363, 364t
    conflict management, 375–377
    contemporary issues, 358–359
    cosmopolitanism, 359–360
    cultural appropriation, 358–359
    cultural relativism, 357
    decision-making ethics, 357
    ethical checkpoint, 372
    ethical competencies, 357–377
    ethical diversity challenges, 356–357
    ethical diversity characteristics, 360–370
    ethnocentrism, 357–359
    feminine cultures, 361, 363
    future orientation, 365
    Global Business Standards Codex, 373
    Global Compact (United Nations), 371–372
    globalization impacts, 355–356
    HKH conflict resolution model, 376–377
    humane orientation, 365
    human rights declaration (United Nations), 371–372
    hunger bonds (Venezuela), 380–381
    hypernorms, 375–376
    individualism, 361, 362, 363, 364t
    Individualism/Collectivism Scale, 362
    integrated social contracts theory, 375–376
    masculine cultures, 361, 363
    moral common ground, 370–375
    Moral Foundations Questionnaire, 369
    moral foundations theory, 367–370
    moral free space, 375
    performance orientation, 364–365
    power distance, 361, 363
    programmed value patterns, 361–364
    Project GLOBE, 364–365
    right-to-privacy, 379–380
    trolley problem, 370–371
    uncertainty avoidance, 362–363
    universal dilemmas, 365–367
    worldliness, 360
Goldman Sachs, 274, 380–381
Golem effect, 146
Google, 262, 288, 289, 337, 347, 351–352, 379–380
Gore and Associates, 150
Greed, 66
Greenberg, Hank, 307–308
Green Zone (Sweden), 340
Griffin, Robert, III, 186
Griner, Brittney, 186
Groupe Diageo, 342

Group ethics:
- Abilene paradox, 242–243
- aggressors, 230
- application projects, 251
- behavioral responsibilities, 229–238
- behavioral risks, 238–250
- blockers, 230
- case studies, 252–256
- chapter takeaway, 250–256
- closed-mindedness, 239
- collective effort model (CEM), 233
- concertive control, 246–247
- Concertive Control Scale, 247
- contemporary issues, 245
- cooperative orientation, 229–231
- credit risks, 256
- dominators, 230
- escalation of commitment, 244–245
- ethical checkpoint, 234–235
- group pressure, 239–240
- groupthink, 238–241, 254–255
- *Gunsmoke* myth, 243–244
- intergroup cooperation, 231
- minority position, 237–238
- mismanaged agreement, 242–244
- moral exclusion, 247–250
- open group climate, 235–237
- overconfidence, 239
- players, 230
- polythink, 241–242
- premature abandonment, 245
- psychological safety, 237
- recognition-seekers, 230
- risky shift, 244
- self-assessment, 232–233, 247
- social loafing, 231–235
- social loafing in virtual teams, 234–235
- Social Loafing Scale, 232–233
- supportive group climate, 235–237
- team denial, 252–253
- unobtrusive control, 246
- virtual teams, 234–235

Group pressure, 239–240
Groupthink, 238–241, 254–255
Guanxi (China), 18–19
Guerrilla bureaucrats, 206–208
Guiding behavior of followers, 212
Gunsmoke myth, 243–244

Habitat for Humanity International, 262
Habits, 41–43
Halden prison (Norway), 30–32
Hanjin, 184
Hard power, 125
Harley-Davidson, 262
Harmonic Wealth (Ray), 254
Harvard Business Review, 325
Hayward, Tony, 196
Head, Payton, 224
HealthEast, 48
Helmsley, Leona, 195–196
Henkel, 342
Herman Miller, 48
Hewlett-Packard, 234–235, 245, 262, 342
High Plains Bank (Oklahoma), 256
HKH conflict resolution model, 376–377
Hobby Lobby, 335
Holbrooke, Richard, 241
Holder, Eric, 290
Holmes, Elizabeth, 190, 225–227
Honest ingratiation, 140–141
Hooker, Tom, 273
Hoover, J. Edgar, 197
Hostile work environment, 178–179
Huckabee, Mike, 337
Huddy, Juliet, 179
Humane-oriented cultures, 365
Human resource management (HRM):
- activities of, 311–312
- application projects, 320–321
- case study, 324–326
- chapter takeaway, 319–326
- code of ethics, 316–317
- commodification of people, 313
- contemporary issues, 319
- defined, 311
- distancing tactic, 318
- distributive justice in, 315
- economic view of people, 313–314
- employment-at-will doctrine, 313
- ethical issues, 311–314
- exploitation, 313
- gig economy, 313
- guidelines for, 314–318
- harmful decision-making, 317–318
- interactional justice in, 315
- just-cause doctrine, 313

    Kantian approach, 314
    moral hazards of, 313–314
    organizational justice perspective, 315–316
    Organizational Justice Scale, 316
    procedural justice in, 315
    refusal tactic, 318
    Robin Hood Effect, 319
    self-assessment, 316
Human rights, 11, 371–372
Hunger bonds (Venezuela), 380–381
HURIER model, 100–101
Hypernorms, 375–376

IBM, 234–235, 277
I-It communicators, 94–95
Imperial Food Products, 194
Implementer followers, 216
Implicit prejudice, 68
Impression management, 136–141
Impulsive leaders, 199
Incivility, 172
Incompetent leaders, 195
Incrementalism in organizational culture, 284
Independence climate, 281
Individualism:
    cultural ideology, 361, 362, 363, 364*t*
    followership, 216
Influence:
    application projects, 149–150
    case studies, 150–154
    chapter takeaway, 148–154
    coercive power, 122–125
    communication of expectations, 145–148
    concentration of power, 125–126, 191–192
    contemporary issues, 140–141
    deception strategy, 139, 141–143, 152
    deep acting, 144
    emotional labor, 143–145, 153–154
    empowerment, 130–133
    ethical checkpoint, 137–138
    expert power, 122–125
    framing strategy, 133–134
    Galatea effect, 148
    Golem effect, 146
    hard power, 125
    honest ingratiation, 140–141
    impression management, 136–141
    impression management tactics, 137–138
    legitimate power, 122–125
    negative political power, 127, 128*f*
    organizational strategies of, 133–148
    Personal Power Profile, 123–125
    political power, 127–130
    political skills, 128–130
    Political Skills Inventory, 129–130
    positional power, 125, 126
    positive political power, 128–130
    power bases, 122–125
    power dynamics, 122–133
    powerlessness, 126
    proactive tactics, 134–136
    Pygmalion effect, 145–148
    referent power, 122–125
    reward power, 122–125
    self-assessment, 123–125, 129–130
    self-fulfilling prophecy, 145–148
    self-management technique, 150–151
    soft power, 125
    surface acting, 144
    veracity, 142
Information management in leadership, 193
Insecurity, 66
Instrumental climate, 281
Insular leaders, 196
Integrated education model, 41
Integrated social contracts theory, 375–376
Integrative negotiation, 168–169
Intel, 234–235
Intelligent disobedience of followers, 206
Intemperate leaders, 195
Interactional justice, 315
Interface, 332, 342
Internalized moral perspective in leadership, 203
Internal Revenue Service, 262
International Container Terminal Services Inc. (ICTSI), 183–184
International Longshore and Warehouse Workers Union (ILWU), 183–184
Interpersonal communication:
    application projects, 116
    betrayal, 113–114
    case studies, 117–120
    chapter takeaway, 115–120
    confirmation process, 105–106
    contemporary issues, 108–109
    default dialogue index, 95

dialogue, 95–96, 117–118
discourse ethics, 113–114
emotional analysis questions, 110–111
emotional intelligence, 106–111
ethical checkpoint, 101, 112
ethical competencies for, 96–115
ethical framework for, 94–96
HURIER model, 100–101
I-It communicators, 94–95
inappropriate self-disclosure, 104
I-Thou communicators, 94–95
listening skills, 98, 100–103
listening styles, 102
Listening Styles Profile, 102–103
Mindful Attention Awareness Scale (MAAS), 99
mindfulness, 97–98
mindlessness, 97
monologue, 95
moral argument, 113–115
self-assessment, 99, 102–103
self-disclosure, 103–105
stem cell research, 119–120
technical dialogue, 95
trait approach to emotional intelligence, 108–109
trust, 111–113
Invulnerability fallacy, 307–308
Irving, David, 252–253
Issues management, 330–332
I-Thou communicators, 94–95

James Ray International, 254–255
Jazz Pharmaceuticals, 321
Jet Blue Airlines, 153
Jindal, Bobby, 336
Johnson, Lyndon, 239
Johnson & Johnson, 282
Jones, Jeff, 288
Jordan, Michael, 335
Journal of Business Ethics, 48
Journal of Organizational Change, 48
J. Sainsbury (Great Britain), 262
Just-cause doctrine, 313
Justice:
    distributive justice, 300–301, 315
    in human resource management (HRM), 315
    interactional justice, 315
    in marketing ethics, 300–301
    procedural justice, 315
Justice-as-fairness theory, 12–14

Kalanick, Travis, 190, 288, 289–290
Kant, Immanuel, 10–11, 314
Kennedy, John, 239
Kennedy, Robert, 75, 240
Khosrowshahi, Dara, 192
Kickstarter, 353
Kilpatrick, Kwame, 196
Klatsky, Bruce, 134
K-Mart, 269, 306
Kony, Joseph, 196
Kooks Burritos, 358, 359
Koop, C. Everett, 43
KPMG, 87–88, 272–273, 308, 346
Ku Klux Klan, 55–56

Labor unions, 183–184
Landrieu, Mitch, 55, 56
Lang, Josiah, 152
Language, 274
Law and code climate, 281
Leadership ethics:
    application projects, 220–221
    authentic leadership theory (ALT), 203–204
    bad leadership behaviors, 195–197
    bullying, 191
    callous leaders, 195–196
    case studies, 221–227
    challenges of, 191–194
    chapter takeaway, 219–227
    consistent leaders, 193–194
    corrupt leaders, 196
    evil leaders, 196
    impulsive leaders, 199
    incompetent leaders, 195
    information management, 193
    insular leaders, 196
    intemperate leaders, 195
    loyal leaders, 194
    Machiavellian leaders, 199–200
    narcissistic leaders, 199
    normative leadership theories, 200–204
    power dynamics, 191–192
    privileged leaders, 192
    recommendations for, 196–197
    responsible leaders, 192–193
    rigid leaders, 195
    self-assessment, 202
    selfish leaders, 199–200
    servant leadership, 201–202

Servant Leadership Questionnaire, 202
toxic leaders, 197–199
unethical behaviors, 194–200
Leadership Quarterly, 48
Lee, Robert E., 55
Legitimate power, 122–125
LeMessurier, William J., 210
Lesbian, gay, bisexual, transgender (LGBT) community, 178
LG Corporation, 17
Life Values Inventory, 38
Lipstadt, Deborah, 252–253
Listening skills, 98, 100–103
Listening styles, 102
L.L. Bean, 336–337
London, Scott, 87–88
Los Angeles Times, 291
Lost souls, 214
Lotus Development, 81–82
Loveless, Tom, 118–119
Loyal leaders, 194
Lumosity, 298
Luther, Martin, 46
Lyft, 313
Lynch, Stephen, 322

MacFarquhar, Larissa, 25
Machiavelli, Niccolo, 199
Machiavellian leaders, 199–200
Macy's, 336–337
Madoff, Bernie, 87, 196
Maduro, Nicolas, 380–381
Manby, Joel, 350
Marketing ethics:
  ABCs model, 297–298
  ambush marketing, 298
  of American Marketing Association, 298–299
  application projects, 320–321
  case study, 321–322
  chapter takeaway, 319–326
  distributive justice, 300–301
  ethical issues, 296–297
  guidelines for, 297–302
  mutuality principle, 299–300
  nondeception principle, 300
  nonmalfeasance principle, 300
  placement, 296
  price, 296
  product, 296
  promotion, 296
  standards, 300–301
  stewardship principle, 301
  virtues, 301–302
  for vulnerable populations, 300
Marriott Corporation, 132
Marshall, George, 127
Marsh USA, 303
Masculine cultures, 361, 363
Masiello, Steve, 139
Materialism, 39
Maximin rule, 13
May, Sally, 152
Mayer, Marissa, 195
Mayer-Caruso-Salovey Emotional Intelligence Test, 109
Mbeki, Thabo, 195
McChrystal, Stanley, 241
McDonald's, 66, 267
Medtronic, 48
Merck Pharmaceuticals, 68
Method, 353
Microsoft, 29–30, 234–235, 245, 337, 347
Midwestern Community Action, 152
Milgram, Stanley, 205
Milken, Michael, 197
Mill, John Stuart, 8–10
Mindfulness, 97–98
Mindlessness, 97
Mismanaged agreement in groups, 242–244
Mission statement, 261–263
Mobbing, 172
Modeling behavior of followers, 211
Monologue, 95
Moonves, Leslie, 192
Moral argument, 113–115
Moral character, 74–78
Moral compass, 81–82
Moral confrontation, 44
Moral courage, 75
Moral crisis, 44
Moral disengagement, 67–68
Moral efficacy, 75
Moral emotion, 71–72
Moral episode, 44
Moral exclusion, 247–250
Moral experts, 2–3
Moral foundations theory, 367–370
Moral free space, 375
Moral hypocrisy, 71

Moral identity, 46–47
Moral imagination, 60
Moral intensity, 61–62, 180–181
Morality, 7
Moral judgment, 64–71
Moral motivation, 71–74
Moral muteness, 61
Moral potency, 75–77
Moral project, 44
Moral sensitivity, 60–63
Moral values, 38–39
Moral work, 44
Morning Star, 150–151
Motivated forgetting, 67–68
Motorola, 277
Moyers, Bill, 239
Mueller, Matthias, 164
Mugabe, Robert, 197
Mulkey, Kim, 187
Mullen, Jim, 84
Munoz, Oscar, 153
Mutuality principle, 299–300
Mylan Pharmaceuticals, 321–322

Narcissistic leaders, 199
NASDAQ Stock Market, 262
National Aeronautics and Space Administration (NASA), 67
National Basketball Association (NBA), 335
National Security Agency (NSA), 29–30, 217
NCR, 234–235
Negotiation strategy, 165–170, 184–185
Nelson, Willie, 350
Nestlé Company, 60
New Leaf Paper, 353
New York Stock Exchange (NYSE), 263, 269
New York Times, 288
Nike, 262, 263, 337, 341
Nondeception principle, 300
Nonmalfeasance principle, 300
Normative leadership theories, 200–204
Norms, 274–275
Novo Nordisk, 331
Nuremberg principle, 205–206

Obama, Barack, 241, 242
Obedient followers, 205–206
Obligatory followers, 205

Oliphant, Marjorie, 119
Omnipotence fallacy, 307
Omniscience fallacy, 307
Open group climate, 235–237
Opportunistic followers, 214
O'Reilly, Bill, 179, 337
Organizational citizenship:
    in agency theory, 329
    altruism, 21
    animal activism, 349–350
    application projects, 348–349
    case studies, 349–354
    CERES principles, 338–339
    chapter takeaway, 347–354
    characteristics of, 327–343
    components of, 328–332
    consumer boycotts, 336–337
    contemporary issues, 336–337
    corporate activism, 335–336
    corporate citizenship stages, 340–343
    corporate social responsibility (CSR), 332–335
    covenantal relationship, 343–345
    Covenantal Relationship Questionnaire, 344–345
    defined, 328
    ethical checkpoint, 334–335, 338–339
    fake news stories, 351–352
    issue management, 330–332
    Issue Maturity Scale, 331
    profit-with-purpose business, 353–354
    promotional strategies, 343–347
    public benefit corporation, 353–354
    public opinion on, 327–328, 336
    self-assessment, 331, 344–345
    self-audits, 345–347
    social performance measures, 345–347
    stakeholder focus, 328–330
    stewardship mind-set, 343–345
    sustainability, 337–340
    triple-bottom-line measure, 345
Organizational culture:
    anomie, 271
    application projects, 287–288
    board of directors, 267–270
    caring climate, 281
    case studies, 288–294
    chapter takeaway, 286–294
    climate analysis, 280–281
    code of ethics, 263–266

communicating ethics messages, 272
compromise process, 284
contemporary issues, 266
cooptation process, 284
core ideology, 261
core values, 261
corporate executive officer (CEO), 268–269, 282–283
cultural change efforts, 278–286
cyberloafing, 266
duty of care, 267–268
duty of loyalty, 267–268
engaged leadership, 282–283
ethical checkpoint, 262, 269–270
Ethical Climate Questionnaire (ECQ), 280–281
ethical components, 260–278
ethical diagnosis, 278–282
ethical drivers, 278–286
ethically decoupled organizations, 259–260t
ethically transformed organizations, 258–260
ethics audit, 279–280
Ethics Audit Questions, 279–280
ethics-based approach, 258–260
ethics officer (EO), 272–273
ethics training, 285–286
formal cultural elements, 261–273
incrementalism process, 284
independence climate, 281
informal cultural elements, 274–278
instrumental climate, 281
integrity-based governance, 269–270
language, 274
law and code climate, 281
mission statement, 261–263
mission statement examples, 262
norms, 274–275
performance evaluation systems, 270–271
reporting ethical violations, 272
reward systems, 270–271, 290–292
risk assessment, 279
rituals, 275–276
rules climate, 281
safety contracts, 292–294
self-assessment, 279–280, 285
social cocoon, 284
socialization process, 283–285
Socialization Scale, 285
stories, 276–278
structure, 267

technology use (TU) code of conduct, 266
winner-take-all approach, 288–290
Organizational ethics:
altruism, 20–25
application projects, 26–27
care ethic, 22–23
case studies, 27–32
categorical imperative, 10–11
chapter takeaway, 25–32
competencies, 2–5
computer security, 29–30
Confucianism, 16–19
consequentialism, 8
contemporary issues, 24–25
defined, 5–8
ethical checkpoint, 19
ethics attitudes, 3–4
ethics defined, 7
eudemonia, 15
extreme altruism, 24–25
Facebook etiquette, 19
federal employees, 27–29
human rights, 11
justice-as-fairness theory, 12–14
morality, 7
organizational citizenship behavior, 21
Organizational Citizenship Behavior Scale, 21
prison operations (Norway), 30–32
self-assessment, 3–4, 21
theoretical perspectives, 8–25
utilitarianism, 8–10
virtue ethics, 14–16
Orpheus Chamber Orchestra, 150
O'Shannon, Tim, 119–120
Other-condemning emotion, 72
Other-praising emotion, 72
Other-suffering emotion, 71
Overconfidence in groups, 239

Pacific Gas and Electric (PG&E), 132
Pai, Lou, 277
Panama Papers, 194
Parmalat, 306
Partner followers, 216
Passages, 45–46
Patagonia, 190, 342, 353
Patton, George, 127
PayPal, 335

Pell, George, 57
People for Ethical Treatment of Animals (PETA), 349
People-oriented listener, 102
Pepper Hamilton, 186–187
Performance evaluation systems, 270–271
Performance-oriented cultures, 364–365
Personal aggression, 173–174
Personal ethical development:
   application projects, 52–53
   caring for the soul, 48–49
   case studies, 53–58
   chapter takeaway, 52–58
   character development, 39–46, 53–54
   character strengths, 40
   Confederate monuments, 55–56
   contemporary issues, 49–50
   ethical checkpoint, 40
   experiential learning, 41
   habits, 41–43
   integrated education model, 41
   Life Values Inventory, 38
   materialism, 39
   moral confrontation, 44
   moral crisis, 44
   moral episode, 44
   moral identity, 46–47
   moral project, 44
   moral values, 38–39
   moral work, 44
   passages, 45–46
   person-organization fit, 38–39
   positive psychology approach, 39–40
   preferred roles, 36–37
   role models, 43–44
   self-assessment, 36–37
   spiritual dangers, 49–50
   spiritual resources, 47–51
   spiritual well-being, 50–51
   Spiritual Well-Being Questionnaire, 50–51
   stories, 44–45
   unique gifts, 34–35
   Vatican leadership, 56–58
   virtue, 39–40, 43–44
   vocational calling, 33–37
Personal power, 123–125125
Person-organization fit, 38–39
Perspective skills, 60
Petreaus, David, 241

Petro-Canada, 342
Phelps, Fred, 197
Piggybacking, 302–303
Pillmore, Eric, 273
Ping An Insurance, 17
Pinkel, Gary, 224
Players in groups, 230
Plum Organics, 353
Political power, 127–130
Polythink, 241–242
Positional power, 125, 126
Positive psychology approach, 39–40
Power distance, 361, 363
Power dynamics:
   of influence, 122–133
   of leadership, 191–192
Powerlessness, 126
Preferred roles, 36–37
Premature abandonment in groups, 245
Price, Norman, 277
Prince, The (Machiavelli), 199
Principled negotiation, 169–170
Prison operations (Norway), 30–32
Privileged leaders, 192
Proactive influence tactics, 134–136
Procedural justice, 315
Proctor & Gamble, 370
Profit-with-purpose business, 353–354
Prohibitive behavior of followers, 211, 212
Project GLOBE, 364–365
Promotive behavior of followers, 211
ProQuest, 88
Protective impression management, 137, 138
Pruitt, Scott, 207
Psychological capital in leadership, 204
Psychological safety, 237
Public benefit corporation, 353–354
Puzder, Andy, 313
Pygmalion effect, 145–148

Quid-pro-quo harassment, 178, 179

Radio Shack, 318
Ragghianti, Marie, 43
Rawls, John, 12–14
Ray, James Arthur, 254–255
Recognition-seekers in groups, 230
Redstone, Sumner, 191

Reell Precision Manufacturing, 48
Referent power, 122–125
Refusal tactic, 318
Relational transparency in leadership, 203
Repetition in followership, 209
Resource followers, 216
Responsible leaders, 192–193
Revlon Company, 277
Revson, Charles, 277
Reward power, 122–125
Reward systems, 71, 270–271, 290–292
Right-to-privacy, 379–380
Rigid leaders, 195
Ringling Brothers Barnum & Bailey Circus, 349–350
Risk assessment, 279
Risky shift, 244
Rituals, 275–276
Robin Hood Effect, 319
Rodgers, T. J., 134
Role models, 43–44
Roof, Dylann, 55
Rousseff, Dilma, 190
Ruckelshaus, William, 43
Rufer, Chris, 150–151
Rules climate, 281

Salesforce, 335, 336
SandFan, 118–119
Sarbanes-Oxley Act (2002), 217, 218, 269, 303–304
Schemas, 64–65
Schiff, Adam, 350
Schlesinger, Arthur, 239–240
Schultz, Howard, 190
Schutz, Dana, 358, 359
Schwartz, Morrie, 117–118
SC Johnson, 330
Scott Paper, 134
Sealed Air Corporation, 261
SeaWorld, 349–350
Securities and Exchange Commission (SEC), 263, 272, 273, 305–306
Self-awareness in leadership, 203
Self-conscious emotion, 72
Self-disclosure, 103–105
Self-fulfilling prophecy, 145–148
Selfish leaders, 199–200
Self-management technique, 150–151
Sensemaking behavior of followers, 212

Servant leadership, 201–202
Sexual assault, 186–188
Sexual coercion, 178
Sexual harassment, 177–181
Shadow Brokers, 29–30
Shinseki, Eric, 222
Shoreham Nuclear Power Plant, 244
Shriver, Eunice, 190
Shultz, George, 225, 226, 227
Shultz, Tyler, 225–227
Singh, Albert, 152
Sinyi Real Estate, 17
Situational aggression, 174–175
Skilling, Jeffrey, 277, 307
Slippery slope, 68
Smith, Bert, 256
Smith, Brad, 30
Smith, Greg, 274
Smith, Samantha, 256
Snowden, Edward, 217
Snyder, Rick, 164
Social Accountability 8000, 345
Social advocacy, 335–336
Social aggression, 174
Social cocoon, 284
Socialization in organizational culture, 283–285
Social loafing, 231–235
Society for Human Resource Management (SHRM), 316–317
Soft power, 125
Soltes, Eugene, 87–88
Solution presentations in followership, 209
Sotheby's, 197
South Shore Bank (Chicago), 60
Southwest Airlines, 190, 262, 276, 325
Special Olympics, 190
Spiritual resources, 47–51
Spiritual Warrior Retreat (Arizona), 254–255
Spiritual well-being, 50–51
Springfield Remanufacturing, 132
Staats, Elmer, 43
Starbucks, 190, 335, 336, 345, 370
Starr, Kenneth, 187
Stem Cell Research Alliance, 119–120
Stewardship principle:
 in marketing ethics, 301
 in organizational citizenship, 343–345
Stockland (Australia), 262

Stories:
  in organizational culture, 276–278
  in personal ethical development, 44–45
Strangers Drowning (MacFarquhar), 25
Stress, 67
Strong Capital Management, 273
Stumpf, John, 190, 290–291
Styles, Harry, 350
Sugihara, Chiune, 206
Sullenberger, Chesley, 43–44
Sunbeam-Oster, 134, 197
Supportive group climate, 235–237
Surface acting, 144
Sustainability, 337–340
Symbol Technologies, 88
Synovus, 201

TaskRabbit, 313
Taubman, A. Alfred, 197
TD Industries, 48, 201
Technical dialogue, 95
Technology use (TU) code of conduct, 266
Tesco (Great Britain), 262
Theranos, 125, 225–227
Thomson, Scott, 139
Threatening resignation in followership, 209
3M, 262
Till, Emmett, 358, 359
Timberland, 332
Time-oriented listener, 102
Times Mirror, 262
Tindell, Kip, 190
Title VII, Civil Rights Act (1964), 178
Tom's of Maine, 48
Tom's Shoes, 332, 342
Toro Company, 201
Toxic leaders, 197–199
Toyota, 282
TransCanada, 262
Trigger events in leadership, 203–204
Triple-bottom-line measure, 345
Trolley problem, 370–371
T. Rowe Price, 381
Truman, Harry S., 239
Trump, Ivana, 153
Trust, 111–113
Tuesdays With Morrie (Albom), 117
Turing Pharmaceuticals, 321
Tyco, 269, 273

Uber, 190, 288–290, 313
Ukwuachu, Sam, 187
Uncertainty avoidance, 362–363
Unilever, 342
United Airlines, 153
United Nations:
  Global Compact, 371–372
  Universal Declaration of Human Rights, 371–372
Unobtrusive control in groups, 246
Unrealistic optimism fallacy, 308
Unwanted sexual attention, 178
U.S. Department of Defense (DoD), 27–29
Utilitarianism, 8–10
Utility, 8

Valeant Pharmaceuticals, 321
Valukas, Anton, 293
Van Huesen, 134
Vatican leadership, 56–58
Veil of ignorance, 13
Veracity, 142
Verizon, 195, 337
Veterans Administration, 222–223
Veterans Affairs, 221–223
Veterans Choice, 222–223
Viacom, 191, 192
Victoria's Secret, 358, 359
Virtual teams, 234–235
Virtues:
  in marketing ethics, 301–302
  in organizational ethics, 14–16
  in personal ethics, 39–40, 43–44
Vocational calling, 33–37
Volkswagen, 164, 347
Vulnerable populations and marketing, 300

Walmart, 277, 325, 337
Washington Mutual Savings and Loan, 208, 270
Watson, Thomas, 277
Wegner, Dave, 207
Weiner, Anthony, 195
Weizhan Garment Company, 17
Wells Fargo, 290–292
Wendy's, 267
West Point Military Academy, 53–54
Wheatley, Margaret, 201
Whistleblower Protection Act (1989), 217
Whistle-blowers, 217–219
White-collar crime, 87–89

Whitney Museum, 358, 359
Whole Foods, 150
Why Do They Do It? (Soltes), 87–88
Wigand, Jeffrey, 44
Wiley, Harvey W., 43
Wolfe, Timothy, 224
World Bank, 325
WorldCom, 208, 269, 306
Worldliness, 360

Xerox, 340

Yahoo, 84, 139, 195
Yang, Jerry, 84
Yum! Brands, 66
Yves Chouinard, 353

Zappos, 150
Zuckerberg, Mark, 352